CHANGE
Your Future, Now!

Questions, Reflections & Answers

Germain Decelles

With a special contribution from
Yvan Poirier

Change Management series
La gestion du changement en affaires. (Change management in business). 2006
ISBN 978-0-9783667-3-5
Le changement POUR TOUS. (Change made easy). 2007
ISBN 978-0-9783667-4-2
LA RECONNAISSANCE, une question de respect! (Recognition, a question of respect!). 2009
ISBN : 978-0-9783667-5-9
Information : www.webtechpublishing.com

Special contribution: Yvan Poirier.

Editing: WebTech Management and Publishing Incorporated
Revision: Catherine Barrier
Cover photo: Collection: Le changement (Change)
Setting: WebTech Management and Publishing Incorporated

Printing and Distribution: http://www.lulu.com

Quotations, short texts, and photographs in this book remain the property of the authors concerned. For other notices, please refer to the section entitled SELECTED BIBLIOGRAPHY & PHOTO CREDITS.

© 2013 by Germain Decelles, WebTech Management and Publishing Incorporated

All rights reserved. No part of this book may be reproduced in any form or by any means whatsoever without the prior written permission of the publishers.

CHANGE Your Future, Now!
Paperback
ISBN: ISBN 978-0-9783667-7-3

E-book format : epub
ISBN: ISBN 978-0-9783667-8-0
E-book format : PDF
ISBN: ISBN 978-0-9783667-9-7

Copyright: first quarter 2013
National Library of Québec
National Library of Canada

17, Marien Avenue, Montréal, Québec, Canada H1 B4T8
www.webtechmanagement.com
www.webtechpublishing.com

CHANGE
Your Future, Now!

Questions, Reflections & Answers

Germain Decelles

With a special contribution from
Yvan Poirier

Everyone thinks of changing the world, but no one thinks of changing himself.

Lev Nikolayevich Tolstoy
Russian writer;
His two most famous works, the novels
War and Peace and *Anna Karenina*,
are acknowledged as two of
the greatest novels of all time and
as pinnacles of realist fiction.

The Illuminated Crowd
by artist Raymond Mason
BNP Tower – Laurentian Bank Tower
Montreal, Canada
Photo: WebTech Collection

Photo: WebTech Collection

CONTENTS

CONTENTS	5
PROLOGUE	15
PROJECT TOMORROW	19
INTRODUCTION	21

What about authenticity?
What is wrong with in authenticity?
What is an authentic person?
What should I consider?

CHAPTER 1 – The Journey   27

How about our needs? 30
Can we avoid death? 32
Do simplicity and effort work? 34
Can I use short cuts in life? 35
How can I use these benefits? 36
What are the steps along the way? 38
How can I get rid of my guilt? 41
What about walking around in a circle? 42
Is life a journey? 43
Am I living in the present? 44
Am I at the right place at the right time? 46
Can I expect many false journeys? 50
Does my journey have a meaning? 52
What do I owe my parents? 52
Is life reliable? 54
How many times a day should I say thank you? 55
How can I ask for help? 56
Should I drop the ego? 57
What should I consider? 58

CHAPTER 2 – Mind Setting   63

What about a productive mindset?
Can I keep an open mind? 63
Can I keep an open mind? 65
Do I think for myself? 66
Can I cultivate the ability to think for myself? 67
Could I not be thinking for myself? 69
Can I think critically? 69
Can I put subjects and things in perspective? 71
How can I make my heart and mind work together? 73
What about imagination and vision? 76
Can I develop courage? 77
How can I stop making excuses? 78
How can I be an original or my true self? 79

Contents

Am I an interesting person? 80
Can I think positively? 81
Can I expand my comfort zone? 82
What does it mean to take control of my life? 83
Can I balance my life? 84
Who is the person I want to be? 84
What should I consider? 85

CHAPTER 3 – Learning & Change 89
Why do we learn? 90
How can I become a more effective learner? 91
Is learning a process? 95
What is a life development program? 96
What do I want to know and learn about? 97
Is reading important? 97
How can I find the right mentor? 99

Do I want to be a Mentor? 100
What is Change? 102
How do individuals and organizations respond to change? 104
What about a plan for change? 105
Do I need to think ahead? 107
What are the reasons for resisting change? 109
What are the change processes? 111
What is the downside of change? 113
What should I consider? 115

CHAPTER 4 – Becoming Great 119
What about the talent myth? 119
What does all this mean? 121
Do I already know how to be Great? 122
What does it take to be Great? 123
Why the extra step? 125
What is a Hero? 126
How can I be patient? 129
How can I become a great Person? 131
How can I become a great Finisher? 131
Do I want to become a great Leader? 132
Do I want to become a great Follower? 135
How might I become miserable? 136
Can I become a strategic Thinker? 139
Is Life a call for action? 142
Can I simplify any problem? 144
How can I become a great Friend? 145
How can I become a great Facilitator? 146
How can I become a great Parent? 148
How can I become a great Mentor? 149
How can I become a great Seller? 151
How can I become a great Communicator? 153
Do I need to surround myself with people better than myself? 154
Is success an accident? 156
What about accidental success? 157

What should I consider? 158

CHAPTER 5 – Communicating 161
Should I be sensitive to other people's feelings? 164
Can I develop effective listening skills? 165
What determines my personality? 167
How can I have the courage to say what I think? 171
Do men and women communicate differently? 174
How can I organize my communications? 177
How do I make eye contact? 178
Should I be aware of what my body is saying? 180
What are others seeing? 181
Should I be aware of conversation pointers? 183
How can I have great conversations? 184
What about nonverbal communication? 188
How can I address an audience? 190
How can I communicate with children? 191
How can I achieve effective inter-generational communication? 192
How can I reach a consensus? 195
How can I be polite? 197
How should I Apologize? 198
How can I forgive? 202
Do you want to live a long, happy life? 202
How can I make my personality stand out? 204
How can I expand my vocabulary? 205
What should I consider? 206

CHAPTER 6 – Networking 209
When should I start networking? 209
How should I act when attending networking activities? 210
How can I improve my networking skills? 213
How can I look approachable? 217
How can I be charming? 218
How can I start a conversation with a stranger? 222
Can I create a friendship in 60 seconds? 224
What about the power of social media? 226
What should I consider? 227

CHAPTER 7 – Knowledge & Wisdom 229
What is the difference between being knowledgeable and being wise? 229
How can I search for the unknown? 231
So how do I continually learn new things in life? 232
Can our general knowledge be updated? 234
Can I gain wisdom? 235
How can I learn from failure? 236
Should I believe I have tried all possible approaches? 238
Is there a technique for learning a subject better? 239
What is reason and how do I use it? 240
How do I strengthen my character? 244
What should I consider? 250

Contents

CHAPTER 8 – Plan Ahead — 253
How can I set goals for life? 255
How can I be bold? 257
How can I reach for my dreams? 259
How can I visualize? 261
How can I solve a problem? 263
What about a goals-setting methodology? 266
How can I form a plan? 267
How can I switch careers? 268
What should I consider? 270

CHAPTER 9 – Influence & Inspire — 273
How can I influence others? 275
How can I be positive? 277
How can I erase a negative influence? 279
How can I get inspired? 282
How can I be an inspiration? 284
How can I be a good role model? 285
How can I choose a role model? 286
How can I be a leader? 287
What should I consider? 290

CHAPTER 10 – Dealing with Change — 293
How can I deal with the fear of change? 295
How can I change my personality? 297
How can I change other people's opinions of me? 298
How can I accept criticism? 299
Can I change people's lives for the better? 302
How can I deal with negative people? 303
How can I deal with people who always complain? 305
Can I change my attitude at work? 307
How can I improve my change management skills? 309
What should I consider? 313

CHAPTER 11 – Negotiate — 315
How do I ask a question intelligently? 317
Can I detect lies? 319
How can I negotiate effectively? 324
Can I control my emotions when I negotiate? 325
How can I win a negotiation? 326
How can I negotiate more effectively? 331
How can I negotiate with parents? 333
How can I argue fairly? 334
Can I control anger outbursts? 336
How can I handle people who are angry with me? 339
What should I consider? 341

CHAPTER 12 – Disagree — 343
How to argue in a positive way? 344
How can I defuse an argument? 346
What can I do to resolve a disagreement? 348
How can I stay out of an argument? 350

How can I walk away from a fight? 352
How can I lose an argument gracefully? 355
How can I say no to the boss? 356

How can I form an opinion? 358
How can I avoid misspeaking? 360
How can I show empathy? 361
What should I consider? 364

CHAPTER 13 – Good Citizen 367
How can I be a world citizen? 368
How can I be nice? 370
How can I learn about other cultures? 374
How can I preserve my culture? 376
How can I be honest? 377
What about imposters? 380
Can I improve my personal integrity? 381
What should I consider? 383

CHAPTER 14 – Power 387
Do people have power over you? 389
How can I identify manipulative behavior? 395
How can I respond to a bully? 403
How can I be captivating? 406
What should I consider? 410

CHAPTER 15 – Health & Stress 413
How can I be healthy? 413
How can I eat healthy? 416
Should I drink plenty of water? 419
What is stress? 420
How can I handle stress? 422
How well do I sleep? 431
How do I meditate? 433
It is time to start planning a vacation? 436
Can I manage stress in the workplace? 440
Am I suffering from depression? 441
How can I leave the past behind? 443
Can I smile for better health? 447
What should I consider? 450

CHAPTER 16 – Common Sense 453
How does the brain work? 454
How can I reason? 458
How can I build character through integrity? 460
Do I need to learn things that are basic common sense? 462
How can I put new common sense thinking habits into place? 465
How can I think outside of the box? 467
How can I think clearly and logically under pressure? 471
How can I think before speaking? 472

Contents

How can I think ahead? 475
What should I consider? 478

CHAPTER 17 – Recognition & Thankfulness   483
My support to this book - 484
New vision - 486

LOVE   487
    How can we get rid of prejudices that we have held on to for thousands of years? 490
    How do I see unconditional love expressed daily? 491
    How can I see love in the future? 496

AUTHENTICITY   496
    How can I stop comparing things by relying on the past? 497
    How can I be authentic when I express my gratitude and my thankfulness? 497
    How can I be conscious that I must be transparent, as much as possible? 498

AUTONOMY   499
    Why do people lack autonomy? 500
    How can I express my autonomy more? 500
    How can I meet my need to feed my autonomy? 500
    How can I reach autonomy while still being myself? 501

DETACHMENT 502
    How can I avoid indifference in detachment? 503
    How can I free myself from sad things or events that are still harmful for my mind? 503
    How can I realize the importance of detachment every day? 504

HUMILITY   505
    What is it to be humble in this kind of process? 505
    How can I be humble, no matter what the circumstances? 506

SIMPLICITY   507
    How can I keep things simple? 507
    How can I remain composed with simplicity during the difficult situations in which we live? 508
    How can I ensure being myself? 508

PERSONAL AND PROFESSIONAL ETHICS   509
    What are personal and professional ethics in terms of thankfulness? 509
    What are the basic principles of personal and professional ethics? 510
    What can we see? 511
    How can we detach ourselves from the former to deal with the new? 511
    How can we trust ourselves to gain the confidence of others? 512
    How can we discern what we can observe? 512
    How can we forgive and to be forgiven? 513
    How can we appreciate others – and be appreciated ourselves? 513
    How can we use our energy correctly for things we are involved in? 514

How can we surround ourselves with people who will help us to see things more clearly? 515
How can we give our opinions without wanting to be absolutely right? 515
How can we use our sense of humor wisely? 516
How can we use what we have in ourselves better? 516
How can we acknowledge ourselves in order to be acknowledged by others? 516
How can we love what we do in order to love what we wish to achieve? 517
How can we choose ourselves above all in order to receive according to our true value? 518
How can we give without expecting to receive anything? 519
How can we help without any expectations? 519
How can we communicate with simplicity and humility? 520
How can we evaluate our personal and professional ethics? 520

THE WORKPLACE 522
How do I see the importance of the workplace in relation to Thankfulness? 523
How can I promote thankfulness in the workplace? 525
How can I get more motivation and satisfaction in the workplace? 526
How can I obtain the participation of management and employees in the organization of ceremonies? 528
What should I understand on a personal level about the thankfulness? 529
What tips and tricks should I suggest? 531
Conclusion 535

CHAPTER 18 – Humor   539
How can I be funny? 540
What about humor in the workplace? 548
How can I socialize, be funny, and make friends? 550
Should I smile? 552
What should I consider? 555

CHAPTER 19 – Intuition   557
How can I develop my intuition? 557
How can I follow my intuition? 560
What can I do about fear and intuition? 561
How can I think ahead? 563
How can I develop the *Sherlock Holmes* intuition? 565
What should I consider? 572

CHAPTER 20 – Success   575
How can I make decisions? 579
How can I be bold? 581
How can I be proactive? 584
How can I be ambitious? 586
How can I be resourceful? 588

Contents

Can I get the collaboration of others? 592
How can I make money? 594
What should I consider? 598

CHAPTER 21 – The Future   601
What about imagination? 603
Can innovation play a part in my life? 606
Is creativity as good as it sounds? 607
How can I overcome anxiety using future visioning? 608
How can I visualize? 610
How can I create a vision of my future? 614
Can I understand the generation gap? 616
What will the 2020 organization be like? 618
What should I consider? 624

ABOUT THE AUTHOR   626
About the contributing author 627

SELECTED BIBLIOGRAPHY & PHOTO CREDITS   629

Photo: WebTech Collection

Special tanks for their wisdom and support to:
Mr. & Mrs. Leonard J. Messineo
Grand Chancellor,
Sovereign Order of Saint John of Jerusalem ®
New-Jersey, U.S.A

Sovereign Order of Saint John of Jerusalem ®
※ Knights of Malta ※

www.sovereignorderofsaintjohnofjerusalemknightsofmalta.com

This book in our change
management series
is addressed to thoughtful
students, parents, workers,
educators, artists, athletes,
physicians, managers,
leaders, retirees, writers, or
coaches, whether they work
alone or belong to a team or
organization struggling with
and committed
to responsible change
for a better future.

Our hope, or goal, is to
spark new intellectual capital
by sharing ideas.

In short we aim to publish a
book that disturbs the
present in order to bring
forth a better future.

WebTech
MANAGEMENT and PUBLISHING

PROLOGUE

Change is important. It matters a great deal to organizations and institutions, to the people who work in them, and to the people who are served by it. For our society to function effectively, we need authentic people who can encourage others to perform at their best and step up and lead themselves.

I wrote *Change Your Future, Now!* because I have a passion to see more people in all walks of life embrace change. I wanted to help people like you discover their potential, so they could help themselves to evolve in life and help the people around them.

Change Your Future, Now! enable you to take the ideas from the book and apply them to your personal development. This will enable you to become a more effective and authentic person, one who can evolve and change from within in order to realize a better future.

Becoming an authentic person takes hard work! To become great at any endeavor, whether in your career, your family, or your community, you must use unique strengths you were born with and develop them to the fullest, while acknowledging and learning from your shortcomings. In the majority of cases, people have to work hard to shape their futures. They endure disappointing defeats and rejections and search for many years to find the right place to flourish. They are each required to make the journey to his or her own soul, in order to find out who they are, where their real passions lie, and how they can become more effective, so they can shape their futures.

Prologue

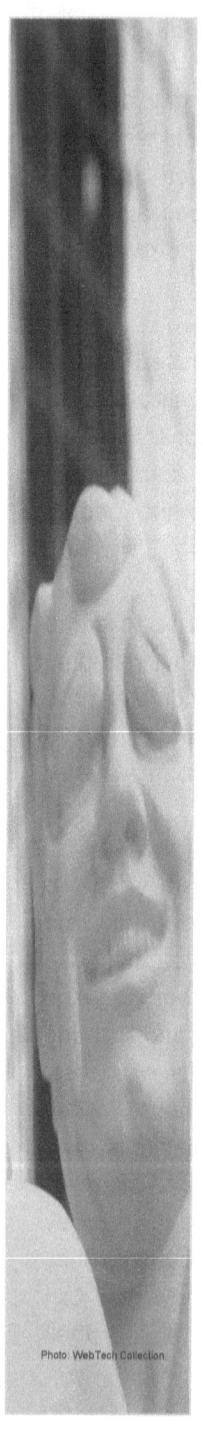

Personally, I did not have a distinctive reference text like this book to help me when I was young, so I made up my development plan as I went along, with the help of my father, employers, close friends, my wife, my son, and some important mentors along the way.

After searching for role models for many years, I learned that I could never become a great person by emulating someone else or by minimizing my shortcomings. If you are aiming to be like somebody else, you will be merely a copycat because you will think that is what people want you to do. You will never be a real person with that kind of thinking. However, you might be a real person, unpredictable by following, your passions.

Many self-help books offer a quick fix, or provide the reader with seven or more easy steps to follow. Unfortunately, in reality a person's development does not usually work that way, and one rarely becomes a great person simply by reading a book.

To realize your potential in life, you need a detailed development program that will enable you to shape your future. That is the purpose of *Change Your Future, Now!* - to help you to develop a clear and detailed program for your personal growth and happiness in life. I encourage you to have as many experiences early in life as you can. Do not sit back and wait for these experiences to come to you. Seek them out! Then after each experience, you should process it by going back to your development plan to see what changes you need to make and/or to determine the future experiences you should have.

Remember the following fundamentals; they will help you to change your future: You will need to discover your authentic self as soon as possible; you will need to remember that you do not have to be born with certain characteristics to be able to shape your future; you will not need to wait for a tap on your shoulder to start; you will not need to wait to be at the top of an organization to start; and the most important, you will need to remember that you are never too young or too old to change your future.

I encourage you to be completely open and transparent as you look inside yourself and answer the very challenging and difficult questions posed about what you think you should be in the future. You need to explore your life's story at a deep level in order to understand who you are as a human being, where you fit in in this world, how you can impact the world in a positive way, and how you can leave a lasting legacy.

I hope that you and many others can transform business organizations and institutions, the nonprofit world, governments, education, and religion, as you bring authenticity to the world and encourage others to do the same. Your enthusiasm to become authentic will indeed make this world a better and richer place for all of us to live in.

At this point, it is important to keep in mind that changing your life for a better future is your sole decision!

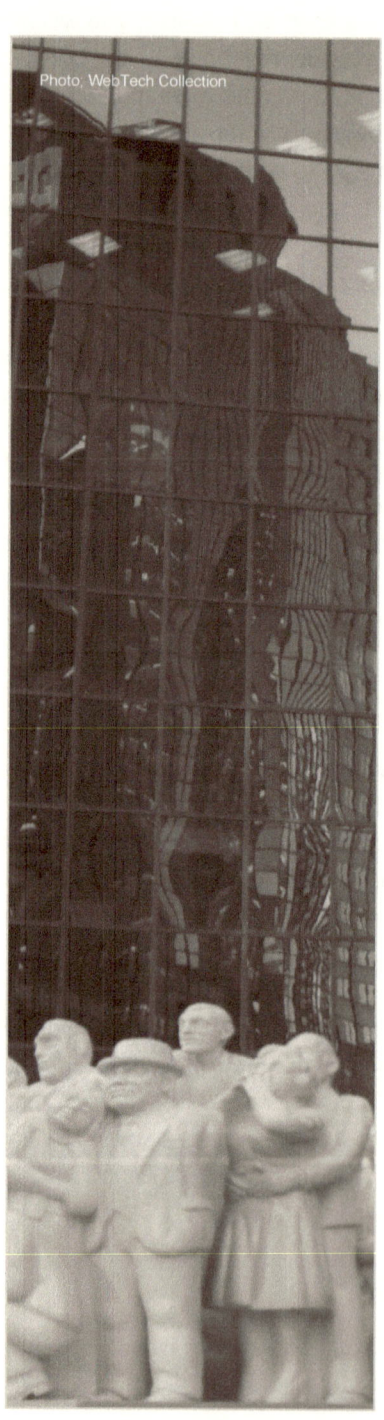

- TOMORROW -

The sun'll come out
Tomorrow
Bet your bottom dollar
That tomorrow
There'll be sun!

Just thinkin' about
Tomorrow
Clears away the cobwebs,
And the sorrow
'Til there's none!

When I'm stuck a day
That's gray,
And lonely,
I just stick out my chin
And Grin,
And Say,
Oh!

The sun'll come out
Tomorrow
So ya gotta hang on
'Til tomorrow
Come what may
Tomorrow! Tomorrow!
I love ya Tomorrow!
You're always
A day
A way!

ANNIE, THE MUSICAL
Music by: Charles Strouse
Lyrics by: Martin Charnin
Book By: Thomas Meehan
Based on: Tribune Media
Service Comic Strip
Little Orphan Annie

PROJECT **TOMORROW**

This book is the result of a four-year project called *Project Tomorrow*. During the four-year period, we followed more than 500 trainees, aged from 16 to 72. The trainees were form colleges and reinsertion programs in administration and computer science.

Some of the trainees implicated where dropouts from school districts, and others were new immigrants or unemployed workers from different economic and social backgrounds.

To graduate, the trainee had to perform during a period of three months in a business environment. At the end of that time, an appreciation evaluation was performed to determine both the amount of change the trainee experienced during the period and the impact of that change on the trainee.

Many of the questions, reflections, and answers presented in this book are issued from our findings during this period. We would like to thank all the trainees for their efforts and determination during the process.

We would like to acknowledge Mrs. Helen Power, who helped to select most of the trainees and who followed their development during the project as well. We are grateful for her help.

In addition, I would like to thank the Adhoot Brothers (Robert & David) from Hypertec Group for providing research and manufacturing environments, as well as administrative support, for the project.

Introduction

Our best thoughts come from others.

Ralph Waldo Emerson
(1803 – 1882)
American essayist, lecturer, and poet.

We have also drawn from thirty years of international experience gathered from our change and transition management consulting services.

I would particularly like to thank all of our professional colleagues for their friendship and support: Bernard Berthiaume, Normand Forgues, Yvan Poirier, Georges Klein, Jean-Louis Richard, and The Hon. Gerry Weiner. We had numerous discussions with them on many of the subjects found in this book. Their guidance and suggestions made this project possible.

Acknowledgement would not be complete without mentioning my wife, Patricia, who supported my career - and my son, Frédéric-Alexandre, who served, during his university and business development years, as the test subject to confirm many of the questions, reflections, and answers for the project and the writing of *Change Your Future, Now!*

Germain Decelles
CEO & Senior Consultant Associate
WebTech Management and Publishing, Inc.

Special thanks to my little *brother Michel*
for is particular knowledge of the manufacturing sector.

INTRODUCTION

> Today is the first day of the rest of your life.
>
> Anonymous

People can change!
You have in your hands a tool that can change your life. The following pages will guide you to determine the path necessary to explore your willingness for a better future.

This book is for people who are actively engaged and open to challenging their own assumptions and to listening to their deepest inner voice, for it is only through this kind of listening that a better future will be "unlocked".

Your motivation to use this book may be that you have thoughts about finding new ways to flourish in life. Maybe you are 18 years old and want to explore ways to advance your career. Or, you may be retiring in a few years, and be looking forward to helping the next generation succeed you.

Perhaps you are 40 years old and are confronted with young aggressive coworkers, and you feel that you need to examine ways of coping with such a situation. Or you may be 70 years old and want to leave a good impression by assisting others to cope with changes by sharing your experiences.

If we are to grow and progress in our lives and careers, we obviously must equip ourselves with the skills and knowledge needed to be proactive in the face of threats and ready for future. Our very survival and well being depend on our ability to anticipate and determine future problems and threats, as well to perceive, evaluate, and control the effects of our actions in order to imagine and create more desirable futures. This book describes how to improve our ability to pursue these goals.

> Nobody can go back and start a new beginning, but anyone can start today and make a new ending.
>
> Maria Robinson
> American Author

The future is the only part of our lives that we can change by what we do or do not do. In particular, being authentic to ourselves is the most important thing!

What about authenticity?

Authenticity refers to the truthfulness of origins, attributions, commitments, sincerity, devotion, and intentions. There are many people who, while being anything but authentic in their ways of doing things, do get ahead in life. Surely, you have met some of them. They are all around us.

> Authenticity is the alignment of head, mouth, heart, and feet - thinking, saying, feeling, and doing the same thing - consistently. This builds trust, and followers love leaders they can trust.
>
> Lance Secretan
> born in 1939. UK, He is best known for his work in leadership theory and how to inspire teams.

Usually, you will recognize them as they try to dominate a situation by using their power to take advantage of people in order to get ahead. They may be constantly directing, controlling, and dealing with others in an aggressive way.

Often, you will recognize these people because they seem incapable of accepting honest feedback. Sometimes they will willingly use others to achieve their goals without respecting them. Some of them might even stretch the truth or see the political advantage in authenticity, and use it, if it makes them look good.

What is wrong with in authenticity?

Although such individuals may be successful in the short-term, over time, their behavior catches up with them. At that point, they either move on or watch their surroundings and/or organization steadily decline. Such people are incapable of building trust around them. In short, they are ineffective people. Worse, such people destroy good people as well as great organizations.

The question to ask yourself is, "Can I be an effective and authentic person who can sustain success over an extended period of time?"

People today seek people whom they can trust. You need to understand that people are not so easily fooled or so quick to offer their loyalty.

In giving advice, seek to help, not please, your friend.
Solon
(638 BC – 558 BC)
Athenian statesman, lawmaker, and poet. He is remembered particularly for his efforts to legislate against political, economic, and moral decline in archaic Athens.

It is a competitive world out there - and not only in the business sector. There are very ambitious people in the social and political arenas. People today are very knowledgeable and may often know more about something than you do. And like you, they may be eager to have the opportunity to step up and lead immediately; they may not wish to wait in line for five to ten years. They are willing to work extremely hard, but will do so only for a cause they believe in, as they are seeking meaning and significance in their work.

It is important to remember that people are willing to trust you only if you prove yourself worthy of their trust by being authentic!

What is an authentic person?
Authenticity is required to be genuine. A person that wants to be honest with herself must practice good values, lead with her heart, develop connected relationships, and have the self-discipline to get results. An authentic person must stay on course in the face of the most severe challenges, pressures, and seductions.

To be an authentic person means being true to yourself and to what you believe in, which will enable you to generate trust and develop genuine

Introduction

Hard times arouse an instinctive desire for authenticity.

Gabrielle Bonheur "Coco Chanel"
(1883 – 1971)
She was an influential French fashion designer.

connections with others. Because people trust you, you will be able to motivate them to a higher-level. Rather than let the expectations of others guide you, you must be prepared to be your own person and do things the way you think is best. As you develop as an authentic person, you will be more concerned about serving others than about achieving success or receiving recognition.

To be an authentic person does not mean you have to be perfect. Far from it. Like all of us, you can have your weaknesses and be subject to the full range of human frivolities and potential to make mistakes. These do not render one inauthentic.

However, by acknowledging your shortcomings and admitting your errors, you will connect with people and empower them. Essentially, to change your future, you need to discover your authentic self!

To change, you need purpose, respectable moral values, a good heart, excellent relationships, and self-discipline. To find your purpose in life, you must first understand yourself and your actions. In turn, your passions will show the way to your individual purpose. As an authentic person, you are defined by your values, which are the deeply held beliefs that guide your actions.

Your values are personal; they cannot be determined by anyone except you. The test of your values is not what you say, but how you behave under pressure. If you are not true to the values you profess, people will quickly lose confidence in you.

To be your authentic self, you must lead with your heart as well as your head. This means having a passion for your work, compassion for the people you

serve, empathy for people with whom you work, and the courage to make difficult decisions. Long-lasting and enduring connections with other people, in all types of relationships enable you to build trust and commitment through the openness and depth of your relationships. These also help wake commitment from others.

Self-discipline enables you to set high standards for yourself when you fall short and you will and to hold others accountable for their performance. It is equally important to admit your mistakes and initiate immediate corrective action. High-level self-discipline on your part will inevitably produce positive results.

What should I consider?
Please go anywhere inside this book! I have tried to make every page count. Each page contains at least one practical piece of information that can assist you in improving your skills to cope with change for a better future. It is important that you be at ease with the material, so please begin wherever you feel most relaxed.

Once you have made yourself comfortable with the book, it will be easier for you to start working to *Change Your Future, Now!*

Our moral responsibility is not to stop the future, but to shape it... to channel our destiny in humane directions and to ease the trauma of transition.

Alvin Toffler

Photo: Vern Evans, Los Angeles, California, USA

THE JOURNEY

CHAPTER 1

We are living at the greatest time in all of human history. We are surrounded by abundant opportunities that we can take advantage of to realize our dreams. The only real limits on what we can be, do, or have are the limits we place on ourselves by our own thinking. Our future is virtually unlimited.

Life is a remarkable journey that takes us up and down a road of happiness, growth, interaction, love, fear, and sometimes pain and hardship, which comes with all the good we are blessed with.

Our journey will begin with our cry at birth and end with our last breath at death. Each of us has his or her own journey, yet all will experience the same emotions and struggles that are synonymous with life. From birth to death, we are always experiencing sensations from the world we live in.

Life is either a daring adventure, or nothing.

Helen Adams Keller
(1880 - 1968)
American author, political activist, and lecturer. She was the first deafblind person to earn a Bachelor of Arts degree.

We are nurtured, loved, taught, and grow, through every form of good and bad we encounter. Every stage of our lives prepares us for the next. We learn to be social beings by interacting with everyone who crosses our paths. We learn about each other through communication, intellect, and emotions.

If we don't change, we don't grow.
If we don't grow, we aren't really living.

Gail Sheehy
(1937 –)
American writer and lecturer, most notable for her books on life and the life cycle.

The journey will not always be smooth; in fact, throughout our lives, we will encounter many challenges. Life is a journey filled with lessons, hardships, heartaches, joys, celebrations, and special moments that will ultimately lead each of us to a particular destination, to a specific purpose in life.

Along the way, we may stumble upon obstacles that will encumber the paths that we are destined to take. Some of these challenges will test our courage,

Chapter 1

Insanity is doing the same thing over and over and expecting different results.

Albert Einstein
(1879 - 1955)
German-born theoretical physicist who developed the theory of general relativity, effecting a revolution in physics. For this achievement, Einstein is often regarded as the father of modern physics and one of the most prolific intellects in human history.

If you could choose one characteristic that would get you through life, choose a sense of humor.

Phylis Lee Isley
(1919 -2009)
Better known by her stage name, Jennifer Jones, was an American actress.

strengths, weaknesses, and faith. In order to follow the right path, we must overcome these obstacles. Sometimes these obstacles are really blessings in disguise, only we do not realize that at the time.

Every person living has two things in common regardless of race, gender, location, social status, or sexuality from the richest to the most impoverished beggar: he or she was born and will die. The distance between those two events measures life.

All the events between birth and death are part of the experience. The beginning is always the same. The ending is always the same. The middle, those moments of living or letting life slip past you, is what defines what life is truly about.

Many people live as if life were a race to get to the grave as smoothly as possible with few detours. At the end of their lives, they are worn out, and left feeling as if like they never accomplished anything. They may become bitter, realizing that the gift of life they were given is almost over without having been enjoyed.

The moments meant to be savored and shared with those closest to you are not about whether or not you go to heaven. They are simply about living, existing, and having a part and a place in the world, if only for a moment.

When you live your life focused only on what happens when it is over, you miss out on all the things that make life worth living.

Life is a journey you take with the people around you. Each choice you make to let an experience pass you by is one more thing you miss out on. It is one more

Dream as if you'll live forever.
Live as if you'll die today.

James Byron Dean
(1931 - 1955)
American film actor.

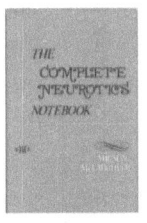

Just when I think I have learned the way to live, life changes.

Mignon McLaughlin
(1913 - 1983)
American Journalist and Author.

memory that you did not take the opportunity to make. Believe in anything you want, just do not let your beliefs become the excuse you use to be afraid of living your life.

The existence of Heaven, Hell, Limbo, and everything in between does not change the fact that you are living today. Where you end up does not change the fact that you have to live now. If you let this life go by without getting the most you can out of it, you are letting the most precious thing you have go unused.

Life is measured in death. That does not mean that life is about death, but just the opposite really. Life is about not being dead; it is about being aware of the world around you and being there in those moments that can slip past without even being noticed. Be the kind of person you wish you were because this is the only chance you have to live the kind of life you dream of.

The journey through life is divided into childhood, man and woman hood, and old age. In childhood, we lay the foundation upon which our future life is to be built. In both man and woman hood, we carry out those early aims and ambitions, completing the edifice we began in childhood, and then we enter the final stage of human life; old age. In old age, we await the final call that must come at last to each on of us.

Along the journey of life, we come to where one path leads in one direction and the other in the opposite one. Which path we choose will determine the future course of our life. Whether we succeed or fail depends entirely upon which path we take.

One path leads to success and happiness, while the other leads to heartaches, disappointment, ultimate

Chapter 1

failure. The path to success is more difficult to travel at first, but it becomes smooth and is easy farther on. The other path starts out downhill and is easy to take, but the farther we travel on it, the rougher it gets.

Remember; life is precious, and seemingly short. It is best to begin on the right path. Should we err for a moment, we can change directions correcting our course, changing from the downhill journey to the successful one.

How about our needs?

A journey begins with a small step, and so as we take our small step of being born into this world, we begin our journey. We initially have people who help us on this journey: our parents and other family members.

Just as treasures are uncovered from the earth, so virtue appears from good deeds, and wisdom appears from a pure and peaceful mind. To walk safely through the maze of human life, one needs the light of wisdom and the guidance of virtue.

Siddhãrtha Gautama Buddha
(563 BCE to 483 BCE)
A spiritual teacher from the Indian subcontinent, on whose teachings Buddhism was founded.

Some people have great friends helping them, and their journeys seem to be easier for them, while others are not so blessed, and so their journeys are not as easy.

Choosing to make good decisions will determine how others treat you, and this will make your journey easier.

This is not to say life's journey will be easy. Quite the contrary. We are tested and then tested again to see how we handle life's obstacles.

Advancing along our journey requires that we correctly learn and grow from the obstacles we have in our lives. In order to do this, we must pass tests, and once we have passed them, then we move on to the next level in life's journey.

THE JOURNEY

Everything has been figured out, except how to live.

Jean-Paul Sartre
(1905 - 1980)
French existentialist philosopher, playwright, novelist, screenwriter, political activist, biographer, and literary critic.

It's not easy being a parent. This is neither a process nor a natural talent. It is a skill that develops throughout the days.

Patricia Goodrum Decelles
40 years as a kindergarten teacher at Boucher-De La Bruère School in Montreal.

In order to achieve our goals in life, the demands of nature and social life must also be considered. We all have needs as human beings that must be satisfied! A need is a requirement of nature or of social life for which we assume a possible quick satisfaction.

This is the kind of definition that you usually find in dictionaries. To promote understanding, consider the hierarchy of needs developed from observations regarding motivation made in the 1950s by the psychologist Abraham Maslow.

Maslow's "pyramid of needs" is well known and used by psychologists, educators, researchers, and behaviorists as well as managers and marketers. This hierarchy of motives, based on the needs of the individual, consists of five main levels:

1. *Physiological needs:* eating, drinking, sleeping, etc.
2. *Physical security needs:* a roof over one's head, clothes, etc.
3. *A need for belonging and affection:* receiving signs of recognition, belonging to a group.
4. *Esteem needs:* self-esteem.
5. *A need of self-realization*.

According to Maslow, we seek first to meet every need at a given level before considering the needs at of the next level of the pyramid. Not surprisingly, as an example, we search to meet the physiological needs above the needs of security. That is why in a situation where our survival is at stake, we are willing to take risks.

A need will help with the motivation of the person after the lower-level needs are met. Everyone moves

Chapter **1**

If you plan on being anything less than you are capable of being, you will probably be unhappy all the days of your life.

Abraham Harold Maslow
(1908 - 1970)
American professor of psychology at Brandeis University, Brooklyn College, New School for Social Research and Columbia University who created Maslow's hierarchy of needs.

Life belongs to the living, and he who lives must be prepared for changes.

Johann Wolfgang von Goethe
(1749 - 1832)
A German writer, pictorial artist, biologist, theoretical physicist, and polymath. He is considered the supreme genius of modern German literature.

from the satisfaction of a given need to the aspiration of a need that is yet to be realized.

Self-realization begins at childhood. Physiological needs are met. It is urgent to consider the person as more than an object that needs to be cared for and fed. The satisfaction of the need for security and belonging comes from outside - own and belong - only develop the confidence we have gaps that outside can fill out.

With membership, identity is constructed; it is equally important to lay the foundation for who the person is at the psychological level, which accompanies the development of uniqueness.

How does Maslow's theory apply to you?
All living organisms, whether it be a microscopic amoeba, a whale, or a child, they all have inherent needs.

In the case of a child the realization of these needs, by the person or with the help of family and community, leads to a healthy development and a solid foundation for adulthood.

Any deficiencies in these requirements can cripple a person, preventing his or her performance at home, at school, and in adult life.

Can we avoid death?

The cessation of life is a scary proposition for most people. In order to think about life in any sort of rational way, we must first come to terms with the reality of death. Nobody can avoid it, and there is no negotiating your way out of it when your time comes. If we do not find a way to deal with this, then our entire lives will be focused on that one moment. For

THE JOURNEY

Andrea Jung (right) with Reese Witherspoon, Michelle Obama, and Hillary Clinton at the International Women of Courage Awards, March 10, 2010.

> There is purpose in my work... At the end of the day, that trumps all things.
>
> Andrea Jung, (1959 -)
> She is a Canadian-American businesswoman. She is the executive chairman and former CEO of Avon Products Inc.

> I have just three things to teach: simplicity, patience, compassion. These three are your greatest treasures.
>
> Lao Tzu
> (6th century BCE)
> Philosopher of ancient China, best known as the author of the *Tao Te Ching*.

people like that, life has become a destination rather than a journey.

There are religions based on the principle that this life is little more than a test to determine where we will go when we die. There are others who think that we must cleanse ourselves of all material connections and desires in order to achieve a peaceful afterlife. The problem with either of these views is that they devalue the experiences we are having in the here and now.

It may be very comforting to think that when we are done living here there is a wonderful place where we will go or a new state of being we will attain where death will no longer trouble us, but to focus on death is to ignore life. Whatever you believe, we are here. We are physical creatures.

We have needs and desires and the capacity to experience pleasure and pain. To ignore these facts is to ignore the truth of who we are.

I, too, have thought about what happens when we die, and I have formulated my own opinions on the matter. I do not believe, though, that it is possible to know anything for sure.

Therefore, I believe that any philosophy that tells us we must sacrifice happiness in this life, so that we can attain it in the next, is leading us down a road to bad time on Earth paved with good intentions.

I am not suggesting that people should do whatever feels good and that everyone should try everything at least once, or any such nonsense. I am simply saying that we should not let our fear of the afterlife rule our decisions in this life.

Chapter 1

Focus on Excellence instead of Success –
When you focus on success, you can easily fall into the trap of comparing yourself to others, looking over your shoulder, feeling envious, playing office politics, and /or competing against coworkers instead of collaborating. However, when you focus on excellence, you measure yourself against your own growth and potential. You strive to be the best you can be. You simply focus on getting better every day, and this makes work more meaningful and rewarding.

Try to be a good person. Do not harm others or yourself on purpose. Help your fellow man when he is in need. Just do not make yourself miserable in the hope that it will gain you entrance into Heaven. A lot of people will be there who enjoyed their lives.

Remember that while final the destination of life may be important, it is not the only thing of importance. Live a good life. Do not focus so much on what is to come that you are unable to enjoy what you have.

Do simplicity and effort work?

Our daily challenges consist of making changes within ourselves. Dare to venture out and grow, explore nature, and expand your horizons. Take bigger steps, and do not be fearful about the risks you take. Experience the brighter side of life, where opportunities appear, and reconnect you to discovering a "new world".

Change is obviously a slow process! Finding your place within the universe is not only a course of study, but is rather, something that follows from commitment time and energy.

Simplicity and effort work if we, in general, believe in the concept of sudden transformation. Time and patience are prized within all of us. All the details of life are presented in daily lessons. We face the everyday routines of living.

We each have our own purpose. The meaning of life is different for everyone. Being your *authentic self* allows you to be open to grow, and when you see that you have control over how to choose to deal with your own true path, choices to explore will appear.

Remember that getting in touch with our authentic self is a lifelong process. Those unwilling to accept the learning process will never progress. In order to improve, we need to learn what life has to teach us. We never graduate from life, but we are students of life. Striving to learn all the lessons we can is a year-round "school of challenges" that enables us to continue to grow.

Can I use short cuts in life?

Many students, after completion of their secondary school, see going on to higher education as a long process and prefer to start work immediately. At the time, yes, it might seem like a great short cut in life to get a job and start earning a salary at an early stage, but when one wants to be successful in life, then it is actually the longest route to accomplishment.

One of the greatest pains to human nature is the pain of a new idea.

Walter Bagehot,
(1826 - 1877)
British Political Scientist.

A person who did not complete a specialty trade, college, or university education has to, in most cases, work twice as hard in life, if not more, than those that completed these education levels.

Uneducated people are more likely to fail at what they do since they do not have the educational know-how to effectively use their own knowledge. To be more realistic, it is difficult to secure employment without a proper educational background in this new economy.

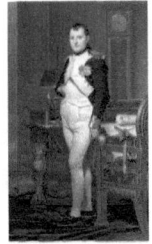

The infectiousness of crime is like that of the plague.

Napoléon Bonaparte
(1769 - 1821)
French military and political leader during the latter stages of the French Revolution.

The sooner people realize that there is no such thing as short-cuts to life the better they can secure proper living standards for themselves and their loved ones. The only shortcut in life is to use the right channels diligently and operate within the limits of the law, while respecting others.

When we use a right and possible available path, it ensures fewer hurdles and lets everything in life run

Chapter 1

A journey of a thousand miles begins with a single step.

Lao Tzu
(6th-century BCE)
A philosopher of ancient China, best known as the author of the Tao Te Ching.

If you do not think about the future, you cannot have one.

John Galsworthy
(1867 - 1933)
English novelist and playwright who won the Nobel Prize in Literature in 1932.

smoothly, but this does not mean that someone should not do things the trouble-free way, as long as that path keeps the person within the limits of good conscience.

Remember that as human beings mostly, we like to take short cuts in life in order to reach our destination, but when we do this, we usually ignore procedures, or rules, that are in place - and sometime the life lessons from those who have traveled the path before us. Regarding wealth, people often turn to crime as a way of getting rich overnight, but what we, as human beings, should understand is that wealth acquired through criminal activities does not really last, and in most cases, it has a lot of sacrifices involved, which end up claiming our lives or the lives of our loved ones.

How can I use these benefits?
You are responsible for choosing your journey and your path to success. Your whole life is challenging you to accept many carefully timed journeys and paths, so you can become the person you know you can be in your world.

Only when you take the time to slow down and appreciate each moment will you truly find those things that you are searching for.

One-day happiness may be found in a blue sky or in watching a bird from your window. It may come in the form of a giggling baby or a smile from a stranger.

Receiving, or even giving, a sincere compliment may be the highlight of one day, while waking up beside the person that you love may be the best part of another.

THE JOURNEY

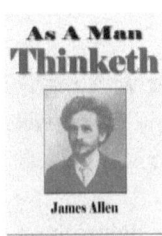

As A Man Thinketh

James Allen

All that you accomplish or fail to accomplish with your life is the direct result of your thoughts.

James Allen
(1864 – 1912)
British philosophical writer known for his inspirational books and poetry and as a pioneer of the self-help movement.

Many people are so focused on what is going to be coming in the future that they miss what is happening around them. They rush forward and end up missing many special moments. Worse yet, some people brush these moments off as insignificant in the grand scheme of things. They fail to realize that these moments are the wealth of life.

People wander through their lives searching for things' such as happiness, wealth, and love, etc. They rush from point A to point B looking for these things and always thinking about where they are going to go tomorrow.

Life has become very task-orientated for the vast majority of the population. The term "Rat Race" comes to mind when thinking about how it is that many people approach life.

I am not saying that you should walk through life without a destination in mind. If your greatest goal is to look for little moments to collect, you will never move forward in your life. Everybody needs a dream to work towards.

During this journey, it is important to remember to slow down and take time each day to reflect on what was good with that day's journey. One should be careful not to focus on the negative things that happened during the day, unless there is a significant lesson in them, which would then actually be a positive thing: a learning experience.

Remember that when you slow down and appreciate the journey, life is going to seem so much more enjoyable. You will reduce your stress and be able to walk through life with a smile on your face. You will be able to focus on events that are significant to you.

Chapter 1

The world is a dangerous place to live; not because of the people who are evil, but because of the people who don't do anything about it.

Albert Einstein
(1879 - 1955)
German-born theoretical physicist who developed the Theory of General Relativity, effecting a revolution in physics. For this achievement, Einstein is often regarded as the Father of Modern Physics and one of the most prolific intellects in human history.

Wishing to be friends is quick work, but friendship is a slow ripening fruit.

Aristotle
(384 BC – 322 BC)

But be careful not to live your life in a way that pleases somebody else but doesn't please you. At the end of the day, you are the only one you have to answer to.

What are the steps along the way?

Along our journey, we will be confronted with many situations. Some will be filled with joy, and some will be filled with heartache.

How we react to what we are faced with determines what kind of outcome the rest of our journey through life will be like.

When things do not always go our way, we have two alternatives to choose from in order to deal with the circumstances. We can focus on the fact that things did not go as we had hoped they would and let life pass us by. Or, we can make the best out of the situation and know that these are only temporary setbacks.

Time stops for no one, and if we allow ourselves to focus on the negative, we might miss out on some really amazing things that life has to offer. We cannot go back to the past, but we can learn, experience, and gain from it – and then move forward. It is the heartaches, as well as the hardships, that in the end help to make us stronger people.

The people that we meet on our journey are people that we are destined to meet. Every person comes into our lives for some reason, or another, and we do not always know the purpose until it is too late. Each one plays some kind of role. Some people we meet may stay throughout a lifetime; others may only stay for a short while.

THE **JOURNEY**

It is often the people who stay for only a short time that end up making a lasting impression, not only in our lives, but in our hearts as well. Although we may not realize it at the time, they will change our lives in a way we never could imagine.

Accomplish something every day of your life.

Walter Annenberg
(1908 - 2002)
American publisher, philanthropist, and diplomat.

To think that one person can so profoundly effect your life forever... well... that one person can do that is truly a blessing. It is because of these encounters that we learn some of life's best lessons, and sometimes we even learn a little about ourselves.

People tend to come and go in our lives quickly, but sometimes we are lucky enough to meet that one special person that will stay in our hearts forever, no matter what. Even though we may not always end up being with that person, that other individual remain for as long as we would like, the lessons that we learn from them - and the experiences that we gain from meeting that person - often stay with us forever.

Look back at the person you were a few years ago and compare it to the person you now have become. By looking deep into your soul, you may realize that the person you are today could not exist if it were not for the things that have happened in the past or for the people you have met.

There are very few people who can get through life based on their brillance and their top performance that can ignore relationships. And if they do, you don't wanna know' em anyway.

Jeff Maurer
Author of the book
Rich in America:
Secrets to Creating and Preserving Wealth.

Everything that happens in life happens for a reason, and sometimes that means we must face heartaches in order to experience joy.

Think back! We grow rapidly as babies and prepare for many years of school and learning. We sometimes move from one house to another, date different people, travel or stay in our local area. As we age, and our body goes through the many transformations

Chapter 1

The dictionary is the only place that success comes before work.
Hard work is the price we must pay for success. I think you can accomplish anything if you're willing to pay the price.

Vince Lombardi
(1913 - 1970)
American football coach.

from birth to death, we can visually observe these changes that take place in our lives.

We start out vulnerable and dependent, and before the journey is completed, we can easily end up in a similar situation once more as we age, that is when it becomes harder to do the particular things we once did. The path seems to come full circle as we become elderly and once again need the kind of assistance we needed as infants.

We work hard to accomplish our goals and discipline ourselves to be productive people who can cause positive change in this wonderful world we live in. We start out learning from others, and if we are lucky enough, down the path, we can teach others the information we have obtained, as we pass through certain stages of development.

We go from student to teacher as we start learning from others and then, with knowledge behind us, we can begin to give advice and help others because of the experiences we have had.

We should not rush through our journey because every stage along the way can never be taken back or relived. We need to continue moving forward because life does not give us time to do things over.

Life is short, and as we look back, it sometimes seems as if it was only yesterday, that we were in a particular place and time, feeling a certain emotion, when in reality, it may have been many years before.

Remember that life is a continuous journey of wonderful experiences that shape us. We should always embrace our joys and sorrows, knowing that they are all part of where we are going and who we are. The happiness we feel and the many emotions have taken us up and down this magnificent road of beauty, love, peace, joy, and loss that together are all part of life's journey. Every step along the way should be savored, understood, and enjoyed as it is meant to be in order to make this unique remarkable journey complete.

How can I get rid of my guilt?

Guilt is the signal that you have a working conscience, and some guilt is appropriate. If you have done something wrong, it is good that you feel guilty. If you do not, it is likely you are a sociopath. If your guilt is from a wrong action on your part, set about making it right, so that you avoid guilt's nasty relative: shame.

Sometimes guilt is obvious because it occupies our minds and can reveal itself in the form of stress. Make sure that you are feeling guilt and not worry. When we feel guilty, we focus intently on events that have already happened. When we worry, it is about events that are presently happening or may happen in the future.

Do not dwell on negative, guilty feelings; they lead to inappropriate levels of shame and self-loathing. You should move on with your life. Recognize that nobody's perfect and that we all make mistakes, and determine that this is one mistake you will not repeat.

Engage in activities that are positive and affirming, and where you have opportunities to do good; allow yourself to see how the same mistake that made you feel guilty has now resulted in your being a better, more conscientious person.

Food, love, career, and mothers, the four major guilt groups.

Cathy Guisewite
(1950 -)
The cartoonist who created the comic strip *Cathy*, about a career woman facing the issues and challenges of eating, work, relationships, and being a mother. As *Cathy* put it in one of her strips, "The four basic guilt groups."

Glory, built on selfish principles, is shame and guilt.

William Cowper
(1731 – 1800)
English poet and hymnodist.

Chapter 1

> All life demands struggle.
> Those who have everything given to them become lazy, selfish, and insensitive to the real values of life.
> The very striving and hard work that we so constantly try to avoid is the major building block in the person we are today.
>
> Ralph Ransom
> American author of
> *Steps on the Stairway.*

Remember that most of the guilt comes from other people telling us directly or insinuating that we should feel guilty. No one has the right to make you feel culpable. Realize that many people who attempt to play on your guilt are controlling or manipulating you. True friends, with your best interests at heart, will not try to make you feel guiltier. They will offer you the opportunity to confess and unburden yourself, help you make amends, and then bolster you positively; they will not use your guilt as a weapon against you.

What about walking around in a circle?

Life is a journey, but not a very dazzling one if all we do is keep walking around in a circle. Which ever of life's paths we journey down, the road is going to be laced with disappointments and tribulations that come and go. It could be a ten-year old job, where you realize that you have gained one year's experience and repeated the work ten times over. In some ways, it is very hard to leave something like that behind despite its evaporating challenges.

The journey to overcome such an event is always hard. It is painfully difficult to move on in life from something that was once appreciated. The decision to move forward though - toward something fresh and desired will surely be beneficial and will most likely bring new situations where you can find a new potential relationship.

Remember that you have gotten lazy and started to walk in circles, if there is no enthusiasm, if life does not tingle, and if you keep seeing the same scenery repeatedly. There is always a fresh view available in life to spark one awake and quicken his or her pace. Life can be chosen to be lived like a journey that moves forward into striking possibilities.

Is life a journey?

A journey is not just a voyage, walk, run, drive, or flight from one place to another. The passing of time is the biggest journey that any of us will undertake, and the best thing is, it is unavoidable.

It is impossible to stop time, so you need to treat life as a journey because life is a journey. Sure, there are some destinations along the way, such as graduation, marriage, childbirth, and more, but when you get down to it, life is ever changing, and there is nothing you can do to stop it.

Even if we do not exactly know what we want out of life, we know what we need to do in order to make ourselves content with our existence.

From the time we are children, we are told to try hard in school, so we can get into a respectable college, and we are told to get into a good college, so we can get a lucrative job, and we are then told to get a well-paying job, so we can make a lot of money.

College, occupations, and money are all destinations that we want to reach in life, but we must understand the journey behind them in order to live fully.

Though it may seem off-topic, people who embark on journeys often learn much more than they originally intend to. When you treat life like a journey and pay attention to everything that is going on, instead of simply wishing that you were already at your destination, you tend to learn more than expected by picking things up along the way.

Life does not just stop after you reach your destination. The truth is, each destination only continues your journey through life. When you finally

All the information will never be in. You'll never know in advance whether a decision is right or wrong. Most often you have to choose one of the roads and make it the right choice by your actions after the decision is made.

Albert J. Bernstein, Ph.D.
American author of *How To Deal With Emotionally Explosive People*, *Dinosaur Brains*, *Emotional Vampires*, *Neanderthals at Work*, and *Sacred Bull*.

Chapter 1

All things are difficult before they are easy.

Thomas Fuller
(1608 – 1661) English churchman and historian. He is now remembered for his writings, particularly his *Worthies of England*, published after his death.

You must live in the present, launch yourself on every wave, find your eternity in each moment.

Henry David Thoreau
(1817-1862) American author, poet, philosopher, abolitionist, naturalist, tax resister, development critic, surveyor, historian, and leading transcendentalist.

get what you want, you realize that there is something else for you to do, a new set of problems to deal with, or a new set of desires tugging at your heart. You cannot expect to be completely finished with life once you have accomplished a goal and reached a destination because life still goes on.

The focus on destinations, on outcomes, is rewarded in our culture. To live life as a journey goes against the values of this culture, a culture that rewards those who set and reach goals and those who achieve " great " things, including position and wealth. We even reward those who are celebrities, with our time and attention, regardless of whether or not they make real contributions to society.

When society's values are strongly focused on destination consciousness, it is hard for an individual to live with a different set of values. Summoning it up, when people are given whatever they want without earning it, they never learn the true value of it because they do not experience the hard work that goes into getting it.

Remember that this is the journey of your life. Work for your goals and do everything you can to be successful at whatever you wish to do in life. Just do not forget how you succeeded. Do not forget the people you meet along the way, the memories you create, the tricks you learn, or the thoughts brewing in the back of your head. Embrace your entire life by willingly accepting that it is one long journey. When you do accomplish your goals you will not just remember what you did, you will recall how you did it.

Am I living in the present?

A common notion in world religions, one that is at least thousands of years old, has to do with the idea of living in the present. This is another way of expressing the idea of life as a journey. To live fully in the present could be called " enlightenment," because doing so results in gaining understanding and in the spreading of knowledge.

Thinking big has led to all of humankind's greatest achievements.

Donald Trump
(1946 -)
American business magnate, television personality, and author.

When we do not spend our time thinking about our past, regretting past experiences or decisions, holding grudges against those who have wronged us, or nursing old wounds, we have an amazing amount of energy available to us in the present.

When we do not spend our time thinking about the future, worrying about how our life is going to be tomorrow or next year, or fearing that we will not accomplish certain things, that our life might get worse, that we might get sick, or that our relationships might end, we have an amazing amount of energy available to us in the present.

It is said that the present is pregnant with the future.

François-Marie Arouet–Voltaire
(1694 - 1778)
French Enlightenment writer, historian and philosopher famous for his wit and for his advocacy of civil liberties, including freedom of religion, freedom of expression, free trade, and separation of church and state.

Most of us are unaware of how much of our energy is drained from our bodies and from our psyches every day, so-to-speak sucked into the past or into the future. Some of us worry a lot. We experience a sense of low-level stress in our bodies at various times throughout the day. It almost feels as if some part of us is trying to hold the world together.

Most of us walk around with this tension. It goes away from time to time. When we are really focused on some project, we are in the present, and our worries disappear.

When we are having fun with friends or family, we are focused on the present, and our worries recede. This means that we know how to live in the present. We just do not know how to do it habitually!

Chapter **1**

> The hottest place in Hell is reserved for those who remain neutral in times of great moral conflict.
>
> Martin Luther King, jr
> (1929 - 1968)
> American clergyman, activist, and prominent leader in the African-American Civil Rights Movement.

> We all talk to ourselves.
> A major key to success exists in what we say to ourselves, which helps to shape our attitude and mindset.
>
> Darren L. Johnson
> Business Coach.
> Life Guide. Speaker.
> Author.

Living in the present, focusing on the journey, is probably one of the most important things any person can do to make his or her life satisfying and joy-filled. It is obviously not easy to do, especially in this fast-spaced culture, but it can be done.

Ironically, living life as a journey is a destination worth seeking, a goal worthy of our time and attention.

Remember that as the wise teachers of the past have said, the present moment is all that really exists. Neither the past nor the future has any reality in the present, except in our minds and imaginations. Only those who have actually experienced living in the present on a day-to-day basis can fully understand the incredible freedom that comes from such action.

Am I at the right place at the right time?

There are many of us who take life for granted, and who believe that the path we most take is set before us. There are many who believe that some of us " are born with silver spoons in our mouths," that we want for nothing, and that we are lucky to have what we have. However, for the majority, it is not the case.

Sometimes it is about being in the right place at the right time and grabbing, with both hands, the opportunities that present themselves. Living is all about decisions!

What happens if you take the left path instead of the right? What happens if you turn down the opportunity of marriage and a potential family? What happens if you decide to go abroad? What happens if you decide to try your hand at something completely new?

So many decisions, and that is what life is about, from beginning to end, a series of decisions and decision-making.

Life is all about making those choices that we think are right for us, at particular points in time. Whether or not there is some kind of *Guide* helping us, gently persuading us to take the left path instead of the right, we will never know for sure. However, the whole of life is all about *decisions.* Indeed, we will never know what we are capable of unless we try.

There's place and means for every man alive.

William Shakespeare
(1564 - 1616)
An English poet and playwright, widely regarded as the greatest writer in the English language and the world's pre-eminent dramatist.

Life is what you make it, and those words are true to a point. However, there are some who may believe otherwise. Such people are stuck with their "lot." Through no fault of their own, they may not have any ambition to rise above their circumstances. They fulfill their own self-fulfilling prophecy, and it is normally a negative one.

Some people may be poor financially or in spirit and may have very low self-esteem. Most of them find it extremely difficult, nearly impossible, to change their circumstances. They may look upon life as not a life filled with opportunity and hope, but instead filled with drudgery and with the absence of any hope at all.

Their journey upon life's path is filled with heartache and despair, and one has to wonder whether some people have been dealt annoying or stupid for their actions. Life is unfair when one looks at the whole picture. However, at the same time, life is a destination, which all those who are born must all travel to and, there are so many unanswered questions to life: Why are some children born into famine and forced to starve to death? Why are some children born into poverty and destitution? Why is it

Chapter 1

that some people are born into such wealth that they are, in some cases, richer than some countries?

Life is unfair, and for some questions, there are no know answers.

Suffice it to say that life is, for better or worse. For those of us who are lucky enough to witness a sunset or sunrise, to see the full moon, and to witness the beauty of this world, life must never be underrated. For all those who are born into poverty, there is always hope that people can rise from their abject and dire situation.

There are numerous examples of this time and again, and it is the *mindset* of a person that can trap someone into their present predicament. To change that *mindset* can be the hardest thing to do, for it seems that we have been conditioned to think a certain way about ourselves, according to who we are. However, there are many people who have broken free from such conditioned thinking and have gone on to higher achievements and goals.

In life, anything is achievable if you really want it. It is all about taking that first step in the journey of life. See where that first step leads, for there is not one of us who can be held down if we really set out to get what we want out of life. Just be prepared to accept that life may have other plans for you as well on your journey.

It has to be noted, too, that anyone who shows the determination to rise above his or her lot, no matter how bad the circumstances and surroundings, quite often receives the needed help to do so. Their mindset and willingness to help themselves is such that they seem to attract like-minded people, and to

My greatest challenge has been to change the mindset of people.
Mindsets play strange tricks on us.
We see things the way our minds have instructed our eyes to see.

Muhammad Yunus
(1940 –)
Bangladeshi economist and founder of the Grameen Bank, an institution that provides microcredit (small loans to poor people possessing no collateral) to help its clients establish creditworthiness and financial self-sufficiency.

THE **JOURNEY**

Courage is not the absence of despair; it is, rather, the capacity to move ahead in spite of despair.

Rollo May
(1909 - 1994)
American existential psychologist.
He authored the influential book *Love and Will* during 1969. He is often associated with both humanistic psychology and existentialist philosophy.

A lot of times people look at the negative side of what they feel they can't do.
I always look on the positive side of what I can do.

Chuck Norris
(1940 -)
American martial artist and actor.

get the help they need. This often works in reverse too.

For example, those people who, through no fault of their own, find themselves stuck in circumstances in which they feel there is no hope often become trapped in a mindset of hopelessness and despair.

Depression sets in, and they lose all hope in life and in what life has to offer. Very often, such people attract similar types of people, that is people who, like them, are negative, and only too willing to stay "down."

In many respects in life, human beings are like magnets, attracting positive or negative people toward themselves, depending on the kind of mindset they have. This happens time and again, and it is amazing to see.

By a simple change in a person's philosophy and view of life, opportunities suddenly become available, where one might have thought that there were none before. Doors begin to swing open where once they stayed firmly shut.

And people who are of a positive frame of mind suddenly find others attracted to them and willing to help, too.

It is all about a change in how you view your life, and with this in mind, life can be managed for the good or bad. Circumstances that we may find ourselves in can be changed, but to change them, we have to have an absolute determination to manage life to suit ourselves. With life comes vibrations, which we, as human beings, can control. However, one must know

Chapter **1**

We can't let wrong mind-sets, a negative past, or other people's opinions discourage us or cause us to give up and quit pressing forward.

Joel Osteen
(1963 -)
American author, televangelist, and the senior pastor of Lakewood Church in Houston, Texas.

A desire to be in charge of our own lives, a need for control, is born in each of us.
It is essential to our mental health, and our success, that we take control.

Robert Foster Bennett
(1933 -)
Former United States Senator from Utah and a member of the Republican Party.

how to do this in order to escape from the kind of life that we may otherwise find ourselves in.

Overall, life is a journey, and our destination is never really known. The only certain thing in life is death. So with that in mind, we must make the best of what we have now, while we are here. We need to change whatever we do not like, and every kind of circumstance can be changed if the determination to do so is there.

Remember that the more positive vibes we send out upon our journey in life, the more we will attract the kind of help we want and need but if we send out negative vibes, we will reap different results. Until we realize that we can change the circumstances we may have been born into, we human beings will remain trapped in the belief that we cannot change our journey in life for the better.

Can I expect many false journeys?
Life is a journey, and each part of your life is a separate, shorter journey. Your success determines the quality of the destination.

What are the benefits of my destination? How can I use these benefits?

You are responsible for choosing the journey and the destination. Your whole life is made up of challenging yourself to accept many carefully timed journeys and destinations. Become the person you know you can be in your world!

Everyone should expect many false journeys in life. Many of these journeys are filled with high expectations and journeys that were undertaken without realizing first how long it would take to

It is not what we get, but who we become, what we contribute... that gives meaning to our lives.

Tony Robbins
(1960 -)
American self-help author and motivational speaker. He became well known through his infomercials and self-help books.

Children begin by loving their parents; after a time, they judge them; rarely, if ever, do they forgive them.

Oscar Wilde
(1854 – 1900)
An Irish writer and poet.

complete them, that is, to be successful. A fortunate journey requires not only the feeling of that one has the necessary talent to accomplish the work or the feeling that it will be easy. Such a journey is a lot more then a feeling. We all learn from it!

Catalogue your skills, talents, abilities, experiences, and knowledge about yourself. Your journeys should be well planned before you start them. Ask yourself these questions:
Do I have the desire to do the necessary work to finish the journey? What will I learn along the journey? What will I learn about myself during the journey? What skills will I master? What financial and spiritual benefits will I obtain?

Life is short. Commit to a plan after doing a full evaluation of how you expect to benefit from your actions and your work – for and of how your loved ones will most likely benefit.

Each destination makes you a better person. Ideally, each of your destinations will give you more self-confidence, happiness, and self-control, which will help you succeed, and prepare you for even better selections of journeys and destinations in the future.

Remember that you are in charge of your life. Building a successful life takes a great deal of planning, action, and the opening of doors along the journey, so that you can arrive at your destination on time, prepared for whatever is necessary to make it successful. To be successful during your life, you need to evaluate all the potential journeys and destinations available to you. In so doing, your life will be meaningful, exciting, thrilling, and successful.

Chapter 1

Does my journey have a meaning?

Yes, life is a journey through time, not space, and most of us are conscientiously trying to avoid reaching our destination. However, it seems that too many people forget that a journey is to be enjoyed. Otherwise, what is the point of taking the trip?

I don't think my parents liked me. They put a live teddy bear in my crib.

Woody Allen
(1935 -)
Award-winning American screenwriter, director, actor, comedian, author, and playwright, whose career spans over half a century.

During the journey, one must take time to smell the flowers that spring up unexpectedly by the roadside. One must always be mindful to stop at the places one come across along the way and fully explore them, seeking out all the attractions that each has to offer.

The love of your journey's companion, the birth of a child, the recognition of peers, the doing of small acts of kindness that cost you nothing and bring happiness to another, and those times of serene contemplation when you feel the journey has been worthwhile, those are the times that are the fuel that gives you the energy to take the next step and continue on the journey.

When I was a kid my parents moved a lot, but I always found them.

Rodney Dangerfield
(1921 – 2004)
American comedian, and actor.

Remember that your journey should have a purpose to provide your spirit with meaning, for aimless questioning is a waste of time and energy. Granted, there can, on occasion, be moments when even pointless wandering can fill the spirit with the sights of unexpected and unplanned for beauty, but those times are even more glorious when stumbled upon by the purposeful mind that is aware of the path being traveled and of why it is being traveled.

What do I owe my parents?

Parents' skills often determine our perception of what we owe our parents, and one's perception can range from nothing at all to respect and gratitude. The relationship between a parent and child is based only on emotions, which can become healthy or unhealthy as a child grows and matures.

If human beings were perfect, parents would have children who grow up with unconditional love, respect, and appreciation for their parents.

Because family history as well as economic, educational, and societal circumstances have an impact on us, there is a domino effect on everyone's parenting skills. Thus, when we are asked what we owe our parents, the answers are based on personal experiences, and on the relationship between the child and parent.

Children who are raised by emotionally abusive parents may have low self-esteem and an internal resentment for their parents, and if that contempt grows, that child may very well grow up to be disrespectful and rude towards the parents.

Single parenting may result in a child feeling that he or she owes his or her life to the parents regardless of how the child was treated or raised. On the other hand, a responsible parent who is strict yet loving and instills a healthy set of values and morals in the child will earn the respect, love, and gratitude of the child. However, with so many teen parents, who are not mature enough to understand fully the emotional and psychological needs of a child, the number of children who are growing up unruly is increasing.

We should love, respect, and honor our parents despite the fact that things have changed, and the family unit is almost non-existent now. Today, many single parents raising children alone are struggling to pay the bills and keep a roof over their heads, and stress is part of every day. Many parents today are,

It's nice to go to small places where we had a lot of fans. They followed our career and it's kind of a way to say thank you to them and do it for a good cause.

Guy Lafleur
(1951 -)
Former Canadian professional ice hockey player who is widely regarded as one of the most naturally gifted and popular players ever to play professional ice hockey. Between 1971 and 1991, he played in an NHL career-spanning 17 seasons and five Stanley Cup championships.

intentionally by choice, focused on earning a living, rather than on parenting.

We also have an epidemic of legal and illegal drug use and addiction. This affects parenting skills and how kids feel about their parents. Some children feel neglected, angry, and as if they need to stand up for themselves, while other children of addicts take on the responsibility of their parents, and the reverse-role parenting leads the child to feel obligated to take care of his or her mom or dad.

Remember that there is really no single answer to what we owe our parents, unless we become judgmental and impose our beliefs on society as a whole. The question is rather personal one, based on each child's reality.

Is life reliable?

No one owes you anything; you are not entitled to a free ride at work, at home, in school, on the playing field...whatever your playing field may be, or in your relationships with others, or with your God. What you receive are gifts. What you do with those gifts is up to you, be they financial, spiritual, intangible, or tangible.

Some of those gifts may have double edges, but they are still viable sources of learning and growing if you accept what this life has in store for you, at full face value, and ride with it to the end. The best thing to do is simply to take 100% responsibility for your life!

No one owes you anything, and past deeds do not always guarantee future deeds. Just because someone does and has been doing something does not mean the person will continue to do so. Perhaps you have not considered that everyone has the right to change and to do or not do anything at anytime for

Refusing to ask for help when you need it is refusing someone the chance to be helpful.

Ric Ocasek
(1949 -)
American musician and music producer.

anyone. Not realizing this is perhaps the source of all our frustrations regarding others.

Our expectations concerning others frustrate us because we are creatures of habit; people tend to assume that the habits one has today are going to be the habits he or she will have forever, but this is seldom so.

The people around us get used to our habits because they make them feel comfortable. They are the "familiar things" about us. They are observable, but you also have to remember that they are unreliable. Life is unreliable!

Remember that you do not know what the next day will bring; life is unreliable. At the same time, people can be deceptive because you do not know whether or not they will still be around tomorrow. This does not mean you should lose faith and trust in people. It simply means that people are under no obligation to you or anyone. So, let others live so that you too may live.

How many times a day should I say thank you?

When someone does something for you, you should say thank you and mean it. When someone wishes you well, you should say thank you. When someone makes your life just a little bit easier or brighter, you should say thank you. When someone helps you get back on your feet after you have stumbled, you should say thank you. When someone shows you right from wrong, you should say thank you. When someone corrects your mistake, you should say thank you. When someone makes way to let you pass, you should say thank you. When someone sacrifices her own comfort, so that you may enjoy yours, you should say thank you.

The best thing about
the future is
that it comes
one day at
a time.

Abraham
Lincoln
(1809 - 1865)
16th President of the United States, serving from March 1861 until his assassination in April 1865. He successfully led his country through a great constitutional, military, and moral crisis – the American Civil War – preserving the Union, while ending slavery, and promoting economic and financial modernization.

Chapter **1**

It is a simple phrase, and said sincerely, "thank you" can mean so much to the person you intend it for. It will make her feel as though you appreciate her, that you genuinely care that she is there, and that you recognize her efforts to make your life better.

If you really mean it, you might also tell her that you love her. It is easy to forget that no one ever needs to do anything for you. No one owes you anything. You do not have a right to be treated kindly.

God gave you a gift of 86,400 seconds today. Have you used one to say "thank you?"

William Arthur Ward
(1921 – 1994)
Author of *Fountains of Faith*, and one of America's most quoted writers of inspirational maxims.

If you are treated well, it is because someone cares for you enough to give you that privilege. It does not hurt anyone to lower your pride, if pride is the reason why you do not say thank you in the first place. Just say it: Thank you!

Remember that nobody owes you anything. You do not deserve a break. Work for it.

How can I ask for help?

Asking for help is fairly easy, once you understand that it must come in the context of a dialogue between people, not just in a question and answer format.

There is so much to accomplish throughout the day that life can become overwhelming. Getting help is often the solution, but asking for help can be difficult. Some people feel as if it will bruise their egos to ask for help, while others are just too shy or feel too awkward to ask.

Learn to take the pressure off yourself and to ask for what you need. You will save yourself a lot of stress and gain more time. And ask for help before frustration and anger take over. This is the first and most important step. If you are someone who tries to do everything and who wants to handle things by himself, it may not be as easy to identify what exactly you need help with. Take a few minutes to think about this.

You should also leave behind feelings of shame and embarrassment. Just because you are asking for help does not mean you are a failure. It is actually wise and a very successful strategy because it will make you less stressed and save you time.

If you feel a bit intimidated asking for help, talk to someone who you are close to, such as a friend or family member. Maybe that person will be able to point you in the right direction. Think about what will happen if the situation is not dealt with and all the weight is on your shoulders.

People generally want to help. They just need to know exactly what is expected of them. State clearly what it is that would be helpful, and be specific.

Abstain from whining. Ordinarily, it will turn people away. Be positive, and you will have the support of people around you. They will often pitch in on their own if they feel you are deserving of help because of the kind of person you are. Then when they do, do not forget to say thank you!

Remember always to be grateful and appreciative when someone has done something to help. That way, if you need to ask for help again, the person will be happy and willing to give you assistance. Furthermore, remember to make yourself available to help others.

Should I drop the ego?
Every human being evolves, and each of us is not only one self but two. One self is the person or

Our prime purpose in this life is to help others. And if you can't help them, at least don't hurt them.

14th Dalai Lama
(1935 -)
He won the Nobel Peace Prize in 1989 and is also well known for his lifelong advocacy for Tibetans inside and outside Tibet.

Chapter 1

Avoid having your ego so close to your position that when your position falls, your ego goes with it.

Colin Luther Powell
(1937 -)
American statesman and a retired four-star general in the United States Army. He was the 65th United States Secretary of State, serving under President George W. Bush from 2001 to 2005. He was the first African-American to serve in that position.

community we have become as a result of a journey that took place in the past. The other self is the person or community we can become as we journey into the future. The other self is the highest future possible. When these two selves talk to each other, we experience the essence of "presencing."

"Presencing" is connecting to the source; who you are and what you need to accomplish. It is the fundamental threshold that you must pass, so that all change efforts do not remain somewhat superficial.

To change, we must touch our essential core, our best future self. To achieve this state of mind, we must learn to drop our egos and our habitual selves in order for the new selves to emerge.

When our two selves begin to communicate, we establish a subtle but very real link to our highest future possibility that can then begin to help and guide us in to situations in which the past cannot offer us useful advice.

Remember that you are the important one to implement change in your life. So drop the ego!

What should I consider?
Will you wait a lifetime for someone somewhere to come to your rescue, wave a magic wand, and instantaneously change your life for the better? Are you praying that one day you will win the lottery and dramatically alter the financial quality of your life? Are you the type of person that sits behind a desk, daydreaming, and hoping to one day rise to top level management without much effort and hard work? Are you hiding in the background, silently praying and

hoping that you will find favors, get noticed, and be thrust into the limelight of your destiny?

These strategies rarely work. Instead, make a deliberate decision to take charge of your life and begin to lead a fulfilled and productive life. Once you have decided to change your life for the better, look first to value yourself, and then take responsibility for your own destiny. Stop doing what does not work and take action.

Value yourself, your life, and your time. Value what you represent. Do not compromise what you are worth for anything. Your current position may not accurately define who you are, but if you place a high value on yourself, you will not only have greater expectations for yourself but also be open to more possibilities and opportunities.

Courage is rightly esteemed the first of human qualities... because it is the quality which guarantees all others.

Sir Winston Leonard Spencer-Churchill
1874-1965
British Conservative politician and statesman known for his leadership of the United Kingdom during World War II.

People who place a high value on themselves can confidently walk into any arena of success and take their place comfortably. They fit right in because this is what they have been waiting for their whole lives, and they know that they deserve it!

Be practical, and stop expecting other people to rescue you from your current distress. People can only do so much. The rest is up to you and your God-given abilities and resolve. Get rid of the dependency syndrome. It incapacitates and blinds you. It keeps you from doing great things with your life and getting the success you have so yearned for.

If you are not going to be the recipient of a large inheritance, or if you have not yet won the lottery, begin to do the right thing by charting your own road's map to success and work intelligently, meticulously, and persistently to achieve your success.

Chapter 1

You only have one life to live. If you plan to live a fulfilled life, stop doing what does not work, and start doing the things that work and change your life for the better. In other words, do something today that produces results!

Remember that if you cannot take radical steps, take small deliberate steps towards the change you desire. One of the greatest impediments to success is procrastination. It is often used as an excuse for inaction to the point that it becomes mind numbing. No one wants to hear that the only reason why you have not managed to turn your idea into reality is because you have been procrastinating! People want to stand and cheer for the doer and the achiever who has taken positive steps to improve the quality of their lives. These are the inspiring stories that we read about everyday, and you too can be the subject of such a story.

Change your life for the better – and why not start now!

Procrastination is one of the most common and deadliest of diseases and its toll on success and happiness is heavy.

Wayne Gretzky
(1961 -)
Canadian former professional ice hockey player and former head coach. He is the leading point-scorer in NHL history, as well as the only NHL player to total over 200 points in one season.

Recommended Reading & References
We suggest consulting the works identified below in order to learn more about the particulars contained in this chapter.

BUTLER-BOWDON, Tom. 50 PSYCHOLOGY CLASSICS: Who we are, How we think, What we do. Gildan Media.
ISBN 1-59659-119-6.

COLLARD, Nathalie. À LA RECHERCHE DU BONHEUR,
Le Quotidien la Presse, Forum, avril 2007. ISBN 0317-9249.

FILLIOZAT, Isabelle. L'INTELLIGENCE DU COEUR, confiance en soi, créativité, aisance relationnelle, autonomie. Marabout, Paris, 40-2625-8.

GEORGE, Bill et al. FINDING YOUR TRUE NORTH.
Jossey-Bass publisher. ISBN 928-0-470-26136-1.

HUSTON, John. 50 FAÇONS DE CHANGER VOTRE VIE.
Amerimag. ISBN 0-65385-575451-1.

ISAACSON, Walter. EINSTEIN, His life and universe.
SIMON & SCHUSTER. ISBN-13-978-0-7432-6473-0.

KENNEDY, John F. Profile of Courage. Harper Classic.
ISBN-13: 978-0-06-085493-5.

MONTEFIORE, Simon Sebag. 101 WORLD HEROES:
Great Men and Women who Changed History.
Metro Books. ISBN-13: 978-1-4351-0509-5.

OSTEEN, Joel. BECOME A BETTER YOU:
7 keys to improving your life every day.
Free Press. ISBN-13: 978-0-7432-9688-5.

PETERS, Thomas J. RE-IMAGE! Business Excellence in a
Disruptive Age. Dorling Kinderly. ISBN 0-7894-9647-X.

ROBBINS, Anthony. UNLIMITED POWER.
Simon & Schuster. ISBN 0-671-62146-7.

ROBINS, Stephen. PRENEZ LA BONNE DÉCISION : améliorez
votre processus décisionnel pour mieux travailler et mieux vivre.
Pearson Éducation France. ISBN 2-7440-6067-4.

SCHMITT, Bernd H. BIG THINK STRATEGY. How to Leverage
Bold Ideas and Leave Small Thinking behind.
Your Coach in a Box. ISBN 1-59659-162-5.

SILLS, Judith. OSER CHANGER.
Stanké Publication. ISBN 2-7604-0481-1.

SMITH, Hyrum W. THE 10 NATURAL LAWS OF SUCCESSFUL
TIME AND LIFE MANAGEMENT.
Warner Books. ISBN 0-446-51741-0.

SULLIVAN, A.M. HUMAN VALUES IN MANAGEMENT: The
Business Philosophy. Dun & Bradstreet Library.
Library of Congress card number: 73-89913.

THE PHILOSOPHY BOOK.
Dorling Kindersley. ISBN 978-2-7613-4125-7.

TOFFLER, Alvin. LE CHOC DU FUTUR.
Médiations. De Noël & Gonthier. Paris, 1971.

TOFFLER, Alvin. THE THIRD WAVE.
Bantam Books. ISBN 0-553-14431-6.

TOFFLER, Alvin & Heidi, REVOLUTIONARY WEALTH.
Alfred A. Knopf. ISBN 0-3-375-40174-1.

TRACY, Brian. CHANGE YOUR THINKING, CHANGE YOUR
LIFE. How to Unlock Your Full Potential for Success and
Achievement. Willey & Sons. ISBN 0-471-73538-8.

TRUDEAU, Pierre Elliott. AGAINST THE CURRENT.
McClelland & Stewart. ISBN 0-7710-6979-0.

TRUDEAU, Pierre Elliott. MEMOIRS.
McClelland & Stewart. ISBN 0-7710-8587-7.

Any man who can drive safely while kissing a pretty girl is simply not giving the kiss the attention it deserves.

Albert Einstein

Official 1921 photograph

MIND SETTING

CHAPTER 2

The skill to do comes from the doing.

Marcus Tullius Cicero
(106 BC – 43 BC)
A Roman philosopher, statesman, lawyer, orator, political theorist, Roman consul and constitutionalist.

No one can persuade another to change. Each of us guards a gate of change that can only be opened from the inside. We cannot open the gate of another, either by argument or emotional appeal.

Marilyn Ferguson
(1938 – 2008)
American author, editor and public speaker.

Change is an inevitable part of life. If we fight or resist it, we will be engaging in a losing battle. Your first step in changing your future is to learn to understand change and to accept it.

When you invest in personal development, you take responsibility for your life, circumstances, and happiness. Change is your ally - and a great tool to help you remain flexible, stay positive, and put your life both in perspective and in control. Embracing personal development will surely make changes easier for you in the future!

Start going over the following reference points and questions to gain experience and wisdom. Make the decision to invest in yourself; it will be the best and most important investment you will ever make to *Change your future, now!*

What about a productive mindset?
Curiosity, desire, motivation, vision, critical thinking, self-confidence, persistence, positive attitude, open-mindedness, and balance are the elements of a productive mindset.

A productive mindset is one that makes the best use of resources, time, energy, and efforts. It is not trying to do everything and be everything, or even doing it in the quickest way possible. It is making the most and the best of what one has while enjoying the process.

In order to acquire the necessary skills to improve who we are and what we have, certain qualities or characteristics are needed. Having a productive mindset means one possesses the willingness to ask questions and find answers - new and better ways of

Chapter 2

Empowerment means taking responsibility for getting something done, and being willing to be held accountable.

Bill George
Professor at IMD International and Ecole Polytechnique in Lausanne, Switzerland, and Executive-in-Residence at Yale School of Management.

A year from now you will wish you had started today.

Karen Lamb
American Author.

doing things. To have a productive mindset, one must train his mind to visualize the outcome. It is all about being able to accomplish the seemingly impossible by envisioning the outcome.

Mind setting is also acquiring the ability to assess a situation in an objective manner. Look at the pros and cons and be willing to make the appropriate adjustments. Even so, mind setting cannot be achieved without faith and belief that you are fully capable and able to do what you set out to do. Without self-confidence and faith, you cannot reach your full potential.

Most things do not come easily. The productive mindset must include being willing to overcome obstacles and adversity. It is the notion of persisting in order to reach a particular goal without letting any circumstances, the opinions of others, or setbacks, lessen one's determination to succeed.

A productive mind setter cannot function without a positive attitude that allows for any possibility. Having a negative one defeats him, even before he gets started. It is all about being either positive or negative. One leads to success. The other will break you and lead to failure or defeat.

Donald Trump in is book, *Think Big and Kick Ass in Business and Life*, formulates a clear definition. "Another thing you can do is to think positively and expect the best. My positive attitude has brought me a lot of luck. In the very beginning of my career, when I was trying to buy the huge abandoned Penn Central rail yard on Manhattan's West side, I was new to the city. I had no money, no employees, and no contacts. The city was in the middle of a financial crisis, but I was optimistic and enthusiastic. Because I was so

MIND **SETTING**

Each time we
ask more of
ourselves than
we think
we are able to
give, and then
manage to give
it, we grow.

– Anonymous

*young, I could not sell the banks on my experience or
my accomplishments, so I sold them on my
enthusiasm. It is important to think positively.
Negative thinking, especially about yourself and
about your prospects for success, will kill your focus
and destroy any chance you have of being
successful.*

There is nothing like an open-mind for generating new and innovative ideas. However, ultimately, to function well and get the most from life, we must maintain balance. Working towards goals is important, but we must also take time to rejuvenate and recharge. Doing too much, or pushing too hard, can lead to "burn out" and frustration.

Remember to integrate these elements into your thought processes, for they will not only cultivate a productive mindset but will also set you up to reach your goals more effectively, develop positive habits and sharpen your mind to function at its best.

A man who
dares to
waste one
hour of time
has not
discovered
the value of
life.

Charles Robert
Darwin
(1809 -1882)
English naturalist.
He established that
all species of life
have descended over
time from common
ancestry and
proposed the
scientific theory that
this branching
pattern of evolution
resulted from a
process that he
called "Natural
Selection."

Can I keep an open mind?

To wait until you know all the facts before forming an opinion or making a judgment is keeping an open mind. It should be the first step in your quest to *Change your future, now!*

To have an open mind means to be willing to consider or receive new and different ideas. It means being flexible and adaptive to experiences and ideas. Now, more than ever, we live in a world that is constantly changing, and we need to keep an open mind!

In order to keep up with our changing world, we must be open to experiences and ways of looking at things. People who are open-minded are willing to change

Chapter 2

We are shaped by our thoughts; we become what we think. When the mind is pure, joy follows like a shadow that never leaves.

Siddhārtha Gautama Buddha
(563 BCE - 483 BCE)
A spiritual teacher from the Indian subcontinent, on whose teachings Buddhism was founded.

Great minds have purposes, others have wishes.

Washington Irving
(1783 – 1859)
American author, essayist, biographer, and historian of the early 19th century. He is best known for his short stories "The Legend of Sleepy Hollow" and "Rip Van Winkle"

their views when presented with new facts and evidence. Those who are resistant to change will find life less rewarding and satisfying. To change now, you need to seek new ways of doing and looking at things. Change is all about expanding our intellectual capability, finding life more exciting, and broadening our experiences by being open-minded.

Remember that being open-minded will help us with problem solving. It will help us look at more than one way to approach a problem. When we give ourselves more options, better solutions are undoubtedly more available to us. Keeping an open mind is how to think for yourself, think critically, put subjects and things in perspective, develop courage, be an original and interesting person, and think positively to expand your comfort zone.

Do I think for myself?

We all live in societies or cultures where the norms and customs are already established. We are expected - to conform to a large degree to what is in place. This is not necessarily a bad thing. However, it can be confining and controlling if we accept everything blindly and never question the status quo.

Societies, cultures, fast media, and the Internet influence today's thinking. For most of us, unless we are discerning and very aware people, we most likely do not even know when our thinking is not our own. Assuredly, not all outside influence is bad or detrimental to forming our views.

Does this mean that all of your ideas can be original and unlike everyone else's? It means choosing not to compromise the facts for the sake of consensus or just to "fit in." It encompasses a broader scope of choices and decision-making in your life. It does not

MIND **SETTING**

Most people give up just when they're about to achieve success. They quit on the one yard line. They give up at the last minute of the game one foot from a winning touchdown.

Henry Ross Perot
(1930 -)
U.S. businessman best known for running for President of the United States in 1992 and 1996.

I think it's good to identify with your role, but at the same time you have to understand who likes you for yourself and who likes you for what you've got.

Esther Dyson
(1951 -)
American journalist, angel investor, entrepreneur, philanthropist, and commentator focused on breakthrough innovation in healthcare, government transparency, digital technology, biotechnology, and space.

require being contrary and argumentative just to be defiant or to stand out.

Group thinking is another trap we fall into when we do not think for ourselves. Ordinarily, an exchange of ideas takes place within a group of people who try to avoid conflict and reach agreement without critically evaluating options or alternative ideas. The problem with group thinking is that it interferes with finding the best solutions, obstructs creative ideas, and prevents independent thinking.

Remember that not being able to think for yourself can make you miserable, at best, or it can make you the puppet of someone else's programming, at worst. To think for yourself means that whatever opinions you hold, you can carefully think them through and arrive at conclusions from a position of thorough investigation and thoughtful analysis.

Can I cultivate the ability to think for myself?

Finding out who you are, what you want, and what is best for you is how you can cultivate the ability to think for yourself. Do not let others tell you how you should look, feel, and act. Work at what is best for you by cultivating your own tastes and enjoying your preferences. Not knowing yourself leads to confusion, lost time and missed opportunities. When we do not know who we are or where we are headed, it is hard to set goals, get motivated, and determine the best course of action for an optimistic future. To be able to change, we need to establish who we are!

In today's world, everyone wants to provide opinions about subjects. Before forming an opinion of your own, gather as much information about the subject as possible. Build your mental resources by reading, observing, and listening. Then take time to reflect and evaluate.

Germain Decelles

Chapter 2

Decisions are easy for a dinosaur.
If it's food, eat it. If it's an enemy, kill it or run away. Every creature or object is either dealt with immediately or ignored. More than anything else, reptiles can't wait. All Lizard Logic patterns are immediate. Dinosaur Brain thinking is always short-term, with high emotional involvement.

Albert J. Bernstein, Ph.D.
American author of *How To Deal With Emotionally Explosive People, Dinosaur Brains, Emotional Vampires, Neanderthals at Work,* and *Sacred Bull.*

Being well informed will enable you to be more flexible to propose as many perspectives as you can. Determine the pros and cons in any given situation.

Are there other possibilities? Would it harm a person or benefit her? What are the potential consequences?

Becoming informed about and reflecting on the subject will also enable you to Identify possible biases. Many times we make poor decisions because we begin with the wrong premise. If we take time to evaluate and judge something based upon what we observe first hand rather than by what we have been led to believe, we can arrive at a more appropriate and practical conclusion.

Have the courage to stand up for what you really believe. Do not fold under pressure, fear, or guilt. If you go along with the crowd for the sake of keeping peace, avoiding confrontation, or because of a fear of failure, you do everyone a disservice, especially yourself.

You may have a brilliant idea, or maybe your view happens to be the right thing to do. If no one hears about it, a healthy discussion cannot take place, and all the possibilities will not be considered. A good idea has the potential to evolve into a better one with input from a variety of sources.

Recognize that you will need to compromise intelligently when facing certain situations. Concessions are necessary in all aspects of life: in matters of business, relationships, and so on. Even in one's personal life, an individual may have to compromise with others in order to reach the most workable arrangements for living.

A compromise is a negotiation in view of an agreement where each person participating in the agreement must make the decision to surrender some of the things he, she, or they would want in order, hopefully, to get the things most desired or most beneficial to everyone involved.

Remember that people who are open minded are more easily accepted by others, have fewer prejudices, and tend to suffer less stress because they are more receptive to change, have enhanced problem-solving skills, and want to learn more; therefore, they are more interesting.

Could I not be thinking for myself?

You are not thinking for yourself when you let others, the media, or conventions sway you from doing what is right for you.

When you continue to "buy into" negative, one-dimensional stereotypes based on sex, race, or culture, or you do something because it has always been done that way even if it no longer works, you are not thinking for yourself.

When you follow old wives' tales, superstitions, or fallacies that defy common sense, you are not taking the necessary time to think things through carefully and fully.

As you may have already concluded, thinking for yourself is not easy. It requires deliberate, mindful, and at times courageous application. However, the personal rewards are endlessly gratifying.

Can I think critically?

When we are aware that we can choose and direct our thinking, we realize that we have the ability to

When we encounter a natural style we are always surprised and delighted, for we thought to see an author and found a man.

Blaise Pascal
(1623 - 1662)
French mathematician, physicist, inventor, writer, and Catholic philosopher.

Informed decision-making comes from a long tradition of guessing and then blaming others for inadequate results.

Scott Raymond Adams
(1957 -)
American creator of the *Dilbert* comic strip.

Chapter 2

Our problems are man-made; therefore they may be solved by man. And man can be as big as he wants. No problem of human destiny is beyond human beings.

John F. Kennedy
(1917 - 1963)
35th President of the United States, serving from 1961 until his assassination in 1963.

The difference between what we do and what we are capable of doing would suffice to solve most of the world's problem.

Mohandas Karamchand Gandhi
(1869 - 1948)
The pre-eminent political and ideological leader of India during the Indian independence movement.

control better the circumstances of our lives, improve our decision-making processes, and generally live more productive lives. This in no way suggests that we need to downplay the many feelings and emotions in life. We as humans enjoy; thinking critically is simply a way for us to manage and balance our emotions with our cognitive abilities.

We are thinking critically, and have a problem-solving mindset, when we rely on reason rather than emotion, evaluate a broad range of viewpoints and perspectives, maintain an open mind to alternative interpretations, accept new evidence, explanations and findings, and are willing to reassess information. We should put aside personal prejudices and biases, consider all reasonable possibilities, and avoid hasty judgments.

Like any other skill, learning to think critically takes time, perseverance, and practice. Knowing which steps to take and how to apply them will help you master the process!

The first task is to determine if a problem exists. Sometimes when you think this point through, you may come to the conclusion there is really no problem, just a misunderstanding. Fine, if that is the case. If not, and you determine that there is indeed a problem you need to identify exactly what it is.

Once you have determined the problem, analyze it by looking at it from a variety of perspectives.

Sometimes by looking at it from many angles, you can come up with a resolution right away. You may also discover a bias or a narrow point of view that needs to be broadened.

MIND **SETTING**

Problems can be solved in many ways. Start by brainstorming a list of several possible solutions. Put down anything that comes to mind, and then go over the list and narrow it down to the best possibilities. Having several viable options leads to obtaining the best results.

A little perspective, like a little humor, goes a long way.

Allen Klein
(1938 -)
Pioneer in gelotology and the therapeutic humor movement. He is an American author and lecturer on the stress relieving benefits of humor and on gallows humor.

Go over your list of possible solutions. Different situations call for distinctive solutions. Quite often what works in one situation may not work in a similar one. Take the time to determine what will work best for the problem at hand. One solution usually does not fit all. Implement your solution.

Remember that every problem has a solution, even if it is only to accept the situation and move on. Instead of approaching problems and challenges as insurmountable obstacles, we can view them as opportunities. Every problem we are able to resolve increases our self-confidence and self-worth, and thinking critically not only helps us handle future challenges more skillfully, it also broadens our life experience and helps us gain perspective.

Can I put subjects and things in perspective?

Perspective is how we perceive things in the context of the whole and how we judge the importance of one thing in relation to others. It is important to understand that everything that happens in your life is in accordance with how you perceive it. When a positive, healthy self-concept exists, putting things in perspective becomes an exercise in critical thinking and reasoning, rather than an emotionally centered on event.

Each person's task in life is to become an increasingly better person.

Lev Nikolayevich Tolstoy
(1828 - 1910)
Russian writer who primarily wrote novels and short stories.

In order to possess a positive or healthy self-concept, you must know yourself, love yourself, and be true to yourself. In addition, critical thinking is the mental

Chapter 2

Do one thing every day that scares.

Anna Eleanor Roosevelt
(1884 – 1962)
First Lady of the United States from 1933 to 1945. She supported the New Deal policies of her husband, distant cousin Franklin Delano Roosevelt, and became an advocate for civil rights.

Canada is a good country to be from. It has a gentler slower pace - it lends perspective.

Paul Albert Anka
(1941 -)
Canadian singer, songwriter, and actor.

process of analyzing or evaluating information. By thinking critically, instead of reacting emotionally to a problem, we employ strategies, which help us learn from an experience, help us to prevent it from occurring again, and help us to put forward reasonable and effective solutions.

A perspective thinking process, even though we cannot help but react emotionally to some difficult situations, can help us to control or change them. Practicing the perspective thought process can also help us to decide how we should allow them to affect us.

Moreover, how we experience or interpret events in our lives depends on our attitude. As we all probably know by now, attitudes can be positive or negative. Attitude, which is an aspect of perspective, is a way of thinking or looking at things.

We have the ability to choose how we think or our attitudes. If we choose to view our good, bad, or indifferent experiences with a positive attitude, we will probably see them as opportunities for personal growth and development.

Understand that if we let ourselves get caught up in negativity when things do not go our way, we will miss out on the opportunities for growth and set ourselves up for similar situations until we comprehend how to deal with them.

Certainly not everything in life goes smoothly and without incident. Sometimes the challenges we face can drive us to the brink and make us question, "why is this happening, and how could it have been avoided?"

MIND **SETTING**

The quality of a person's life will be determined by the depth of their commitment to excellence, no matter what their chosen field.

Vince Lombardi
(1913 - 1970)
American football coach.

During those times, we would probably prefer not to have to deal with the obstacles that are thrown in our path. It is in these moments that we really have to think and choose how we are going to approach the situation at hand. When we operate from the perspective or attitude that we are here to learn, develop, and work to reach our potential, we cannot help but have a positive, progressive outlook.

Remember that, ultimately, life is a subjective experience, and it is up to each of us to decide how we choose to view and experience it.

How can I make my heart and mind work together?

We are friendly with people we only kind of like. We do and say things to fit in and seem cool that really go against what we feel is right in our hearts. Unfortunately, it is typical in our society to feel a conflict between what we want to do in our hearts and what we feel is practical in our minds.

Is your heart at fault? Are your feelings just silly and frivolous?

Or, maybe it is your mind that is to blame. It might seem like it is always coming up with conflicting messages anyway.

He has a right to criticize, who has a heart to help.

Abraham Lincoln
(1809 – 1865)
16th President of the United States.

Even if you really feel like something is the right choice, how do you know for sure? How do you know it is not just what you think you should do?

All this might sound a bit unrealistic, but it is a real problem. People's inability to make up their minds about whether or not the paths they end up living merely shadows of the possibilities they could have, all because they could not make up their minds.

Chapter **2**

> This is my simple religion. There is no need for temples; no need for complicated philosophy. Our own brain, our own heart is our temple; the philosophy is kindness.
>
> 14th Dalai Lama
> (1935 -)
> He won the Nobel Peace Prize in 1989, and is also well known for his lifelong advocacy for Tibetans inside and outside Tibet.

The main reason we suffer from this illness of indecision is that we have mistaken the purposes of the heart and mind. The heart is like a compass. Its purpose is to guide the direction our lives should take. Our heart takes a bird's eye view on our life and shows us the direction we need to go.

Our mind, on the other hand, is not made for making purpose-driven decisions. The nature of the mind to conceptualize, organize, and compare information. It does this as best it can when hearing the facts from both sides of an issue or proposal.

The reason we are so troubled by this conflict of "head vs. heart" is that the mind is not only playing the prosecutor and the defense but has taken over the role of the judge as well. The mind should never be the judge. The mind's job is to compare. However, more often than not, our minds are not doing that. Our minds are making our choices.

Worse even is when we do not need our minds to be working but they are still comparing and contrasting everything. Most of the time they are mediating.

Have you ever noticed that even when it is completely unnecessary to think about anything, your mind is still doing so? Have you noticed that when this happens your mind is getting in the way of your experience?

> A good head and a good heart are always a formidable combination.
>
> Nelson Rolihlahla Mandela
> (1918 -)
> President of South Africa from 1994 to 1999 and was the first South African president to be elected in a fully representative democratic election.

If we want to end the conflict of head and heart we have got to figure out a way to "marry" this disparate pair. It will not be easy at first because we have been doing thing a certain way for so long.

When deciding you will need to consider the following:

MIND **SETTING**

Do what you feel in your heart to be right- for you'll be criticized anyway. You'll be damned if you do, and damned if you don't.

Anna Eleanor Roosevelt 1884-1962 First Lady of the United States from 1933 to 1945. She supported the New Deal policies of her husband, distant cousin Franklin Delano Roosevelt, and became an advocate for civil rights.

Gain information:
What is the implied benefit of the decision? Will it be something you will ever regret?

Although your mind may be telling you that the temporary benefit of a bad decision will be a wise one, in your heart you may still know that it is not the best thing to do. Seek information about it and evaluate it in your mind.

Identify problems:
What might go wrong? Will you feel good after making the decision?

Explore options:
Think about what is best for you, and most of the time doing what your heart tells you to do is the best choice.

Make a choice and implement a plan:
Learn from your mistakes and try, try again.

By listening to your heart, you can train your mind to think like it and eventually get them to work in harmony.

Donald Trump, in his book *Think Big and Kick Ass in Business and Life*, formulates a down-to-heart definition: *"You have to love what you do or you are never going to be successful no matter what you do in life. If you love what you do, you are going to work harder, you are going to try harder, you are going to be better at it, and you're going to try harder, you are going to be better at it, and you're going to enjoy your life more. The most important things are knowing your business and loving what you do, both of which solve a lot of problems."*

Chapter **2**

I am captivated more by dreams of the future than by the history of the past.

Thomas Jefferson
1743-1826
Founding Father who was the principal author of the United States *Declaration of Independence* (1776).

A rock pile ceases to be a rock pile the moment a single man contemplates it, bearing within him the image of a cathedral.

Antoine Marie Jean-Baptiste Roger, Comte de Saint Exupéry
(1900 – 1944)
An aristocrat French writer, poet, and pioneering aviator. He is best remembered for his novella *The Little Prince* (*Le Petit Prince*) and for his lyrical aviation writings, including *Night Flight* and *Wind, Sand and Stars*.

Remember that the important thing here is to keep practicing in this new decision – making habit.

Have you ever wondered how to tell whether a decision is right?

You will find that the right choice is immediately evident. It becomes so easy when you think, "Is this choice going with me, or against me?"

If you can learn to practice this every time you make a choice, you will start to regain your personal power. Make the choice today. Just try it out and trust yourself.

What about imagination and vision?
Imagination and vision can be inspirational and can spark your creativity in life. Imagination is something to use in abundance in life. Our vision and what we see in our minds are very important to us.

We need to have this inspiration to tackle and manage the changes we experience throughout our lives. This can help us develop and maintain our creativity in the face of the challenges of life.

We need to be responsible and determined to see our vision become reality. This can inspire our creative side and allow our vision to become reality.

Then we need not just imagine our future; we can go forward and claim it - and take any changes in stride as we manage to achieve our dreams and goals.

Remember that in meeting the challenges and rigors of life, the ability to imagine continues to be an important element. This vision, creativity, inventiveness should not be dismissed easily. If it is, we will be limiting not only our impact on life but also our ability to be constructive and productive in life.

Can I develop courage?

Courage is the mental and emotional preparedness and ability to deal with difficult, challenging, and sometimes seemingly impossible circumstances. It is the ability to confront fear, pain, danger, uncertainty, intimidation, and other threats. It does not necessarily require doing something dramatic or heroic. On a day-to-day basis, many ordinary people summon the courage to conquer both physical and psychological barriers to accomplish what they need to do.

Developing courage arms us with the power to confront problems and to deal with adversity head on. It helps us deal with life's challenges. By developing courage, we strengthen ourselves and build resistance and resilience to hardship. This means we can continue with everyday tasks, remain balanced, and bounce back quickly from hard times. Today, when so many resort to various harmful and counterproductive substances to deal with problems, a healthy supply of courage is without doubt the wiser alternative.

Making the effort to develop courage is an exercise in building additional strategies to live a productive, happy, and meaningful life. A large part of developing courage is having faith in oneself, faith in a higher power, and faith that things will work out. This type of confidence comes from maintaining a positive attitude and visualizing a favorable outcome. A courageous mindset is the product of faith, self-confidence, and useful thinking.

There can be no great courage where there is no confidence or assurance, and half the battle is in the conviction that we can do what we undertake.

Orison Swett Marden
(1850 – 1924)
American writer associated with the New Thought Movement. He also held a degree in medicine and was a successful hotel owner.

All our dreams can come true, if we have the courage to pursue them.

Walter Elias "Walt" Disney
(1901 - 1966)
Disney is particularly noted as a film producer and a popular showman, as well as an innovator in animation and theme park design.

Chapter **2**

I think a lot of people are afraid to fail, so they don't try. They talk, but don't do. That's a great formula for failure. My advice is to take some risks, even if you fail. There has never been and there will never be an Olympic ice skater who hasn't taken a spill on the ice, no matter how much she knew about ice-skating. She's acquired her skill by doing, not by watching.

Donald J. Trump
writing in *Inside Trump Tower Newsletter*

The person who is waiting for something to turn up might start with their shirtsleeves.

Garth Henrichs
Poet

Remember that visualization will help you to imagine, through pictures or mental imagery, how to create visions of what you want in life and how to make it happen. With focus and emotion, visualization becomes a powerful, creative tool that will help you to achieve your goals.

How can I stop making excuses?

The only difference between being responsible and being irresponsible comes down to two things: accountability and adaptability.

A dependable person owns up to his or her role in any situation and learns from mistakes. An irresponsible person will shift the blame to someone or something else and makes the same mistakes repeatedly.

Understand that responsibility is earned. It is not something you are entitled to. If someone is hesitant to give you additional responsibility, it is probably because you have been nonchalant with the responsibilities you already have.

A classic characteristic of irresponsible people is that they do things as long as they are challenging, fun, and new, and when these things fade, they lose interest.

A responsible person follows through with what he or she committed to do. Period. So if you want to be seen as more reliable, think about the responsibilities you already have, and take them more seriously, no matter how pointless they might seem.

In any situation, there are always some factors we cannot control. Irresponsible people tend to shift the blame onto those factors and vocalize them as excuses.

MIND **SETTING**

Take the risk! It's all over in 30 seconds anyway!
TSufit
Canadian Author.

Anytime you make an excuse it is like saying, "I am not responsible for this because..." and what you are really saying is, "I am not responsible." Pay attention to how you think and talk. Excuses come in many shapes and sizes, but the most common is, "I would/would've, BUT..."

When you see something that needs doing or needs to change, do not wait for somebody else to do it. View yourself as a creator, not a victim of circumstances and make a positive difference. Once you see yourself as making a positive change, it will get easier to be a creator instead of a victim of circumstances.

Remember to always follow through. You will struggle with losses of confidence and motivation along the way, and that is normal. The important thing is that you get back on course and finish what you started.

How can I be an original or my true self?

Life is too short to live trying to be anything other than your true, original self. Be who you are, and be it the best way you know how. Celebrate your individuality and uniqueness. Dare to be an original!

Be regular and orderly in your life, so that you may be violent and original in your work.

Gustave Flaubert
(1821 – 1880)
French writer who is counted among the greatest Western novelists. He is known especially for his first published novel, Madame Bovary (1857) and for his scrupulous devotion to his art and style.

The best way to be your true self is to know how you are, trust your intuition and instincts, express and cultivate your own style, tastes and personality, believe in yourself, and do not worry about how others will perceive you.

The benefits are great in finding your true self if you are ready to take risks, think originally, and be creative; therefore, be open to greater life opportunities.

Chapter **2**

Always be yourself, express yourself, have faith in yourself, do not go out and look for a successful personality and duplicate it.

Bruce Lee
(born Lee Jun-fan)
(1940 – 1973)
Chinese American, Hong Kong actor, martial arts instructor, philosopher, film director, film producer, screenwriter, and founder of the Jeet Kune Do martial arts movement.

We continue to shape our personality all our life. If we knew ourselves perfectly, we should die.

Albert Camus
(1913 – 1960)
French author, journalist, and philosopher of the 20th century.

Remember that when you dare to be an original, you dare to be courageous, strong, and vibrant and are willing to realize the full potential of your unique skills and talents.

Am I an interesting person?

Everyone wants to be attractive to others. To that end, having a pleasant personality is vital, probably even more so than good looks. In fact, most of your success and happiness will be the result of how you interact well with others.

Ultimately, it is your personality that determines whether others are attracted to you or shy away from you. While we can only enhance our looks, to a certain extent, we have the ability to improve our personality as much as we want. Develop all aspects of yourself - your mind, body, intellect, and spirit. It is never too late to start!

A simple definition of the word "personality" is:
Personality is the particular combination of emotional, attitudinal, and behavioral response patterns of an individual.

When we say that someone has a "good personality," we mean that he or she is likeable, interesting, and pleasant to be with.

You can be a more interesting person by being a better listener, taking a genuine interest in others, reading and cultivating a variety of interests. You can also develop excellent communication skills, be a good conversationalist, and expand your knowledge in the arts, music, literature, and sports.

MIND SETTING

Somewhere along the line I made the switch and was able to look at the bright side rather than the dark side all the time. Now I look at everything I have and think how lucky I am.

Michelle Marie Pfeiffer
(1958 -)
American actress. She made her film debut in 1980 in *The Hollywood Knights* but first garnered mainstream attention with her performance in Brian De Palma's *Scarface* (1983).

Change is the law of life. And those who look only to the past or present are certain to miss the future.

John F. Kennedy
(1917-1963)
35th President of the USA

Remember that you can have an uncommon point of view or differing opinion, meet new people, express your informed opinions, have a positive outlook and attitude, be funny and see the humorous side of life, be supportive of others having integrity and, treat people with respect.

Can I think positively?

Negative feelings and circumstances do exist and often serve as an indication that something is not working or needs to be attended to. In such cases, we must employ positive thinking and use it as a strategy for interpreting everything that happens to us in a useful, constructive way, in order to make our lives work.

Of course, this does not mean we should deny pain and discomfort. It means we need to make sense of them and use what we can to strengthen our resolve.

We can develop a useful active mindset by thinking positively and productively and by accepting the fact that we are on this earth to grow and evolve, and to look for the lessons to be learned in every situation.

Positive thinking also comes by not feeling sorry for yourself when things do not go your way, by avoiding falling in to the same traps and repeating the same mistakes, and by knowing you have what it takes to succeed. You need to recognize you have a unique contribution to make, set your mind to not giving up and read about and study the triumphs of others.

Remember that the next time a well-meaning person tells you to think positively, just smile back confidently and let the person know that it is part of your everyday, productive mindset.

Chapter 2

> The important thing is this: to be able at any moment to sacrifice what we are for what we would become.
>
> Charles Du Bos
> (1882 – 1939)
> French critic.

Can I expand my comfort zone?

Many unhappy or unfulfilled people have a natural inclination to stay within their comfort zone simply because it is familiar and safe. Many stay in occupations, relationships, and situations that have long since lost their relevance only because they are afraid of the unknown.

The truth is that security does not reside in anything outside of ourselves; instead, it lies within us.

Unfortunately, if you choose to remain in your comfort zone, you will never find out what your true potential is or what you are capable of achieving. Nor can you really succeed at anything without venturing out of the comfort of your safety net.

> The events of your past do not reduce your potential.
> How somebody has treated you or what he or she said about you doesn't change your potential.
>
> Joel Osteen
> (1963 -)
> American author, televangelist, and the senior pastor of Lakewood Church in Houston, Texas. His ministry reaches over seven million broadcast media viewers weekly in over 100 nations around the world.

Remember that you must make the decision to move beyond the circumstances, people, and experiences you are familiar with. You need to move out of your comfort zone and onto the path of personal development. It is a path that forces you to stretch yourself, push your limits, and become more than you were.

When you take a new subject in school, learn a language, take up a sport, or start a new job, you operate out of your comfort zone in the beginning. Once you start to familiarize yourself with the tasks, people, and environment, you rapidly once again enter your comfort zone. After all, it is a simple, natural mindset adaptation process!

Sometimes breaking out of our comfort zones can be an arduous process. By experimenting with changing small everyday routines at first, you might be able to expand your mindset?

MIND **SETTING**

The most commom complaint of businesspeople is that they have no time.
I've seen lots of time-management courses, and I've realized that even the title is misleading because you really can't manage time. No matter what you do, there will always be 24 hours in the day. What you can do is manage yourself and decide how you're going to use the 24 hours. So time-management is really self-management.

Albert J. Bernstein, Ph.D. American author of How To Deal With Emotionally Explosive People, Dinosaur Brains, Emotional Vampires, Neanderthals at Work, and Sacred Bull.

Some people look forward to breaking from a routine or habit they have had for a long time and to finding a different, perhaps better way to do things. Others, typically sedentary can take a break from reading or from sitting in front of the computer and find a physical activity they can enjoy. Very active people, on the other hand, could learn to wind down, read, or relax.

Remember that stretching yourself and expanding your comfort zone is an important part of personal development. Each step that you make advances you to the next level and keeps you on the path of self-improvement. By moving forward, you will challenge yourself and improve yourself, enhance your enjoyment and experience of life, stimulate brain activity and therefore, boost your mental health, increase your self-confidence, and more.

What does it mean to take control of my life?

Each day, you have the ability to make the choice to take control of your life or to let it control you. You can either be proactive, or you can let circumstances follow their course. When you take responsibility for yourself and for every area of your life, you become more productive, more optimistic, and more able to solve problems more easily – and you ultimately have less stress in your life.

To take control of your life means that you need to determine your values and what is important to you. Develop a roadmap that will spell out your overall goals. What will drive your actions and your decision-making process?

When you state your objectives succinctly, you cannot help but be focused and take the right actions to help you be where you need to be. This also helps

Chapter 2

keep you from being aimless and scattered and from missing situations.

Remember that one of the hardest things to do is to remain positive when your best efforts to take control of your life do not go as planned. Living a full, productive life requires maintaining a balance between work, relaxation, and recreation. So take time to have some fun!

Can I balance my life?

To live a successful and productive life, you need to factor in moderation. Know yourself and how much rest, food, and exercise you need to function at your best. Keep your mind alert and in shape by always trying to learn something new.

I believe that being successful means having a balance of success stories across the many areas of your life.
You can't truly be considered successful in your business life if your home life is in shambles.

Hilary Hinton "Zig" Ziglar
(1926 -)
American author, salesman, and motivational speaker.

Stay connected with family and friends; we should never be too busy to connect with a parent, sibling, or friend. You can do spontaneous things, such as take a walk or a drive in the countryside one afternoon, and most important, make time at the end of each day to unwind. Decide what works best for you, and add it into your routine!

Remember that while we cannot anticipate and plan for everything in our lives, we can decide how, where, and when to concentrate our energies. This may require some critical thinking and problem solving, but in the end, it will lead to much less stress and a well-balanced life.

Who is the person I want to be?

You need to learn how to program and reprogram your self-concept, so that your inner world is consistent with the person you want to be and the life you want to experience on the outside.

MIND **SETTING**

The two most powerful things in existence: a kind word and a thoughtful gesture.

Ken Langone
Co-founder of Home Depot.

There is a law in psychology that if you form a picture in your mind of what you would like to be, and you keep and hold that picture there long enough, you will soon become exactly as you have been thinking.

William James
(1842 – 1910)
Pioneering American psychologist and philosopher who was trained as a physician. He wrote influential books on the young science of psychology, educational psychology, psychology of religious experience and mysticism, and on the philosophy of pragmatism.

- Define your ideals clearly. If you could be an excellent person in every way, what qualities would you have, and how would you behave?

- Identify one or more areas of you life where your thinking is having a major influence on your emotions, attitudes, or actions. You become what you think about most of the time.

- In what area of activity do you perform at your best? How do you visualize yourself in that area? How could you extend this act of visualization to other areas?

- What kind of people do you most admire and respect? Why? How could you change your behavior so that it is more consistent with the behavior of the best people you know?

- In what areas of your life do you like yourself the most? What kinds of activities give you the highest levels of self-esteem and personal value? How could you do even more of these things?

- See yourself as the very best you can be, and refuse to accept any limitations on your possibilities.

- Change your self-concept by continually thinking, talking, and acting as if you were already the person you would like to be, enjoying the life that you want and deserve.

What should I consider?

Everyday, we are confronted with various decisions that need to be made. Some decisions are small and of minor consequence, while others are huge and potentially life changing. Certainly, you can never

Chapter 2

Courage is resistance to fear, mastery of fear, not absence of fear.

Mark Twain
(Samuel Langhorne Clemens)
(1835 – 1910)
American author and humorist. He is most noted for his novels, The Adventures of Tom Sawyer (1876) and its sequel, The Adventures of Huckleberry Finn (1885).

You are the storyteller of your own life, and you can create your own legend or not.

Isabel Allende Llona
(1942 -)
Chilean writer. In 2004, Allende was inducted into the American Academy of Arts and Letters, and in 2010, she received Chile's National Literature Prize.

know in advance whether a decision will be correct. In life, there are no guarantees, so be prepared to take risks.

If you make a mistake, view it as an opportunity to learn. Many times decisions are reversible, and you can change your mind. If you have done everything you can to make a good decision and still cannot make up your mind, do not delay making an important decision for fear that you do not know enough or will make the wrong choice.

Sometimes people become so paralyzed with the fear of making a wrong decision that they panic and lose sight of what they are trying to accomplish. This prevents them from making any decision. Second-guessing yourself also undermines what you are trying to accomplish. Once you have made the decision, let the chips fall where they may. At the very least, you will have learned important lessons.

When all is said and done, all you can do is the best with what you have to work with. Incidentally, do not underestimate the power of intuition, or your gut feeling. After all the facts are weighed and evaluated, it can be the final determinant. Quite often it may be all you have to go on.

Remember that change is an inevitable part of life. Everything will not invariably go your way; there will be both losses and wins. Always "give your best shot" and learn the lessons along the way. You will come out a winner, and by investing in your personal development, you will have initiated the actions needed to *Change Your Future, Now!*

Recommended Reading & References

We suggest consulting the works identified below in order to learn more about the particulars contained in this chapter.

BENNIS, W. & NANUS B. LEADERS. THE STRATEGIES FOR TAKING CHARGE. Harper Press. ISBN 0-06-015246-X.

BERNSTEIN, Albert j. Ph.D. DINOSAUR BRAINS, DEALING WITH ALL THOSE IMPOSSIBLE PEOPLE AT WORK.
Wiley & sons ISBN0-471-61808-X.

BLANCHARD, Ken & collective. KNOW CAN DO!
ISBN-10-1-4272-0251-6.

DEL, Michael. DIRECT FROM DELL, strategies that revolutionized an industry. Harper, ISBN 0-694-52023-3.

KAWASAKI, Guy. THE ART OF THE START, the time-tested, battle-hardened guide for anyone starting anything.
ISBN 1-59184-056-2.

KRAUSE, G. Donald. THE ART OF WAR FOR EXECUTIVES. Penguin Books, ISBN 0-399-53150-5.

PETER, L.J & HULL, R. PETER'S PRINCIPLE.
ISBN 70-11-682-850-1580.

PETERS, Thomas J. THRIVING ON CHAOS/ A PASSION FOR EXCELLENCE. Random House. ISBN 0-517-14816-1.

SIMMONS, Harry. HOW TO TALK YOUR WAY TO SUCCESS. Prentice-Hall. 1954 – 43526.

TAYLOR, William C. MAVERICKS AT WORK. Why the most original minds in business win.
Harper. ISBN-13: 978-006-11-252-1.

THATCHER, Margaret. THE DOWNING STREET YEARS. Harper Collins. ISBN 0-06-017056-5.

TSUFIT. STEP INTO THE SPOTLIGHT! Beach View Books. ISBN 978-0-9781913-0-6.

TRUMP, Donald J. THINK BIG AND KICK ASS.
Harper Collins. ISBN 978-0-06-154783-6.

VENTRELLA, Scott W. THE POWER OF POSITIVE THINKING IN BUSINESS. Simon & Schuster. ISBN 0-7435-1810-1

WALKER, Harold Blake, POWER TO MANAGE YOURSELF. Harper & Brothers Publishers. Library of Congress catalog card number: 55-8529.

Anyone who stops learning is old, whether at twenty or eighty. Anyone who keeps learning stays young. The greatest thing in life is to keep your mind young.

Henry Ford

Artist: Hans Wollner, 1937

CHAPTER 3

LEARNING & **CHANGE**

We are in a new age, the age of information, of global competition! We have no choice but to prepare for this new age in which the key to success will be the continuous education and development of the human mind and imagination. I like to call it the "Learning Age."

In the 21st-Century, the new disadvantaged will be those who do not have the capacity to learn. They will sink, unable to change and adapt, as they are flooded with ever more information and change.

However, learning is about more than just getting by in a changing world. Our ability to learn is what makes us human; we are born curious and our ability to continue learning is what defines us as individuals, as communities, and as societies.

He who learns but does not think, is lost! He who thinks but does not learn is in great danger.

Confucius
(551 BCE–479 BCE)
Chinese thinker and social philosopher of the Spring and Autumn Period. The philosophy of Confucius emphasized personal and governmental morality, correctness of social relationships, justice and sincerity.

Learning can bring you, your family, your organization, and your community any number of benefits. Just some of them include: personal growth, and expanded horizons, increased employability, improved career development prospects, a broader range of interests, and a wider social life, that is, the ability to create your own future.

Every day, people around the world are changing their lives through learning. Learning something new can help you to earn more money, get a better job, and do something you really enjoy. It can be a way to gain confidence and discover talents you never knew you had. It can be a way to meet new people and have a bit of fun. If you feel you are in a monotonous routine, it could help you escape. Even if you did not like learning when you were at school, you must find a way to enjoy it now.

Chapter 3

A human being is not attaining his full heights until he is educated.

Horace Mann
(1796-1859)
American education reformer.

We now accept the fact that learning is a lifelong process of keeping abreast of change.
And the most pressing task is to teach people how to learn.

Peter F. Drucker
(1909-2005)
American writer and management consultant.

Why do we learn?

Learning is acquiring new or modifying existing knowledge, behaviors, skills, values, or preferences and may involve synthesizing different types of information.

All kinds of people can learn all kinds of things. It does not matter if you have worked for years or have just left school. Young, old, male, female, working, non-working, all can achieve trough learning.

When we ask students, workers, professionals, or retired people what they understand by learning, responses such as these are received:

- Learning is a quantitative increase in knowledge.
- Learning is acquiring information.
- Learning is memorizing.
- Learning is storing information that can be reproduced.
- Learning is acquiring facts, skills, and methods that can be retained and used as necessary.
- Learning is making sense of something or abstracting meaning from it.
- Learning involves relating the parts of a certain subject matter to each other and to the real world.
- Learning is interpreting and understanding reality in a different way.
- Learning involves comprehending the world by reinterpreting knowledge.

In a constantly changing world, it is important that we embrace our role with optimism. A life's journey is all about development, improvement, growth, and particularly learning. It is also, for the most part, all about our work, which will permit us to be at peace with others and ourselves.

LEARNING & CHANGE

Better to be proficient in one art than a bungling in a hundred.

Japanese Proverb. Japanese opera mask.

Tell me and I forget.
Teach me and I remember.
Involve me and I learn.

Benjamin Franklin
(1706-1790)
Founding Father of the United States. A noted polymath, Franklin was a leading author, printer, political theorist, politician, postmaster, scientist, musician, inventor, satirist, civic activist, statesman, and diplomat.

Formal education will make you a living; self-education will make you a fortune.

Jim Rohn
(1930 – 2009)
American entrepreneur, author, and motivational speaker.

We approach work according to guiding principles, such as:

- We work to earn the position of trusted family member, community member, partner, educator, advisor, coach, consultant, and facilitator.
- We respect the confidentiality of the people with whom we work.
- We look for and act upon opportunities to foster collaboration with others in the community by promoting cooperative goals, making connections, and providing support, advice, and thoughtful leadership.
- We offer solutions that are driven by the goals, needs, and agendas of the people we work with.
- We involve others through a consultative engagement process that involves robust assessment and diagnosis, design, development, implementation, and evaluation.

Work is to be embraced as a positive factor in realizing our life's journey. Including learning in our day-to-day activities as part of our positive philosophy enables us to capture the essence of the world surrounding us.

Learning cannot be seen as something we've already completed before we start a career. It must be viewed as an element integrated into our life's journey.

Remember that without learning stagnation will install itself, and any effort to change will be automatically stopped.

How can I become a more effective learner?

We are all interested in finding new ways to learn better and faster. The amount of time we have to spend learning new things is limited. So, it is

Chapter 3

Live as if you were to die tomorrow. Learn as if you were to live forever.

Mohandas Karamchand Gandhi
(1869-1948)
The pre-eminent political and ideological leader of India during the Indian independence movement.

We must teach our children to resolve their conflicts with words, not weapons.

William Jefferson "Bill" Clinton
42nd President of the United States, from 1993 to 2001.

We now accept the fact that learning is a lifelong process of keeping abreast of change. And the most pressing task is to teach people how to learn.

Peter F. Drucker
(1909-2005)
American writer and management consultant.

important to get the most educational value out of our time as possible. However, retention, recall, and transfer are also critical. We need to remember accurately the information we have learned. For the recall part, we will utilize it effectively, at a later time, in a wide variety of situations.

Using memory improvement basics is one of the best ways to improve memory. Improving focus, avoiding educative session that are compressed, and structuring your study time are good places to start. There are also lessons to be taken from psychology that can dramatically improve your learning efficiency.

One proficient way to become a more effective learner is simply to keep learning. So, if you are learning a new language, it is important to keep practicing the language in order to maintain the gains you have achieved. This use-it or lose-it phenomenon involves a brain process known as *pruning*.

Certain pathways in the brain are maintained, while other are eliminated. If you want to retain the new information you just learned, keep practicing and rehearsing it.

You need to focus on learning in more than one way. Instead of just listening, which involves auditory learning, find a way to rehearse the information both verbally and visually. This might involve describing what you learned to a friend, taking notes, or drawing a mind map.

By learning in more than one way, you are further cementing the knowledge in your mind!

Educators have long noted that one of the best ways to learn something is to teach it to someone else.

LEARNING & CHANGE

> An educated person is one who has learned that information almost always turns out to be at best incomplete and very often false, misleading, fictitious, mendacious - just dead wrong.
>
> Russell Wayne Baker
> (1925 -)
> American Pulitzer Prize-winning writer known for his satirical commentary and self-critical prose, as well as for his autobiography, *Growing Up*.

Share your newly learned skills and knowledge with others. Start by paraphrasing the information into your own words.

This process alone helps solidify new knowledge in your brain. Next, find some way to share what you have learned. Some ideas include writing about the subject learned or participating in a group discussion.

Another great way to become a more effective learner is to use relational learning, which involves relating new information to things that you already know.

Learning typically involves reading textbooks, attending lectures, or doing research in the library or on the Web. While seeing information and then writing it down is important, actually putting new knowledge and skills into practice can be one of the best ways to improve learning. If you are trying to acquire a new skill or ability, focus on gaining practical experience.

Learning is not a perfect process. Sometimes, we forget the details of things that we have already learned. If you find yourself struggling to recall some information, simply look up the things you need to know at the moment.

Furthermore, the longer you spend trying to remember answers, the more likely you will be to forget those answers again in the future. Why?

Such attempts to recall previously learned information actually result, more often than not, in merely recalling superficial, out of context information, or simply in making an error instead of arriving at the correct response.

> Learning never exhausts the mind.
>
> Leonardo di ser Piero da Vinci
> (1452 – 1519)
> Italian Renaissance polymath, painter, sculptor, architect, musician, scientist, mathematician, engineer, inventor, anatomist, geologist, cartographer, botanist, and writer whose genius, perhaps more than that of any other figure, epitomized the Renaissance humanist ideal.

Chapter 3

> Have you invested as much this year in your career as in your car?
>
> Molly Sargent,
> Consultant and trainer.

> It takes nine months to have a baby, no matter how many people you put on the job.
>
> American saying.

> Change is the end result of all true learning.
>
> Felice Leonardo "Leo" Buscaglia
> (1924 –1998)
> Also known as "Dr Love."
> He was an author and motivational speaker, and a professor in the Department of Special Education at the University of Southern California.

Another great strategy for improving your learning efficiency is to recognize habits and styles. There are a number of different theories about learning styles which can all help you gain a better understanding of how you learn best. Gardner's theory of multiple intelligences describes eight types of intelligence that can help reveal your individual strengths. Looking at Carl Jung's learning style dimensions can also help you better see which learning strategies might work best for you!

Research has demonstrated that taking tests actually helps us better remember what we have learned, even if something we've learned is not specifically covered on the test. Students who study and are then tested tend to have improved long-term recall of the material, even of information that was not covered by the tests.

Research also tells us that students who had extra time to study but were not tested had a significantly lower recall of the material.

For many years, it was thought that people who multitasked, or performed more than one activity at once had an edge over those who did not. However, research now suggests that multitasking can actually make learning less effective.

By switching from one activity to another, we learn more slowly, become less efficient, and make more errors. We can avoid the dangers of multitasking by focusing our attention on the task at hand and continuing to work for a predetermined amount of time.

Remember that the key to learning is active engagement with the information through a mediating

LEARNING & CHANGE

process that entails the exploration, discussion, and implementation of the material.

There is a significant difference between information and knowledge. Knowledge occurs once information is applied or used. The learning process must take into account the needs, concerns, and interests of the learners or potential users of information in order for it to be applied effectively. Learning takes place through two-way interaction in which the users of information are engaged with the information in a meaningful way.

Is learning a process?

Learning takes time and patience. It is a process part of our life's journey. A self-directed learning process is arguably the most powerful model for facilitating and inspiring individuals and groups.

A learning process empowers individuals to guide themselves through their personal education cycles and development throughout life's journey. Such a process should be built upon principles that will help identify gaps between one's "ideal self" and "real self."

These gaps represent a primary motivator to learn and improve. Even so, you will need to create and implement a challenging and realistic action plan for development that follows a recognized formula, enabling you to evaluate your progress and to compete with others.

Remember that the most important element to achieve constant success during your life's journey is facilitating ongoing development dialogue between learners and teachers. Both parties have a responsibility to ensure that the entire learning process happens.

> **Beyond your formal schooling:** There is a whole new universe of learning called "professional development" – these are the things that will give you the job - the specific skills to be successful. The sooner you become aware of the fact that you need to demonstrate continuous learning by taking classes, training, workshops, and attending conferences / tradeshows / conventions, as well as by gaining industry certifications, the sooner you will be light years ahead of anyone else in your graduating class. This process does not end until you retire. And if you ignore this area, you will have a much more difficult time with career advancement because employers then to hire subject matter experts. How can you build your knowledge?

Chapter **3**

Get as much experience as you can so that you're ready when luck works.

Henry Jaynes Fonda
(1905 –1982)
American film and stage actor.

Education is what remains after one has forgotten what one has learned in school.

Albert Einstein
(1879-1955)
German-born theoretical physicist who developed the Theory of General Relativity, effecting a revolution in physics.

What is a life development program?

All successful learners and teachers encourage you to grow personally and professionally throughout your life's journey by embracing many educational opportunities and benefits to acquire new skills and knowledge.

As a member of society, you must be committed to supporting your personal and professional development, because your abilities, skills, and contributions will provide essential support to your family, organization, and community.

Any process behind a life's journey development program needs to explore and understand your individual capabilities and aspirations. It needs to be a continuous life learning philosophy, to surround you with people that will provide on-going support and motivation, and to identify goals to help you achieve your potential and contribute to society.

A life's journey development program can enhance your performance and on-going personal and professional development. It will need to help you obtain the necessary information and tools to take advantage of current or future growth opportunities.

Search for individual coaches who are respected in the community and who will help you explore your interests and value your personal and professional ambitions. They should be able to identify the next steps that you should take to move forward in the right direction.

Remember that in today's rapidly changing environment, to be successful, you need to augment your learning capacity constantly to exceed the rate of change imposed on you. You play the most integral

LEARNING & CHANGE

role in your career development process. All successful people believe learning and development occur from self-directed real life and on-the-job experiences, tasks, and problem solving opportunities which are necessary for a thriving life journey.

What do I want to know and learn about?

You should establish what you need to know. Step back for a moment. Identify a few major trends that will affect your social life and your business ventures in the coming 2-3 years.

Ask yourself how much you know about those trends. Create a little curriculum list for yourself, and monitor your progress against that learning agenda. This will help you find the opportunities to amass this new knowledge - perhaps a book, a training course, a seminar, reading certain blogs, or simply sitting down to lunch with people who are really smart about that topic.

Immerse yourself in the subject you want to learn more about. Keep your mind open to new tools, ideas, and techniques. Challenge your conventional wisdom, and ask yourself how the new knowledge changes your existing worldview.

Remember that learning is a lifelong activity. The minute you stop learning, you die.

Is reading important?

Books are the source of a multitude of ideas, innovations, experiences, and knowledge. Reading will enable you to think better and open your mind to change.

Read fiction: Fiction gives your mind a break from what you might normally read but it does even more.

A person who won't read has no advantage over one who can't read.

Mark Twain
(Samuel Langhorne Clemens)
(1835-1910)
American author and humorist. He is most noted for his novels, The Adventures of Tom Sawyer (1876) and its sequel, The Adventures of Huckleberry Finn (1885).

The things I want to know are in books; my best friend is the man who'll get me a book I ain't read.

Abraham Lincoln
(1809-1865)
16th-President of the United States, serving from March 1861 until his assassination in April 1865.

Chapter 3

If I'm honest I have to tell you I still read fairy-tales, and I like them best of all.

Audrey Hepburn
(1929 –1993)
British actress and humanitarian.

Autobiographies are only useful as the lives you read about and analyze may suggest to you something that you may find useful in your own journey through life.

Anna Eleanor Roosevelt
(1884-1962)
First Lady of the United States from 1933 to 1945.
She supported the New Deal policies of her husband, distant cousin Franklin Delano Roosevelt, and became an advocate for civil rights.

Good fiction not only tells a story, it develops interesting characters. So, as you read good fiction, you can learn about human nature while enjoying yourself.

Read a classic: There is a book you have always wanted to read, or a book it seems everyone else has read that you have not. You know what it is. Read it! Then you will cross it off your list, feel better about yourself, and likely learn something very useful!

Read older books: With so many new books with flashy covers and clever titles, it is easy to go to your favorite bookstore and be sucked into buying the latest and newest tome. Any master of a topic is a student of the past. Want a fresh perspective on your area of interest? Find a book from 30, 40, or 100 years ago on that topic and read it. The writing style might be a challenge, but what you learn will be worth the effort.

Read biographies: In short, biographies are written by and about people who have succeeded in some way. Learning from them is like adding mentors to your life, over distance and time. Pick one and read it.

Read history: We can learn about the future by reading about the past. The context may change, but people remain pretty much the same. As you understand things from the past, you create new patterns in your mind, giving you new insights and creating that feeling of *déjà vu* when you most need it.

Read outside your industry: Trade magazines, journals, and blogs are important. However, reading within your industry or discipline will never create a breakthrough idea. Reading something from a completely different industry will, however, spur new thinking and help you create a new and deeper understanding of the world around you.

Read randomly: Stop at a newsstand and pick up a magazine you have never heard of. Read the novel your teenager just finished. Read what your best friend recommends. Go to your reading stack and choose randomly. Go to a used bookstore and have someone pick out a book for you. Do something to spice up your reading in a creative way. You will be surprised what you might learn.

Remember that we read to learn, grow, and enjoy ourselves. When you read more broadly, you will find new perspectives, new ideas, and new solutions in unexpected places. What more could you ask for?

How can I find the right mentor?

Look for someone in your same, or in a similar, field or industry. If you are looking forward to breaking into another industry, find a mentor who already works in your desired field. In addition, you should look for someone who has goals similar to your own.

Take the initiative to contact the individual, as you will benefit the most from the relationship, but do not think that your potential mentor will not benefit at all from the experience. He or she will.

Be prepared to dedicate time for the relationship to grow as not much is gained from a relationship with when little effort and time are put into it. Having a mentor is a truly great way to excel in your chosen career path.

Learn from an experienced professional. A mentor has worked in your industry and can "show you the ropes." Such a person can provide wisdom about

The mediocre teacher tells. The good teacher explains. The superior teacher demonstrates. The great teacher inspires.

William Arthur Ward
(1921–1994)
Author of *Fountains of Faith*, is one of America's most quoted writers of inspirational maxims.

I am not a teacher, but an awakener.

Robert Frost
(1874–1963)
American poet. He is highly regarded for his realistic depictions of rural life and his command of American colloquial speech; received four Pulitzer Prizes for Poetry.

Chapter 3

When you need to transfer knowledge, the method must always suit the culture.

Thomas H. Davenport
(1954-)
American academic and author specializing in analytics, business process innovation, and knowledge management.

Mentoring is a brain to pick, an ear to listen, and a push in the right direction.

John C. Crosby
(1859 –1943)
American politician from the U.S. state of Massachusetts.

workplace issues and career challenges and help you look at things in a new light. A mentor can help you navigate your career and job search by giving you advice and guidance based on his or her past experiences.

Ever feel like you cannot solve a problem when you are too close to the source? A mentor is a great third-party resource to turn to when you are stuck on a project, having a conflict with a superior or co-worker, or facing a hurdle in your career. In addition, a mentor can help you solidify your ideas and goals by talking them through out loud.

Remember that you are more prone to follow through with goals when you have shared them with someone who will hold you accountable. Furthermore, a mentor will help you look at projects and issues in a new way. They will challenge you to think about your career.

Do I want to be a Mentor?

Did you know that there could be great satisfaction in formally mentoring others? It is a way of *giving back* and can also be a way for you to learn some new things. To enjoy your role as a mentor, it is preferable to discuss the roles and responsibilities at the beginning of the relationship with the protégé. Doing so will increase the odds that you will enjoy the time in your mentoring role.

First make your role as a mentor explicit:
First, your role as a mentor should include being a confidante, guide, encourager, advice-giver, and perhaps introducing your protégé to various people and opportunities. Make sure you describe what your role will be clearly at the outset in order to avoid misunderstandings.

LEARNING & CHANGE

It is not the strongest of the species that survives, nor the most intelligent, but the one most responsive to change.

Charles Darwin
(1809 -1882)
English Naturalist.

Second, start out slowly. This will protect your time and allow both of you to see if you have a good fit in your relationship. You can always increase or decrease the frequency and duration of your time together, but begin with some explicit time frames in mind. Let the protégé know if he or she can contact you between regularly scheduled meetings and your preferred method of contact, such as phone, e-mail, text message, etc.

Third, you may not yet know if you recommend this person to others for new opportunities. Make this clear. And if this is a purely business transaction, make that clear, too. For example, you may not want to invite the protégé to your home for dinner and to meet your family. If not, make sure the limits, or scope, of the relationship, are understood.

Next, make your expectations for the protégé clear:
First, the protégé must take responsibility for his or her own learning and growth; you cannot force it on anyone. If the protégé does not take personal responsibility in theses areas, frustration is likely to be right around the corner. In addition, let the protégé take primary responsibility for setting up your meetings. They should also prepare the agenda for the meetings. This saves you time and effort and helps them to be accountable for your time together.

Second, it is important that the protégé know that he or she is responsible for his or her own actions and career. When a promise is made, it should be followed through on - especially if it will further the individual's career. The protégé's follow through will show the level of commitment he or she has to self and to the relationship.

Chapter **3**

People change what they do less because they are given analysis that shifts their thinking that because they are shown a truth that influences their feelings.

John Kotter & Dan Cohen

All is flux, nothing stays still.
Nothing endures but change.

Heraclitus
Pre-Socratic Greek philosopher, famous for his insistence on ever-present change in the universe, as stated in his famous saying, "No man ever steps in the same river twice."

Third, you should make it clear that this is not a *forever* thing. The end date of your time together should be agreed to, or later extended if both parties agree and make sure you both understand the situations that would cause you to terminate the relationship. For instance, a lack of follow through on actions the protégé has committed to may reveal that you are wasting your time; that might be one big reason for terminating a mentor – protégé relationship.

Remember that you can gain a lot of satisfaction from mentoring others; it is wonderful to watch people change and achieve their career goals. You may also personally learn and grow through the relationship. Make sure you "start off on the right foot;" the mentoring relationship will tend to be hassle free when you agree to some guidelines at the beginning of your relationship.

What is Change?

Is change a constant in life or something that occurs from time to time, disturbs our equanimity, and should be resisted? Why does it bother us so much? Why do we regard Change as a cause of strain and hassle? Maybe it depends on how we respond to the question *what is Change?* And maybe that response is driven by how we perceive life?

Simply put, most of us see life from one of two perspectives: we either see life as fixed or we see it as fluid. This is significant because societies are a reflection of personal attitudes. Alternatively, to put it bluntly, your environment will reflect your attitudes.

This matters; it is not a mere philosophical abstraction because it goes straight to the root of all resistance to

LEARNING & **CHANGE**

The problem is habit. We've spent more than a century developing and polishing a management paradigm that resists change. As much as we talk about the horrors of bureaucracy, as much as we poke fun at red tape, as much as we rail at the slowness of officialdom, we still try to get most things done through the same tired, bureaucratic means. Habit haunts us even when we ought to know better.

Robert H. Waterman, Jr.
Co-author, with Tom Peters, of *In Search of Excellence*.

or acceptance of change. It brings us to the ultimate question: What is in it for me?

If we regard life as fixed and static, we tend to think of it in terms of *my* life, *my* job, *my* business, and all nicely packaged up with clear boundaries defining a personal inner *map of reality*. This is the process of cognition, which we use to record, categorize, and interpret our life experiences.

In this perspective, things are seen as separate and in stasis. Time proceeds in a linear manner from past to the future, and the human experience from this perspective is one of the dualities and separation. In other words, there is *me here* and the world *out there*.

So what is Change? This is answered and illustrated by events such as recessions; things that we do not like and that happen to us.

This is how we as human beings are hardwired to behave. It is the *default setting,* and much of what we do is motivated by this inbuilt need to keep things as they are, to preserve the boundaries around *my life*, to preserve our individual survival, safety, and comfort.

What is change but something to be avoided, unless it is on my terms and within my control? It brings us back to the ultimate question: What is in it for me?

"Change is something to be avoided " is normally the default setting for most societies or businesses. A model that works is established and perpetuated for as long as possible, with the same organizational motivations of survival, safety, and comfort.

Chapter 3

Only in growth, reform, and change, paradoxically enough is true security to be found.

Anne Morrow Lindbergh, (1906 –2001) American author, aviator, and the spouse of fellow aviator Charles Lindbergh.

Change is inevitable – except from a vending machine.

Robert C. Gallagher

Change should instead be seen, perceived, and experienced as something that is inter-connected, constantly in movement and changing, even though the linkages may not always be apparent. We live in a world of change, movement, and evolution.

One's life's journey should be seen as fluid. In this perspective, life is regarded as a *process* and not as a *thing,* and the "What is change" question is answered simply with: "Change is life, and life is change."

Remember that, the only current certainty about change is that there is no certainty about change. Charles Darwin said that, *"*It's not the strongest of the species that survive, nor the most intelligent, but the ones who are most responsive to change.*"*

How do individuals and organizations respond to change?

It is preferable to accept reality. Denial only makes matters worse when the evidence of a change becomes overwhelming. Denying reality is simply retreating to the comfort of the world we know.

When a change affects us, a major step in dealing with that change is to understand its impact and longevity. Is it indeed a trend, something temporary or a long-term change?

Possibly it is something that will become a new "normal," and failure to respond to it may be final or fatal? Many people fail because they do not fully grasp the impact of change that is upon them.

Learning to change is all about why a change is taking place. When we are on the receiving end of change, it is critically important to understand the

LEARNING & CHANGE

genesis of that change. Only then can we move forward positively and proactively.

Remember that when a change is inevitable, we have one of two options. First, we can complain about the new reality and fight it for as long as possible. Or, more positively, we can learn how we can better move forward with original ideas, new creativity, and new hope.

By changing nothing, nothing changes.

Tony Robbins
(1960 -)
American self-help author and motivational speaker. He became well known through his infomercials and self-help books.

The second option is admittedly more challenging. However, the first one is a formula for decline, and in some circumstances, even death. We need to learn how to move forward with new realities!

What about a plan for change?

Opportunity usually requires change, and change is scary. The starting point in all planning is two-fold: to eliminate fears and realize your potential.

A good plan always includes new, positive, constructive, and courageous beliefs about yourself and your future.

Faced with the choice between changing one's mind and proving that there is no need to do so, almost everybody gets busy on the proof.

John Kenneth Galbraith
(1908 –2006)
Canadian-American economist. Among his most famous works was a popular trilogy on economics, *American Capitalism* (1952), *The Affluent Society* (1958), and *The New Industrial State* (1967).

For most people, fears govern their lives. Everything is organized around avoiding failure and criticism. They think continually about "playing it safe," rather than striving for their goals. They seek security instead of an opportunity. You need to be responsible to yourself!

Being responsible means preparing a workable personal plan. To achieve this crucial goal, you will need to ask yourself several questions.

The advantage of asking questions will help you think through your plan and put it into practice.

Chapter **3**

Be pliable enough to adjust to changing circumstances.

Donald Trump
(1946 -)
American business magnate, television personality, and author.

We are shaped by our thoughts; we become what we think. When the mind is pure, joy follows like a shadow that never leaves.

Siddhãrtha Gautama Buddha
(563 BCE - 483 BCE)
A spiritual teacher from the Indian subcontinent, on whose teachings Buddhism was founded.

What is it that you want to be different when you have made a change?
You will need to define success and specify your target, or you will not know when you have "hit" it. Decide how you are going to measure and track your progress. Tracking progress is motivational.

What is your current situation?
You should take a hard look at your current situation because it is an important component of changing it. If you do not know where you are, you are not ready to move. It is important to take your time and figure this out thoroughly. This is your starting point.

What is the major benefit of the change?
You would not be setting out to change if your current situation was fine and the new situation did not offer anything better. Identify the benefit, or benefits of the change, and write it up somewhere where you will see it. Add pictures if possible. If you picture in your mind what you would like to be, and you keep and hold that picture there long enough, you will soon become what you have been thinking. This is what you should keep in front of you to motivate you through the change.

What are you already doing now that you can use to your advantage?
Incorporate into your daily routine the desired changes, so that you are regularly reminded of them. This will become a positive habit that you use every day to keep your life functioning.

What other resources do you have?
You have skills, experience, knowledge, and creativity. You have access to knowledgeable people and economic resources. As an adult human being,

you solve problems all the time, so how are you going to use all that?

What is preventing you from making the change?
Identify as many obstacles as possible that may be preventing you from making the change, and figure out how you are going to deal with them: Is it a lack of knowledge, motivation, resources, or opportunity?

Is there something in your life that is actively preventing you from making the change?
If part of the problem is that you have resistance to the change, you need to confront that. You do not need to understand why the resistance is occurring in order to overcome it, but you do need to acknowledge it and do some introspection work in order to make it dissipate. For example, make a list of the fears and solutions you have or a similar resource to open your subconscious mind to the change.

What are you prepared to do in order to make this change?
Having answered the above questions, you should now have a good grasp of the benefits, and also the costs, of making the change. Now you can simply decide whether the benefits outweigh the costs or not?

Do I need to think ahead?
Normal, intelligent people organize each area of their lives to avoid failure and disappointment as mush as possible. It is all about taking the necessary precautions, balancing different options and selecting the course of action that offers the greatest likelihood of success.

Nonetheless, no matter how well you think and plan things will not always turn out the way you expect.

> Nothing ever happens the way it's supposed to. Count on the fact that the job will change. You will always have to do things that aren't in your job description just to be allowed to do the things that are.
> All instructions that you will ever be given will leave out at least one or two crucial items. Many of the most important questions will never be answered.
>
> Albert J. Bernstein, Ph.D.
> American author of *How To Deal With Emotionally Explosive People, Dinosaur Brains, Emotional Vampires, and Neanderthals at Work.*

Chapter 3

Disappointment may still arrive uninvited. Disappointment comes in spite of your best efforts to avoid it, and in many cases, may be inevitable and unavoidable.

During your life's journey, you are going to experience disappointments, and the more goals you set, and the more things you try, the more difficulties and problems you will have. Murphy's law says:

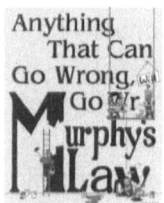

A supposed law of nature, expressed in various humorous popular sayings, to the effect that anything that can go wrong will go wrong.

" Whatever can go wrong will go wrong. Of all the things that can go wrong, the worst possible thing will go wrong at the worst possible time and cost the most amount of money."

Since you cannot always avoid disappointment, no matter what you do, the only thing that matters is how you deal with the disappointment when it comes.

Do you let disappointment overwhelm you? Do you become angry and blame or attack others? Or, do you respond effectively? Unsuccessful people allow disappointment to stop them; they quit and go backwards, while the successful ones recover and continue forward.

Develop the quality to extrapolate. This is the ability to think and plan several moves ahead in whatever you are doing. This way of thinking involves your considering every possible event that could occur and then making provisions for them well in advance. Thoroughness and depth of preparation, carefully considering every detail, is the key to success. Be a great thinker and develop in advance a well thought out plan that will take into consideration every possible eventuality.

LEARNING & **CHANGE**

People will not do what they should do. The rules that you follow are not necessarily those that the universe follows. People will do what they are sufficiently rewarded to do. (This is where virtue beings it's own reward comes in.) Or they will do what is easiest. A corollary to this is, tasks that are not checked will not be done. Most people will leave most things until the last minute. If there is no time limit, then the task will await judgment day for completion.

Albert J. Bernstein, Ph.D.
American author of How To Deal With Emotionally Explosive People, Dinosaur Brains, Emotional Vampires, Neanderthals at Work.

Remember not to react with impatience and anger if something you wish, hope, or plan to happen in a certain way does not happen, or does not happen as you had planned. Frustrated expectations are triggered mostly by negative emotions, and this is quite normal. You can have very little control over your emotions and reactions at this point if something happens to you – or does not happen.

One of the best ways to change your thinking, and your life, is to prepare for disappointment in advance. Set yourself up to bounce back quickly by practicing mental preparation. Always prepare by mentioning to yourself that you are going to face all kinds of problems and difficulties when you decide to proceed with your plan. It is better to prepare yourself for possible negative eventualities, rather than to think of naively attaining automatic success. Simply think of disappointment as a learning process, a positive value, or additional knowledge which is needed to comprehend the necessary future steps in your life's journey. Then try again and again and again!

What are the reasons for resisting change?
It is a fact of life that people change, like seasons change. We must understand why people resist the inevitable or sometimes the absurd.

Misunderstanding the need for change/when the reason for the change is unclear: If people do not understand the need for change, you can expect resistance - especially from those who strongly believe the current way of doing things works well and has for the past for twenty years!

Fear of the unknown: One of the most common reasons for resistance is fear of the unknown. People will only take active steps toward the unknown if they

Chapter 3

God grant me the serenity to accept the things I cannot change, the courage to change the things I can, and the wisdom to know the difference.

Karl Paul Reinhold Niebuhr
(1892 –1971)
American theologian and commentator on public affairs.

All changes, even the most longed for, have their melancholy; for what we leave behind is part of ourselves; we must die to one life before we can enter into another.

Anatole France,
(1844 –1924)
French poet, journalist, and novelist.
He won the Nobel Prize for Literature.

genuinely believe - and perhaps more importantly, feel that the risks of standing still are greater than those of moving forward in a new direction.

Lack of competence: People will seldom admit it, but sometimes change in organizations necessitates changes in skills, and in such situations, some people will feel that they will not be able to make the transition very well.

Connected to the old way: If you ask people in an organization to do things in a new way, as rational as that new way may seem to you, you will be setting yourself up against a certain degree of "hard-wiring," that is all those emotional connections to those who taught your audience the old way, and that is not a trivial thing.

Low trust: When people do not believe that they, or the organization, can competently manage the change, there is likely to be resistance.

Temporary trend: When people believe that the change initiative is a temporary measure.

Not being consulted: If people are allowed to be part of the change, there is less resistance. People like to know what is going on, especially if their lives may be affected.

Poor communication: When it comes to implementing change, there is no such thing as too much communication.

Changes to routines: When we talk about comfort zones, we are really referring to routines. We love them. They make us feel secure. So there is bound to

LEARNING & CHANGE

be resistance whenever a change requires us to do things differently.

Exhaustion and saturation: People who are overwhelmed by the continuous changes resign themselves to them and go along with the flow. You get them to comply in the present, but you do not have their hearts. The usual result is that motivation is low.

Change in the status quo: People who feel they will be worse off after the change are unlikely to give it their full support. Similarly, if people believe the change favors another group, department, or person, there may be unspoken anger or resentment.

Benefits and rewards: When the benefits and rewards for making the change are not seen as adequate for the trouble involved.

What are the change processes?

Everyone during his or her life's journey is subject to change. Understanding the process behind change is crucial to any success. Whether you are implementing a change in a school, factory, office, or technical or commercial environment, you must recognize the phases involved in change.

In order to successfully manage the change processes, it is necessary to analyze the phases of this process. We need to know in which phase to expect what types of situations and problems.

Most successful people are those that are able to adjust themselves to new conditions quickly.

This requires planned learning processes that lead to improved organizational effectiveness. Normally,

Don't say you don't have enough time. You have exactly the same number of hours per day that were given to Helen Keller, Pasteur, Michelangelo, Mother Teresa, Leonardo da Vinci, Thomas Jefferson, and Albert Einstein.

Life's Little Instruction Book.

Chapter 3

If you have always done it that way, it is probably wrong.

Charles Franklin Kettering
(1876 –1958)
American inventor, engineer, businessman, and the holder of 186 patents.

All great changes are preceded by chaos.

Deepak Chopra
(1946 -)
Indian medical doctor, public speaker, negotiator, and writer on subjects such as spirituality, Ayurveda, and mind-body medicine.

people perceive change process in seven typical stages.

Shock and surprise: Confrontation with unexpected situations can happen as a result of accidental or planned events. These situations make people realize that their own patterns of doing things are unsuitable for new conditions. Thus, their perceived competence decreases.

Denial and refusal: People activate values as support for their conviction that change is not necessary. Consequently, they believe there is no need for change; their perceived competency increases again.

Rational understanding: People realize the need for change. According to this insight, their perceived competence decreases again. People focus on finding short-term solutions; thus, they only cure the symptoms. There is no willingness to change their own patterns of behavior.

Emotional acceptance: This phase, which is also called *crisis*, is the most important one. Only if a willingness to change certain values, beliefs, or behaviors is created can someone tap into people's real potentials. In the worst-case scenario, however, the change process will be slowed down or stopped here.

Exercising and learning: The acceptance of change creates a new willingness to learn. People start to try brand new behavior and processes. They will experience success and failure during this phase. Early wins usually come with easier projects, and these will lead to an increase in the way people perceive their own competence.

Realization: People gather more information by learning and exercising. This knowledge has a feedback-effect. People understand which behavior is effective in which situation. This, in turn, opens up their minds for new experiences. These extended patterns of behavior increase organizational flexibility. Perceived competency has reached a higher level than prior to the change.

Change before you have to.

John Francis "Jack" Welch, Jr.
(1935 -)
American chemical engineer, business executive, and author. He was Chairman and CEO of General Electric between 1981 and 2001.

Integration: People totally integrate their newly acquired patterns of thinking and acting. The new behaviors become routine.

Remember that only if we understand these phases of change, and we act accordingly, will we be able to successfully manage the change process without destroying people's motivation and commitment.

What is the downside of change?

What was true more than two thousand years ago is just as true today. Whenever human communities are forced to adjust to shifting conditions, pain is ever present. But a significant amount of the waste and anguish witnessed in the past is avoidable.

I always like to look on the optimistic side of life, but I am realistic enough to know that life is a complex matter.

Walter Elias "Walt" Disney
(1901-1966)
Disney is particularly noted as a film producer and a popular showman, as well as an innovator in animation and theme park design.

According D^r. John P. Kotter, in is book entitled *The Heart of Change*, the most common errors in implementing change in organizations, whether they be social, political, administrative, commercial, or manufacturing are:

Failing to develop a sense of urgency around the need for change. This may help you spark the initial motivation to get things moving.

Failing to create a sufficiently powerful guiding coalition. Convince people that change is necessary. This often takes strong leadership and visible support from key people within your organization. To lead in implementing change, you need to bring together in a coalition, or team, of influential people whose power comes from a variety of sources.

Underestimating the power of vision. When you first start thinking about change, there will probably be many great ideas and solutions floating around. Link these concepts to an overall vision that people can grasp easily and remember. A clear vision can help everyone understand why you are asking him or her to do something. When people see for themselves what you are trying to achieve, then the directives they are given tend to make more sense.

Undercommunicating the vision. What you do with your vision after you create it will determine your success. Your message will probably have strong competition from other day-to-day communications within the organization, so you need to communicate your vision frequently and powerfully, and embed it within everything that you do. When you keep it fresh in people's minds, they will remember it and respond to it.

Permitting obstacles to block the new vision. If you follow these steps and reach this point in the change process, you have been talking about your vision and building acceptance at all levels of the organization. Put in place the structure for change, and continually check for barriers to it. Removing obstacles can empower the people you need to execute your vision, and it can help the change move forward.

Failing to create short-term wins. Nothing motivates more than success. Give your organization a taste

I'm not afraid of death; it's just that I don't want to be there when it happens.

Woody Allen
(1935 -)
Award-winning American screenwriter, director, actor, comedian, author, and playwright, whose career spans over half a century.

LEARNING & **CHANGE**

of victory early in the change process. Within a short time frame, you will want to have results that your people can see. Without this, critics and negative thinkers might hurt your progress. Create short-term targets, not just one long-term goal.

Declaring victory sooner. Dr. Kotter argues that many change projects fail because victory is declared too early. Real change runs deep. Quick wins are only the beginning of what needs to be done to achieve long-term change. Launching one new product using a brand-new system is great. However, if you can launch 10 products, that means the new system is working. To reach that 10th success, you need to keep looking for improvements.

Neglecting to anchor changes firmly. To make any change stick, it should become part of the core of your organization. Your organizational culture often determines what gets done, so the values behind your vision must show in day-to-day work.

Remember that people do not really change just because they see a series of points from a plan and receive some new information. Rather, they change because the change messages communicated reach their hearts and minds.

What should I consider?

We are all, to some extent, creatures of habit. We rely upon and trust routines to guide many of our actions and decisions. These habits, routines, guides, pathways, and traditions combine with beliefs to create a culture, a way of living, which serves the very desirable purpose of pulling us together.

I believe that if you show people the problems and you show them the solutions they will be moved to act.

William Henry "Bill" Gates III
(1955 -)
American business magnate, investor, philanthropist, and author. Gates is the former CEO and current chairman of Microsoft, the software company he founded with Paul Allen.

The illiterate of the future will not be the person who cannot read. It will be the person who does not know how to learn.

Alvin Toffler
(1928 -)
American writer and futurist, known for his works discussing the digital revolution, communication revolution, corporate revolution, and technological singularity.

Chapter 3

Much of our adult life is devoted to the development of reliable routines and habits, which will operate smoothly and predictably to produce the outcomes we seek. We seek to figure out the system. We are careful about not to rock the boat. We become experts. We dwell comfort zones. We know what we are doing.

We know we will do it well. The rules are clear. The expectations can remain unspoken. We can rely upon what has worked in the past. The secrets of success are public knowledge. We need no magic or sacrifice. We can ignore omens and signs. The future has been decided. We have its picture in hand.

Then enter rapid change and turbulence, and what worked yesterday may not work today. In such times, the comfort zone is much like the sand into which the ostrich sticks its head.

In fact, the majority of people prefer the safety and predictability of a settled environment. Most, it turns out, prefer their comfort zones. Change is all about commitment to a better future!

Leaving one's comfort zone is part of one's life journey and needs to be addressed with good values of leadership. Leaders always turn toward danger! This is as true for a human being as it is for animals. You become a leader to the degree to which you force yourself to turn toward danger.

Remember that a good leader is a change agent, an influencer, but most of all an achiever. A change agent identifies the areas that cause fear and stress, and instead of avoiding them and hoping that they will go away, confronts them directly.

> Change will not come if we wait for some other person, or if we wait for some other time.
> We are the ones we've been waiting for.
> We are the change that we seek.
>
> Barack Hussein Obama II
> (1961 -)
> 44th President of the United States.
> He is the first African-American to hold the office.

Recommended Reading & References

We suggest consulting the works identified below in order to learn more about the particulars contained in this chapter.

COHEN, Dan S. THE HEART OF CHANGE FIELD GUIDE.
Harvard Press. ISBN 1-59139-775-8.

GEORGE, Bill et al. FINDING YOUR TRUE NORTH.
Jossey-Bass publishers. ISBN 928-0-470-26136-1.

HOPKINS, Tom. HOW TO MASTER THE ART OF SELLING:
How to persuade others positively.
Champions Press. ISBN 0-938636-03-0.

KOTTER, John P. LEADING CHANGE.
Harvard Press. ISBN13: 978-0-87584-747-4.

KOTTER, John P. THE HEART CHANGE.
Harvard Press. ISBN-1-57851-254-9.

KOTTER, John P. A SENSE OF URGENCY.
Brilliance Audio. ISBN-13: 978-1-4233-6935-0.

LIEBERMAN, David J. HOW TO CHANGE ANYBODY.
Audio Renaissance. ISBN 1-59397-803-8.

MAURER, Rick. CHANGE WITHOUT MIGRAINES, Solving the middle manager's dilemma, www.beyondresistance.com

PATTERSON, Kerry et al. INFLUENCER, THE POWER TO CHANGE ANYTHING.
VitalSmart. ISBN-13:978-0-17-148499-2.

PETER, L. J & HULL R. LE PRINCIPE DE PETER, Pourquoi tout va toujours mal. Éditions Stock. ISBN 70-11-682-850-1580.

THE NEW YORK TIMES. GUIDE TO ESSENTIAL KNOWLEDGE.
St-Martin's Press. ISBN 0-312-31367-5.

TRACY, Brian. CHANGE YOUR THINKING, CHANGE YOUR LIFE: How to unlock your full potential for success and achievement. Willey & Sons. ISBN 0-471-73538-8.

WATERMAN, Robert H. ADHOCRACY. The Power to Change.
Norton & Co. ISBN 0-393-03414-3.

ZIGLER, Philip. MOUNTBATTEN. Collins. ISBN 0-00-216543-0.

Do what you feel in your heart to be right-for you'll be criticized anyway. You'll be damned if you do, and damned if you don't.

Anna Eleanor Roosevelt

Source: White House

CHAPTER 4

BECOMING GREAT

To become great, you must focus your attention on developing your unique and dominant gifts. Do you love to sing, fix broken things, talk to people, or sell things? Whatever it is you like to do, you must focus your attention on doing it to the best of your ability. Give that dominant talent your focus, and allow it to develop through training. Given sufficient time, and enough focus, we will consider you great.

Martin Luther King, Jr. provided us with a wonderful thought about greatness: *If a man is called to be a street sweeper, he should sweep streets even as Michelangelo painted, or Beethoven composed music, or Shakespeare wrote poetry. He should sweep streets so well that all the hosts of heaven and earth will pause to say, here lived a great street sweeper who did his job well.*

Martin Luther King, Jr.

Remember that there is always room at the top for those who are dedicated to greatness, so whatever you do, do it well or not at all. I believe life is too short only to give 50 percent. You only get one bite at the apple. You only live once, so why not live life to the fullest? Why not play life to the hilt? Why not die empty, with no regrets? You have everything you need inside of you to succeed.

You just need to put yourself in the right environment, so you can grow and become all that you were destined to become. Life is too short for you not to be great!

Nothing great was ever achieved without enthusiasm.

Ralph Waldo Emerson
(1803 –1882)
American essayist, lecturer, and poet, who led the Transcendentalist movement of the mid-19th century.

What about the talent myth?

Think of the greatest athlete, musician, artist, or business professional that inspires you, such as Michael Jordan, Frederick Chopin, Albert Einstein,

Chapter **4**

Luck, that's when preparation and opportunity meet.

Joseph Philippe Pierre Yves Elliott Trudeau
(1919 – 2000)
15th Prime Minister of Canada
"Reason before passion" was his personal motto.

Professor K. Anders Ericsson

Victory belongs to the most persevering.

Napoléon Bonaparte
(1769 –1821)
Emperor of the French from 1804 to 1815.
His legal reform, the Napoleonic Code, has been a major influence on many civil law jurisdictions worldwide, but he is best remembered for his role in the wars led against France by a series of coalitions, the so-called Napoleonic Wars.

Napoleon Bonaparte, Winston Churchill, or today, Bill Gates or Steve Jobs. Each of them was born with a special gift. Each was given talents and abilities at birth that most of us do not have access to, right?

Research shows that it is not that simple. In fact, many child prodigies do not go on to major success in the area of their early gifts. And many of the greatest performers, athletes, and business people never showed any early signs of aptitude. So, how did they become great at what they do?

Professor K. Anders Ericsson and his colleagues from the Florida State University published a paper in 1993, on *expert performance,* which along with the additional studies around the world that it inspired, made some very interesting discoveries:

Nobody is *great* without lots of hard work. Early aptitude is not a predictor for greatness in a given field without consistent practice over a long period of time. The most accomplished people in any field need about ten years of hard work before they become of *world class* quality. They call this the Ten Year Rule.

Many of these scientists are now saying that *targeted* natural gifts do not exist at all. You are not born a CEO or chess grandmaster. Rather, greatness is achieved by hard, focused work over many years.

However, you and I both know people who work very hard. Many work for decades at a job or hobby without approaching greatness. Why do they not become *world class* then?

It turns out that only hard work is required. Focused, consistent practice over a long period of time is also

BECOMING GREAT

The key to success is to focus our conscious mind on things we desire not things we fear.

Brian Tracy
(1944 -)
Canadian author and motivational speaker.

It's all to do with the training: you can do a lot if you're properly trained.

Queen Elizabeth II
(1926 -)
Constitutional monarch of 16 sovereign states known as the Commonwealth realms, head of the 54-member Commonwealth of Nations, and, in her role as the British monarch, Supreme Governor of the Church of England.

needed, something the researchers are calling *deliberate practice*.

Truly great people in any field devote many hours to deliberate practice. Deliberate practice is an activity that goes beyond repetition. It is consistent practice where the goal is continually to improve performance, reach beyond current capabilities, and seek feedback on results.

Whatever it is that you do and have a passion for, you can improve and become truly great at, if you are willing to put in the work, that is. Approach each critical task with an explicit goal of getting much better at it. Set goals that are just beyond your level of competency.

As you do a task, focus on what is happening and why you are doing it the way you are. After the task is completed, get feedback on your performance from multiple sources. Do not get emotional about the feedback, and make changes in your behavior as necessary.

Remember to continually build mental models of your situation, of your career, your organization, and your industry. Expand the models to encompass more factors, and do those steps regularly, not sporadically. Occasional practice does not work. Consistency is the key here.

What does all this mean?

We do not have to be born with a special talent in order to be great at something. We just have to have the desire to work constantly at it and to improve our skill.

Chapter 4

The true measure of a man is how he treats someone who can do him absolutely no good.

Samuel Johnson
(1709 – 1784)
English author who made lasting contributions to English literature as a poet, essayist, moralist, literary critic, biographer, editor, and lexicographer.
(Practical lexicography is the art or craft of compiling, writing and editing dictionaries.)

This is very important because it means that you can learn to be good, or even great, at nearly anything!

Most people will not go through the long and difficult process of deliberate practice. Nevertheless, this is what can separate you from the pack.

This is what makes grand performance rare: most people either do not believe they can do a certain thing or are not willing to do the work to become truly great at their passion.

So ask yourself what your mastery skill is? What should you work on to improve regularly - practicing, getting feedback, or improving and pushing yourself to higher levels of excellence? Is it your career? Is it a sport? Is it art or music? Now that you know that excellence is a choice, a whole world of possibilities opens up. Are you ready to pursue your dream and become *world class* at it?

Do I already know how to be Great?

One of the hardest things we will attempt to do is to act on what we already know to do. It is the difficulty that lies behind much of our search for the next big thing; some way to get around or make easier what we know we should be doing. It is never easy, but by applying some new thinking, we can get out of our own way.

Alan Fine states in *You Already Know How to Be Great*, that performance improvement is most often an issue of reducing the interference that is getting in the way of using the knowledge we already have.

Fine says that we have to get right the three elements that facilitate the use of the knowledge we already have. They are:

Faith: Beliefs are all about ourselves and what we believe about others. High performance is more likely to be achieved when we believe that we can learn and do better. The absence of *Faith* could be described as insecurity.

Fire: Fire includes energy, passion, motivation, and commitment. High performance is more likely to be delivered when we are excited about learning and doing. The absence of *Fire* could be described as indifference.

Focus: This is what we pay attention to and how we pay attention to it. High performance is more likely when we pay attention in a way that will quiet our minds. The absence of *Focus* could be described as inconsistency.

High performance happens when we get rid of the interference that blocks these natural, inherent human gifts. *Focus* is the most powerful tool for removing distractions, and thus it is the most effective way to release *Faith* and *Fire*.

Remember that if we create a singular focus on one or more critical variables of the task, we are far more likely to create the flow that creates high performance.

What does it take to be Great?

As parents, teachers, managers, leaders, or coaches, we find it hard to believe, or more likely, it never even occurs to us to think that without our excessive instructing, regulating, controlling, directing, and intervening, people might actually be able to perform with greater confidence, more enthusiasm, and more effective focus.

Continually remind yourself that you have the gift on the inside.

Joel Osteen
(1963 -)
American author, televangelist, and the senior pastor of Lakewood Church in Houston, Texas. His ministry reaches over seven million broadcast media viewers weekly in over 100 nations around the world.

Even if you stumble, you're still moving forward.

Anonymous

Chapter 4

Always remember, your focus determines your reality.

George Walton Lucas, Jr.
(1944 -)
American film producer, screenwriter, director, and entrepreneur. He is the founder, chairman and chief executive of Lucasfilm. He is best known as the creator of the space opera franchise *Star Wars* and the archaeologist-adventurer character Indiana Jones. Lucas is one of the American film industry's most financially successful directors/producers, with an estimated net worth of $3.2 billion as of 2011.

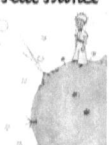

A goal without a plan is just a wish.

de Saint-Exupéry
(1900-1944)
He was an aristocrat French writer, poet and pioneering aviator. He is best remembered for his novella *The Little Prince* (*Le Petit Prince*) and for his lyrical aviation writings, including *Night Flight* and *Wind, Sand, and Stars*.

Rather than instructing, we should be trying to determine what is blocking our family members, individual performers, teams, and organizations.

We tend to approach most situations by providing more information. We actually nourish the expectation that we are supposed to tell people what to do, when we really need to work to help them get what is inside of them out. It is less about providing more knowledge and more about releasing what is already there in the performer.

The result is frequently a lack of engagement and accountability on the part of the people - and little or no performance improvement. You will also observe, when you simply tell people what to do, which is often the case, one of the primary observable signs of your approach to the real outcome is that people are constantly asking you what to do, and that is not good!

The best way to create focus is by asking yourself: What is my goal? What is the reality here? What are my options? What is the best way forward?

To be great is all about removing the interference that is blocking performance!

Focus will help reduce interference, clarify thinking, identify options, and break down the challenge into doable tasks. It will help you believe in yourself and use the knowledge you already have.

We must also practice relentlessly. The best people in any field are those who devote the most hours to what the researchers call deliberate practice. It is an activity that is explicitly intended to improve performance, one that reaches for objectives just beyond one's level of competence, provides feedback on results, and involves high levels of repetition. More deliberate practice equals better performance. Tons of it equals great performance.

Remember that nobody is tremendous without work. It is nice to believe that if you find the field where you are naturally gifted, you will immediately be great at what you do, but it does not happen that way. There is no evidence of high-level performance without experience and/or practice. Reinforcing this "no-free-lunch finding" is vast evidence that even the most accomplished people need about ten years of hard work, a pattern so well established that researchers call it the ten-year rule before they become world class.

> Follow your compass and not your clock.
>
> Anne Moore
> CEO, Time, Inc.

Why the extra step?

For most people, work is tough enough without pushing even harder. Those extra steps are so difficult and painful that they almost never get done. That is the way it must be. If great performance were easy, it would not be rare, which leads to possibly the deepest question about greatness.

While experts understand an enormous amount about the behavior that produces great performance, they understand very little about where that behavior comes from.

The critical reality is that we are not held hostage to some naturally granted level of talent. We can make of ourselves what we will. Strangely, that idea is not popular.

People hate abandoning the notion that they would coast to fame and riches if they found their one special talent. Even so, that view is tragically

> Never in the history of human conflict has so much been owed by so many, to so few. It was perhaps their finest hour.
>
> Sir Winston Leonard Spencer-Churchill
> (1874 –1965)
> Statesman and orator, Churchill was also an officer in the British Army, a historian, a writer, and an artist. He is the only British prime minister to have received the Nobel Prize in Literature and was the first person to be made an Honorary Citizen of the United States.

Chapter 4

These are the times in which a genius would wish to live. It is not in the still calm of life, or in the repose of a pacific station, that great characters are formed. The habits of a vigorous mind are formed in contending with difficulties. Great necessities call out great virtues. When a mind is raised and animated by scenes that engage the heart, then those qualities, which would otherwise lay dormant, wake into life and form the character of the hero and the statesman.

Abigail Adams
(1744 – 1818)
Wife of John Adams, the second President of the United States. Remembered for the many letters she wrote to her husband during the Continental Congresses. Adams frequently sought his wife's advice on many matters.

constraining, because when they hit life's inevitable bumps in the road, they conclude that they just are not gifted and give up.

Recognize that we cannot expect most people to achieve greatness. It is just too demanding. However, the striking, liberating news is that greatness is not reserved for a preordained few. It is available to you and to everyone.

Everybody has talent; you only need to discover what yours is. What do you desire? What are you good at? Find out and do it, and do not just read about it. Do not buy a single product or book or magazine that claims to teach you something in minutes, hours, and days.

They are lying to you, with a hand in your pocket at the same time. Just keep working at what you want to do, or at what you're good at and then keep doing it again. It is the only way to become great, but the good news is anyone can do it. It just takes some time and persistence.

Remember that when the world tells you to give up, try it one more time. The only way to master something is to devote yourself to it with all your strength and soul. For this reason mastery demands all of a person.

What is a Hero?

We are talking about heroism, greatness, that special something that wins your admiration, adoration, and maybe even your face on a postage stamp.

Heroes may seem *passé* in a cynical era where we seem to relish tearing down icons more than we do creating new ones or cherishing the ones we already have. Some folks, moreover, find the very idea of heroes objectionable, arguing that there is something elitist about exalting individuals who, after all, are nothing more than flesh and blood, just like the rest of us.

Nevertheless, we sorely need heroes to teach us, to captivate us through their words and deeds, to inspire us to greatness. And if we seem today to be in short supply of them, the good news is that the pool of potential heroes has never been greater.

That is, every one of us has heroic potential, and there is plenty we can do to develop that untapped greatness, to ensure that the next generation gets the heroes it needs. Though our personal heroes differ, we all share a common vision of what a hero is and is not. So, if you seek greatness, either in yourself or your children, you would do well to nurture these aspects of personality, courage, and strength.

Whatever a hero is, he is not a coward or a quitter. Heroes maintain their composure, and even thrive, under adversity, whether it be a life-threatening event facing a war hero or the psychological or emotional strain that a politician or businessman must endure.

Honesty: Deceit violates our culture's concept of heroism.

Kind, loving, generous: Great people may fight fiercely for what they believe, but they are compassionate once the battle is over, toward friend and foe alike.

Skill, expertise, and intelligence: A hero's success should stem from his talents and smarts, rather than from mere chance. Although for the sake of modesty, a hero might well attribute his hard-earned achievements to luck.

Be patient. Today's graduates are used to the fast pace of technology and in a way, this has built up a low tolerance for being willing to wait. Especially for job promotions or advancement. But unfortunately, the big wheels of business do not move that quickly and sometimes the opportunity simply is not there yet. Take a deep breath. It will happen, but not necessarily on your timelines. It is all in the timing…great things come to those that wait!

Chapter **4**

Every post is honorable in which a man can serve his country.

Letter to Benedict Arnold (14 September, 1775)

George Washington

Source: Metropolitan Museum of Art

Risk-taking: Even though many people will not take risks in their own lives, they admire risk-taking in someone else. No matter what they are called, heroes are willing to place themselves in some sort of peril.

Objects of affection: We might be impressed, on an intellectual level, by somebody's deeds. However, admiration is not enough; heroes must win our hearts as well as our minds.

Remember that heroes also exhibit depth. Depth is that timeless, mythical, almost otherworldly quality that marks a hero. It is hard to articulate exactly what this is, but we all know it when we see it. It is what makes even physically diminutive heroes seem larger than life.

How can I be patient?

In a world where messages and information can be sent across the world instantly, everything is available with only a few clicks of a mouse. Fortunately, patience is a virtue that can be cultivated and nurtured over time.

People who are impatient are people who insist on getting things done now and do not like to waste time. However, some things just cannot be rushed.

Think about your happiest memories. Chances are such as they were instances when your patience paid off, like when you worked steadily toward a goal that was not immediately gratifying or took a little extra time to spend leisurely with a loved one.

Would you have those memories if you had been impatient? Probably not because almost anything really good in life takes time and dedication, and if

He that can have patience can have what he wills.

Benjamin Franklin
(1706-1790)
Founding Father of the United States. A noted polymath, Franklin was a leading author, printer, political theorist, politician, postmaster, scientist, musician, inventor, satirist, civic activist, statesman, and diplomat.

Chapter 4

The two most powerful warriors are patience and time.

Lev Nikolayevich Tolstoy
(1828-1910)
Russian writer who primarily wrote novels and short stories.

I have never thought of writing for reputation and honor. What I have in my heart must come out; that is the reason why I compose.

Ludwig van Beethoven
(1770-1827)
German composer and pianist. A crucial figure in the transition between the Classical and Romantic eras in Western art music, he remains one of the most famous and influential of all composers.

you are impatient, you are more likely to give up on relationships, goals, and other things that are important to you. Pleasant things may not always come to those who wait, but most good things that do come do not come right away.

However, not focusing on what matters most in life will assuredly fuel impatience. When other less important things fuel our impatience, taking time to remember any one of these more important things in life reduces our tendency to want something different right now.

While it may be true that, if you work hard at something, you will eventually get what you want, most of the time you have to be patient about what you want. For some, this may be easy, but the only thing that matters is that you know how to keep yourself busy, even when nothing seems to be happening.

Just remember that patience is a mental skill that you will never forget, so cherish patience as a major step for you in life. Impatience is not something to be proud of, but something that you should try to get rid of before it harms you in life. Always keep a positive outlook. Remember that life is not a race, but a journey to be savored each step of the way.

We all have plans, but things do not always work out as planned. Accept the twists and turns in life gracefully. Keep your expectations realistic. This applies not only to circumstances, but also to the behavior of those around you. Even if the occasion is not an isolated incident but is, instead, caused by their repeated neglect and carelessness, losing your patience is not going to make it any better. Rather, address the issue with discussion and self-control.

Remember to give yourself a break. Stop holding yourself and the world around you to unreachable standards. Sure, we would all be more patient if babies did not cry, dishes did not break, computers did not crash, and people did not make mistakes. However, that is never going to happen. Expecting the world to run smoothly is like beating your head against the wall. Give yourself a break!

How can I become a great Person?

Being a great person is not difficult. Start loving everyone you know at home and at work. Whenever someone gives you a good reason not to love him or her, "be great" and love him or her anyway. Whenever someone invites or provokes you to hate him or her, refuse to play the game. Instead, generate some understanding for the person and, if possible, some love. Eliminate revenge as a purpose in your life.

A great person shows greatness by the way he or she treats little people.

Thomas Carlyle
(1795–1881)
Scottish satirical writer, essayist, historian, and teacher during the Victorian era.

Whom do you want to get even with? Change that decision to something positive, such as the desire for prosperity for yourself and others. Whenever you feel depressed or a loss of hope, find someone to love. Make yourself thrilled by loving people. If you ever feel happy and then unhappy, look for where you let some hate slip in.

Remember that your happiness will remain intact if you do not feel revenge or hate. Make yourself mentally tough and strong by loving people. To maintain that strength, do not seek revenge or agree with reasons to hate.

How can I become a great Finisher?

More than anything else, becoming a great Finisher is about staying motivated from a project's beginning to

Chapter **4**

Stick to a task 'til it sticks to you...for beginners are many, but finishers few.

Thomas Spencer Monson
(1927-)
American religious leader and author.

If your actions create a legacy that inspires others to dream more, learn more, do more and become more, then, you are an excellent leader.

Dolly Rebecca Parton
(1946 –)
American singer-songwriter, author, multi-instrumentalist, actress, and philanthropist, best known for her work in country music.

its end. It is easy to stay focused on the progress that has already been made.

When we focus on the progress already made, we are more likely to try to achieve a sense of balance, by making progress on other important goals. If, instead, we focus on how far we still have to go, motivation is not only sustained, it is heightened.

Fundamentally, this has to do with the way our brains are wired. We are tuned in subconsciously, to the presence of a discrepancy between where we are now and where we want to be. When the brain detects a discrepancy, it reacts by throwing resources at it: attention, effort, a deeper processing of information, and willpower.

In fact, it is the discrepancy that signals that an action is needed. You might feel good about what you have already accomplished, but you probably will not do much more if you stay focused on that.

Remember that great Finishers force themselves to stay focused on the goal, and never congratulate themselves on a job half-done. Great managers create great Finishers by reminding their employees to keep their eyes on the prize, and they are careful to avoid giving effusive praise or rewards for hitting milestones along the way. Encouragement is important, but to keep your team motivated, save the accolades for a job well, and completely, done.

Do I want to become a great Leader?

Regardless of whether you are new to management at work, lead a troupe of boy scouts, or whether you have just been made the captain of your local football team, these points should help you become a great leader.

BECOMING GREAT

Confidence: Confidence is a strong belief in your ability to succeed. Arrogance is excessive, often rude, and an obnoxious quality that will not make people like you. If you want to be a strong leader, having confidence is important because people need to feel secure and confident about what their leader is doing.

The greatest leader is not necessarily the one who does the greatest things.
He is the one that gets the people to do the greatest things.

Ronald Wilson Reagan
(1911–2004)
40th President of the United States, serving from 1981 to 1989. Prior to that, he was the 33rd Governor of California from 1967 to 1975 and a radio, film, and television actor.

Any sign of uncertainty will likely unsettle your team. It will make them nervous and unable to perform to the highest standards. Even if you are not feeling one hundred percent confident yourself, it is important that you do not make it obvious to those around you. This does not mean you should not ask for help and advice, but you should not come across like someone who does not know where he or she is going next.

Listen: You must be able to listen to, and understand, any problems or worry your team has. Being strong and a good talker are important, but almost secondary when compared to the importance of being able to listen.

Proactive: As a leader, you must be aware of what is going on around you and try to find potential problems, so you can stop them before they actually manifest.

Focus: It is important for everybody around you that you are always aware of what is going on. If anything does go wrong, then it will be you that your team turns to, and they will need you to know what is going on.

Do not lose your head: In a pressured situation, a good leader will remain calm and collected. If you start to panic, then things could rapidly fall apart.

Decisive: Similar to confidence, being decisive relates

Chapter 4

The new leader is a facilitator, not an order giver.

John Naisbitt
(1929 -)
American author and public speaker in the area of future studies. His first book *Megatrends* was published in 1982.

A leader leads by example, not by force.

Sun Tzu
(544 BCE– 496 BCE) Ancient Chinese military general, strategist, and philosopher who is traditionally believed, and who is most likely, to have authored *The Art of War*, an influential ancient Chinese book on military strategy. Sun Tzu has had a significant impact on Chinese and Asian history and culture, both as an author of *The Art of War* and through legend.

to being sure of what you are doing, or being able to instruct your team to do what is necessary. Half-hearted decisions will leave your team feeling unsure or confused. If you are not certain of how to deal with a situation immediately, take some time to think it over first before delivering a firm, decisive course of action.

Respect: It is very hard for anyone to respect, or admire, someone who is rude, short of temper, and obnoxious. It is vital you treat everybody around you with grace and respect. Leaders who treat people fairly and generously are those who people really want to work with, and do a good job for.

Nevertheless, inscribe in your memory the following aspects that great leaders nurture:

- *Genuineness.* Be open, straightforward, comfortable in your skin; no BS or sugarcoating.
- *Passion.* You love and feel strongly about what you do and how you do it.
- *Clarity.* Communicate thoughts, feelings, and insights in crystal clarity and simplicity.
- *Intelligence.* No way around this one, and yes, it shows through.
- *Insight.* Ability to boil complex factors and mounds of data down to rare conclusions.
- *Determination.* Be driven and full of purpose, determined to achieve and succeed.
- *Confidence.* Do not be overconfident, but have enough self-doubt to be objective.
- *Humility.* Having willingness to admit mistakes, misjudgment, fear, and uncertainty is endearing.
- *Courage.* Have the willingness to take risks and take a position against considerable odds.
- *Humor.* Have the right measure of humor, for it brings down other's defenses.

Do I want to become a great Follower?

Even the most powerful leaders have to answer to someone; so at some point, we all have to be followers. And great leaders cannot be great unless they have great followers. Here are some things followers will want to practice.

Imagine a place where everyone chooses to bring energy, passion, and a positive attitude every day.

The Hon. Gerald "Gerry" Weiner (1933 -) Canadian politician, Minister of State for immigration. In 1988, he became Minister of State for Multiculturalism and served in that position until 1991.

Inform: Leaders throughout history have made wrong decisions based on a lack of information or bad information. Great followers keep their leaders abreast of key projects, even if they are not asked.

A leader cannot recognize and reward if he does not know what his followers are doing. Leaders also hate finding out about bad news from a third party. If something happens, give your leader a heads-up that there may be trouble coming.

Support: It means do not criticize your leader, particularly behind his back. For one thing, it is unprofessional. It is also a safe assumption that whatever you say, good or bad, will get back to the leader.

Deliver: When a follower consistently delivers extraordinary results, most leaders end up giving him or her more trust and latitude. And when a leader does not have to waste time cleaning up after mistakes or following up, he or she has more time to spend on vision, strategy, recognition, resource allocation, and other good things that benefit the entire team. Do what you say you are going to do, and do it well.

Admit: When you make a mistake, admit it. Be accountable; do not make excuses; do not point fingers; and do not act like a victim. Tell your leader

Chapter 4

what happened, what you are doing to fix it, and what you have learned, so that it will not happen again.

Be a Team Player: Be an advocate for the leader in the background. Leaders cannot stand back-stabbers, and they inevitably discover what you have done no matter how subtle you think you have been.

Offer Solutions: Do not bring problems to your leader; bring solutions. It is a tired *cliché*, but it is true. In addition, do not delegate upwards.

Prioritize work: Great followers never have to ask their leader to help prioritize their work for them. New followers might need to do this, or average followers, but not the great ones. They always seem to know what is important and urgent and what can wait.

Be an Optimist: Positive attitude and energy are contagious, and everyone loves being around optimists.

Embrace change: A great follower can see the possibilities in someone else's idea. Be the early adopter; do not be the time waster.

Love what you do: If you do not like what you do, it will show up in your work and attitude. You are not doing yourself, your leader, or your co-followers any favors by hanging on to what you consider to be a lousy job. Life is too short; find something that you can be passionate about.

How might I become miserable?

A few years ago, I finally came to the conclusion that some people like to be unhappy, that they actually feel happier when they are miserable. I am sure that it

---

The extra mile.
Be willing to work longer hours and go for as many miles as it takes.
90% of your life and career is about showing up and participating in person.
The remaining 20% is the longer hours, passionate vision and personal effort required to go 110% of the distance required.

You can turn painful situations around through laughter.
If you can find humor in anything, even poverty, you can survive it.

William Henry "Bill" Cosby, Jr.
(1937-)
American comedian, actor, author, television producer, educator, musician, and activist.

You can be smart and happy or stupid and miserable. . . it's your choice.

Gordon Bitner Hinckley
(1910-2008)
American religious leader and author.

is an oxymoron, but I am guessing you know the kind of people I mean and that we agree.

I like to think that I align with people's belief systems rather than trying to change them, so I thought it was remiss of me not to offer advice to those folks that thought wallowing in self-pity and gloom would result in a good day.

Of course, we all understand that this does not apply to you, but if you know somebody who likes to work on feeling bad about things, please feel free to help them out by passing on the following handy tips.

Always whine and complain about stuff that is out of your control. Great examples are the weather, other people's actions, and the housing market. Do not ever miss an opportunity to remind people that life is much worse and a lot harder than they think it is.

Keep up to date on celebrity culture. We all know that celebrities lead charmed, perfect lives. They do not ever get sick and they have lots of money and are all perfectly balanced human beings. Read up on them, yearn to be them, and above all, idolize them as the gods they are. Never forget that your life is a meaningless travesty compared to theirs.

Be a martyr and never ever put your own needs first. Make sure that you put your spouse, kids, even the mailman's happiness above yours. These people are far more important than you, so show them so by neglecting yourself. Do not worry if you get sick and die because that will just cement your position in the Martyr's Hall of Fame.

Judge others. Do not listen to people that say you cannot judge a book by a cover. You do not have

Chapter **4**

You know the message you're sending out to the world with these sweatpants. You're telling the world, "I give up. I can't compete in normal society. I'm miserable, so I might as well be comfortable."

Jerome Allen "Jerry" Seinfeld (1954 -) American stand-up comedian, actor, writer, and television and film producer, best known for playing a semi-fictional version of himself in the sitcom *Seinfeld*.

time to read books, so how else are you supposed to make up your mind (about someone) other than by glancing at the cover?

If a person is fat, then he eats too much; if he smokes, he is stupid; and if he is out of work, it is obvious he is lazy.

Local news. Make sure you know who has murdered whom, and more importantly, which drug-crazed lunatic is on the rampage in your neighborhood. Do not go to bed feeling cheerful when you can watch stories about the worsening economy and rising crime rates.

Eat junk food, drink lots of beer, and never exercise. Stick to your guns and ignore those fitness fascists like the plague. After all, if you get fit, you have to stay fit, and that requires time, time that you need to watch TV.

Watch more TV. If you are watching eight hours of TV per day, that is not enough. Watch more and aim for a diet of reality TV, local news, soap operas, and anything that humiliates people. Avoid programs that are remotely informative like the plague.

Refuse to see other people's points of view. If you have an opinion, stick to it. You have spent years fine-tuning your belief system, so hang on to it tightly. Even if you realize you are wrong, stick to it regardless, and look confident. If that does not work, shout a lot.

Be Catastrophic. You have not been sick, you have been violently ill. You have not had a bad day at work you have had a nightmare. You do not have a tough boss, you have the boss from hell. Get the message?

BECOMING **GREAT**

Whether you think you can, or you think you can't-- you're right.

Henry Ford
(1863 –1947)
American industrialist, the founder of the Ford Motor Company, and sponsor of the development of the assembly line technique of mass production.

It is amazing what you can accomplish if you do not care who gets the credit.

Harry S. Truman
(1884 –1972)
33rd President of the United States (1945–1953)
Truman's presidency was also eventful in foreign affairs, with the defeat of Nazi Germany and his decision to use nuclear weapons against Japan, the founding of the United Nations, and the adoption of the Marshall Plan to rebuild Europe.

Drift into your job. Take a job that pays an O.K. amount of money and then spend every day despising it. Do not think about developing a career plan.

Understand you are worthless without a degree. Believe that in the history of the world, nobody has ever been successful without first doing well at school. If you have not got at least one degree, be convinced that you are unemployable in anything other than flipping burgers. Give up trying to get a decent job now to avoid future disappointment.

Do not accept compliments. If somebody compliments you on something, you need to find out what they are after. They could not possibly be genuine. They are trying to manipulate you. Do not rest until you find out what it is.

Can I become a strategic Thinker?

Strategic thinking will create a structured and progressive path forward to your vision. It is essential in order to improve your performance in order to improve. And in order to raise the bar of performance in what ever your endeavor is from where you are now to where you want to be will require a level of strategic thinking that is in perfect harmony with your vision for the endeavor.

We believe that the following requirements are essential to the success of all your endeavors:

- *You must have a vision.* And you must be great at thinking with a strategic purpose and creating a visioning process. Great strategic thinkers are visionaries.
- *You must learn from experience and commit to being a lifelong learner.* You must use your

Chapter 4

It is easier to criticize than to praise.

Germain Decelles
La gestion de projet d'affaires.
(Business Project Management)

Happiness is when what you think, what you say, and what you do are in harmony.

Mohandas Karamchand Gandhi
(1869-1948)
The pre-eminent political and ideological leader of India during the Indian independence movement.

experiences to think well about strategic issues. Great strategic thinkers strive for continuous improvement in all they do.

- *You must learn to use your time efficiently and effectively.* Great strategic thinkers place a high value on time and are masters of strategic time management.

- *You must have an extremely high level of awareness* of what is happening around you and be open to absorbing all that you can. In any endeavor, there are clues, often subtle, ones both internal and external, to help guide future directions and to identify opportunities. Great strategic thinkers take all of this in, and then they set aside time to think about all the experience and information to help guide them in planning and working on the issues, challenges, and opportunities that lie ahead.

- *You must be patient.* It is so important to remember that strategic thinking is about the longer-term future, rather than about today, tomorrow, or next week.

- *You must have clearly defined and focused milestones and goals.* And these must be subject to frequent review to ensure your thinking is validated. Great strategic thinkers have an innate ability to identify the potential twists and turns that could destroy the possibility of reaching the desired milestones.

- *You must be open-minded.* Great strategic thinkers do not bind themselves by constantly judging their thinking as they think up ideas. They keep open minds and test the details later.

I think the way to change it is to handle issues individually when it's essential to do so.

Stephen Joseph Harper, PC MP
Prime Minister of Canada

Source: World Economic Forum - Remy Steinegger

Chapter **4**

You must be realistic in creating your ideas and be honest about what is achievable in the longer term. This will facilitate and ensure a higher probability of delivering success. The great strategic thinker will under-promise and over-deliver.

- *You must reserve and set aside time for yourself.* In highly competitive and intense dealings, it is important to take time out. This could be to go on a retreat, or to get away for a day to a creative relaxing place to do some strategic thinking, without undue distractions. Great strategic thinkers set aside time to "think!"

- *You must seek the advice and perspective of others.* This may take the form of bouncing ideas off a team of people, participating in a peer advisory group, or working with a strategic thinking advisor to achieve that needed advice and other perspectives.

Remember that if you can acquire the above essential elements, then you will become a great strategic thinker. We encourage you to fully realize the benefits of strategic thinking.

Is Life a call for action?

Life is about creating yourself. It is about realizing that we have the ability to craft and shape who we are and what we experience in this world. We have the ability to decide what we believe in, what we do, and also how we perceive and absorb those things around us.

We get to choose how we will act on our desires and interests and what actions to take to become that person we envision and desire to be. All of that boils down to the reality that we actually do have the ability

The only limit to our realization of tomorrow will be our doubts of today.
Let us move forward with strong and active faith.

Franklin Delano Roosevelt
(1882 –1945)
32nd President of the United States (1933–1945) and a central figure in world events during the mid-20th century, leading the United States during a time of worldwide economic crisis and world war.

to create ourselves. We just have to find a way to believe in that alternate view and act on it.

We must continually ask ourselves if we are taking advantage of our ability to create ourselves?
To respond affirmatively to that question, we have to be willing to do anything and everything we can to determine what our true interests and desires are and where we should be going with them. We need to have the will to devote the time and energy that are required to get there and to ask ourselves tough questions repeatedly until we find our answers.

What is my purpose? What am I supposed to be doing? What am I interested in? What are my unique skills, and what can I contribute?
We have to be willing to figure things out for ourselves. We have to be open to reprogramming ourselves. We need to be willing to clear away any thoughts that may be holding us back.

A common barrier for people is limiting their thoughts, and you have to commit to removing them and chipping away at any thoughts that may be holding you back. If life is all about creating yourself, then there is really no reason to assume anything about yourself based on the traits you think you inherited. Allow your desires to shape your reality, without being limited by what you may have thought in the past was realistic.

Dedicate yourselves to the journey. Be willing to do anything and everything you can to move forward. This means you need to keep your vision at the forefront of your mind and everyday do something in support of it. You should continually make progress and commit to completing the things you need to do.

> Obstacles are things a person sees when he takes his eyes off his goal.
>
> Joseph Cossman
> Cossman International Marketing

> Your work is to discover your world and then with all your heart give yourself to it.
>
> Siddhārtha Gautama Buddha
> 563 BCE - 483 BCE
> A spiritual teacher from the Indian subcontinent, on whose teachings Buddhism was founded.

Chapter **4**

When you're in trouble and all your defenses get stripped away, you realize what matters and who matters. That's when you need to get back to your roots and to your values.

David Richmond Gergen
(1942 -)
American political consultant and former presidential advisor who served during the administrations of Nixon, Ford, Reagan, and Clinton.

Each problem has hidden within it an opportunity so powerful that it literally dwarfs the problem.
The greatest success stories were created by people who recognized a problem and turned it into an opportunity.

Joseph Sugarman
Marketing Specialist

You must be ready to do whatever it takes, consistently and continuously.

Remember that you have the ability to take control, figure out what you were really meant to do, believe that you are more than capable of achieving it, and then do everything to make that vision a reality. You have the ability to create the life you desire. All you have to do is realize that that is indeed the case and then continually choose to do something about it. Life is a call to action!

Can I simplify any problem?

Simplifying it is all about realizing that the more we break a problem down, the easier it will be to work towards an answer. The more we examine everyone's part, his or her purpose, and then rebuild the puzzle with each part, the more the problem or issue will become answerable.

Break it down: If you have a problem with a life issue, break down the problem to its basic form. Do not destroy your potential by thinking of "eating" the whole thing. Rather, look at each piece, one at a time.

Ask for help: Do not be afraid to ask for help. It never hurts to learn, and people who look down on you for asking for help should not be significant to you and your life anyway.

It is not the end of the world: If you cannot solve a problem, do your best and learn from a possible correction. Most problems we have are smaller than we tend to make them out to be.

Be kind to yourself: Just try to understand the issue on a simpler level and go from there. Diminishing your confidence will not solve the problem.

> I think the next best thing to solving a problem is finding some humor in it.
>
> Frank Howard Clark
> (1888 –1962)
> American screenwriter.
> He wrote for 100 films between 1913 and 1946.

Slow down: The more time you waste thinking about how hard the problem is, the longer it will take to solve it. Take a step back and refocus on just one part of the problem.

Take a walk: Get your blood flowing and the carbon dioxide out of your system and bring in some healthy new oxygen. This will help clear your frustration.

Do not be analytical: Try not to make the problem more complex than it needs to be, and the answer or solution will present itself. The answers to life's problems are usually easier than you would expect.

How can I become a great Friend?

Being a great friend is usually intuitive, but sometimes we need a reminder about how to go above and beyond when it comes to friendships. Here are five ways to be the type of friend you would want in your own life.

> Friendship is to be purchased only by friendship. A man may have authority over others, but he can never have their hearts but by giving his own.
>
> Thomas Woodrow Wilson
> (1856 –1924)
> 28th President of the United States.

Make time for friends: A great friend is busy, but still manages to make time for their pal. Do not look at friendships as a waste of time, or something to pay attention to only when you need a favor. Make time even when you are busy by proactively keeping in touch.

Give support freely: A great friend will rally behind you without prompting when you need a few words of encouragement, and he will stand by you when you make a life-changing decision. While friends might not always agree with the things you are doing, they will support you nonetheless. This means that when you need a shoulder to cry on, or somebody to celebrate with, they will be right by your side.

Chapter **4**

> Real friendship is shown in times of trouble; prosperity is full of friends.
>
> Anonymous

Know how to have fun: Having a great time might mean something slightly different to each of us, of course, but your best pals know exactly how to make you kick back and enjoy yourself with some fun activities.

Be honest: Your pal might not always tell you what you want to hear, but he will be honest with you, and that is valuable in today's world. More than that, his honesty will always be meant to help you rather than hurt you.

Respectful: When a friend disagrees with you, he does so in a respectful way that allows for you both to come to an understanding; it does not force one of you to change his mind or allow only one of you to win. Your level of trust is high with a good friend because he respects you too much to ruin your relationship.

How can I become a great Facilitator?

We can all instinctively tell if a person is putting on a show or being honest. People know if you are being real. If you can be authentic, acknowledge your mistakes, ups and downs, fears and joys, problems and successes, you will be considered credible and trustworthy.

> If you want to lift yourself up, lift up someone else.
>
> Booker Taliaferro Washington
> (1856 –1915)
> African-American educator, author, orator, and political leader. He was the dominant figure in the African-American community in the United States from 1890 to 1915.

Being real means you get to be imperfect. You are entitled to make mistakes, not to know all the answers, to be occasionally angry, or to have a bad day. You can have personal problems, complicated feelings, and decide when and how much of yourself to share. You get to be a group-member, and like everyone else in the group, you can and should be held accountable for your behavior.

An important message to all group members is that who are you, right now, is really great. That is a good message for facilitators, too. Being authentic, imperfect, and self-accepting, as well as being very clear about your limits in working with people, is a great combination of facilitator attributes.

Tolerate emotional intensity: It is a gift to be able to experience a full emotional life. However, that capacity develops fully only when people are supported in experiencing the complete range of emotional options. It is very helpful if a facilitator can hang in there when group members are having strong feelings. To the degree that you can be comfortable with expressions of anger, joy, love and other emotions, your value to the group will be greatly enhanced.

Children have to be educated, but they have also to be left to educate themselves.

Ernest Dimnet
(1866-1954)
French priest, writer, and lecturer, he is the author of *The Art of Thinking*, a popular book on thinking and reasoning during the 1930s.

Grow "big ears": Big ears imply the ability to be a good listener, a person who can be non-judgmental and comfortable with the long silences that are sometimes necessary while people figure things out. Having big ears mean, you will be able to hear the unasked questions.

Be satisfied with small success: Under the best of conditions, it can take a long time to feel safe enough and supported sufficiently to try a new behavior and risk failure or looking foolish. The facilitator, who can recognize this fact, preferably from personal experience, will have the necessary empathy and patience to wait. Real patience often means celebrating the smallest hint of movement in a self-affirming direction.

Be consistent: By being consistently affirming, supportive, and fair with all members of a group, you

Chapter 4

As I saw it, my job was to create the climate that enabled people to unleash their potential. Given the right environment, there are few limits to what people can achieve.

Captain D. Michael Abrashoff U.S.N.
Former *captain*, Commander D. Michael Abrashoff, the commanding officer from 1997 to 1999, wrote the best-selling book *It's Your Ship*.

become worthy of trust and of a reciprocal commitment.

Avoid personal agendas: The quickest way to disqualify yourself as a trustworthy person is to have all the answers to their problems, know how they should behave, or make their decisions for them.

Share power: Sometimes you will need to exert control. However, when you share power, you demonstrate your belief in the group's competence. Being consistent and avoiding personal agendas, as well as practicing a healthy sharing of power, makes a facilitator really great!

How can I become a great Parent?

Using simplicity is the best way to become an excellent parent. A great parenting skill is to understand how the mind of the child works and to integrate some of this simplistic fun into your own life.

Children love to play, and they know quite nicely how to entertain themselves. So, take pleasure in the children's fun and participate in their activities.

Attempt newer activities in order to increase your parenting abilities, and let your children know that they may do the same thing. Parents ought to enable their children to try many more various activities, such as hockey, basketball, playing the piano, dancing, etc. This is a way that young children can experience what they really get pleasure from and what they are excellent at.

Children are curious about many new things, and it is excellent to have them explore a brand new activity.

Parents should take their kids to the library or to a museum to pick out some new books or to learn other educational things that they can enjoy.

Encourage your children to meet new friends, particularly in their kindergarten. It is so gratifying to see how open a child is to meeting an unknown individual. It is a great way to enhance their communication abilities and help them turn out to be sociable.

Remember that it is especially important to teach your child that a *genuine smile* can get them anywhere in life.

How can I become a great Mentor?

A good mentor is first a teacher. Instilling a desire to learn and encouraging the ability to take the risks involved with learning are two of the mentor's greatest goals. Mentoring facilitates the sharing of knowledge, experience, and wisdom.

Mentoring is a "two-way street" and an active collaboration between committed individuals. It is a partnership dedicated to empowering both parties to achieve personal and professional growth.

Understand the potential of the person you are mentoring. When you are aware of a person's natural abilities and talents, you can guide that person forward into areas that will truly interest him.

Identify the personality traits that will help you better understand what drives a person to learn. Establish in the beginning whether you and the person you may be mentoring are compatible and can make the relationship work.

Real knowledge is to know the extent of one's ignorance.

Confucius
551 BCE – 479 BCE
Chinese thinker and social philosopher of the Spring and Autumn Period. The philosophy of Confucius emphasized personal and governmental morality, correctness of social relationships, justice, and sincerity.

Do you share similar values and beliefs? Are your work ethics basically the same? Do you share a mutual respect for each other?

And as basic as it may sound, in order for a mentor/protégé relationship to work, you must like each other.

A good mentor is able to share personal experiences and achievements openly, so that the protégé can learn from both the failures and successes.

As a mentor, it is also your responsibility to help your protégé believe in his, or her, own potential and encourage him to develop his own personal interests and follow his own dreams. Many people find it much easier to adapt to the goals and directions of others, rather than to develop their own.

You will be there to instruct and to teach but also to encourage, reward, and inspire. You will be the one to help your protégé up when he falters and to offer encouragement and reinforcement whenever he begins to doubt himself.

A mentor will encourage a protégé to venture out of his natural comfort zone and to try brand new things and take new risks in order to broaden his horizons and expand his realm of experiences.

Understand that a mentor/ protégé relationship will require quite a large investment of both time and energy in order to be successful. It can be enormously rewarding and fulfilling for the mentor and an enriching and even life-changing experience for the protégé.

Your greatest challenge may be in maintaining the right balance of friendliness and familiarity. It is essential to provide sufficient support, encouragement, and respect, while being able to teach, counsel, and recommend ideas for change and improvement without becoming too personal or to involved.

And finally, be open to the possibility that a relationship may not be working. Not every pairing will be a good match, and it is far better to part as friends than to try and force a relationship.

Remember that eventually protégés need to leave the nest and strike out on their own. If you have done your job, the protégé will stand on his or her own with conviction and confidence. As a mentor, you can feel good about the fact that you helped someone enhance his or her career. Often, a mentoring relationship can have a lifetime positive impact on each person involved. A great mentor is a great person.

How can I become a great Seller?

Everyone lives by selling something, but that does not mean everyone is good at it. However, it is possible to hone your sales skills if you want to improve your ability.

I haven't spoken to my wife in years.
I didn't want to interrupt her.

Rodney Dangerfield
1921 –2004
American comedian and actor.

You can be technically good at what you do, but not good at selling. And while you can learn to sell, you also need to make sure that you are not trying to be something you are not, because with sales, it is all about authenticity.

The biggest mistake made by many folks is falling into the *lock and load* approach. You see this all the time as a customer. The salesperson has learnt their product knowledge really well, can explain why it is a great product and rattle off all the product

Chapter 4

specifications. However, this is all immaterial until you know what the customer wants.

Another common mistake is to interrupt the customer repeatedly when he is trying to tell you what he needs in order to do the sales pitch. Some people think this is a dialogue, and in some ways it is, but it is not an effective way to sell.

You need to ask all your questions before you start the selling process, so you understand the customer's needs. What you want to do is extract key pieces of information from the customer.

You need to make sure you have a valid reason for speaking to someone you want to sell to. And you need to have some degree of confidence, courage, drive, and ambition to be an effective seller.

As human beings, we do change, grow, adapt, perhaps even learn, and become wiser.

Understand that the most important way to improve your sales skill is by studying language:

Wendy Carlos
American composer and electronic musician.

First, you should know that the language you use is uniquely shaped by your personality and is influenced by your background and experiences.

Second, recognize that customers speak a variety of languages, depending on their role in the organization and the decision-making process.

Finally, the conscious ability to adapt your language to mirror the customers is the best way to build a winning rapport.

Remember that you need to ascertain whether the customer is enjoying the social interaction side of the sale, or if he is in a hurry, and then respond in a like fashion. And lastly, if you find that you are unable to help the person, make sure you refer him to someone who can whenever possible.

BECOMING **GREAT**

How can I become a great Communicator?

There are two sides to any communication, and if the person listening, reading, or seeing gets a different message than the one that you intended, then you have messed up just as much as they have. There is a duty of care for both parties to try and understand at a deeper level what the other person is trying to say.

Any problem, big or small, within a family always seems to start with bad communication. Someone isn't listening.

Emma Thompson
(1959 -)
British actor, comedian, and screenwriter.

Communication, or rather the lack of it, is one of the biggest problems facing mankind today. We all generalize, distort, and delete information when we are communicating. This is an absolute necessity to staying sane, but it breaks down when we start to interpret other people's communications.

So, how do you learn to communicate well? Like any skill, it takes patience and practice. Take the time to listen to the language you are now using.

Is it always clear what you want? Do you expect people to mind read you by leaving out crucial information? Are you aware of your tonality and the impact that can have? Now think about your body language. Are your words, tonality, and body language congruent? By that I mean, is your voice saying yes while your shoulders slouch and you sound as if it is a real effort, which suggests you are thinking no?

Bad human communication leaves us less room to grow.

Rowan D. Williams
(1950 -)
Anglican bishop, poet, and theologian.

Listen actively and pay attention. Too many people are listening purely for a gap in delivery, so they can dive in and give their own opinions, or worse still, not listening at all because they are multi-tasking or their minds are elsewhere. Try to understand what the other person means by staying engaged. The easiest way to succeed in life is to study great communicators. Look for what they are doing that you are not, and then just do it! You will screw up from

Chapter **4**

Whenever you find yourself on the side of the majority, it's time to pause and reflect.

Mark Twain
(Samuel Langhorne Clemens)
(1835-1910)
American author and humorist. He is most noted for his novels, *The Adventures of Tom Sawyer* (1876), and its sequel, *The Adventures of Huckleberry Finn* (1885).

It is not love that is blind, but jealousy.

Lawrence George Durrell
(1912 –1990)
British novelist, poet, dramatist, and travel writer, though he resisted affiliation with Britain and preferred to be considered cosmopolitan.

time to time, but who cares, as long as you are working towards your goals.

Remember not do take it for granted that you are a good communicator because if you do, you probably are not. If you cannot communicate properly, you are destined to be misunderstood, and trust me, it is not the rest of the world's fault; it is yours.

Do I need to surround myself with people better than myself?

Greatness happens when you let go. It is the ultimate *stone soup*. You bring only your true self and others actually provide all the other ingredients you think you need when the time comes. It takes an incredible amount of self-confidence and faith to play this game.

Let go of judgment. You can only do this if you are able to put aside your own issues and prejudices and see others for who they are.

Let go of ignorance. Sifting through the self-promoters to get to what is real requires that you have some education about the world around you.

Let go of jealousy. If you are jealous of what someone else has, you will feel it, they will feel it, and discord will probably be inevitable.

Let go of need. Needing others is only fractionally better than being jealous of them. Needing people leads you to make demands, which makes things awkward and usually ends painfully.

Let go of labels. Strong people do not need anyone to define a relationship with labels. Trying to label a relationship can scare a strong person off. If you are not comfortable with ambiguity, keep that to yourself.

BECOMING GREAT

Let go of doubt. Great people want people around them who are even better than them. If you do not believe you belong, you do not belong.

Let go of control. Great people will do things you do not understand and cannot explain. Insisting on living in a world you fully understand will keep you from experiencing people who can open you up to new and bigger ideas. Great people approach their worlds with innocence, wonder, and curiosity.

Let go of you. Help the people around you shine brighter. The strong ones will keep you around and start feeding your gift back to you. The weak ones will show their true colors by trying to take advantage or assuming malice on your part.

Let go of work/life distinctions. When the relationship comes first, it is sometimes difficult to know if it is going to grow into friendship, business, or both. This is especially true with great people who jump from idea to idea with ease, and make no distinction between projects that make money and those done for fun. Always be professional.

Let go of self-esteem. The thing about surrounding yourself with awesome people is you are always being challenged. It is with love and support, but they are challenges, nonetheless, and you must win, without help, without cheating, without rationalizing. And when you do not win, you must bounce back quickly and confidently because you do not want to fail twice in a row.

Let go of ego. You need to accept that you are just one small part of other's success and help them get recognition anyway. Let others claim successes.

It isn't until you come to a spiritual understanding of who you are – not necessarily a religious feeling, but deep down, the spirit within – that you can begin to take control.

Orpah Gail Winfrey
(1954 -)
American media proprietor, talk show host, actress, producer, and philanthropist.

A change in bad habits leads to a change in life.

Jenny Craig
(1932 -)
American weight loss guru and founder of Jenny Craig, Inc.

Chapter **4**

> The top personal attributes employers say would make them less likely to extend a promotion include:
> *Piercings* –
> 37 percent
> *Bad breath* –
> 34 percent
> *Visible tattoo* –
> 31 percent
> *Wrinkled clothes* –
> 31 percent
> *Messy hair* –
> 29 percent
> *Dresses too casually* –
> 28 percent
> *Too much perfume or cologne* –
> 26 percent
> *Too much makeup* –
> 22 percent
> *Messy office or cubicle* –
> 19 percent
> *Chewed fingernails* –
> 10 percent
> *Too suntanned* –
> 4 percent

Let go of negative. Awesome people fix things or laugh about them. They see no third option.

Let go of safe. Surrounding yourself with extraordinary people guarantees one thing: change. You know, the scary, risky, life-altering change. Yes, it means no-more-comfort-zone change. A great person requires us to abandon the safe harbor of our routines.

Is success an accident?
Those who achieve success do so by making the right choices and cultivating good habits. Those with the best habits succeed in life. Before a person can succeed in life, he or she must understand the real nature of success. In addition, she or he must recognize that true success is not so much the result of correct decisions but of right habits.

A person may decide to go on a diet. In fact, millions of people make that decision every day. But how many stick with it? The key is not in the making of decisions. The key to success lies with those daily decisions that form habits. People with the right habits are the ones who will succeed in life.

- People who wish to succeed in life must take care of their minds and bodies. They must eat right, stay in shape, and maintain spiritual and mental, health as well as physical health.

- Successful people decide to focus on the positive and express gratitude for the many things for which they can be thankful.

- Be careful not to make too many assumptions about life. Be thorough. Pay attention to detail.

We make a living by what we get, but we make a life by what we give.

Sir Winston Leonard Spencer-Churchill (1874 –1965)

Successful people practice this attentiveness with respect to tasks and also people.

- Successful people pay attention to the words they use and do not throw accusations or generalizations around carelessly.

- Successful people understand that feelings are real and most of the time relevant. Feelings, however, should never drive decisions. On the contrary, decisions should drive feelings.

- Successful people understand the critical value of time. They do not waste time in social situations that will bring them down. Instead, they invest their time in people they can help and in people who can help them.

What about accidental success?

Accidental success means taking advantage of opportunities as they arise, including a willingness to act boldly and decisively and to take risks without overanalyzing possible outcomes.

Successful invention requires a lot of trial and error. It also means not using social networking, but the "old boys club" from your past school and college days to enable you to network in a friendly and persuasive manner, especially to gain favor, business, or connections.

You can be presented with all the opportunities in the world, but if you are a negative person, always seeing the glass as half empty, the fly in the ointment, why something cannot or should not be done, you will never capitalize on any of it.

Chapter 4

Few will have the greatness to bend history itself, but each of us can work to change a small portion of events, and in the total of all those acts will be written the history of this generation.

Robert Francis "Bobby" Kennedy
(1925 –1968)
American politician, a Democratic senator from New York, and a noted civil rights activist. An icon of modern American liberalism and a member of the Kennedy family, he was a younger brother of President John F. Kennedy and acted as one of his advisors during his presidency. From 1961 to 1964, he was the U.S. Attorney General.

Smart, successful people are attracted to those who are genuine and open. Being genuine entices others to open up and share their thoughts and feelings.

Be inquisitive and search for answers about how things work.

A place in the world can be difficult to explain or quantify, but I think it comes down to a genuine need to figure things out, understand how things work, or do something important. It drives certain people, and one thing is for sure: we do not stop until we find what we are looking for.

Remember that truly successful people are not infatuated with themselves. They are primarily givers and not takers. They make decisions and cultivate habits designed to bring value to others. While there are certainly situations that some people seem just to have coming their way: *lucky breaks* or inherit large sums of money or great health, these kinds of things do not constitute success.

True, meaningful success does not come by accident, but by our own deliberate choices and constructive habits. Those who wish to have success in life must choose to succeed in life and live that way every single day.

What should I consider?

Greatness requires significant planning and even bigger effort. From personal achievement to business success, the potential for greatness is in direct relationship to the way you live your life. Greatness is about understanding what you wish to accomplish and why the accomplishment is worth the effort, time, and sacrifice. Look at the venture from many perspectives and measure the risk/reward ratio for your participation. Be realistic and evaluate the potential for crisis, success, or lasting chaos associated with the new venture, investment, commitment, or structural change, and only then should you proceed accordingly.

Know your strengths and weaknesses. Utilize your strengths and strengthen your weaknesses. Build on high-performance skills as you strengthen areas of great weakness or instability. Use areas of proficiency to balance your general ability.

If you are a great problem solver, but lack listening skills, learn to investigate the comments of others, as if you would be a puzzle or complex problem. Actively listen to discover the *who, what, when, where* and *why* of the story. Focus your attention on how to solve the problem.

Learn how to be a more effective communicator, negotiator, problem solver, and general team player. Think in terms of the greatest benefit to the greatest number of people and work to implement efficient change. State the desired goal and work to find a means to that end.

Remember to be positive. Work to solve problems and find a happy solution to every crisis. Think in terms of results, not obstacles.

Recommended Reading & References
We suggest consulting the works identified below in order to learn more about the particulars contained in this chapter.

REHKOPF, Ed. LEADERSHIP ON THE LINE.
Clarity Publications. ISBN 0-9722193-1-5.

ROBINS, Anthony. UNLIMITED POWER.
Simon & Schuster. ISBN 0-671-62146-7.

TRACY, Brian. CHANGE YOUR THINKING, CHANGE YOUR LIFE. How to Unlock Your Full Potential for Success and Achievement. Willey & sons. ISBN 0-471-73538-8.

Before you can inspire with emotion, you must be swamped with it yourself. Before you can move their tears, your own must flow. To convince them, you must yourself believe.

Sir Winston Leonard Spencer-Churchill

CHAPTER 5

COMMUNICATING

No matter what your age, background, or experience, effective communication is a skill you can learn. Developing good communication skills is an important part of living a fulfilled life.

Effectively communicating your career, personal, and everyday needs in a way that comes across clearly, persuasively, and thoughtfully is crucial. Even so, not everyone knows how to communicate.

Knowing how to communicate well is not innate, and many bright, talented, and dedicated people do not get where they should, all because they fail to adequately communicate their points. With a little self-confidence and knowledge of the basics of good communication, you would be able to communicate your message effectively in both conversations and presentations, in all walks of life.

Communication is the process of transferring signals/messages between a sender and a receiver through various methods, such as written words, nonverbal cues, and spoken words. Communication is the mechanism we use to establish and modify relationships.

Communication is selling; after all, we are all selling something. Some of us sell products, other ideas. Some will sell a viewpoint, and surely we all sell ourselves. At every stage of our private lives or careers, whether it be management, sales, training, education, politics, church, home, or parties, we are all engaged in selling something.

The two most powerful things in existence:
a kind word and
a thoughtful gesture.

The Hon.
Gerald "Gerry" Weiner
(1933 -)
Canadian politician; Minister of State for immigration. In 1988, he became Minister of State for Multiculturalism, and served in that position until 1991.

Chapter 5

> Communication is a skill that you can learn. It's like riding a bicycle or typing.
> If you're willing to work at it, you can rapidly improve the quality of every part of your life.
>
> Brian Tracy
> (1944 -)
> Canadian author and motivational speaker.

> Without feelings of respect, what is there to distinguish men from beasts?
>
> Confucius
> (551 BCE – 479 BCE)
> Chinese thinker and social philosopher of the Spring and Autumn Period.
> The philosophy of Confucius emphasized personal and governmental morality, correctness of social relationships, justice, and sincerity.

Moreover, the idea of selling can be used interchangeably with the idea of persuasion and reaching an agreement.

So, if communication is selling, then what we want is for our listener to "buy in," to agree. We want to influence him, or her, to make a decision in our favor. Our listener will base his, or her, decision primarily on how he or she feels about us, on information received at an emotional level, and on whether we have made emotional contact.

The first thing to understand about communication is that we are all selling something. The second and even more crucial thing to understand is that people buy emotion and justify with fact.

The attitudes you bring to communication will have a huge impact on the way you compose yourself and interact with others. Choose to be honest, patient, optimistic, sincere, respectful, and accepting of others.

Honesty is always the best policy. You will never regret being honest. It sounds like the simplest thing in the world, but being truly honest with others and with yourself, can be a real challenge. Communication is also about being sensitive to other people's feelings and facing uncomfortable truths about yourself. This usually requires lots of patience, vigilance, and hard work.

Patience is never easy, but it is probably even harder now than at any time in history. In a world where messages can be sent across the world instantly, seemingly everything is available with a few clicks of the mouse. It is very hard not to expect instant satisfaction.

COMMUNICATING

Faced with the choice between changing one's mind and proving there is no need to do so, almost everyone gets busy on the proof.

John Kenneth "Ken" Galbraith
(1908-2006)
Canadian-American economist.

When people saw me opening myself to criticism, they opened themselves up. That's how we made dramatic improvements.

– Captain D. Michael Abrashoff, U.S.N.

Nevertheless, patience remains a valuable tool in life. Fortunately, patience is a virtue that can be cultivated and nurtured. It does take time to fulfill this goal, but once this has grown into an ordinary skill for you, you certainly will not be disappointed at what life can offer you with a little patience.

Optimistic people are the real communicators. Seeing only the pessimistic aspects of any situation can cause you to miss opportunities, neglect problems that need to be solved, and fail to take action that would otherwise improve your relationships and quality of life.

Always assuming the worst can have major negative consequences on your life. In fact, studies show that pessimists are more likely to develop chronic illnesses later in life than optimists. Optimists look for the light at the end of the tunnel.

Sincerity is all about being genuine, having faith and trust in yourself, and just being rather than trying to project something that you are not. No other formula exists for sincerity than to be sincere.

Respect should be incorporated into your everyday lifestyle and be part of your regular social skills. You should always remember that it takes respect to earn respect.

Being respectful tells people you not only care about others, but you care about yourself. Respect is shown in many more ways than by just using *please* and *thank you*. Listening and responding intelligently and seriously will show a great amount of respect.

Accepting others is the most important value in the communication process. We can find it challenging to

Chapter 5

Personal relationships are the fertile soil from which all advancement, all success, all achievement in real life begins.

Benjamin Jeremy "Ben" Stein
American actor, writer, lawyer, and commentator on political and economic issues.

To understand, listen to what is beneath the words.

Anonymous

accept other ways of life and rituals. However, closed-mindedness and intolerance are not helpful, especially when there is so much we can learn about other cultures. Learning to accept and respect them is an important step that opens your mind to the world around you and everyone's unique differences.

Remember that the wonderful thing about character and integrity, which are intimately related, is that they are some of the few things in life that no one will ever be able to take away from you force ably. Your choices are your own. Even if someone can take your life, he cannot force you to make a choice that you believe is wrong. To be a good communicator is to learn about your own virtues and values and about how they correspond to your life and the world around you.

Should I be sensitive to other people's feelings?

People can be irritating, annoying, and baffling in life. Nevertheless, before striking back at them about how pestering they are, or ignoring them because you do not particularly like them, remember that you have to be considerate of how that person feels and why they do and say certain things. Before you can judge, you need to understand that person's feelings and thoughts.

It is especially important not to judge people before "stepping into their shoes." Before you judge them and label them, think about how he or she must feel. You should not label a person before trying to make sense out of why they act or say the things they do.

How would you feel if someone you were not familiar with came up to you and said something mean to you, just because you looked, sounded, or acted differently than what the person expected or thought you should? You would be pretty hurt, wouldn't you? Do not put someone through that kind of pain if you would not want to be put through it yourself.

Sometimes people can seem to be in a bad mood when you talk to them. This does not mean they are constantly angry and depressed. You should not let one encounter ruin your perception of a person. Maybe he or she was having a bad day, or not feeling well. Try to speak to people more often and see how they act. You have to be around them frequently to see how they really are.

The deepest human need is the need to be appreciated.

William James
(1842-1910)
Pioneering American psychologist and philosopher who was trained as a physician.

You will also find it common to meet people with different beliefs, likes, and dislikes than you have, so do not be frustrated if the person you are talking to does not like something you do, or like something you do not do. They feel that way for a reason, and you should respect that. You should talk to them and not let your insecurities or beliefs get in the way.

Remember that when you start to feel irritated, it is good to stop yourself from saying anything. Think to yourself that there is a reason this person is acting this way, and realize that you should respect how he or she feels at the moment, even if it bothers you.

Can I develop effective listening skills?
People often think they are listening, but they are really thinking about what they are going to say next when the other person stops talking.

Truly effective communication goes both ways. Not only should one be able to speak effectively, one must listen to the other person's words and engage in communication about what the other person is speaking about.

Chapter 5

Avoid the impulse to listen only for the end of their sentence, so that you can let out the ideas or memories that come to your mind while the other person is speaking.

> **Listen before you speak.**
> How often have you said or done something, and then noticed that it was neither well understood nor followed? We often continue policies because *"we've always done it that way,"* and then fail to notice that people, practices, or acceptable norms have changed. Ask people what they think; ask follow-up questions; and listen carefully for truths or inconsistencies within the answers. And once you have found the answers that work, thank and praise those who participated in the dialogue.

Listening is an essential part of communication, and it is different from hearing. Do not interrupt. Do not get defensive. Just hear others and reflect back on what they are saying, so they know you have heard them. Then you will understand them better, and they will be more willing to listen to you. In addition, you will learn a lot from listening. But as simple as listening to and acknowledging other people may seem, doing it well, particularly when disagreements arise, takes sincere effort and lots of practice and patience.

Being a good and patient listener will help you not only solve many problems at home, school, or work, but also to see the world through the eyes of others, thereby opening your understanding and enhancing your capacity for empathy.

However, you should postpone a conversation if you are not in the mood to listen. It is better not to talk about something if you are not ready rather than to try to force through a conversation when you are too distracted by emotions, worries, and other things that prevent you from listening.

It is often too easy to wonder about how what the other person is telling you is impacting you. It is not a good idea to consider yourself as smarter than the speaker and to assume that if you had been in his or her shoes you would have seen your way through the problem much faster.

Active listening is not about inward thinking. Instead, you must look at the problems from the other person's

COMMUNICATING

Nature, which gave us two eyes to see and two ears to hear, has given us but one tongue to speak.

Jonathan Swift
(1667 –1745)
Irish satirist, essayist, political pamphleteer. He is remembered for works such as *Gulliver's Travels*, and *A Modest Proposal*, *A Journal to Stella*.

perspective and actively try to see his or her point of view.

Remember that when your interlocutor feels that he or she has been listened to, he or she is much more likely to listen to your ideas. Never criticize while listening, and at no time should you attack another person for his or her feelings. In addition, keep in mind that sometimes we need to listen *between the lines*, but there are times when we need to absorb things at face value. When we listen intensively, our minds are often busy placing what we hear into both the situation and our emotions, which creates barriers to our ability to listen fully to what is being said. This is similar to making judgments and drawing conclusions before all has been said. Do not do that. Take what is being said at face value and go on.

What determines my personality?
To communicate properly and adequately, you will need to evaluate your current personality.

Are you outgoing, laid-back, friendly, funny, shy, etc.? In which category do you fit? How do others like you? Do you like your current personality position?
If you want to change from one to another, you must think about the following things.

Do you recognize yourself?
The Know-It-Alls. They are arrogant and usually have an opinion on every issue. When they are wrong, they get defensive.

The Passives. These people never offer ideas or let you know where they stand.

The Dictators. They bully and intimidate. They are constantly demanding and brutally critical.

To become different from what we are, we must have some awareness of what we are.

Eric Hoffer
(1902-1983)
American philosopher and author.

Chapter 5

> It is a psychological fact that you can influence your environment and thoughts. If you do so consciously and with high purpose, you can change your habits and attitudes for the better.
>
> — Anonymous

The "Yes" People. They agree to any commitment, yet rarely deliver. You cannot trust them to follow through.

The "No" People. They are quick to point out why something will not work. What is worse, they are inflexible.

The Gripers. Is anything ever right with them? They prefer complaining to finding solutions.

Are you extroverted or introverted?
All of us wonder why we do not get along with some people. It may well be because we have different personalities than them. Find out whether you are an introvert or an extrovert.

EXTROVERTS ARE MORE LIKELY:	INTROVERTS ARE MORE LIKELY:
To energized in a group: "*I create fun at a party!*"	To be drained by a group: "*I'd talk to a friend.*"
To move forward! "*I'm assertive and aggressive!*"	To be recessive. "*I'm less assertive, non-aggressive.*"
To be driven by anger under stressful emotion.	To revert under stress or to be cautious.
To be Ready to communicate: *I think on my feet.*	To deliberately communicate: *I plan ahead.*
To talk first: *I'll talk; then I'll summarize.*	To talk later: *I'll clarify it; you summarize.*
To have a talkative pace of speech: *Pressing on!*	To have a slower pace of speech: *I'm thorough...*
To be rapidly moving on: *Let's go!*	To be deliberately moving; *Let's prepare.*
To share opinions easily: *I'm confident!*	To reserve opinions; *I'm figuring it out first.*

COMMUNICATING

EXTROVERTS ARE MORE LIKELY:	INTROVERTS ARE MORE LIKELY:
To be confrontational: *I'm rather decisive!*	To be non-confrontational; *I'll decide thoughtfully.*
To be impatient listeners; *I'll interject this!*	To be patient, attentive Listeners : *You finish.*

In a relationship, each person should support the other; they should lift each other up.

Taylor Alison Swift
(1989 -)
American country pop singer-songwriter, musician, and actress.

It is impossible to get anything made or accomplished without stepping on some toes; enemies are inevitable when one is a doer.

Edith Norma Shearer
(1902 –1983)
Canadian actress. In the 1930 film *The Divorcee*, for which she won an Oscar for Best Actress; she played sexually liberated women in sophisticated contemporary comedies.

Are you task or relationship oriented?

Task-oriented people: Dress more formally; their topics of speech are current issues and tasks at hand. Their body posture is more rigid. Their facial expression is more controlled. Their general attitude is on the serious side. They have controlled and guarded emotions. They are filled with facts and data. They are less interested in small talk. Their decisions are fact based. They are disciplined about time. They are strict and disciplined about rules. They are harder to get to know and seem preoccupied.

Relationship-oriented people: Dress more informally; their topics of speech are people and stories. Their body posture is more relaxed. Their facial expression is more relaxed. Their general attitude is more on the playful side. They are free to share their emotions. They are more interested in small talk. Their decisions are gut based. They are less disciplined about time. They are more lenient about rules. They are easy to get to know and are more carefree.

What is your social style?

Sanguine: The sanguine temperament personality is fairly extroverted. People of a sanguine temperament tend to enjoy social gatherings and making new friends. They tend to be boisterous. They are usually quite creative and often daydream. However, some alone time is crucial for those of this temperament. Sanguine can also mean very sensitive, compassionate, and thoughtful. Sanguine personalities generally struggle with following tasks

Chapter 5

If you don't like something, change it. If you can't change it, change your attitude.

Maya Angelou
(1928 -)
American author and poet who has been called "America's most visible black female autobiographer" by scholar Joanne M. Braxton.

all the way through, are chronically late, and tend to be forgetful and sometimes a little sarcastic. Often, when pursuing a new hobby, interest is lost quickly when it ceases to be engaging or fun. They are very focused on people. They are talkative and not shy. People of sanguine temperament can often be emotional.

Choleric: A person who is choleric is a doer. This kind of person has a lot of ambition, energy, and passion, and tries to instill these in others. Choleric person can dominate people of other temperaments, especially phlegmatic types. Many great charismatic military and political figures were choleric. They like to be leaders, in command of everything.

Melancholic: A person who is a reflective thinker has a melancholic disposition. Often very considerate, this is the kind of person that gets rather worried when he or she cannot be on time for an event. Melancholics can be highly creative in activities such as poetry and art. They can become preoccupied with the tragedy and cruelty in the world. They are also occasionally perfectionists. They are frequently self-reliant and independent; one negative part of being a melancholic is sometimes that they can get so involved in what they are doing that they forget to think of others.

Phlegmatic: Phlegmatics tend to be self-content and kind. They can be very accepting and affectionate. They may be very receptive and shy and often prefer stability to uncertainty and change. They are very consistent, relaxed, calm, rational, curious, and observant, making them good administrators. They can also be very passive-aggressive.

Remember that if you want to change your personality, you must change your attitude. If you want to be peppy and happy about things, or funny and clever, or you want to be spunky, it may take time. So take the time to change, taking it step by step. You will see that this changes the way you talk - and eventually think. It will even change your characteristics, such as what values you hold as a person. Your change in attitude will be most evident when you "look the part." You do not have to go out and get a new wardrobe, but maybe adding some new jewelry or changing the way your hair looks, or changing the way you smile, laugh, hold yourself, or anything else may help.

How can I have the courage to say what I think?

The courage to say what you think can afford you the opportunity to learn more than you knew before. Individuals who are hesitant to speak because they do not feel their input would be worthwhile need not fear. What is important or beneficial to one person may not be to another - and may be more so to someone else.

We are all-human and have flaws. Even if your physical appearance or social skills are not what you wish they were, that does not have to stop you from being confident. Now that you know you can make worthwhile contributions to the conversation, think about the good things that may happen if you succeed.

Do not compare yourself with other people. It is a wasteful pursuit, and you could be doing something better with your time and energy. Know what you, personally, want and expect from yourself, and focus on attaining those things. The things that you want and expect from yourself do not have anything to do with how you measure up to others.

In giving advice, seek to help, not please, your friend.

Solon
(638 BCE – 558 BCE)
Athenian statesman, lawmaker, and poet. He is remembered particularly for his efforts to legislate against political, economic, and moral decline in archaic Athens.

Chapter 5

Joan was a being so uplifted from the ordinary run of mankind that she finds no equal in a thousand years. She embodied the natural goodness and valour of the human race in unexampled perfection. Unconquerable courage, infinite compassion, the virtue of the simple, the wisdom of the just, shone forth in her. She glorifies as she freed the soil from which she sprang.

Sir Winston Churchill,
in *The Birth of Britain*

Centre Historique des Archives Nationales, Paris

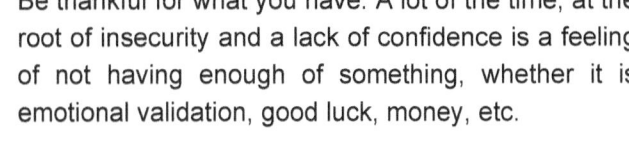

I am still learning every day not to watch other people's careers and compare.

Joely Fisher
(1967 -)
American actress.

Be thankful for what you have. A lot of the time, at the root of insecurity and a lack of confidence is a feeling of not having enough of something, whether it is emotional validation, good luck, money, etc.

By acknowledging and appreciating what you do have, you can combat the feeling of being incomplete and unsatisfied. To find that inner peace will do wonders for your confidence.

Having the courage to say what you think is when you feel strongly about something, speak loudly and clearly, and make eye contact with people. Let go of your fear of being perceived as annoying or overbearing. People will judge you all the time, and usually they will misjudge you anyway, so why bother trying to indulge in their opinions at all?

If people put you down, then let them know that everyone, most of all you, does not hold the same opinion of you. This may, at first, be hard to do. However, once you stick up for yourself a few times, your confidence builds, and you get more adept at it.

The strongest principle of growth lies in the human choice.

Mary Anne Evans
(1819 –1880)
Better known by her pen name George Eliot, she was an English novelist, journalist, and translator, and one of the leading writers of the Victorian era.

Do not be afraid to ask questions. It will keep you in the conversation and will make your interlocutor reflect indirectly on your point of view by exposing his own. But do not forget that there is a fine line between confidence and arrogance. Being confident means recognizing your inherent value. Being arrogant means thinking you are more valuable than other people.

Every now and then, listen to yourself and notice how you are doing. Be conscious of your speech. When you are saying what you think, have the confidence to say it to be heard.

Chapter 5

But behavior in the human being is sometimes a defense, a way of concealing motives and thoughts, as language can be a way of hiding your thoughts and preventing communication.

Abraham Harold Maslow
(1908-1970)
American professor of psychology at Brandeis University, Brooklyn College, New School for Social Research, and Columbia University who created Maslow's hierarchy of needs.

An appropriate tone and volume can inform listeners that you mean what you say, you have thought about what you are saying, and what you are saying is worth hearing. Using proper inflection helps ensure that your listeners hear exactly what you are saying and reduces the possibilities for misunderstanding.

Remember that the greatest acts of kindness are those done by choice, not out of fear or guilt. It is noble to want to help others, but it is something you should do because you want to, not because you feel you have to. While helping others can be a source of confidence, for some people it can be a symptom of a lack of confidence, especially when it comes to basing your self-worth on how much you do for other people.

Do men and women communicate differently?

Two men having a conversation communicate effectively and clearly with each other. They often use matter-of-fact language, and the exchange is simple and logical.

Two women conversing together also communicate effectively and clearly, but the exchange has added nuances that allow the conversation to expand and deepen into something broader.

Since men and women communicate differently, conversations between the two genders can be misunderstood, frustrating, and sometimes argumentative. As someone discovers how to communicate with the opposite sex, he or she can start to understand the others and have enjoyable conversations.

But communication is two-sided - vital and profound communication makes demands also on those who are to receive it... demands in the sense of concentration, of genuine effort to receive what is being communicated.

Roger Huntington Sessions
(1896 –1985)
American composer, critic, and teacher of music.

How do men communicate?
Men often communicate using their intellect, that is, the rational, analytical part of the brain. This is why they frequently jump into solving problems. Men obviously embody the masculine, yang. Action oriented, they create and destroy energy, so this comes into play in their conversations. They are typically not raised to develop their feminine nurturing and emotional side, so their conversations involve discussing the what, how, and why of a situation and that is about it. They like simple, clear, bottom-line conversations. They do not want long-winded stories with emotional drama. Most men also do not like to be interrupted.

How do women communicate?
Women often converse from the heart, sharing memories that touched them and explaining the details in stories. They are not afraid to express emotions, and they know how to listen. This represents the feminine, yin, and nurturing, creative energy. They also know how to multitask, so they can have a conversation with several layers without missing a beat. It becomes like a dance, where both women take turns leading and following. When two women have a conversation, one creates a picture, complete with color, shapes, and texture, and places it down in front of the other. The other woman either adds to this picture or creates her own to place beside it. Neither destroys her picture, but instead keeps adding to both of them, weaving an increasingly complex design. Sometimes they create and add pictures so quickly that it might look like a blur to a nearby male, but the women are so immersed in the flow of their "dance" that they understand each other completely.

Chapter **5**

Debate is masculine, conversation is feminine.

Amos Bronson Alcott
(1799 –1888)
American teacher, writer, philosopher, and reformer. As an educator, Alcott pioneered new ways of interacting with young students, focusing on a conversational style, and avoided traditional punishment.

How can men and women communicate more easily? It is obvious that men and women communicate differently, but it does not mean they cannot understand each other. If each accepts how the other communicates and takes time to learn a new way of communicating, the differences can be bridged.

When conversing with a male, a woman should remember how men like to communicate their ideas simply and fully before letting them go and hearing the other's ideas. Women should give them time to complete their thought before adding theirs. Women should break their ideas down into sizable chunks and communicate these ideas one at a time - to ensure that the men understand each piece before moving on. Women should think "bottom-line" when giving details.

When speaking with a woman, a man should try to communicate from the heart and soul. Connect with your heart and listen for the emotional aspect of what she is saying. Avoid the temptation to rationalize and solve any problems. Instead, just listen and empathize. If a story with lots of details is unfolding, enjoy envisioning it, instead of trying to compartmentalize it.

Effective communication is 20% what you know and 80% how you feel about what you know.

Jim Rohn,
(1930 – 2009)
American entrepreneur, author and motivational speaker.

When speaking with a significant other about an important subject, it can be helpful to tell the person what you need. The woman may say she needs to express her emotions and be listened to fully without being given "solutions." A man may say he needs to have a simple conversation without going into deeper details. Agreeing on how you will communicate before the conversation begins can save frustration and heartache.

Remember that when you communicate with the opposite sex, whether it is from the head or heart, it is important to follow basic rules for communicating effectively. Practicing acceptance, non-judgment, and compassion will lead to easier and more enjoyable conversations, whether you are a male or a female.

How can I organize my communications?

It is important to be clear from the outset as to the purpose of what you wish to convey. For example, your purpose could be to inform others, to obtain information, or to initiate action. You need to know in advance what you expect from your communication.

If you are feeling passionate about a topic, you may become garbled if you have not already thought of some key points to stick to when communicating it.

Organize and clarify ideas in your mind before you attempt to communicate them. A good rule of thumb is to choose three main points and keep your communication focused on those. That way, if the topic wanders off course, you will be able to return to one or more of these three key points without feeling flustered.

Think about setting the listener at ease before launching into your conversation or presentation. It can help sometimes to begin with a favorite anecdote.

Not only does it help the listener identify with you as someone who is like him or her, but it can also help ease you into the conversation or presentation.

Once you start addressing your three main points, make sure all facts, stories, allusions, etc., add to the conversation or debate. If you have already thought through the issues and the essence of the ideas that

An eye can threaten like a loaded and leveled gun; or can insult like hissing and kicking; or in its altered mood by beams of kindness, make the heart dance with joy.

Ralph Waldo Emerson
(1803 –1882)
American essayist, lecturer, and poet, who led the Transcendentalist movement of the mid-19th century.

Chapter 5

you wish to communicate, it is likely that some pertinent phrases will stick in your mind. Do not be afraid to use these to underline your points. Even very confident and well-known speakers re-use their key lines repeatedly for major effect.

You've got to be believed to be heard.

Bert Decker
American Author

Remember that no matter what the outcome of your communication, even if the response to your talk or discussion has been negative, it is good manners to end it politely and with respect for everyone's input and time. Thank the person or group for the time taken to listen and respond.

How do I make eye contact?

Eye communication is your number one skill. It ranks first because it has the greatest impact in both one-on-one communications and large group communications. It literally connects mind-to-mind, since your eyes are the only part of your central nervous system that is in direct contact with another human being.

A gentle word, a kind look, a good-natured smile can work wonders and accomplish miracles.

William Hazlitt
(1778 –1830)
English writer, remembered for his humanistic essays and literary criticism, and as a grammarian and philosopher.

When your eyes meet the eyes of another person, you make a First Brain-to-Brain connection. When you fail to make that connection, it matters very little what you say.

Eye contact conveys an interest and encourages your interlocutor to be interested in you in return. Whether you are speaking or listening, looking into the eyes of the person with whom you are conversing can make the interaction more successful.

In smaller intimate settings, when giving a speech, focusing on the eyes of different members of your audience can personalize what you are saying and maintain attention.

Eye contact is considered a basic component of social interaction in many cultures. Some people struggle to make eye contact with others. Failing to make eye contact suggests to some that you are shy; to others, it indicates rudeness or boredom.

Some people have the opposite problem. Making eye contact for a long time can indicate you are very outgoing; to others, it indicates aggression and over-confidence. Although engaging in this process is as natural as breathing for many people, it is difficult for many others.

When you make eye contact, as with anything else, the more you think about it, the more self-conscious, you will become. Your nervousness can then be misinterpreted. Learning how to relax is key to good communication and should be a permanent part of your lifestyle.

When you initiate eye contact, you should concentrate on one eye. Switching from left to right and back all the time will make you appear insecure, inattentive, and confused. It may help to prefer the left eye, because the right side of the brain controls emotions. You should also avoid staring.

Just look directly into the person's eye in a relaxed manner. You should not be anxious and remind yourself that you are hoping to have a pleasant conversation with this person.

During the conversation, if you focus completely on what that person is saying, you will not have to worry about making eye contact correctly; if you are truly listening, you will just naturally focus your eyes on his or her eyes. Maintaining eye contact is how you quietly prove to a person that you are interested in

Body language is a very powerful tool. We had body language before we had speech, and apparently, 80% of what you understand in a conversation is read through the body, not the words.

Deborah Bull
(1963 -)
English dancer, writer, and broadcaster and Creative Director of the Royal Opera House.

Chapter 5

what he or she is saying. It is a vital way to demonstrate respect.

It is also important to try not to look away instantly when something else calls for your attention. If somebody calls you, do not look away as if you just got rescued from a boring conversation. Instead, slightly hesitate before looking at your caller. Looking away then quickly looking back is also a good idea.

Remember that smiling with your eyes makes people feel more relaxed, which is needed for a nice casual conversation to take place. Hostile eyes or false smiles tend to make for uncomfortable conversations, and the other person will probably try to end the conversation. A real smile arises from your own personal joy, not from someone else's. A genuine smile comes from genuine happiness. So learn how to be optimistic and real smiles will follow. After all, think about who has the most genuine smiles: children! They never worry, and life is one big game to them. Follow their lead. Be laid-back and playful!

Should I be aware of what my body is saying?

We all speak with body language, and actual words are not necessary to communicate a message to others.

Unfortunately, your body may not always say what you want it to. If your gestures and posture are saying, "I'm too busy," or "Leave me alone," it is not likely people will approach you. People watch your body for cues, so it is important to pay attention to what cues you are displaying.

An open pose, with arms relaxed at your sides tells anyone around you that you are approachable and open to hearing what they have to say.

Always write angry letters to your enemies. Never mail them.

James Fallows
(1949 -)
American print and radio journalist, visiting professor at a number of universities in the U.S. and China, and holds the Chair in U.S. Media at the United States Studies Centre at University of Sydney. He is the author of nine books, including *National Defense*, for which he received the 1983 National Book Award, *Looking at the Sun* (1994), *Breaking the News* (1996), *Blind into Baghdad* (2006), and *Postcards from Tomorrow Square* (2009).

Body language can say so much more than a mouthful of words. Arms crossed and shoulders hunched, on the other hand, suggest a disinterest in the conversation or an unwillingness to communicate.

Appropriate posture and an approachable stance can make even difficult conversations flow more smoothly.

> Humor can alter any situation and help us cope at the very instant we are laughing.
>
> Allen Klein
> (1931–2009)
> American businessman, talent agent, and record label executive. His clients included The Beatles and The Rolling Stones.

There are various estimates on how much of our communication is verbal and how much is non-verbal. In any case, body language is very important in all aspects of our lives to help us get our messages across and to interpret the messages of others.

It is easy to find books that attempt to decipher the meaning such as the blink or a muscle twitch. The meanings of signals differ from one person to the next. However, there are vast cultural differences as well. Moreover, it is impossible to control all your muscles so that each gesture and facial expression delivers the meaning you want it to deliver. Even if you were to succeed in controlling your body language "by the book," you would look phoney.

Remember simply to be natural!

What are others seeing?

People spend a lot of time looking at your body language. Make a conscious effort to think about what your body is doing in different interactions with diverse people. The important thing here is to examine your facial expressions and posture.

> Humor is richly rewarding to the person who employs it. It has some value in gaining and holding attention, but it has no persuasive value at all.
>
> John Kenneth "Ken" Galbraith
> (1908-2006)
> Canadian-American economist.

Nevertheless, you will mostly just want to pay attention to what your body does when you are angry, nervous, and happy.

Chapter 5

Learn how to control anger, so you can lead a happier life. Anger can be very destructive to you and others; it can even cause you to break the law!

Not only can it harm your external environment, but it can damage you internally as well. Anger is a feeling, a destructive emotion that can, and will, take over without warning.

Conversation about the weather is the last refuge of the unimaginative.

Oscar Fingal O'Flahertie Wills Wilde (1854 –1900) Irish writer and poet. After writing in different forms throughout the 1880s, he became one of London's most popular playwrights in the early 1890s. Today he is remembered for his epigrams, plays, and the circumstances of his imprisonment, followed by his early death.

There are many ways to control anger, so that you do not become angry in the first place, but even the calmest of us loses his or her patience sometimes.

So what do you do when that anger has already developed? How do you release it without hurting others or yourself, emotionally or physically? Before your anger gets the best of you, take it down a notch. The neurological process that triggers anger lasts just two seconds. The rest is up to you. Either the anger response can be amplified, or it can be defused.

Examine thoughts about memories as the possible causes and reasons for the anger arising. Understand the reasons for your anger and understand its causes. Limit this examination to one source or cause at a time, and isolate it from the numerous other things that may make one angry.

Many times, when we look back at what we were furious about, it really is ridiculous and silly, even though we certainly did not see it that way at the time! Injecting a little humor into the situation can help you break out of your angry mood.

Getting nervous can be a burden. First, relax and take deep breaths, and remember that the people you are in front of are not going to do anything to you. Secondly, keep in mind that you are human, and the people you are presenting in front of are also, so relax.

Remember that relaxing is the most important thing you could ever do to break the nervous cycle. In addition, knowing the importance of relaxation and knowing how to relax are vital for ensuring your ongoing health and well being, as well as for restoring the passion and joy in your life.

Should I be aware of conversation pointers?
If you are joining a conversation and have no clue what the people are talking about, do not say anything until you have figured out what they are discussing. If you know the people who are talking, they will be more likely to let you join in.

However, if anyone hints that you should go away, you should. Personal conversations are usually best avoided. In addition, do not linger near anyone for too long, as you might be deemed nosy.

Conversation between Adam and Eve must have been difficult at times because they had nobody to talk about.

Agnes Repplier, (1855 –1950) American essayist born in Philadelphia, Pennsylvania. Her essays are esteemed for their scholarship and wit.

Nevertheless, read the body language of the people talking. Before you join in, see if the people are talking closely or in hushed tones. If the conversation seems to be a serious one, you might want to leave the people alone.

If the group seems more open, take the opening. If the members of the conversation try to nudge you out, take the hint and assume the conversation was personal in nature.

"Small talk" may be defined as a very short conversation to either: kill time, make the other person feel relaxed in your presence, get a date, have a discussion with a client, get to know somebody you meet that could be a potential friend, or just to make oneself feel comfortable. Do not force people into having small talk with you.

Some people are introverts, and everyone is social at certain times and with certain people. Some may not care about the weather or where you get your shoes. Always retain as much as possible about what the other person says. And if she emphasizes a certain subject, try your best to be interested and to talk about it.

Have you ever found yourself stuck in a boring conversation and not being able to think of a way to escape? Be careful when telling someone you are not interested. He or she may be talking to you because of loneliness or have little experience in conversation making. Do not just stop talking to the person or ignore him. This is mean, and it could result in the person becoming an enemy.

Remember that while ignoring the person can sometimes be effective, the nature of "kidding" is to get a reaction out of you. The trick is to give them a reaction, but not an expected one.

How can I have great conversations?
The art of conversation takes practice, but it is not as hard as you might think. Forget yourself.

Dale Carnegie
(1888-1955)

Dale Carnegie once said, *it's much easier to become interested in others than it is to convince them to be interested in you.*

If you are too busy thinking about yourself, what you look like, or what the other person might be thinking, you will never be able to relax.

The best conversations come from gaining new understanding about the topic discussed or the person. Try to lead into personal stories and anecdotes. These give limitless conversation and are revealing about the character of a person.

In addition, it is fine to talk about yourself as long as the person listening is interested and getting new information about you or the topic. People do not like to rehash things they already know or have thought about, so try to give a fresh perspective or way of thinking.

Understand that you want to have a conversation, not be a story-teller. While you want to talk about a topic, make sure you pause in between sentences, which allows for the other person to ask a question to clarify if he or she understood you and/or for the other person to interject with a thought of his or her own.

You do not want to venture into overly private issues. Choose carefully when asking personal questions. Even if the other person might be willing to talk about it, you may end up learning things that you really do not want to know. You certainly do not want the other person to think afterwards that you coerced them into revealing confidential information.

Find out about the person you will be talking to before you actually talk to them, if you can. The information you get can be good for starting conversations. In addition, ask questions.

What does the person like to do? What sort of things has the person done in life? What is happening in the person's life now? What did he or she do today or last weekend? Identify things about the person that you might be interested in hearing about, and politely ask

Like religion, politics, and family planning, cereal is not a topic to be brought up in public. It's too controversial.

Erma Louise Bombeck
(1927 –1996)
Born Erma Fiste, American humorist who achieved great popularity for her newspaper column that described suburban home life from the mid-1960s until the late 1990s. Bombeck also published 15 books, most of which became best-sellers.

Chapter 5

I like to listen. I have learned a great deal from listening carefully. Most people never listen.

Ernest Miller Hemingway
(1899 –1961)
American author and journalist. His economical and understated style had a strong influence on 20th-century fiction, while his life of adventure and his public image influenced later generations. Hemingway produced most of his work between the mid-1920s and the mid-1950s, and won the Nobel Prize in Literature in 1954. He published seven novels, six short story collections, and two non-fiction works. Three novels, four collections of short stories and three non-fiction works were published posthumously. Many of these are considered classics of American literature.

questions. It is important for you to remember that there was a reason that you wanted to talk to the person, so obviously there was something about him or her that you found interesting. However, try to space out your questions, or the other person may feel as if you are conducting and interrogation, which is very bad and closes off friendships.

Try to get the person to talk about something he enjoys thinking about and something that you are interested in hearing about, or else the conversation will not be fulfilling and one of you will feel unsatisfied with it. If the topic seems to be one he is interested in, ask him to clarify what he thinks or feels about it. If he is talking about an occupation or activity you do not know much about, take the opportunity to learn from the person.

Everyone loves having a chance to teach another person who is willing and interested about his or her hobby or subject of expertise. Make sure your questions are good ones – nothing personal, or the person may think ill of you.

Topics such as religion and politics can be inflammatory. Try to avoid venturing into them unless you know the person has roughly the same convictions as you, or the circumstances may, otherwise, allow for pleasant discussion.

Again, it is fine to disagree, it and can be nice to talk about differences, but it can also be a quick step toward an argument. Always remember the *Golden Rule*: Treat others the way you want to be treated. And respect others for who they are. Do not try to change them. Even though some people may not be nice to you at first, they will come around eventually.

COMMU**NICATING**

Listening is the most important part of any conversation. Pay attention to what is being said. Try to avoid interrupting a person in mid-sentence, or when she naturally pauses between sentences or tries to remember a detail. It seems disrespectful, and it makes it seem as if you think that what you have to say is more important than what others have to say. Let the person finish her thoughts and then carry on with your thoughts.

A conversation will go nowhere if you are too busy thinking of anything else, including what you plan to say next. If you listen well, the other person's statements will suggest questions for you to ask. Allow the other person to do most of the talking. He or she will often not realize that it was he or she who did most of the talking, and you will get the credit for being a good conversationalist.

A man never knows how to say goodbye; a woman never knows when to say it.

Helen Rowland
(1875-1950)
American journalist and humorist.

However, if you do not give people the chance to make up their own minds, they will contradict you. Always include in your statement the opportunity for your interlocutor to add an opinion by asking questions such as: What do you think about that? Do you think that could be right? Is that how you see it?

Most importantly, consider your response before disagreeing. If the point was not important, ignore it rather than risk appearing argumentative. On the other hand, agreeing with everything can kill a conversation just as easily as disagreeing with everything. If the topic seems to have been exhausted, use the pause to think for a moment and identify another conversation topic or question to ask the other person.

Moreover, sometimes if a conversation is not going well, it might not be your fault. Now and then the other person is distracted, lost in thought, is not willing to contribute to the conversation, or is having a bad day. If he does not speak or listen, subsequently he is the one not using good conversation skills, not you.

Remember that it is important to know when the conversation is over. Even the best conversations will eventually run out of steam or be ended by an interruption. Smile if you are leaving, tell the person it was nice talking to him, and say goodbye. Ending on a positive note will leave a good impression.

What about nonverbal communication?

When the term nonverbal communication is used, most people think of facial expressions and gestures, but while these are important elements of nonverbal communication, they are not the only ones. Nonverbal communication can also include vocal sounds that are not words, such as grunts, sighs, and whimpers.

Even when actual words are being used, there are nonverbal sound elements such as voice tone, pacing of speech, and so forth.

Clothes make the man. Naked people have little or no influence on society.

Mark Twain
(1835–1910)
He achieved great success as a writer and public speaker. His wit and satire earned praise from critics and peers, and he was a friend to presidents, artists, industrialists, and European royalty.

In our society, a person wearing a police uniform is already communicating an important message before he says a word. Another example is a man's business suit, which is perceived by some as communicating an air of efficiency and professionalism. Informal attire in today's society can imply a relaxation of professional standards. While each of these signs conveys a message, so does its absence.

In some settings, failing to express a nonverbal sign also communicates meaning. A policeman out of uniform is called *plainclothes* and is seen as deliberately trying to conceal his role. To some, this may make him seem smart or efficient, while others may consider him sneaky or untrustworthy. In addition, a businessman who does not obey a certain dress code will convey an air of nonchalance, which some would consider slightly less professional.

Many signs are based on learned cultural standards, but there are some elements of nonverbal communication that are universal. Paul Eckman's landmark research on facial expressions in the 1960s found that the expressions for emotions such as anger, fear, sadness, and surprise are the same across all cultural barriers.

Some nonverbal communication accompanies words and modifies their meanings. For instance, our speed of speaking and the pauses we place between our words form nonverbal element in our speech. If someone asks you a question in a hurried manner, you will probably get the feeling that she wants a similarly quick reply.

A people without the knowledge of their past history, origin and culture is like a tree without roots.

Albert Camus
(1913 –1960)
French author, journalist, and philosopher of the 20th century. Specifically, his views contributed to the rise of the philosophy known as absurdism. He wrote in his essay "The Rebel" that his whole life was devoted to opposing the philosophy of nihilism while still delving deeply into individual freedom.

The use of personal space constitutes a form of nonverbal communication. Depending on the social nuances of the situation, a person leaning forward as he speaks may be seen as offering a sign of friendship or as providing an unwanted invasion of space.

The use of touching is very culturally dependent. In North-American society, a handshake or pats on the shoulder have certain definite meanings understood by practically everybody. In other societies, these might be enigmatic acts or an embarrassing invasion of personal space.

Chapter **5**

The use of eye contact is also highly dependent on the culture of the participants. A prolonged stare may establish a bond of trust, or destroy it. It may elicit a reply from the person being stared at, or it may make the person become uncommunicative and embarrassed.

Remember that when we consider the amount of nonverbal communication that passes between us, compared to the mere words we say, it is obvious that the nonverbal part is by far the largest influencer in the communication process.

How can I address an audience?

Listening is the key to addressing an audience. When you address an audience, no matter what size, you have to meet its needs to communicate effectively. To know the needs of your audience, you have to listen. This is true no matter whether you are speaking to a crowd of thousands or to a party of one. When you are addressing an audience, always begin by knowing your listeners. This is perhaps the most important piece of advice you will receive.

For example, if you are speaking to a small gathering of people, the best tool in your arsenal is the ability and willingness to listen to what the others have to say, as well as to what they are not saying. When you plan to speak to a larger group, it will be to your advantage to find out beforehand as much as possible about those you will be speaking to, in the audience.

Try to find out the burning questions your audience might have. It pays to do your homework!

Find out how much they know about the subject you plan to introduce. Find out if they hold any opinions

It is my experience that labeling yourself "shy" is inaccurate and misleading. If you change the setting to a situation you're comfortable in, you'll be surprised to find your shyness fall away.

TSufit
Canadian Author
TSufit is a Dean's List graduate from University of Toronto Law School and was once named a "Super-achiever" by *Canadian Lawyer* magazine. Her music CD *Under the Mediterranean Sky* has made Top Album lists all over North America and is played on the radio internationally.

about the topic, and if so, which ways those opinions lean. Learn how the audience is likely to communicate; some audiences will listen to everything you say whether they agree with you or not. Other audiences will be full of challengers and interrupters.

Knowing your audience is not enough; you need to know your subject. You would be surprised if you knew just how many people are willing to stand in front of audiences and deliver unprepared or poorly prepared presentations or performances each day. Gather and prepare your information and remember that the Internet offers more information than has previously been available at any other time in human history; take advantage of it as well as or better than, your audience.

> All great speakers were bad speakers at first.
>
> Ralph Waldo Emerson
> (1803 –1882)

You need to do your reading and your listening. Find out as much as you can about your topic, so you can become an expert in it. Think about how you feel about the issue you plan to discuss. Think about why you hold the opinions you do. Think of all the potential questions people might ask you about your topic, and think about ways to answer them effectively.

Remember that preparing your plan to speak will help you deliver a more prepared, competent, and confident presentation. Your success in life should be founded on these two suggestions: read and listen.

How can I communicate with children?

Let the child feel absolute acceptance. Let him know that you accept him completely the way he is and love him for what he is. This will enhance his confidence, and he will interact better with others. You can do this by a positive body language, appreciative looks, and of course, verbal motivation.

> Tell the children the truth.
>
> Robert Nesta "Bob" Marley
> (1945 –1981)
> Jamaican singer-songwriter and musician.

Chapter **5**

Every generation laughs at the old fashions, but follows religiously the new.

Henry David Thoreau
(1817 –1862)
American author.

Each generation wants new symbols, new people, new names. They want to divorce themselves from their predecessors.

James Douglas "Jim" Morrison
(1943 –1971)
Lead singer and lyricist of the rock band The Doors, as well as a poet.

Readily listen to the child and let him know that you are interested in what he is saying and want to know all about it. Keep the conversation going by asking him questions and being a part of it. Make it a point to address the child personally before telling him to do anything. Get is name and make sure you have his serious attention and are not just seen as somebody ratting of something in the background.

A very important key to effective communication is eye contact. It is important to look into his eyes and talk, not just when you are giving him some command but at all times, even when he is narrating his playground experience to you.

Use polite language with children. Using words like "please," "sorry," "thank you," will not only make them courteous but will also make them feel important. Always use motivating words. Do not ever discourage a child by telling him that he is not good at something. Always tell him that you have absolute faith in his capabilities and that he is doing a good job.

Remember that communicating effectively with a child will make him perform better and try harder to achieve his goals. It will make him grow into a positive and matured person with the right approach towards life.

How can I achieve effective inter-generational communication?

The Baby Boomers are delaying retirement. Generation X is sandwiched between the Baby Boomers and the millennial generation, waiting for its turn at formal leadership. And through the occurring clashes of generational differences, the need for

COMMUNICATING

effective communication has never been more important.

Even though people in different generations often do not agree, there is one thing they all agree on: Respect for each of them in general simply does not exist. Those in the older generations, the Silent Generation and the Baby Boomers, think the younger people of today are lazy and disrespectful.

On the other hand, the younger generations, Generation X and the millennial generation, think the older people are stuck in their ways and too closed-minded.

Despite these differences, people from the varying generations must live and work together productively to succeed. If they let their generational outlooks get in the way, conflict will result.

In a nutshell, the Silent Generation and the Baby Boomers prefer in-person communication. They do not like conflict and will avoid it at all costs. They like consensus, and they expect everyone to respect authority. Generation X and the millennial generation are not afraid to confront others; they want their voices heard. They twitter each other and e-mail the majority of the time. They dislike being on teams and prefer to work alone.

While we cannot automatically assume every single person in a particular generation behaves and thinks the same way, knowing the generalities is a great first step. Therefore, take the initiative to learn about the other generations you socialize or work with. The more you understand their points of view and what events shaped their lives, the more you will be able to work with them without conflict.

Don't handicap your children by making their lives easy.

Robert Anson Heinlein
(1907 – 1988)
American science fiction writer.

Each generation goes further than the generation preceding it because it stands on the shoulders of that generation. You will have opportunities beyond anything we've ever known.

Ronald Reagan
(1911 –2004)
40th President of the United States,

Chapter 5

The greatest discovery of my generation is that human beings can alter their lives by altering their attitudes of mind.

Lido Anthony "Lee" Iacocca
(1924 -)
American businessman known for engineering the Mustang.

Two basic rules of life:
1- Change is Inevitable
2- Everyone resists change.
Remember this: When you are through changing... you're through.

Anonymous

Simply knowing each other's preferences is one thing; it is another thing to spend actual time learning from another person. Remember that learning and mentoring is a two-way street. Just as younger people can learn things from older people, the older generation can definitely learn from the younger generation.

As you do this, realize that you will likely have to make compromises. For example, a younger person can teach an older person about some of the latest computer communication tools. The younger person will need to employ patience during the training, and the older person will need to keep an open mind to the new technology. You will also have to confront your own personal biases and work through them. Only then can you truly benefit from the interaction.

The older people do not understand what all the pierced noses and tattoos are about, while the younger people cannot comprehend how someone can be so loyal to a company. Instead of just wondering in silence, it is time to talk things out - with the very people you do not understand. As long as the conversation stays respectful and does not turn into an accusatory yelling match, it will be a healthy way to gain a broader understanding of each other. The sooner you start the conversation, the quicker you will resolve differences.

Remember that it is important to know each other's preferences, to spend time with each other, and to be open to talking things out. Generational differences can be tough. However, when you are open and honest and take the time really to listen to each other, you can overcome any perceived differences, real or otherwise. A little generational understanding can go a long way to boosting moral in your life, to improving a company's output, or bottom-line.

How can I reach a consensus?

Consensus decision-making is the process used to generate widespread agreement within a group. These instructions will guide you through that process. Consensus decision-making involves a collaborative discussion, rather than an adversarial debate. Thus, a consensus process is more likely to result in all parties reaching common ground. The benefits include:

Better decisions - because all perspectives in the group are taken into account. The resulting proposals are, therefore, able to address all the concerns affecting the decision as much as possible.

A consensus means that everyone agrees to say collectively what no one believes individually.

Abba Eban
(1915 2002)
Israeli diplomat and politician. In his career, he was Israeli Foreign Affairs Minister, Education Minister, Deputy Prime Minister, and ambassador to the United States and to the United Nations.

Better group relationships - through collaborating rather than competing, group members are able to build closer relationships through the process. Resentment and rivalry between winners and losers is minimized.

Better implementation of decisions - when a widespread agreement is achieved and everyone has participated in the process, there are usually strong levels of cooperation in follow through. There are not likely to be disgruntled losers who might undermine or passively sabotage effective implementation of the group's decision.

A consensus process allows a group to generate as much agreement as possible. Some groups require everyone to consent if a proposal is to be passed. However, other groups allow decisions to be finalized without unanimous consent.

Chapter 5

Diversity in the world is a basic characteristic of human society, and also the key condition for a lively and dynamic world as we see today.

Hu Jintao
(1942 -)
He was until November 2012 the Paramount Leader of the People's Republic of China. He has held the titles of General Secretary of the Communist Party of China since 2002.

Be polite; write diplomatically; even in a declaration of war one observes the rules of politeness.

Otto Eduard Leopold, Prince of Bismarck, Duke of Lauenburg
(1815 –1898)

Often, a super-majority is deemed sufficient. Some groups use a simple majority vote or the judgment of a leader. They can still use a consensus process to come up with their proposals, regardless of how they finalize a decision.

Consenting to a proposal does not necessarily mean it is your first choice. Participants are encouraged to think about the benefits for the whole group. This may mean accepting a popular proposal even if it is not your personal preference. In consensus decision-making, participants voice their concerns during the discussion, so that their ideas can be included. In the end, however, they often decide to accept the best effort of the group rather than to create factions.

It is important to outline clearly what needs to be decided. You may need to add something or take something away. You may need to start something new or amend something current. Whatever it is, make sure that the entire issue is clearly stated for everyone to understand. This sets the groundwork for collaboratively developing a proposal that most people will support.

Sometimes a solution is reached by finding middle ground between all parties. Even better, however, is when a proposal is shaped to meet as many needs as possible (win-win) rather than through compromise. Remember to listen to every single dissenter in the effort to get full agreement.

And remember to make certain that everyone understands what is meant by *consensus* since everyone will want to know when consensus is reached. You must be patient with people as they learn about the consensus climate. It is often much different for people, especially for individuals from

Europe and North America who are from a different democratic lifestyle background. Nevertheless, set aside some time for silence during the discussion.

Participants will give more measured and well-reasoned opinions if they have time to think before they speak. And lastly, keep in mind that the goal is to reach a decision the group can accept, not necessarily a decision that fulfills every member's wishes.

How can I be polite?

Being polite is all about being considerate and appreciative, but for many people, it remains a challenge!

Be gentle, not forceful or insistent. This does not mean you need to act like a meek, quiet pushover. It means that when you do something, offer something, or make a request, you do it without pressuring the people around you and making them feel like they are being pushed into a corner. If you are having a conversation, it is one thing to ask a question or offer your opinion, but it is rude to push the matter when someone has expressed discomfort, verbally or non-verbally, about the subject.

When you are in doubt, observe others. How are they greeting and addressing each other? What are they doing with their coats? What kinds of topics are they discussing? Different settings require distinctive standards of formality, and those standards often define what is polite and what is not. A work-related dinner, a holiday gathering, a wedding, and a funeral will all demand different polite behavior.

Treat everyone the same way, even if you are not fond of him or her. Never make any enemies. Always

For me, politeness is a *sine qua non* of civilization.

Robert Anson Heinlein
(1907 –1988)
American science fiction writer.

One of the greatest victories you can gain over someone is to beat him at politeness.

Josh Billings
was the pen name of 19th century American humorist Henry Wheeler Shaw (1818 –1885)
He was perhaps the second most famous humor writer and lecturer in the United States in the second half of the 19th century, after Mark Twain, although his reputation has not endured so well with later generations.

Chapter 5

The only true source of politeness is consideration.

William Gilmore Simms
(1806 –1870)
Poet, novelist, and historian from the American South.

It is the highest form of self-respect to admit our errors and mistakes and make amends for them. To make a mistake is only an error in judgment, but to adhere to it when it is discovered shows infirmity of character.

Dale Turner
American trumpet player, best known for being a member of the American new wave band *Oingo Boingo*.

be courteous. You might meet this person again in another setting and would not want to have created negative memories that would give you a bad standing. If someone annoys or even insults you, do not get into an argument. Change the subject, or simply excuse yourself from the conversation.

Start a conversation by asking questions about the other person. Try not to talk about yourself too much. Be confident and charming. Do not hog the conversation, which is arrogant. Look interested and listen to the answers. Do not look over the person's shoulder or around the room when he or she is talking. That implies you are distracted, not interested - or that what the person is sharing is not important to you.

Remember to say please and thank you. Tailor your behavior to the occasion. Be polite to the servers, and tip appropriately if you are the host. Try not to interrupt people when they are talking to someone else or in the middle of something. Do not put your elbows on the table or reach over people for the salt, pepper or sauce. Always ask someone to pass it to you. Never help yourself unless whomever it is you are with says you may.

How should I Apologize?

It can be difficult to swallow our pride and say, "I'm sorry." However, if the other person ever meant anything to you, or had a major impact on your life, you should apologize. An apology is an expression of remorse or guilt over having said or done something that is acknowledged to be hurtful or damaging. It is also a request for forgiveness.

Do you have a difficult time making amends for mistakes or repairing the effects of angry words? Did you say something insensitive, the accuracy of the comment notwithstanding? Did you fail to come through on a promise? Was the offense recent or long ago?

You cannot apologize effectively if you do not know what you are apologizing for. If you do not think you did anything wrong, then express regret or sadness for the feeling that someone is experiencing as a result of what you did. Presuming the effect was unintended, the basis of the apology often lies in not having foreseen how your actions would affect this person and in realizing that the benefits of the action did not outweigh the unforeseen consequences. An apology indicates a wanting to compensate for your oversight.

It is important to admit that you were wrong emphatically, unreservedly, and immediately. An incomplete apology often feels more like an insult. An apology with an excuse is simply *not* an apology. It may very well be that other people or circumstances contributed to the situation, but you cannot apologize for them; you can only apologize for yourself, so leave them out of it.

Simply take full responsibility for the offense, without sharing the blame with anyone else, and without presenting mitigating circumstances.

Do not try to think of or offer an excuse. An apology with an excuse is not an apology. Take full responsibility for what you did. Apologizing is realizing that there are no excuses. A true apology implies you have to carry out your promise action in order for the apology to be sincere and complete. Otherwise, your apology will lose it's meaning, and trust may disappear for good.

Canadians can easily "pass for American" as long as we don't accidentally use metric measurements or apologize when hit by a car.

Doug Coupland
Canadian novelist and visual artist.

There is no waste of time in life like that of making explanations.

Benjamin Disraeli, 1st Earl of Beaconsfield
(1804–1881)
He was a British Prime Minister.

Chapter 5

Sometimes apologizing immediately after your mistake is best, but sometimes it is better to wait. The sting of a harsh word can be cooled right away with a quick apology, but other offenses might need the other person to cool down before he or she will be willing to even listen to your next sentence. However, the sooner you apologize for your mistake, the more likely it will be viewed as an error in judgment and not as a character flaw. That being said, never forget that a direct and honest apology is best. Do it face to face, if possible. A phoned, e-mailed, or recorded apology may show a lack of sincerity and effort.

When making amends, be specific about the incident, so that the other person knows exactly what you are apologizing for. Make it a point to avoid using the word *BUT*. "I am sorry, but..." means, "I am not sorry." Also, do *not* say, "I'm sorry you feel that way" or, "I'm sorry if you were offended." Be sorry for what *you* did! "I'm sorry you feel that way" makes it seem as if you are blaming the other person; it is not a real apology.

Validate the other party's feelings or discomfort by acknowledging your transgression's potential effects, while taking responsibility.

Think about what caused you to make the offense. Is it because you are a little too laid back about being on time, or about remembering important dates? Is it because you tend to react instantly to certain comments, without pausing to consider an alternative point of view? Is it because you are unhappy with your life, and you unknowingly take it out on others? Find the underlying problem, describe it to the person, as an *explanation*, not as an *excuse*, and tell the person what you intend to do to rectify that problem, so that you can avoid this mistake in the future.

A wise man is superior to any insults which can be put upon him, and the best reply to unseemly behavior is patience and moderation.

Jean-Baptiste Poquelin, known by his stage name Molière (1622–1673) French playwright and actor who is considered to be one of the greatest masters of comedy in Western literature. Among Molière's best-known works are *Le Misanthrope* (*The Misanthrope*) and *L'École des femmes* (*The School for Wives*).

It is important to emphasize that you do not want to jeopardize or damage the relationship and to express your appreciation for the role that he or she plays in your life.

This is the time to recount briefly what has created and sustained the bond over time and to tell loved ones that they are indeed loved. Describe what your life would be missing without their trust and their company.

Nevertheless, you need to ask the person if he will give you another chance to make up for what you did wrong. Tell him you have learned from your mistake, and that you will take action to change and grow as a result if he will let you. Make a clear request for forgiveness and wait for the answer. This gives the injured party the well-deserved *power* in determining the outcome of the situation.

Remember that patience is always of the essence. If an apology is not accepted, thank the individual for hearing you out and leave the door open for if and when he wishes to reconcile. Be conscious of the fact that just because someone accepts your apology does not mean she has fully forgiven you. It can take time, maybe a long time, before the injured party can completely let go and fully trust you again.

There is little you can do to speed this process up, but there are endless ways to bog it down. If the person is truly important to you, it is worth it to give him or her the time and space needed to heal. Do not expect the person to go right back to acting normally immediately. At the same time, do not let someone hang this over your head for the rest of your life. The same way you need to learn how to apologize, the other person needs to learn how to forgive.

Adopt the pace of nature: her secret is patience.

Ralph Waldo Emerson
(1803 –1882)
American essayist, lecturer, and poet.

Always forgive your enemies - nothing annoys them so much.

Oscar Fingal O'Flahertie Wills Wilde
(1854 –1900)
Irish writer and poet. After writing in different forms throughout the 1880s, he became one of London's most popular playwrights in the early 1890s. Today he is remembered for his epigrams, plays, and the circumstances of his imprisonment, followed by his early death.

Chapter 5

A man is not old until regrets take the place of dreams.

John Barrymore
(1882 –1942)
actor of stage and screen.

There are two ways of being happy: We must either diminish our wants or augment our means - either may do - the result is the same and it is for each man to decide for himself and to do that which happens to be easier.

Benjamin Franklin
(1706-1790)
He invented the lightning rod, bifocals, the Franklin stove, a carriage odometer, and the glass "armonica."

How can I forgive?

One of the thorniest and most difficult things we humans are ever called upon to do is to respond to evil with kindness, and to forgive the unforgivable.

We love to read stories about people who have responded to hatred with love, but when that very thing is demanded of us personally, our default seems to be anger, anguish, depression, righteousness, hatred, etc.

Remember that study after study shows that one of the keys to longevity and good health is to develop a habit of gratitude and to let go of past hurts.

Do you want to live a long, happy life?

Forgive the unforgivable. It really is the kindest thing you can do for yourself. Your enemy may not deserve to be forgiven for all the pain and sadness and suffering purposefully inflicted on your life, but *you* deserve to be free of this evil.

Chances are your enemy has gone on with life and has not given you another thought. Realize that the hate you feel toward your enemy does not harm him or her in the slightest.

Understand that the best revenge against your enemies is to live a successful and happy life. Want to get even with someone who tried to destroy you? Show them, yourself, and the world that the obstacles they tried to create were not significant enough to disable you and/or destroy you.

Think of your enemy as someone who has helped you to grow. Even though unfortunate things happen to us, the best thing we can do is take those opportunities as tests that will either destroy or

> You will never be happy if you continue to search for what happiness consists of. You will never live if you are looking for the meaning of life.
>
> Albert Camus
> (1913 –1960)
> French author, journalist, and philosopher of the 20th century.

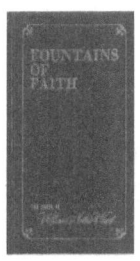

> A well-developed sense of humor is the pole that adds balance to your steps as you walk the tightrope of life.
>
> William Arthur Ward
> (1921–1994)
> Author of *Fountains of Faith*, he is one of America's most quoted writers of inspirational maxims.

strengthen us. If you have been through something, it did not destroy you. Take what you learned and become a better person because of it.

Make a list of the good things that emerged as a result of this awful experience. You have probably focused long enough on the negative parts of this experience. Look at the problem from a completely new angle; look at the positive side. Look at the bigger picture!

If you have ruminated over this problem for a long time, forgive yourself. Be patient and kind to yourself. Extreme emotional pain has a profound effect on the body.

Give yourself time to heal, physically and emotionally. Eat well. Rest. Focus on the natural beauty in the world. Give yourself permission to feel the emotions and process them. Do not bottle up the pain.

The fastest way to free yourself from an enemy and all associated negativity is to forgive. Untie the bindings and loosen yourself from that person's ugliness. Your hatred has tied you to the person responsible for your pain. Your forgiveness enables you to start walking away from him or her and the pain. Forgiveness is for you and not the other party. Freeing yourself through forgiveness is like freeing yourself from chains of bondage or from prison.

Learn how to balance trust with wisdom. It is a fact that not all of our fellow humans are trustworthy. Painful memories can serve to protect us from future hurts. Forgiveness is not acceptance of wrong behavior. If you must continue to interact with someone who has wronged you, who has offered a

Chapter 5

> Distance not only gives nostalgia, but perspective, and maybe objectivity.
>
> Robert Morgan
> (1944 -)
> American poet, short story writer, and novelist.

> Personality is only ripe when a man has made the truth his own.
>
> Søren Aabye Kierkegaard
> (1813 –1855)
> Danish philosopher, theologian, and religious author.

lame apology only to follow it up with more bad behavior, nothing requires you to trust such a person.

This person is not likely to ever be trustworthy. You must keep some distance between the two of you. While it is fruitless to torment yourself over this person's actions, you should not be his or her willing victim. Acknowledge what as taken place and move on! An offender who wants reconciliation must do his or her part by offering a sincere apology or a promise not to repeat the offense, by making amends, and by giving time for healing to take place. If you do not see repentance, understand that according forgiveness to that person is a benefit to yourself, not to the offender.

Unless those who have harmed us have truly repented of whatever they have done, we need to use wisdom and avoid allowing the hurt to be repeated. This may require avoiding those who are unrepentant of the harm that they have inflicted upon us. It would be wise to balance forgiveness against the certain knowledge that evil exists and that some people enjoy harming others.

Remember that you need to maintain perspective. While the *evil* actions of your *enemy* are hurtful to you and your immediate surroundings, the rest of the world goes on unaware. Validate the meanings of these evil actions in your life, but never lose perspective that others are not involved and do not deserve anything to be taken out on them. Your enemy is someone else's beloved child, someone's employee, or a child's parent.

How can I make my personality stand out?

Many people want to be noticed and stand out. You, too, can make your personality stand out in a good way. Do not be afraid to be different. People will admire you for your unique personality. Be kind and considerate. People who truly practice these virtues with everyone they meet can be true to themselves and still stand out.

Remember to keep a smart head and to keep cool. Do not shout or be aggressive. Do not doubt yourself. Be executive-like in dress and create your own personal style. Do not copy anyone. Be creative and do different things, but do not make people think you are weird. Most importantly, have a good sense of humor!

How can I expand my vocabulary?

Expanding your vocabulary is achievable. It can improve your communication skills and develop reading and writing ability. It does not matter at what stage of your career, your education, or your personal growth you are presently at. Vocabulary development can benefit everyone.

It's like learning a language; you can't speak a language fluently until you find out who you are in that language, and that has as much to do with your body as it does with vocabulary and grammar.

Fred Frith
(1949 -)
English multi-instrumentalist, composer, and improvisor.

Vocabulary development is often pursued for a variety of reasons. Individuals may seek to communicate more effectively at work, or college students may be searching for a richer vocabulary to assist in understanding material and in obtaining better grades. To facilitate your vocabulary increase, it should always be combined with other types of activities to obtain maximum learning.

Wide reading is extremely important when developing your vocabulary, the richer and more varied the text, the more opportunities you have for vocabulary increase.

Many people have extensive knowledge of words. That is, they can recognize a significant number of

Chapter **5**

One forgets words as one forgets names. One's vocabulary needs constant fertilizing or it will die.

Arthur Evelyn St. John Waugh
(1903–1966)
Known as Evelyn Waugh, he was an English writer of novels, travel books, and biographies. His best-known works include his early satires *Decline and Fall* (1928) and *A Handful of Dust* (1934).

You cannot open a book without learning something.

Confucius
551BCE–479 BCE
Confucius' principles had a basis in common Chinese tradition and belief. He championed strong familial loyalty, ancestor worship, respect of elders by their children (and, according to later interpreters, of husbands by their wives), and the family as a basis for an ideal government.

words, but when it comes to demonstrating meaning, it is often another story.

"Knowing a word" means understanding its different meaning depending on the context, the surrounding words and situation, in which it is used. Words can have several different meanings.

Our verbal vocabulary is often less sophisticated than our written vocabulary. This is because verbal communication relies heavily upon non-verbal cues and gestures. As such, it is important that we experience vocabulary in both environments.

Vocabulary development can also occur through exploring similarities and differences among related words and keeping written documentation of the words learned, their definitions, and the different ways the words can be used.

Learning new vocabulary words helps keep your mind sharp and makes you sound intelligent during a conversation. An expanded vocabulary will also help you communicate more clearly and to avoid the frustration of lacking the right word to express your thoughts.

Remember that expanding your vocabulary will take effort and patience. At first, you may grow frustrated as you try to memorize all the new words you are learning. Stick with it, and soon you will have a larger repertoire of words at your disposal.

What should I consider?

Communication is essential in relationships. Learning to communicate effectively from the heart and soul deepens the connection between people. Most people know how to share their thoughts and express

COMMU**NICATING**

The way we communicate with others and with ourselves ultimately determines the quality of our lives.

Anthony "Tony" Robbins (1960 –) In is books, *Unlimited Power: The New Science Of Personal Achievement* and *Awaken The Giant Within*. Robbins writes about subjects such as health and energy, overcoming fears, persuasive communication, and enhancing relationships.

their feelings, but there is much more to communication than a mind-body connection. Communicating from the intellect offers a rational and logical perspective, but on its own it can lead to judgmental opinions and right and wrong arguments.

Remember that sharing feelings brings intimacy, but it can also lead to emotional reactions and outbursts that are hurtful if not balanced with a heart and soul connection.

Recommended Reading & References
We suggest consulting the works identified below in order to learn more about the particulars contained in this chapter.

DECKER, Bert. YOU'VE GOT TO BE BELIEVED TO BE HEARD. St-Martin's Press. ISBN 0-312-06935-9.

GRAY, John. Ph.D., MEN ARE FROM MARS, WOMEN ARE FROM VENUS, A Practical Guide for Improving Communication and Getting What you Want in your Relationships. Harper. ISBN 1-55994-878-7.

LIEBERMAN, David J. YOU CAN READ ANYONE. Never be Fooled, Lied to, or Taken Advantage of Again. Audi Coach. ISBN 1-59659-153-6.

LICHTENBERG, Ronna. IT'S NOT BUSINESS IT'S PERSONAL, The 9 Relationship Principles that Power your Career. Hyperion. ISBN 0-7868-6594-6.

You can fool some of the people all of the time, and all of the people some of the time, but you can't fool all of the people all the time.

Abraham Lincoln

Artist: George Peter Alexander Healy (1818–1894)

CHAPTER 6

There are four ways, and only four ways, in which we have contact with the world. We are evaluated and classified by these four contacts: what we do, how we look, what we say, and how we say it.

Dale Breckenridge Carnegie
(1888 –1955)
American writer, lecturer, and the developer of famous courses in self-improvement, salesmanship, corporate training, public speaking, and interpersonal skills.

NETWORKING

Networking involves making connections and maintaining relationships with people who support you throughout each phase of your life. Your network of contacts may help you to choose the right career and people in your life, find rewarding opportunities, develop your skills, and achieve your goals.

Making connections and maintaining relationships with the people who support you, can be the key to your success. By effectively building a network of friends, colleagues, and business associates, you are ensuring that whenever you need a social contact, a new job, a new client, or to develop your skills further, you can call upon your network to help you.

Networking is perhaps more crucial than ever, as an established relationship can make you stand out against the competition. Take advantage of the access you have been given. Go out of your way to meet other intelligent individuals and build up a network of contacts.

When should I start networking?

Networking should not start just when you begin to look for a job; you should build up your contacts and friendships as soon as possible, even if you are happy in your long-term job and are not thinking of changing. You never know when you are going to need these contacts in the future. Or may be you will need them to help a friend or family member being introduced to one of who would benefit from them.

Whom should you talk to? Talk to anyone and everyone. This includes family, friends, neighbors, work colleagues, old school and university friends, and people that you meet by chance when out and

Chapter 6

about. Even though one person may not be able to assist you in the future or vice versa, his or her son, brother, sister, neighbor or even their cleaner might. You never know who a person might know, which is why it is best to talk to as many people as possible. This is not done in one day; it takes time and a lot of effort.

Remember that in many cases, you may not even realize that you are networking. Striking up a conversation with a stranger in the dentists' waiting room or on the train is networking, as is attending trade meetings and career fairs. Networking is fantastic, not only because you have your own personal network of friends, work associates, and family, but because each of them will have his or her own network of contacts. It is no wonder that networking is consistently quoted as the most effective way of getting a job or meeting interesting people.

How should I act when attending networking activities?

When attending networking groups, trade fairs or trade discussions, there is certain etiquette that everyone should follow in order to make the best impression.

Before walking in the door, you should be prepared to:

Determine how often you should be networking in a given week, month, or quarter. This will help you narrow down where to go. Attend events with a plan to learn something new. All venues are not right for all people. You owe it to yourself to do your research and find the venues that make sense for your business.

Etiquette means behaving yourself a little better than is absolutely essential.

William Jacob "Will" Cuppy (1884–1949) American humorist and literary critic, known for his satirical books about nature and historical figures.

NETWORKING

In conversation, humor is worth more than wit and easiness more than knowledge.

George Herbert
(1593 –1633)
Welsh born English poet, orator, and Anglican priest. Throughout his life, he wrote religious poems characterized by a precision of language, a metrical versatility, and an ingenious use of imagery or conceits that was favoured by the metaphysical school of poets.

Identify where you should go. Decide which organizations you should join and which you do not have to join in order to gain value from their events. You need to register for the event and schedule it as a business meeting. Many people either do not sign up for events or sign up for them and then forget to go.

Prepare yourself physically and mentally for the event. Dress appropriately. Arrive early so that you get to talk to some people in more depth before the event becomes too hectic. Make sure that you have business cards with you - and possibly a notebook and pen. Develop open-ended questions you can use to start a conversation. Try to find unique questions; do not ask, if you can help it, the same old "So, what do you do?"

Listen to other people, ask questions about their businesses, and offer to help them in any way you can. Networking is a two-way relationship; it is not all about you. This will keep you from talking too much about yourself and your business. Be yourself, and do not put on any kind of act. People will more than likely be able to see through it. Turn your cell phone off, and be on your best behavior from the time you enter the room.

When you walk into the room, step to the side, take a deep breath, and scan the room. This will give you a chance to regroup and focus before you approach anyone. If you go to an event with someone you know, split up once you get there. Do not sit down until the program begins. If there is no program, you can sit once you have connected with someone.

Sit with strangers, not with people you know. When you see someone sitting alone, go up to the person

Chapter **6**

Luck
is believing,
you're lucky.

Thomas Lanier
"Tennessee"
Williams III,
(1911 –1983)
American writer who
worked principally as
a playwright in the
American theater.
Two Pulitzer Prizes
for Drama for *A
Streetcar Named
Desire* (1948) and
*Cat on a Hot Tin
Roof* (1955).

and introduce yourself. You may be "saving the person's life"! After all, he was alone and may be nervous. You can even take the person with you to mix and mingle with others.

Have a firm but not too firm handshake. Your handshake is a key indicator of your level of confidence. If it is weak, you are signaling, unintentionally, your intentions. If it is strong, you are sending a signal that you are probably more aggressive than assertive or cooperative. Either way, it does not lend itself to building relationships. Do not give your business card to everyone you meet. Rather, give it to anyone who asks you for it. Do get the business card of everyone you meet.

"Be present." When you are talking with someone, look him or her in the eye and really pay attention to what the individual is saying. Do not look around the room or over someone's shoulder when you are talking with someone. It is rude. You are letting the person know that you are not really interested in him. Share information. People love to learn things. Use social networking as a way to share relevant information with other people. Be a giver. Whenever you can connect people, or help someone with a question, do it.

Disengage politely. How do you get away from someone graciously? There are a couple of tactics. You can tell the person you do not want to monopolize their time. You can say you see someone you need to speak with. You can excuse yourself to go to the restroom. You can tell the person you would like to continue meeting people.

Follow up; it is critical to your networking success. If you are going to take the time to network, then please

NETWORKING

take the time to follow up with the people you meet. You can send them a handwritten note or reach out to them to schedule a time to meet for coffee or to get together in some other way. This depends on how well you connected at the networking event. Do not assume that just because you met someone you have the right to gain a referral from them, use them as a resource, or give them your promotional and sales materials.

Remember do not pitch too early. Quite frankly, do not *pitch* at all. When you build relationships, it will become apparent to you and the other person when it makes sense to do business with each other. Limit the self-promotion. You can let people know what you are up to as long as that is not your only topic of conversation. Remember that business networking is about relationships, not selling.

How can I improve my networking skills?

Success in networking requires that you know what other people know but also who other people know. However, building a circle off contacts or business associates requires planning, and you have to work at it continually.

How do you get started? Most importantly, how do you make sure you are not turning people off or damaging your reputation? Here are some pointers to consider improving your networking skills:

There is really no single formula. However, It is recommended to start with a specific goal and time frame. Once you "program" that goal into your brain, you will be amazed at the number of opportunities that come your way. Sign up for seminars, attend presentations, take a class, or ask a friend to introduce you to someone. Just get going. And do not

If you learn anything from showbiz, learn how to work a room. Entertainers do it naturally. The independent music scene in Toronto has a networking event appropriately called " The big schmooze".

Tsufit
Canadian singer, television actress, and comedienne.

Chapter 6

Authentic values are those by which a life can be lived, which can form a people that produces great deeds and thoughts.

Allan David Bloom
(1930 –1992)
American philosopher, classicist, and academic.

Without feelings of respect, what is there to distinguish men from beasts?

Confucius
(551 BCE–479 BCE)

worry about imposing; people are generally very nice and like to help each other out.

Networking is about being authentic, unselfish, genuine and honest. The key to successful networking is to be a decent and honorable person even when you are not networking. Be yourself. Do not hide behind a persona. Remember that people do business with people they trust. You have to be you in order for people to get to know you. You need to be cheerful, hard working, well put together and well thought of. You have to demonstrate that you are worth building a relationship with.

Whatever happened to "Please" and "Thank you"?
People of all ages fail to use the basic" Please" and "Thank you" and this is not appealing. Use an appropriate level of formality and a respectful tone. Over time, you can become more relaxed, but never, ever lose basic courtesy. If you are sending an email, watch your grammar and spell check it before sending it. If you are leaving a voicemail, remember that your verbal and written communication reflects who you are.

You need to demonstrate respect for process and position. Do not ask people to go around their company's internal processes or to leap over organizational levels for you. This puts them on the spot. Instead, ask them to explain what their company's process is and whom they recommend that you contact. Always ask for permission to use their name before doing so. This approach shows that you are a responsible and trustworthy person.

Self-confidence is most important. Try to ignore any negative self-talk. You may feel understandably self-conscious and uncomfortable when meeting people more powerful and successful than yourself, but successful networking requires you to do it anyway. It is important for you to keep the conversations productive. Be completely professional and upbeat in your networking activities.

Networking is not a vehicle for you to whine, complain, or badmouth. It is an opportunity for you to learn from others and to help them out as well. Anybody who is a quality individual for you to know will not be interested in listening to garbage. In networking circles, word travels fast about which people to avoid.

Human behavior flows from three main sources: desire, emotion, and knowledge.

Plato
(348 BCE-347 BCE) Classical Greek philosopher, mathematician, student of Socrates, writer of philosophical dialogues, and founder of the Academy in Athens, the first institution of higher learning in the Western world.

Be on your best behavior at all times. The world is a small place, and people have long memories. You never know who you will run into and whose assistance you will need. You cannot go wrong by being kind and respectful of everyone all the time.

Protect your good name and reputation. Do not feel obligated to let just anyone into your personal network. Be especially careful if you have any doubts about how a person's behavior will reflect upon you, even if you have known this person since childhood, or if she is your second cousin. It can take someone less than five minutes to ruin the good reputation you have spent years building.

Reach out to people in a warm and sincere way. Be friendly and generous. Smile, shake hands firmly, make eye contact, and ask them open-ended questions, questions, which require more than a yes or no. Resist the urge to dominate the conversation. Listen intently, be present, and focus on their concerns, not yours. Learn their names and use them so you begin to associate the names with the faces.

Chapter **6**

The price of greatness is responsibility.

Sir Winston Leonard Spencer-Churchill
(1874-1965)
Born into the aristocratic family of the Dukes of Marlborough, his father, Lord Randolph Churchill, was a charismatic politician who served as Chancellor of the Exchequer; his mother, Jenny Jerome, was an American socialite. As a young army officer, he saw action in British India, the Sudan, and the Second Boer War. He gained fame as a war correspondent and wrote books about his campaigns.

I've learned to walk into a room like everyone there is already a friend.

Tsufit
Canadian singer, television actress, and comedienne.

At meetings or conferences, go out of your way to meet people. Physically move around and work the room; do not get stuck talking to one person just to be polite. Show genuine interest in everyone you meet and form relationships that are meaningful. If you are meeting someone for the first time, let him or her do most of the talking. People love to talk about themselves. Ask them about their interests, professions, whatever. First, you will learn pretty quickly if a person is someone you want to keep in touch with. Second, if you do ask someone for a business card or contact information, he or she will gladly give it to you because you are viewed very favorably as being "a good listener." Make sure you ask for permission to contact the person in the future.

Introduce new friends to old friends. Become a resource to others. Look for ways you can help other people make useful contacts. Put in a good word for others. Build a reputation as an unselfish, decent person, the sort of person that others want to work with. Treat everyone with respect and courtesy, especially those less powerful than you.

Before attending a conference, think strategically about your goals. Write down the specific results you want to achieve and have a game plan. Make a list of whom you want to meet. Write or call them ahead of time to schedule a meeting. Prepare specific questions and offers of assistance. At conferences, do not compare yourself to others. Do not waste time and energy fretting over someone else that may be having more success at networking than you.

When you talk about your work, talk passionately. Prepare a one-minute description of what you do or want to do, so that you are ready to talk in a succinct, enthusiastic, and inspiring way about your work and ideas. Be a sponge. Write down all the inspiring ideas and information you gather so you do not forget them.

Remember that after meeting an interesting person send him or her a thank-you note. Suggest ways you might be able to help the person in some way. Fulfill any promises you made. Show people that you actually do what you say you are going to do.

How can I look approachable?

Parties and other social functions can really be a drag sometimes. You stand by the punchbowl or sit down on a sofa and watch everybody else mingling, but nobody seems to want to chat with you. You are attractive, witty, and interesting; what is wrong with these people?

A good listener is not only popular everywhere, but after a while, he knows something.

Wilson Mizner
(1876 –1933)
American playwright, raconteur, and entrepreneur. His best-known plays are *The Deep Purple*, produced in 1910, and *The Greyhound*, produced in 1912.

It could be that you are sending out the wrong signals. No matter how beautiful you are or how good a conversationalist you can be, if you look intimidating, preoccupied, or scared, people might not be inclined to talk to you.

Aside from body language, other elements of your appearance can affect how approachable you look. Think velvet, cashmere, angora, corduroy, it will make you stand out more in a crowd and look more accessible.

In a social situation, such as a party, you should offer to help out in some way. Your host or hostess will likely be appreciative, and sometimes having a specific task may help you feel more focused than just standing around feeling awkward. It is a great way to meet others and be sociable without having to feel you do not know what to do. Excellent tasks: cutting vegetables, washing dishes, keeping the music going, picking up used plates, etc. At the same

Chapter **6**

time, do not over-focus and use the task as an excuse for not engaging in conversation.

Reading a newspaper or wearing headphones can ease the monotony of a long train ride, but in situations where you want to look approachable, lose these props. Position yourself for conversation. If you are standing up, but everybody else is sitting down or vice versa, people will find it difficult and somewhat awkward to talk to you. If you want to talk to someone, or if you are already talking with someone, position yourself so that you can comfortably talk.

Remember that there may indeed be times when you do not want to look approachable. Closed body language can be useful to fend off potential attacks, to get rid of unwanted suitors, or to tell panhandlers you do not want to be bothered.

How can I be charming?

Charm is the art of having an attractive personality. This characteristic can only be achieved over a period of time. While everyone is born with differing amounts of natural charm, much can be acquired and honed through practice and patience. As with dancing, the more you practice, the better you will become.

Improve your posture. Throw those shoulders back and let them drop so you can relax. When you walk, imagine you are crossing a finish line; the first part of your body to cross should be your torso, not your head. If you have poor posture, your head will be pushed forward, which makes you seem timid and insecure.

Smile with the eyes. Scientists have pinpointed more than 50 types of smiles, and research suggests that the sincerest smile of all is the Duchenne smile, a

> Silence... can be one of the best attention getters!
>
> TSufit
> Canadian Author
> *TSufit* is a Dean's List graduate from University of Toronto Law School and was once named a "Super-achiever" by *Canadian Lawyer* magazine. Her music CD *Under the Mediterranean Sky* has made Top Album lists all over North America and is played on the radio internationally.

smile that pushes up into the eyes. The reason it is more genuine is because the muscles needed to smile with our eyes are involuntary; they only become engaged in an authentic smile, not in a "courtesy" smile. In addition, research shows that if you look at someone and then smile, it instantly charms him or her.

Remember people's names when you meet them for the first time. This takes an enormous amount of effort for most people. Repeating the person's name when stating your name to that person will help you to remember it better. The more you say a person's name, the more that person will feel that you like him or her and the greater the chance that the person will warm up to you.

A smile is the universal welcome.

Max Forrester Eastman
(1883 –1969)
American writer on literature, philosophy and society, a poet, and a prominent political activist.

Be genuinely interested in people. You do not have to love everyone, but you should be curious or fascinated by people in some way. Learn how to ask questions based on your interests, while being polite, and you will make people feel interesting.

Take into account topics that interest those around you, even if you are not so keen on them. Sometimes you can build rapport just by asking questions and not caring if you seem naive. There are people who like talking about and explaining their interests, and these people will like you for listening. It is your level of interest and willingness to engage in topics that make you an interesting person to be around. Exercise an open mind. Let others do the explaining. If someone mistakenly thinks you know more about the topic, be genuine and simply say that your knowledge is limited, but that you are hoping to learn more about it.

Praise others instead of gossiping. If you are talking with someone, or you are talking in a group of people,

Chapter 6

Sincerity is not only effective and honourable, it is also much less difficult than is commonly supposed.

George Henry Lewes
(1817 –1878)
English philosopher and critic of literature and theatre. He became part of the mid-Victorian ferment of ideas which encouraged discussion of Darwinism, positivism, and religious scepticism.

and the subject of another person comes up in a positive or negative way, be the one to mention something you like about that person. Praise is the most powerful tool in gaining charm because it is always viewed as 100% sincere. It has the added benefit of creating trust in you. The idea will spread that you never have a bad word to say about anyone. Everyone will know that his or her reputation is safe with you.

Issue compliments generously, especially to raise others' self-esteem. Try to pick out something that you appreciate in any situation and verbally express that appreciation. If you like something or someone, find a creative way to say it, and say it immediately. If you wait too long, it may be viewed as insincere and badly timed, especially if others have beaten you to it. Because you waited, you are most likely not confident in saying what you thought, so waiting will only result in a less than enthusiastic presentation. If you notice that someone is putting a lot of effort into something, compliment the effort, even if you feel that there is room for improvement. If you notice that someone has changed something about himself or herself - a haircut, a manner of dress, etc., notice it, and point out something you like about it. If you are asked what you thing about something, be charming and deflect the question with a very general compliment.

Be gracious in accepting compliments. Get out of the habit of assuming that the compliment is being given insincerely. Even when someone makes a compliment contemptuously, there is always a germ of jealous truth hiding in his or her own heart. Be effusive in accepting the compliment. Go beyond a mere "Thank you" and add, "I'm glad you like it" or "It is so kind of you to have noticed." These are "*compliments in return*".

Control your tone of voice. The tone of your voice is crucial. Your tone of voice should be gentle and peaceful. Speak clearly and project your voice. When you say, "You look nice today", it should be in the exact same tone that you would use to say, "It's a nice day." Any variation from your normal tone will arouse suspicion about your sincerity. Practice giving compliments into a recorder and play it back. Does it sound sincere? Practice until you get it right!

Sometimes being charming means simply being a good listener. Charm is not always an outward expression, but an inward one, too. Engage the other person in conversation about his or herself - About something that the person likes or is passionate about or about him or herself. This makes him or her more comfortable to share and express things with you.

Assume rapport. This simply means talking to a stranger or a newly met acquaintance in a very friendly manner, as if the person is a long-lost friend or relative. This helps break down the awkwardness and speeds up the "warm-up" process when meeting new people, making them feel more welcomed and comfortable around you.

Kindness coupled with respect makes others feel as if they are loved and cared for. This is a powerful tool during interaction.

Watch the way you phrase things. Be mature and have a touch of wise, polite language.

There are only three things women need in life: food, water, and compliments.

Christopher Julius "Chris" Rock III
(1965 -)
American comedian, actor, screenwriter, television producer, film producer, and director.

Chapter 6

Remember that the degree of charm that you possess depends on the creativity of your praise. Say something that is not immediately obvious, and say it in a poetic way.

It is good to have some premeditated compliments and phrases, but the most charming people are able to invent them on the spot. This way, you can be sure that you are not repeating it. If you cannot think of anything to say, bring up a current event that is interesting.

Charm is a way of getting the answer yes without asking a clear question.

Albert Camus
(1913 –1960)
Awarded the 1957 Nobel Prize for Literature for his important literary production, which with clear-sighted earnestness illuminates the problems of the human conscience in our times.

Empathy is at the core of charm. If you cannot tell what makes people happy or unhappy, you have no way to assess whether you are saying the right thing or not.

However, when you greet someone, make him or her feel like the most important person to you. The response you receive will probably be a nice one, and the person will discover what a great person you are.

Remember that every so often, you will have no choice but to express an opinion that few others hold. That is fine. Consider expressing it in a humorous way. Humor is the spoonful of sugar that helps the medicine go down. Be patient. Something may be obvious to you but not so simple to others. Understand that and help them out. Do not confuse being charming with being a people pleaser.

How can I start a conversation with a stranger?

Greet the person, and smile in an amiable way. Ask in a general, friendly tone, "How are you? How are things with you?" Or say, "Wonderful weather we're having today!"

Broach general topics that you may have in common, such as current news, weather, interests, friendly topics, such as food, music, weather, computers, movies, books, sports, fashion, etc.

Avoid touchy topics, such as religion, politics, sex, philosophy, world problems, death, divorce, and other potentially sensitive topics. Ask the person what genre of music he or she likes. Ask what his or her favorite food is. If you are talking to teenagers or certain adults, they generally like to talk about music, sports, TV, celebrities, video games, cool websites, etc. Younger children like to talk about their toys, video games, music, TV shows, food, etc.

Listen to the reply. The key to an enjoyable conversation is the feeling that someone is interested in what we have to say. Ideally, you will take turns speaking, but to start a conversation, ask a question and then listen. This is also a great way to figure out whether the person wants to talk or not.

Sometimes, a simple way to strike up a conversation is to compliment the person, and then ask a question.

Do not ask any personal questions, such as, "What is your address?" Instead, ask where the other person lives. This allows them to be as general or specific as they choose.

If you choose to introduce yourself, use only your first name. While you may have the best intentions, the stranger you have just met might not. Be safe. If you are young, do not talk to suspicious-looking people. On the other hand, do not go overboard and be paranoid. Observe body language.

A friend to all is a friend to none.

Aristotle
(384 BCE – 322 BCE) Greek philosopher and polymath, a student of Plato and teacher of Alexander the Great. Aristotle's views on the physical sciences profoundly shaped medieval scholarship, and their influence extended well into the Renaissance, although they were ultimately replaced by Newtonian physics.

Remember that you do not want to strike up a conversation with someone who is angry or busy. In addition, it is important not to approach people if you are not seriously interested in being friends with them, or else it may come back later to haunt you. Do not swear.

Can I create a friendship in 60 seconds?
You may be missing a chance to talk to someone who could become your best friend! It is all about being confident. If the other person does not start the conversation, then you should try to start it. Look around and see what is the most interesting thing to talk about.

Most people will judge you on first impressions, so always follow good hygiene and dress nicely. You should not be too fancy. You just have to look decent, and that will make people like you more. Even if friendship is not based on clothing style, a fashionable combination could be a fun thing to talk about.

Maybe you will find a friend with a similar clothing style. In addition, it is important to know that looks are not everything, so follow all of these other techniques as well.

If you want friends, you must be willing to associate with people who may not have an aura of confidence and popularity around them. If you pick ugly/unsociable/eclectic friends, they will be more faithful than someone who has people falling over them to impress them.

Have common decency. Befriend the creeps. It will benefit you in the end. However, do not move away from a "normal" or popular person just to do. It is

Friendship is a plant of slow growth and must undergo and withstand the shocks of adversity before it is entitled to the appellation.

Gen. George Washington
(1732- 1799)
the first President of the United States of America.
His leadership style established many forms and rituals of government that have been used since, such as using a cabinet system and delivering an inaugural address.

NETWORKING

better to make a friendly acquaintance and cut it off later if the person proves to be treacherous or unfriendly, rather than to pass up starting a great friendship because of labels.

A big smile is a sign that you are a fun person, and that makes it easy for the others; and they will come to you faster. A smile is important, but you have to smile on the inside, too. Think about positive things, and your mood will make everyone feel good.

If you judge anyone before meeting the person, it will show on your face. There are a number of new friendships coming your way, so always be equally nice and friendly to everyone, and you will surprised. Your life will soon be overflowing with friends. In addition, do not forget to ask for their phone numbers or their e-mail addresses and to make sure you follow up with some kind of contact afterwards.

Recollect that everyone you know today was once a stranger. When you see the person that you want to be friends with, smile and say, "Hi!" That is all it takes, and before you know it, you might start hanging out more often, and the friendship will simply take off. Just be a good person.

Give compliments to others about their clothes, shoes, hair, etc. But be careful not to overdo it. Flattery is a nice icebreaker, but should not be used just to benefit you. The best compliments are true and honest; do not lie to people. Just point out what you think is nice about them and do not get upset if they disagree.

Remember that to find out what you have in common with the other person and to determine whether sure you want to have him or her as a friend. You do not

The media doesn't need to be informed every time you've had a haircut.

TSufit
Canadian Author
TSufit is a Dean's List graduate from University of Toronto Law School and was once named a "Super-achiever" by *Canadian Lawyer* magazine.

want to later find that the person is annoying and hurt the individual. Furthermore, watch what you say and be cheery.

What about the power of social media?
We can no longer consider the social media phenomenon a *new thing*. Google, Twitter, Facebook, MySpace, LinkedIn, and other sites have been around long enough for an entire generation of people to know nothing except these tools as communication media.

That generation is a growing part of the workplace. That generation is making decisions about how the workplace operates and how we communicate within the workplace. Those from the generation born in 1985 and beyond will be in decision-making positions before we know it, if not they do not already own their own businesses. When they are decision-makers, rather than *just influencers*, the pace of change in the workplace will really take off.

Take the time to get to know people you meet via social networking. Social networking is just like in-person networking. You want to approach it as a way to learn things. When you pay attention to the chatter, the events, groups, and conversations, you will learn an awful lot about the people in your network. You will also learn about people you should be connected to. You do not have to connect with everyone.

Remember that you can make decisions about whom you connect with on different platforms. Just be consistent. If you decide that you do not want to be connected to business associates on Facebook, then do not. If someone whom you do not know requests a connection to you, you are under no obligation to connect with him or her.

The greatest discovery of all time is that a person can change his future by merely changing his attitude.

Gen. George Washington
(1732- 1799)
The first President of the United States of America.

NETWORKING

What should I consider?

Understand how *social* is different for someone born in 1990 than for someone born in 1950, and yet it is the same. Start small. A sustained effort over the long run is better than making a one-time big effort and then burning out.

Remember that networking requires maintenance; so do not bite off more than you can chew. It always helps to look approachable and be charming. Over time, it will get easier for you to start a conversation with a stranger.

Can you find a local club or group relating to your interests or career? If not, start one!

You can make great contacts with politicians and their aides by volunteering in an election or being involved with their party outside of election time.

Remember to use every Internet tool at your disposal to build your social network in real life. Instant messaging applications, for instance, are sometimes better than phone calls. The Internet is very useful to meet and keep in contact with a large number of people worldwide.

Recommended Reading & References

We suggest consulting the works identified below in order to learn more about the particulars contained in this chapter.

INGLE, Sud. QUALITY CIRCLES MASTER GUIDE. Prentice-Hall. ISBN 0-13-745000-1.

MACKAY, Harvey. HOW TO BUILD A NETWORK OF POWER RELATIONSHIPS. Conant. ISBN 0-7435-2659-7.

QUICK, Thomas L. UNDERSTANDING PEOPLE AT WORK. Executive Enterprises publications Co. ISBN 0-917386-17-5.

TSUFIT. STEP INTO THE SPOTLIGHT! Beach View Books. ISBN 978-0-9781913-0-6.

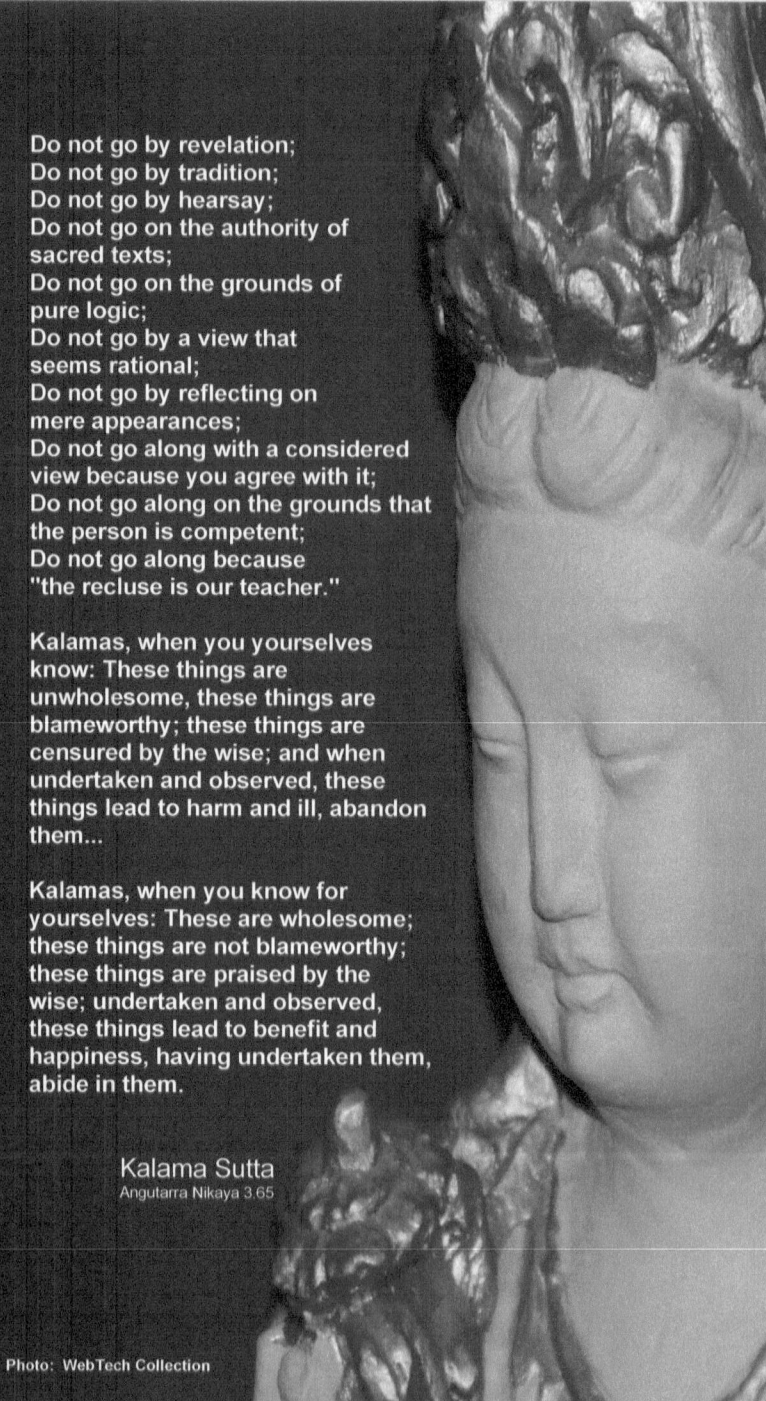

Do not go by revelation;
Do not go by tradition;
Do not go by hearsay;
Do not go on the authority of sacred texts;
Do not go on the grounds of pure logic;
Do not go by a view that seems rational;
Do not go by reflecting on mere appearances;
Do not go along with a considered view because you agree with it;
Do not go along on the grounds that the person is competent;
Do not go along because "the recluse is our teacher."

Kalamas, when you yourselves know: These things are unwholesome, these things are blameworthy; these things are censured by the wise; and when undertaken and observed, these things lead to harm and ill, abandon them...

Kalamas, when you know for yourselves: These are wholesome; these things are not blameworthy; these things are praised by the wise; undertaken and observed, these things lead to benefit and happiness, having undertaken them, abide in them.

Kalama Sutta
Angutarra Nikaya 3.65

Photo: WebTech Collection

CHAPTER 7

The beginning of wisdom is to call things by their right names.

Chinese proverb
Ceremonial mask

The struggle is constant, as the trade-offs and choices don't get any easier as you get older.

John Donahoe
(1960 -)
CEO. eBav

KNOWLEDGE & **WISDOM**

Knowledge refers to the information, understanding, and skills that you gain through education or experience. It refers to the hard facts and the data that can be available to anyone if he or she has the right resources. For example, you can have practical, medical, or scientific knowledge.

Wisdom, on the other hand, refers to the ability to make sensible decisions and give good advice because of the experience and knowledge that you have.

Someone may have all the knowledge about a subject but may not have the wisdom to utilize this knowledge properly to be able to act in a sensible manner.

You can gain knowledge by educating yourself, but you can gain wisdom only by experience.

Growth has its many forms and manifests itself in human beings. Knowledge about growth can lead to wisdom of sorts.

Remember that if you are born with this deep-rooted desire to grow from within, you need to set your priorities right. Your aims and ambitions all need to be clear concerning what you want to do in life, along with the experience that gets attached to it all.

What is the difference between being knowledgeable and being wise?

When you grow, you grow in two ways: one in terms of volume and the other in terms of qualitative knowledge. I have often noted that there is a thin line of difference between being knowledgeable and

Chapter 7

> Develop a passion for learning.
> If you do, you will never cease to grow.
>
> Anthony J. D'Angelo
> American Author

being wise. It is seldom that you find a combination of both. When you grow in experience, you may or may not understand the need for it, until after you have learned from it.

You might have wanted to be a painter. If so, spending a little time painting billboards can help you gain some knowledge that you may otherwise be devoid of. And it is this experienced that can help make you wise.

So what does any experience entail? Your experience gives you knowledge; it empowers you with those things that you have learned. Instead of merely accepting the facts that you are not familiar with, you are enticed into acquiring first-hand information about those areas. This in turn leads to growth. "I don't know" and "I am not sure" are mere words that make you search for more.

Once you have reached this stage, growth occurs automatically. Acceptance of what you do not know, in short, leads to growth. Your aims and aspirations are stepping-stones to knowledge; following unfamiliar paths leads to growth and thus towards wisdom.

You have experienced your body, to a degree, your mind to a point, and you have experienced the world, to some extent. You might have also experienced the energy which makes this body and mind function. Beyond this, you have not experienced anything at all.

Remember that everything else is just pure, unadulterated imagination, and your imagination functions in whatever way society has taught you. Take stock of what experience you have and have

> Data is not information, information is not knowledge, knowledge is not understanding, understanding is not wisdom.
>
> Clifford Stoll
> U.S. astronomer and author. He is best known for his pursuit of hacker Markus Hess in 1986 and the subsequent 1989 book detailing his investigation.

not had, and all that is not there in your experience accept it as, "*I do not know*". This is very, very essential. Otherwise, your whole life may pass by in pretensions.

How can I search for the unknown?

An important aspect about this growth is that it leads to an unending search for the unknown. This in turn may make you "move mountains". Human life has always been a search for understanding the unknown.

To exist is to change, to change is to mature, to mature is to go on creating oneself endlessly.

Henri-Louis Bergson, (1859 –1941) French philosopher, influential especially in the first half of the 20th century. Bergson convinced many thinkers that immediate experience and intuition are more significant than rationalism and science for understanding reality.

The reason why we focus on the past is because it helps us "live through" the experiences that the historical figures went through. They have gained knowledge we can learn from, and knowledge makes us much more mature and wiser people. Half-baked knowledge leads to an inflated ego. More importantly, the search and zeal for knowledge make us dig deep.

Acknowledge this is one subject that builds your patience; your assimilation powers and a combination of these makes you wise. In a situation where you are searching; you will notice that the human mind is not completely satisfied with others' results. And curiously, when you are involved in this research, there comes a time when you are no longer really interested to obtain a conclusion, just as you have gathered sufficient knowledge to put into perspective your approach.

Remember that the journey towards gaining knowledge is so overpowering that the search just continues on.

Chapter 7

The only source of knowledge is experience.

Albert Einstein
On the eve of World War II, he helped alert President Franklin D. Roosevelt that Germany might be developing an atomic weapon, and recommended that the U.S. begin similar research; this eventually led to what would become the Manhattan Project.

So how do I continually learn new things in life?
Constantly increasing our knowledge is essential if we are to progress further or develop ourselves. Whatever field we are involved in, we always have to look for ways and means to expand our knowledge. To increase in knowledge in a particular subject can lead to better understanding, to a better grasp on things, to better judgment, to more intelligence and to ability in that area. It can expand our thinking and heighten our expertise on a topic.

So how do we go about gaining knowledge? What are the sources of knowledge? I think people are the biggest source of knowledge for anybody. From childhood, we have learned things by watching others. Whatever field you want to gain knowledge in, there must be many who have enough experience in that field.

So make use of this valuable source of information by learning from the experience, accomplishments, mistakes, and expertise of others. Study carefully and associate with people who are experts in the field you want to gain knowledge about.

Donald Trump, in his book *Think Big and Kick Ass in Business and Life,* formulates a down to heart definition. *The formula of knowledge is the best way to learn because learning from someone else's mistakes is faster and easier than making them yourself. For example, you don't have to go through an early 1990s real estate crash like I did to know what to do in that situation. Because of the way things go in life, lots of times life forces you to learn from your own mistakes, but it is much better if you can learn from others' mistakes rather than your own.*

KNOWLEDGE & **WISDOM**

Other sources of knowledge can come from the millions of books written throughout the world in every language and on almost any topic imaginable.

An investment in knowledge pays the best interest.

Benjamin Franklin
(1706-1790)

Somebody else before must have faced whatever problem you are facing, and its solution is likely to have been preserved in the form of a book. If you are serious about gaining knowledge on a topic, then read any book, magazine, article, etc. you can lay your hands on related to that topic. Read as much as you can.

This is another important resource for the seeker of knowledge. It is said that experience is a great teacher, so learn from your experiences and the experience of others. Learn from your and others' past and present achievements as well as mistakes.

Bad times have a scientific value.
These are the occasions a good learner would not miss.

Ralph Waldo Emerson
(1803 – 1882)

Experimentation is trying out new things and observation is paying attention to small and big details. If you want to learn something new, you may have to experiment and observe a lot. You will need to explore in depth and try out new things to see what works and what does not. Observe not just your own efforts, but also those of others.

Experimenting with new things and observation can help you learn very quickly. People who do not experiment or observe much may take a long time to learn. Keep in mind though, that while experimenting, you may encounter a few failures, too.

Do not become discouraged, as failures are a part of the learning curve, especially while attempting something new.

Try to learn from failures instead of becoming disheartened!

Chapter **7**

Remember that while learning a new thing, you need to concentrate a lot. Just reading lots of books is not sufficient, as you need to grasp fully what you are reading. Deep understanding about a subject is likely to come only through deep thinking and contemplation. Ponder over what you have read, observed, experienced, or experimented with. It is wise to make sure you have fully understood a thing before moving on further.

Can our general knowledge be updated?
General Knowledge is an integral part of our lives. It helps us to communicate and build social networks. Due to technological advancements, general knowledge is much more accessible. It is no longer confined to a particular group of people but has spread its wings throughout the world.

Real knowledge is to know the extent of one's ignorance.

Confucius' principles had a basis in common Chinese tradition and belief. He championed strong familial loyalty, ancestor worship, respect of elders by their children (and, according to later interpreters, of husbands by their wives), and the family as a basis for an ideal government.

General knowledge is found in our educational system – especially in entrance exams, where general knowledge is given great importance.

For some careers, it has become the pre-requisite for recruitment. Thus, it has become very important for us to stay updated. Today, there are various ways to gain general knowledge.

The oldest and best accessible way to gain information on the on-going events and occurrences is to read the newspaper. It is the most preferred option by the majority of people.

Television is also an entertaining way to gain general knowledge. Not only news channels, but channels like Discovery, the History channel, or National Geographic can provide useful information and also entertainment at the same time. It is a proven fact people can retain information for a longer time if they watch it or hear it. Thus, television is a viable option as a way to gain general knowledge. Radio is another option, where you can hear about the on-going activities around you.

The Internet is the treasure box. In this technologically advanced world, the Internet has made peoples' lives much easier. You will find all the general knowledge on any subject, person, place, organization, event, etc. on the Internet.

Quizzes are another entertaining medium that can be used to gain overall knowledge. They also help you test your general awareness level. They are usually in a questionnaire format with multiple answers. The ascending difficulty level makes it interesting for the user, providing information at the same time.

Remember that if you want to achieve anything in life, hard work is the only way. In the case of gaining general knowledge, being in constant touch with these media forms, or with some of them, can be very beneficial. The important thing is that you stay updated and aware.

Can I gain wisdom?

Wisdom is generally thought of as keen insight that helps in navigating life. Believing in wisdom carries the assumption that there is a best way of doing things. There are many ways to gain wisdom and learn how to navigate the storms of life. Generally, wisdom is best gained from your own personal experience, but you can also learn by watching others and even through reading and meditation.

You need to determine the source or sources of wisdom you find most consistent and trustworthy. To do so, ask those you consider wise how they have

We can be knowledgeable with other men's knowledge, but we cannot be wise with other men's wisdom.

Lord Michel Eyquem de Montaigne
(1533 –1592)
One of the most influential writers of the French Renaissance, known for popularising the essay as a literary genre and is popularly thought of as the father of Modern Skepticism.

Chapter 7

learned what they have learned, where they studied or how they changed their mindsets throughout their lives to gain wisdom.

Right thinking will produce just action. Consistency in carrying out appropriate action over time is the basis of wisdom. Realize that every situation you go through is an opportunity for change and for developing right thinking. However, you will need to think about your actions both present and past. Ask yourself what these situations and actions could have taught you, if you had let them. Notice any patterns you might be experiencing or if the same thing keeps happening to you. There is likely a lesson waiting for you to learn and gain wisdom from.

> A wise man changes his mind, a fool never will.
>
> Anonymous

As you become more refined in asking yourself why you do the things you do, you may notice that a higher truth is guiding you into right thinking and correct behavior. Constantly seek out higher wisdom.

Remember that the wisdom you possess lays a foundation for the revelations you have and developments you will go through in your lifetime. Reflecting on your progress helps you to gain perspective and thus more wisdom. Keep a journal of your progress.

> I can accept failure, everyone fails at something. But I can't accept not trying.
>
> Michael Jeffrey Jordan
> (1963 -)
> Former American professional basketball player, active entrepreneur, and majority owner of the Charlotte Bobcats.

How can I learn from failure?

Failures are said to be stepping-stones to success, but they can only be so when you learn from them and avoid them in the future. It is bad enough to fail, but worse if you do not learn from failure.

You can make each failure count by learning something from it. Whenever you fail, take a piece of paper and write down the important lessons that you learned from this failure.

KNOWLEDGE & **WISDOM**

Such an exercise will force you to think about your failures and focus on the lessons you can learn from them, which you may otherwise miss.

Once you have learned some things from your failure, it is time to forget about it and move on in life. Do not dwell on your past mistakes. If at anytime thoughts of previous failures come into your mind, read the papers that list the important lessons you learned from each of these mistakes. Reminding yourself of the lessons learnt from your mistakes helps to take your mind off the failures and to help dwell you on positives instead.

Because you have failed, do not be afraid to try out new things. Remember the lessons and attempt new things in the future. When you keep in mind the lessons learnt from previous mistakes, you lessen your fear of trying out new things because you know that you are now more prepared than you were before.

Remember that you can gain knowledge and wisdom by educating yourself through your failures. If you still feel negative or resentful about your failures, think about a time when you achieved some worthwhile success.

Think about how many times you failed and how many mistakes you made before finally succeeding. This will help you realize that failures are a part of the learning curve and that there will be obstacles and disappointments along the way of most endeavors you undertake. Learn to accept them as part of life and to use what you learn from them rather than to get disheartened about them.

> It is essential to employ, trust, and reward those whose perspective, ability, and judgment are radically different from yours.
> It is also rare, for it requires uncommon humility, tolerance, and wisdom.
>
> Dee Ward Hock
> (1929 -)
> Founder and former CEO of the VISA credit card association.

> The struggle is constant, as the trade-offs and choices don't get any easier as you get older.
>
> John Donahoe,
> (1960 -)
> American businessman and the President and CEO of eBay, Inc

Chapter **7**

A little more persistence, a little more effort, and what seemed hopeless failure may turn to glorious success.

Elbert Green Hubbard (1856 –1915) American writer, publisher, artist, and philosopher. He and his second wife, Alice Moore Hubbard, died aboard the *RMS Lusitania*, which was sunk by a German submarine off the coast of Ireland on May 7, 1915.

Should I believe I have tried all possible approaches?

Time and again, we have seen the value of persistence in the lives of successful people in whatever field they were in, whether in business, politics, sports, etc. But there may be a lot of men and women who persisted in trying to achieve something yet failed.

You may be among them. You may have tried to achieve something for many years and still have not succeeded. So what is the difference between people who persist and finally succeed and people who fail despite persisting tirelessly?

People who persist and still fail in achieving their desired goals are usually those who keep on doing the same thing repeatedly and yet expect a different result.

Persistence is not about repeating the same thing over and over and hoping for a different result each time. That is stupidity, not persistence. Such persistence is misguided and not likely to succeed.

People who have tasted success are usually those who have learned from their mistakes, changed their approach, tried new things, and kept trying until they have finally achieved their desired result. Such people are open-minded, willing to learn, ready to try new approaches, and they do not assume they know everything.

So remember the following points while pursuing your goals: Be persistent; try another approach if the earlier one did not work and keep an open mind and be willing to learn, especially from your mistakes.

KNOWLEDGE & **WISDOM**

Most importantly, do not assume that you know everything!

Remember not to think that you have tried all possible approaches. You may have tried all the approaches that you are aware of, but there may be things that you do not currently know. So focus on finding newer approaches. By not being a quitter, you are giving your mind strong signals that you are determined to achieve your goal. Your mind no longer has any excuses. This is the kind of persistence that is needed.

Is there a technique for learning a subject better?

Do you want to know about a technique which can help you learn things faster and better? The teaching technique can do so.

When you read something, or whenever you are trying to learn about any topic or subject, you can get a better grasp of the subject by teaching it to somebody. The important thing is not whom you are teaching it to. It is to go through the motions of teaching. Keep doing it even though you may find it silly in the beginning.

What happens when you go through the motions of teaching?

- You repeat what was just learnt, which helps you remember the information.
- You put the information in your own words, which helps you clear up any confusions that you might have about the subject.
- You organize the information you just studied in your head.
- You may also notice that there are some points that you did not understand as perfectly as you

Flaming enthusiasm, backed up by horse sense and persistence, is the quality that most frequently makes for success.

Dale Carnegie
(1888 –1955)
Written in 1936, *How to Win Friends and Influence People* is still a popular book to date in business and Business Communication skills. Dale Carnegie's four part book is packed with advice to create success in business and personal lives.

Learning without thought is labor lost; thought without learning is perilous.

Confucius
(551 BCE–479 BCE)

Chapter 7

thought you did. You can write down which points you did not fully understand, and then re-read those points to get a better understanding.
- While teaching, you may get new thoughts and ideas about the subject. If so, stop teaching for a few moments and write down the ideas that have come to mind.

Anyone who stops learning is old, whether at twenty or eighty. Anyone who keeps learning stays young. The greatest thing in life is to keep your mind young.

Henry Ford
(1863 – 1947)
The Model T was introduced on October 1, 1908. It had the steering wheel on the left, which every other company soon copied.

Remember that it does not matter whom you are teaching, whether it is to humans, animals, or to the walls of your house, just go through the motions of teaching. Simply try to explain the subject as clearly as possible in your own words. This will help you grasp the information more firmly and remember it. If you feel silly or embarrassed using this technique, only imagine doing it in your mind. Furthermore, you can write down what you have learnt in an organized manner as if you were trying to write a chapter on the subject that you have just studied. This can help as well.

What is reason and how do I use it?
Reason is the mental powers and processes concerned with forming conclusions, judgments, or inferences. Proper use of reasoning is extremely important in making daily decisions.

We are all short sighted and very often see only one side of a matter; we fail to see the whole picture. We see now but in part, and therefore, we may draw erroneous conclusions, inferences, and judgments from our partial views. Narrow-mindedness is a great fault of reasoning that we must all strive to avoid.

Never imagine that you know all there is to know about any subject and that there is no more truth to know. Seek the truth earnestly. Dispel all prejudices from your mind. Do not think that there is no truth

A good head and a good heart are always a formidable combination.

Nelson Rolihlahla Mandela
(1918 -)
President of South Africa from 1994 to 1999, and was the first South African president to be elected in a fully representative democratic election.

Humor is perhaps a sense of intellectual perspective: an awareness that some things are really important, others not; and that the two kinds are most oddly jumbled in everyday affairs.

Christopher Morley
(1890 – 1957)
American journalist, novelist, essayist, and poet.

except in the sciences you study. If you prejudge another's notions before examining them, you have not discovered what might be wrong with them but have only turned a blind eye to them. Be eager to discover the truth in subjects unfamiliar to you. Read widely and take an interest in many different subjects.

You can always learn something from others, be it parents, siblings, friends, neighbors, ministers, etc. If you see something someone does well, learn from it by following his example. If you see something a person does poorly, learn from that as well, by finding a way to improve, so as not to repeat the mistake yourself. Distinguish truth from appearances of truth. Discernment skills come with repeated and frequent practice in seeking the truth without any prejudices or presumptions.

Refuse to be offended easily, but learn to view things from others' perspectives. Some people hold on so tightly to their own beliefs' and they will not even reconsider them when others question those beliefs because they believe them to be infallible or sacred. They don't accept that they could be wrong about what they believe. No man is infallible. Each of us could be wrong about something. To suppose one is infallible is to refuse reason.

Therefore, accept criticism with eagerness, as convenient means to examine your own beliefs, ideas, and views. Be humble, and dispel any biases or errors you chance to uncover immediately, unreservedly, and wholeheartedly. Note that this includes all subjects and areas of your life, even in matters of religion or politics.

Furthermore, passion is a major bias that blinds us to the facts, and distorts reason, insomuch that as you

Chapter 7

Bad reasoning as well as good reasoning is possible; and this fact is the foundation of the practical side of logic.

Charles Sanders Pierce
(1839 – 1914)
American philosopher, logician, mathematician, and scientist. An innovator in mathematics, statistics, philosophy, research methodology, and various sciences, Peirce considered himself, first and foremost, a logician.

Socrates
(469 BCE – 399 BCE)
A classical Greek Athenian philosopher.

become incapable of using your own or listen to others' reason. To reason appropriately, you must adopt a spirit of unbiased disinterest. Get all the facts by seeking out the best books on every science, search the Internet for all the reliable sources, and learn from the most knowledgeable people on the subjects.

Should you study and apply logic in reasoning?

Deductive reasoning is drawing conclusions from the general to the specific. In deductive reasoning, if a logical sequence is followed, the argument is valid, and the conclusion must be true if the premises are true. For instance, if "*All men are mortal*" is the major premise, and "*Socrates is a man*" is the minor premise, then "*Socrates is mortal*" is the valid conclusion, which must be true if the premises are true. Deductive reasoning is to be contrasted with inductive reasoning.

Inductive reasoning is drawing a conclusion from the specific to the general, and is mostly used to formulate theories. In inductive reasoning, the specific facts do not necessarily lead to the general conclusion. For instance, if you reach your hand into a bag of stones of unknown colors, and all the stones, you draw out are white. You might induce that all the stones in the bag are white. This may or may not be true; the next non-white stone you draw out of the bag would disprove the conclusion. The more facts you gather, and the larger the sample size, the stronger the inductive reasoning process becomes. Using inductive reasoning is also called making a conjecture.

Your conclusion is more probable, in such a conjecture, that all the stones in the bag are white if you draw out a thousand stones, rather than if you only draw out ten stones. The collection of such data is part of the process of reasoning by statistical inference and probability.

Abductive reasoning is drawing conclusions or making an argument to select a better explanation, as in medical diagnosis; this is related to inductive reasoning since the conclusion in an abductive argument does not follow with certainty from its premises and concerns something unobserved. What distinguishes abduction from the other forms of reasoning is an attempt to favor one conclusion above others, by attempting to falsify alternative explanations or by demonstrating the higher likelihood of the preferred conclusion, given a set of more or less disputable information and assumptions. In addition, abductive reasoning is used to explain a conclusion or an outcome. "*The grass is wet. Therefore, it may have rained.*" Detectives as well as diagnosticians are commonly associated with this style of reasoning.

Analogical reasoning is drawing comparisons by analogy, either explicitly or implicitly. This form of logical reasoning infers that a given similarity of one thing to another thing means a similarity exits between the things in other respects as well.

Remember that just as you would not make a major purchase without finding out more about the product, you would not begin to reason without obtaining the facts. However, do not go to extremes about it. It is unnecessary to visit every mountain, river, and creek upon the face of the earth and to survey all the land in order to be a good geographer, but it is desirable to know the land better by traversing it up and down,

Logic: The art of thinking and reasoning in strict accordance with the limitations and incapacities of the human misunderstanding.

Ambrose Gwinnett Bierce
(1842–1913)
American editorialist, journalist, short story writer, fabulist, and satirist. Today, he is best known for his short story, "An Occurrence at Owl Creek Bridge" and his satirical lexicon, *The Devil's Dictionary*.

Chapter 7

rather than limiting yourself to just a particular field of the land.

Learn to strike a balance between reason and passion. There is a time for Reason and a time for Passion. Use the one that is appropriate in any given situation.

How do I strengthen my character?
Character is known as the sum of all the attributes, such as integrity, courage, fortitude, honesty, and loyalty, in a person. Character is perhaps the most important essence a person can possess, as it defines who a person is. To strengthen one's character is to mold oneself into a productive person within one's sphere of influence.

Strength in character consists of having the qualities that allow you to exercise control over your instincts and passions, to master yourself, and to resist the myriad temptations that constantly confront you. Moreover, strength in character is freedom from biases and prejudices of the mind and is about displaying tolerance, love, and respect for others.

Strength of character allows you to exercise your will freely while enabling you to cope with setbacks. It assists you in accomplishing your goals. It allows you to inquire into the causes of ill fortune, instead of just complaining about it, as many are inclined to do. It gives you the courage to admit your own faults, frivolousness, and weaknesses. Moreover, it gives you the strength to keep a foothold when the tide turns against you, and to continue to climb upward in the face of obstacles.

A wise man is superior to any insults which can be put upon him, and the best reply to unseemly behavior is patience and moderation.

Jean-Baptiste Poquelin, known by his stage name Molière.
(1622 –1673)
Hi best-known works are Le Misanthrope (The Misanthrope), L'École des femmes (The School for Wives), Tartuffe ou L'Imposteur, (Tartuffe or the Hypocrite), L'Avare (The Miser), Le Malade imaginaire (The Imaginary Invalid), and Le Bourgeois Gentilhomme (The Bourgeois Gentleman).

KNOWLEDGE & **WISDOM**

The most important way to strengthen your character is to empathize with others, especially the weaker individuals, and to love others as yourself.

This may come at some cost, causing you to examine your own motives, so that you can empathize ungrudgingly. Empathizing differs from sympathizing in denotation, as empathizing requires you to project yourself and engage as needed, that is to walk in and help clear the other person's pathway, whereas sympathizing implies, having an emotional but passive reaction, such as listening, looking, and mimicking without extending oneself.

Favor reason over pure emotion and seek the truth. The person with a strong character will examine all the facts using his or her head and will not be biased by emotions from the heart. Settle all matters upon reason alone, and avoid entangling yourself in the chaos of your feelings.

Character may almost be called the most effective means of persuasion.

Aristotle
(384 BCE – 322 BCE)

Be a leader, neither a pessimist nor an optimist. A pessimist complains about the wind. An optimist expects the adverse wind conditions to improve. But the leader takes action to adjust the sails and ensure that they are ready to cope with whatever weather exists.

Thomas of Aquin or Aquino, (1225 –1274) Italian Dominican priest of the Catholic Church, and an immensely influential philosopher and theologian in the tradition of scholasticism.

Aristotle and Aquinas considered that there are seven human passions: love and hatred, desire and fear, joy and sadness, and anger. While good in and of themselves, these passions can bypass our intellect and cause us to love the wrong things, eat too much food, fear things irrationally, or become overwhelmed in sadness or by anger. You must guard against irrational impulses.

Chapter 7

The answer is found in always looking before you leap and in practicing good habits to free yourself from the enslavement of your own passions. Inordinate, sensual appetites are the marks of a weak character; the ability to delay gratification and practice self-control is a sign of strength.

Change yourself and your work will seem different.

Dr. Norman Vincent Peale
(1898 –1993)
Minister and author (most notably of The Power of Positive Thinking) and a progenitor of the theory of "positive thinking".

Appreciate your own values and what you have. Imagining that the grass is greener somewhere else is a recipe for lifelong unhappiness; remember that doing so is actually projecting your assumptions about how others live.

It is better to focus on how you live. If you shun the battle of life, you must forgo the victory, and the joy associated therewith. Be brave enough to take calculated risks. Neither be cowardly, nor aloof, nor evade your rightful duties, but be courageous to contribute your part to the progress of humankind.

Albert. J Bernstein, Ph.D., in his book: *Dinosaur Brains: Dealing with All Those Impossible People at Work,* noted the following: *People will consider their own feelings and best interests before they consider yours. This is true even of close friends and family. Never assume malicious intent when ignorance is sufficient to explain. People will come to you for favors but will not be as ready to do favors for you when you come to them, as you were to do favors for them when they came to you.*

People will tell you their problems but will never be available to listen to yours. If you tell somebody at work something in confidence and it's of any importance, it will get out. If you are abrasive and aggressive, nobody will ever come and tell you. That's because they're afraid of you. If you want to form an alliance, make a group cohesive or start a

KNOWLEDGE & **WISDOM**

It is easy to hate and it is difficult to love. This is how the whole scheme of things works. All good things are difficult to achieve; and bad things are very easy to get.

Confucius
(551BCE–479 BCE)
He was a Chinese teacher, editor, politician, and philosopher of the Spring and Autumn Period of Chinese history.

Perspective:
As our days move by us faster and faster, it becomes that much more important to take a breath, and reflect on what happened during the day. Without the perspective of our days, we cannot really take satisfaction in our big wins, nor can we learn from our mistakes.

friendship, you will have to do all the work. It will seem that you're the one who always has to do all the phone calling, planning or grunt stuff. If you feel that way, it means you're doing it right. If you're on a committee, you'll have to do most of the work, but you'll have to divide the credit.

Every individual has his or her interests foremost in mind, whether consciously or unconsciously. Neither impose your will upon others, nor allow others to impose their wills upon you. Remain aware and accepting of the fact that different people will have distinctive suggestions, and that you cannot please everyone. Find the right path, and walk therein, neither turning to the right nor the left. Govern yourself, and never abandon the right path.

Seek peace and pursue it earnestly. Learn to do good and eschew evil. Aim not for personal goals that trample on others' needs, but aim after noble and worthy motives to benefit society as a whole. If you seek personal gains, you will run into conflicts with others, and, in the end, you will inevitably fail. If you seek the mutual good, everyone will benefit, and you will also find satisfying personal gains as well.

Avoid letting anything other than sound reason dictate your decisions in the conduct of everyday life. Learn to master your feelings. It might often be difficult, and at times impossible, not to yield to feelings deep within your soul, but you can learn to suppress their manifestations and to overcome them through relying on common sense and sound judgment.

The ability to seek the middle ground is the mark of a strong character capable of resisting extremes. Be neither prodigal, nor miserly, but seek the middle ground.

Chapter 7

> You do things when the opportunities come along. I've had periods in my life when I've had a bundle of ideas come along, and I've had long dry spells.
> If I get an idea next week, I'll do something. If not, I won't do a damn thing.
>
> — Warren Edward Buffett
> (1930 -)
> American business magnate, investor, and philanthropist. He is widely regarded as one of the most successful investors in the world.

> Comfort in expressing your emotions will allow you to share the best of yourself with others, but not being able to control your emotions will reveal your worst.
>
> — Bryant Harrison McGill
> (1969 –)
> American editor and author who was born in Mobile, Alabama.

Calmness is a state of quietude that enables you to concentrate and reassemble your divergent thoughts and to benefit from doing so. Be calm in all things.

Contemplation leads to ideas, and ideas lead to opportunities, and opportunities lead to success. Calmness is a *sine qua non* of a strong character.

Without calmness, there can be no strength in character. Without calmness, passion can easily become overheated, turning into an intense desire and interfering with sound reason. Calmness is not the foe of feelings, but its regulator, permitting their proper expression.

Everyone is responsible for his or her own development and fortune. We must focus on the positives in life and spare little time for the negatives. To accept fatalism, that is, to believe that destiny is somehow immovable, is to discourage you from attempting all initiatives to improve your life and self.

Destiny is blind and deaf; it will neither hear us nor regard us. Instead, remember that fixing calamities and changing destiny for the better are ways to strengthen your character and improve your lot in life. Work out your happiness; do not wait for someone or something else to do it for you because it will never happen unless you persevere.

An individual with a strong character will not quit when faced with obstacles but will persevere to the end and overcome them all. Learn to delay gratifications in life, learn to wait, and learn that time is your friend. It also helps to know which battles are worth fighting, and when to let things rest; sometimes letting go is more important than clinging to a "sinking ship."

KNOWLEDGE & **WISDOM**

Economy, prudence, and a simple life are the sure masters of need, and will often accomplish that which their opposites, with a fortune at hand, will fail to do.

Clarissa Harlowe "Clara" Barton (1821 –1912) Pioneer American teacher, patent clerk, nurse, and humanitarian. She is best remembered for organizing the American Red Cross.

By constant self-discipline and self-control you can develop greatness of character.

Grenville Kleiser (1868-1935) Canadian author. He was the author of a long list of inspirational books and guides to oratorical success and personal development.

Timidity is a stumbling block to success. You must conquer all your fears. Entertain no superstitions based upon superficial observations, but accept facts based upon solid reason.

Avoid building your foundation upon sand, preferring instead to build upon a rock. Once you overcome fear, you will have the strength of character to think, to have resolve, and to act victoriously.

You need to guard against excessive emotions and attribute to them their exact significance. Whenever you find yourself preoccupied with some overwhelming emotion, immediately get busy doing something else for fifteen minutes, or more.

Many great warriors have lost their lives when they reacted too brashly to insults and hot-headedly went to fight prematurely against their tempters without adequate preparations. Learn to overcome such a weakness with practice, remembering that anger is a common vice in all those of weak character.

In business, as in life, we need to exercise coolness, circumspection, discernment, and prudence. Cultivate your mind with logic, and conduct your affairs accordingly.

If you are dishonest, you are untruthful with yourself, and that is an assault upon your own character. Always be truthful in all things and about every aspect of life.

Work hard, and shun idleness like the plague. By the same token, learn to appreciate quality leisure time, for its ability to rejuvenate and inspire you to return to your good deeds. Most of all, excel wherever you are, and do your best at whatever you do.

Chapter **7**

Remember, happiness is health. Happiness gives you strength to overcome the monotonous and dispel boredom in life. It allows you to make the best of everything. Happiness is a state of mind. You need to do physical exercise to train your endurance. The mind and the body interconnect. So train your physical endurance to strengthen your mental endurance. Have discipline and self-control. Devote yourself to your friend, and be willing to sacrifice. Never hold grudges, and dismiss all petty incidents. Live in harmony with others. Do not be egotistic; always think in terms of others' interests.

What should I consider?
The wonderful thing about character and integrity, which are intimately related, is that they are some of the few things in life that no one will ever be able, forcefully, to take away from you. Your choices are your own. Even if someone can take your life, they cannot force you to make a choice that you believe is wrong.

Be conscious every day of the decisions you make, no matter how big or small and how close they bring you to be the person you really want to become. You will probably feel your self-confidence and personal strength growing as you face and overcome challenges while sticking to your values, whatever they may be.

Beware of people who will try to convince you to forfeit on your character or integrity, saying that nobody is perfect and taunting you for being such an idealist. The fact that nobody is perfect does not mean you should violate what you believe is right. It is good to learn from our mistakes, but we do not always need to make mistakes in order to learn.

A man with convictions finds an answer for everything. Convictions are the best form of protection against the living truth.

Max Rudolf Frisch
(1911 –1991)
Swiss playwright and novelist, regarded as highly representative of German-language literature after World War II.
In his creative works Frisch paid particular attention to issues relating to problems of human identity, individuality, responsibility, morality and political commitment.

Remember that striving to be perfect and being perfect are two different ideas; the former is integrity. The latter is futility. Your character is unique. It may not match with anybody else's. So do not try to copy others. Build your character assuming your own aptitude and inner light. Self-assessment, self-evaluation, introspection, etc. are all good, but never get disheartened by petty failures and criticism revolving around failures.

Stand firm on your convictions. You are bound to succeed with the assistance of the knowledge you have gathered and the wisdom of your life experiences.

Recommended Reading & References
We suggest consulting the works identified below in order to learn more about the particulars contained in this chapter.

BERNSTEIN, Albert j. PhD. DINOSAUR BRAINS, DEALING WITH ALL THOSE IMPOSSIBLE PEOPLE AT WORK.
Wiley & sons. ISBN0-471-61808-X.

BUTLER-BOWDON, Tom. 50 PSYHOLOGY CLASSICS. Who We Are, How We Think, What We Do.
Gildan Media. ISBN 1-59659-119-6.

DAVENPORT, Thomas H. – PRUSAK Laurence. WORKING KNOWLEDGE. Havard Press ISBN 1-57851-301-4.

GIULIANI, Rudolph W., LEADERSHIP.
Miramax Books. ISBN 0-7868-6841-4.

Kennedy, John F. PROFILE OF COURAGE.
Harper Classic. ISBN-13: 978-0-06-085493-5.

LIEBERMAN, David J. YOU CAN READ ANYONE. Never Be Fooled, Lied to, or Taken Advantage of Again.
Audi Coach. ISBN 1-59659-153-6.

MACHIAVELLI, Niccolo. THE PRINCE.
Penguin Classics. ISBN 0-14-044107-7.

MACKAY, Harvey. SWIM WITH THE SHARKS WITHOUT BEING EATEN ALIVE. Ballantine Books. ISBN 0-8041-0426-3.

MICHAELSON, Steven W. SUN TZU FOR EXECUTION.
Adams Business. ISBN-13: 978-1-59869-052-1.

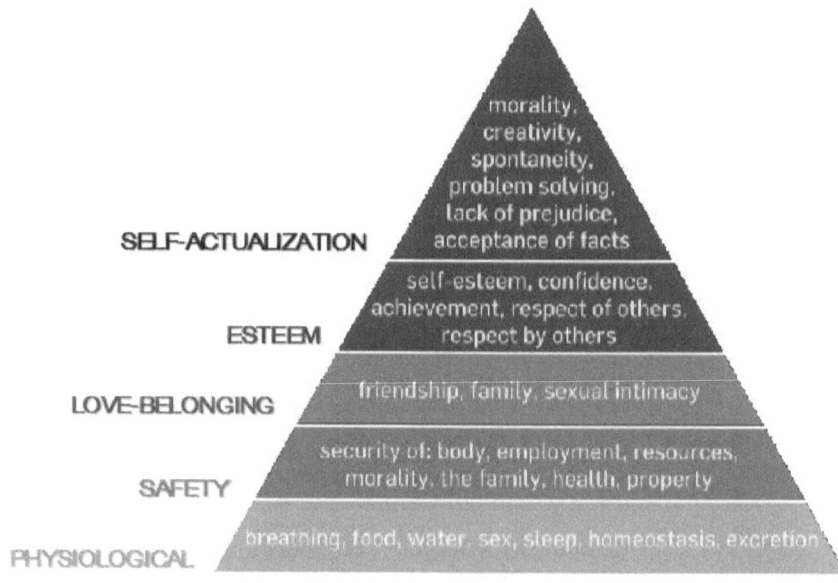

If you plan on being anything less than you are capable of being, you will probably be unhappy all the days of your life.

Abraham Maslow

Maslow's hierarchy of needs is a theory in psychology, proposed by Abraham Maslow in his 1943 paper *A Theory of Human Motivation*.

PLAN **AHEAD**

CHAPTER 8

Life is a journey. How will you get there if you do not have an itinerary? Goals tell you where you are going, how you are going to get there, and what you will do when you get there.

You have to decide what you want, first of all. The problem with so many people is that they do not know what they really want. In other words, they are not at all clear about what they want in life. Setting your goals requires you to decide what you want and to determine by when you want to have achieved that thing. For instance, you must put a deadline on what you currently want.

Get clear about what you want. Have a good plan of attack. Ask yourself: What do I know about this? What information do I have? What information do I need, and where can I get it? What skills do I need to master? What other resources should I use? Is this the best way to do it, or is there some other way?

> Just as any successful business owner has a business plan, every successful professional should have a career plan.
>
> Anonymous

Start small, but keep moving forward. Goals do not necessarily have to be big ones. When you set your goals too high, you might find things becomes overwhelming and time-consuming and just give up. Set goals in small increments, complete with time, dates, amount, and some other details. By breaking down your goals in to smaller, workable units, you are more likely to realize them.

Remember that even great people had to start somewhere.

Be positive when stating your goals. Stating your goal positively will help you view it as a good thing to do, and not as a by-product of what you had to avoid.

Chapter **8**

However, spread out your goals and try to make tiny goals for different aspects of your life; for example, one or two for each aspect, or more if you like.

Areas for goal-setting include: family and home, career, social, physical, mental, and spiritual. If you say, "I want to be a successful dad", then try to make goals towards the development of your family life while still keeping an eye open for ways to improve your career and other areas of your life.

Do not underestimate yourself. It is tempting to sometimes just slack off, or let yourself off too easy.

In order to succeed, your desire for success should be greater than your fear of failure.

William Henry "Bill" Cosby, Jr.
(1937 –)
American comedian, actor, author, television producer, educator, musician, and activist.

The fear of failure is sometimes to blame for setting our goals too low. Remember that some fears are unfounded. How do you know you will actually ruin something? And how do you know for sure your coworkers will laugh at your effort? If you try to reason with your fears, more often than not, you will realize that there really is no reason for you to be reluctant and that, in fact, you can do whatever is challenging you.

Putting your goals down on paper is more than just having a way to memorize them. You are actually confirming your willingness to make them come true. A written list of goals is an effective reminder of what you need to do, and once you have met them, a good review of your accomplishments. This process helps you affirm your goals.

Affirmation is really more than writing down, "I am going to buy my $750,000 home by Christmas" twenty times. It is actually being conscious not only of your thought processes, but also of your acts during the day.

PLAN AHEAD

Nothing can stop the man with the right mental attitude from achieving his goal; nothing on earth can help the man with the wrong mental attitude.

Thomas Jefferson
(1743 –1826)
American Founding Father who was the principal author of the United States *Declaration of Independence* (1776). .

My philosophy of life is that if we make up our mind what we are going to make of our lives, then work hard toward that goal, we never lose - somehow we win out.

Ronald Reagan
40th President of the United States, serving from 1981 to 1989.

Stop procrastinating. If you are used to procrastination, being bull-headed about a goal can seem scary at first. Try to set a schedule, and then reward yourself each time you meet it. Start inculcating the habit of liking something. The most difficult thing is to like something useful. Our minds generally reject any conscious attempt to focus on any worthwhile goal. Some really lucky souls subconsciously liked these worthy goals and had great success in the areas.

Many of us focus subconsciously on petty things such as entertainment, celebrities, etc. and when the time comes for focusing on big things, we back out because we have an already loaded negative image of that goal. It is simply a misinterpreted relativity. There is no reason to feel worthless before a big goal just because we have put our attention on petty goals. You need to think big when you are setting goals; think great thoughts. You must also crystallize your thinking and make it clear to you first. Then write them down. Plan ahead, so you can get ahead!

Remember to try visualizing the outcome at a time in the future when it will become apparent that to set definite times in the future is obtainable. Setting huge impossible goals can and will ruin the want or need for goals, which may be important during your life. So please start small and work your way up!

How can I set goals for life?

We set goals for the near future, and we think in terms of six months, or at a maximum five years, while setting any goal. Life is bigger than that, and if you want to achieve something magnificent in your life, you have to set goals accordingly, so that during your life you always are in perspective.

Chapter 8

> If you are not willing to invest in your career, why would any organization be willing to invest in you?
>
> Anonymous

> Don't be afraid to fail. A lot of people have to fail to be successful. A lot of people on top have had things happen to them.
>
> Michael Jeffrey Jordan
> He played on two Olympic gold medal-winning American basketball teams.

Visualize yourself being 70-75 years old and at the end of your lifespan. What do you think your achievements should be? What would make you happy at this age, so that you can die in peace? Find the answers and ponder a little more. This way, you will figure out the ultimate purpose of your life.

Once you have got the purpose of your life, take one more step and plan your life up to that age starting from today. How do you want to achieve your life's purpose? Start with today and feel better when you think that you have completed 0.001% of your goal today. That is what you need to do. The mystery of your life and the uncertainty of your life will then be over, and you will be sure that you will die in peace.

Furthermore, disregard and ignore any unimportant things and distractions in your life because you know what exactly you are looking for and you know the purpose of your life. The best point is, when you follow this strategy, you are happy everyday. You do not ever run out of happiness. Its effects are great. You are always in perspective, and you never can think of committing suicide. You are rock stable!

Planning is all about time. People up to 21 years old might not find a point in this strategy because they have no direction. They still have to find a stable direction in which to go, work, and achieve something. They also tend to be a little childish - to the point that they might find this strategy insane.

People between 24 and 30 are the best subjects for this strategy. They already know the directions of their professional and personal careers.

A period of 40 years is a long time. If you miss one day, you do not run out of time. You can always recover it the next day or the day after. Regardless of what age you are, the fact of the matter is that setting goals can be a very difficult thing. Just do it, write down anything you want to be, want to achieve, or even what you want to possess.

Remember that every single breath you take is helping you move toward that goal or goals, and it makes no difference if you are 16 or 60. Once you have reached that goal, there is always the next one that is ready to take its place. If you find that this strategy does not work, and you cannot figure out what you want to be at 60 or 65, then please leave this strategy for a while, and give it another try after a few months to see if you can comprehend what the strategy asks for. Do you still not know what you want to be when you are 70 or 75? Think about that for a while. You may find that the answer is "Accomplished."

Once you articulate an agenda, you have to follow it.

Martin Brian Mulroney
(1939 –)
18th Prime Minister of Canada from September 17, 1984 to June 25, 1993 and was leader of the Progressive Conservative Party of Canada from 1983 to 1993. His tenure as Prime Minister was marked by the introduction of major economic reforms, such as the Canada-U.S. Free Trade Agreement and the Goods and Services Tax.

How can I be bold?

If you are shy, hesitant, or passive, you run the risk of leading a boring life marked by routine and unfulfilled goals. People who were bold scientists, public servants, artists, entrepreneurs, and others who did not wait for opportunities have led interesting lives and made the most progress; they created opportunities.

Do you want to be bold and unstoppable? If you were to switch places with somebody who is as bold as can be, what do you think he or she would do in your shoes? If you have already known someone who is bold, imagine how he or she would act if you do not know anyone like that, think of a character from a movie or book, a character who is daring and brave.

Chapter 8

A good plan violently executed now is better than a perfect plan executed next week.

George Smith Patton, Jr.
(1885–1945)
United States Army officer best known for his leadership while commanding corps and armies as a general during World War II.

It's all right to aim high if you have plenty of ammunition.

Hawley R. Everhart

Spend one hour a day, or one day a week, pretending to be them. Go through the motions and see what happens. You might discover that amazing things happen when you are bold, and you might be convinced to carry this daring behavior into your everyday life. Whenever you are feeling hesitant, especially in your interactions with others, swallow your pride and make the first move.

Bold people are not afraid to try new things, and one of the reasons they are so exciting to be around is that they keep you guessing. You can start small, perhaps by wearing a color or style of clothing that you do not normally wear, or visiting a place you ordinarily would not visit.

Eventually, you may get to the point where you entertain ideas that make other people's eyes widen when you mention them.

Rather than wait to be recognized for your efforts, or expect someone to consider your needs, step right up to the plate and ask. Some people feel that asking for things is greedy, selfish, and rude, and it is, if you are asking for something you do not deserve.

However, if someone is withholding something that you have rightfully earned, he or she is the one being greedy, selfish, and rude. Besides, what is the worst that could happen? The person could say no. Life goes on. There is a difference between being reckless and accepting risks. Impulsive people do not accept risks. They do not even think about them.

A bold person, on the other hand, is aware of the risks, and has decided to go through with the decision anyway, ready and willing to accept the consequences if things do not work out. You might make a mistake; we all do. Even so, inaction can be a mistake as well, one that leads to emptiness and regret. For many people, having taken risks and fallen flat on their faces was far more fulfilling than having done nothing at all.

Ultimately, boldness comes from within you, from what you believe. It is not about what you do. It is about who you are. If you do not know who you are, you can never be truly bold.

It is strange that modesty is the rule for women when what they most value in men is boldness.

Anne "Ninon" de l'Enclos
(1620 –1705)
French author, courtesan, and patron of the arts.

Start really appreciating your uniqueness. Discover what makes you different, and then parade it around for all to see. Put flags on it, call attention to it, and love yourself for it no matter what others think. That is the heart of boldness.

Remember, do not confuse being bold with being aggressive. Aggressiveness often involves imposing your viewpoints or actions on others. Boldness has nothing to do with the people around you; it is about overcoming your fears and taking action. Do not worry about rejection. Embrace the failure; it is not the opposite of success. It is a necessary component. The opposite of success is sitting still. Even so, there is a difference between being bold and being stupid. If you know doing something will hurt you, it does not matter how daring you are; do not do it!

How can I reach for my dreams?
Everybody has dreams, even if they are buried deep inside childhood fantasies. Remain in touch with your dreams. What do you fantasize about doing with your spare time? What extraordinary future makes you feel a little more alive when you imagine yourself in it? What did you dream about when you were a child? Think about all this and write it all down.

Chapter 8

Read books or check out websites related to your dreams. Steep yourself in the stories of people who have done or are doing what you want to do. See how they approached following their own dreams. Make sure you have other people to talk to about your goals, people that will support you and not discourage your realizing your dreams. However, no matter what, have someone near by that truly cares.

> **Define what freedom means.**
> Is it freedom of place, so you can work wherever you want?
> Is it freedom of time, so you can keep your own schedule or work fewer hours?
> Is it freedom of decision, so you have autonomy to work independently or you have responsibility of a specific area or team?
> Is it variety, so you work on different projects or clients and not feel constrained by repetitive tasks?
> Is it several or all of the above?

Ask yourself honestly: What is more important - achieving my dreams getting respect from my peers, or being financially secure? If you had to choose between your dreams and your other concerns, what would you choose?

Identify mental obstacles that stand in the way of your dreams and break the negative cycles. If you are not already working towards your dreams, you are probably trapped in a cycle that keeps you locked away from them. For a lot of people, this means making some necessary changes. Set clear, inspiring goals. Goals are like pillars that support your dreams.

Remember that as you try to make your dreams a reality, you learn more about what you want. Do not be scared to adjust your course as you learn more about yourself and what you want out of life. Discovering your dreams is an ongoing process.

Believe in yourself, and never let someone fill your head with doubt. Keep moving forward and live in the here and now. Never lose focus if something that appears better comes along. Most people give up without realizing how close they were to accomplishing their dreams. Do not be this kind of person!

How can I visualize?

Visualization is a technique used by winners in all walks of life. If you really want something to come to fruition, put your imaginative mind to work. See the result in front of you, play the game you are going to play in the future in your mind, or watch yourself accepting your degree at college. You are only limited by your own mind.

The way to get good ideas is to get lots of ideas and throw the bad ones away.

Linus Carl Pauling
(1901 – 1994) American chemist, biochemist, peace activist, author, and educator. He was one of the most influential chemists in history and ranks among the most important scientists of the 20th-century. Pauling was among the first scientists to work in the fields of quantum chemistry and molecular biology. Pauling is one of only four individuals to have won more than one Nobel Prize.

You can use visualization to acquire new habits, such as eating healthier or eating slowly, which prevent overeating and obesity. Have you ever seen an aerobatic pilot visualizing his or her routine on the ground using only the hands and imagination? Have you ever rehearsed a job interview in your mind?

Think, "*What you see is what you get*" and be ready for creativity and mind synthesis to take the lead. Dream of your project, work it through your mind, and let it evolve in pictures. After you have spent a moment, day, month, or even years visualizing the possibilities, then shift to focus mode. Right at the moment before you perform the activity, task, or event that will achieve an outcome or even the outcome toward your goal, focus clearly on the picture of the action you are about to make. Then do it for real.

A positive mindset will be readjusting an erring period of bad luck. Nothing is going to get better when you feel lousy about yourself and your chances in life. Positive thinking will turn that half-empty glass into the half-full glass the rainy day into the silver-lined cloud. Seize opportunities to change and move on.

Anybody who wants to change overnight will be disappointed. Think long term. Even if you won a fortune in the morning, you would be as dissatisfied

Chapter 8

Visualization is daydreaming with a purpose.

Robert "Bo" Bennett

He knows about success. By the age of 29, he had developed, built up, and sold an innovative technology company during the peak of the tech boom and sold it for $20,000,000 -- and he got to keep most of it! He now gives back information and inspiration that can lead others to live a successful life in his debut book, Year To Success.

Make sure you visualize what you really want, not what someone else wants for you.

Jerry Gillies
American Author

with your life in six months' time as you are now unless you look inside to what ails you. Instead, plan to make the realization of your hopes and dreams long term.

Visualize where you will be in five, ten, and fifteen years time - and the sorts of outcomes you want. However, do not just make a shallow photo of you in a Cadillac surrounded by a large house, a massive diamond collection, and fawning friends.

That is artificial and will not prove healthy nor satisfying in the long run. Instead, visualize what you want to achieve as a human being and what legacies you will leave your community and world.

Visualization solely works when you are calm, at ease, and willing to give yourself time to focus in peace, free from immediate worries.

Visualization is a technique very close to meditation only it is more active and vivid. In visualization, you are encouraged to think actively about the possibilities, but with meditation, you must put aside anything extraneous to your dreams and goals and only focus on them.

Visualize the personality traits needed to get you where you want to be. It is not enough to want to be the president. You need to think about the qualities that will assist you in reaching this goal.

Visualize not only the presidency but also the skills of open communication, persuasiveness, smiling, sharing, listening, discussing, being able to deflect criticism with skill and respect, etc. It is likely there will be skills you need to work on, but again, use

PLAN **AHEAD**

visualization to focus on separate skills to bring them up to par.

Remember that visualization takes practice. Everyone has the power to do it, but not everyone has the belief in it. If you are skeptical, you may want to convince yourself that this is a waste of time. Do not give into this temptation because everyone, skeptics included, can benefit from visualizing. It is about our brain's ability to synthesize results, a scientifically proven fact.

To accomplish great things we must first dream, then visualize, then plan... believe... act!

Alfred A. Montapert
He wrote the book *The Supreme Philosophy of Man: The Laws of Life*.

Beware of people who think this technique is self-fooling. Usually, these are people embedded in negativity who could use some seeing the glass half full for a change. Be kind to them and listen to them, but do not be swayed by their negativism.

How can I solve a problem?

Problem solving is one of the most essential skills in life. Regardless of who you are or what you do, you will face obstacles. How you deal with such challenges will often be a determining factor in how successful you are in life.

Most people change careers 3 to 7 times in their lives.
That does not mean you will. Layoffs happen. You may get fired. You may be *"forced out"* for reasons beyond your control. You will survive. And you will be stronger for it.

Anonymous

This is the first and most important component to problem solving. While action and energy can often assist you in overcoming challenges, these must be focused correctly.

The first step is always to approach any issue in a clear and logical manner, even if under time constraints or pressure. Once you are appropriately focused, you need to run through the problem. What are the components of the issue? What aspects are vital to a solution and which are extraneous? Once you have broken down a problem into its vital aspects, sort through any cause and effect

Chapter 8

You can never solve a problem on the level on which it was created.

Albert Einstein
(1879 –1955)
He published more than 300 scientific papers, along with over 150 non-scientific works. His great intelligence and originality have made the word "Einstein" synonymous with genius.

No problem can withstand the assault of sustained thinking.

François-Marie Arouet de Voltaire
(1694 –1778)
French Enlightenment writer, historian, and philosopher famous for his wit and for his advocacy of civil liberties, including freedom of religion, freedom of expression, free of trade and separation of church and state.

relationships or patterns and cycles at work. Basically, you will want to make a good assessment of what is going on.

After you have a good grasp of the problem, begin to plan out a solution. In most cases, this is a simple relationship of cause and effect. In dealing with a problem, you desire to achieve a particular result. Consider what steps must be taken to achieve the said result, given the parameters posed by the problem.

Once you have outlined the logical steps toward your desired result, execute them! If you are dealing with an issue where conditions change upon execution, do not be afraid to reevaluate your strategy. Is something going vastly awry?

This is important. You should approach any new developments in the same logical manner in which you approached the original problem. You must make a critical decision as to whether or not your plan warrant's alteration. Remember that changes in the parameters of the issue do not necessarily mean the steps you have outlined will fail!

In addition, it is sometimes necessary to execute your original plan fully to gain more insight into the problem. Unless this is a one-shot deal, trial-and-error is often an excellent approach.

Upon seeing your plan through, consider the results. Optimally, you successfully tackled the dilemma. However, if the results you expected were not achieved, consider your approach. Was there an error in the planning or execution? Did new parameters present themselves?

PLAN AHEAD

Reevaluate in light of these discoveries and approach the problem again. Sometimes you can repeat your original plan if the error was in the execution. However, if the parameters have changed, then a new strategy is often necessary.

Several attempts may be necessary to solve the issue. Each time, however, keep logic, clarity, and focus in mind. These are the elements that ultimately lead to resolution. Even if you are checked by failure, clear thinking usually leads to a successful resolution. Do not turn away from your problems. They will come back sooner or later, and they will be more difficult to solve.

If you only have a hammer, you tend to see every problem as a nail.

Abraham Harold Maslow (1908 – 1970) Maslow based his study on the writings of other psychologists, Albert Einstein and people he knew who clearly met the standard of self actualization. Maslow used Einstein's writings and accomplishments to exemplify the characteristics of the self actualized person.

Remember to try always to remain calm and logical when approaching a problem; resolution ultimately lies in this approach. Naturally, common sense is vital to solving any problem. And keep in mind the role others can play in problem solving. The threats of personal tension in such situations merely underscore the importance of promoting clarity and logic within the group.

Attitude is the key. The more problems you solve, the greater your experience with problem solving will be. You can apply a solution from one area to another only by gaining experience. Be open to new problems. If you start feeling overwhelmed or frustrated, take a breather. Realize that every problem has a solution, but sometimes you are so wrapped up in it that you cannot see anything but the problem. If you feel as if you cannot do anything, stop thinking about what you cannot do, and start thinking about what you can do. Even if it is something small or it seems unimportant, that little step might just lead to another, bigger step. Be brave!

Chapter **8**

You can never plan the future by the past.

Edmund Burke
(1729 – 1797)
Irish statesman, author, orator, political theorist, and philosopher who, after moving to England, served for many years in the House of Commons of Great Britain as a member of the Whig party. He is mainly remembered for his support of the cause of the American Revolutionaries, and for his later opposition to the French Revolution.

Management by objectives works if you know the objectives. Ninety percent of the time you don't.

Peter Drucker
(1909 – 2005)
American management expert.

What about a goals-setting methodology?

The basis for sound goal setting for a long period of time is using a methodology. It is the simplest way to reach your goals realistically and consistently. Using a method should also permit you to have enough room to adjust for unforeseen circumstances.

Make your goals as specific as possible. If you set a goal to own your own home, be definite about it.

Answer the questions *Who, What, When, Where, Which,* and *Why?* The more specific a goal is, the more you can find ways of reaching your target.

When setting goals, make sure you set a goal where you can measure the progress. This will help you see progress and motivate you to keep pushing forward.

And you will want to set a goal that is attainable. Based on the present restrictions, such as your schedule, workload, and knowledge, do you believe you can attain the objective you set? If not, then set a different goal, one that is attainable for you in the present. Set goals that are realistic! Set a goal you have a rational chance of achieving.

All smart goals should be time-bound, meaning they should have a deadline, or there should be a date specified for the completion of the goal. Setting a deadline reinforces the seriousness of the goal in your mind. It motivates you to take action. When you do not set a time-line, there is no internal pressure to accomplish the goal, so it gets put on the back burner.

Remember that time is the true price paid for your dreams; the earlier the dream can be achieved, the more time you have to enjoy it. Do not let other

PLAN AHEAD

people rob you of your goals. Use the method and share it with others, so you can help each other reach your goals.

How can I form a plan?

We all have problems in lives we would like to overcome. Sometimes we can go straight to the solution with little thought beforehand. Other times, a plan is the better option, especially if the goal is complex and involves many steps. If you set out a plan, then make clear what work must be done, and even if you do not make the progress you want, you will at least know how far you have progressed. Whatever happens, you had your own plan, and even if it all goes wrong, you will learn from it for the next time.

Is something happening that is wasting your time in life? Maybe you would just like to do better at something and feel you can form a plan to make a difference. Write down the problems that you want to solve. Sometimes this is the most difficult step. A crucial step, it is important to never self-censor here. You can always cut things later. Right now, it is important to get everything down on paper.

One thing will lead to another. Things you have not thought of will appear, and you will start to form an idea of the steps it will take to realize your goal and solve your problem. You may even come upon the solution while brainstorming.

Determine what is different about your current situation from where you want to be. In other words, start thinking about your goals and how you want to achieve them. Your goals will be the solutions to your problems. Set a time limit for your plan by choosing a realistic date by when you want to achieve a given

Whether you have someone managing your bottom line or if you're doing it yourself, money, like anything, takes maintenance and planning to grow.
Don't ignore it, because if you do, you're going to lose it.

Donald J. Trump
with
Meredith McIver

Chapter **8**

In preparing for battle I have always found that plans are useless, but planning is indispensable.

Dwight David "Ike" Eisenhower
(1890 – 1969)
34th President of the United States, from 1953 until 1961.

goal. Make sure to think about how "big" your goal is and the amount of change that will have to happen. Congratulate yourself on your plans, and be excited about your goals. Visualize how your life will be different once you have accomplished these goals.

Remember do not get bogged down in details during the brainstorming stage. When adding to the detail of your plan, try to guess what could go wrong and develop contingency plans. Do not forget to check off the steps of your plan as they are completed so you can see your progress.

How can I switch careers?

Making a big career change is never easy, especially if you have children to support, a mortgage to pay, and a car to worry about. Nevertheless, if you have the motivation, you can do it!

If you had all the money in the world, what would you be doing with yourself? This is brainstorming time. Make a list of all the things you would rather be doing with your time. Ask yourself if you are content with stringent working hours, accounting to higher authorities, etc. If this is what you do not like, then strive for a self-actualizing job that gives you exactly what you desire or hope to achieve. Your first step should be to evaluate your skills and talents. Ask yourself: What am I good at? What do I most enjoy doing? Write down every skill you are capable of. Do not be shy. Check to see if your current job gives you satisfaction and utilizes all your potential.

We all have big changes in our lives that are more or less a second chance.

Harrison Ford
(1942 –)
American film actor and producer.

Your second step will consist of identifying your transferable skills. After deciding what career best suits you, and having listed all your known skills and talents, identify what skills will transfer well over into your new line of work.

Choice.
Have a cash stash so your salary is not you're only access to money.
Maintain an active network so your job is not your only professional support.
Take care of yourself – exercise, get enough sleep, pursue personal passions – so that you have the energy, will, and discipline to launch a job search or a start-up as needed.
Freedom can be defined in many ways, but ultimately it is about having choices. You may love your job, but you do not want to need it.

The longer the list, the easier will be the transition. If you have only a few or no transferable skills, do not be discouraged. Pursue your passion to find happiness.

Always remember that new skills can be easily learned. Other life experiences can also make this transition easy. Some basic life skills may have already been acquired. Give yourself a boost and some credit.

Now be creative and open-minded. Focus on what your inner feelings guide you to do. Think of jobs that allow you to do what you really want to do, at least in some form, and apply your skills and talents every day.

Like any plan, you will need to consider your financial situation. How much does it cost, on a monthly and annual basis, to support your current standard of living? Are you willing to lower your standard, so that you can take a job that pays less? It takes a great deal of courage to do something your heart desires at the cost of some financial loss.

Make a list of everything you want in your new job, and one of everything you do not want. Work gradually towards your needs and wants. Stay focused and do not allow yourself to be distracted along the way. Go for it if this makes you happy.

Once your decision is made to move ahead, talk to people in your desired field. Explain your situation. Ask them for advice. Give them your contact information. If what they say is true, "It's not what you know, it's whom you know," then cover all your bases in this department.

Chapter 8

Never too old, never too bad, never too late, never too sick to start from scratch once again.

Bikram Choudhury
(1946 –)
Indian yoga guru.

If you love your life, you have to fight. If you believe in life and progress and possibilities, you have no choice.

Michael Joel Zaslow
(1942 — 1998)
American actor.

Remember to consider your present career and the amount of time you need to retire. It may be better to stick with the job you have, retire a bit before time, then take up something more rewarding. Bailing out early when you have a good retirement plan may compromise some of your other goals.

What should I consider?

New possibilities are happening all the time. In all our lives, these situations, circumstances, and chances are occurring. What makes a difference between some people and others is that some take advantage of these possibilities while others do not. Grab your chances in life.

Opportunities, they come and go, or so they say!

When a venture appears, which may change things for you, what do you do? Do you run away and hide, or do you step forward with confidence and motivation and manage the obstacles and the good luck in equally skilful ways.

The chances are that we welcome these new possibilities. We see the excitement that they bring to life and the options for the future. These help to motivate us to give extra effort and application to enable these new possibilities to come to fruition, so we can achieve our ambitions and have greater freedom in our lives.

Once we have done this, or after a few times, we can "get on a roll," and we can really see that life is "taking off" for us. We can feel fortunate and grateful that life is giving us these extra chances to make something of ourselves.

Remember that the time may well feel ripe for us to apply ourselves to new ventures and opportunities. These moments can be very special and really personal. If we give ourselves a chance, the possibility, and feel that we can grow and develop in new and exciting ways, than life for us can be a wonderful experience.

Recommended Reading & References
We suggest consulting the works identified below in order to learn more about the particulars contained in this chapter.

BLANCHARD, Kenneth & JOHNSON, Spencer. THE ONE MINUTE MANAGER, Berkley Books, ISBN 0-425-09847-8.

CLEMMER, Jim. FIRING ON ALL CYLINDERS. Macmillan of Canada. ISBN 0-7715-9133-0.

GRAY, Collin S. WAR, PEACE AND VICTORY: Strategy and Statecraft for the Next Century.
Simon & Schuster. ISBN 0-671-60695-6.

Kawasaki, Guy. THE ART OF THE START. The Time-Tested, Battle-Hardened Guide for Anyone Starting Anything.
Portfolio. ISBN 1-59184-056-2.

Krause, G. Donald. THE ART OF WAR FOR EXECUTIVES. Penguin Books. ISBN 0-399-53150-5.

LOGAN, John R. EVOLUTION NOT REVOLUTION. Aligning Technology with Corporate Strategy to Increase Market Value. McGraw Hill. ISBN 0-07-138410-3.

PEACH, Robert W. The PROJECT MANAGEMENT. Handbook. CEEM Information Services. ISBN 1-883337.

PORTNY, Stanley E. CPMP. PROJECT MANAGEMENT FOR DUMMIES. Hungry Minds. ISBN 0-7645-5283-X.

Project Management Institute. A GUIDE TO THE PROJECT MANAGEMENT BODY OF KNOWLEDGE.
PMBOK®. Guide 2000 Edition. ISBN 1-8804110-25-7.

ROHN, Jim. & TRACY, Brian. SMALL BUSINESS SUCCESS. Topics. ISBN 159150915-7.

The herd seeks out the great, not for their sake but for their influence; and the great welcome them out of vanity or need.

Napoléon Bonaparte

Artist: Madelaine Delfosse, private collection

CHAPTER 9

INFLUENCE & **INSPIRE**

The ability to influence people is a vital skill in the real world. You cannot make others do things, unless they want to. As the saying goes, you can only lead the horse to the water, but you cannot make the horse drink. In order to influence people, you first need them to like you and respect you.

Be genuinely interested in others. A typical person cares more about the small cut on his finger then about a flood in China that kills thousands. Why should anyone be interested in you or what you have to say unless you are interested in him or her first?

Be kind, outgoing, and smile a lot to make a good impression. Remember other people's names by using them in conversations. People like to hear their names, and the use of their names makes your messages more personal to them.

Be a great conversationalist. Engage others to talk about themselves and listen attentively to what they have to say. This is the most important thing you can do to make others feel important, and they will like you and respect you for showing interest in what they have to say.

Never talk about your own interests, but instead talk only about the other person's interests. That will make what you have to say more relevant to them, and they will listen. The key to influencing people is to cause them to desire the change for themselves, not to change themselves so they can please you and satisfy your interests.

You always need to respect others' opinions and avoid arguments like the plague. Arguments will go

Life is measured by the rapidity of change, the succession of influences that modify the being.

George Eliot
(1819-1880)
British writer.
She used a male pen name, she said, to ensure her works would be taken seriously. Female authors were published under their own names during Eliot's life, but she wanted to escape the stereotype of women only writing lighthearted romances.

Chapter 9

There are three kinds of men, ones that learn by reading, a few who learn by observation, and the rest of them have to pee on the electric fence and find out for themselves.

William Penn Adair "Will" Rogers
(1879 –1935)
American cowboy, vaudeville performer, humorist, social commentator, and motion picture actor.

Do the act and the attitude follows.

William James
(1842 – 1910)
Pioneering American psychologist and philosopher who was trained as a physician.

nowhere. If you "win" an argument, you will cause ill feelings in others and alienate them as a result, so you lose. And if you lose an argument, well, you lose. So do not argue. A quick way to generate animosity is by failing to admit your mistakes when you are obviously at fault. So if you want to build credibility and respect, be sure that you are swift to admit your errors as soon as you realize them.

Always begin in a friendly manner if you want to try to change others to your way of thinking. Start by asking questions that they will quickly say yes to, in order to get cooperation. Let others feel the idea is theirs. This is very important in trying to influence others to your way of thinking. People can be critical of others' ideas, but if they believe something is their idea, they will be much more in favor of it.

Try to see things from other's points of view and sympathize with their beliefs. Ask yourself what motivates them to do such and such? By seeing things from others' points of view, you can influence them accordingly. However, reciprocity works in such away that if you respect others' beliefs, they will appreciate you and your beliefs as well. However, if you cannot sympathize with their beliefs, why should they sympathize with yours?

People are more likely to change their behaviors if the change benefits society as a whole, rather than just you. You must appeal to noble motives. Always assume good faith, and call attention to others' mistakes indirectly.

Begin with genuine praise and appreciation; smile; and just briefly mention something that you think they did incorrectly. Do not say that they are wrong, but rather seek to clarify, so you can understand and learn from what they did. And before you talk about others' mistakes, talk about yours first.

Nevertheless, never give orders, even with the word *please*. Instead, ask questions. For example, instead of saying, "Please don't smoke here," say something like "Isn't it a nice day outside? Would it be preferable to smoke outside instead?"

If the person says no, do not argue. Try not to reprimand in public, and assume good faith, even when it seems clear that he or she has done wrong. Let the other person save face. Encourage him or her by making the faults seem very easy to correct.

Remember that praise is the best motivator for behavior, so be lavish with your praise and praise even the slightest improvement. Give others a fine reputation to live up to. Make others feel happy about following your suggestions. In addition, give honest appreciation and praise for every good work. Do not argue. Do not condemn. Do not criticize.

How can I influence others?

Make a clear plan of what you want. Establish what you are trying to achieve by establishing rapport. This means mirroring their body language, their posture, breathing rate, language patterns, and other minutia. Note that this does not mean mimicking them. Rapport puts you and the other person in a similar mindset, establishing a helping friendship.

You can then lead the person, for example, to be relaxed by matching his or her breathing rate and gradually slowing your breathing down. To create better rapport with people, research – more on the topic.

It is not enough to do your best; you must know what to do, and THEN do your best.

William Edwards Deming
(1900 –1993)
American statistician, professor, author, lecturer, and consultant.

The secret of my influence has always been that it remained secret.

Salvador Domènec Felipe Jacinto Dalí i Domènech, Marquis de Púbol
(1904 –1989)
He is known as **Salvador Dalí.**
A prominent Spanish surrealist painter.

Chapter 9

Never, never, never, never give up.

Sir Winston Leonard Spencer-Churchill (1874 - 1965)
He said... "we shall fight in France, we shall fight on the seas and oceans, we shall fight with growing confidence and growing strength in the air, we shall defend our island, whatever the cost may be, we shall fight on the beaches, we shall fight on the landing grounds, we shall fight in the fields and in the streets, we shall fight in the hills; we shall never surrender."

Example is not the main thing in influencing others, it's the only thing.

Albert Schweitzer (1875 –1965) French Philosopher-Physician.

People are in one of three categories of mindsets; visual, auditory, or kinesthetic. You will notice that these mindsets have certain language traits. For example, visual people will say something such as "Have you seen the news lately?"; an auditory person would say, "Have you heard the news lately?"; and a kinesthetic person would say, "I cannot grasp how they must be feeling" contrary to "I just can't begin to picture what they must be going through". All these forms of rapport.

Actively listen to people. This enables us to gain insight into other people's perspectives, and usually helps us to foster trust. Take into account their body language, tone of speech, facial expressions and gestures. All these help us make sense of their emotions, as this makes up the bulk of non-verbal language.

When you express your views, use " I " instead of " you." Using " I " makes you take ownership of what you say. In addition, be objective and express the broad sense of what you think the person is trying to get at.

When you are giving some advice, use "we" whenever possible. This gives you a sense of having something in common and suggests support for the other person.

Using "You" tends to separate the advice-giver from the advice-taker, which can be intimidating at times. Make sure the advice-receiver actually understands what you are saying. Getting the person to try and say what they understand helps.

When trying to gain support, use scenarios or day-to-day activities that your target audience can relate to.

INFLUENCE & **INSPIRE**

The mind is everything. What you think you become.

Siddhārtha Gautama Buddha

Gautama is the primary figure in Buddhism, and accounts of his life, discourses, and monastic rules are believed by Buddhists to have been summarized after his death and memorized by his followers. Various collections of teachings attributed to him were passed down by oral tradition, and first committed to writing about 400 years later.

Always bear in mind that your own resolution to succeed is more important than any other.

Abraham Lincoln

The *Gettysburg Address* was delivered at the dedication of the Soldiers' National Cemetery in Gettysburg, Pennsylvania, on the afternoon of Thursday, November 19, 1863. In 272 words, and three minutes, Lincoln asserted the nation was born not in 1789, but in 1776, "conceived in Liberty, and dedicated to the proposition that all men are created equal."

This helps to bring heightened interest because people like to "be in the know." The results are gradual, so expect change to occur slowly but surely.

Remember that *With great power comes great responsibility*, according to Spiderman's Uncle Ben. Anyone with great power, whether or not he is Spiderman, should use it with caution and not be caught up in personal greed.

How can I be positive?

We must learn to be more positive. The environment and all the experiences in life are the result of habitual and predominant thoughts. Negative thoughts can tell us about something that needs attention. So, thoughts lead to discovering what needs to be done, and one can think positively or negatively to take care of it.

Many people fail to see a negative occurrence as a learning experience and continue to feel victimized and helpless, ultimately blaming others for what they brought on themselves. Instead, embrace the facts, if you have been negative or inactive. This will make it easier for you to become positive!

Goals give you a more positive outlook on life. Those who are bored with life and feel stuck usually feel depressed in those areas where they have no goals and so, no progress.

Start small with your goals. Do not "shoot for the moon" right away! Appreciate the people in your life who have stood by you through thick and thin. Enlist their support to help you become more positive, and in the process, you will probably help them, too. Friends help each other through the good times and

Chapter 9

Positive thinking will let you do everything better than negative thinking will.

Hilary Hinton "Zig" Ziglar (1926 –) American author, salesman, and motivational speaker.

Never believe that a few caring people can't change the world. For, indeed, that's all who ever have.

Margaret Mead (1901 –1978) American cultural anthropologist, who was frequently a featured writer and speaker in the mass media throughout the 1960s and 1970s.

bad. Feel positive about them and feel lucky to have good friends in your life.

Realize that the negativity is really all in our mind! What goes on in your mind can really determine your actions and whether you are positive or negative. If you always think negative thoughts, you are constantly going to turn out to be a negative person. It is better to think positive thoughts. Avoid negative influences. Even if they come from a family member or close friend, do not tolerate the person's bad behavior. Steer clear of the negativity, so that it will not rub off on you.

It is much easier to affect change if you just put your mind to it and change your thoughts. Focus your imagination and efforts on becoming this new positive person. We cannot always control things that happen in our lives, but we can, with some effort, control what we think in our minds.

If you want more success, focus on all the ways that you are already successful. If you want more love, focus on all the people that already care about you and the abundance of love you have to give to others. If you want to create greater health, focus on all the ways that you are healthy, and so on and so forth.

The only thing between you and your desire to be happy is one single fact: You are not happy because of the way you think. This little-known fact keeps many from reaching their goal of happiness.

If you keep thinking things such as "*My life sucks!*", then your life will seem like it really is that bad. Imagine that you are already a positive person and that you love your life.

> There are a lot of ups and downs, but you can ride them out if you're prepared for them. "Learning to expect problems saved me from a lot of wasted energy, and it will save you from unexpected surprises. It's like Wall Street; it's like life. The ups and downs are inevitable, so simply try to be prepared for them. Sometimes I'll ask myself why I want to take on some new, big challenge. A substantial loss is always a possibility. Can I handle it if it doesn't go well? Will I be asking myself later, Why did I ever do that? What was I thinking? I'm actually a very cautious person, which is different from being a pessimistic person. Call it positive thinking with a lot of reality checks.
>
> Donald Trump
> *How to Get Rich*
> by Donald J. Trump
> with Meredith McIver.

Know that you are in control of your thoughts. If you are thinking negatively, you can change this at anytime by thinking about something positive. Now that you realize this and are inspired to accomplish something, what do you really desire in life?

Think of the glass as not half empty but as half full and filling up!

Remember to beware of those who do not want to be positive. Look to positive people and do not blame your past; accept it and forgive it. Do not look back. There will always be someone who looks downward to your positive outlook. Do not let that attitude bother you. You should simply look beyond these people and let them wallow in their past and unhappiness. They will not change until they are ready. In addition, do not go overboard while thinking positively. Make sure that you are constantly learning from your past mistakes and the negative things that have happened to you in the past.

How can I erase a negative influence?

All of us have at one time or another lived negatively or are still living negatively. There is a lot of defeatism within many of us, and some people are afraid to express themselves because they are tearful of negative response. Everything that we as human beings do is for ourselves, and we cannot afford to make anyone happy if we are not happy. Positive change has to start with the individual first, and then what the person wants in life cannot be taken away by anyone.

Anything that happens in your life affects you, and the outcome depends on you and how you choose to overcome the situation. You can make yourself happy by changing negative thoughts into positive thoughts.

Chapter 9

20 years from now you will be more disappointed by the things you didn't do rather than by the one's you did. So throw off the bowlines. Sail away from the safe harbor. Catch the trade winds in your sails.
Explore.
Dream.
Discover.

Mark Twain's
(1835-1910)
views became more radical as he grew older. He acknowledged that his views changed and developed over his life.

Wise men don't need advice. Fools won't take it.

Benjamin Franklin
(1706-1790)

You can make yourself happy by the choices you make, both ethical choices and practical choices.

If a tornado blows your house down, you can be glad to be alive or miserable because you lost all your stuff, or you may feel both ways. However, paying more attention to being pleased you are alive is a way to pick yourself up and rebuild more easily. There is always a positive side and always a funny side, even if sometimes the two are the same.

It is up to you to find happiness by changing your behavior if something does indeed bother you. Setting, and doing your best to achieve, goals will allow your dreams to come true.

Set goals reasonably. Set a lot of small goals in steps along the way to achieve big goals. Having at least one little achievement a day does wonders for having a good attitude in life and gives one something to look forward to. Do not put a hard deadline on the big goals. Life happens, and sometimes goals get put off or come into reach sooner. Success in the little day-to-day goals will get you going in the right direction.

Taking advice from others is good. However, you are the only one that knows whether the advice will help you or not. If you tried it and it did not work, trying again might not be a bad idea. If you tried it many times, and it never worked, stop and rethink it. Try something else and test it with small daily goals, to see what you get with other ways to achieve your goals.

Positive thinking will absolutely make your life better, and you should keep that in mind. All or nothing is not positive thinking. Positive thinking is something else.

INFLUENCE & **INSPIRE**

The key to successful leadership today is influence, not authority.

Kenneth Hartley Blanchard
(1939 –)
American author and management expert.

A good teacher can inspire hope, ignite the imagination, and instill a love of learning.

Charles Bradford "Brad" Henry
(1963 –)
26th Governor of the U.S. state of Oklahoma.

It is looking at things as they are and choosing to pay a little more attention to the good things, little kindnesses, small beauties in life and to share those rather than sharing the equally inevitable gripes.

When you are happy, look inside yourself to understand why. If you understand why you are thrilled, you can learn to control and arrange your life to maximize situations in which you will be happy.

People question themselves when things go wrong. It is a natural desire to want to figure out what went wrong, so it does not happen again. Do that when you are happy to figure out how to make yourself happy again, too!

However, when you are sorting out what went wrong in a situation, stand back from it a little and do not just look at it two-dimensionally. Look at it from all sides!

Remember to forget about everybody else and think about yourself first. If you do not take care of yourself, you will not have the resources to take care of anybody else. So balance your love of others with your own real needs and do not neglect either. To have a fruitful, happy life and give joy to others as well, you have to make yourself contented first. Even so, nobody can take away your happiness without your permission. If you agree with the oppressor, you are helping them oppress you. Know your own ethics; build a sense of right and wrong for yourself, looking at all the moral questions in life and holding on to your integrity. Avoid those who always pull you down. Avoid those that add negativity to your life. Avoid those that never give you valuable advice and most of all, never attempt to satisfy an immediate desire by compromising your integrity.

Chapter **9**

How can I get inspired?

First, take a moment to breathe and reflect on one of your goals. This step may take some time, and you should be relaxed while you think. You will not be able to think properly if you are anxious about something or if you just generally have other things on your mind. Try to be comfortable physically and emotionally, as much as you can. Try to recall thoughts that you have had that you found particularly interesting, and branch out from those thoughts with a more complex analysis. Look around you, wherever you are, and see if you notice anything that stands out to you as interesting. Try not to be "*looking for something*". Just think deeply about your surroundings. Remember that if something causes any emotion whatsoever, it is probably a good source of inspiration. Furthermore, you can focus on other things while waiting for inspiration to come. You do not need to sift through thousands of inspirational quotes or motivational documents. Simply relax!

Do you think corporate tycoons think up their million-dollar business plans in 5 minutes? Of course not! Do not go desperately hunting for such an easy way. You will only end up stressed with a headache, or at best a sloppy idea.

Often, the most inspirational of concepts or ideas can be found only in your mind. Think of a certain memory you have of a circumstance or situation. Also, think of things that you feel strongly about or of moral opinions that you may have such as: *war, religion, politics, relationships, death, etc.*

All ideas start as tiny seeds in a person's mind. Of course, many of them die quickly. Try to plant as many of these seeds as you can by enriching yourself with media. Listen to music, watch videos, read

Remembering you are going to die is the best way I know to avoid the trap of thinking you have something to lose. You are already naked. There is no reason not to follow your heart.

Steven Paul Jobs
(1955 –2011)
American businessman, designer, and inventor.
Stanford commencement address 2005.

books, analyze articles, and try new things every day. If you have an idea or feel inspired, hold onto that. Keep what you have simple. Do not be constantly trying to expand it. Just relax and think about it in its current form.

I must govern the clock,
not be governed by it.
Golda Meir
(1898 –1978)
Teacher, *kibbutznik,* and politician who became the fourth Prime Minister of the State of Israel.

Once you have an idea that you find interesting or emotional, close your eyes and picture exactly what it is that you are thinking about. Then imagine yourself observing this idea from the outside. See the idea as a whole, and note how it makes you feel. Do not pursue your inspiration if it does not interest you. Once you feel that you have captured the essence of your idea, produce a rough outline on paper with more ideas relating to your main idea.

When something gets hard or tedious, or you just decide you have had enough of it, leave it alone and come back to it later. Do not just abandon it.

Nothing is so contagious as enthusiasm.
Samuel Taylor Coleridge
(1772 –1834)
English poet, Romantic, literary critic, and philosopher who, with his friend William Wordsworth, was a founder of the Romantic Movement in England and a member of the Lake Poets. He is probably best known for his poems *The Rime of the Ancient Mariner* and *Kubla Khan,* as well as for his major prose work *Biographia Literaria.*

This way, if you feel like doing so at another time, you can always come back to it. Keep all of these ideas in one place, and in no time, you should have a reservoir of old, interesting ideas that you can look back on.

If you are messy with your time, you are going to end up with a messy head. Create a timetable for yourself to manage your time and organize what you need to do. This will help you to get on top of everything, even in those sticky situations where your "to-do" list is sixteen pages long.

Do not get in over your head. Think about what is achievable, and think about which of these things you would be proud of achieving. Come up with a reasonable solution for reaching your goals and then set out to reach them. By accomplishing these goals, you will be proving that you can accomplish the things you want to, and you will hopefully have something to show for your efforts.

Remember that diving deeply into things that bring on emotion may be painful or upsetting. If you feel that you are becoming too emotional or stressed out, you may want to consider meditating on a particular subject, or discussing something with a close friend or family member first. This will help you to learn more about the subject and be more honest in your creativity. Whatever you do, do NOT run from the emotion or avoid facing it in any way.

How can I be an inspiration?
Becoming an inspirational person requires acknowledgment of your own talents, skills, and worth in this world. You will need to be someone who is willing to beat a path that may be rarely trodden, but you will light the way and show others how things can be done, and usually for the better.

To put the world in order, we must first put the nation in order; to put the nation in order, we must put the family in order; to put the family in order, we must cultivate our personal life; and to cultivate our personal life, we must first set our hearts right.

Confucius
(551 BCE - 479 BCE)
Chinese philosopher.

Being inspirational is about speaking to other people from your heart, so that no matter how many people you touch in your life, each of them will come away thinking about your verve for life, your energy, and your faith in their ability to be great, too.

Being an inspiration begins within you. First you must inspire yourself to inspire others. Find something that makes you happy and do it. However, remember that no one will care about what you do until you care! When you find something that you love or happen to be very passionate about and care for, take pride in it.

Be polite to everyone you come across. Be helpful. If someone asks you a question about yourself or about what you do, then always do your best to

INFLUENCE & INSPIRE

answer. Work hard; never do half a job, because that is not inspirational at all. If you are going to attempt something, then do it to the best of your ability, and when you are done, be proud of yourself.

Remember not do try to target one person to inspire, and do not try to inspire everyone individually. Take on everything eagerly, and always smile and be happy and proud of yourself. Furthermore, do not put others down by making them feel that they can never be you because the whole point is to let them know they can be whatever they like, or more! Most of all, never give up!

How can I be a good role model?

You would be surprised if you found out how many people look up to you. Think about how many people in your life have inspired you to get to where you are today. By being a good role model, you can help others to achieve success in their own lives.

Realize that somebody is watching you most of the time. Be aware of your actions. Whether you are working diligently or doing nothing, chances are somebody is noticing. So be careful about what actions you show to society. Furthermore, identify your bad habits and problems. Once you have discovered them, fix them.

A role model shows off his or her high qualities; chances are people will see everything good that you do. Whether you are a parent, teacher, coach, athlete, artist, or anything else, do what you do best and be an inspiration. People you have never met and may never meet are watching you perform. It is up to you to meet their expectations and show them the right way through example. It is fun to be a good

Never forget your effect on people. Leaders need to understand how profoundly they affect people, how their optimism and pessimism are equally infectious, how directly they set the tone and spirit of everyone around them.

— Captain D. Michael Abrashoff
U.S.N

role model and have the leadership skills to help others follow in your footsteps.

Remember that if you are a bad role model, it will hurt those around you. Turn your life around, and you will be turning around more than one life.

How can I choose a role model?
Role models are important. They help us become the people we want to be and inspire us to bring about change. Choosing wisely means that you have been influenced correctly, and doing so will help you to be the best person you can be.

Choose someone who has a lot of confidence in him or herself and his or her abilities. A good role model would be someone who knows who they are. You do not want someone who is down and who will bring you down. You want someone who will not pretend to be someone he is not and will not be fake just to suit other people.

You should consider someone who will make you feel good about being yourself, a role model who should not make you compare yourself to her.

You should consider someone who interacts well with others or who is kind and can communicate well with people, such as a teacher. Look for someone who is living life the way you would like to. Choose a role model who may have done something you find admirable, such as having raised a lot of money for charity, saved lots of lives, helped people in need, or discovered the cure for a disease.

Furthermore, find someone who does not always take credit for what they do. Some poorly chosen role models may take advantage of their position and

The best thing you can do is the right thing; the next best thing you can do is the wrong thing; the worst thing you can do is nothing.

Theodore "Teddy" Roosevelt
(1858 –1919)
26th President of the United States of America (1901–1909). He is noted for his exuberant personality, range of interests and achievements, and his leadership of the Progressive Movement, as well as his "cowboy" persona and robust masculinity.

make you do things to make you look bad or to make you be an awful influence to others. They also can direct you to a wrong place, to somewhere you don't want to be, and you will follow their leads because you want to please them.

Remember that the true role models are those who possess the qualities that we would like to have and those who have affected us in a way that makes us want to be better people. We often do not recognize our true role models until we have noticed our own personal growth and progress. Keep in mind that having a role model does not mean you become exactly like that person; remember to retain your individuality. Emulate them, but put your own individuality into the things you do.

How can I be a leader?

A leader is someone who others consistently want to follow for new trends and ideas. Someone having a fancy title can make that happen temporarily, at least, but a true leader inspires steadfast loyalty with the steps below!

The first step towards becoming a leader is to look around and find ways to make the world a better place. Observe your surroundings and listen to people!

How can you help?
Discover what your talents are, develop them, and focus on applying them towards making a difference. Think of problems in the broader sense. They are not always easy to define. Look for needs, niches, conflicts, or gaps that need to be filled, and for inefficiencies. The solutions will not always be creative or cutting edge; sometimes they are the simplest things.

Stay vigilant.
Being in charge is never easy, and doubly so when you are managing people with whom you used to pal around. Do not expect to be invited to post-work gatherings. It might occur, but if it does not, be prepared. Recall how you and your colleagues might have complained about the boss. Well, now you are the boss. Your presence might be uncomfortable. When a manager is in charge of former peers, it does not mean he or she must stop being friendly. It simply means the peer-to-peer relationship forged in the workplace is over. It is time to develop a new professional relationship. A friendship might be strained, but if it is true friendship, it will not only survive but also be strengthened.

Chapter 9

A leader is a dealer in hope.

Napoléon Bonaparte
(1769-1821)
Bonaparte instituted lasting reforms, including higher education, a tax code, road and sewer systems, and established the Banque de France (central bank). He negotiated the Concordat of 1801 with the Catholic Church, which sought to reconcile the mostly Catholic population to his regime.

The greatest revolution in our generation is that of human beings, who by changing the inner attitudes of their minds, can change the outer aspects of their lives.

Marilyn Ferguson,
(1938 –2008)
American author, editor and public speaker, best known for her 1980 book *The Aquarian Conspiracy* and its affiliation with the New Age Movement in popular culture.

As you are solving problems, you might notice patterns and wonder if many of those problems are not symptoms of a deeper, bigger problem. Take a step back and try to find the root of the problem. The thing about the deeper problem is that it is not something anybody can solve alone; it will require a group effort, which is where your role as a leader comes into play.

If you have got these ideas in your mind about what the deeper issues are, you can probably predict the problems that will crop up as a result. Instead of waiting for those problems to appear, take steps to prevent them. If you cannot prevent them, then you can at least prepare for them.

That is the core difference between a leader and a manager. A good manager responds well to a variety of situations; a good leader takes effective action to prevent and create situations before they actually happen.

In order to exert influence and tackle bigger problems, you are going to need decision-making power, and those decisions will affect the people who grant you that power.

Having decision-making power is a responsibility as well as an honor. Not only do you need to be able to make sound decisions, but you also need to be willing to be held accountable to people for your decisions. If things go wrong, people will assume it is your fault, whether it is or not.

Think of yourself as the captain of a ship; the fate of the ship is essentially in your hands, and it is up to you to steer everyone in the right direction.

INFLUENCE & **INSPIRE**

So exercise wisdom when calling the shots; hope for the best, and prepare for the worst. If you are not prepared to take responsibility for your decisions, if you struggle with hesitation and self-doubt, it might be a good idea to step down. An insecure leader often becomes a tyrant.

Great leaders are almost always great simplifiers, who can cut through argument, debate, and doubt, to offer a solution everybody can understand.

Colin Luther Powell
(1937 –)
His last military assignment, from October 1, 1989 to September 30, 1993, was as the 12th Chairman of the Joint Chiefs of Staff, the highest military position in the Department of Defense.

As a leader, you can see the bigger issues at hand, but you can also see how things could be so much better if only certain obstacles were removed. To get people to help you to change things, you need to share your positive vision with them. Inspire them. Motivate them. Guide them.

Show them how their actions are bringing everyone closer to a chosen dream. Leaders conceive and articulate goals that lift people and unite them in pursuit of objectives worthy of their best efforts.

The greatest leaders saw their roles as means to an end, and themselves as instruments of deeper purpose; any glory, prestige, or wealth was a side effect rather than a motivation. If you want to realize a vision, the most effective way to do it is not with an army of puppets; that army will only last as long as you do. For long-lasting results, share your vision and let people adopt it as their own, and let it spread like wildfire.

A leader should think of him or herself as the beginning of a chain reaction. Once it is begun, he or she can step away, so that it continues to happen without any effort on his or her part.

Remember that people need to trust you, and to be inspired by you. What you will need is good communication skills, so that you can articulate your vision. Do not forget to practice what you preach at all

Chapter **9**

Leaders don't create followers, they create more leaders.

Thomas J. "Tom" Peters
(1942 –)
American writer on business management practices, best-known for *In Search of Excellence* (co-authored with Robert H. Waterman, Jr).

times. There is no better way to lose your credibility as a leader than to be a hypocrite.

What should I consider?

You will never be able to control people, but you will be able to let people control themselves in ways that benefit you. If you tell people what to do, they may not listen to you and will probably resent you. You must get people to do what they want to do, while you influence their control over themselves.

The things you discover to inspire others do not have to be overwhelming or grand; in fact, they usually are not. They might be as seemingly insignificant as listening better to those around you, becoming more inclusive in your leadership, or expressing your heartfelt gratitude for others' work.

These are the things that will matter, even if they seem small. Now infuse them into the lives of those around you.

Remember to practice ways to inspire daily with the help of a mentor, coach, or friend, and continuously look for inspiration. Mysteriously, inspiration is a wonderful self-fulfilling cycle; the more you "breathe it in", the more you will "exhale it" out to others.

Recommended Reading & References
We suggest consulting the works identified below in order to learn more about the particulars contained in this chapter.

ABRASHOFF, Michael D. IT'S YOUR SHIP.
Warner Books. ISBN 0-446-52911-7.

BLANCHARD, Ken *et al*. KNOW CAN DO!
Audio renaissance. ISBN-10-1-4272-0251-6.

BRIAN, Denis. A LIFE, PULITZER.
Wiley & Sons. ISBN 0-471-33200-3.

BYHAM, W. C. Ph.D. & COX, Jeff. EMPOWER YOURSELF, YOUR COWORKERS, YOUR COMPANY.
Harmony Books. ISBN 0-517-59860-4.

CARTER, Jimmy. SOURCES OF STRENGH.
Times books. ISBN 0-8129-2944-6.

HOGUE, J-Pierre. L'HOMME ET L'ORGANISATION.
Édition Commerce. ISBN 2-7616-0048-7.

HOWARTH, David & Stephen. NELSON: The Immortal Memory.
Conway Classics. ISBN 0-85177-720-1.

ISAACSON, Walter. EINSTEIN, His Life and Universe.
SIMON & SCHUSTER. ISBN-13-978-0-7432-6473-0.

KEEGAN, John. L'ART DU COMMANDEMENT ; Alexandre, Wellington, Grant, Hitler.
Éditions Perrin. ISBN 2-262-00615-6.

PATTON, Arch. MEN, MONEY AND MOTIVATION.
McGraw-Hill, Library of Congress Catalog card number: 61-7845

PATTERSON, Kerry *et al*. INFLUENCER, THE POWER TO CHANGE ANYTHING.
Vital Smart. ISBN-13: 978-0-17-148499-2.

PELL, Dr. Arthur R. ENCADRER ET MOTIVER UNE ÉQUIPE.
Simon & Schuster. ISBN 2-7440-0427-8.

PETERS, Thomas J. THRIVING ON CHAOS/ A PASSION FOR EXCELLENCE. Random House, ISBN 0-517-14816-1.

REHKOPF, Ed. LEADERSHIP ON THE LINE.
Clarity Publications. ISBN 0-9722193-1-5.

RYE, David E. 1001 WAYS TO INSPIRE YOUR ORGANIZATION, YOUR TEAM AND YOURSELF.
Castles Books. ISBN 0-7858-2094-9.

THATCHER, Margaret. THE DOWNING STREET YEARS.
Harper Collins. ISBN 0-06-017056-5.

VALLÉE, Danielle. WHIZ TEENS IN BUSINESS.
Truman Publishing Co, Missouri, ISBN 0-9663393-2-0.

VENTRELLA, Scott W. THE POWER OF POSITIVE THINKING IN BUSINESS. Simon & Schuster. ISBN 0-7435-1810-1.

Few will have the greatness to bend history itself. But each of us can work to change a small portion of events, and in the total of all these acts will be written the history of this generation.

Robert F. Kennedy

Artist: Murphy Elliot. Plant City, Fl- USA

CHAPTER 10

DEALING WITH **CHANGE**

Changes are never far away, whether it is breaking up with an ex, having a best friend move away, facing the death of a relative, the loss of a job, or a demotion, or living through disappointment about something that once meant a great deal but that has not turned out as hoped for.

Being prepared for a changing world involves flexibility, strength of self-purpose, and belief in one's own worth.

Life is full of unexpected surprises; do not let this be a lesson you refuse to learn. Death, loss, and strange situations will be a part of your life, no matter how much you may try to shelter or protect yourself from them. The major key to coping with change is to accept the reality of change and its inevitability.

Once you have accepted the reality that you cannot change others and that the only way they can change you is if you let them, then you suddenly find yourself empowered.

Empowerment is a key element of change acceptance and change management. When you feel empowered, in command, and not bothered by events but conscious of a need to roll with the surrounding effects to lessen their impact, it is easier to accept change.

If you are grieving after a death, be it for a person or a pet, do not let anyone tell you how long to grieve for. That decision is yours, but your life cannot meander in sorrow forever.

Do the things your fear and death of fear is certain.

Ralph Waldo Emerson
(1803 –1882)
When asked to sum up his work, he said his central doctrine was "the infinitude of the private man."

Chapter 10

If things seem under control, you're just not going fast enough.

Mario Gabriele Andretti
(1940 –)
He is a retired Italian American world champion racing driver, one of the most successful Americans in the history of the sport.

Learning to tolerate uncertainty is the key factor in building great self-confidence. Unfortunately fear of "what might happen next"
– The feeling of uncertainty
– Can be very unpleasant.

Anthony Charles Lynton Blair
(1953 -)
Prime Minister of the United Kingdom from 2 May,1997 to 27 June, 2007.

However, it is most clear that those who avoid grieving do end up worse off and can sometimes experience breakdowns and be left with an inability to cope at unexpected times. With grief for death, there will always be a piece of your heart missing, but if you accept this and are willing to keep the memories alive as best you can for the rest of your life, this will help you reach some acceptance of what has happened.

If you have had job loss or some other non-depth-related personal loss you still need time to mourn and to assuage your sadness and grief over the loss of the thing that once filled a large part of your life. Perhaps a small ending ceremony of some sort will help to give you a sense of closure and allow you to move forward.

Change occurs, but you do not need to be buffeted by it. Have a purpose in life, no matter what it is, that serves as your own personal anchor. While it is important to be open to change and to be flexible as to the possibilities that change open up for you, it is also important to remain true to yourself and the dreams that you hold in life. This self-belief and your dreams serve as your anchor.

Whatever else life throws your way, these are the barometers by which you can measure your progress in the world and how you are reacting to change. Be prepared to question your methods of getting to where you wish to go, but be less prepared to change your destination if it means dismantling the person you are inside.

Look for the opportunities that you can make use of when change occurs rather than continuously viewing the change as a deep loss or as something making you think nothing will ever be the same.

Remember the adage every cloud having a silver lining. There is a reason for this saying - wise humans of the past knew well that change could herald both fear and opportunity. Once the fog of shock, despair, and anger passes, look for the opportunities that exist in the change.

How can I deal with the fear of change?

Life is a constant journey through variables we cannot control; however, be well prepared. We fear change because we do not know what change will bring us. All we know is that it will cause us to move into the unknown. If we are not prepared to accept change, we will never know if change is good or right for us.

When we experience change and find out it is not appropriate for us, we can always take action to change it. Change must begin from within our own selves. It is only when we change our inner world that we can change the outer world.

Changing ourselves starts with self-discovery that exposes our personal weaknesses, so that necessary corrections can be made. Understanding our fears, which are the root causes of our weaknesses, is an essential step towards eliminating the fears.

Understanding our fears allows us to know the truth about the kind of people we are, and it helps to facilitate a change in our personalities. However unpleasant the truth is, it will not dissuade us if we have decided on a change for the better. Fear appears when we resist change due to our failure to understand it correctly.

We avoid change because we feel pretty comfortable in our comfort zone. We do not want to take risks and venture out from where we feel comfortable and are

Adapt or perish, now as ever, is nature's inexorable imperative.

Herbert George "H.G." Wells
(1866 –1946)
English author, now best known for his work in the science fiction genre.

When in doubt, choose change.

Anonymous

Chapter 10

To exist is to change, to change is to mature, to mature is to go on creating oneself endlessly.

Henri Bergson
(1859-1941)
French philosopher. He was awarded the 1927 Nobel Prize in Literature "in recognition of his rich and vitalizing ideas and the brilliant skill with which they have been presented".

He who fears being conquered is sure of defeat.

Napoléon Bonaparte
(1769-1821)
His set of civil laws, the *Code Civil*—now often known as the Napoleonic Code—was prepared by committees of legal experts under the supervision of Jean Jacques Régis de Cambacérès, the Second Consul.

familiar with things to move into unfamiliar territory. It is a lot easier and safer to stay where we are, even if it is not a pleasant place. Simply put, we face no risks, if no change takes place.

However, to make some progress, we need to bring about positive change, and this is only possible if we free ourselves completely from the fear of change. To be able to secure change, we must act courageously and decisively in challenging all feelings of fear.

We fear change because it requires the surrender of old habits and beliefs. Understandably, we are unwilling to give up completely the beliefs that we have rigidly followed clung to for so long. However, when we discover new information that is entirely incompatible with our beliefs, we must accept change as inevitable.

We should invariably focus on being the kind of people who hold the right belief, which is the truth. We must also understand that we have to subject ourselves willingly to the truth, even though it is the veracity that we fear. The more we do that, the more familiar fears come to be, and the once fearful situations stop causing us to be afraid.

Furthermore, most of our beliefs are mistaken beliefs, and we still follow our mistaken beliefs thinking they are true, whether our beliefs are benefiting us or causing us to suffer. We should get rid of our beliefs in favor of change. Even so, our fear of change keeps us where we are – in a state of being completely certain of things.

Even if we experience positive change, we will still be feeling uncertain as we generally lack optimism. Our fearful anxiety is caused by what we imagine may

DEALING WITH **CHANGE**

result. We think if we cannot get a promotion, we will look for another job.

However, if we get that promotion to a higher position, with a higher salary and better advancement prospects, there is still the fear of insecurity and doubt about whether we can manage in the new position. Likewise, we would have similar feelings had we gotten another job.

Remember that we can bring about really personal change. All it requires is our will power to make a firm and irreversible decision to carry on with change in our lives. We do that by removing the greatest obstacle from our life, which is the feeling of fear. If we are resolutely determined to chase away our feelings of fear, nothing can keep us from the personal achievement that we have always wished for.

How can I change my personality?

Do you want to be preppy and happy about things, or funny and clever, or do you want to be spunky and hard? It may take time to get used to that, so take your time changing it and take it step-by-step. You will see that this changes the way you talk, and eventually think.

It will even change your characteristics, such as what values you hold as a person. Your change in attitude will be most evident when you look the part. You do not have to go out and get a new wardrobe, but maybe adding some new jewelry or changing the way your hair looks or changing the way you smile, laugh, or hold yourself, will help.

Only the wisest and stupidest of men never change.

Confucius
(551BCE–479 BCE)
Although Confucianism is often followed in a religious manner by the Chinese, arguments continue over whether it is a religion. Confucianism discusses elements of the afterlife and views concerning *tian* (Heaven), but it is relatively unconcerned with some spiritual matters often considered essential to religious thought, such as the nature of the soul.

Success consists of going from failure to failure without loss of enthusiasm.

Sir Winston Leonard Spencer-Churchill
(1874 –1965)
He was an accomplished artist and took great pleasure in painting, especially after his resignation as First Lord of the Admiralty in 1915.

Chapter 10

We continue to shape our personality all our life.
If we knew ourselves perfectly, we should die.

Albert Camus
1913–1960
French author, journalist, and philosopher of the 20th-century.

Imagine for yourself a character, a model personality, whose example you determine to follow in private as well as in public.

Epictetus
(AD 55 – AD 135)
Greek sage and Stoic philosopher.

Did you really achieve what you wanted to achieve? Do other people think more positively about you now that you act and wear different thing? Are you willing to sacrifice yourself for a fake imitation of the ideal person? Many people, at this stage, will realize that what they need is not a personality change, but an acceptance of who they are and a willingness to try to improve themselves instead of hiding behind an artificial public image of themselves.

You want to change yourself completely, and it will take some time before you actually do it. Do not get frustrated if you do not change right away. Simply do it step-by-step. Is there something you absolutely love that you can't sacrifice? Then keep it!

Practice makes perfect. If you are suffering from being "anti-social" or "depressed," it is really difficult to change. Focus on what you are doing. Do not focus on the negatives, and you will get through the difficult time before you know it.

Remember that it is most important to feel good about your new self. Most importantly, never change who you are because other people do not like you. If you think you cannot change who you are because of parents or other people in your life, change yourself in small ways. Sometimes, it might be hard to change completely, but do not worry. You can do this step-by-step and make sure that people around you like the way you behave. If they do not, it will be hard for you to make friends like that.

How can I change other people's opinions of me?

If people do not like you at all, that may be a problem. Here is one possible solution to this common problem experienced in everyday life. It is important to relax. Do not get worked up if people do not appear to like

DEALING WITH CHANGE

you right away. Sometimes, it takes others a while to adjust to new people in their lives.

You should find out a little more information about the person who seems not to like you. Try to see if the person is naturally shy because this might be the cause.

Change your opinions,
keep to your principles;
change your leaves, keep intact your roots.

Victor-Marie Hugo
(1802 – 1885)
French poet, playwright, novelist, essayist, visual artist, statesman, human rights activist, and exponent of the Romantic movement in France.

You may need to get a friend to do this for you since most people will not give answers to questions directly. It could be that the person might consider some of your strong points flaws. For instance, if he or she does not enjoy your sense of humor, then the person might think that you are annoying while others love your ability to share jokes. If the "flaws" appear to be a big part of you that others also dislike, you can consider changing this part about you. Hopefully, the person who did not like you before will now have a new opinion of you.

Remember that such a process may take a long time to be fully complete, so do not rush it. If this does not change the person's opinion, then do not give up. Keep trying until you accomplish what you want, assuming you still want to change to get the person to like you.

Example is not the main thing influencing others.
It is the only thing.

Albert Schweitzer
(1875 –1965)
German and then French theologian, organist, philosopher, physician, and medical missionary.

How can I accept criticism?

If your first reaction is to lash back at the person giving the criticism, or to become defensive, take a minute before reacting at all. Take a deep breath, and give it a little thought. For example, let a critical email sit in your in-box for at least an hour before replying.

That is like walking away from someone instead of saying something you will regret later. That cooling-off period allows you to give it a little more thought beyond your initial reaction. It allows logic to step in

Germain Decelles

Chapter 10

Boredom, after all, is a form of criticism.

Wendell Phillips
(1811 –1884)
American abolitionist, advocate for Native Americans, orator, and lawyer.

Criticism and pessimism destroy families, undermine institutions of all kinds, defeat nearly everyone, and spread a shroud of gloom over entire nations.

Gordon Bitner Hinckley,
(1910 – 2008)
American religious leader and author. Hinckley was awarded ten honorary doctorate degrees, and in 2004, he was awarded the Presidential Medal of Freedom by George W. Bush.

and for you to get past just the initial emotional response.

One of the keys to success in anything you do is the ability to find the positive in things that most people see as negative. You can do the same thing with criticism: find the positive in it.

Sure, it may be rude and mean, but in most criticism, you can find a nugget of gold: honest feedback and a suggestion for improvement. See it as an opportunity to improve. Improvement is a good thing!

Even if someone is harsh and rude, thank him or her. He or she might have been having a bad day, or maybe just be a negative person in general. However, even so, your attitude of gratitude will probably catch them off-guard. Thanking a critic can actually win a few of them over - all because of a simple act of saying thank you for the criticism. It is unexpected, and often appreciated. And even if the critic does not take your "thank you" in a good way, it is still excellent for you. It is a way of reminding yourself that the criticism was a good thing for you, a way of keeping you humble.

After seeing criticism in a positive light, and thanking the critic, do not just move on and go back to business as usual. Actually try to improve.

That is a difficult concept for some people because they often think that they are right no matter what. Even so, no one is always right.

You, in fact, may be wrong, and the critic may be accurate. So see if there is something you can change to make yourself better. And then make that change.

DEALING WITH **CHANGE**

... the whole earth hangs in the air... a thing so strange and seeming so far against nature and reason... which is yet now found true by experience of them that have in less than two years sailed the world round about.

Thomas More
Dialogue Concerning Heresies (1529)
Referring to Magellan's 1519 voyage.

Legend: (Ferdinand Magellan, you overcame the famous, narrow, southern straits.)
Source: The Mariner's Museum Collection, Newport News, VA

Remember not to confuse criticism with insults. Insults are personal conflict, such as off-topic descriptions of a person, but criticism may change your life for the better because you may use it to redirect your communication and efforts. Stay engaged and active while not allowing the criticism to stagnate you. Rather, use the stirring-up to prompt a flow of more appropriate input and output.

Can I change people's lives for the better?

Do you wish you could change people? There is a small problem with wanting to change people; in general, you cannot. You can inspire, lead, motivate, impress, show by example, etc., but changing another person is not something we are meant to do or capable of.

If you run you stand a chance of losing, but if you don't run you've already lost.

Barack Hussein Obama II
(1961-)
44th President of the United States. Signed economic stimulus legislation in the form of the American Recovery and Reinvestment Act of 2009 and the Tax Relief, Unemployment Insurance Reauthorization, and Job Creation Act of 2010.

With a refocus of your perspective though, it is just possible that you may make changes in your own situation and surroundings that can help others make changes for themselves.

People need to reach their own decisions to change and to put into place the effort required to perform the changes. By being realistic, you do not set yourself up for great disappointment, but you adjust your expectations to the realities.

Think of change in constructive ways. For example, you might ask questions about what you can do to make the change process easier. Constructively suggest ways that people can change undesirable behaviors.

Be a facilitator to remove obstacles to change and provide incentives for change!

DEALING WITH **CHANGE**

To improve is to change; to be perfect is to change often.

Sir Winston Leonard Spencer-Churchill
(1874–1965)

The world hates change, yet it is the only thing that has brought progress.

Charles Franklin Kettering
(1876–1958)
American inventor, engineer, businessman, and the holder of 186 patents.

Part of wanting people to change means wants them to conform to your viewpoint of the world, so that it is easier for you to cope and do the things you want to do. Trying to manipulate your surroundings and social interactions in this way is doomed to fail. Instead, seek to accept the person as he or she is with the undesirable behaviors.

Provide support and motivation to the extent that you have the energy to do so; otherwise, find ways to move away from the aspects of their behavior that are impacting you. At that point, you will need to consider forming new habits that do not involve them or require their input.

Remember that by changing peoples' lives for the better, you also improve your own life! The more people you help the better you feel! Do not give bad advice! It will come back to harm you and make matters worse!

How can I deal with negative people?

Sometimes you cannot avoid negative people in life. If you live with them, try to spend as much time as possible with other family members or with friends outside the home. Simply do something that does not involve the other person too much. You do not want to learn their ways of thinking and add them to your own thoughts.

When you do spend time with them, try to have a positive attitude yourself. Balance it out! Try to think of good qualities about that person. Pay proper attention to him or her. Everyone likes a bit of attention, whether they think they do or not!

If the person has a problem that you know you may be able to solve, jump in, and give the person a hand.

Chapter 10

Do something unexpectedly sweet, such as taking a walk with the person, or taking a brake from doing something that annoys.

Be constructive; offer the person ideas for action or change. Encourage, do not force. Most people do not like lectures on how to behave, especially when they are pointed towards them and suggest that they are horrible, etc. In addition, try to understand why an individual acts the way he or she does. There may be many hidden issues that you do not know about.

Progress is impossible without change, and those who cannot change their minds cannot change anything.

George Bernard Shaw
(1856-1950)
Irish playwright and a co-founder of the London School of Economics.

Think that there can be many different reasons for negativity, including insecurity, low self-esteem, an abusive past, frustration in life, low confidence, etc. Try to get close to these people; open your heart. Inspire them to change.

Let them see the bright side and how it is to be an optimistic person. Include them in your life; make them feel needed. Most people are negative because of low self-esteem, and by making them feel needed, you make them feel unique. Be a singular individual yourself and help let them breathe more easily!

These people may have a hard time seeing the positive side or the positive outcomes of life. Understand that these people have to want to change their way of thinking of themselves. Just keep your positive attitude, and hopefully it will rub off on them. Most of all, do not let them become a killjoy to you. In addition, someone who is negative all the time may be depressed.

Ensure that the person is not planning to harm themselves or others. Someone who is suicidal should be encouraged to seek professional help. In addition, be aware of your presence and how the other person feels when you are around him or her. Perhaps the person may be envious of you and what you have. Prove to that individual that you are not a threat, and that you can be a loyal friend he or she can come to when life gets hard.

Remember that you also need to protect yourself. If trying to help the other person hurts you too much, if it exhausts you or depresses you, maybe you need to step back. You do not always have to be there for that person. Do not let negativity from people like this turn you into a pessimist! Nothing ruins the happiness in one's life more than anxiety and letting a depressing imagination take over. Be yourself; love optimism!

How can I deal with people who always complain?
There are a lot of annoying people out there that like to whine and complain about others for no reason. Many of these people are passive-aggressive sorts.

Accept it when you are being complained about for something you are sure you did not do, and then it is not your problem. Realize that you are not the problem; it is the one complaining who has a problem.

Do not let this person complaining get to you. Ask the complainer to put the complaint in writing. Tell the person that it is important that he or she only state the facts, not their feelings. Then encourage them to give their comments to you – or the person or people he or she is complaining about. This can actually do something about his or her complaint. Nine times out of ten, he or she will stop complaining and will not write anything down.

People whose thinking has gotten out of shape automatically distrust the unfamiliar or different. When someone suggests a new idea, their immediate reactions tend to be negative. They cover up their fear by marshalling facts to prove that the suggested change would do no good. "We tried that in 1968 and it didn't work."

Albert J. Bernstein, Ph.D.

Chapter 10

I find people very impertinent when they say I am deep and then try to get to know me in five minutes. Between you and me, I am not deep but very wide, and it takes time to walk around me.

Honoré de Balzac
In a letter to Countess Maffei (1837)

Source: Daguerreotype by Louis-Auguste Bisson, 1842

Complainers may have a big ego, or think they are better than the rest of us, and that is usually not true.

In addition, normally people who complain are unhappy. They are unsatisfied with life. They are not getting what they need or want to be happy, so they complain. If they are complaining about you and demand an apology, and you have no idea what you have done wrong, do not give it to them!

The world does not owe you anything; you have to work for it.

Donald Trump
(1946 -)

Remember that people who complain excessively are miserable, and they take their misery out on everyone. Never say, "Well that's your problem then!" It will get you into trouble. However, you need to put some distance between you and the subject. Do not try to put your view forward as this would fuel the complainant, but keep a cool head and listen without getting your emotions involved.

Can I change my attitude at work?

The type of attitude you have at work plays an important role in your productivity and job performance.

A positive attitude is conducive to your occupational success, while a negative attitude is counter-productive. Therefore, if you do not have a positive attitude towards work, you may want to consider an attitude change in order to improve your work experience.

The only people who like change are wet babies.

Anonymous

You may find some of the things that are affecting your attitude in a negative way are things you can change. Make the necessary changes. Once you figure out what is causing your counter-productive attitude, determine what you can do to remedy those causes. For example, if your work is not challenging enough, then you may change your attitude by taking

Chapter **10**

The greatest discovery of all time is that a person can change his future by merely changing his attitude.

Oprah Winfrey
(1954 -)
Born in rural poverty, then raised by a mother on welfare in a poor urban neighborhood, Winfrey became a millionaire at age 32 when her talk show went national. Winfrey was in a position to negotiate ownership of the show and start her own production company because of the success and the amount of revenue the show generated. At age 41, Winfrey had a net worth of $340 million.

on some new tasks. It is important that you approach work with a realistic mental image of what your relationship with your work should be.

Accept the fact that certain tasks associated with your job may be less fulfilling than others. Recognize that a lack of motivation does not mean that you cannot complete your tasks. Rather, it means that you would prefer not to. You must acknowledge that an attitude change is your own responsibility, and something that you must proactively work toward.

Avoid comparing yourself to others who seem to enjoy the parts of their jobs that you do not enjoy, as this will only make you feel insufficient. Remember that it is likely that your coworkers dislike parts of their jobs that you actually enjoy.

Explain to your supervisor that you have identified some ways in which you would like to improve your productivity at work. Ask for suggestions regarding how you may change your attitude for the better. When you involve your supervisor, you are not only improving that relationship, but you also assert yourself as someone who takes your job and performance seriously, which can reap positive job-related benefits and further contribute to a constructive attitude. If there is a person in your workplace who has a good attitude, you could learn a lot by spending some time working alongside that person. Ask to work with someone who inspires you.

Remember to take your strengths and weaknesses into account and focus on accomplishing your tasks in a way that is tailored to your personal work style. Working towards goals and seeing them come to fruition is a natural and productive way to change your attitude on the job for the better.

How can I improve my change management skills?

Change management is a systematic method of transition for individuals from a current mode of operation into a new one. Because change is so common in the business world today, effective change management skills are necessary for a business to succeed.

Change management skills include leadership development, marketing and sales abilities, and communication abilities.

Furthermore, beneficial to an effective change management is knowing the psychological stages people go through in the midst of change, as this will allow you to know if you have managed a successful transition or if you need to address additional problems.

Solid leadership skills are much more important during a transition rather than strict business procedures. You will need to focus on your leadership ability first. Being a good leader will get people to believe and trust in what you are doing, which in turn will allow you to begin your campaign for change. To be an effective leader in the change management process:

- As head of your business, others turn to you for a direction in business needs, behavior, ethics, and standards. If others in your business are to change, you need to set an example.

- Perks suggest division and thought processes typical in a hierarchy. Removing your perks shows that you are willing to level the playing field.

Don't forget your boss is human. Because your boss is human, there may be times when he or she is grouchy, frustrated, or frazzled, or when he or she would appreciate hearing that he or she handled something well.

Plus, realize that in the same way you might have sensitivities about the relationship, he or she might, too. For instance, if you are taking on responsibilities that used to be his or hers, he or she probably would not appreciate hearing that they used to be a disaster until you came along. In other words, be thoughtful.

Chapter 10

- Today's business leaders manage their employees better though in-person interactions and learning more about their problems on an individual basis. Walk around and talk to people.

- To be a leader of change. It is critical to be honest in your interactions with other people. You do not have to open yourself up like a book, but being a leader also does not mean you need to hide your emotions. Just let people get to know you. Doing so allows you to build trust and rapport.

- Being a strong leader requires passion behind your vision for change. Without passion, you will face frustration and lose the desire to continue moving forward. Leadership requires lots of energy; so make sure you are passionate about what you are doing.

Target every group within your business regarding your campaign for change, explaining to each group why change is necessary. For example, the board of directors may be curious about the long-term effects of the change. On the other hand, your employees may want to know how they will personally be affected by your proposed changes.

Fill your employees in on what is happening. Communicate with everyone who has been affected once the change occurs. It may help to set up a formal way of communicating with everyone.

By keeping everyone informed, you reduce the chances of low productivity and low morale.

The great growling engine of change - technology.

Alvin Toffler
(1928-)
He explains, "Society needs people who take care of the elderly and who know how to be compassionate and honest. Society needs people who work in hospitals. Society needs all kinds of skills that are not just cognitive; they're emotional, they're affectional. You can't run the society on data and computers alone.

Realize that no matter how much effort you invest into making the transition seamless, you will experience at least some resistance.

The reason for this is that different people adjust to change at different rates. To reduce your frustration, it is helpful to know the six phases people undergo when changes occur.

1. *Anticipation.* This is the waiting phase when people do not know what to expect and wait for what the future has in store.

2. *Confrontation.* At this stage, people begin to realize that change is imminent, or in some cases, already under way.

3. *Realization.* People enter Phase 3 once change has occurred. This is where the realization sinks in that things will always be different.

4. *Depression.* As well as realizing the change intellectually, people are now realizing the change emotionally and are mourning the past.

5. *Acceptance.* Now people comprehend the change emotionally as well. It is not uncommon for people to maintain some reservations about the change, but at this phase, little effort is made to fight the change. Benefits from the change are acknowledged but not always fully supported.

6. *Enlightenment.* People are now fully accepting of the change and often wonder how they ever managed under the "old" way.

Understand that there is no way of predicting how long it will take to implement a change fully. The

---

Things do not change; we change.

Henry David Thoreau
(1817 – 1862)
Civil Disobedience (Resistance to Civil Government) is an essay by American transcendentalist Henry David Thoreau that was first published in 1849. In it, Thoreau argues that individuals should not permit governments to overrule or atrophy their consciences, and that they have a duty to avoid allowing such acquiescence to enable the government to make them the agents of injustice. Thoreau was motivated in part by his disgust with slavery and the Mexican–American War.

Chapter 10

> Commitment is the enemy of resistance, for it is the serious promise to press on, to get up, no matter how many times you are knocked down.
>
> David McNally is an activist and Professor of Political Science at York University in Toronto, Ontario, and past chair of the university's Department of Political Science. He is a member of the New Socialist Group.

reason for this is that people go through the above phases at different rates of speed.

One person may require three months to reach Phase 6, while another, a full year. Moreover, people do not undergo these phases in a linear order, but rather jump around. For example, an individual may go from 4 to 6 and back to 2.

Let the challenges of managing change management inspire us! We meet challenges every single day. They come in all shapes and sizes. Some of these highlight the resistance we have to change. Some are known and some creep up behind us and surprise us. However, how often do you change, have you ever thought about that?

The whole area of managing change can bring out the best in us, or the worst. Management is something we really need to think about. After all some of the time changes are easy, yet other times we experience resistance, heartache, and problems before they drift away. Change is all around us every single day. How we tackle it helps us make our mark on life.

Remember that confrontations are a part of our everyday lives. They have the ability to test us and to "keep us on our toes". They can be exhilarating and exciting. They can be dull and boring. They can be complex and difficult. They can be simple and straightforward. They can be all things to all people.

We find each different thing to be confrontational or a test of resources or resolve. What one of us thinks is difficult is a breeze, or a joy, for another, and vice versa. Always recognize that your attitude will help you succeed in life!

What should I consider?

We Are Change! Change is everywhere!

For us to make the most out of life, we have to realize that we are in command and we can adapt and evolve. In fact, we are doing it all the time.

We just have to step back a little at times and see the bigger picture. We have to recognize it first, see things for what they really are, and then we can act and achieve.

Remember that adapting to life and meeting these challenges head on are some of the things that we all need to experience, work at, and get a feeling for.

Recommended Reading & References
We suggest consulting the works identified below in order to learn more about the particulars contained in this chapter.

BENNIS, W. & NANUS, B. LEADERS, THE STRATEGIES FOR TAKING CHARGE. Harper Press. ISBN 0-06-015246-X.

BRIDGES, William. MANAGING TRANSITIONS. Perseus Group. ISBN –13: 978-0-7382-0824-4.

COHEN, Dan S. THE HEART OF CHANGE FIELD GUIDE. Harvard Press. ISBN 1-59139-775-8.

DRUCKER, Peter F. MANAGING IN TURBULENT TIMES. Harper Business. ISBN 0-88730-616-0.

KOTTER, John P. LEADING CHANGE. Harvard Press. ISBN-13: 978-0-87584-747-4.

KOTTER, John P. THE HEART CHANGE. Harvard Press. ISBN-1-57851-254-9.

LIEBERMAN, David J. HOW TO CHANGE ANYBODY. Audio renaissance. ISBN 1-59397-803-8.

MAURER, Rick. CHANGE WITHOUT MIGRAINES, Solving the Middle Manager's Dilemma, www.beyondresistance.com

TRACY, Brian. CHANGE YOUR THINKING, CHANGE YOUR LIFE. How to Unlock your Full Potential for Success and Achievement. Willey & sons. ISBN 0-471-73538-8.

Business people see me as a master negotiator because I usually wind up with what I am aiming to get. In other words, I negotiate to win and then I win. Pretty simple from the outside looking in, but I can tell you that I spend time preparing for any negotiation.

Donald J. Trump

Photo: WebTech Collection

CHAPTER 11

NEGOTIATE

Many people think they do not like to negotiate because it can feel too much like being in conflict, but the truth is that we negotiate every day with our co-workers, family members, and friends.

Conflict is a natural byproduct of human interaction, and how we handle it can determine what kind of success we experience in our lives. In contrast to unresolved conflict, effective negotiation can build trust between people or companies and make it easier to communicate in the future.

Effective negotiation is not a contest of wills to determine who has the most power. It is not a game in which each party seeks to best the other. However, there are rules that make the dialogue respectful and the outcomes fair.

There is no need to personalize the issues with remarks about the person on the other side of the table. You simply need to stick to the issues. Separate the people from the issues. Recognize that there are emotions and investment on both sides, and be prepared to listen well.

Let us never negotiate out of fear.
But let us never fear to negotiate.

John Fitzgerald "Jack" Kennedy
(1917 – 1963)
35th President of the United States, serving from 1961 until his assassination in 1963.

First, you will need to understand the point, of view of the others before you can expect to be understood. Be soft on people and hard-on issues. This way, you can maintain the relationships and mutually satisfying outcomes.

You will need to focus on the interests of the other, rather than his or her position. Behind each position lies compatible as well as conflicting interests.

Chapter 11

If there is no struggle, there is no progress.

Frederick Douglass
(born **Frederick Augustus Washington Bailey**)
(1818 –1895)
American social reformer, orator, writer, and statesman. After escaping from slavery, he became a leader of the abolitionist movement, gaining fame for his dazzling oratory and incisive antislavery writing.

Do you know the difference between education and experience? Education is when you read the fine print; experience is what you get when you don't.

Peter "Pete" Seeger
(1919 -)
American folk singer whowas an iconic figure in the mid-20th century American folk music revival.

Negotiations do not take place in a vacuum. Each person has a real life going on, with actual needs and interests.

Work with the other party to generate a variety of options from which to create a solution, and brainstorm possibilities without judgment or comment. You would be surprised how many good ideas can surface when this is allowed to occur. Make no decisions until you have exhausted your list of possibilities. Then look for areas of agreement.

Where are your shared interests? Explore options that are of low cost to you and high value to the other party and vice versa.

It is imperative to negotiate within mutually agreed-upon standards of fairness. Otherwise, negotiating can turn toward street fighting!

These criteria may range from current market value to procedures for resolving conflict. They will allow you to create an equitable solution while keeping your relationship intact.

Before beginning to negotiate decide on the ground rules and stick to them. Negotiating fairly builds trust. Demonstrations of power erode it.

You are setting the standard for future conversations as well.

Remember that you teach people how to treat you in two ways: you know, set, and enforce your boundaries, and you demonstrate your values in the ways you treat others.

Bargaining and maintaining strong positions are best left for those fun holiday moments when you do not really care whether or not the street vendor sells you that black velvet painting.

In the business world, those tactics may bring you short-term results; however, the long-term damage to the relationships involved may be irreparable. Remember that wherever there is a winner, there must be a loser. Hard-nosed bargaining usually leaves both sides exhausted, resentful, and dissatisfied. You may know this from bitter experience. You will especially relate to this if you were on the losing end!

Remember to be clear about the outcome you prefer, before entering into a dialogue of negotiation. Be able to express this preference well with supporting statements that will make sense to your partner. Be prepared to listen more, or, at least, as much as you speak. Listen for common interests and possible options. Know what you are willing to give as well as what you would like to receive. When you are focused this way, you will get more of what you want, often while winning friends and influencing people. This is a compelling reason for integrating these rules into your next negotiation!

How do I ask a question intelligently?
There are two elements that you need to be concerned about in asking questions. Those elements are processes and outcomes. The two sides of the process element are perspective questions and evaluative questions. The outcome elements involve knowledge questions and action questions.

Never interrupt your enemy when he is making a mistake.

Napoleon Bonaparte (1769-1821)
Is biggest influence was in the conduct of warfare. Antoine-Henri Jomini explained Napoleon's methods in a widely used textbook that influenced all European and American armies. Napoleon was regarded by the influential military theorist Carl von Clausewitz as a genius in the operational art of war, and historians rank him as a great military commander. Wellington, when asked who was the greatest general of the day, answered: "In this age, in past ages, in any age, Napoleon.

Chapter 11

He must be very ignorant for he answers every question he is asked.

François-Marie Arouet de Voltaire (1694-1778)
He was one of several Enlightenment figures (along with Montesquieu, John Locke, Jean-Jacques Rousseau, and Émilie du Châtelet) whose works and ideas influenced important thinkers of both the American and French Revolutions.

To raise new questions, new possibilities, to regard old problems from a new angle, requires creative imagination and marks real advance in science.

Albert Einstein (1879-1955)

The best questions involve both process and outcome elements in the question. Asking something simple first lets the information provider know you are about to state your opinion, but you fully realize you do not comprehend the whole story, and you are hoping they can fill in some gaps. It is suggested not to use huge words. They will make you sound pretentious. Just tap into your thoughtful but friendly side, and do not worry too much about sounding brilliant.

Before you pose a question, it is important to have a concept of what is unclear about the information in your head; otherwise, you risk creating confusion and not getting an answer that satisfies what you seek to know.

On the other hand, if you are asking questions in a leadership role, it is significant that you do not specifically ask a question to which you already have an answer. Doing so will only frustrate those you work with, and they will begin to see you as a game player. Questions are not only about knowledge; they are also about action.

It is important not to ask a question in an aggressive manner. Doing so indicates that you are only asking the question to prove to the other person you are right and they are wrong, meaning you will appear argumentative and not open-minded. Ask because you are genuinely interested. Otherwise, you will receive a defensive-and-less than helpful response.

Furthermore, take care to make sure that the other person is fully aware of exactly what your current thinking is and why you think it. Recognize also that you are seeking information to fill a gap in your

NEGOTIATE

> Judge a man by his questions rather than his answers.
>
> François-Marie Arouet de Voltaire
> (1694-1778)

> Successful people ask better questions, and as a result, they get better answers.
>
> Anthony "Tony" Robbins
> (1960 -)
> Author of:
> *Awaken The Giant Within*.

> The most common lie is that which one lies to himself; lying to others is relatively an exception.
>
> Friedrich Wilhelm Nietzsche
> (1844 –1900)
> German philosopher, poet, composer, and classical philologist.

knowledge and that the person in front of you may be one who may have the answer, so be polite!

If appropriate, if you do not really feel comfortable with the response or feel that it does not respond to what you have asked, proceed gently by asking how the person knows this information.

If you find the information provider is beginning to feel uncomfortable and maybe out of his or her area of expertise, do not press the issues, unless you are questioning in a professional capacity. It is rare that public grilling amounts to any good. In most situations, it is better to back down and thank the person. Often, there will be time afterwards to find the individual and discuss things privately. Never ask a question that you are not willing to answer!

Remember never to ask a question just for the sake of it, whether it be to bring attention to yourself or to appear smart. That is the worst possible motivation for asking a question. Void becoming aggressive at the response you get if you do not like it. If you are not willing to receive the answer(s), do not ask the question(s). Sometimes a person can answer aggressively to your innocent query. Do not worry.

Can I detect lies?

You have to learn the little facial and body expressions that can help you distinguish a lie from the truth. Watching facial expressions in order to determine whether a person is lying might just save you from being a victim of fraud, or it could help you figure out when somebody is being genuine. A base line is what someone acts like when they are not lying. You have to get a base line before you proceed with anything.

Chapter 11

Those who honestly mean to be true contradict themselves more rarely than those who try to be consistent.

Oliver Wendell Holmes Jr.
(1841 –1935)
American jurist who served as an Associate Justice of the Supreme Court of the United States from 1902 to 1932.

One may sometimes tell a lie, but the grimace that accompanies it tells the truth.

Friedrich Wilhelm Nietzsche
(1844-1900)
He wrote critical texts on religion, morality, contemporary culture, philosophy, and science, displaying a fondness for metaphor, irony, and aphorism.

To establish a baseline, you need to see the person when he or she is not lying. Try asking what his name is, and what she does for a living. If any of the signs below pop up when you know the individual is telling the truth, then those signs are not indicative of lying.

Learn to recognize deflections. Usually when people are lying, they will tell stories that are true but are deliberately aimed at not answering the question you asked. If a person responds to the question "Did you ever hit your wife?" with an answer such as "I love my wife; why would I do that?", the person is technically telling a truth, but he is avoiding answering your original question. This may indicate that he is lying or trying to conceal something from you.

Notice the behavior of the person's other body parts. Watch his hands, arms, and legs, which tend to be limited, stiff, and self-directed when the person is lying. His hands may touch his face, ear, or the back of the neck. These are, however signs of nervousness, not signs of deceit. He might not necessarily be nervous because he is lying.

Look out for micro expressions. Micro expressions are facial expressions that flash on a person's face for a fraction of a second and reveal the person's true emotion underneath the façade. Some people may be naturally sensitive to them, but almost anybody can easily train herself to be able to detect micro expressions. Typically, in a person who is lying, the micro expression will exhibit the emotion of distress, characterized by the eyebrows being drawn upwards towards the middle of the forehead, sometimes causing short lines to appear in the skin across the forehead.

NEGOTIATE

Above all, I would teach him to tell the truth. Truth-telling, I have found, is the key to responsible citizenship. The thousands of criminals I have seen in 40 years of law enforcement have had one thing in common: Every single one was a liar.

J. Edgar Hoover
(1895–1972)
The first Director of the Federal Bureau of Investigation (FBI) of the United States.

Someone who knows too much finds it hard not to lie.

Ludwig Josef Johann Wittgenstein
(1889–1951)
Austrian-British philosopher who worked primarily in logic, the philosophy of mathematics, the philosophy of mind, and the philosophy of language.

Check for sweating. People tend to sweat more when they lie. However, this is not always a reliable indication of lying. Some people may sweat a lot more because of nervousness or shyness.

Mind-exaggerated details. See if the person is telling you too much, such as "My mom lives in Toronto. Isn't it nice there? Don't you like the CN tower? It's so clean there." Too many details may tip you off to the speaker's desperation to try to get you to believe what he or she is saying.

Notice the person's eye movements. Contrary to popular belief, a liar does not always avoid eye contact. Humans naturally break eye contact and look at non-moving objects to help them focus and remember. Liars may deliberately make eye contact to seem more sincere. You can usually tell if a person is remembering something or making something up based on the eye movements displayed. When someone is remembering details, his eyes move to the right (your right). When someone is making something up, his or her eyes move to the left. It is usually reversed for lefties. Remember that eye contact is considered rude in some cultures, so this may explain why the individual is reluctant to look you in the eye consistently.

Be aware of the person's emotional responses. Timing and duration tend to be off when someone is lying. If you ask someone a question, and she responds directly after the question, there is a chance that the person is lying. This can be because she has rehearsed the answer, or he is already thinking about the answer just to get it over with and move forward.

Additionally, you should pay close attention to the person's reaction to your questions. A liar will often

Chapter 11

A lie gets halfway around the world before the truth has a chance to get its pants on.

Sir Winston Leonard Spencer-Churchill
(1874-1965)

Hard conditions of life are indispensable to bringing out the best in human personality.

Alexis Carrel
(1873 –1944)
French surgeon and biologist who was awarded the Nobel Prize in Physiology or Medicine in 1912 for pioneering vascular suturing techniques. In 1972, the Swedish Post Office honored Carrel with a stamp that was part of its Nobel stamp series.

feel uncomfortable and turn his head or body away, or even subconsciously put an object between the two of you. For her part, an innocent person would go on the offensive, usually responding with anger, which will generally be revealed in a micro expression directly after you say you do not believe her.

A guilty person will immediately go on the defensive, normally by saying something to support his facts, some kind of deflection.

Listen for a subtle delay in responses to questions. An honest answer comes quickly from memory. Lies require a quick mental review of what people have told others to avoid inconsistency and to make up new details as needed. However, when people look up to remember things, it does not necessarily mean that they are lying.

Be conscious of how people use words. Verbal expression can give many clues about whether a person is lying, such as: Using and repeating your exact words when answering a question, speaking in muddled sentences, using humor and sarcasm to avoid the subject, and allowing silence to enter the conversation. If someone is lying, he or she will become uncomfortable if you stare at the person for a while with a look of disbelief. If he or she is telling the truth, the individual will usually become angry or just frustrated.

Change the subject quickly. While an innocent person would be confused by the sudden shift in the conversation and may try to return to the previous subject, a liar will be relieved and welcome the change. You may see the person become more relaxed and less defensive.

Make the lie big, make it simple, keep saying it, and eventually they will believe it.

Adolf Hitler
(1889 –1945)
Austrian-born German politician.

Dictator of Nazi Germany (as Führer und Reichskanzler) from 1934 to 1945. Hitler is commonly associated with the rise of fascism in Europe, World War II, and the Holocaust.

It takes a wise man to handle a lie, a fool had better remain honest.

George Norman Douglas
(1868 –1952)
British writer, now best known for his 1917 novel *South Wind*.

Watch his or her throat. A person may constantly be either trying to lubricate his or her throat when he/she lies by swallowing or clearing their throat to relieve the tension built up. A person's voice can also be a good lie indicator; the person may suddenly start talking faster or slower than normal, or the person's tension may result in a higher-pitched speaking tone. Many of the signs that a person is lying can also simply be signs that someone is nervous. This can especially be the case if they are uncomfortable with the subject being discussed.

Follow through. If you have the means, check the validity of what the liar is saying. A skilled liar might give some reason why you should not talk to the person who could confirm or deny a story. Perhaps the liar will imply that the person is particularly favorable to the liar, or that the person would have little time for you. These probably lie themselves, so might be worthwhile overcoming your reluctance and to check with the person you have been warned against.

Notice it when the speaker repeats sentences. If the speaker uses almost the exact same words over and over, then it is probably a lie. When a person makes up a lie, he often tries to remember a certain phrase or sentence that sounds convincing. When asked to explain the situation again, the liar will repeat the very same 'convincing' sentence.

Remember that some people are extremely experienced or even professional liars. These people have told their made-up stories so many times that they are actually believable, getting all their days, dates, and times down perfectly! Sometimes, you may need simply to accept that you cannot catch every lie all the time.

Chapter **11**

If you don't like something, change it.
If you can't change it, change your attitude.

Maya Angelou
(1928 -)
With the publication of *I Know Why the Caged Bird Sings*, Angelou was heralded as a new kind of memoirist, one of the first African-American women who was able to publicly discuss her personal life.

I'd like to add that negotiating is not something to be avoided or feared - it's an everyday part of life.

Leigh William Steinberg
(1949 –)
American sports agent and sports lawyer.

How can I negotiate effectively?

Negotiation is a fact of life. Little children learn about it early. You did, too.

Were you effective? Are you now? Do you want to improve your abilities? Do you want to feel better about both the outcome and yourself when negotiating? You can!

Learn everything you can about the issue to be negotiated and the person with whom you will negotiate. In addition, come to the negotiation with a clear understanding of what you really need or want. Pre-establish a reasonable plan that your research will support. For instance, if you are negotiating the price of a car, consult a consumer magazine to learn about the car, and do not start by offering a ridiculously low price.

Because it is assumed that the first offer will not be the final offer, this puts you in a strategic position to move the outcome closer to your goal. Encourage the other person to offer the first term of negotiation.

Offering a fair price or reasonable compromise will strengthen your standing as an effective negotiator. Be honest in your negotiations. Do not threaten to quit a job, cancel a deal, or end a relationship if you do not mean it. This will only hurt your ability to negotiate successfully in the future.

Letting a negotiation drag out too long can result in losing ground. Politely end the meeting by offering a legitimate reason to do so such as another meeting date to continue the discussion. Close the discussion when you are happy with the terms.

Negotiating means getting the best of your opponent.

Marvin Pentz Gaye, Jr.
(1939 –1984)
American singer-songwriter and musician with a three-octave vocal range.

Number one, that it is smart to communicate and negotiate with your enemy instead of just waging war with bombs and weapons of mass destruction.

Theodore Chaikin "Ted" Sorensen,
(1928 –2010)
American presidential advisor, lawyer, and writer, best known as President John F. Kennedy's special counsel, adviser, and legendary speechwriter.

Remember to congratulate your opponent for completing a good negotiation. Do not offer false flattery, but a sincere handshake and a complimentary comment will help the person look forward to negotiating with you in the future and will help build your reputation as a credible negotiator.

Can I control my emotions when I negotiate?

When negotiating, do you let emotions get in the way of your goals? During the negotiations, most people experience different emotions. The ways you control your emotions have a major influence on the progress and outcome of the negotiation.

Before the negotiations, consider what could possibly lead you to become emotionally and mentally prepared for such situations. Consider a possible recourse you may adopt to keep emotional control. Assess the other negotiator to determine what may cause him or her to become emotionally unglued.

Evaluate the emotions: Every time you encounter an emotion, evaluate it. Try to uncover whether the emotion is real or contrived. It may be described as genuine but may actually be a mask of deceit in order to provoke a calculated reaction in you. If you suspect such a trick is being used, consider displaying no emotion in return. By doing so, the perpetrator will cast doubt on his or her actions, which in turn can give the person cause to reflect upon whether his or her trick is working.

Control the emotions: You must control your emotions and try to control those of the other negotiator. To control the other negotiator's emotions, you must have a strong sense of what might lead him or her to one action versus another. Then during the negotiation, strike the proper chord to motivate the

Chapter 11

During a negotiation, it would be wise not to take anything personally. If you leave personalities out of it, you will be able to see opportunities more objectively.

Brian Koslow
Founder and President/CEO of Breakthrough Coaching, Inc., a company that provides business training to professionals who aspire to become top earners in their fields.

Unreality is the true source of powerlessness. What we do not understand, we cannot control.

Charles A. Reich
(1928 -)
American legal and social scholar, as well as writer who was a Professor at Yale Law School.

person to move in the direction you want. Your success will be determined by how well you predict the other person's reaction(s).

Display appropriate emotion for the environment: The emotions you show must be aligned with the outcome you are looking for from the negotiation. So the proper mannerisms, connected with the fitting emotions, will lend cohesiveness to your position.

The body language and emotion: As you progress through negotiations, monitor the connection that a displayed emotion has with a person's body language. If there is an incongruity between the emotion and the body language, perhaps the emotion is contrived and has less importance than what is being conveyed.

Learn that even if an emotion is genuine, you must not give credence to it. You can choose to ignore it if it does not serve your purpose of moving the negotiation towards a positive result.

Remember that regardless of how you react to the emotions during a negotiation, if you are aware of the role they play and adjust to them accordingly, you will have greater control of the negotiation and will, in the process, be more successful.

How can I win a negotiation?

Whether it is buying a house, disputing your cell phone bill, scoring more frequent-flier miles, haggling in China, or paying off your credit card, the basic principles of negotiation are the same. Just remember that even the most skilled and experienced negotiators will feel discomfort when negotiating. The only difference is an experienced negotiator has learned to recognize and suppress the outward signs of these feelings.

As with many endeavors, preparation is essential and often more instrumental to success than the tactics employed tableside. If you do not know what a potential deal is worth to you or have not considered how the other party views it, you simply will have no idea where to begin or how to react to an offer.

The optimal way to evaluate any proposed deal is to weigh it against your best option in the absence of a deal. The value or cost of this alternative helps determine your best alternative to a negotiated agreement. Know what is the most you would pay, or the least you would take, to cut a deal.

Determining your best alternative to a negotiated agreement improves your bargaining power by stiffening your resolve at the table.

You need to know your counterpart. A deep understanding of your counterpart's interests and motives will help you evaluate his strengths and weaknesses and give you a sense of the bargaining zone, which lies between your reservation price and his. In addition, you need to know the standards. Accepted standards and norms, spoken or not, underpin virtually every negotiation.

They serve as benchmarks for the terms, just as the Official Kelley *Blue Book* New Car and Used Car Prices and Values sets prices for a used car, or as an earning's multiple is used to value a company. Even so, negotiators also make decisions based on the principles they have adopted.

Men are moved by two levers only: fear and self interest.

Napoléon Bonaparte (1769-1821) Emancipated Jews (as well as Protestants in Catholic countries and Catholics in Protestant countries) from laws which restricted them to ghettos, and he expanded their rights to property, worship, and careers. Despite the anti-semitic reaction to Napoleon's policies from foreign governments and within France, he believed emancipation would benefit France by attracting Jews to the country given the restrictions they faced elsewhere.

Chapter 11

A company committed to social responsibility, for example, might favor a supplier who pays employees a fair wage or uses environmentally sensitive manufacturing processes.

Donald Trump in his book: *Think Big and Kick Ass in Business and Life,* formulates a straight to heart definition. *Get people to respect you. You have to make sure that people you deal with know that you know what is happening, because, otherwise, they are really going to take advantage of you. You don't want that to happen. Make them respect you for your knowledge. I am good at real estate. I understand real estate, and I love real estate. Nobody can pull the wool over my eyes when it comes to real estate. That is the most important lesson in getting respect: know your stuff.*

Again preparing for negotiation involves deciding on your breakpoint, that is, the lowest amount, or cheapest price, you will accept in the deal, the *worst-case scenario*.

Know what you are worth. How much does the other party need you? Is what you are offering hard to come by, or does it come a "dime a dozen"? How desperate is the other party? Who needs whom more? Do you need them more than they need you; how can you give yourself an edge?

As long as you get there before it's over you're never late.

James John Walker, (1881–1946) He was often known as **Jimmy Walker** and colloquially as **Beau James** and was the mayor of New York City from 1926 to 1932.

Plan how you will move in your proposals. Your moves should be in ever-decreasing steps, which will give the impression that you are being *bled* and there is increasingly less bargaining range to be had.

Preparation is 90% of negotiation. Gather as much information about the deal as you possibly can;

It's not over until it'a over.

Lawrence Peter "Yogi" Berra
(1925 –)
Former American Major League Baseball catcher, outfielder, and manager.

evaluate all the key variables; and understand which concessions you can trade.

Open at your maximum sustainable position, that is, the most you can logically argue for. Ask for what you want, and then some. When starting off a negotiation, do not be scared to make an outrageous request. You never know. You might get it!

And what is the worst that could happen? The other party might think you are vain, or delusional; but he or she will also know you have guts, and you value yourself, your time, and your money.

Are you worried about insulting others, especially if you are making a very low offer to buy something? Remember that this is business, and if others do not like your offer, they can always counter-offer. Just be bold. If your opening offer is too close to your breakpoint, then you will not have enough bargaining range to concede to the other party as a way of giving satisfaction.

What else can the other party give you that is of low value to them and high value to you? Alternatively, what can you offer that is of low value to you and high value to them? This is why retail stores offer employee discounts. Think along the lines of bartering, and be creative.

Take time to deliberate, but when the time for action has arrived, stop thinking and go in.

Napoléon Bonaparte
(1769-1821)

What do you have a lot of or what can you offer with ease that the other party would find valuable? Make a list of your skills and materials things. Calculate how much they cost you, and then find out how much they sell for.

Research their costs, retail versus wholesale. If you are buying a car, and you know the other dealer will

Chapter 11

The first step is to know exactly what you want. You have to be clear about your own goals.
The second step is to know what the other side wants.
Give that some thought.
Whether you're in baseball or in business, you've got to know the strengths and weaknesses of your opponents in order to deal with them effectively.
No two teams are exactly the same, and no two companies or organizations are exactly the same.
Don't rely on generalizations. Find out for yourself.

Donald J. Trump
(1946-)
From is *Inside Trump Tower* newsletter.

sell you the same car for $200 less, tell the salesperson so. Tell him or her the name of the dealer and salesman. If you are negotiating a salary, and you have researched how much people in equivalent positions get paid in your area, print out those statistics and have them handy.

An up front payment is always desirable to a seller, especially in situations where most people do not pay ahead, such as car dealerships. As the buyer, you can also offer to buy in bulk, paying in advance for a certain number of products or services, in exchange for a discount. Finally, paying in cash rather than with a check or credit card can be a useful negotiation tool because it reduces the risk to the seller. There is no fear of a check bouncing or a credit declined.

Always hold back one or two facts or arguments you can use when you sense the other side is close to a deal but needs that final push. If you are a broker and your client is going to buy this week, whether this seller is willing or not, that is a great deal closer.

Be ready to walk away. You know what your breakpoint is, and you know if that is not what you are going to get. Be willing to walk out the door if that is the case. You might find that the other party will call you back, but you should feel happy with your efforts if they do not.

Remember that if someone surprises you with a very appealing offer, do not let on that you expected something less favorable. Even when you are unsure, speak with authority. Speaking louder than usual and giving the impression that you have done this many times before will close deals with people who are not experienced. If someone is totally unreasonable, do not negotiate. Tell the person to keep you in mind if

NEGOTIATE

> Good people do not need laws to tell them to act responsibly, while bad people will find a way around the laws.
>
> Plato
> (423 BCE – 348 BCE
> *The Republic*
> His a Socratic dialogue written around 380 BC concerning the definition of justice and the order and character of the just city-state and the just man.

> Never get angry. Never make a threat. Reason with people.
>
> Don Corleone
> *The Godfather.*

he or she comes down in price or whatever. However, avoid hostility at all costs. Even if there has been hostility in the past, start each contact upbeat, positive, and do not hold a grudge. Watch your body language, a skilled negotiator will pick up on non-verbal signals, which may give away your true feelings.

How can I negotiate more effectively?

What is your best price? This is too expensive! Your competitor is selling the same thing for... Most salespeople and business owners hear statements like this every day. That means it is important to learn how to negotiate more effectively.

Learn to flinch. The flinch is one of the oldest negotiation tactics but one of the least used. A flinch is a visible reaction to an offer or price. The objective of this negotiation tactic is to make the other people feel uncomfortable about the offer they presented.

Recognize that people often ask for more than they expect to get. This means you need to resist the automatic temptation to reduce your price or offer a discount.

The person with the most information usually does better. You need to learn as much about the other person's situation as possible. This is a particularly important negotiation tactic for sales people. Ask your prospect more questions about his or her prospective purchase. Learn what is important to the prospect as well as his or her needs and wants. Develop the habit of asking questions such as:

- What prompted you to consider a purchase of this nature?
- Who else have you been speaking to?

Chapter **11**

- What was your experience with...?
- What time frames are you working with?
- What is most important to you about this?

It is also important to learn as much about your competitors as possible. This will help you defeat potential price objections and prevent someone from using your competitor as leverage.

He is free who knows how to keep in is own hands the power to decide.

Salvador de Madariaga y Rojo
(1886 – 1978)
Spanish diplomat, writer, historian, and pacifist.

It is important to practice at every opportunity. Most people hesitate to negotiate because they lack the confidence. Develop this confidence by negotiating more frequently. Ask for discounts from your suppliers. As a consumer, develop the habit of asking for a price break when you buy from a retail store.

Here are a few questions or statements you can use to practice your negotiation skills: You'll have to do better than that! What kind of discount are you offering today? This is too expensive! Wait for their response afterwards.

Learn to flinch. Be pleasant and persistent but not demanding. Conditioning yourself to negotiate at every opportunity will help you become more comfortable, confident, and successful.

You can hesitate before deciding, but not once the decision is made.

José Bergamín Gutiérrez
(1895 – 1983)
Spanish writer, essayist, poet, and playwright.

Maintain your walk away power. It is better to walk away from a sale rather than to make too large a concession or give a deep discount on your product or service. Remember that there will always be someone to sell to.

Remember that negotiating is a way of life in some cultures. And most people negotiate in some way nearly every day. Apply these negotiation strategies and you will notice a difference in your negotiation skills almost immediately.

How can I negotiate with parents?

Negotiating with your parents is challenging. Most parents get angry at any sign of disrespect, or if you get anxious before them for their not immediately giving you what you want. Know whom you are dealing with. You need to do some serious groundwork to know your parents as individuals. Furthermore, make sure you approach your parents at reasonable times, not when they are stressed or worried, and not when they are busy.

Do you have a tendency to get angry and yell? There is a possibility that you will become disrespectful or say something your parents' will claim is discourteous. Work on trying to avoid these things from surfacing while negotiating. This way, you stay on the positive side. If you do accidentally slip up, remember to apologize immediately. This is going to require that you be in control of yourself and get rid of your pride.

A child who is allowed to be disrespectful to his parents will not have true respect for anyone.

William Franklin "Billy" Graham, Jr.
(1918 –)
American Christian evangelist, who rose to celebrity status as his sermons were broadcast on radio and television.

Spend some time beforehand highlighting your good points to them. Do not fight with them, and every time a fight starts, if you accidentally slip up that is, remember that it is not worth fighting. Apologize, and keep your negotiating goal in mind.

Get some background information on the topic the negotiation will be about; know the positive sides of it and even some of the negative sides that you know will not affect your parent's decision very much. Have explanations as to why they do not need to worry about the negative sides, that is, try to determine what objections they may have and prepare answers to overcome these objections.

Always be polite, but do not "suck up" right before you negotiate; try to do so beforehand if you feel you

Chapter 11

must. You are negotiating, so use your research well, and word it in non-offensive ways, and be, or at least act as if you understand your parents' views.

Never get angry with them for their final decision. Accept it if they deny your request. Ask them why, but be polite. If they say they do not need to explain themselves, tell them it makes it easier for you to accept it. If they still do not explain, then let them know you respect their decision and walk away. You can use this and spend more time coming up with good, positive counters as to why you should get what you want and how it will help you, and even possibly them. In addition, do not be rude if you do not win, for this will only make them sure they made the right choice and not let you have other things as well.

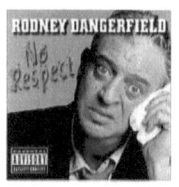

I could tell that my parents hated me. My bath toys were a toaster and a radio.

Rodney Dangerfield (born Jacob Cohen, (1921 –2004) American comedian, and actor, known for the catchphrases "I don't get no respect!", "No respect, no respect at all... that's the story of my life", or "I get no respect, I tell ya" and his monologues on that theme. He is also famous for his 1980s film roles, notably in *Easy Money*, *Caddyshack*, and *Back To School*.

Remember that before entering a negotiation, keep in mind that you may not always get what you want, and explain to your parents that you understand why they do not want you to get or do what you are negotiating for. Even so, be on your best behavior. When negotiating, never bring up old points; parents will keep them in mind. Be polite once again, and be respectful. Avoid certain words that may upset them, calm down, and do not ever give them orders. Avoid telling them what to do.

How can I argue fairly?

Arguing in relationships is natural and healthy, and it is sometimes necessary to work out issues and misunderstandings. A good argument can be beneficial to a relationship. However, it is important to communicate effectively during arguments, and to avoid certain counterproductive behaviors and practices.

Approach arguments with a mindset geared toward understanding and resolution. Fighting fairly involves focusing on understanding what the other is trying to say and on conveying your own message, rather than on reacting emotionally or manipulating the emotions of the other party.

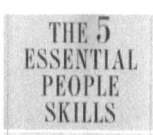

Fear not those who argue but those who dodge.

Dale Breckenridge Carnegie
(1888–1955)

You should set and agree to rules outside of the argument, and then do your best to stay within the preset boundaries while you are arguing. Ground rules may include things such as allowing one party to call a time out when the argument gets too heated, limiting the subject matter, taking turns, speaking, placing restrictions on the type of language used, and/or placing a time limit on the argument.

Inviting outside opinions can complicate matters and demean the validity of the argument. Do not involve others unless you need an unbiased third party to mediate.

In order to argue fairly, you need to leave out references to past arguments that have nothing to do with the present. If you have an unresolved issue that does not pertain to the argument, bring it up at a later time and not in the midst of an argument.

Money talks... but does it tell the truth?

Herb Cohen
(1932-2010)

It is not fair to treat every issue with the same amount of intensity. Make sure the nature of the argument suits the issue you are arguing over. For example, an argument regarding laundry on the floor does not warrant the same passion as an argument over serious financial matters.

Enter each argument with a specific purpose in mind, and end the argument when the issue has been sufficiently discussed.

Chapter 11

Be calm in arguing;
for fierceness makes error a fault, and truth discourtesy.

George Herbert
(1593 –1633)
Welsh born English poet, orator, and Anglican priest.

I never make the mistake of arguing with people for whose opinions I have no respect.

Edward Gibbon
(1737 – 1794)
English historian and Member of Parliament. His most important work, *The History of the Decline and Fall of the Roman Empire*, was published in six volumes between 1776 and 1788. The *Decline and Fall* is known for the quality and irony of its prose, its use of primary sources, and its open criticism of organized religion.

Argue fairly by allowing yourself time to formulate thoughtful replies before responding. Additionally, allow breaks in your speech, so that the other person can respond or ask for clarification.

Name calling, threats, and character bashing only escalate the arguing in relationships; they do nothing to aid in reaching a positive resolution.

Arguing in relationships should never turn to physical violence, or even threats of violence. If the argument begins to take on a violent nature, then it is time for a "time out."

It is okay to take a break from the argument if you or the other person feels that emotions are getting in the way of effective communication. Discuss when and where the argument will reconvene before stepping away for a breather.

Remember to acknowledge attempts to end an argument constructively. Pay close attention to signals that the other person is ready to call a truce, or that a suitable understanding has been reached. In order to argue fairly, you must also be willing to end the argument justly.

Can I control anger outbursts?

Life is filled with situations that can lead you to want to lose your temper and unleash havoc. However, learning to control yourself when you are about to have a tantrum is an important part of anger management and will ensure that your stress levels are reduced. It will also improve your relationships with family, friends, and colleagues.

NEGOTIATE

Lawyer, professor, author, and defender of human rights, this statesman served as Prime Minister of Canada for fifteen years. Lending substance to the phrase "the style is the man", he has imparted, both in his and on the world stage, his quintessentially personal philosophy of modern politics.

Order of Canada citation

The past is to be respected and acknowledged, but not to be worshipped. It is our future in which we will find our greatness.

The Right Honourable
Pierre Elliott Trudeau

Artist: Myfanwy Spencer Pavelic - House of Commons, Heritage Collection

Chapter 11

I learned both as a performer on stage and as a lawyer in court.
You gotta know when to sit down and shut up!

TSufit

Every time you get angry, you poison your own system.

Alfred Armand Montapert
He wrote the book *The Supreme Philosophy of Man: The Laws of Life*.

If you feel that you are about to lose your temper, try to focus and remain grounded by using deep breathing or counting to ten silently to get your brain thinking rationally. Tell yourself that you are not going to explode and repeat, "I am not going to lose it" several times over, so that the message sinks in.

When you are in a situation that makes you angry, or you are in disagreement with someone, try sincerely to listen to the other person and empathize with him or her. Our sensibility to empathize with others is critical in being able to listen well; if you are not able to empathize, you are not really able to hear. Try to understand the conflict from the other person's point of view; people will value and respect you for listening to them.

If you are in disagreement with someone, try not to take it personally. When you take something that someone else has said personally, you lose all form of objectivity. It is critical that you be able to identify if you are taking it personally. Then you have a choice about how you want to respond.

Try to stay objective about the situation, and this will help you not to become angry. Objectivity is an indicator of maturity and helps you to have much healthier relationships.

People with anger management problems tend to react to situations immediately, without taking the time to consider their reactions. If you feel as if you are about to explode or lose your temper, try to take a moment to think and reflect before you react. Use this time to think about what the consequences of an angry outburst will be. Waiting before responding is a very successful indicator that you are managing your anger. You will feel really liberated, and the whole process of managing anger becomes fun.

Know that anger is usually about misplaced expectations: you expected a person to act one-way, and he or she did something else. Alternatively, you expected one outcome from a situation, and the result was a very different outcome. When you put it in perspective, anger becomes much easier to deal with. So what it boils down to is that you need to deal with people or situations without expectations of behavior or outcome. If you do this, and you will generally avoid the anger and disappointment to begin with.

Let reason and reputation guide you, not passion and feeling wounded. In addition, learn the difference between the angry expression of your opinions or issues and assertiveness. Many people never learn this and continue to think that yelling, cursing and blowing their tops mean they are asserting themselves. It is not; it is reacting in a heated fashion and not using reasoned discussion.

Remember that if you have trouble managing this distinction and your anger, seek professional counseling, or join an anger management group to learn coping techniques and to undo bad habits.

How can I handle people who are angry with me?

It can happen virtually anywhere with anyone at work with your boss, at home with your mother-in-law, or in traffic with that mad taxi driver. People start shouting at you or will not talk with you for a while; they make offensive gestures or threaten to beat you up.

How do you handle this kind of thing civilly? You must simply stay calm. Any angry person can cause a

---

Show that you care. Explaining "why" is consistent with a complimentary philosophy: *"People don't often care what you ask them to do as long as they know that you care."*

This creates a more trusting and respectful environment. It is not that they question any less, but the amount of information available to them, their ability to process it at their own pace, and the opportunity to better understand and get comfortable with what is going on around them makes people more flexible and agreeable.

Chapter 11

chemical reaction within you that could make the situation worse. Try to put yourself in the other person's shoes. Assess the reason why the person is angry at you.

What if the other party did to you what you did to them? Do not be afraid to admit you did an injustice in the past. It is an act of courage, as long as it does not become a habit. Accept the fact that this person is angry with you, regardless of whether the reason for the anger is true or not. Let the person vent. Stand back and do not get in their way. Show them you are actually listening to what they are saying. This may already be part of the solution.

Getting angry doesn't solve anything.

Grace Patricia Kelly
(1929–1982)
American actress who, in April 1956, married Rainier III, Prince of Monaco, to become Princess consort of Monaco, styled as Her Serene Highness **The Princess of Monaco**, and commonly referred to as **Princess Grace**.

Normally, people will calm down if they see you have a sincere interest in what they are saying. Communication is the keyword. Hurt feelings can make people unable to reason well. Many people react when they are angry by avoiding the person they are furious with for a while. This is not necessarily a bad thing. It gives them time to reflect and, in many cases, allows them to realize how much they care about the other person. In quicker situations, try to follow the previous steps and stretch out the time as best as you can without being obvious.

Angry people can often repeat themselves when they are not thinking rationally or think you do not get what they mean. Find a way to stop the repetition by telling them you understand, repeating what they said in another way, or by simply changing the subject slightly.

Give up for the moment if the person is still angry with you even though you think it is not your fault, and you have tried to tell the person that. If it is a stranger, you might tell him or her you are sorry in any case and just move on. It is more useful and easier to educate people you know rather than a stranger you might not ever see again. In quicker situations, this may very well be the only option. Sometimes, there is nothing you can do.

Remember that giving an apology may help if the person seems to blame you. "Kill them with kindness". It is hard to continue being angry with someone who is agreeing with you sincerely. Furthermore, do not resort to violence! This can lead to legal action, and that is only good for lawyers and nobody else. If you suspect aggressive behavior from the angry person, step back. Be ready to defend yourself or to back away. Your safety comes above getting your way.

What should I consider?
Empathize with the other person's feelings and share your own; explicitly identify the underlying needs that you are each trying to fulfill; and then request what you would like the other person to do.

Remember that this shifts the conversation from "*who's right and who's wrong*", or from demanding that the other person back down, to getting what you each really want.

Recommended Reading & References
We suggest consulting the works identified below in order to learn more about the particulars contained in this chapter.

COHEN, Herb. YOU CAN NEGOTIATE ANYTHING.
Bantam Book. ISBN 0-553-23455-2.

COHEN, Herb. NEGOTIATE THIS!
Warner Books. ISBN 0-446-52973-7.

HINDLE, Tim. NEGOTIATING SKILLS.
Fenn Publishing. ISBN 1-55168-172-2.

Opinion has caused more trouble on this little earth than plagues or earthquakes.

François-Marie Arouet de Voltaire

Artist: Catherine Lusurier (vers 1753-1781) ;
d'après Nicolas de Largillière (1656-1746)

CHAPTER 12

DISAGREE

Accepting and embracing disagreement is difficult for some people who seek harmony and cooperation all the time. However, without dissent and differing opinions, the world would be a very bland and conformist place indeed.

Embracing disagreement is a valuable way of learning new ideas, tempering your own ideas into workable outcomes, and reaching solutions that everyone can benefit from.

Sometimes disagreement can lead to conflict, but it can also lead to discussion and learning. Remember that disagreement does not equal conflict.

Recognize that it is important to exercise an open mind. Ask a lot of questions. Try to understand why and how the person drew the conclusion that you disagree with. You might find he or she has experienced things you have not, and those experiences can shed light on your own beliefs.

To prevent the discussion from escalating into any kind of argument, communicate empathetically by stating observations, feelings, needs, and requests in that order.

Somewhere in there, be sure to thank the other person for expressing his or her opinion. Disagreement means that the person you are dealing with is bringing a different perspective into the mix and offering you a chance to broaden your horizons.

You can appreciate someone's viewpoint without agreeing with it. If the discussion drags on in a stalemate of sorts, it is probably better to move on

The people to fear are not those who disagree with you, but those who disagree with you and are too cowardly to let you know.

Napoléon Bonaparte
(1769-1821)
He was born in Corsica to parents of noble Genoese ancestry, and trained as an artillery officer in mainland France.

Chapter **12**

We may disagree on some things, but we can do so without being disagreeable.

Christine O'Grady Gregoire
(1947 -)
22nd and current Governor of the state of Washington.

An argument is a connected series of statements intended to establish a definite proposition.

The Python troupe
in 1969.
On Arguments.

and talk about something that you do agree on. Know when to agree to disagree.

Remember that you must confront the problem, not the person. Embrace the other person's point of view and actively seek for a solution. Emphasize the reconciliation. It is not about winning or getting your demand met. It is about reconciling the relationship. If you have to express disagreement, do not become a passive person.

How to argue in a positive way?

It can be difficult for people to get their points across without hurting one another in the process. Arguing can either be a good way to get to know a person better or, sometimes, it can lead to the end of your relationship.

Try to be more flexible. You should never stick to your opinion. Instead, listen carefully to what the other person has to say. Be more understanding.

Everyone goes through some tough days, when he or she is not in the mood to talk, smile, or even listen to you.

However, this is okay if it does not become a habit of course. Give the other person some space. Tomorrow, things will be better. Do not characterize everything a person says. Instead, agree with him or her, showing that you like his or her idea.

First, take things on one at a time. It is also a good idea to plan ahead, so if you must argue you are prepared.

Secondly, value the argument by listening to what the other person has to say. Try not to become angry, but

DISAGREE

I like to listen. I have learned a great deal from listening carefully. Most people never listen.

Ernest Miller Hemingway
(1899 –1961)
American author and journalist. His economical and understated style had a strong influence on 20th-century fiction, while his life of adventure and his public image influenced later generations.

Change happens by listening and then starting a dialogue with the people who are doing something you don't believe is right.

Dame Jane Morris Goodall
(1934 –)
British primatologist, ethologist, anthropologist, and UN Messenger of Peace. Considered to be the world's foremost expert on chimpanzees.

just listen quietly until it is your turn to speak. Do not try to cut off or interrupt the other person. When it is your turn to speak, use your words to convey your feelings, not your tone. This makes the other person feel as if he or she is not at fault, and so the person does not have to become defensive. Try to choose your words carefully. Remember that you are trying to express to another person what it is that you are thinking and feeling. You have to convey that with your words.

Thirdly, respect what the other person has to say. If you do not like it, that does not matter. The person has a right to an opinion and you should respect it, whether you agree with it or not. Indeed, if opinions were truly subjective and never wrong, there would be no reason to debate in the first place.

Fourthly, keep the dialogue going, with each person taking turns, speaking and saying what he or she feels and thinks in the way described above. You will both eventually understand what the other is trying to say, and you will both see a clearer picture of the other's feelings. However, never let him or her take advantage of you.

Everything has its limits.

Remember that sometimes one of you may need a few minutes alone to absorb what has been said. That is okay. If the other person asks for a few minutes alone, you should respect that and agree upon a time to continue the conversation. If you need a few minutes, you should be granted the same respect. Recognize that people can be good friends, although they have different opinions. You should also avoid arguing about politics or religion, unless you are very close to the other person and you know

Chapter 12

that the person will respect your opinion. Most people cannot agree on these topics.

How can I defuse an argument?

At some point, most people have been involved in a flaming row: each of you convinced the other was wrong, and neither of you backing down. You tried everything: ironclad logic, tearful manipulations, shouting louder and longer than the other person, and neither side budged. So, what can we do to defuse an argument?

Beginnings are always messy.
John Galsworthy (1867–1933) English novelist and playwright. Notable works include *The Forsyte Saga* (1906–1921) and its sequels, *A Modern Comedy* and *End of the Chapter*. He won the Nobel Prize in Literature in 1932.

People's higher reasoning abilities shut down when they are angry. If either you or the other person is hot with anger, take a few quiet minutes to cool off, half an hour or more if necessary.

Find out what the other person wants you to hear. You do not have to agree with it. Many arguments go on unpleasantly and without progress because each side is trying to be heard but neither side is listening. By listening, you break the deadlock.

Summarize your understanding of the other person's position by stating it in your own words, and ask if your understanding is accurate. You create an opportunity to correct misunderstanding, and if you do understand correctly, the other person now sees this.

Making an honest effort to understand show's good faith. The heat of an argument often derives from each party doubting that the other is acting in good faith.

Now, ask the other person if he or she is willing to summarize your position. If the person cannot, or he or she has not heard it yet, ask if the person would be willing to listen to what you have to say now.

Phrase your request in a way that avoids blaming or shaming the other person for misunderstanding you. You can do this by wording it so you are the one responsible for communicating your point, rather than making the other person responsible for understanding you.

After people listen and confirm understanding, most arguments dissolve immediately; there was no actual disagreement. If there is still disagreement though, take a moment to list the main points you already agree on.

The man who never alters his opinions is like standing water, and breeds reptiles of the mind.

William Blake
(1757 –1827)
English poet, painter, and printmaker. Largely unrecognised during his lifetime, Blake is now considered a seminal figure in the history of both the poetry and visual arts of the Romantic Age.

You would not be having an argument if there were not some underlying agreement. If parts of what the other person has said have moved you to change your mind, now is a good time to say so. If they have enlightened you or corrected an error of yours, thank the other person.

Do not use agreement on these other points as a tactic to logically *checkmate* the other person into admitting he or she was wrong. That is the kind of tactic that keeps the argument burning. Genuine agreement will come when and if it comes. It cannot be forced.

Now that you have clarity about each other's positions, and you know what you already agree on, take a moment to put into words the point you disagree on.

Many arguments go on fruitlessly because neither side even knows what the argument is about!

Remember that when you put the disagreement into words, either you will both agree very quickly on what the disagreement is, or you will not. If the latter, you

Chapter 12

I have never developed indigestion from eating my words.

Sir Winston Leonard Spencer-Churchill
(1874-1965)
After the Conservative Party lost the 1945 election, he became Leader of the Opposition. In 1951, he again became Prime Minister, before retiring in 1955. Upon his death, Elizabeth II granted him the honour of a state funeral, which saw one of the largest assemblies of world statesmen in history. Named the Greatest Briton of all time in a 2002 poll, Churchill is widely regarded as being among the most influential persons in British history.

open up an opportunity to hear something important that you have not heard yet. Alternatively, perhaps you will discover that there is no actual disagreement.

What can I do to resolve a disagreement?

If it is a disagreement about who should do some work, how to use limited resources, how to do something, or about whether a plan will work, you have simply to negotiate and compromise. One thing that often works is to delay in order to let your mind work on the disagreement. Now that you have each heard the other and understand the disagreement clearly, your mind has new material to work on, and this may take some time.

By now, you have probably resolved the disagreement. If not, then agree on a plan for how to resolve it. You might go to a third party, flip a coin, meet again the next day after thinking about it or check out some facts that you think will settle the matter. Agreeing to a way of resolving the disagreement often tends to be easier than resolving the disagreement directly. You can both agree right now that the way of deciding needs to be fair.

You started angry over what looked like an insoluble stalemate. You heard each other, and you broke the logjam. This calls for a ritual to mark your shared success: a laugh, if it was only a silly misunderstanding, or perhaps a handshake or a drink. Importantly, let go of being *right*. Wanting to be right in an argument is the surest way to keep it going.

People will argue about who is right and who is wrong for years if they do not decide to do something else with their energy. It is a no-win situation.

DISAGREE

Empathize with the other person's feelings and share your own, explicitly identify the underlying needs that you are each trying to fulfill, and then request what you would like the other person to do. This shifts the conversation from "who's right and who's wrong," or from demanding that the other person back down, to getting what you each really wants.

If there is anything you can possibly be sorry for, apologize for it. Even if you did not do anything wrong, you can apologize for the way your actions or words affected someone. Sometimes an apology is enough to disarm a person's ego or frustration, or perhaps it was what the person was looking for all along.

Many times, an argument will fizzle as soon as a sincere apology is given. If there is anything the person did to upset or offend you, openly forgive the person, even if he or she did not apologize. Shift the focus to something positive. Suggest doing an activity you both enjoy together.

At first, it might feel unnatural to do so, but that is residual anger...let it go. Cheer up, and before you know it, the argument will be "water under the bridge." If the other person raises his or her voice, a good tactic is to ask the person, "Why are you yelling?" It may take a second and shift his or her focus to self-perception, perhaps forcing the person to ask him-or herself, "Why am I yelling?" It will allow the conversation to proceed more smoothly.

Remember that the quickest way to end any argument is simply to agree with the other person, even if you do not. If you do not desire any further relationship with that person, that may be fine. However, fake agreement is acting in bad faith. In a

An apology? Bah! Disgusting! Cowardly! Beneath the dignity of any gentleman, however wrong he might be.

Stephen Glenn "Steve" Martin
(1945 -)
American actor, comedian, author, playwright, producer, musician, and composer.

Chapter **12**

To fake it is to stand guard over emptiness.

Arthur Herzog III (1927 –2010) American novelist, non-fiction writer, and journalist, well known for his works of science fiction and true crime books. His novels *The Swarm* and *Orca* have been made into films.

After an argument, silence may mean acceptance or the continuation of resistance by other means.

Mason Cooley (1927 –2002) American aphorist known for his witty aphorisms. One of these such aphorisms Cooley developed was "The time I kill is killing me".

relationship, fake agreement can be an avoidance tactic, especially if the issue is crucial to the relationship. It is disrespectful and plants the seeds of resentment, your own resentment, because you are not getting your needs met. If you have arrived at a stalemate situation, one way to bring it to a close is to say, "This is how I feel about the situation right now. You can either accept it or be upset about it, but I am not arguing about it anymore."

How can I stay out of an argument?

People can and do get angry or upset – with children, spouses, co-workers, etc. Once an argument begins, rarely does anything get accomplished besides both parties becoming angrier.

Would it be great just to stay out of an argument right from the start? Is the matter important enough to warrant an argument? Is it appropriate to argue about the matter, or at this time? Can anything be changed, made different, by prevailing in the argument?

If you get no answer to any of these questions, there is no point in arguing. Sometimes realizing there is no benefit to arguing is enough to eliminate the temptation to argue.

Learn to recognize when a discussion is no longer a discussion but is escalating into an argument: Raised voices, flushed face or neck, hairs on the back of your neck standing up, feeling defensive. A good mutual discussion involves both sides listening and attempting to understand each other.

These are the things that typically set a person off: someone saying I hate you, using swear words, slamming doors, making obscene gestures, attacking your beliefs, or someone rolling his or her eyes at you, etc.

If a person really wants to win an argument, he or she will push your "buttons", too. When you recognize someone approaching your buttons, think to yourself, "Ah-ha! This is becoming an argument!" And those others certainly know where to find your buttons.

Anger is never without an argument, but seldom with a good one.

Indira Priyadarshini Gandhi
(1917 –1984)
Indian politician who served as the third Prime Minister of India for three consecutive terms.

Say these words in the calmest tone of voice you can muster: "I love," "I care about," or "I respect you too much to argue with you." If you can, add: "I'll be glad to talk with you when we can both be calm."

Prepare yourself for weird looks, the same ones they usually give you behind your back and be prepared for another attempt to keep the arguing going... like "That's not true!" or "Well, I don't love you."

Try not to listen too much to the content of what the person is saying back to you. Remember that he or she is trying to push your buttons. You may even hear something like "You're so stupid you can only come up with that to say." If warranted, when both of you are calm, ask if this is a good time to finish your discussion.

Behind every argument is someone's ignorance.

Robert Charles Benchley
(1889 –1945)
American humorist best known for his work as a newspaper columnist and film actor.

If a topic needs discussion, do it. You might initiate the conversation this way: "I could see we weren't accomplishing much earlier. Is this a good time to finish our discussion?" Do not respond to the content of their remarks. The less you say, the less likely you are to get drawn into an argument.

If you become angry, know that you will not be able to think calmly, and you will probably say or do something you might regret. Words, once spoken, can never be taken back. You might sincerely

Chapter 12

apologize, but it does not erase the memory. Think before you speak.

When you see this working, you may be tempted to smile or laugh at the excitement of finally finding something that works. Do not laugh. This will just irritate the person and make it worse. Wait until you are alone, and then enjoy the moment.

A man will fight harder for his interests than for his rights.

Napoléon Bonaparte
(1769-1821)
He has become a worldwide cultural icon who symbolises military genius and political power. Martin van Creveld described him as "the most competent human being who ever lived". Since his death, many towns, streets, ships, and even cartoon characters have been named after him. He has been portrayed in hundreds of films and discussed in hundreds of thousands of books and articles.

Remember that it takes two or more to argue. By politely refusing to argue, you stay out of it. Be the adult and apologize when necessary. Walk away! Sometimes it is a simple as that. If you want to get away from it, just walk away and do not look back. Be the bigger person and have the willingness to do the right thing.

How can I walk away from a fight?

Yes, it is true fights can be a tough predicament, especially trying to get out of one. So just walk away and don't make the situation worse than it already is. Keep your distance from the person that wants to fight with you.

Talk to the person about why he or she wants to fight with you, and quickly acknowledge the person's freedom to want to fight. Back away from the troublemaker. Try to ignore any negative things he or she might have to say about you or others as you are walking away.

The important thing is to avoid a fight and not to argue about petty points you both have. Do not insult your opponent or become angry with him or her, but just be calm and try to convince the person that a fight is a bad idea. If necessary, acknowledge that the other person has a valid argument for whatever it is that is instigating the fight, even if you are in the right. Do not escalate the argument.

Keep an eye out for danger signs, such as high tension, the presence of alcohol, the (late) hour, or the person being upset over something else already, and stay away. Attempt to defuse the situation as soon as it arises. Foremost, avoid getting into situations that threaten fights.

When all else fails, remember that there is no shame in running away; you did your best. After all, the alternative could be much worse: You could die, get crippled, or end up in jail.

Remember what is important to you and how a fight could impact your life. When trying to avoid a fight, keep eye contact with the person and also try to keep an eye on the person's hands. Discuss the problem and apologize for anything you have caused, even if you are right.

While attempting to defuse the situation, it is important to keep your hands in a defensible yet non-aggressive position. Some people are scared and do not want to confront their opponent, but you should never assume your opponent will not fight.

For people unfamiliar with adrenaline bursts, walking away can be nearly impossible. People who get their adrenaline pumping regularly in a peaceful manner have more control of themselves in a stressful situation.

Regardless, try to keep a level and clear head. If you cannot get away, just tell someone that you want to get away with out giving many details. When someone threatens to kill, you just find the closest

Don't fight a battle if you don't gain anything by winning.

Erwin Johannes Eugen Rommel (1891 –1944) Popularly known as the **Desert Fox,** he was German Field Marshal of World War II. He won the respect of both his own troops and the enemies he fought.

Feedback is the breakfast of champions.

Kenneth Hartley Blanchard (1939 –) American author and management expert. His book *The One Minute Manager* (co-authored with Spencer Johnson) has sold over 13 million copies and has been translated into 37 languages.

Chapter 12

> **You have the right to disagree, but you should never be disagreeable.**
> It is good to have opinions, and it is better to be encouraged to speak your mind. Not every decision is going to be popular, but if people have a chance to voice their concerns, listen to others and their views, and to process both sides of an issue, then they just might be more accepting of decisions that are made.
> In life, people should be encouraged to participate in the discourse. Once a decision is made, everyone should be encouraged to support it.

responsible person and tell him or her. If you are in a car or vehicle, lock the doors and refuse to get out. Drive away if possible. Remember that walking away from a fight does not make you a coward; it makes you mature and a responsibly thinking person.

Be careful when and if you do try to walk away. If the other person is very angry, he or she may simply attack you from behind. When walking away, face the person who is causing you trouble in order to prevent the person from attacking you from behind while you are walking away. In addition, make sure to glance back a bit to check for potential escape routes. Do not turn your head as you look back.

In a truly dangerous situation, the most important thing is to put your ego aside. Tell him what he wants to hear.

He or she wants ego gratification, and if you can do that without taking a beating, so much the better. Think of the people who are important to you, and swallow your pride.

Sometimes the person that wants to fight with you is looking for it and will hit you anyway. Your best option is always to walk away, but if the person is a threat to you, and backing off isn't an option, you must defend yourself. Usually, the first hit can be the strongest and can also catch the person off guard. A follow up can quickly end the fight if it is well timed and delivered.

If there is an authority figure around you, do not hesitate to alert the person. Fighting is not a game and should not be used to resolve petty conflicts. Serious legal, as well as physical, consequences may result. The worst thing that could happen in a fight is that someone may end up dead. There are no rules or referees on the street, and the person who ends up dead could be you.

Remember always to keep in mind that there is no shame in turning down a fight. If other people are around, this is still the case. People calling you yellow is not something to make you have to fight. Remember that it is what you think of yourself when a fight is about to start, and when you turn it down, that is important. Besides, there is more maturity in turning down a fight.

How can I lose an argument gracefully?

Being graceful under pressure is an art, and being able to put forth a refined attitude even when someone has clearly gained the upper hand in an argument is to be admired and respected, even by the argument's winner.

At twenty a man is full of fight and hope.
He wants to reform the world.
When he is seventy he still wants to reform the world, but he knows he can't.

Rodney Dangerfield
(1921 –2004)

Bring out the objectiveness in you. Once you remove your emotional attachment to your argument and look critically at what your opponent is saying, it may be that you will begin to see things his way.

Honestly re-evaluating your position regularly will help you to realize all points of view.

In addition, losing gracefully can win you big points. If you show your willingness to hear others out without getting hostile and really, truly, honestly evaluate an argument, regardless of your initial opinions, others will come to respect your advice and counsel.

They will know you have the ability to think critically without taking things personally rather than just making up your mind and then refusing to reconsider. They will see that you do not dismiss the opinions of others and new information without even bothering to listen. If you get a reputation that once you have made up your mind it is set in stone, it makes you appear stubborn and narrow-minded.

Remember not to be condescending. People will recognize it and get annoyed with you.

How can I say no to the boss?
Give yourself some time to think about your boss's request before immediately saying no. If the request arrives via email or some other means besides a phone or in-person conversation, do not reply right away.

Trust, but verify.

Ronald Reagan (1911-2004) He was first elected to the Board of Directors of the Screen Actors Guild in 1941, serving as an alternate. Following World War II, he resumed service and became 3rd Vice-president in 1946.

Set the request aside and think about it for a while. If your boss asks you in-person or on the telephone, request some time to give it some thought and tell her you will get back to her by a specific time. Consider the request carefully to determine if it is really unreasonable and whether you have to say no.

Prepare your answer before telling your boss no. Anticipate questions she or he might ask in response to your refusal, and decide how you want to answer them. Rehearse your conversation with your boss out loud to help build your confidence before the real conversation.

Choose the right time and place to speak with your boss. Have the conversation in private if your work situation allows you to get a moment alone with your boss. Keep in mind your boss's workday pressures and work style. If she or he is a morning person be sure to speak with her before lunch.

If your boss is asking you to take on more responsibility, that shows you that she, or he has faith in your ability to do the job. Acknowledge that the boss's confidence in being able to do a good job means a lot to you before telling him or her that you feel you cannot do it. It is preferable to pay your boss a compliment while denying her, or his, request.

Assuming that you have a legitimate reason for saying no, you have no reason to lie. Most employers respect honesty in their employees and will be grateful that you answered honestly, rather than simply took on a project you could not handle. Simply tell your boss why you have to say no to the request.

Offer an alternative solution. For example, if your boss asks you to serve on a committee, suggest someone else in the company that you think may be interested and capable of serving.

Perhaps you cannot do exactly what your boss asks of you, but it might be possible for you to do some of it. For example, maybe you could offer to share the workload with someone else. Try a compromise!

Remember to stay calm and speak with an even tone when telling your boss no. Approaching your boss with your temper flaring is never a good idea. Do not turn the conversation into a gripe session, providing your boss with a laundry list of all the things you already do. Chances are good that she or he already knows what your workday involves and will be put on the defensive if you take this approach. However, if your boss asks you to do something that is illegal, you have every right to say no. Contact the proper authorities to file a complaint legally to protect yourself from a retaliatory firing.

SUCCESS THROUGH A POSITIVE MENTAL ATTITUDE
NAPOLEON HILL

Have the courage to say no.
Have the courage to face the truth.
Do the right thing because it is right.
These are the magic keys to living your life with integrity.

— William Clement Stone (1902–2002) Businessman, philanthropist, and New Thought self-help book author. Stone teamed up with Napoleon Hill to author *Success Through a Positive Mental Attitude*.

Chapter 12

He who does not trust enough, Will not be trusted.

Lao Tzu
(6th century BCE)
A central figure in Chinese culture. Both nobility and common people claim Lao Tzu in their lineage. He was honored as an ancestor of the Tang imperial family and was granted the title *Taishang xuanyuan huangdi*, meaning "Supreme Mysterious and Primordial Emperor". *Xuanyuan* and *Huangdi* are also, respectively, the personal and proper names of the Yellow Emperor. Throughout history, Laozi's work has been embraced by various anti-authoritarian movements.

Everyone is entitled to his own opinion, but not his own facts.

Daniel Patrick Moynihan
(1927 –2003)
American politician and sociologist.

How can I form an opinion?

Most of us enter a number of discussions each day where ideas are floated around, topics are debated, and controversial issues are discussed.

To have a solid basis for your opinions on these issues and topics, you should know how to form an opinion on the subject, and here are a few steps which may help.

Choose the subject, or issue, you feel the need to have an opinion about. Opinions come in many levels of importance. Look at the process of forming an opinion as an internal argument with yourself, a mental debate, so to speak. This means looking at all sides of the issue, pro and con.

You may be satisfied to read only one article at an online website, or you may research for hours, but until you understand all the sides of this hypothetical argument, your opinion should not become a conviction. Talk to other people, get their opinions on the subject, and weigh the reasons they feel as they do. Be careful not to get a one-sided view. Listen to discussions, debates, and even arguments.

Opinions on topics of social significance generate public debate everywhere you go, from the editorial pages of newspapers, to national television news, and to many points in between. Find out what recognized experts and professionals have to say about the subject.

The man on the street does not always have access to all the pertinent information on issues such as homeland security, the stock market, or major health issues. The man on the street will usually have an opinion though, if he is aware of the issue.

DISAGREE

Talk about the issue or subject with your friends. Friends often share your view about many social or local issues, and if they have formed a solid opinion, they may have reasons for what they believe, which will help you form your own.

Learn to throw out sensationalized or motive generated stories on the subject. If you only read the headlines on an issue, especially in a biased media outlet, you will be led into thinking the way that that media outlet wants you to think. Often, headlines are worded in such a way as to grab attention, and only in the fine print will you find any reasoned, substantially accurate information on the topic.

Too often we... enjoy the comfort of opinion without the discomfort of thought.

John Fitzgerald "Jack" Kennedy (1917-1963) He was the first of six presidents to have served in the U.S. Navy, and one of the enduring legacies of his administration was the creation in 1961 of another special forces command, the Navy SEALS, which Kennedy enthusiastically supported.

Ask yourself if what you hear or read is reasonable, logical, and realistic. If someone says that in his or her opinion a certain stock will triple in value in a short time, you may obviously question the person's opinion. Often, this "shading" of facts is much more subtle, so educating yourself is the best foundation for forming a coherent view on a topic.

Decide what your opinion is on a subject, be willing to state it, defend it, and stand by it, but have an open mind unless you are thoroughly convinced and willing to argue your point of view. Keep your opinion to yourself until you reach the point described above, unless you are asked for it, or choose to reveal it in friendly discussion.

Remember that when talking about controversial subjects such as abortion, religion, and politics, it is important to realize that there are many different paths to the same conclusion. In addition, if you feel strongly about something it is O.K. to state that you do not agree with the other party and to take a break from that topic for a while. Chances are you can

Chapter 12

It is easier to get forgiveness than it is to secure permission.

Jesuit saying
The **Society of Jesus** is a Catholic male religious order that follows the teachings of the Catholic Church. The members are called **Jesuits** and are also known colloquially as "God's Marines".

We have no right to express an opinion until we know all of the answers.

Kurt Donald Cobain
(1967 –1994) American singer-songwriter, musician, and artist, best known as the lead singer and guitarist of the grunge band Nirvana.

come to an agreement based on factual evidence. Finally, also be open to involving a third party in the discussion.

How can I avoid misspeaking?

"I misspoke" is often heard on the news being used by politicians or government officials to explain away guilt when they have been accused of lying. Misspeaking can also be an unintentional act committed if one does not have all the facts, but it still creates an uncomfortable social situation. Learn how to avoid misspeaking, so your integrity is never questioned.

Avoid misspeaking by getting all the facts about the topic you will discuss before you talk about it. Being well informed will help you convey your message or position clearly, and then you will be able to defend yourself if someone accuses you of lying or misspeaking.

Prevent misspeaking or being accused of misspeaking by knowing who could be listening when you talk. You are less likely to be accused of misspeaking by trusted colleagues or friends and family members, but it would be wise to speak more carefully around competitors or individuals who have reasons to try to damage your reputation.

People who misspeak often use complicated language or complex technical terminology to cover up their errors or fallacies, so use ordinary language and a straightforward approach. Keep misspeaking from occurring by using simple speech that cannot be misconstrued and by getting right to the point you are trying to make.

Prevent accusations of misspeaking by backing up what you say with trustworthy documented sources. Utilize quotes or statistics from experts on the topic you will discuss and research references or case studies that back up what you're saying. You cannot be accused of lying if you have documented proof.

Commit to the facts that you know for sure when you are speaking, and focus more on them than on what you are unsure about. If you stick to what you know, you will be less likely to misspeak about things of which you are not as knowledgeable.

Everything we hear is an opinion, not a fact. Everything we see is a perspective, not the truth.

Marcus Aurelius
(121 –180 AD)
Roman Emperor from 161 to 180 AD. He ruled with Lucius Verus as co-emperor from 161 until Verus' death in 169. He was the last of the "Five Good Emperors", and is also considered one of the most important Stoic philosophers.

Avoid misspeaking by being you and not trying to impress anyone. It is important to act in a natural and confident way regarding your knowledge or opinions when you speak. If you look as if you know what you are talking about, people will be more likely to believe that you really do, and that you are telling the truth.

Remember that if you only talk about the things you know to be true and have proof of being accurate, you will not be misspeaking. Avoid elaborating on topics you are less knowledgeable about because vague statements could be construed as misspeaking. If you only discuss what you know for sure, you will not misspeak.

How can I show empathy?

You are talking to someone, and suddenly he or she tells you something emotional, such as "I just lost my job." How do you respond? Respond with empathy, and you will greatly improve your relationship with the other person. However, if you respond as if you do not really care, you could ruin the relationship. Empathy, literally "in feeling," is the ability to appreciate, understand, and accept another person's emotions.

Chapter **12**

"Reasonable accommodation" means necessary and appropriate modification and adjustments not imposing a disproportionate or undue burden, where needed in a particular case, to ensure to persons with disabilities the enjoyment or exercise on an equal basis with others of all human rights and fundamental freedoms.

Jean Charest, P.C. MNA
29th Premier of Quebec
Deputy Prime Minister of Canada
from June 25 until November 3, 1993.

Photo: Assemblée Nationale du Québec.

DISAGREE

Anyone who has experienced a certain amount of loss in their life has empathy for those who have experienced loss.

Anderson Hays Cooper
(1967 -)
American journalist, author, and television personality.

The great gift of human beings is that we have the power of empathy.

Mary Louise "Meryl" Streep
(1949 -)
American actress who has worked in theatre, television, and film. She is widely regarded as one of the most talented film actresses of all time.

Showing empathy genuinely is one of the most important interpersonal skills that anyone must master. Listen attentively to what the other person is saying. This will allow you to absorb what he or she says and be able to respond appropriately. Eliminate distractions: put down the book you are reading; turn off the TV; etc. Focus all your attention on what the other person says.

Pay attention not only to the words spoken, but also to the way these words are communicated - the tone, inflection, mannerism, etc.

Establish comfortable eye contact. Let your body language convey empathy and maintain good body posture. Do not fidget or do other things that show disinterest, but rather direct 100% of your attention toward the other person.

Reflecting upon what the other person has said helps to show that you are understanding and interpreting what was said. Give the other person a chance to elaborate further on the feelings being experienced, and demonstrate your concern for the other person. For example, say something such as, "Sorry to hear you just lost your job; I see this is upsetting to you", "you look a little sad right now", or "this is hard to talk about, huh?"

Validate the other's emotions; immediately agree with what the other person just said. Validating, or justifying the other person's emotions, helps to convey your acceptance and respect for the feelings the other person is experiencing. For example, "I can understand why you would be upset under these circumstances", or "Anyone would find this difficult," or "Anyone would have felt the same way", or "Your reactions are totally normal".

Chapter 12

Offering personal support goes beyond mere words to enhance rapport by letting the other person know that you want to help. For example, "I want to help in any way I can; please let me know what I can do to help."

A sense of partnership helps the other person to feel that he or she can be part of the solution, and that you are willing to be there to help. For example, you can say, "Let us work this out together" or "After we talk a little more, perhaps we can work out some solutions that may help."

Showing respect by focusing on the positive aspects further enhances rapport and fosters effective coping skills. For example, you can say, "Despite your feeling so bad, you are still coping so well. That is quite an accomplishment. I am very impressed by how well you are coping with the uncertainty."

Remember to make sure you show empathy genuinely. The other person can see through insincerity, and your relationship may be harmed by it. Do not be discouraged if you do not succeed in empathizing with people immediately. Like anything else, showing empathy effectively takes practice to make it a habit. Avoid "why" questions. Sometimes this comes across as accusatory. Do not tell the person what he or she should have done or should do. Often, he or she already knows this.

What should I consider?

When you are mad at someone, it is hard to see his or her side of the story. And for some people, it can be very difficult and can lead to them losing friends. Empathy is an important thing to have, so with a few easy steps, you can put things in perspective.

When you start to develop your powers of empathy and imagination, the whole world opens up to you.

Susan Sarandon
(1946 -)
American actress. She has worked in movies and television since 1969 and won an Academy Award for Best Actress for her performance in the 1995 film *Dead Man Walking*.

DISAGREE

The state has no business in the bedrooms of the nation.

Joseph Philippe
Pierre Yves
Elliott Trudeau
(1919 –2000)
15th Prime Minister of Canada.
Established the Charter of Rights and Freedoms within Canada's constitution.

When you get in an argument, take a deep breath and count to ten. Do not resort to violence or screaming. Do whatever you can to calm down. Put yourself in that person's shoes. Think about all the hardships that the other person has been through.

Then think about exactly what you are arguing about. Try as hard as possible to imagine why the person thinks that what he or she is saying is true. If you feel disagreement, find a way to go outside, go home, or move at least thirty feet away from the person. Talk to each other again when you both are calmer. This will help you sort all this out.

Remember that no argument is worth losing a friend.

Recommended Reading & References
We suggest consulting the works identified below in order to learn more about the particulars contained in this chapter.

BERNSTEIN, Albert J. Ph.D. DINOSAUR BRAINS: DEALING WITH ALL THOSE IMPOSSIBLE PEOPLE AT WORK.
Wiley & Sons ISBN0-471-61808-X.

ELGIN, Suzette Haden. Ph.D. HOW TO DISAGREE WITHOUT BEING DISAGREEABLE. MJF Books. ISBN-10: 1-567731-739-1.

LIEBERMAN, David J. HOW TO CHANGE ANYBODY.
Audio renaissance. ISBN 1-59397-803-8.

LIEBERMAN, David J. YOU CAN READ ANYONE. Never be Fooled, Lied to, or Taken Advantage of Again.
Audi Coach. ISBN 1-59659-153-6.

SELLS, Scott P. Ph.D. PARENTING YOUR OUT-OF-CONTROL TEENAGER. St-Martin's Press. ISBN 0-312-26629-4.

I have found that being honest is the best technique I can use. Right up front, tell people what you're trying to accomplish and what you're willing to sacrifice to accomplish it.

Lido Anthony "Lee" Iacocca

Reference: www.leeiacocca.com/

CHAPTER 13

GOOD CITIZEN

We all want to be known as good citizens. Being a good citizen is all up to you.

What do you do best? Help out. You can help out in almost any way! Do you have a green thumb? If so, then you can take the time to help plant things at your community garden. Do you have a lot of clothes in your closet that you do not wear anymore? Give them to charity! Do you have $10 you do not plan to spend? Donate it to an animal shelter, school, or hospital! There are so many things you can do! There has to be something for you.

You cannot give people dirty looks and be rude if you want to be a good citizen. Smile and treat everyone with respect. If you see trash laying around, do not just stare at it and walk by or step over it. One day, get a shopping bag and pick up all the trash that you see.

Even if you are just encouraging the little seven-year-old down the street to learn to ride a skateboard...it is still giving encouragement and being a good citizen.

Would you do anything that would ruin your or anyone's reputation? You cannot be known as a good citizen if you have done something stupid that would make you known as a bad person.

Remember that this can be done in so many ways that there has to be something you can do. You can donate canned food to the homeless, or you can even stuff teddy bears and give them to children for Christmas.

True leadership is often the antithesis of popularity.

Martin Brian Mulroney,
PC, CC, GOQ,
(1939 –)
18th Prime Minister of Canada. His tenure as Prime Minister was marked by the introduction of major economic reforms, such as the Canada-U.S. Free Trade Agreement.

Chapter **13**

How can I be a world citizen?

We are in a global age. The world has become a global village due to technological advances in communications and other spheres of human endeavor.

In a progressive country change is constant; change is inevitable.

Benjamin Disraeli, 1st Earl of Beaconsfield (1804 –1881) British Prime Minister, parliamentarian, Conservative statesman, and literary figure. He is exceptional among British Prime Ministers for having gained equal social and political renown.

Being a world citizen can foster international cooperation on all levels, uniting people and making the world a better and safer place for all; the mentality of *us against them* has caused untold, useless suffering worldwide. Is it a utopian vision of society? Let's follow the steps, and find out!

Understand that the world does not encompass only your home village, town, city, state, or country. Recognize that events happening on the other side of the world can have a real impact on your life, things such as a war, global warming, or an economic recession.

Learn about other countries and cultures. Get interested in international news. Be curious about the life and struggles of other people and cultures, and find out how you can help others. Participate in international discussions, such as those on the BBC, CNN, CBC, or the Internet.

You can also learn some new major language or languages. Be tolerant and respectful of other people's cultures. Resist, react, repeal, and speak against xenophobia and intolerance in all their forms. Oppose racism, tribalism, regionalism, religious bias, and all kinds of segregation of any kind. Value each human life as you value your own.

Consider everyone on his or her own merits, and repeal unfounded popular myths about certain nations and people.

GOOD **CITIZEN**

Democracy is a difficult kind of government. It requires the highest qualities of self-discipline, restraint, a willingness to make commitments, and sacrifices for the general interest...

John F. Kennedy
Speech in Dublin (28 June, 1963)

Photo: Alfred Eisenstaedt - White House Press Office.

Chapter 13

Education is a better safeguard of liberty than a standing army.

Edward Everett
(1794 –1865) American politician and educator from Massachusetts. Everett was one of the great American orators of the antebellum and Civil War era. He is often remembered today as the featured orator at the dedication ceremony of the National Cemetery in Gettysburg in 1863, where he spoke for over two hours — immediately before President Abraham Lincoln delivered his famous, two-minute Gettysburg Address.

Do not say, for example, that Americans are arrogant, Africans are ignorant, Muslims are evil, atheists are Satanists, or that Germans are Nazis, that the Jews killed Jesus, or that Foreigners increase crime, etc.

Teach other people in normal conversation. For example, if someone says something ignorant, simply mention that he or she should not generalize. There is no reason to include a whole race. And do not refer to your special group if you intend your message to be universal.

Find the best way you can to help in a concrete way. Be active and contribute. Learn from wise people and redistribute your knowledge. Learn about the past in order to help build a better future.

Remember that to become a world citizen requires a conscious effort. Not all people consider themselves world citizens. They consider the world to be the next visible hill and taunt you as a stranger. Be understanding. It is a matter of education and culture. In addition, you will have to give up racism.

How can I be nice?
You have been told to be nice since you were a child. Even so, what exactly does that mean for an adult?

Nice may be a vague term to you if your parents never gave you a definition of it. Were your parents nice to you? Being nice to people, especially your friends, can "pay off" big time.

A smile will let people know that you are pleasant. If you smile at someone, look him or her in the eye. For the most part, if you smile at someone, the person will not do anything but smile back. If the person does not, then maybe he or she is just having a bad day.

> **Thank those that help you.** Manners do matter, and those that have made the effort to help you remember if you thanked them or not. This can have far-reaching impacts on your career. Your biggest supporters (and this is reinforced by taking the time to thank them) can open doors you cannot even imagine... both now and in the future.

It is up to you to set the mood of the encounter. Make it happy by being the first to smile. Normally, making faces at or offering moody looks to someone is not nice.

When you are walking past someone, a stranger, try to acknowledge the person's presence with a simple "Hello" or "Hi!", or even just a wave or a nod in their direction. Adding a smile to this can make it all the more friendly.

Take the time to ask someone how things are going in his life, without being nosy or intrusive. If he seems resistant to talking, just let him know that you are always around to talk to, and that you want him to be all right. He will understand that you are trying to care for him and not assume that you are a prying person.

Listen when other people are talking to you. It is not nice just to ignore other people's opinions and stories. If you find that someone is becoming rude or pushy, acknowledge his or her opinion, issue a compliment, and excuse yourself politely.

Always say, "please," "thank you", and "you're welcome." You can also address people by "Sir" or "Ma'am," depending on the occasion. Be patient, observant, and considerate. Treat people with respect. Even if you do not particularly like someone at first, he or she could end up being a really interesting and kind person.

Do not forget "Excuse me!" instead of "MOVE!"

Remember that people are not dogs or the ground you spit on. They are living beings like you. If you are respectful of another person, that person will usually

Chapter 13

Be nice to people on your way up because you meet them on your way down.

James Francis "Jimmy" Durante
(1893–1980)
Italian American singer, pianist, comedian, and actor.

act the same way. Why would she be mean to you when you are being a good person?

Do not be negative or critical. Keep looking for the positive in any given situation. Cheer others up. There are two sides to things: the positive side and the negative side. Mention the positive side of the thing first before mentioning the negative side - and in a nice way.

The key to being nice is remembering that you are not "better" than someone else. You are an individual, but everybody has his or her struggles, and being nice to one another makes life better for everyone. Do not brag or have a big ego. Everybody is equal. So, be positive and "bright."

If you see someone struggling or doing something difficult, offer to help, even by doing something as simple as carrying a bag of groceries, or holding the door for someone. You can also be nice to the community and the world by volunteering.

Do not be nice as a means to an end. If you just want to be nice so that you can gain preferential treatment, it is quite the opposite of being nice. In fact, it is deceptive, shallow, and cruel. Be nice because you want to look back on your life and know that you were a nice person, no matter what. Be nice because you feel like you willingly want to.

Do not talk about other people, and do not be a "back stabber". Try to be nice to everyone and do not pick favorites. And do not be two-faced or talk about people who trust you. Do not ever gossip about other people you do not like. Just think about all the positive things about them and the negative opinions

> There are three faithful friends - an old wife, an old dog, and ready money.
>
> Benjamin Franklin
> (1706-1790)
> His colorful life and legacy of scientific and political achievement and his status as one of America's most influential Founding Fathers have seen Franklin honored on coinage and money; warships; the names of many towns, counties, educational institutions, namesakes, and companies; and more than two centuries after his death, countless cultural references.

> Do good to your friends to keep them, to your enemies to win them.
>
> Benjamin Franklin
> (1706-1790)

about them will slowly fade, leaving you no excuses to gossip.

Always try to make friends with people who are nice. If you make friends with those who are rude, that will make you look rude - because you associate yourself with rudeness. If you have friends who are like you, your life will be much better. However, you can try to be nice to a rude friend. Maybe that friend will start to be nice too.

Those little, everyday things, such as holding a door for a teacher you do not know, or smiling at someone who is not always nice to you, those little tiny things that do not seem to matter much are, in the end, very important. They help you appear to be a much nicer person and they also help you show that you sincerely and genuinely care.

If your friends give you a present, say something honestly positive about it even if you do not like it, and make sure you do not tell anyone that you do not like it. Doing so may lead to a fall out with the person, and make sure that if you have not gotten them presents, do not tell them so in a horrible voice. I would not mention it at all!

If someone is being mean to you, still be nice to him or her. Do not bring yourself down to the other person's level by being mean to him or her. The person might "get your drift" and stop being unkind to you. Be mature!

If you and your brother are fighting, do not beat him up to the point where he starts crying. Be nice to him and let him have his way.

Chapter **13**

Old friends pass away, new friends appear. It is just like the days. An old day passes, a new day arrives. The important thing is to make it meaningful: a meaningful friend - or a meaningful day.

The Dalai Lama
(17th century)
He is a high lama in the Gelug or "Yellow Hat" branch of Tibetan Buddhism.

Try to compliment people. Do not compliment the same people daily or else they will think you are trying to *butter them up* before asking for a favor. And only compliment them if you truly mean it.

Remember the *Golden Rule*: Treat others the way you want to be treated. And respect them for who they are. Do not try to change them. Even though some people may not be nice to you at first, they will probably come around eventually.

Be optimistic about everything, even when you do not particularly feel like it. Always look on the bright side! Never underestimate the power of optimism, and at the same time, you might try cracking a joke in a funny way to do something unexpected, so long as you counteract it with a lot of positive behavior as well. Funny, I find, is nice.

While being nice, do not be a total pushover. Compromise is good, but expect to be treated fairly. Do not be afraid to stand up for what is right, and do not hesitate to defend someone. If you find that you are being considerate of someone's time, but he or she is not being considerate of yours, "bow out" as respectfully as you can and "make yourself scarce."

Remember to stand up for others, and do not gossip about them. In addition, be careful about smiling or saying "Hi!" to someone with whom you have a bad rapport for... it can backfire, and the person may think you are being sly, and he or she may reply with an unkind comment.

How can I learn about other cultures?
There are a lot of ways to experience other cultures without having to take a long plane flight. You can travel via the Internet, without ever leaving your

GOOD **CITIZEN**

house and without having to go broke, and learn about other countries.

You can also visit the library and check out travel books. Reading through travel books and travel journals gives you great ideas about local and international destinations and begins to expose you to new cultures.

You could also visit nearby museums and cultural centers, especially when they are exhibiting works from other countries.

Volunteer to practice English with people in your community who speak English as a second language. In exchange for practicing English, you can ask them to help you learn more about their cultures and languages. Taking a class at your community college to learn about another culture might be a good idea, too.

Realize that if you would still like to travel, investigate exchange programs in your community. Many cities have *sister city* exchange programs for which they select young people to visit the town's sister city for a week. Other travel options include Rotary, church programs, and volunteer organizations. Many of these groups offer supervised travel and travel grants.

Remember that it is always good if you have a friend from another culture. This way, you can learn more about how people look, act, etc. in that culture. For the younger ones, make sure your parents know why you want to travel and learn more about other cultures. They might be able to help you, and, by keeping them informed, you are more likely to be able to make a trip.

A people without the knowledge of their past history, origin and culture is like a tree without roots.

Marcus Mosiah Garvey, Jr.
(1887 –1940)
Jamaican publisher, journalist, entrepreneur, and orator who was a staunch proponent of the Black Nationalism and Pan-Africanism movements, to which end he founded the Universal Negro Improvement Association and African Communities League.

The highest possible stage in moral culture is when we recognize that we ought to control our thoughts.

Charles Robert Darwin
(1809 –1882)
Proposed the scientific theory that the branching pattern of evolution resulted from a process that he called natural selection.

Chapter 13

How can I preserve my culture?

Culture is an important factor in everyone's life. It is the foundation of a prosperous lifetime. In order to keep it alive, doing your part to preserve it is extremely necessary.

Speak your mother language. People from your country will respect you. As well, you will have a chance to get a high-paying job because of your language skills, and your parents will be very proud of you. Another benefit of being able to speak your mother language is that when you go outside, nobody will be able to eavesdrop on your private conversations.

No people come into possession of a culture without having paid a heavy price for it.

James "Jim" Baldwin
(1886 -)
He was an American football player, track athlete, coach of football, basketball, and baseball, and college athletics administrator in the United States.

It is never too late to whip up some recipes from your mother's cookbook. Bringing your native food home reminds you about where you came from and helps you appreciate those old memories. If you cannot find any ethnic recipes in your family's cookbook, or on the Internet, going to a local cultural restaurant occasionally is the next-best option.

Religion is the most vital key factor in any culture. It brings you inner peace. Going to a mosque, synagogue, church, or temple is a great way to keep your cultural spirit alive. Read your holy book. Try to understand it by buying books with footnotes in them. See how your culture relates to your religion. You will find that they both have a few things in common.

Attending your country's national festivals will help you see more of your traditions. This will also help you make new friends. If you live in a foreign country, having a gathering with your ethnic community is a fabulous idea.

GOOD CITIZEN

Remember that people who abandon their culture usually have an unpleasant life. Their own people are not satisfied with them. If you have more than one cultural background, blend some of your ideas and beliefs together. At least you will be preserving some of the key factors. Do not forget that extreme cultural bias can lead to oppression and violence. Be proud of your culture, but let others be proud of theirs, too.

How can I be honest?

Webster's dictionary says that trust is *the absolute certainty in the trustworthiness of another* and *absolute confidence in the truthfulness of another*. Where do you find the word *truth* in the dictionary? Right after the word trust!

If you tell the truth, you don't have to remember anything.

Mark Twain
(1835 –1910)
The Prince and the Pauper, despite a storyline that is omnipresent in film and literature today, was not well received. Telling the story of two boys born on the same day who are physically identical, the book acts as a social commentary as the prince and pauper switch places. Pauper was Twain's first attempt at historical fiction, and blame for its shortcomings is usually put on Twain for having not been experienced enough in English society and also on the fact that it was produced after a massive hit.

You will never regret being honest. It has been said that honesty is the best policy. It sounds like the simplest thing in the world, but being truly honest with others and with yourself can be a real challenge.

Political correctness, being sensitive about other people's feelings, and facing uncomfortable truths about yourself usually require lots of patience, vigilance and hard work.

Most of us learned to be dishonest as children. The process often began with the realization that unusual behaviors resulted in different outcomes. For example, saying certain things, or not saying certain things, garnered desirable approval and praise or undesirable disapproval and censure, if not punishment. Adopting dishonest behavior to get desired results was just a small step away.

With time, the thought processes behind such actions get so entrenched in our subconscious minds that one is not even aware of them. A time comes when

Chapter 13

Say what you mean and mean what you say.
People are fed up with half-truths and spin, which are so prevalent that people automatically discount the accuracy of what they are told. This ultimately leads to the assumption that playing fast and loose with the truth is acceptable. Well, it is not, and people need to stand for accuracy, honesty, openness, and transparency. This raises the bar on behaviors and people's expectations, and ultimately it changes everyone's behavior.
If people believe that everyone around them is being honest, then trust will grow.
People who trust one another have fewer disputes.

one loses the capacity to know when and where to draw the line and how negatively dishonesty affects our lives. Dishonesty often becomes a tool that may help us pretend that there is nothing wrong with us, or help us shift blame to others, avoiding embarrassment, distracting ourselves, minimizing conflict, and avoiding responsibility or work.

Be willing to address issues that you have been less than honest about in the past, whether you took a cookie and then denied it or blatantly lied about whose fault an automobile accident was.

While reviewing your past transgressions can create discomfort and guilt, recognizing where you have been dishonest in the past can help you identify patterns and stop them from continuing.

If you feel guilty for having been dishonest in the past, apologize to the person you lied to and/or find a creative way to make things right. Moreover, list your weakness. It may be as simple as having a tendency to make up excuses for failures, or as complicated as having a penchant for stealing.

Do not forget that dishonesty is rooted in fear, so you must look for and face those fears. By listing areas where you have a problem, and then working to deal with them, you can consciously battle these habits. If you find yourself lying because you fear disapproval from someone, for example, perhaps you need to learn how to stop being a people pleaser and be yourself.

Most importantly, admit your errors, so that you can forgive yourself and use those experiences to reinforce your determination to do better. You cannot fix what you do not acknowledge as a problem.

This may sound silly, but if you do not think honestly, you will not be honest. Prejudices and preconceived ideas can make it difficult to distinguish what the truth really is.

When you read, see, or hear something, do not make assumptions. Offer the benefit of the doubt, and be skeptical if necessary.

When you make a commitment to communicating and understanding the truth, it can be humbling to realize that most of what we think we know is actually just based on assumptions rather than facts.

Practice being honest about the simple things. This is especially important in situations where "coloring" the facts would make no difference in the world, and these situations covers a good bit of life - from speaking the truth to avoiding thoughtless acts, such as picking up someone's pencil or grabbing an apple off the neighbor's tree to snack on without thinking what you are doing.

Abraham Lincoln became famous for going to great lengths to return a few cents that did not belong to him, hence the nickname *Honest Abe*. By applying honesty to the little things, you will get in the habit of being honest in general.

We all know that being literally honest can hurt feelings and turn friendships sour. It can also be misinterpreted as criticism or a lack of support. It is very tempting to tell a *white lie* when dealing with sensitive loved ones, especially children, but you can still be honest by being creative in how you express the truth.

People do not like to feel they are being conned, and no one is going to support the career of a subordinate who is a little too secretive, a little too clever for his or her own good.
If you feel the only way to get ahead is to con the people you work for, you'd better be very good at covering yourself because over the long term there are so many different ways you can be found out.

Mark Hume McCormack
(1930 –2003)
American lawyer, sports agent for professional athletes (particularly in golf and tennis), and a prolific writer.

Chapter **13**

Find a balance between full disclosure and privacy. Just because you are honest does not mean you have to reveal all of your or anybody else's business.

There are some things that we do not talk about because it is not information that the person asking may be entitled to. On the other hand, withholding information that you know should be disclosed is lying by omission.

It is a fine thing to be honest, but it is also very important to be right.

Winston Churchill
(1874–1965)
He had been among the first to recognize the growing threat of Hitler long before the outset of the Second World War, and his warnings had gone largely unheeded.

Remember that not telling a romantic partner that you have a child, or that you have been married in the past, is objectionable as far as most people are concerned. Deciding what information an individual should or should not know is a personal decision. Just because you believe a person is better off not knowing something does not mean you are acting in the person's best interest by hiding that information. Follow your gut, and put yourself in that person's position; ask yourself: "If I was in his or her shoes, would I rightfully feel betrayed if this information wasn't shared with me at an appropriate time?"

What about imposters?

Bill George, Andrew N. McLean, and Nick Craig in *Finding Your True North, a Personal Guide* propose a definition of imposter: *Imposters frequently lack self-awareness and self-esteem. They may have little appetite for self-reflection and consequently defer personal development. They rise through the organizational ranks with a combination of cunning and aggression. Imposters use these strategies to achieve positions of powers but then have little sense of how to use that power for the good of the organization. In effect, they have been too busy besting competitors to learn how to lead. Leaders who succumb to this hazard embrace the politics of getting ahead and letting no one stand in their way.*

GOOD **CITIZEN**

He who mistrusts most should be trusted least.

Theognis of Megara
Ancient Greek poet active sometime in the sixth century BC.

Ethical problems often are the result of the way the Dinosaur Brain operates. Ethics of all kinds are based on balancing the needs of several different constituencies and deciding which is highest. When the Dinosaur Brain focuses on only one set of needs at a time, sometimes that leads to decisions that have ethical implications.

Albert J. Bernstein, Ph.D.

They are the ultimate political animals, adept at figuring out who their competitors are and then eliminating them one by one.

Remember that being honest is not easy. At its core, being truthful is difficult because it makes us vulnerable. It shows people who we really are, and that we make mistakes, which gives them a chance to criticize and reject us in a more hurtful way than if we had hidden the truth or lied to begin with. And sometimes, the truth just hurts. Although honesty develops character, as well as credibility and trust, all of which are the building blocks of high self-esteem and healthy relationships, being honest is not a goal that you can check off on a list. It is an ongoing process that will both challenge and benefit you throughout your life. Nothing is as liberating as having nothing to hide.

Can I improve my personal integrity?

Personal integrity is essential for success in life. You have likely met, at some point in your lifetime, the kind of person who made your skin crawl.

On the other hand, you may have had the pleasure of meeting the kind of person who made you feel as though he or she genuinely cared about your problem and authentically wanted to solve it.

In many cases, the professional who instantly comes across as trustworthy and honest is the one who possesses a high level of personal integrity. Increasing one's personal integrity involves bringing consistency and congruency into all areas of life.

You cannot maintain personal integrity only in part of your life. It is everywhere, or it is nowhere. Besides being truthful in your dealings with clients, you must

Chapter 13

also practice honesty in dealing with relatives, friends, neighbors, and perfect strangers.

Do what you say you will do, by when you say you will do it. Again, this cannot work in just one or two areas of your life. Personal integrity means consistency across the board. Do not over promise. Only commit to what you can actually deliver.

Donald Trump, in is book *Think Big and Kick Ass in Business and Life,* formulates a straight to the heart definition: *Your word is golden. That is another very important thing: when you shake somebody's hand, go with it. It is very important. Shaking hands with someone means you are making a deal. You are giving your word. If you back out after you have shaken hands on a deal, then people will never trust you again.*

Notice when you stray from personal integrity, and recommit to getting back on track. Set wrongs right again. Make a fresh start immediately.

It is very difficult to increase your personal integrity if you spend a lot of time with unscrupulous individuals. Strive to surround yourself with people of high integrity, and they will uplift you and support you in your quest for personal improvement.

Remember that it is impossible to maintain personal integrity on part time basis. In other words, you cannot be honest and forthcoming in your job and not in your personal relationships and still expect to maintain personal integrity. It is about demonstrating consistency across the board, especially when no one is watching. Truly great people are always striving to improve themselves and raise their level of personal integrity.

If someone knows they made a mistake and they apologize, forgive them and move on, but never trust them again.

Donald J. Trump
(1946 -)

What should I consider?

We live in a world where selfishness seems to be the rule of the day, and personal gain the objective of most relationships and endeavors. One of the most honorable character traits a citizen can develop is the ability to be loyal, whether to family, friends, an employer, or clubs and organizations to which he or she may belong. You must be willing to allow your own interests to take second place to being truly loyal to another person or cause. Loyalty is simply the act of putting someone or something else ahead of oneself.

Value loyalty above everything else.

Donald J. Trump
(1946 -)

Being loyal in a patriotic sense, as in loyal to one's country, has placed millions in harm's way in wars throughout history. The citizens who serve in the modern military are loyal to their nation, its flag, and the reason they serve. Being loyal to a friend or your own family can also require sacrifice.

To take steps toward becoming loyal, you need to recognize that it is a deliberate effort, and that to be truly loyal to someone, you have to be willing to invest yourself, your time, and your energy in the person. Take time to look at the needs of whomever will have your loyalty.

Ask yourself if to what or whom you are offering your loyalty is worthy of the investment. Is the person or organization that asks for your loyalty worthwhile? Depending on what philosophy or religion you may follow, you might find guidance there. In the Judeo-Christian religion, the order of loyalty may be summed up as *God, Family, and Country*, putting loyalty to God first, then family, and finally, to one's country.

Chapter 13

This may be most obvious in the case of employment. Being a loyal employee often creates its own rewards, with increases in pay, job security, and respect from your employer. Being a loyal employer who is willing to look after his or her employees will give your workers the incentive to be more dedicated and productive for you.

You should always structure the hierarchy of your loyalties according to your evaluation of their importance. If being loyal to a group or club causes you social ostracism or creates negative influence in your family or in a social circumstance, it may not be worthwhile to continue that loyalty.

Being loyal to a volunteer group or social organization at the expense of taking time for your family may result in suffering loss in your personal relationships. Always balance your loyalties with the day-to-day needs of your own life and your family.

Being loyal to an unappreciative person or group is not very rewarding, and although this implies a selfish motivation for your loyalty, it is a practical thing to expect the person or group to which you give your allegiance to be loyal to you in return.

Remember to be realistic in extending your loyalty and to keep in mind the costs associated with doing so. Be aware that it is not unusual to be rewarded for your loyalty and dedication with additional demands for more and more of your time and energy.

Recommended Reading & References
We suggest consulting the works identified below in order to learn more about the particulars contained in this chapter.

JENNINGS, Warren. DEVENIR UN MEILLEUR LEADER. Ce que tout leader devrait savoir.
Les Éditions Québecor. ISBN 2-7640-0858-9.

QUICK, Thomas L. UNDERSTANDING PEOPLE AT WORK.
Executive Enterprises Publications Co. ISBN 0-917386-17-5.

ROCHE, Daniel. Dossier : UNE RÉVOLUTION TOTALE.
Revue l'Histoire. N° 307, mars 2006.

SAMSON, Guy. L'ENFANT-TYRAN, SAVOIR DIRE NON À L'ENFANT-ROI.
Les Éditions. Québécor. ISBN 2-7640-0851-1.

SELLS, Scott P. Ph.D. PARENTING YOUR OUT-OF-CONTROL TEENAGER. St-Martin's Press. ISBN 0-312-26629-4.

STERNELL, Zeev. Dossier : ILS ONT INVENTÉ LA LIBERTÉ.
Revue l'Histoire. N° 307, mars 2006.

THE PHILOSOPHY BOOK.
Dorling Kindersley. ISBN 978-2-7613-4125-7.

TOUS PSYCHOLOGUES.
Dorling Kindersley. 2012. ISBN 978-2-7613-4873-7.

TREMBLAY, Jacinthe. LE MYTHE DU TRAVAIL D'ÉQUIPE.
Le quotidien La Presse, section affaires. ISSN 0317-9249.

TRUDEAU, Pierre Elliott. AGAINST THE CURRENT.
McClelland & Stewart, ISBN 0-7710-6979-0.

TRUDEAU, Pierre Elliott, MEMOIRS.
McClelland & Stewart. ISBN 0-7710-8587-7.

ZIGLER, Philip. MOUNTBATTEN.
Collins. ISBN 0-00-216543-0.

Allow me to introduce myself. My name is Wile E. Coyote... Genius. I am not selling anything, nor am I working my way through college, so let's get down to cases. You are a rabbit, and I am going to eat you for supper. Now, don't try to get away! I am more muscular, more cunning, faster, and larger than you are... and I'm a genius. Why, you could hardly pass the entrance examinations to kindergarten. So, I'll give you the customary two minutes to say your prayers.

The Bugs Bunny/Road Runner Movie (1979)

CHAPTER 14

POWER

Power is the ability to get things done your way. Sometimes it involves asking for a favor, making a suggestion or a request, or giving a direct order; but the result is always that the other person acts, and you derive a benefit from the other person's actions. The condition is that you have power!

You have it over your employees because you pay their salaries. If you are an expert in a special field, it is because you know the best way to handle matters. In a legal dispute, it is because you have the law on your side. In politics, it is because folks will give you their votes, hoping that you will work and succeed in getting the government to serve them in their areas or areas of interests. If you have credit cards, it can be part of your lifestyle to go into a store, hotel, or restaurant, in any city, and order whatever you wish.

All the forces in the world are not so powerful as an idea whose time has come.

Pierre Corneille
(1606–1684)
French tragedian who was one of the three great 17th-century French dramatists, along with Molière and Racine. He has been called "the Founder of French Tragedy" and produced plays for nearly forty years.

And there is the power that derives from being talented, captivating, and capable from being up-to-the minute and knowledgeable, so that people know that if they let you handle things for them, or listen to your advice, they will probably come out ahead. If everybody in the world were fair and equal, we would not have the need for power. However, of course, they are not, which often means that in a competitive situation, you cannot merely settle for an equal chance.

You must keep your eyes and ears open for and alert to any clue or other tips that will move the balance in your favor. Whenever possible, make sure you get more than an equal chance. When the struggle for power gets more intense, some other methods are needed. When you are dealing with someone whose mind is closed to your ideas and influence from the

Chapter 14

Ambition is the immoderate desire for power.

Baruch de Spinoza (1632 –1677) Dutch Jewish philosopher. Revealing considerable scientific aptitude, the breadth and importance of Spinoza's work was not fully realized until years after his death. By laying the groundwork for the 18th-century Enlightenment and modern biblical criticism, he came to be considered one of the great rationalistsof 17th-century philosophy.

start, or who feels he is in direct competition with you, then things must be handled somewhat differently. The issue becomes what kind of power a person has and how someone uses that power. Here are some of the common types of power you will encounter in society.

Coercive power: It is associated with people who are in a position to punish others. People fear the consequences of not doing what is asked of them.

Connection power: It is based upon whom you know. This person knows, and has the ear of, other powerful people within the society.

Expert power: It comes from a person's expertise. This is commonly a person with an acclaimed skill or accomplishment.

Informational power: It is about the value or importance of information and knowledge.

Legitimate power: It comes from the position a person holds. This is related to a person's title and responsibilities.

Referent power: The ones who are well-liked and respected hold this kind of power.

Reward power: It is based upon a person's ability to bestow rewards.

Remember that power is something that can be used in different ways. When a person has an unbelievable amount of power and abuses it, then you have a problem. When the person can brandish the power in order to achieve great exploits that benefit a cause larger than himself or herself you often have a positive outcome from the use of that same power.

POWER

Being powerful is like being a lady. If you have to tell people you are, you aren't.

Margaret Hilda Thatcher, Baroness Thatcher
(1925 -)
British prime minister of the 20th-century, and the only woman to have held the post. Dubbed the "Iron Lady" for her firm opposition to the Soviet Union, she implemented a number of conservative policies that have come to be known as Thatcherism.

You must welcome change as the rule but not as your ruler.

Denis E. Waitley
(1933 -)
He is an American motivational speaker and writer, consultant, and best-selling author.

Do people have power over you?

Those who try to control other people are, simply put, neither nice nor respectful. While a controlling personality belongs to someone who probably has deeper issues, such as codependency, narcissism, sociopath tendencies, or just sheer stubbornness, you should shoulder none of these negative traits.

Controlling people are selfish to the core, immature at heart, and likely to put the brakes on your leading a fulfilling life if you are in constant close proximity to them. In order to spare yourself getting too entangled with a controlling personality, or to awaken yourself to the fact that the controlling person is the one with the problem and not you, here are some questions to ask to help you recognize a controlling person.

Do you have any relationships in which you feel suffocated, bossed around, confused, or distressed?
Is there someone in your life around whom you feel that you have to tiptoe and be super careful to mollify or not anger? Do you know someone who seems to have *buttons* that when *pushed* make the person go off at you - at the simplest of things you say or do, often without rhyme or reason? If you feel that any of these situations has a ring of familiarity to it, then you may be dealing with a controlling person.

Controlling people can be both male and female, and you find them in both romantic and platonic relationships. Be just as wary of a jealous friend who hates your significant other as you are of your significant other, especially if your friend is unhappy with his or her romances. Just because someone has a forceful personality does not make him or her a controlling personality.

Chapter 14

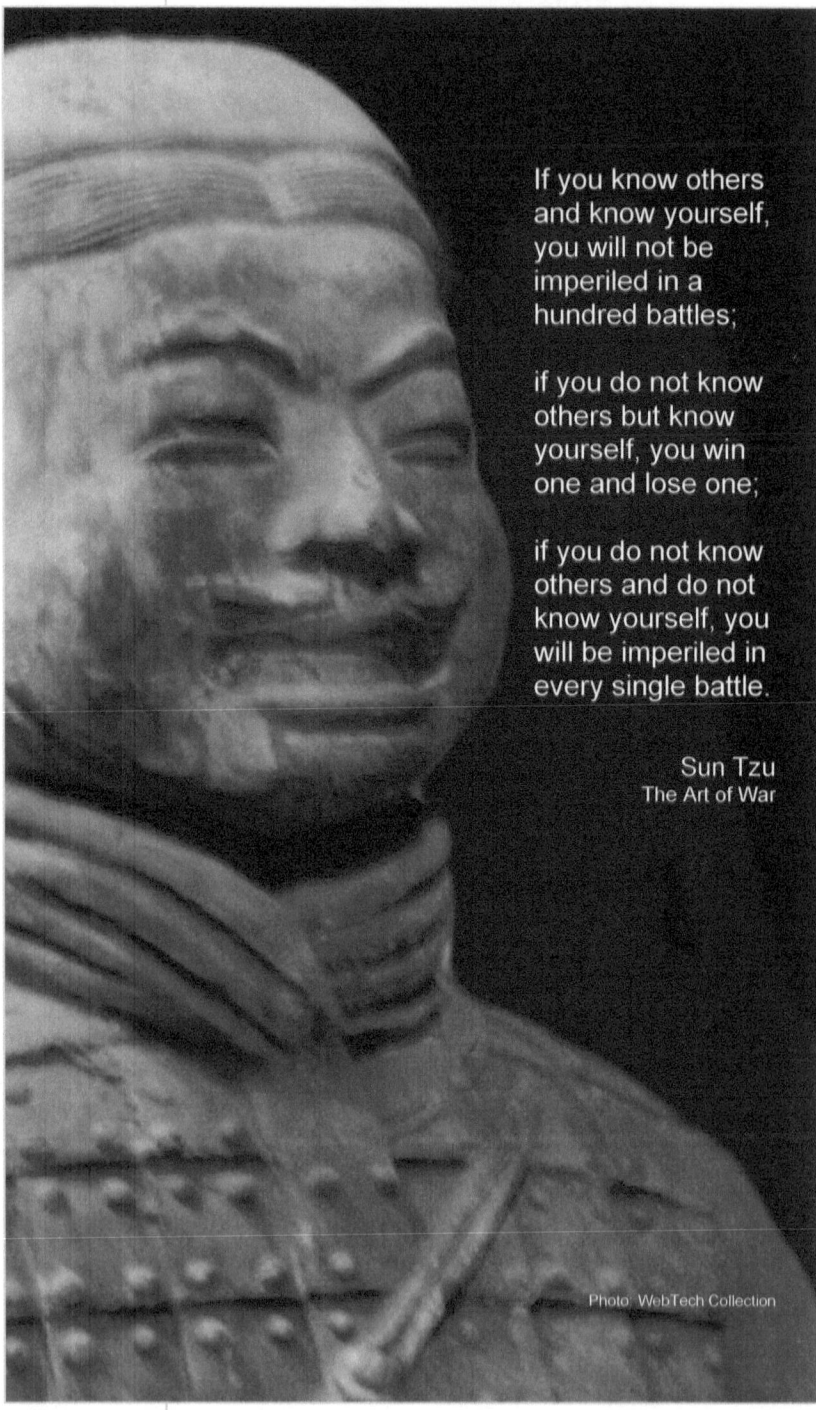

If you know others and know yourself, you will not be imperiled in a hundred battles;

if you do not know others but know yourself, you win one and lose one;

if you do not know others and do not know yourself, you will be imperiled in every single battle.

Sun Tzu
The Art of War

Photo: WebTech Collection

Character is power.

Booker Taliaferro Washington (1856 –1915) African-American educator, author, orator, advisor to Republican presidents, and black political leader. He was the dominant figure in the African-American community in the United States from 1890 to 1915.

Circumstances are beyond human control, but our conduct is in our own power.

Benjamin Disraeli, (1804 –1881) 1st Earl of Beaconsfield. According to some interpretations, a supporter of the expansion and preservation of the British Empire in the Middle East and Central Asia.

The test is: *Does he or she allow you to be yourself, or exert undue influence over your behavior?* You should know this instinctively.

Moodiness is a key signal of a controlling person, precisely because those with moody personalities tend to be mulling over perceived hurts and injustices that have happened to them personally and to be seeking to remedy their internal pain and to improve their situations by controlling others.

Moody people tend to withdraw or "to throw a depressing darkness" right into the middle of a moment of happiness. Narcissists will frequently throw an abusing attack when inadequate attention is being paid to them and their needs.

This is a manipulative way of controlling that can be hard to say no to because the person will often say they are in pain, upset, hurting, and the like, trying to make the other person feel bad for them.

Frequent temper outbursts, especially those accompanied by bullying or threats, are a sign of a controlling personality type. Temper outbursts often happen when you disagree with them or do not do exactly what they want you to do.

In their minds, you are challenging their authority over you when you either disagree with them or do not comply with their wishes.

Questions can reveal several things in terms of a controlling person when he or she responds in a frustrated or condescending way. As I already alluded to, a controlling person thinks that you can read his or her mind. If you ask basic questions about what to do together, where to go, what he or she want, etc., the

Chapter 14

Knowledge is the most democratic source of power.

Alvin Toffler
(1928 -)
He explains, "Society needs people who take care of the elderly and who know how to be compassionate and honest. Society needs people who work in hospitals. Society needs all kinds of skills that are not just cognitive; they're emotional, they're affectional. You can't run the society on data and computers alone."

Never underestimate the power of human stupidity.

The Number of the Beast is a science fiction novel by Robert A. Heinlein, published in 1980.

person can become easily frustrated because they expected you to have all of their needs thoroughly understood and accounted for and placed ahead in priority over yours.

Asking questions means a decision still needs to be made, and when the controlling person thinks, the decisions have already been made, all about the person himself or herself for the convenience of that person.

Controlling people often assume that they understand how you think, even when they actually do not. They may become frustrated because they have constructed an image of you that is at odds with what you say and who you are.

Questions can irritate a controlling person because the person would rather be in control of the questioning, not have anybody else in control.

Questions can verify for a controlling type of person that the questioner is in need of guidance and control because they do not know the answer.

This may actually make things worse over time because the controller is seeking to have the controlled person second-guess his or her own decision-making abilities.

It is often the case that people with control issues are not very good at giving sincere compliments. They do not want you to feel pleasant about yourself because it may take away control from them and draw attention away from them. Compliments, when given, are backhanded, sneaky, and actually point out some flaw or defect in the other person.

A controlling person may try to control the way you dress and speak, or he or she may even criticize your opinions.

Be wary of any person who seems incapable of understanding or accepting the word "NO." Controlling or not, this person is a problem but coupled with controlling tendencies, he or she is bound to walk all over. This person will tend to insist on something under he or she wears you down and makes you give in, changing your firm no to a weak yes, and leaving you feeling guilt-ridden and ashamed of yourself.

Remember that it is your right to make decisions, including ones that are in the negative and that refuse to do what this person asks.

You should review how this person sees difficult situations, mutual decision-making, or issues of responsibility. It is in these areas that you can truly spot the controlling person more fully.

Unlike a highly opinionated person, a controlling person lacks the ability to tolerate or accept differences between the two of you. Indeed, a controlling person is always seeking ways to change some part of your core traits or personality, to reshape you as part of his or her feeble attempt to control the surrounding world.

While it can be said that relationships are not democracies, neither are they dictatorships. It is important to seek a balance that the parties are comfortable with within any relationship, and the ability to compromise, tolerate, and be flexible - and give mutually and take are essential to healthy relationships.

Power acquired by violence is only a usurpation, and lasts only as long as the force of him who commands prevails over that of those who obey.

Denis Diderot
(1713 -1784)
French philosopher, art critic, and writer. He was a prominent person during the Enlightenment and is best known for serving as co-founder and chief editor of and contributor to the *Encyclopédie*.

Chapter 14

It's our nature: Human beings like success but they hate successful people.

Scott Thompson
(1965 -)
Better known by his stage name, **Carrot Top**, he is an American comedian known for his bright red hair, prop comedy, and self-deprecating humor.

Power is dangerous unless you have humility.

Richard Joseph Daley
(1902 –1976)
He served for 21 years as the mayor and undisputed Democratic boss of Chicago and is considered by historians to be the "last of the big city bosses."

Remember that we teach people how to treat us. If you find yourself constantly "giving in" to the other person on things that matter to you, then you are not being yourself but are being controlled.

Look at what happens in your other relationships. When the controlling person is around your friends and supporters, watch out. The controlling person will often try to cause trouble between you and your friends, spreading rumors, attempt to create divisions, divide and conquer, and will even tell lies about you to them or about them to you to try to break your attachment to them.

The ultimate aim is to isolate you from others, so that he or she can have your exclusive attention inside the reality he or she is trying to structure for you. Stay alert; any attempts to remove or downgrade your friends or supporters from your life are red flags.

Controlling people often do not have close friends, and they are rarely friends with others who are more attractive, intelligent, or well liked than themselves.

They tend to be jealous of popular, successful people and will criticize those held in high-regard by others. A lack of close friends may be one additional sign of their inability to tolerate others and their need to control relationships tightly.

Relationships and friendships are not built on who is in control. They are mutual interactions based on shared give and take and people always seeking balance.

A controlling person tends to keep up social and legal connections, such as threats of litigation, divorce, manipulating marriage, roommate tenancy contracts, shared cell phone plans, misuse of divided credit, and similar contracts, especially if administrative rights are included.

Even in social networks, one may block and unblock a person rather than delete the connection, as another attempt to control a difficult or failed relationship.

The longer that you allow other people to control you, the weaker you may become. In time, this softer self may become your new personality, and you can find yourself only dreaming of your former strong self.

Suspect excessive generosity from a controlling personality as an attempt to impress and control you. By seeming to give you lots of things, so that you always feel as if you are benefiting in some way, you end up feeling as if you owe the person something, perhaps even long term. The controller then uses that obligation you feel towards him or her to control you.

Remember that if you are a person who likes to control others, step back and take a long look at the stress that you may be causing someone else while you are breaking down your own mental health and happiness.

How can I identify manipulative behavior?
Manipulation refers to making attempts at indirectly influencing someone else's behavior or actions. As human beings, our emotions often cloud our judgments, making it difficult for us to see the reality behind hidden agendas or motives in different forms of behavior.

The controlling aspects, or shrewdness, linked to manipulation are sometimes very subtle and may be

You only have power over people as long as you don't take everything away from them. But when you've robbed a man of everything, he's no longer in your power - he's free again.

Alexander Solzhenitsyn,
(1918-2008)
Novelist and Nobel laureate.

Chapter 14

easily overlooked and buried under feelings of obligation, love, or habit.

The characteristics of a manipulative personality are not always obvious because the person plays a silent game of building up obligations toward him or her, and that results in you feeling guilty, pressured, and/or obliged to carry out things for him or her even though you are still wondering how things got to this point. Here are some of the characteristics:

A martyr style personality: This personality type behaves as if he or she is being considerate toward others but is actually mixing up consideration with a need to be significant to you. By "martyring" themselves, they are doing things nobody has asked of them or wants them to do, but in the process, this creates binds when they do them. In "doing you a favor," the expectation increases that you will have to return the favor. This kind of person may also complain constantly about all the things he or she does for you and wonder rhetorically when you are going to return the favors.

Excessively needy and dependent personalities: People who feel uncomfortable in their own skin, putting forth their personal opinions and ideas, can often hide behind manipulative behavior, so that it seems as if you are responding of your own accord even though they have set up everything to have you respond directly to their neediness.

Narcissists: In lay terms, basically means that a person is totally absorbed in self. The extreme narcissist is the center of his own universe. This is the archetypal manipulative personality, and it is very hard to deal with this master manipulator.

Power is the great aphrodisiac.

Heinz Alfred "Henry" Kissinger
(1923 -)
German-born American academic, political scientist, diplomat, and businessman. A recipient of the Nobel Peace Prize, he served as National Security Advisor and later concurrently as Secretary of State in the administrations of Presidents Richard Nixon and Gerald Ford. After his term, his opinion was still sought by many subsequent presidents and many world leaders.

POWER

Silence is the ultimate weapon of power.

Charles André Joseph Marie de Gaulle
(1890 –1970)
French general and statesman
who led the Free French Forces during World War II.
He later founded the French Fifth Republic in 1958 and
served as its first President from 1959 to 1969.

Author: Office of War Information. Overseas Picture

Chapter 14

The greater the power, the more dangerous the abuse.

Edmund Burke
(1729–1797)
He was praised by both conservatives and liberals in the 19th- century. Since the 20th- century, he has generally been viewed as the philosophical founder of modern Conservatism, as well as a representative of classical liberalism.

The only power you have is the word no.

Frances Louise McDormand
(1957 -)
American film and stage actress. She has starred in a number of films, including her Academy Award-winning performance as Marge Gunderson in *Fargo*, in 1996.

Manipulative behaviors: At one time or other, every single one of us practices manipulative behaviors in one form or another. It is just that, for most people, cunning actions tend to be only occasional instances rather than a purposeful map for daily living and interaction with others. Know the possible ways people try to manipulate one another. There are some key behaviors that can end up being manipulation, and it is helpful to know how to spot them before walking right into them.

The guilt trip: This manipulative behavior seeks to make you feel guilty and is aimed at sending you into the land of *should* rather than allowing you to stand up for your own values.

The assumption statement: This manipulative tactic seeks to turn your behavior into what the beholder perceives it as, whether or not his or her interpretation is accurate. It soon leads to a guilt trip because no matter what, your refutation is proof of the assumption.

He said; she said: This manipulative ploy is pseudo-sociology in action. The manipulator takes it upon himself or herself to tell you what someone else said was the right thing to do. It is a handy way for the manipulator to push aside his or her responsibility while loading it all onto you.

The confronting statement: This manipulative approach is about causing an argument. That way, the provoker will end up making you feel terrible about something you did not do or say but for which you ought to feel guilty anyway, and the person will get a huge chunk of sympathy with which to manipulate you all over again.

Self-pity: At times, each one of us really needs some tender self-care, but long-term manipulators can make a habit of being the victim or the one needing special attention.

Learn that there is a big difference between being in control of oneself and trying to control other people. Let's elaborate:

The guilt trip: Guilt trips are really high on the list of manipulative tools. If you can get someone else to feel guilty, then you are a manipulator. The trouble is people wear out after being made to suffer guilt trip after guilt trip, and the manipulator who thinks that he or she is on to a good thing here risks losing respect, friends, and being distanced from those who cannot get away, such as family and co-workers. One of the key things to keep in mind when escaping the guilt trip bind is that the sooner you can recognize it, the better, and that it is the manipulator's guilt trip, not yours.

Unlimited power corrupts the possessor.

William Pitt, 1st Earl of Chatham (1708–1778) British Whig statesman who led Britain during the Seven Years' War (known as the French and Indian War in the United States). He again led the country (holding the official title of Lord Privy Seal) between 1766–68.

Furthermore, take a return-to-sender approach with guilt trips, and do not let the manipulator's interpretation of your behavior determine the situation. You can give the other person a little of his or her own medicine, so that he or she understands how it feels to be made to feel guilty. This approach involves taking what the manipulator has said and telling him or her how he or she is not respecting, appreciating, caring for, etc. your behavior in return, and in the process, you dissolve the need to meet the obligation he or she is aiming to impose on you. In addition, shorten the hold the person has on you. When a manipulator tries to guilt-trip you by suggesting that he or she does not matter, do not buy into it. Instead, answer with a quick retort that breaks this hold instantly.

Chapter 14

The mind games: The use of third party "authority" is thoughtlessly rampant in much of everyday life because we like to defer to these generalizations as a way of backing up our own vague and often unexplored preferences. While most of us know it is a bad habit, in the hands of a manipulator, it becomes a weapon. This tactic is used to try to compare the perceived lack in your responsiveness with the way other people apparently would behave more appropriately than you. While some of this has to do with the manipulator fantasizing that the grass is greener in someone else's life, it is far more about being a tool that lets the manipulator abdicate his or her own responsibility for making the statement.

The confrontation and dispute: Determine whether someone is deliberately using a ploy or "game" to bring about a dispute or conflict. This frequently happens among friends or in relationships when one-member wishes to have influence over or to control the other. Confrontational statements are designed to upset you immediately and to cause an argument to occur. For example, "How dare you leave me alone tonight!" Rather than engaging in an argument with this kind of manipulator, learn simply to say "NO".

The self-pity: The manipulator who finds everything unfair and "falls to pieces" is attempting to gain your sympathy in order to use it to further the satisfaction of his or her needs. In such a case, the manipulator will rely on a sense of "helplessness" and will seek financial, emotional, or other forms of help from you. In dealing with a "meltdown of self-pity", be compassionate but wary, as you do not want to establish an obligation as a result.

The twist and distort facts: Generally, people who use this tactic will lie to the ends of the earth in order to

Those who desire to rise as high as our human condition allows must renounce intellectual pride, the omnipotence of clear thinking, and belief in the absolute power of logic.

Alexis Carrel
(1873 –1944)
French surgeon and biologist who was awarded the Nobel Prize in Physiology or Medicine in 1912 for pioneering vascular suturing techniques.

What it lies in our power to do, it lies in our power not to do.

Aristotle
(384 BCE – 322 BCE)
His views on the physical sciences profoundly shaped medieval scholarship, and their influence extended well into the Renaissance, although they were ultimately replaced by Newtonian physics. In the zoological sciences, some of his observations were confirmed to be accurate only in the 19th-century. His works contain the earliest known formal study of logic, which was incorporated in the late 19th-century into modern formal logic. In metaphysics, Aristotelianism had a profound influence on philosophical and theological thinking in the Islamic and Jewish traditions in the Middle Ages, and it continues to influence Christian theology, especially the scholastic tradition of the Catholic Church.

get what they want. This often happens in the work environment, simply to get others on their side or to gain favor with management and higher authorities. When responding to distorted facts, seek clarification. Explain that this is not how you remembered the facts, and say that you are curious to get a better understanding of the other's view of them. Remain polite and feel free to say that you wish to know to clarify your confusion. Ask the person simple questions about when you both agreed to an issue, how he or she believed the approach was formed, etc. When you meet on common ground again, take this as the new starting point, not their distorted one. Beware of people with "selective memories." This is a manipulative tool for wriggling out of obligations they do not want to meet, while still managing to remember obligations that they expect you to meet, or to have met.

The bargaining tool of love: People who display this type of attitude will often make you feel indebted, or that you owe them something. Instead of letting them manipulate your love for them, try to point out how what you are doing is proof of your love for them.

The pretended illness: Unfortunately, some people use illness as a way of manipulating others. There are people who feign a little illness and symptoms on a small scale, and then there are people who suffer from Factitious Disorder. Faking illnesses is the intentional production of false and exaggerated physical symptoms designed to achieve an ulterior motive. People who do this may be trying to avoid responsibilities, have more leisure time, obtain medical benefits, or they are lazy enough to want someone else to do everything for them. Not all illnesses or excuses for being unwell should be looked upon with doubt or suspicion. People may be

Chapter 14

> Whatever you fear most has no power over you. It is the fear that has the power.
>
> Anonymous

> When you start to develop your powers of empathy and imagination, the whole world opens up to you.
>
> Susan Sarandon
> (1946 -)
> American actress. In 2006, Sarandon received the Action Against Hunger Humanitarian Award. She was honored for her work as a UNICEF Goodwill Ambassador, an advocate for victims of hunger and HIV/AIDS and a spokesperson for Heifer International.

genuinely sick. Likewise, some people may have a slight illness that they greatly exaggerate in order to get "sympathy." The key is to watch for a pattern of recurring symptoms or a lack of treatment for the said condition.

The false rumors: Individuals who use this tactic will tell you the opposite of what you wish to hear. They may do so hoping that you will correct them and that they will force out the real story from you. Very private people often fall prey to this type of tactic because it is targeted at eliciting information from you directly when you have been reticent about something.

The emotional outbursts: Some people will use crying, sorrow, screaming, and other forms of emotional release to further their own ends or simply to get what they want. This is common among children and teenagers who will "test the waters" to see how far they can get with this form of manipulation.

Remember that in all the possible manipulative situations outlined above, whether or not the signs are easy for you to spot, it is very important to listen to yourself and to know how you feel about the situation. Do you feel oppressed, pressured, obliged to do things for this person that you would rather not do? Does his or she behavior seem to impact you endlessly, so that after one form of assistance, you are expected to grant yet more help and support? Your answers should serve as a true guide to where your relationship with this person is headed next. In addition, look for a pattern in a particular behavior. If you can safely predict how someone will behave, in order to achieve certain ends, you are most likely on the right track to picking up on cunning behaviors.

POWER

Recognize also that bullying behavior has manipulation as its goal. It also is very evident and is not something that you or your children should tolerate. You may need to seek help from someone else if you are being bullied.

How can I respond to a bully?

Often people have the idea that "bullying" is something which only occurs among some children until eventually they grow out of this behavior. However, unfortunately, this is not always true. Adults can be just as capable of employing bullying tactics as any young child or teenager.

You only have power over people so long as you don't take everything away from them. But when you've robbed a man of everything, he's no longer in your power - he's free again.

Aleksandr Isayevich Solzhenitsyn (1918 –2008) A writer, who, through his often-suppressed writings, helped to raise global awareness of the gulag, the Soviet Union's forced labor camp system – particularly in *The Gulag Archipelago* and *One Day in the Life of Ivan Denisovich*, two of his best-known works. Solzhenitsyn was awarded the Nobel Prize in Literature in 1970.

If you suspect that either you or anyone else you know is on the receiving end of bullying from an adult, here are some suggestions on how to respond to the bully. If you have been on the receiving end of bullying treatment from an adult for some time, it is possible that you will be blaming yourself for how this person has reacted to you. However, you are not responsible for how the other person reacts.

Everyone is responsible for how he or she chooses to treat others. This is easy to say, but sometimes the bully can arouse strong feelings of anger in you. Do not let the bully see this, as a reaction such as this will simply prove to the bully that he or she has succeeded in getting to you, which is what the bully wants.

The majority of bullies feed off negative emotions, because, deep down inside, in some way, they feel inferior and insecure about themselves, and it is solely by making others feel bad that they can raise their self-esteem. Reacting to a bully by showing negative emotions is likely to only further encourage

Chapter **14**

Courage is fire, and bullying is smoke.

Benjamin Disraeli, 1st Earl of Beaconsfield (1804 –1881) Although born of Jewish parents, Disraeli was baptised in the Christian faith at the age of twelve, and remained an observant Anglican for the rest of his life. Adam Kirsch, in his biography of Disraeli, states that his Jewishness was "both the greatest obstacle to his ambition and its greatest engine." Much of the criticism of his policies was couched in anti-Semitic terms. He was depicted in some antisemitic political cartoons with a big nose and curly black hair, called "Shylock" and "abominable Jew," and portrayed in the act of ritually murdering the infant Britannia.

and possibly worsen their unwanted behaviors towards you. The adult bully is a coward.

See if "killing them with kindness" helps. This does not always work. However, in circumstances when you have not known the bully long, such as if, for example, you have just been introduced to them at work, it can.

Often, what inspires a bully to be nasty to others is an assumption that he or she target is personally threatening in some way, or a bully may act out of the experience of a lack of kindness from others throughout his or her life.

By demonstrating that you do not intend any harm towards the bully and are willing to be friendly, you can encourage more positive responses from him or her. You might do anything from giving him or her an amicable good morning *hello* to offering to help him or her with something.

But, if after trying this two or three times, the bully still continues with his or her behavior, cease this approach. This will not work on every bully, and being nice to him or her every time he or she chooses to bully you is likely to send the message that you reward bullying and find it acceptable.

Try assertive responses against the bully. Choosing an appropriate decisive behavior will, to a certain extent, be dependent on the specific bullying situation. What might be effective in a work-bullying situation might not work so well in a family or cyber bullying situation.

For example, this could include assured body language, looking at the bully firmly in the eye while standing straight, having a confident tone of voice that is clear and firm without sounding threatening and assertively choosing your words. You might say, "I've recently noticed signs that you are trying to bully me, and I want this behavior to stop."

If all else fails, consider enlisting somebody's help. This might be a trusted colleague or supervisor if it is a work bullying situation or a family relative or friend if it is a family bullying situation.

A liar begins with making falsehood appear like truth, and ends with making truth itself appear like falsehood.

William Shenstone
(1714 –1763)
English poet and one of the earliest practitioners of landscape gardening through the development of his estate, *The Leasowes*.

Speaking to your doctor is also an option if you feel the situation is heavily impacting upon your physical and or mental health. If you are a teenager, tell a trusted adult, such as parent, a friend of a parent, another family relative, or a teacher. You should do this as soon as you suspect the adult bully is regularly showing cruel and nasty behavior towards you.

Recognize that assertive behavior can be very effective if used in the early stages of bullying. However, if the bullying has already been going on for a long time, it might not have the desired effects. Sometimes the only thing to do in a bullying situation is to walk away.

You may not be able to walk away and may be forced to engage the person. Always ask yourself if there is a way to outflank the bully; that is, without confronting him or her head-on, is there a way you can force the person to back off by applying pressure elsewhere?

Keep in mind possible adverse consequences down the road. For example, you may use alternative methods to get your adversary to back off now, but the consequence is that you will have made a permanent enemy out of a simple bully, with the

Chapter 14

possibility that he or she will "up the ante" when it comes time to serve out a cold dish of revenge.

Remember that when dealing with such a person, who has some power over you, caution is the key, and sometimes you may have no choice but to appear to go along with their demands for the time being, as you build strength, connections, power, etc. in anticipation of being able to turn the tables on the person.

How can I be captivating?

Have you ever noticed how some people captivate everyone they speak to? No matter what they look like or how much money they have, they can just walk into a room and instantly be the center of attention. When they leave, people think highly of them and want to emulate them.

Some people die at 25 and aren't buried until 75.

Benjamin Franklin
(1706-1790)
He was a prodigious inventor. Among his many creations were the lightning rod, glass armonica (a glass instrument, not to be confused with the metal harmonica), Franklin stove, bifocal glasses, and the flexible urinary catheter. Franklin never patented his inventions; in his autobiography he wrote, "... as we enjoy great advantages from the inventions of others, we should be glad of an opportunity to serve others by any invention of ours; and this we should do freely and generously."

That is charisma, a sort of magnetism that inspires confidence and adoration. Like beauty, luck, and social position, charisma can open many doors in life. Unlike these other qualities, anyone can become more charismatic.

Charm is the art of having an attractive personality: This characteristic can only be achieved over a period of time. While everyone is born with differing amounts of natural charm, much can be acquired and honed through practice and patience.

Be genuinely interested in people: You do not have to love everyone, but you should be curious or fascinated by people in some way. If you are empathic, maybe you are intrigued in by how people feel. Alternatively, you could be fascinated by people's psychology, or by what people know. Learn how to ask questions based on your interests, while

POWER

being polite, and you will make people feel interesting. Do not confuse being charming with being a people pleaser.

Remember people's names: This takes an enormous amount of effort for most people. Repeating the person's name when stating your name to that person will help you to remember the person's name better. The more you say a person's name, the more that person will feel liked by you and the greater the chance he or she will warm up to you.

Assume rapport: This simply means talking to a stranger or a newly met acquaintance in a very friendly manner, as if the person is a long-lost friend or relative. This helps break down the awkwardness and speed up the warm-up process when meeting new people, making the person feel more welcomed and comfortable around you. Kindness coupled with respect makes others feel as if they are loved and cared for. This is a powerful tool during interaction.

A good stance and posture reflect a proper state of mind.

Morihei Ueshiba
(1883 –1969)
A famous martial artist and founder of the Japanese martial art of aikido.

Furthermore, the degree of charm that you possess depends on the creativity of your praise. Say something that is not immediately obvious, and say it in a poetic way.

It is good to have some premeditated compliments and phrases, but the most charming people are able to invent them on the spot. This way, you can be sure that you are not repeating the same things. If you cannot think of anything to say, bring up a current event that is interesting.

Smile With the Eyes: Smiling with the eyes is a genuine smile. Research shows that if you look at someone and then smile, it instantly charms him or her.

Chapter 14

Control your tone of voice: The tone of your voice is crucial. Your voice should be gentle and peaceful. Articulate and project your voice. Any variation from your normal tone will arouse suspicion about your sincerity.

Improve your posture: Throw those shoulders back and let them drop to show that you are relaxed. When you walk, imagine you are crossing a finish line; the first part of your body to cross should be your torso, not your head. If you have poor posture, your head will be pushed forward, which makes you seem timid and insecure.

Women are never disarmed by compliments. Men always are. That is the difference between the sexes.

Oscar Fingal O'Flahertie Wills Wilde
(1854–1900)
Irish writer and poet.

Topics of interest: Take into account topics that interest those around you, even if you are not so keen on them. Sometimes you can build rapport just by asking questions and not caring if you seem naive. There are people who like talking about and explaining their interests, and they will like you for listening to them. It is your level of interest and willingness to engage in topics that make you an interesting person to be around. Let others do the explaining. If someone mistakenly thinks you know more about the topic, be genuine and simply say that your knowledge is limited but that you are hoping to learn more about it.

Watch the way you phrase things: Be mature and have a touch of wise, polite language. Of course, do not overdo it, but try to be polite and turn every negative towards a positive. Every so often, you will have no choice but to express an opinion that few others hold. That is fine. Consider expressing it in a humorous way. Humor is the spoonful of sugar that helps the medicine go down.

Issue compliments generously: If you like something or someone, find a creative way to say it and say it immediately. If you wait too long, it may be viewed as insincere and badly timed, especially if others have beaten you to it. Because you waited, you are most likely not confident in saying what you thought, or so people will think so waiting will only result in a less than enthusiastic presentation. If you notice that someone is putting a lot of effort into something, compliment the person, even if you feel that there is room for improvement. If you notice that someone has changed something about himself or herself, make mention of it, and point out something you like about it.

Accept compliments: Get out of the habit of assuming that compliments you receive are given without sincerity. Even when someone makes a compliment out of contempt, there is always a germ of jealous truth hiding in his or her own heart. Be enthusiastic in accepting the compliment. Avoid diminishing a compliment.

Praise others instead of gossiping: If you are talking with someone, or you are talking in a group of people, and the topics turns to another person in a positive or negative way, be the one to mention something you like about that person.

Positive hearsay is the most powerful tool in gaining charm because it is always viewed as 100 percent sincere. It has the added benefit of making people trust you. The idea will spread that you never have a bad word to say about anyone. Everyone will know that his or her reputation is safe with you.

Remember that sharing feelings is at the core of being captivating. If you cannot tell what makes

Fire and swords are slow engines of destruction, compared to the tongue of a Gossip.

Sir Richard Steele
(1672 –1729)
Irish writer and politician, remembered as co-founder, with his friend Joseph Addison, of the magazine *The Spectator.*

people happy or unhappy, you have no way to assess whether you are saying the right or wrong thing. Furthermore, when you greet someone, make him or her feel as if he or she is the most important person to you. The person will respond more nicely and always think what a great person you are.

What should I consider?
We need power, whether it is physical, personal, financial, mental, emotional, or spiritual, to achieve what we desire. Most people abuse it, while others have learned how to use it responsibly. It is like water; you can drink it, or you can share it. You can also purify it or let it be contaminated.

Don't abuse your friends and expect them to consider it criticism.

Edgar Watson Howe (1853 – 1937) Sometimes referred to as **E. W. Howe**, he was an American novelist and newspaper and magazine editor in the late 19th- and early 20th-centuries. He was perhaps best known for his magazine, *E.W. Howe's Monthly*. Howe was well traveled and known for his sharp wit in his editorials.

If you want power, you must first learn how to handle it. This is because if you cannot handle it, it can be your worst weakness. Furthermore, if you know how to handle your weaknesses, it can be your best power.

People always crave strength and power, while usually ignoring their weaknesses. Thus, they do not achieve a balanced power, the true power. It is that kind of power that can overcome not only a weakness but also other power.

If you can manage knowledge, the truth, or just your monthly rent, then you have considerable power. Moreover, if you can manage your life even when you are "in the dark," when you are poor, and when you do not have any advantages that is also a great power. If you combine these two, you can have a greater power, a power that can handle almost everything in life.

If power is the rate at which work is performed, you can be prevailing if you work in full. In general, powerful people are the ones who work hard. They are the ones who love fully and serve greatly. And more than that, they are the people who can serve while remaining humble. These are the people who are considered the servant-leaders. They are called great leaders because they serve in great ways becoming proud.

Remember that they do it not for pride, but for the honor and glory of the people they serve.

Recommended Reading & References
We suggest consulting the works identified below in order to learn more about the particulars contained in this chapter.

BARKLEY, Bruce T. & SAYLOR, James H. CUSTOMER-DRIVEN PROJECT MANAGEMENT: Building Quality into Project Process. McGraw Hill, ISBN0-07-136982-1.

FERNANDEZ-ARMESTO Felipe. IDEAS THAT SHAPED MANKIND. Barnes & Nobles Publishing, ISBN 0-7607-7826-4.

FRIDMAN, L. Thomas. The World Is Flat. A brief history of the twenty-first century. ISBN 1-59397-669-0.

GREENE Robert. THE 48 LAWS OF POWER.
Penguin Books. ISBN 978-0-14-028019-7.

LAMARCHE, J. LES REQUINS DE LA FINANCE.
Éditions du jour, 1962.

MACHIAVELLI, NICCOLO. THE PRINCE
Penguin Classics. ISBN 0-14-044107-7.

PETERS, Thomas J. WATERMAN, Robert.
LE PRIX DE L'EXCELLENCE. Les secrets des meilleures entreprises. Inter Éditions, Paris. ISBN 2 7296 0025 6.

ROBINS, Anthony. UNLIMITED POWER.
Simon & Schuster. ISBN 0-671-62146-7.

THATCHER, Margaret. THE DOWNING STREET YEARS.
Harper Collins. ISBN 0-06-017056-5.

Mental tensions, frustrations, insecurity, and aimlessness are among the most damaging stressors, and psychosomatic studies have shown how often they cause migraine headaches, peptic ulcers, heart attacks, hypertension, mental disease, suicide, or just hopeless unhappiness.

Dr. Hans Selye

Artist: Laszio, Montréal.

CHAPTER 15

HEALTH & **STRESS**

Your health, happiness, success, satisfaction, productivity, and fulfillment will be directly proportional to the amount of time you revel in wonderful moments of joy, contentment, inspiration, laughter, and love!

Maintain a healthy outlook through the power of positive thought!

Do the daily rituals that you normally do to take care of your body, and also to care for your mind. How important is your physical shell if you do not have a sharp, positive, encouraging, and affirming mind to blend with it perfectly?

Fill your mind with hopeful, positive, and uplifting thoughts and you will bring about more success, abundance, health, and happiness. Your days are numbered, so fill them with more joy, smiles, fun, and simple happy essentials that you can stream into your life.

How can I be healthy?
Being healthy is a big part of life that you would not want to miss out on. Try to keep an optimistic outlook. It makes everything you do easier, including getting healthy. Think about what you can do that would make you happier. Contrary to popular belief, happiness does not just happen. You have to work at it!

Mental health is greatly aided by physical health. It is hard to feel good about anything if you do not feel excellent physically. Even if other things are going wrong in your life, take care of your health. Getting enough exercise, keeping clean, and eating right are usually some things you have a lot of control over. Do

Start every day off with a smile and get it over with.

William Claude Dukenfield
(1880–1946)
Better known as
W. C. Fields, he was an American comedian, actor, juggler, and writer.

Chapter 15

If you're happy, if you're feeling good, then nothing else matters.

Robin Gayle Wright,
(1966 -)
American actress. She has also been credited as **Robin Wright Penn**.

Over the years your bodies become walking autobiographies, telling friends and strangers alike of the minor and major stresses of your lives.

Marilyn Ferguson
(1938 –2008)
American author, editor, and public speaker, best known for her 1980 book *The Aquarian Conspiracy* and its affiliation with the New Age Movement in popular culture.

not blow it off if you are unhappy. It will just make you unhappier.

A key part of being healthy is not getting sick. Use some common sense about germs. Wash your hands after you use the restroom, or before you prepare food. Use hand sanitizers if you have to deal with the public, and keep up on your vaccinations, etc. Do not make yourself crazy about this. Just be mindful of it.

As far as alcohol: watch it. It is easy to underestimate its ability to screw up your health, partly from its direct effects on your body over time and partly from its effects on your judgment. If you commonly drink more than fourteen drinks a week, you have a problem. Get help. Avoid smoking and using other drugs.

You should get at least three hours of exercise a week, spread out over at least three days per week. Mix it up. Ideally, you should get some cardio, some resistance training, and some stretching. Unfortunately, few single exercises offer all three. Try to find a sport you really think is fun.

Exercising can be as deliberate as jogging around your neighborhood, or as simple as taking the steps instead of the elevator. Anything that increases your heart rate is good exercise.

When you are working out, never overwork yourself. If you know your body is asking for a rest, listen to it. In addition, never exercise without having a bottle of water with you. The average human body should get at least 8 cups of water per day.

Drink enough water so that your urine is clear. It will make your skin clear, and remove toxins from your body as you urinate. Eat water-rich foods, such as

HEALTH & STRESS

"Every stress leaves an indelible scar, and the organism pays for its survival after a stressful situation by becoming a little older."

Dr. Hans Selye
(1907 —1982)
A pioneering endocrinologist. After studying in Paris and Rome, he went on to receive his medical degree from the German University in Prague. In 1945, he began serving as the Professor and Director of the Institute of Experimental Medicine and Surgery at the University of Montreal, a position he held for decades.

fruits like watermelon, which is 92% water by weight. Cranberry juice is another option, but it has a bitter taste. Patients suffering from urinary infection caused by insufficient intake of water should drink cranberry juice and eat watermelon if they do not get enough plain water everyday. A tomato is 95% water. An egg is about 74% water.

If you ordinarily have coffee first thing in the morning, try a glass or two of water instead. Surprisingly, you will get much the same effect as drinking a cup of coffee, with less caffeine, less expense, and fewer hassles. Try to drink at least two liters of water or other fluids a day, a little over two quarts.

Recognize that there is water in many foods, such as soup, stew, oranges, and so on. Consider getting some sort of filtered water setup or one of those filtered carafes you keep in the refrigerator. You are more likely to drink water if it tastes good. You can keep some water in your locker at school, your desk at work, in your car, or in your bag.

Remember that the most important thing is to believe in yourself and - that you can achieve a healthy lifestyle. You are never going to get anywhere without believing in yourself, and positive thinking will make everything seem less difficult!

Everyone gets sick or injured sometimes, particularly as they get older. If you get sick or injured and you do not heal on your own, especially if it is something serious, see a doctor or nurse practitioner. Protect yourself. Take the usual safety precautions. Wear your seat belt. Wear a helmet if you are riding a bicycle, motorbike, or motorcycle. Lift heavy things with your thigh muscles, not your back. Take care of yourself.

Chapter 15

The only way to keep your health is to eat what you don't want, drink what you don't like, and do what you'd rather not.

Mark Twain

Ultimately this issue is on us. We're the ones who make the decisions about what our kids eat.

Michelle LaVaughn Robinson Obama
(1964 -)
The wife of the 44th- President of the United States.

How can I eat healthy?

There are many popular diets on the market today, but most of them are unhealthy and sometimes even dangerous. How to eat a healthy, balanced diet and avoid unhealthy diets is the secret to being healthy.

You need to determine how many calories your body needs to function each day. This number can vary widely, depending upon your metabolism and how physically active you are. If you are the kind of person who puts on 10 pounds just smelling a slice of pizza, then your daily caloric intake should stay around 2000 calories for men, and 1500 calories for women.

Your body mass also plays a part in this: More calories are suitable for naturally bigger people, and fewer calories for smaller people. If you are the kind of person who can eat without putting on a pound, or you are physically active, you may want to increase your daily caloric intake by 1000-2000 calories, a little less for women.

Furthermore, consider that the more muscle mass you have, the more calories you need to function. The bad fats are saturated and trans fat. Someone on a 2000-calorie diet should consume fewer than 20 grams of saturated fat a day, and trans fat can and should be avoided altogether.

The good fats are poly - and monounsaturated fats, which should make up about 30% of your daily calorie intake.

You need to consume fat from foods for your body to function correctly. However, it is important to choose the right kinds of fats: Most animal fats and some vegetable oils are high in the kind of fats that raise your LDL cholesterol levels, the bad cholesterol.

HEALTH & STRESS

As much as we thirst for approval we dread condemnation.

Dr. Hans Selye
(1907 —1982)
A proud Canadian living in Montreal, Hans was granted Fellowship of the Royal Society of Canada along with 42 other Honorary Fellowships around the world. In addition to these things, he received numerous honorary citizenships and medals, including the highest distinction of the Canadian Medical Association, the Starr Medal, and the highest distinction of Canada, a Companion of the Order of Canada.

Worthless people live only to eat and drink; people of worth eat and drink only to live.

Socrates
(469 BCE – 399 BCE)
Classical Greek Athenian philosopher.

Contrary to popular belief, eating cholesterol does not necessarily raise the amount of cholesterol in your body. If you give your body the right tools, it will flush excess cholesterol from your body. Those tools are monounsaturated fatty acids, which you should try to consume regularly.

These are the good fats, and they help lower the bad cholesterol in your body by raising the good cholesterol. Foods that are high in monounsaturated fatty acids are olive oil, nuts, fish oil, and various seed oils.

Adding these "good" fats to your weekly diet can lower your cholesterol and reduce your risk of heart disease. Consider sautéing vegetables in small amounts of olive oil, and grabbing a hand-full of mixed nuts for a snack instead of a candy bar. There are also various supplements that contain these good fats that you can take daily.

You need to eat foods high in carbohydrates since they are your body's main source of energy. The trick is to choose the right carbohydrates. Simple carbohydrates like sugar and processed flour are quickly absorbed by the body's digestive system.

This causes a kind of carbohydrates overload, and your body releases huge amounts of insulin to combat the overload. Not only is the excess insulin bad on your heart, but it also encourages weight gain.

Insulin is the main hormone in your body responsible for fat storage. Eat plenty of carbohydrates, but eat carbohydrates that are digested slowly by the body, such as whole-grain flour, hearty vegetables, oats, and unprocessed grains like brown rice.

Chapter 15

Around age 40 I put on twenty pounds.
I had always had a perfect metabolism. But, my metabolism betrayed me as it does most people, except a very rare few who will always be thin.

Suzanne Somers (born **Suzanne Marie Mahoney** (1946 -) American actress, author, singer, and businesswoman, known for her television roles as Chrissy Snow on *Three's Company*.

These kinds of food not only contain complex carbohydrates that are slowly digested by the body, but they are usually higher in vitamins and other nutrients that are beneficial to the body, and they are higher in fiber, which keeps your digestive system running smoothly.

Your metabolism slows down towards the end of the evening and is less efficient at digesting foods. That means more of the energy stored in the food will be stored as fat, and your body will not absorb as many nutrients from the meal. Many North American families tend to have their big meal at dinnertime.

The problem with this is that your day is basically over, and your body's need for energy is not as great as it was earlier in the day. This large meal, late in the day, can also make you feel tired. Try eating a medium-sized meal for breakfast, a large meal for lunch, and a small meal for dinner.

Better yet, try eating four or six small meals over the course of your day. That keeps your body fueled for the whole day without dumping a large amount of food into your stomach, which your body might have a hard time digesting.

Read the labels on everything you eat. Do not just buy something because it is marketed as being "healthy." Lots of companies try to sell their food as healthy when really it is full of high-fructose corn syrup, hydrogenated oils, trans fats, and hidden sugars.

Remember that reading the label is also the best way to learn about a product. It gives you almost all the information about that product you will ever need. If you are trying to lose weight, try to choose foods with

HEALTH & STRESS

low calories. Avoid processed foods. They are unnatural, and so are more difficult for your body to break down, which means they will lie in your gut making you feel bloated and lethargic. Eat things which are not altered, such as raw fruits and vegetables, brown rice, whole-wheat pasta, and so on.

Water is the driving force of all nature.

Leonardo di ser Piero da Vinci (1452 –1519) Renaissance humanism recognized no mutually exclusive polarities between the sciences and the arts, and da Vinci's studies in science and engineering are as impressive and innovative as his artistic work.

Should I drink plenty of water?

Drinking water makes you feel more alive and energized, does wonders for your skin, and makes you feel fuller, so you end up eating less!

There are a variety of reasons to drink plenty of water each day. Adequate water intake prevents dehydration, cleans out the body, and promotes healing processes. Substituting water for alcohol can also help control weight.

Drink water before, with, and after every meal; it will help you to prevent overeating and obesity. Eat slowly, drink water, and you will be satisfied with less food. However, as with everything else, be careful and do not overdo it. Drinking too much water can be toxic, so exercise in moderation.

Water, air, and cleanness are the chief articles in my pharmacy.

Napoléon Bonaparte (1769 –1821)

Water is not a substitute for food, and you can indeed create severe health issues if you drink too much water daily, including severe heart and endocrine system problems. And make sure that you consult your physician before you make any radical lifestyle changes!

Eliminating soda and replacing it with water will do wonders for your weight loss.

Recognize that avoiding simple carbohydrates and fatty foods does not need to be boring. Have fun, not only with the food, but also with the meal. Eating with family and friends makes the meal more satisfying than eating in front of the TV or in the car on the way home from work. You will also eat more slowly when enjoying your meal, which gives your body time to feel full before you burst a button; your brain needs about 20 minutes to get the signal that you are satisfied. To be more precise, it is a region in the brain called the hypothalamus that receives the signal. If you eat too fast, you will overeat; your stomach will get bloated, and you will still feel hungry.

Remember that there are also more creative cooking resources available to us than ever before. You can find great-tasting recipes in magazines, books, and on the Internet. Eating baked fish three or four times a week can get boring, so do a little recipe hunting to find more exciting ways to prepare your meals.

What is stress?
We all experience stress from time to time. When stress gets to be too much, it can take a toll on our health and well-being. That is why effective stress relievers are essential in restoring inner peace and physical health.

Adopting the right attitude can convert a negative stress into a positive one.

Hans Selye
(1907 – 1982)
Austrian-Canadian endocrinologist.

Stress can be defined as any type of change that causes physical, emotional, or psychological strain. However, not all types of stress are harmful or even negative. There are different types of stress that we encounter:

Eustress is a type of stress that is fun and exciting and that keeps us full of life, for example, skiing down a slope or racing to meet a deadline produces this kind of stress.

HEALTH & **STRESS**

Get-well cards have become so humorous that if you don't get sick you're missing half the fun.

Clerow Wilson, Jr.
(1933 –1998)
He was known professionally as **Flip Wilson** and was an American comedian and actor

Man should not try to avoid stress any more than he would shun food, love or exercise.

Dr. Hans Selye
(1907 – 1982)

Acute stress, a very short-term type of stress that can either be positive, eustress, or more distressing, is what we normally think of when we think of stress; this is the type of stress we most often encounter in day-to-day life.

Episodic acute stress is where acute stress seems to run rampant and be a way of life, creating a life of relative chaos. For example, the type of stress that coined the terms 'drama queen' and 'absent-minded professor' is episodic acute stress.

Chronic stress is the type of stress that seems never-ending and inescapable, such as the stress of a bad marriage or that of an extremely taxing job. This type of stress can lead to burn out.

Stress can trigger the body's response to perceived threat or danger, the Fight-or-Flight response. During this reaction, certain hormones, such as adrenalin and cortisol are released, speeding the heart rate, slowing digestion, shunting blood flow to major muscle groups, and changing various other autonomic nervous system functions, giving the body a burst of energy and strength.

Originally named for its ability to enable people to fight physically or to run away when faced with danger, it is now activated in situations where neither response is appropriate, such as in traffic or during a stressful day at work.

When the perceived threat is gone, the body's systems are designed to return to normal functioning via the relaxation response, but in our times of chronic stress, this often does not happen enough, causing damage to the body.

Chapter **15**

Being in control of your life and having realistic expectations about your day-to-day challenges are the keys to stress management, which is perhaps the most important ingredient to living a happy, healthy and rewarding life.

Mary Lucy Denise "Marilu" Henner
(1952 -)
American actress, producer, and author. She is best known for her role as Elaine O'Connor Nardo on the sitcom *Taxi* from 1978 to 1983.

Illness strikes men when they are exposed to change.

Herodotus
(484 BCE – 425 BCE)
Greek Historian.

Remember that when faced with chronic stress and an over activated autonomic nervous system, people begin to see physical symptoms. The first symptoms are relatively mild: chronic headaches and increased susceptibility to colds. With more exposure to chronic stress, however, more serious health problems may develop. These stress-influenced conditions include, but are not limited to: depression, diabetes, hair loss, heart disease, hyperthyroidism, obesity, obsessive-compulsive or anxiety disorder, sexual dysfunction, tooth and gum disease, ulcers, and even possibly cancer. In fact, it is been estimated that as many as 90% of doctor's visits are for symptoms that are at least partially stress-related!

How can I handle stress?

Knowing the importance of relaxation and knowing how to relax are vital for ensuring your ongoing health and well being, as well as for restoring the passion and joy in your life. Your health is your responsibility!

Allowing life's stressors to impact your health negatively will result in your feeling under par in everyday activities and could eventually lead to illness. Learning how to relax is one of the keys to good life balance and self-respect. Relaxing should be a permanent part of your lifestyle.

Obviously, some stress is good for us. It adds interest and excitement to life and motivates us, in good ways. It is when the level of stressors in your life causes you to put up with things that are harming or distressing you constantly that you risk sliding into being too stressed. You might be too stressed if:

- All you do and think about is work, non-stop, be it your own business, a career, a salaried position, a stay-at-home mom or dad position, or anything

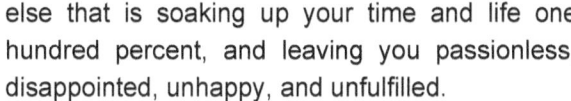

I believe that stress is a factor in any bad health.

Christopher Hunter "Chris" Shays
(1945 -)
American politician.

else that is soaking up your time and life one hundred percent, and leaving you passionless, disappointed, unhappy, and unfulfilled.

- You experience constant body tension, including headaches, neck aches, backaches, soreness all over, etc.

- You are always irritable, short-tempered, and perhaps unable to focus on completing tasks. If trivial things set you off easily, you are too stressed.

- You feel as if you have too much going on, and that you cannot *get off the merry-go-round*.

- Your sleep is a battlefield, and you wake up feeling less rested rather than refreshed. If insomnia has become your norm rather than an unusual event, you are too stressed.

- You are eating too much or too little. Alternatively, if you are choosing unhealthy food options.

If I had no sense of humor,
I would long ago have committed suicide.

Mohandas Karamchand Gandhi
(1869–1948)
The pre-eminent political and ideological leader of India during the Indian independence movement.

- You cannot remember the last time you had a good laugh, and your sense of humor seems to have disappeared.

Once you have accepted that there are negative stressors impacting your life, it is important to make room for relaxation amid all those busy things you are doing. Adding relaxation to your day will improve your productivity, not lessen it, while not adding relaxation to your life could lead to burn out, fatigue, stress-related illnesses, and/or constant insomnia. Ways to prepare for adding relaxation back into your routine include:

Chapter 15

Letting go of guilt. Many religious and cultural beliefs instill the value of hard work very deeply. Over time, and increasingly so with the advent of smart technology that keeps us hyper-wired 24/7, many of us have come to believe that being *on-the-go* constantly is the only way to prove our value. Having an unrealistic interpretation of *hard work* will end up wearing you down. Hard work is giving your tasks the attention they deserve when needed, not letting them fill all the hours of your day!

Accepting that sleep is a very important part of life. When you sleep, your mind continues learning in ways that are impossible during your waking hours. Sleep restores and refreshes your body in a myriad of ways that do not occur when you are awake.

I've chosen to treat my life more like a party than something to stress about.

Martin Hayter Short
(1950 -)
Canadian actor, comedian, writer, singer, and producer. He is best known for his comedy work, particularly on the TV programs *SCTV* and *Saturday Night Live*.

Not being tempted to devalue the worth of sleep. Moreover, the alleged ability that some people have to thrive on four hours of sleeps per night is the exception, not the rule; most of us need a six-or eight-hour sleep cycle to experience full restoration.

Recognizing that finding your own optimal ways to relax may take time, and some trial and error. Do not give up. Keep searching until you find the right combination of activities that relax you and rejuvenate your enthusiasm for living fully. For example, regular moderate exercise can boost energy and reduce stress. Walking outdoors is a good aerobic exercise for both the body and the mind. You can try simple exercises, such as jogging, walking, swimming, biking, aerobics, etc. In addition, stretching loosens muscles and facilitates deeper breathing; thus, it can be good for overcoming stress. Exercise releases mood-enhancing chemicals, such as endorphins, the mind-body's natural painkillers and mood calmer.

Stress is not a specific reaction. The stress response is, by definition, not specific, since it can be produced by virtually any agent.

Dr. Hans Selye
(1907 – 1982)

Using visualization techniques. While you might not feel calm and relaxed, imagining a calm and relaxed scene in your mind can do wonders to improve your outlook. Picture beaches, lying down resting, going for a hike, etc. to help you stay relaxed.

Using affirmations to change your outlook on life, to stop yourself from always jumping to negative conclusions. Affirmations are short, powerful statements that build you up and increase your confidence, helping you to expect positive outcomes.

Being careful about the words you choose. If you repeatedly say things about yourself, you will soon believe your own rhetoric. Use positive, believable, and caring words about yourself.

Teaching yourself to step back and see the big picture when you are in a difficult situation. Change your ways. If the problem is something you are doing, then change the way you act or react.

Stopping and listening to those around you to figure out and correct what it is you might be misunderstanding or doing wrong. Focus on the beauty in everything.

Developing an invisible shield between you and stressed folk. This is really a visualization technique, one in which you imagine that you are cocooned against the negative vibes of overly stressed people around you.

See their behavior and attitudes for what they are; recognize what their stress is doing to them, but refuse to let this penetrate your shield. Do not carry the world's weight on your shoulders.

Chapter **15**

If I can get you to laugh with me, you like me better, which makes you more open to my ideas. And, if I can persuade you to laugh at a particular point that I make, by laughing at it you acknowledge it as true.

John Cleese,
as quoted in <i>What Winners Do to Win!
The 7 Minutes a Day That Can Change
Your Life</i> (2003) by Nicki Joy, p. 113.

This image shows John Cleese on The Muppet Show in 1978. The copyright is owned by the makers of the show. No free image could be found that would convey the same information. It's inclusion here is believed "fair use".

HEALTH & STRESS

These people are making a choice to behave in this way, and you do not have to go along for the ride. Disengaging yourself from others' stress can be hard at first, especially if you are empathic by nature, but keep practicing until not allowing their negativity in becomes second nature.

Guilt is a potent source of stress.

Stop feeling culpable. Get rid of the source of guilt by behaving yourself; stop engaging in behaviors that make you feel guilty. Seek professional help, if necessary, but do not allow destructive behavior to escalate and sabotage your life and health.

Avoid feeling panicky. It may be natural to feel a little tension and to have a case of nerves prior to an important meeting, interview, exam, etc., but there is no point worrying unnecessarily. Worrying too much may prevent your mind from thinking clearly.

Resist comparisons with others. Very often the common cause of stress for people is that they compare their own performances to those of other people, and if their performance is a little inferior, it destroys their confidence and creates stress for them. Instead of comparing yourself with others, use your own previous performance as a standard against which to set future goals for yourself.

Keep competing with yourself and not with others. Competition with self can lead to improvement, but too much competition with others can lead to stress.

Sports psychologists have known for a long time that visualizing success can make an enormous difference to the performance of players. However, most people do the opposite; instead of focusing on

In times of great stress or adversity, it's always best to keep busy, to plow your anger and your energy into something positive.

Lido Anthony "Lee" Iacocca
(1924 -)
One of the most famous business people in the world, Iacocca was a passionate advocate of U.S. business exports during the 1980s.

Chapter **15**

Its not stress that kills us, it is our reaction to it.

Dr. Hans Selye
(1907 – 1982)

success, they visualize and focus on failure. You can minimize stress and build up confidence by focusing on your strengths and on what you know, rather than focusing on your weaknesses and what you do not know.

Be sure to include time for relaxation in your daily schedule. Learn to prioritize. Make a list of tasks for the day. Organize the items on the list by importance. Learn to be proactive and to take care of things before they become a big problem. Time spent more productively means more time to relax. Although the above may sound counteractive to your goal of relaxing, procrastination never feels as good as having nothing to do, so get done what needs doing and then you can truly relax. Avoid trying to hurry. Always try to be relaxed and composed while doing things. Hurrying will result in worry and anxiety. Try to maintain a schedule that does not make you have to hurry to get things done.

Running is a great way to relieve stress and clear the mind.

Joan Van Ark
(1943 -)
American actress.
Received a Theatre World Award and was nominated for a Tony Award for her stage work.

Avoid toxic people. Spend less time with people who try to make you feel guilty to try to get you to do things or who tell you that you are not good enough. Yes, even if they are family members. Avoid people who are constantly complaining or miserable. Stress can be contagious, so avoid "transmitters." Understand that there is always a solution to a problem even if someone else does not, or will not, accept that that is so.

Avoid people who practice the art of wondering, and avoid practicing it yourself!

Wallowing in misery is an art form for some people. You do not need their negativity, nor their rapacious need for making the worst of every situation. Spend

HEALTH & **STRESS**

time with people who radiate warmth and with whom you can truly connect.

Contact with positive-thinking and joyous people broadens your capacities enormously and helps you to feel more relaxed and happy.

Know when to let go of a relationship. If you value your relationships, as do most people, it can be challenging to realize that there are people who are just too toxic or overly needy to keep in your inner circle because they sap your energy and stress you out constantly. Sometimes it is best to let go of relationships with such people, provided you only do so after thinking everything through carefully. Avoid being judgmental, hurtful, or blunt; just move on, as you need to.

Try at least thirty minutes per day of moderate activity. Walk in the park, in the woods, or on a treadmill. Take the stairs instead of the elevator. Park a little further away from the entrance of a store. Increase your activity, once you've built endurance, if desired.

You should do activities or hobbies that relax you. Get your mind off the things that normally stress you out. You may just need a break every now and then. Go fishing, sew, sing, paint or take photographs.

Try singing a song using numbers instead of words. Singing can distract you from stress and help you to relax. Use music as relaxation therapy. Play it as loudly or as softly as you like, whichever calms you the most.

Spend time with your pet. Cuddle or play with your pet. They will love it and so will you. Talk to your pet

Adopting a new healthier lifestyle can involve changing diet to include more fresh fruit and vegetables as well as increasing levels of exercise.

Linford Cicero Christie
(1960 -)
Former sprinter from the United Kingdom. He is the only British man to have won gold medals in the 100 metres at all four major competitions open to British athletes: the Olympic Games, the World Championships, the European Championships, and the Commonwealth Games.

Chapter 15

about all the stress and anxiety you have been going through, and you will feel a lot better. Pet therapy is a genuine way to relax; you can also learn from watching how your pet relaxes. Note: animals do not carry guilt around!

Walking in a garden or looking at green trees can have a soothing effect on you. Spend time looking at trees and plants, watching birds or animals, sitting by the seaside watching the waves, or enjoying beautiful or natural scenery. All these can take your mind off everyday problems and help calm you. Try being absorbed in nature for some time everyday. You can also develop gardening as a hobby. Besides feeling calmer, your health will benefit from the fresh unpolluted air while you are in the natural surroundings.

Never forget that laughter is the best medicine. Rent, buy, or see a hilarious movie. This is guaranteed to help. Smiling and laughing release's endorphin, which fights stress, helps you to relax, and reminds you that life is more than just work. Even if it feels strange at first, make it a point to smile more often.

Remember that most things that you worry about have not actually happened. What was the thing that worried you the most last year or two years back?
Most likely, you will not even remember it. The same thing will probably be true of your current fears in the future. Do not try to be perfect. By trying to be flawless in everything you do, you may be creating unnecessary stress in your life. Instead of that, try to do the best that you can with everything you do, and if you make a mistake, embrace it, forgive yourself, and learn from it. Do not be too hard on yourself, and do not criticize yourself excessively for making mistakes. Instead, learn from mistakes and move on.

The greatest weapon against stress is our ability to choose one thought over another.

William James
(1842 –1910)
Pioneering American psychologist and philosopher who was trained as a physician. He wrote influential books on the young science of psychology, educational psychology, psychology of religious experience and mysticism, and on the philosophy of pragmatism.

HEALTH & STRESS

How well do I sleep?
A good night's sleep is an important part of a healthy lifestyle. Your sleep can affect other areas of your life, such as how you feel during the day, how active you are, your studies, career, relationships, etc. Sleep is one of the most important things that your body needs in order to be healthy.

Man should forget his anger before he lies to sleep.

Mohandas Karamchand Gandhi's
(1869-1948)
His complete works were published by the Indian government under the name *The Collected Works of Mahatma Gandhi* in the 1960s.

Sleep is also essential in order to have a sharp mind, to be able to learn, to be in a good mood, and even to stay safe and maintain a healthy weight. It is an important part of just about every part of your life.

Have a bed that is comfortable. In addition, maintain a regular schedule for when you go to bed and wake up, even on weekends.

Maintaining this time schedule is very important. This will help you overcome sleep problems. This will help you avoid that time you often spend trying to sleep but failing to do so. Keep your bedroom at a comfortable temperature, neither too hot nor too cold.

Create a sleep-conducive environment that is dark, quiet, comfortable, cool, and relaxing. Make sure your bed and mattress are comfy. There are many things that can keep people awake at night, with stress being just one of them. To start, avoid working right up until bedtime. Then to alleviate stress, create a bedtime routine where you do something calming leading up to bedtime such as reading or taking a bath. This should help you fall asleep faster.

Finish your dinner at least two or three hours before going to bed. If you feel hungry before going to bed, nutritional food such as green vegetables and fresh fruits can help improve the quality of your sleep. Avoid nicotine, caffeine, and other stimulants, which

Chapter 15

can be found in coffee, tea, soft drinks, cigarettes, chocolate, etc.

Regular exercise can help in maintaining good health and can also be useful for getting a good night's sleep. But, remember to finish your workout at least a few hours before your bedtime.

Naps can be an important part of keeping you alert and performing at your best. A power nap of just twenty or thirty minutes can go a long way toward making you feel fresh, alert, and ready to take on the rest of your day.

Do not worry unnecessarily if you feel you are not getting enough sleep, as it might make matters worse. If you have the habit of waking up in the middle of the night and looking at your clock, it is advisable to turn the clock away from you, so that you have to turn it back in order to see the time, and you may decide not to go through that trouble and may soon overcome this habit. If you cannot fall asleep for fifteen or twenty minutes, then get out of bed and do something else. Return to bed only when you feel really sleepy. Repeat this as many times as necessary during the night.

Free your mind from worries as they can prevent you from having a restful sleep. Leave office work at the office; do not spend more than three to five minutes thinking about the day's problems while you are in bed; and avoid having arguments with somebody in the evenings as these can interfere with your sleep at night. If you have a long list of things to do and your mind is constantly thinking about them, then one of the best ways to free up your mind is to write down each important task on a piece of paper. Next to each task you may write down a future date and time when

A good meditation, even when it is interrupted by occasional nodding, is much more beneficial than many outward religious exercises.

Johannes Tauler
(1300 –1361)
German mystic theologian.

HEALTH & STRESS

you want to deal with it. Writing them down will help unclutter your mind, so that you can go to sleep peacefully.

Remember that every person has a specific number of hours of sleep that he or she needs in order to perform optimally. Adults usually need somewhere between seven to nine hours per night. So, if your body needs eight hours per night, and you trim an hour off each day, you are setting yourself up to not be able to perform well. To determine what your body needs, pay attention to how you feel after various amounts of sleep. When you consistently feel your best after a particular amount, that is how much sleep you should normally get.

How do I meditate?

Meditation is a mental discipline by which one attempts to get beyond the conditioned "thinking" mind into a deeper state of relaxation or awareness. There are many different meditation methods!

At the core of meditation is the goal to focus and eventually quiet your mind. As you progress in this mental discipline, you will find that you can meditate anywhere and at any time, accessing an inner calm regardless of the surroundings. You will also find that you can better control your reactions to things as you become increasingly aware of your thoughts. For example, you should be able to let go of anger more easily.

First, you have to learn to tame your mind and control your breathing. Make time to meditate. Set aside enough time in your daily routine for meditating. The effects of meditation are most noticeable when you do it regularly, rather than sporadically. Some people will find a five-minute meditation worthwhile; for

I've learned to relax more. Everybody feels pressure in what they do. Maybe mine is just a little different because there doesn't seem to be enough hours in the day to accomplish what I want to.

Thomas Cruise Mapother IV
(1962 -)
He is known as **Tom Cruise** and is an American film actor and producer.

Chapter **15**

others, the benefits of longer meditation are well worth the time. You can meditate at any time of the day; some people like to start the day off with meditation; others like to end the day by clearing their minds, and some prefer to find refuge in meditation in the middle of a busy day.

Second, find or create a quiet, relaxing environment. It is especially important, when you are starting out, to avoid distractions. Turn off any TV sets, phone(s), or other noisy appliances. If you play music, make sure it is calm, repetitive, and gentle, so as not to break your concentration. Meditating outside can be beneficial, as long as you do not sit near a busy roadway or another source of loud noise.

The main thing to do is relax and let your talent do the work.

Charles Wade Barkley
(1963 -)
American professional basketball player and current analyst on the television program *Inside the NBA*.

Third, sit on level ground. Sit on a cushion if the ground is uncomfortable. You do not have to twist your limbs to a half lotus or full lotus position or to adopt any unusual postures. The important thing is to keep your back straight, as this will help with breathing later.

- Tilt your pelvis forward by sitting on the forward edge of a thick cushion or on a chair that has its back legs lifted off the ground 8 to 10 cm (3 or 4 inches).

- Starting from your bottom, stack up the vertebrae in your spine, so that they are balanced one on top of another and support the whole weight of your torso, neck, and head. Done correctly, it feels as if no effort is required to hold your torso up. A small amount of effort is, in fact, required, but with the right posture, it is so small and evenly distributed that you do not notice it.

HEALTH & STRESS

- Relax your arms and legs. They do not need to be in any special position, just as long as they are relaxed and do not interfere with your balancing your torso. You can put your hands on your thighs, but it might be easier at first to let your arms hang at your sides. The hanging weight helps reveal where things are out of alignment.

Fourth, relax everything, and keep searching for parts of you that are not relaxed. When you find them, and you will, relax them. You may find that you cannot relax them unless you adjust your posture so that you are better aligned and that place does not need to "work" anymore. This commonly happens with muscles near your spine. You may also notice that you are twisted a little and need to straighten out. Little muscles in your face often keep getting tense, too.

Fifth, let your attention rest on the flow of your breath. Listen to it, follow it, but make no judgments about it. The goal is to allow the "chattering" in your mind to fade away gradually and to find an "anchor" on which to settle your mind. Try reciting a mantra, the repetition of a sacred word. A single word such as "om" uttered at a steady rhythm is best. You can recite it verbally or just with the voice in your mind. Beginners may find it easier to count their breaths. Try counting your breaths from 1 to 10, and then simply start again at 1. To circumvent images that keep intruding on your thoughts, visualize a place that calms you. It can be real or imaginary.

Sixth, silence your mind. Once you have trained your mind to focus on just one thing at a time, the next step is to focus on nothing at all, essentially "clearing" your mind.

Sleep is the best meditation.

The 14th Dalai Lama (1935 -) Tibetans traditionally believe him to be the reincarnation of his predecessors and a manifestation of the Bodhisattva of Compassion. In 1578, the Mongol ruler Altan Khan bestowed the title *Dalai Lama* on Sonam Gyatso. However, the 14th Dalai Lama asserts that Altan Khan did not intend to bestow a title as such and that he intended only to translate the name "Sonam Gyatso" into Mongolian.

Chapter 15

There will never be a time of smooth sailing. As soon as one crisis is over, another will move in to take its place. Nature abhors a vacuum.
There will never be a good, quiet time to make a change.
If you're waiting for all your work to be done before you take a vacation or do long-term planning, you'll probably wait forever.
(This is the problem that workaholics have. It's not, as popularly believed, that they like to work all the time; they're just waiting until the work in front of them is done before they stop.)

Albert J. Bernstein, Ph.D.

This requires tremendous discipline but is the pinnacle of meditation. After focusing on a single thing as described in the previous step, you can either cast it away or observe it impartially and let it come and then go, without labeling it as *good* or *bad*.

Take the same approach to any thought which returns to your mind until silence prevails.

Note that for some people, focusing their attention on a single thing or object does exactly the opposite of what meditation is all about. It takes them back to the life of focus, concentration, and strain. In this case, as an alternative to the above techniques, some doctors recommend un-focusing your attention.

Instead of focusing your attention on one thing or an object, this type of meditation is achieved by attaining a state of zero. Focus your attention above all thoughts to a point where you lose all attention and all thoughts.

Remember not to expect immediate results. Meditation works best when it is done for its own sake, without becoming attached to results. If you find your mind is wondering, try not to get upset with yourself about it. Wandering restlessly is the normal state of the conditioned mind. This is the first lesson many people learn in meditation, and it is a valuable one. Simply, gently, invite your attention back to your breath, remembering that you have just had a small but precious "awakening." Becoming aware of your wandering mind is a success, not a failure.

It is time to start planning a vacation?
The beginning of July often marks, for many, the official start of summer, with children being out of school for the summer break paired with the warmer

HEALTH & STRESS

weather and sunny skies that mark this time of the year.

This is also typically the time when most of us start making preparations to take the vacation time we have earned at work. Unfortunately, there is a growing trend among both employees and management to forgo taking any breaks from work in order to deal with the growing demands that fill their plates.

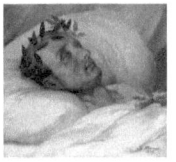

The best cure for the body is a quiet mind.

Napoléon Bonaparte
(1769 –1821)
Forshufvud, in a 1978 book with Ben Weider from Montreal Canada, noted the emperor's body was found to be remarkably well-preserved when moved in 1840. Arsenic is a strong preservative, and therefore this supported the poisoning hypothesis. Forshufvud and Weider observed that Napoleon had attempted to quench abnormal thirst by drinking high levels of orgeat syrup that contained cyanide compounds in the almonds used for flavouring.

Taking time off work recharges your productivity and sharpens your ability to come up with new ideas. Vacation time also allows us to pursue other interests, something many innovative companies encourage their employees to do during the work week in order to see what new solutions or ideas they might come up with that can be incorporated into the organization's goals.

If you are the owner being away from your work environment for a longer period of time will allow you to gain a fresh perspective on the vision you have for your organization, and give you time to think of new ways that you can help your team to transform that vision into reality.

When it comes to good leadership practices, a common axiom that is shared is to *lead by example*, that is, to encourage the behavior and commitments you would like to see in your employees by exhibiting them first in your own actions.

Ironically, by choosing to forgo taking vacation, leaders are not showing support for their employees as much as demonstrating to them how little they value or consider it necessary for their employees to take time off from work.

Chapter 15

I think it was always there and it was maybe a matter of bringing it out. It was harder than I thought it would be and I had to try harder. I had to regain my confidence, maybe the most important thing. I have learned a lot to relax. I know what I can do now, and I do it.

Guy Lafleur
(1951 -)
Canadian professional ice hockey player.

Indeed, employees who do opt to go on vacation can feel ostracized by others in the team, considering how everyone else, from the leadership on down, has decided that current conditions require everyone to sacrifice what he or she might otherwise be entitled to.

That is why leaders should not only take their vacations, but make a point of advising their employees that they expect each of them to do the same as well.

One common assumption all of us like to make is that we are indispensable to our team or organization, that our being away for any given period of time would make things difficult for others who do not know how to manage things in our absence.

While this might make us feel good about our contributions, this is far from a healthy situation for our organization, both in terms of the company's growth and overall morale.

By taking time off from work, leaders will provide their team members with the opportunity to develop their skills effectively as they learn to "manage the fort" while the leaders as they learn are away.

Through such opportunities, leaders can foster within their employees a sense of confidence and assurance that they can manage things just fine, even if only for a short period of time, without direct support or assistance.

In today's economy, many organizations cannot afford to hand out too many raises, while at the same time they are worried that, in not offering such

Chapter 15

rewards, they are at risk of losing key players in their organizations.

By reminding the team members that their vacation time is a part of their remuneration, and more importantly, by allowing them actually to take this time off work, leaders can demonstrate to their employees that they understand the importance and necessity of being able to have "downtime" to relax and enjoy the fruits of their labor.

In today's economic climate, it is easy for us to fall into the belief that we need to sacrifice our free time for the sake of the greater good, or worse, to succumb to the fear that taking a vacation will cast us in a negative light among our peers.

Concern should drive us into action and not into a depression. No man is free who cannot control himself.

Pythagoras of Samos
(570 BCE –495 BCE)
Ionian Greek philosopher, mathematician, and founder of the religious movement called Pythagoreanism.

Remember that the reality, though, is that we need our leaders and employees to bring their full efforts to the process of attaining the organization's goals. The best way to ensure that this happens is to encourage everyone in the organization to take advantage of their vacation break to remove themselves from facing the challenges currently on their plates, thereby allowing them to bring a fresh perspective to the work when they return and with it, new ideas on how to attain these shared goals.

Can I manage stress in the workplace?

Take frequent breaks throughout the day. It will help clear your mind and relieve pressure. A brake can be something as simple as going to the water cooler for a drink or making or getting a cup of tea.

Do more demanding work in the morning, when your energy level is higher, and easier work later in the day, when you may be tired.

This way, your day can go smoothly. Vary your routine getting to work. Get to work early sometimes or stay late once a week. You may be able to accomplish more when you vary your routine.

If you are in an argument with someone, before you say something which you might regret later, get away from the stressor and collect yourself. You can look away for a moment, or put the caller on hold. Use your time-out to take a few deep breaths, stretch, or count to ten.

Boosting your vitamin intake can help you deal better with stress. However, try avoiding stress formulas, which often contain large amounts of randomly formulated nutrients such as the B vitamins, but little else.

Furthermore, try tea, which can be a good stress reducer. Tea contains caffeine in much less quantity compared to coffee. So it should not be harmful to have a few cups of tea per day. Tea is good, but green tea is even better!

Depression is the inability to construct a future.

Rollo May
(1909 –1994)
American existential psychologist. He authored the influential book *Love and Will* during 1969. He is often associated with both humanistic psychology and existentialist philosophy. May was a close friend of the theologian Paul Tillich. His works include *The Courage to Create*, the latter title honoring Tillich's *The Courage to Be*.

Remember that the body affects the mind and vice versa. If the body is relaxed, the mind also follows suit. And the face leads the way for the body. If the face is tense, the muscles in other regions of the body tend also to tense up. So whenever you feel stressed, begin by relaxing your facial expressions; get rid of the frown and smile more often.

Am I suffering from depression?

Depression is defined as an illness that affects your whole body, including your mood and thoughts. It is as much a physical condition as it is a mental one. Depression can affect your eating and sleeping

Chapter 15

habits. It can change the way you feel about yourself and how you view the world around you.

Depression can interfere with your work and personal relationships, and in severe cases, it can be debilitating. Depression is more than just *feeling blue,* and people who suffer from depression cannot just "pull themselves together".

In order to be diagnosed with depression, the patient must have suffered from at least five of the seven main depression symptoms for at least two weeks.

One of the best ways to identify the signs of depression is to be familiar with the major symptoms. They include a change in sleeping habits, reduced interest in activities, feeling guilty, lack of energy, concentration difficulties, sudden change in appetite, and suicidal thoughts.

The reason people find it so hard to be happy is that they always see the past better than it was,
the present worse than it is,
and the future less resolved than it will be.

Marcel Pagnol
(1895 –1974)
French novelist, playwright, and filmmaker. In 1946, he became the first filmmaker elected to the Académie Française.

Whether it is you or somebody else that you suspect is suffering from depression, be observant. Observe behaviors carefully, making note of any changes. The person may be withdrawn and unwilling to discuss his or her feelings, so be sensitive when addressing the issue with them.

Many of the signs and feelings of sadness can be confused with depression. If you have just suffered a loss, such as the death of a friend or family member, or the loss of your job, then your feelings of sadness may be due to that occurrence.

Depression, however, requires no such trauma, although it can begin as a result of an event. Doctors use the two-week rule to differentiate between sadness and depression. If you have been feeling this way for longer than two weeks, and suffer from additional depression symptoms, then you are depressed, not just sad.

Seeing your doctor is the most reliable way to identify signs of depression. If you talk to your doctor, let him or her know that you may be depressed. The doctor will then help you identify the signs of depression, and may well make a diagnosis and help you to start feeling better.

Remember that managing depression can be a lifelong task for some people. Making progress toward a healthier life depends on keeping the positive thinking momentum going.

Do not rest on your laurels, but take time to congratulate yourself for the incredibly hard work of finding a place to express yourself through working and using work as a tool to reduce the negativity that is inherent with clinical depression.

How can I leave the past behind?

There always comes a time when you must cease to stay stuck in the past, or it will define you and mark every step you take from that day forward.

A past left unresolved will continue to haunt you if you do not address the underlying sorrow, pain, or anger. You may not want to revisit aspects of what happened in the past, but if you do not, you allow the part of your mind that conceals and glosses over hurts to dominate in your daily life.

And instead of fully comprehending what happened and learning from it, you live in the grip of the past subconsciously and let it eat away at you. If you cannot get a clear view of the past by self-

Change means that what before wasn't perfect. People want things to be better.

Esther Dyson
(1951 -)
Journalist and Wall Street technology analyst who is a leading angel investor, entrepreneur, philanthropist, and commentator focused on breakthrough innovation in healthcare, government transparency, digital technology, biotechnology, and space.

assessment, seek professional therapeutic assistance to guide you.

What has happened has happened. You will need to accept that you cannot change what happened. It is impossible to rewrite the facts of what you experienced and went through. However, it is possible to rewrite the way you perceive what happened and handle it differently in the future. If you do not, your hurt self-will carries over this emotional pain into all new experiences and relationships, possibly poisoning them and dooming them to failure without any conscious desire on your behalf.

Acknowledge that you are living in real-time carrying the baggage of old-time. And then let go of it.

Are you playing out a past habit in a current relationship? Does your fear of anger, loss, raised voices, silence, etc. now set the tone for how you relate to others?

This requires careful consideration, so that you can untwist the tendrils of who you really are and what experiences from childhood onward have shaped how you react to situations. Most of us feel a deep inner core of who we are at our best. And we are all capable of separating the emotional triggers from the solid core of self if we sit still long enough to tease apart what triggers our habitual behavior and seek that which is truly what we believe ourselves capable of being.

To be better, you will need to remove the past from your future. This simply means that you must learn to stop letting experience morph into future probability.

HEALTH & STRESS

This happens when you have a bad experience, and it immediately conjures up memories of where similar bad experiences have led you in the past. In this case, instead of thinking positively and remembering the means by which you ultimately overcame prior negative challenges, your immediate, habitual reaction is to transfer the bad outcomes from that former experience to a current situation, assuming the worst-case scenario for your current experience, with full-blown expectations that things will only be bad. And with that come the habitual reactions, on cue, rather than a series of chosen proactive actions defined by you as the person you are now.

Combine the knowledge that you cannot change the past with the knowledge that you cannot predict the future.

However, you can make sure that the person you are right at present is strong, whole, and healthy emotionally, that any future negative scenarios are something the person you are now can definitely cope with, no matter what gets thrown at you. This is really about taking responsibility for yourself and how you react.

Once you have faced the challenges from your past and accepted that, while you cannot change the past, you can cease to let it be role played out every time a new challenge arises, you are beginning to remove the fear of worse things happening as directed by your past experiences. Instead, you now learn to embrace the reality that the future is as yet unwritten, and if you want it to be a positive and strong experience, the power lies within you to achieve this.

No overnight transformation will occur when you are trying to move yourself through past habits. It all

Sometimes it's the smallest decisions that can change your life forever.

Keri Lynn Russell,
(1976 -)
American actress and dancer.

Chapter **15**

We all have big changes in our lives that are more or less a second chance.

Harrison Ford
(1942 -)
American film actor and producer. He is famous for his performances as Han Solo in the original *Star Wars* trilogy and as the title character of the *Indiana Jones* film series. Harrison Ford received the AFI Life Achievement Award in 2000.

takes time, and you will only achieve the best and soundest results by allowing yourself the time and space to move on. While you are going through the healing process to strengthen your ability to deal with the past in a reasoned and distanced manner, be aware of the triggers that will send you back to past habits.

Actively aim to put a hold on habitual reactions and challenge yourself to do things differently, while at the same time accepting why you need to do this. This also means avoiding making hasty decisions that you may regret later, such as cutting off all ties with somebody in your family, sending notes filled with vitriol to people, or stepping away from something you have been doing.

While ultimately some of these outcomes might end up being the path you take after reasoning things out with great care, initially, this exercise is about strengthening yourself to make calm and enlightened decisions rather than allowing yourself to make merry with curses and burning your bridges with no care for tomorrow.

Recognize that you can start again any moment you choose. Shift the focus as often as you can from the sadness, disappointment, anger, and broken heart and try, instead, to remember the good times and the best things.

Focusing on negative aspects to try to increase the intensity and duration of the pain from your loss will not change what has happened but will make you feel a great deal worse. Ultimately, you need to question why you would do this, as making yourself unhappier is a recipe for longer-term health problems and risks debilitating you. And be assured that no one or being who has brought you happiness would have ever wanted you to collapse in a heap.

Every single time you feel tempted to become even sadder, angry, down, or full of self petty, grab a diary and write down the good things you can remember about the person, pet, or "dream" that has been lost to you. If you have lost someone, remember such things as what a person said or did, from the small quirky mannerisms to the large generosities, the times that you spent laughing together, and the things this person has taught you about life and yourself. If it is a lost pet, remember the beautiful times you spent together, the happy life you enabled for your pet, and the special traits your pet had. And if it is a lost "dream", or object of desire, remember the good that came of pursuing or having these things, and think about what you learned that could be applied to other experiences in the future.

Can I smile for better health?

Smiling will always play a very important role in maintaining and improving your health, both physically and emotionally.

Phyllis Diller
(1917- 2012)
American actress and comedian.

As Phyllis Diller once said: *A smile is a curve that sets everything straight, and the smile can help you to stand out, improve people's perception of your attractiveness and relieve any stress you might be experiencing. A fun way to improve your physical and mental well-being, the smile is free of charge and always available by choice.*

Stress is easily shown on our faces. Smiling prevents people from looking too tired or overwhelmed. When you are stressed, try to "put on a smile", as it will make you feel happy, and you will appear cheerful. Your feelings of stress will be reduced as the

Chapter 15

A sense of humor is good for you.
Have you ever heard of a laughing hyena with heartburn?

Bob Hope
born **Leslie Townes Hope**;
(1903 –2003)
British-born American comedian and actor who appeared in vaudeville, on Broadway, and in radio, television, and movies. He was also noted for his work with the US Armed Forces and his numerous USO shows entertaining American military personnel.

endorphins associated with the smile are released, and the infectiousness of your smile will help to make others joyful.

When others are happy, you will feel happier, knowing you are helping others to feel better. You may even start laughing, and if so, others might join in. That shows you that from being sad, you can start laughing with the help of a smile. Smiling brings about a sense of relaxation, and it is relaxation that helps your immune system to work more efficiently.

You can reduce the risk of sicknesses, such as the cold and the flu, by smiling, in addition to getting a seasonal flu vaccine, exercising, eating right, and living a healthy lifestyle.

A simple test to show you how smiling keeps you positive is to smile. You will soon see that it is hard to combine the negative thought with the smile!

When we smile, our bodies and minds are sending us a message that everything is okay, and that life is great. Smiling will help to lift depression and sadness, and done frequently, works better than any type of medication to relieve stress. Dozens of studies show that if one is positive, he or she is more likely to live longer - and help to win over sickness.

The muscles used to smile lift your face up, which makes people appear much younger. Do not push for an unnatural and dramatic smile; just try to smile naturally throughout the day. Use your smiles to increase your chances of living longer. Those who smile are thought to live an average of 79.9 years, while partial smilers live an average of 75 years, and non-smilers live an average of 72.9 years.

HEALTH & STRESS

It is impossible for you to be angry and laugh at the same time.
Anger and laughter are mutually exclusive and you have the power to choose either.

Wayne Walter Dyer
(1940 -)
American self-help advocate, author, and lecturer.

The only conclusion to be reached from this is to smile every day. Even if it does not guarantee that you will live longer, you will feel a whole lot better smiling throughout your life!

When you are in pain, physically or mentally, smile. Smiling will release endorphins and serotonin. Endorphins are natural painkillers. Together, these two chemicals make people feel more able to cope when they are in pain.

When someone is sad, and he or she friend comes over and makes the person laugh to cheer the person up, the resulting smiles and laughter relieve pain.

If you are a person suffering from high blood pressure, hypertension, then it is recommended that you smile a lot more. When you smile, you should see a marked reduction in your blood pressure. Of course, smiling is not the answer to hypertension. Be sure to be under your doctor's guidance, receiving all the care and attention required to treat your disease.

People who smile appear more confident, are more likely to be promoted - because they will put their boss into a happy mood, and are more likely to be approached by many people. They also tend to make more friends. Smile at meetings, and you will see that people will react to you differently.

Smile to help put people at ease, and you'll feel a lot more at ease, too. Ultimately, smiling is an easy way to improve your mental well-being through increased confidence and better relationships with other people.

Recognize that a fake smile can make you look phony, nervous, or even dangerous, so do not just try to put on a smile without first practicing or putting

Chapter 15

To truly laugh, you must be able to take your pain, and play with it!

Sir Charles Spencer "Charlie" Chaplin (1889–1977) English comic actor, film director, and composer best known for his work during the silent film era. Chaplin wrote or co-wrote the scores and songs for many of his films. "Smile", which he composed for his film *Modern Times*, hit number 2 on the UK charts when sung by Nat King Cole in the 1950s. It was also Michael Jackson's favourite song.

Always laugh when you can. It is cheap medicine.

George Gordon Byron, 6th Baron Byron, later George Gordon Noel, 6th Baron Byron (1788–1824) British poet and a leading figure in the Romantic movement.

yourself in a happy state of mind. You can spot a fake smile from a genuine smile. A fake smile is one where the corners of the mouth are not turned up, or the mouth is solely smiling, with no change at all in the eyes. You will know it when you see it as you pick up the subtle body language cues that confuse you as to the smiler's intention; and if it is you making the fake smile, check your emotions to know whether or not you mean the smile.

Remember that forcing yourself to smile is better than not smiling at all, and if you persist, a genuine smile can ensue. Furthermore, do not smile to take advantage of people. If you are making someone do everything you ask just by smiling, stop. It is mean, and people will catch on and will not like you as much.

What should I consider?

If you fail, and you will fail, laugh at yourself, kick yourself in the butt and go on. Love yourself.

Do not regret anything. Do not put yourself down because you did not have the chance to say you were sorry, or "I love you", or "goodbye." You can still say it. Do not let the "if-only lies" take over: "If only I'd been nicer" or "If only I'd made time to visit more often".

Life is beautiful, and it has many wonderful surprises in store for you. So go ahead and smile, visit new places, and meet original people.

Music can be a very soothing way to cope when you are feeling loss and pain. Try to move from sad to more upbeat songs though, or you may cause yourself to feel morose just by listening to depressing music for a long time.

HEALTH & STRESS

There are six components of wellness: proper weight and diet, proper exercise, breaking the smoking habit, control of alcohol, stress management and periodic exams.

Kenneth H. Cooper
(1931 -)
Doctor of medicine and former Air Force Colonel from Oklahoma, who introduced the concept of aerobics.

You are free to think of other things. There is nothing that says that you have to keep dwelling on the loss to prove your sadness or to show others how much the loss means to you. People already know that you are devastated; you do not have to prove or explain anything. And remember that the most important thing is to believe in yourself and that you can achieve a healthy lifestyle.

Remember that you are never going to get anywhere without any self-belief, and positive thinking will make everything seem less difficult!

Recommended Reading & References
We suggest consulting the works identified below in order to learn more about the particulars contained in this chapter.

SELYE, Dr. Hans. STRESS SANS DÉTRESSE.
La presse. ISBN 0-7777-0095-6.

SOMER, Elizabeth, M.A., R.D. THE ESSENTIAL GUIDE TO VITAMINS AND MINERALS. Harper-Collins. ISBN 0-06-273345-1.

WEIL, Andrew, MD. 8 WEEKS TO OPTIMUM HEALTH.
Knopf publisher. ISBN 0-679-44715-6.

LONG, M.D. James W. THE ESSENTIAL GUIDE TO CHRONIC ILLNESS. Harper Perennial. ISBN 0-06-273137-8.

THE BURTON GOLBERG GROUP. ALTERNATIVE MEDICINE
Future Medicine Publishing. ISBN 0-9636334-3-0.

GUIDE MEDICAL PRATIQUE.
Québec Agenda. ISBN –2-8929-4115-6.

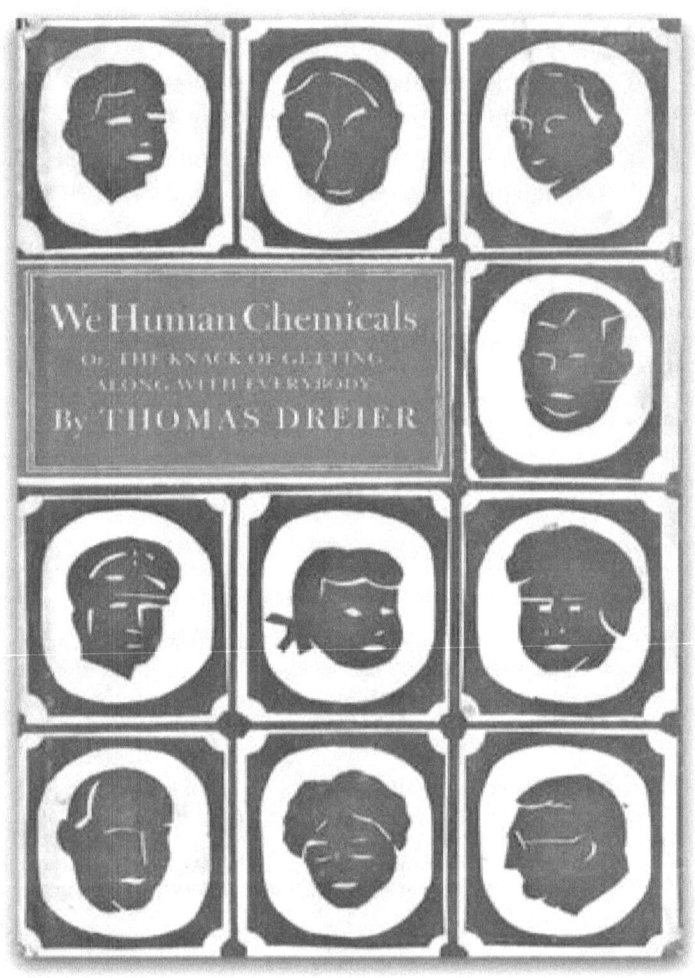

The world is like a great mirror. It reflects back to you what you are. If you are loving, if you are friendly, if you are helpful, the world will prove loving, friendly, and helpful to you.

The world is what you are.

Thomas Dreier

CHAPTER 16

COMMON SENSE

Whatever your background, training, IQ, or experience, common sense can be learned and applied to everyday situations. Smart people do not always do bright things; sometimes-intelligent people can do confoundedly irrational things, such as gambling away all their money on the stock market or forgetting to take adequate clothing for a back-country hike in the middle of very changeable weather. And while it may seem provocative to suggest that people do not use common sense, this deliberate association is merely to highlight that everyone has lapses in common sense.

Furthermore, the more we are trained to think one way, by our workplace, family, culture, etc., the greater the chance we will allow sloppy or autopilot thinking to take the place of common sense. Common sense is not a one-stop-destination; it is a way of thinking that needs constant nourishing.

Common sense is the collection of prejudices acquired by age eighteen.

Albert Einstein
(1879–1955)
His intellectual growth was strongly fostered at home. His mother, a talented pianist, ensured the children's musical education. His father regularly read Schiller and Heine aloud to the family. Uncle Jakob challenged Albert with mathematical problems, which he solved with 'a deep feeling of happiness'.

Common sense is about exercising sound and prudent judgment based on a simple perception of the situation or facts. As to the purpose of common sense, it is basically thinking that prevents you from making irrational mistakes or decisions, a thinking approach that may open your eyes to the possibility that insisting on being right prevents you from seeing the bigger picture.

Common sense can also serve the purpose of keeping you from being a stickler for rules, theories, ideas, and guidelines that would hamper or stifle the best decision in a particular situation. In other words, just because something says so, or it has always been done that way, is not a good reason to abandon common sense about present needs and changed

Chapter 16

The chief function of the body is to carry the brain around.

Thomas Alva Edison
(1847 –1931)
American inventor and businessman. He developed many devices that greatly influenced life around the world, including the phonograph, the motion picture camera, and a long-lasting, practical electric light bulb.

circumstances. Common sense is natural, but things can always go wrong; just do not beat yourself up about the past too much. Some things are inevitable.

Remember that good judgment requires that we ask ourselves two fundamental questions before we act: "What can I say or do that will help me get what I want?" and "What impact will my actions have on others?"

How does the brain work?

We are human; we are fallible. And our brains work in certain ways as a means of providing shortcuts to ensure survival in a world where being chased by predators could end our lives. In a modern world where caves and saber-toothed tigers are no longer constant companions, some of that reactive, split second judging can land us in hot water as we react instead of reflecting, assume instead of teasing apart the realities, and follow habit instead of challenging its continued utility. Some of the things our amazing minds are capable of doing to override common sense include:

Maintaining our own sense of reality out of proportion with identifiable reality. While each of us creates a reality out of our own experiences and makes sense of our world through this "personal lens", for the most part, we understand that our sense of reality is only a small portion of a much larger picture.

For some people, however, their sense of reality becomes the only sense of reality, and they believe that they can manipulate or magically transform situations to turn out the way they want them to be. In such cases, steps irrational behavior for some and insanity for the less fortunate.

Engaging in reflex or associative thinking. This is reactive thinking that is based simply on what we have learned through life, reenacting learned models and applying them to each new situation as it appears, without modifying the thought processes being applied. This type of thinking leads to errors in thinking because we refuse to push beyond standard associations formed in our minds about how things *should be*.

It is common sense to take a method and try it. If it fails, admit it frankly and try another. But above all, try something.

Franklin Delano Roosevelt
(1933–1945)
32nd President of the United States and a central figure in world events during the mid-20th-century, leading the United States during a time of worldwide economic crisis and world war.

When we apply what we know to a present situation by reference to a similar past situation by merely applying our mind's template without adjusting for the context, we are overriding common sense. Even where this template is a bad fit, the insistent or biased mind just ignores the parts of the template that do not fit by trimming them off mentally and only seeing the parts that *match*.

Consequentially, we have our problem solved without thinking it through. This type of thinking tends to make us easily swayed by current popular theories and fads, such as the fashionable tendency in some societies to control social opinion through inflating fears of germs, criminals and terrorists, and job unavailability.

Invoking absolute certainty. Absolutist black and white thinking about the world and others in it in a way that never allows space for doubt is often a cause for forgetting to apply common sense. For such a thinker, the "one true way" is the only way and, therefore, seems like common sense even though it is not.

Embracing pigheadedness. An unwillingness to never be wrong, founded on any number of reasons, including insecurities, fear, incomprehension, anger,

Chapter 16

The brain is a wonderful organ; it starts working the moment you get up in the morning and does not stop until you get into the office.

Robert Lee Frost
(1874 –1963)
American poet. He is highly regarded for his realistic depictions of rural life and his command of American colloquial speech.

and fear of ridicule, pigheadedness is the cause of many an irrational and unjustifiable decision or action.

What you see is what you have programmed your brain to see. This is not an invitation to insanity. This is a request to consider that your sense of reality is not real. And once you start down the slippery slope of self-confirmation that reality is only ever what you see it as, you are open to the possibilities of bigotry, selfishness, intolerance, and prejudice because you will constantly seek to make everyone and everything else conform to your standard of reality and your standard of *what's right*.

By dissociating yourself from this one-sided reality, and learning as much as you can about how other people perceive the world and our place in it; you begin to make room for common sense to grow because your sense is built on *common* experiences, not just your own.

Start by taking a look at your own emotions, beliefs, and practices to make sure they are not overriding your common sense. Test different scenarios in your mind to try and ascertain the sensible consequences of applying the decision or action the way you want to.

Is it practical, have you accounted for everything, and what will happen if things go wrong? If things go wrong, can you fix them, and if you can't, what will be the consequences? If your reality is clouding your judgment too much, reach out and discuss the situation with others to gain a wider appreciation of their perspectives and ideas. This is most important when you are too close to a situation and any decision or action you take might be affected by our being too closely involved.

Familiarize yourself with your reflective mind. This is the part of your thinking where true common sense resides, the part that takes a bit of time out from the cleverness, the brightness, the importance of everything rushing at you at the moment and suggests that it is time to add a dose of cold water to the excitement.

Reflective intelligence is about being able to stand back and view the bigger picture, so that you realistically appraise the situation or environment directly around you rather than end up forcing yourself to conform to its suitability or practicing wishful thinking.

After an accurate appraisal of the situation, a reflective mindset enables you to set goals that are realistic, given the parameters you are working within, and to take sensible actions toward meeting those goals. In other words, just because other people do or use something effectively is not a sign that it will suit you, too; you need to put your own pensive mind to work on each situation to decide whether it will be a fit for you, your lifestyle, and those around you directly impacted by your decisions.

It is man's own mind, not his enemy or foe, that lures him to evil ways.

Siddhārtha Gautama Buddha
(563 BCE - 483 BCE)
According to tradition, the Buddha emphasized ethics and correct understanding.

Recognize the previous step has just suggested that you need to reflect more before you make decisions or act. However, the obvious flip side to reflection is the reality that some things need very fast thinking and swift decisions that will produce sound results.

How do you marry rapid cognition to reflective thinking under the rubric of *common sense*? It is simple; spend your reflecting time intelligently, so that you will react wisely when quick thinking is required. Common sense builds on your reflecting on past experiences, enabling you to refine your

Chapter 16

understanding of the world and how it works time and time again. This contrasts with a person who only ever reacts on gut reactions, biases, and has failed to reflect on prior experiences.

Remember that engaging in reflection will bring about sound "gut reactions" or fast assessments of situations because your reaction is based on having taken the time to work through errors and successes of past experiences.

How can I reason?

Reason is the mental powers and processes concerned with forming conclusions, judgments, or inferences. Proper use of reasoning is extremely important in making daily decisions.

We are all short-sighted, and we very often see only one side of a matter, while failing to see the whole picture. We see partially; we know in part, and therefore, we may draw erroneous conclusions, inferences, and judgments from our partial views. Narrow-mindedness is a great fault of reasoning that everyone must strive to avoid.

Never imagine that you know all there is to know about any subject and that there is no more truth to know. Seek the truth earnestly. Dispel all prejudices from your mind. Do not think that there is no truth except in the sciences you study.

If you prejudge another's notions before examining them, you have not discovered the truth. Be eager to discover the truth in subjects unfamiliar to you. Read widely and take an interest in many different subjects.

You can always learn something from others, from parents, siblings, friends, neighbors, ministers, etc. If

My philosophy of life is that if we make up our mind what we are going to make of our lives, then work hard toward that goal, we never-lose – somehow we win out.

Ronald Wilson Reagan
(1911- 2004)
He was known to joke frequently during his lifetime, displayed humor throughout his presidency, and was famous for his storytelling. His numerous jokes and one-liners have been labeled "classic quips" and "legendary". Among the most notable of his jokes was one regarding the Cold War. As a sound check prior to his weekly radio address in August 1984, Reagan made the following joke as a way to test the microphone: "My fellow Americans, I'm pleased to tell you today that I've signed legislation that will outlaw Russia forever. We begin bombing in five minutes." Former aide David Gergen commented, "It was that humor... that I think endeared people to Reagan."

you see something someone else does well, learn from it by following his example. If you see something he does poorly, learn from that as well, by finding a way to improve, so as not to make the mistake yourself.

Refuse to be offended easily, but learn to view things from other's perspectives. Some people hold so fast to their own beliefs that they would not even consider they might be wrong when others question the beliefs which they hold as infallible or sacred.

No man is infallible. To suppose one is infallible is to refuse reason. Therefore, accept criticisms with eagerness, as convenient means to examine your own beliefs, ideas, and views.

On the other hand, be humble, and dispel any biases or errors you chance to uncover immediately, unreservedly, and wholeheartedly. Note that this includes all subjects and areas of your life, even in matters of religion or politics.

Remember that passion is a major bias that can make one blind to the facts, and distort reason, insomuch as you become incapable of using your own or listening to others' reason. To reason appropriately, you must adopt a spirit of unbiased disinterest. Learn to strike a balance between reason and passion. There is a time for reason and a time for passion. Let one not confound the other. Furthermore, seek out the best books in every science, search the Internet for the most reliable sources, and learn from the most knowledgeable people on all subjects.

Knowledge will give you power, but character respect.

Bruce Lee
(1940-1973)
He is best known as a martial artist, but he also studied drama and philosophy while a student at the University of Washington. He was well-read and had an extensive library. His own books on martial arts and fighting philosophy are known for their philosophical assertions, both inside and outside of martial arts circles.

Chapter **16**

How can I build character through integrity?

The wonderful thing about character and integrity, which are intimately related, is that they are some of the few things in life that no one will ever be able to take away from you forcefully. Your choices are your own. Even if someone can take your life, he cannot force you to make a choice that you believe is wrong. The definitions of character and integrity are often stretched or misrepresented.

Character is the sum of qualities that show up in a person or group, the moral or ethical strength, and the description of a person's attributes, traits, and abilities. Character is who you are. It defines you and guides your actions, hopefully in a positive way.

Integrity is steadfast adherence to a strict moral or ethical code, being unimpaired, sound, whole, and having undivided completeness. It can be summed up simply as "doing the right thing, for the right reason, even when no one is watching."

Choose a set of rules, morals, or principles that you believe will lead to a happy, satisfying, and righteous life, as well as a better world. You can subscribe to the ethics of a particular religion, or you can develop your own, based on your experiences.

You will probably feel your self-confidence and personal strength growing as you face and overcome challenges in sticking to your values, whatever they may be.

Importantly, look at the choices you have made in your past, and observe how much you have or have not lived by those principles. Decide what you must change in your behavior to align your life more closely with what you believe. In addition, be conscious every

Be more concerned with your character than your reputation, because your character is what you really are, while your reputation is merely what others think you are.

John Robert Wooden
(1910–2010)
American basketball player and coach.

day of the decisions you make however big or small, and of how close they bring you to being the person you really want to become.

Beware of people who will try to convince you to give up on your character or integrity, saying that nobody's perfect and taunting you for being such an idealist. The fact that nobody's perfect does not mean violating what you believe is right. It is good to learn from our mistakes, but we do not always need to make mistakes in order to learn. Remember that striving to be perfect and being perfect are two different ideas; the former is integrity; the latter is futility.

What about morality and religion?
Morality comes from a variety of sources, but a supernatural god is not one of those sources. If a modern human were to stone to death an adolescent for not honoring his or her father and mother, we would certainly think him or her amoral. However, these are the prescribed punishments for such acts, according to the Abrahamic texts.

Since modern humans do not follow their religious texts to the letter, they must have some method for determining which prescriptions to follow and which to discard. The reasoning behind this disconnect is the same reasoning from which morals come. Aside from this intuitive denial of a divine moral source, contemporary ethicists tend to point to Plato's *Euthrypo* for an excellent problem that all divine command theorists find difficult to overcome. In this dialogue, we are encouraged to question whether something is good because God tells us it is OR it is good regardless of God's commands.

It was much later that I realized Dad's secret.
He gained respect by giving it.
He talked and listened to the fourth-grade kids in Spring Valley who shined shoes the same way he talked and listened to a bishop or a college president. He was seriously interested in who you were and what you had to say.

Sara Lawrence-Lightfoot
American sociologist who examines the culture of schools, the patterns and structures of classroom life, socialization within families and communities, and the relationships between culture and learning styles. She has been a professor at the Harvard Graduate School of Education since the 1970s.

Chapter 16

Character, in the long run, is the decisive factor in the life of an individual and of nations alike.

Theodore "Teddy" Roosevelt
(1858 –1919)
Historians credit Roosevelt for changing the nation's political system by permanently placing the presidency at center stage and making character as important as the issues. His notable accomplishments include trust busting and conservationism.

Your life does not get better by chance, it gets better by change.

Jim Rohn
(1930 – 2009)
American entrepreneur, author, and motivational speaker.

If you answer with the latter, then religion is irrelevant to morality, and if you answer with the former, then morality is arbitrary; for example, if God commanded that everyone be a serial killer, the killing would be moral, and that seems wrong.

Remember that your character is unique. It may not match with anybody else's. So do not expect it to. Build it assuming your own aptitude and inner light. Self-assessment, self-evaluation, introspection, etc. All work well. Nevertheless, never get disheartened by petty failures and criticism revolving around failures. Stand firm on your convictions. You are bound to succeed.

Do I need to learn things that are basic common sense?

There are things that every human being should know how to do and not leave to another person, things that go to the heart of personal survival, self-knowledge, and long-term health and safety.

You can learn common sense through practical knowledge and application, which both inform you accurately when times are harder or when you must react quickly. Some of the common sense basics that every human should know include:

Knowing how to cook and how the food gets to your table. Knowing how to cook is basic common sense because it will ensure your healthy survival under any condition. Furthermore, no matter how infrequently you use this skill, it is enjoyable and rewarding.

Knowing how to grow your own food. Being able to grow it is an assurance of self-survival. Learn the skill, if you haven't already, and teach it to your children.

Real knowledge is to know the extent of one's ignorance.

Confucius
(551BCE–479 BCE)
His principles had a basis in common Chinese tradition and belief. He championed strong familial loyalty, ancestor worship, respect of elders by their children (and, according to later interpreters, of husbands by their wives), and the family as a basis for an ideal government. He expressed the well-known principle, "*Do not do to others what you do not want done to yourself*", one of the earlier versions of the Golden Rule.

The maxim of the "golden rule" is exemplified in many Christian stories, such as the Parable of the Good Samaritan, which are unadorned replications of the Jewish Torah: "Love your neighbor as yourself: I am the LORD."(Leviticus 19:18 —NJPS)

Knowing about nutrition. If you are cooking for yourself, and perhaps growing your own food, eat healthily most of the time, in moderation, and with an eye to meeting all appropriate nutritional needs for your age, gender, height, and personal conditions.

Knowing and respecting your surroundings. It is common sense to know what local conditions impact your life, from weather to wildlife. Take the time to get to know your local environment, and respond to it appropriately, from adequately weatherproofing your home to removing invasive species from your garden.

Knowing how to budget and not spend more than you are earning. It is common sense only to spend what you have. Over-spending is an irrational habit, as is hiding unopened bills at the back of a closet; reining in the spending with a budget and self-restraint is common sense in action.

Knowing the limitations of your own body. This includes knowing which foods wreak havoc with your body, which foods work for you, how many hours of sleep you need, and the type of exercise that benefits your body and metabolism best. Read widely, but work out for yourself what harms and heals your body, as you are the real expert on this topic. Moreover, you are no super hero. Ignoring bodily injuries is done at your own peril, such as continuing to carry heavy loads with an aching back, or refusing to acknowledge constant pains.

Knowing how to analyze situations and think for yourself. Instead of digesting the pulp media thrown at you every day, and ending up in a state of fear because every second news item is a crime or disaster, look at the reality behind the news feed and

Chapter 16

start thinking with a healthy, open, and questioning mindset.

Knowing how to repair items. In a world heavily dependent on the disposal of items rather than on repairing them, we are adding to the Earth's burden. Those who manufacture items with built-in obsolescence have caused us to lose the ability to tinker and fix things ourselves. Learning how to fix or mend clothes, appliances, household objects, car engines, and many other items that are important to our daily functioning is not only liberating but also an important way to exercise our common sense.

Knowing how to plan in advance. So that you are not doing things haphazardly, more expensively, or without any idea of the consequences, learn to plan ahead. Forward thinking is always a sign of good common sense, as is being able to review the consequences of different outcomes.

Knowing how to be resourceful is about taking small things and making them go a long way with a little imagination and elbow grease. It is about being able to thrive under difficult conditions and still prosper and not feel deprived. Resourcefulness is a key part of using common sense, and again, it is a skill that liberates you from having to consume in order to live.

Knowing how to connect with community. It is common sense to be a part of your community; unfortunately, many people prefer to bunker down and remain aloof or unhindered by the others around them. Connecting with others in your community is part of being human, of relating, and of opening yourself up to sharing and generosity.

Remember you will not always win. Some days, the most resourceful individual will taste defeat. But there is, in this case, always tomorrow - after you have done your best to achieve success today.

Dr. Maxwell Maltz (1899 – 1975) American cosmetic surgeon and author of *Psycho-Cybernetics* (1960), which was a system of ideas that he claimed could improve one's self-image. In turn, the person would lead a more successful and fulfilling life.

Knowing how to keep safe. Whether you are in public or at home, safety is a matter of common sense. Looking both ways before crossing the street, walking with a friend or group in dark areas of the city at night instead of being alone, etc., these are common sense safety actions that can be planned for and put into action before anything harmful happens; and doing so will often avert problems altogether. Think prevention, not disaster.

Remember that common sense is learned through experience. Your friends and family will be more than happy to talk about basic dos and don'ts for any given situation with which they have familiarity if they know it is about ensuring your safety. In addition, manipulative and controlling strategies do not equate to common sense. These are signs of people who wish to change reality and cause other people to fit in with their notions of reality. You cannot change this type of person, so unless you are paid to hear their woes, use your common sense and keep a good distance from them.

How can I put new common sense thinking habits into place?

Take the philosophical, the psychological, and the popular theories behind how we think and add this understanding to the active ways in which you can use your common sense:

Practice mental flexibility. This is the ability to stay open-minded and to listen to other people's notions and ideas, even if they scare you or derail your own thinking. It does you good to practice mental elasticity and to stretch yourself beyond the things you think you already know.

Knowing is not enough; we must apply. Willing is not enough; we must do.

Johann Wolfgang von Goethe
(1749 –1832)
German writer, pictorial artist, biologist, theoretical physicist, and polymath. He is considered the supreme genius of modern German literature.

Chapter 16

The only way to make sense out of change is to plunge into it, move with it, and join the dance.

Alan Wilson Watts
(1915 –1973)
British philosopher, writer, and speaker, best known as an interpreter and populariser of Eastern philosophy for a Western audience.

A lifestyle is what you pay for; a life is what pays you.

Thomas J. Leonard
(1955 – 2003)
Was a key player in the field of personal and business coaching.

Use affirmative thinking. Affirmative thinking is perceiving yourself and others in a positive manner, always looking forward to seeing the best in others and yourself, and making constant conscious decisions about who or what you will allow yourself to be influenced by, and what you will consider worthy of devoting your thinking time to. This is not as simplistic as chanting affirmations or thinking happy thoughts; the mental work required to maintain an affirmative, responsive mindset is hard but rewarding.

Value ideas. Valuing ideas leads you to accept new ideas rather than immediately knocking them down as unfamiliar, insane, or undoable. How do you know they do not match your viewpoint until you have worked through them? And valuing ideas helps one reflect often, and without adequate time for reflection, you will fail to come up with your own ideas. Furthermore, ancient wisdom can be helpful, but it can also hinder. It all depends on the context of when the *wisdom* was developed and whether it stands the test of time or not.

Trust yourself. If you put in the constant hard work of thinking things through carefully for yourself, as well as learning all that you can about the world and other's thoughts about the world, you will be in good shape. You do not have to be highly educated; you do have to be open-minded and curious. And realize that this is a process, not a destination. You will have to make the mental effort throughout your lifetime as to which messages you absorb and which people you allow to influence your thinking. After all, doing so is just plain common sense.

Additionally, common sense dictates that all-important agreements, such as financial and marriage agreements, be in writing. Trust subject yourself to the vagaries of time and faulty memories. Furthermore, do not be paranoid; be wise!

Just think things through beforehand!

Remember to be compassionate. People using common sense can sometimes be impatient with the stupidity of others around them. Shelve this desire, for tomorrow it may be your lack of common sense that is being laughed at or berated. We are all equally stupid at different times in life, just as we are all equally smart at other times. It is contextual, and it is only embarrassing or wrong if we refuse to learn from it.

How can I think outside of the box?

No doubt you have heard of "thinking outside the box." Perhaps you have wondered what that actually meant, or you know what it means but you are so firmly "inside the box" that you do not even notice that you are in the box.

To re-educate yourself and change the way you think is almost a "lifestyle" change. Be prepared for a big change. Basically, you are re-inventing the wheel, and you are the wheel. Indications that it might be time to change your way of thinking include being in a dead end. If you are familiar with the terms, you will be in a great position to do some research into out-of-the-box thinking.

Understand that, for a given problem, some people tend to come up with the more "creative" solutions. The inability to do so does not reflect a person's intelligence. What it does indicate is that people with such solutions are the ones who are more willing, or have needed, to push themselves out of their comfort zone to get the answers they seek.

The potential of the average person is like a huge ocean unsailed, a new continent unexplored, a world of possibilities waiting to be released and channeled toward some great good.

Brian Tracy
(1944 -)
Canadian self-help author and motivational speaker.

Chapter 16

The principal characteristics for those who think outside of the box are usually: A willingness to embrace new perspectives toward day-to-day work, an ability to think differently with an open mind, the capacity to think about the substance of issues, and the openness to be receptive to doing things differently.

In addition, those who think outside the box focus on the value of finding new ideas and acting on them and are ready to strive to create value in newer ways. They are also capable of listening to, supporting, nurturing, and respecting others when they come up with new ideas.

Learn what inhibits your ability to change. Some characteristics lessen your ability to make a positive change in your thinking methods: Negative attitudes, fear of failure, perfectionism, stress, blindly following rules, not being flexible, and an inability to perceive the value in gray areas.

Assumptions are the termites of relationships.

Henry Franklin Winkler
(1945 -)
American actor, director, producer, and author. In September 2011, Winkler was made an honorary Officer of the Order of the British Empire (OBE) "for services to children with special educational needs and dyslexia in the UK".

Furthermore, making assumptions about others, about the world, about the expectations you feel weighing on you, and about your own abilities, all these also hinder change. Relying too much on logic and assuming you have an accurate grasp of what is logical makes change difficult as well.

Just because it has always been that way, does not mean that it has to continue to be that way. In fact, by expecting things never to change, you are setting yourself up for a lot of pain and unhappiness when things, and people, do change around you, without "taking you along". Ways to challenge assumptions include:

- Do not ignore your questions; give them free rein.

- Haste makes waste and can leave you in "hot water". Reflect on things until the better answer arrives. Stop jumping to hasty conclusions.

- Look at something in a different way, literally. Perhaps you have been hammering out a new design for something at work. You have been looking at this design for weeks, always in the same position. Try shifting it. Turn the design upside down, or take it out onto the sunshine under the trees, or project it into the ceiling and have all of your co-workers lie on the floor to observe it. You will be amazed at what a position change can do for assumptions and perspective.

Doing the same thing, day in and day out, will make even the smartest person's mind dull. Break free of dull routine. Find ways of minimizing routine in your life, while still embracing ritual; the two approaches bring very different results.

Ritual is about daily or regular activities that anchor you, keep you well, and give you a sense of place and identity. Routine is about the things that cause you to fall into a rut or respond without thinking, and they often feel imposed upon you from outside.

Change things occasionally; do things differently. Change your appearance and clothes. Walk a different way to work, catch a bus instead of driving, and bring your lunch in instead of eating out or vice versa. Go home early for a change.

Brainstorming can do amazing things to help you think outside the box. Furthermore, it can be really beneficial to help you learn about how people do things in other walks of life. Whether you are a CEO, an engineer, a stay-at-home mom, or a teacher, there

Human beings lose their logic in their vindictiveness.

Elizabeth Cady Stanton (1815–1902) American social activist, abolitionist, and leading figure of the early woman's movement. Her *Declaration of Sentiments*, presented at the first women's rights convention held in 1848 in Seneca Falls, New York, is often credited with initiating the first organized woman's rights and woman's suffrage movements in the United States.

Chapter 16

are ways of thinking laterally that can benefit what you do.

Read about processes and solutions in industries different from the one you work in. Chances are there are some amazing answers for you to uncover and apply to your situations.

The same will be true for cross-disciplinary studies. Instead of staying within your own expertise, branch out and investigate what other disciplines are doing in areas, or topics, that interest you. There may be some surprising connections worth uncovering and adapting. Sit down and talk with others who know nothing about what you are doing but are willing listeners. Explain your situation and challenges, and ask for their thoughts and ideas for possible solutions.

There is no fruit, which is not bitter before it is ripe.

Publilius Syrus
Latin writer of maxims, flourished in the 1st century BC. He was a Syrian who was brought as a slave to Italy, but by his wit and talent he won the favour of his master, who freed and educated him.

There is nothing quite so re-energizing as the fresh, unwearied viewpoint of a child. Take your child to work. It is not that your child is cleverer than you; it is just that your child is less worn down, more open to speaking his or her mind in a forthright manner, and usually unafraid to use what creativity he or she possesses.

You should give your child a look at the situation or problem before you. Ask the child what he or she would do. And listen to the answer very carefully; take it to heart; and use the freshness of perspective the child brings to your thinking to help re-energize your outlook.

Thinking outside of the box, is also taking your vacations. They are given to you so that you can go away and refresh your thinking, your body, your mind, and your soul.

COMMON **SENSE**

The refreshed you is worth infinitely more to the company than the worn-out and irritable, frazzled, in-a-rut you. So if you must sell your soul to the company, at least see vacations as benefiting the company as much as you.

Remember that learning to change your style of thinking is not an easy process, or a quick one. Be patient. Enjoy the journey. Explore faiths beyond your own. Try to find the similarities and connections. And aim to accept each for what it is. Read something that is not in your normally preferred genre. For example, if you think you hate crime fiction why not try reading one? You might be pleasantly surprised. It could challenge your thinking processes. Be sure to read to the end! Read biographies to see how other people overcame ruts in their lives. Adapt their thought-out solutions to your current situation.

How can I think clearly and logically under pressure?

In order to set the stage for clear logical evaluation under pressure, you have to be able to control your panic reaction to a situation for just a few seconds!

A few seconds is all the time you will ever need to come to a clear decision, normally. Perhaps you do not give yourself this breathing space, but you almost always can - unless everything is completely out of your control.

Stop whatever you are doing-just for literally two or three seconds. Look at the cause of the pressure, whatever it is, and begin to ask yourself these questions: What are the pressures I am being put under here? Does the situation require prioritizing or simply time control?

Courage is what it takes to stand up and speak; courage is also what it takes to sit down and listen.

Sir Winston Leonard Spencer-Churchill
(1874 –1965)
He is the only British prime minister to have received the Nobel Prize in Literature, and was the first person to be made an Honorary Citizen of the United States.

Remember not to become overconfident and make mistakes. Think about worst-case scenarios in your free time. Make your mind accustomed to fictitious pressure, so that when pressure hits you, you will not panic. Take deep breaths and assess the situation.

How can I think before speaking?

One of the most obvious and significant attributes of humans is the ability to communicate through speech. An interesting corollary is that we can also communicate our thoughts in real time; we do not need to plan what we are going to say before we say it.

This has both advantages and disadvantages. It would be clearly undesirable for us to have to formulate our thoughts before we issue an immediate warning, and communication would be dramatically slowed if we were unable to respond, naturally, to people in normal conversation.

But generally speaking, I tend to be quiet and introspective.

Rowan Sebastian Atkinson
(1955 -)
British actor, comedian, and screenwriter.
He is most famous for his work on the sitcoms *Blackadder*, *Mr. Bean* and *The Thin Blue Line*.

On the other hand, this innate ability is often the source of consternation when what we say on the spur of the moment is something we later wish we had either not said, ... or said differently; it happens to everyone sometimes. Typically, this happens when we are responding quickly in stressful situations or during a confrontation, although it can happen at any time. The trick is to try to catch ourselves before we say something amiss.

Recognizing that we do not always say what we would like to communicate is an important realization. How to help mitigate that issue is not complex, but it does require some behavioral changes.

The goal is to be aware of when to talk naturally and fluidly and when to think before we speak and when not to speak at all. After we determine what circumstances will most likely produce such miscommunication, we need to be very observant about when those conditions appear to be manifesting. The more skilled we become at recognizing this, the better we will be at changing our approach.

Once you know you are in one of those situations, the goal is for you to process information. Often when we respond in a less than appropriate way, it is because we did not fully comprehend what was being said. This is the time to sit back and listen to what is going on around you. Do not start focusing on what you are going to say; just absorb what is being said. Your mind will process this information in the background.

Who is speaking and how does he or she communicate? Some people are very literal, and some people use examples. Some people use a lot of facial expressions and body language to augment their conversation, whereas others rely on complex verbiage. How people convey information is a very good indicator of how they best absorb information.

Do not consider just one way you might respond, but consider all your options. There are many different ways to say things, and your goal here is to find the best way to convey what you want to say in a way that has a positive impact.

Communication primarily succeeds based on the action of the recipient, so you have to communicate based on the listener. If you are just responding because other people are talking, then it is possible your communication does not fit the *effective, necessary, accurate, timely,* and *appropriate* model. If not, afterwards sit back and continue to listen.

Are we like late Rome, infatuated with past glories, ruled by a complacent, greedy elite, and hopelessly powerless to respond to changing conditions?

Camille Anna Paglia
(1947-)
American author, teacher, and social critic.

Chapter 16

You will want what you say to have an impact, and not just to make noise. Always wait five or ten seconds before responding. This gives you time to determine whether a response is required - and if so, to formulate an appropriate and thoughtful response.

Is the information you are going to present formulated in a way that will make a positive impact? Make sure your comments are relevant and appropriate to the conversation. Do not stray from the topic; stay focused. Creating a negative atmosphere will guarantee failure in communications.

You will want people to understand that you are contributing to the conversation, rather than detracting from it. It only takes an instant to ruin your ability to communicate during that time. Identify first how the listeners will react.

Before entering a room, think about the people involved in the situation and the possible questions you might be asked. Decide how you will respond and what points you want to make before hand.

Positive thinking will let you do everything better than negative thinking will.

Hilary Hinton "Zig" Ziglar (1926 -) American author, salesman, and motivational speaker.

How you say something is, in many ways, as important as what you say. Tone of voice can convey enthusiasm and sincerity, or it can rebuff and show sarcasm, and as many people have experienced, what we say can be taken in the wrong way.

The most likely reason is that the tone of voice, what was said, the body and facial language, as well as the content, were not all thoughtfully combined to integrate with the listener's most effective method of communication. If people are not actually addressing you, they may not want your opinion. Try to refrain from forcing yourself into conversations.

COMMON SENSE

While you are talking, consider what you are saying and keep a close watch on the reactions of your listeners as they emerge. After the conversation is over, review the whole process again in your mind and note what you might have done differently and why.

This is an ongoing process. Over time, you will refine it and improve. You will become a better communicator, and people will accept your responses more openly. This will take time. It should become a part of your life. As you get better, you will be regarded as someone whose opinion is valued.

Remember that the important thing is to think before you speak. When you have said something, if it was something hurtful, make a point to apologize. Whether immediately or in private, it is most appropriate to do so. If you do not know what you are talking about, do not try to be convincing. It is okay to express an opinion, but make sure people know you are speculating. Strictly avoid insults or inappropriate personal references of any kind. You will lose respect, and you are guaranteed a negative result.

How can I think ahead?

No one can see into the future, yet we all must make guesses about it in order to make decisions and be better prepared for what comes our way. The guesses that we make are not based on seeing into the future but on our knowledge and past experiences, with a little insight mixed in.

The future is a big place with many eventualities, but chances are that you will want to address a specific situation, problem, or opportunity. Define this "end" to the best of your ability.

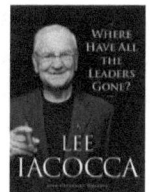

Talk to people in their own language.
If you do it well, they'll say, 'God, he said exactly what I was thinking.'
And when they begin to respect you, they'll follow you to the death.

Lido Anthony "Lee" Iacocca (1924 -) American businessman known for engineering the Mustang, the unsuccessful Ford Pinto, being fired from Ford Motor Company, and his revival of the Chrysler Corporation in the 1980s.

Chapter 16

Not all decisions are rational or carefully analyzed, and intuitive guesses can often be quite powerful. What feels right? What do you think will happen? When you use your intuition, you draw upon your experience and knowledge in a different way than when you make a rational analysis. Listen to your first instinct. Intuition often works best before you have had time to study the details, so pay attention to it, even if you do not act on it immediately.

Intuition may clue you into emotional factors and subtle cues that you might otherwise miss. If something feels wrong about a situation, or you just do not like somebody, do not ignore it, even if you cannot put your finger on the exact problem. Use intuition as a "lead", rather than as a solution. Investigate what might be causing your hunch or gut feeling; dig deeper until you find it.

Take time to deliberate, but when the time for action has arrived, stop thinking and go in.

Napoléon Bonaparte
(1769 –1821)
He ordered a young cavalry officer, Joachim Murat, to seize large cannons and used them to repel the attackers on 5 October 1795—*13 Vendémiaire An IV* in the French Republican Calendar. One thousand four hundred royalists died, and the rest fled. He had cleared the streets with "a whiff of grapeshot", according to the 19th century historian Thomas Carlyle in *The French Revolution: A History*.

Consider what you already know. Prior knowledge comes from many places. Have you tried something similar before? Do you know how somebody is likely to react? Have you seen something done, or could you read about others' experiences with a situation? Could you ask others what they think? Can you try something out or gather data that might suggest what could happen?

People tend to bias their guesses and actions in certain predictable ways. Detect your own biases. For example, recent events may play a larger role in influencing decisions than they warrant. Alternatively, you may be more likely to believe something just because everyone around you believes it. If you think this sort of thing is happening, start looking closely at the hard evidence, such as facts and numbers, and question your own assumptions. Ask yourself "*what if*" for various possibilities and imagine promising outcomes and potential courses of events that could result.

In particular, think about the possible consequences of different courses of action. Consider the worst-case scenario. What is the worst thing that could possibly happen? Evaluate the possible risks. Moreover, consider the best-case scenario. What is the best thing that could possibly happen?

Evaluate the possible rewards. If you are trying to think ahead, it is probably because you want to decide how to respond to some situation or need; consequently, think of possible responses.

Think of potential actions to take based on your experience and knowledge about how such events usually turn out. Choose or narrow down which action(s) to take.

Whatever you have to get ready - be it people, equipment, facilities, plans, or simply courage, get it ready. Be honest with yourself.

No amount of wishful thinking is going to stop the next natural disaster, but the realistic admission that one might happen could lead you to prepare appropriately.

As much as possible, write down your thoughts. Writing can be a powerful tool for preparation. It helps you remember your plans, and it helps you to see them completely.

Then act according to your predictions and your plans, and let life take its course. See what happens. By taking note of the outcome, you will have more experience and knowledge to draw from the next time

The best ideas come as jokes. Make your thinking as funny as possible.

David Mackenzie Ogilvy (1911–1999) British advertising executive. He has often been called "The Father of Advertising". In 1962, *Time* called him "the most sought-after wizard in today's advertising industry". He was known for a career of expanding the bounds of both creativity and morality.

Chapter 16

Very little is needed to make a happy life; it is all within yourself, in your way of thinking.

Marcus Aurelius
(121 AD – 180 AD)
Roman Emperor from 161 to 180 AD. He ruled with Lucius Verus as co-emperor from 161 until Verus' death in 169. He was the last of the "Five Good Emperors" and is also considered one of the most important Stoic philosophers.

you must make a decision in a similar situation. As you see what really does transpire, adjust your actions or responses appropriately. You may not have the opportunity to change course after you begin, but you can acquire new information or continually affect results. Use what you learn to decide how to modify your actions in the present and in the future.

In addition, thinking of the best and worst-case scenarios can help you both establish a range of likely possibilities and make plans and decisions accordingly. Statistics and probability are mathematical ways of analyzing track records. Use them if you need numerical information about how likely an outcome is.

Remember to brainstorm together with others. Thinking ahead need not be done solo, and you will have the insights and ideas of everybody you consult. In addition, ideas generally feed other ideas. Do not get so caught up in thinking ahead that you fail to act. Often, the first thing to do is to try something based on your best guess and see whether it works. Treat your guesses as guesses, and remember that no one can foresee every eventuality.

What should I consider?

Common sense is about exercising sound and prudent judgment based on a simple perception of the situation or facts. As to the purpose of common sense, it is basically thinking that prevents you from making irrational mistakes or decisions, a thinking approach that may open your eyes to the possibility that insisting on being right prevents you from seeing the bigger picture.

COMMON **SENSE**

During a life span, we encounter common sense situations and reflections that may challenge us to endure, and not ignore, the feelings and thoughts that linger. This may drain us of our energy, our peace, our time, our resources, our health, and sometimes our relationships and/or opportunities.

We may get overwhelmed and lose focus, optimism, or peace. This is when we truly have to maintain our calm for the sake of our health, peace, and well-being.

Reflection is the art of pondering on one's virtues and faults. It is, as well, the ability to reflect on the "here and now," on your feelings and thoughts.

This also includes reflecting on the thoughts, emotions, and feelings of others. This can help you to improve yourself as you assess and reflect upon the decisions you make and have made in life.

Use your reflections to make a profound, constructive, or positive change in your life. This may require letting go of some people and retaining others. This will depend greatly on the outcome of your reflections, and on the accuracy and intuitive feelings of these reflections.

Demanding times can steal our joy, our peace, our strength, and our optimism. When you are dealing with a difficult situation, forgive yourself and, as applicable, forgive the other people involved.

When we harbor bitterness, guilt or anger, it hurts us more than anyone. Forgive yourself for the choice that may have placed you in the situation, and free up that space within you to make room for positive energy.

Hammurabi Stone

Hammurabi
(died c. 1750 BCE)
Was the sixth king of Babylon. He is known for the set of laws called Hammurabi's Code, one of the first written codes of law in recorded history.

Then commit to having the foresight to identify what you could do or say differently in the future to minimize the chances of the difficult situation recurring.

Remember that difficult times are not forever; they will pass!

Recommended Reading & References
We suggest consulting the works identified below in order to learn more about the particulars contained in this chapter.

BERNSTEIN, Albert J. Ph.D. DINOSAUR BRAINS, DEALING WITH ALL THOSE IMPOSSIBLE PEOPLE AT WORK.
Wiley & Sons. ISBN0-471-61808-X.

BOUCHARD, Jacques. LES 36 CORDES SENSIBLES DES QUÉBÉCOIS. Éditions Héritage. ISBN 0-7773-3944-7.

BURSK, CLARK + HIDY. Harvard Business School. THE WORLD OF BUSINESS, Selected Library of the Literature of Business from the Accounting Code of Hammurabi to the 20th-century. Simon & Schuster, New York, 1962. Library of Congress catalog card number: 62-14278.

BUTLER-BOWDON, Tom. 50 PSYHOLOGY CLASSICS. Who We Are, How We Think, What We Do.
Gildan Media. ISBN 1-59659-119-6.

ISAACSON, Walter. EINSTEIN: His Life and Universe.
SIMON & SCHUSTER. ISBN-13-978-0-7432-6473-0.

LINOWES, F. David. STRATEGIES FOR SURVIVAL: Using Business Know-how to Make our Social System Work. AMACOM. American Management Association. ISBN 0-8144-5326-0.

MCCORMACK, Mark H. WHAT THEY DON'T TEACH YOU AT HARVARD BUSINESS SCHOOL.
Bantam Books. ISBN 0-553-05061-3.

PETER, L. J. & HULL, R. LE PRINCIPE DE PETER, pourquoi tout va toujours mal.
Éditions Stock, 1970. ISBN 70-11-682-850-1580.

PETERS, Thomas J. THE LITTLE BIG THINGS: 163 Ways to Pursue Excellence.
Harper Studios. ISBN 978-0-06-189408-4.

SULLIVAN, A.M. HUMAN VALUES IN MANAGEMENT.
Dun & Bradstreet library, Library of Congress
card number: 73-89913.

THE PHILOSOPHY BOOK.
Dorling Kindersley. ISBN 978-2-7613-4125-7.

THE NEW YORK TIMES. GUIDE TO ESSENTIAL KNOWLEDGE.
St-Martin's Press. ISBN 0-312-31367-5.

TSUFIT. STEP INTO THE SPOTLIGHT!
Beach View Books. ISBN 978-0-9781913-0-6.

WALKER, Harold Blake. POWER TO MANAGE YOURSELF.
Harper & Brothers Publishers. New York, 1955.
Library of Congress catalog card number: 55-8529.

Recognition and thankfulness,
it is purely a matter of judgment and admiration
for ourselves and others.

Open your heart to thankfulness and you will recognize your fair value.

Yvan Poirier

Photo: WebTech Collection

RECOGNITION & THANKFULNESS

(This chapter is a special contribution by Yvan Poirier.)

CHAPTER 17

During a process of change, it is important that all the participants be willing to modify their ways and their personal and professional approaches to the changes that are taking place.

It is, sooner or later, necessary for them to look objectively at what they have to improve, whether it is the way they do things or how they manage their feelings in reaction to efficiency.

It is essential for them to observe in themselves, through questioning, what can be changed both in terms of respect and empathy for others: You cannot change anything in life as long as you do not change yourself first!

It is very important to speak about thankfulness with regard to everything inside this book. First of all, to have a certain thankfulness in life is something that we all will want to have toward people – workers, friends, family, etc.

Also from Yvan Poirier:
LA RECONNAISSANCE, une question de respect! (Recognition: A Question of Respect!).

WebTech Publishing (2009).

It is necessary to realize that, throughout life, we have many opportunities for thankfulness, each of which allows us to review our commitments, actions, and ways of acknowledging and respecting other people and things.

Being full of thankfulness is a personal choice, a way of living, and it has permanent implications throughout our lives and our careers, no matter what our responsibilities may be.

Chapter **17**

My support to this book

I accepted with great pleasure the opportunity to contribute to the writing of this book on change, which I find very interesting and educational but mostly innovative.

Thankfulness is the beginning of gratitude. Gratitude is the completion of thankfulness. Thankfulness may consist merely of words. Gratitude is shown in acts.

Henri Frédéric Amiel
(1821 – 1881)
He was a Swiss philosopher, poet, and critic.
The one book by which Amiel is still known is the *Journal Intime* ("Private Journal"), which, published after his death, obtained a European reputation.

Furthermore, I want to thank and congratulate the author, Germain Decelles, for his initiative and courage because this book will be very useful for most readers, regardless of their levels of involvement in a process of change. This work, which I consider to have expert advice regarding changes – and the process of change, is an indispensable tool to be used to face these changes, both for the individuals concerned and for the organizations wishing to modify outdated or different mechanisms through a process of change.

However, my concept of thankfulness, under all its forms, represents for me a challenge to demonstrate that it is possible to succeed when we are ourselves, no matter what difficulties or successes we may have to live through. To me, being thankful means considering the process of change as if it were something that we all have to raise awareness about, transcend – no matter what the importance of the change, and execute. I believe my approach is complementary to the rest of this book.

My culture-of-change is not only a system in which we revise the organizational infrastructure but also an opportunity to observe profound modifications in ourselves during the process because everyone has to look at what the development of the re-organizational situation will create within himself or herself in order to understand why we had to go through this turbulent period in which the morale and consciousness undergo an important shock.

Moreover, it is necessary to recognize that the process of change is a relatively abrupt awakening, which stirs not only our values and our personal achievements but especially the vision that we must have according to the current reality and our immediate future.

> We cannot appeal to the conscience of the world when our own conscience is asleep.
>
> Carl von Ossietzky
> (1889 – 1938)
> He was a German pacifist and the recipient of the 1935 Nobel Peace Prize.

With all that we live, nationally and internationally around the globe, and with the chapters on the economy, the workforce at work, and the various social and personal suggestions having already been presented, it is time to move more in-depth towards the innovative systems of change that will be in operation in the near future. While considering what to write for this chapter, I decided to include a new dimension, which is a part of my intrinsic vision of life and my experience: thankfulness, which I explain and assess as completely as I can. It is with humility that I move forward and offer you an introspective facet of change, using criteria which you already know, certainly, but which I hope to elaborate on in several ways.

My goal is to offer you some simple tools that should help you become more aware of your inner source, whether you call it your soul, spirit, or by some other name. This does not mean that I want to indoctrinate you. On the contrary, I simply want to help you examine the inner strength that you already possess when you face a situation that requires a change in your personal life and, subsequently, in your professional life. Perhaps my approach may seem a bit complex, but I believe it will give you a new look at the attitude to have when you face changes in the future.

Of course, you undoubtedly realize that change is part of our daily lives, and we have to face it sooner

Chapter 17

or later, so why not give it a new, conscious meaning. During the change process, it is necessary to learn to free ourselves from the former to reach the new, but we also need to "deepen" our approach, using intuition and instinct, both of which come from the depths of ourselves. In the following pages, I hope to bring you to an awareness that will, I hope, raise your awareness and help you to be more open-minded to face the changes, whatever they may be and whenever they may occur, both effectively and efficiently.

New vision

First, to change our future, we need to renew our way of thinking about the present; we need to see things and look at life differently and in ways we have not yet previously thought of or imagined. We cannot change our immediate future if we do not open our minds and spirits to observe things as they are in the present and as they realistically have been (nowadays often considered outdated or obsolete). But by replacing our external vision with our internal vision, by subtly "putting on new glasses", we can often "see" in innovative and creative ways that can help us change the current organizational realities.

Essentially, there are fundamental criteria which allow us to see our systemic approach to the change with a new consciousness, as I mentioned earlier, wearing "new glasses". So, here in bulk, are these criteria of the basic elements of awarenesses that we must apply to the change to make it successful. There are seven (7) determining criteria to help transform a vision into a real change. At this point, it must be remembered that the changes we make often seem to take place outside of us, but in reality they come from within, and they open our consciousness to new perceptions and visions of life.

Life is one big road with lots of signs.
So when you are riding through the ruts, don't complicate your mind.
Flee from hate, mischief and jealousy.
Don't bury your thoughts; put your vision to reality.
Wake Up and Live!

Robert Nesta
"Bob" Marley
(1945 – 1981)
He was a Jamaican singer-songwriter and musician.

RECOGNITION & THANKFULNESS

A flower cannot blossom without sunshine, and man cannot live without love.

Friedrich Maximillian Müller
(1823 – 1900)
He was more popularly known as Max Müller and was a German philologist and Orientalist, one of the founders of the western academic field of Indian studies and the discipline of comparative religion.

Depend upon yourself. Make your judgement trustworthy by trusting it.
You can develop good judgement as you do the muscles of your body - by judicious, daily exercise.
To be known as a man of sound judgement will be much in your favor.

Grantland Rice
(1880 - 1954)
He was an early 20th-century American sportswriter known for his elegant prose.

The seven (7) criteria are:
- Love
- Authenticity
- Autonomy
- Detachment
- Humility
- Simplicity
- Personal and professional ethics

LOVE
My intrinsic vision of love

In order to add thankfulness to our love, we - and the people we encounter at work, at home – need to realize that sometimes a change in certain attitudes or behaviors but especially in vision and, in where one stands regarding his or her personal values, needs to be made to succeed with discernment and respect.

When I speak about love, I am not talking about being in love with anyone. Rather, we must learn to love ourselves above all, to appreciate with humility, innocence, transparency, and simplicity.

Thankfulness is an inherent part of love that we project from ourselves and to others. Just consider the fact that we usually look for someone or something to love in our lives. It may be a life partner, a friend, or even an activity that we dedicate time and energy to and cherish in our own way.

Indeed, there is no passion swings, everyone finds his or her way to what he or she likes to accomplish so we can never judge any individual, regardless of his or her activity. He or she likes and embraces something, that's it!

Chapter 17

Those who deny freedom to others deserve it not for themselves.

Abraham Lincoln
(1809 – 1865)
The 16th President of the United States.

A man is simple when his chief care is the wish to be what he ought to be, that is honestly and naturally human.

Charles Wagner
(1852 – 1918)
He was a French reformed pastor whose inspirational writings were influential in shaping the reformed theology of his time.

Everybody has the ability to be manipulative, to be hateful and deceitful.

Neil LaBute
(1963 -)
He is an American film director, screenwriter, and playwright.

You know that one of the antitheses of love is judgment!
That an individual collects something he likes, even if it is very commonplace, we cannot judge this because we are not him, much less in his head and his heart!
Each finds his own way from the moment he loves what he does, in spite of its beauty or ugliness. Everything is relative in life to someone.
That is the freedom we have in our world!
It is necessary to remind ourselves that in this world everything is relative. Someone can consider a person handsome, and another can find that same person to be ugly.

Who is right?
Any interpretation is relative and individual. The "viewer" cannot be judged because everything is relative!
The standards for each cannot be weighed in the same way; everything still depends on the education and values society has given the viewer to interpret what he or she sees or perceives. We must respect everyone's vision if we want others to respect ours.

Between you and me, are we more selective than impartial in our vision, in our evaluation of the acknowledgement that we want to identify and share with others? Honestly, I am not sure that we remain fair and objective in our appreciation, our gratitude, and our tributes! These situations are not only the reflection of some convenience but also of morality to give our appreciation regardless of the person or context.

To understand that our way of seeing things is not always impartial, let us look in a relatively broad sense at the love we have in certain situations. Is it

A special contribution by Yvan Poirier

RECOGNITION & THANKFULNESS

It is well, when judging a friend, to remember that he is judging you with the same godlike and superior impartiality.

Arnold Bennett
Enoch Arnold Bennett
(1867 – 1931)
He was an English writer. He is best known as a novelist, but he also worked in other fields, such as journalism, propaganda and film

All too often arrogance accompanies strength, and we must never assume that justice is on the side of the strong. The use of power must always be accompanied by moral choice.

Theodore Meir Bikel
(1924 -)
He is a character actor, folk singer, and musician. He made his film debut in The African Queen (1951).

essential to know how to love, not in terms of being in love, but of appreciating with all our honesty and transparency?

I thought of widening this point of view with you to look at the word "love" or "like" more closely than we usually do in everyday life.

These days, all sorts of concepts tarnish the word "love". Now more than ever, we realize that we have been misled regarding the concept of love by ideas coming from either religious, philosophical, or esoteric institutions. The rulers of the earth have established this "love" on the conditionality of actions, unworthy laws, manipulative expectations, subliminal thoughts, and erroneous corruption.

So, people tried, for the greater part, to love, but under conditions which were unbalanced and especially fearful. So, jealousy, possession, envy, vengeance, and many other things were buried in bitterness, suffering, fear, unforgiveness, non-thankfulness, arrogance, and deep grief at having loved in duality instead of freely, without laws or conditioning.

So, love in human terms has almost always been "a love of battlefields". That is to say that the duality between good and evil, which is either true or false, has always taken precedence over letting go, over having the freedom to live and the compassion to love without the need to condition our love for someone for a situation.

As a matter of fact, it is a love that is paradoxical or contradictory, diverging more than viable, as much for the family and friendly relations as for the level of society that calls itself modern and adaptive. It is in

Chapter 17

Bias and prejudice are attitudes to be kept in hand, not attitudes to be avoided.

Charles Curtis
(1860 – 1936)
He was the 31st Vice-President of the United States (1929–1933).

All historical experience demonstrates the following: Our earth cannot be changed unless in the not too distant future an alteration in the consciousness of individuals is achieved.

Hans Küng
(1928 -)
He is a Swiss Catholic priest, theologian, and prolific author.

total confusion where everyone tries to love in his way, but looking at love as the fashion of the day.

"Today, I love you because you meet my expectations, and tomorrow I will hate you because you will not respond to my requests and requirements."

How can we get rid of prejudices that we have held on to for thousands of years?
Now, when we express our «paradoxical love», it should be based on the connection of two people or more, so the unconditional love, which is the free expression of what we are in our hearts, our natures, and not another way of seeing things. Thus, to live that love so detached from expectations or desires, and in an unconditional way, we must stop judging, comparing, and feeling guilty all the time.

We must learn to love ourselves as we are and also learn to love our friends as much as we despise our enemies. The best way for us to express our unconditional love is to let people be themselves, free in their desires, their needs, their choices, their thoughts, reactions and actions, good or bad; even if they are not in line with our own way of living. It is the same for the affection which we give without expectations - and which we receive with enjoyment and appreciation.

The influence of unconditional love will allow us as individuals, as well as the whole human race, to get rid of the chains that are destroying our freedom to live, our freedom to react to situations or actions.

In these times of revelations, evolution, conflicts of all kinds on the personal and organizational levels, in ethics and morality, we are at the turning point of the

> I refuse to accept the view that mankind is so tragically bound to the starless midnight of racism and war that the bright daybreak of peace and brotherhood can never become a reality... I believe that unarmed truth and unconditional love will have the final word.
>
> **Martin Luther King, Jr.**
> (1929 – 1968)
> He was an American clergyman, activist, and prominent leader in the African-American Civil Rights Movement.

> Love comes when manipulation stops; when you think more about the other person than about his or her reactions to you. When you dare to reveal yourself fully. When you dare to be vulnerable.
>
> **Joyce Brothers**
> (1927 -)
> She is an American psychologist, television personality, and advice columnist, publishing a daily syndicated newspaper column since 1960.

elevation of consciousness, so that everyone finds the intrinsic place, which awaits since millenniums. All of this, to be able to live in freedom without being conditioned by anything or anyone. The unconditional love represents the transmission of providential energy particles that enter our heart, while helping to transcend our fears, our guilt, and our sense of duty, which is sometimes abusive as others created it, to our detriment.

This unconditional love allows us to experience redemption, the resurrection to reinstate our heart, to finally live entirely in the freedom to be; instead of the freedom conditioned by intolerable social laws and exceeded by a new philosophy of the happiness at the present moment. The unconditional love cannot be subjected to conditions, because it is vibratory and detached from deceptive feelings, in the sense that it is a part of the limitless consciousness that runs through the memories of time and space and as the veils of shadows which obsess our limited consciousness. Through this unconditional love, we love our brothers and sisters as they are, without judging them or interpreting their life choices, whatever they are.

How do I see unconditional love expressed daily?
I believe that unconditional love is:

- A Love without expectations from others and without the need to justify anything or anyone;
- A Love where jealousy, possession, hatred, revenge, envy, rivalry, vanity, and pride have no place;
- A Love that can never manipulate, lie, act, mislead or deceive, but rather unites what is best within ourselves: unconditional love;

Chapter 17

Love all, trust a few, do wrong to none.

William Shakespeare
(1564 – 1616)
He was an English poet and playwright, widely regarded as the greatest writer in the English language and the world's pre-eminent dramatist.

Every life is a march from innocence, through temptation, to virtue or vice.

Lyman Abbott
(1835 – 1922)
He was an American Congregationalist theologian, editor, and author.

- A Love without judgment of a certain person or circumstance whatsoever;
- A Love with no need of religion, decadent laws, or drastic measures because it is itself the Absolute in our hearts;
- A Love that feeds the innate impulse of our heart and that, or those, of others without begging for anything because it was always present in us;
- A Love that cannot be relative or paradoxical because it is eternally alive in our hearts;
- A Love that prevents total falling in love, and it makes us rather climb in love;
- A love that transcends and heals all kinds of afflictions, pain, and suffering because it blesses the being instead of rejecting someone and abandoning him;
- A Love that denies nobody, and so anyone can surrender to it with confidence;
- A Love in which we can trust, because it will never repudiate or disown us;
- A Love where time, space, past, and thinking of the future do not exist because it exists in the present;
- A Love that anyone can submit to;
- A love sharing what we have best to offer;
- A Love of liberation, and of salvation, which offers the freedom to be what we are in the reality of our heart;
- A Love that rebuilt inside of us all the faith and innate confidence that we had lost since time immemorial;
- A Love where the power is limitless;
- A Love alchemically made in which only the vibration of light inside our hearts is manifested in its essence;
- A neutral love because it is separated from all forms of polarities, such as good or bad; this love is unconditional;

RECOGNITION & THANKFULNESS

A kind heart is a fountain of gladness, making everything in its vicinity freshen into smiles.

Washington Irving
(1783 – 1859)
He was an American author, essayist, biographer, and historian of the early 19th-century. He is best known for his short stories "The Legend of Sleepy Hollow" and "Rip Van Winkle".

This is my simple religion. There is no need for temples; no need for complicated philosophy. Our own brain, our own heart is our temple; the philosophy is kindness.

Dalai Lama
(1391 – 1474)
In religious terms, the Dalai Lama is believed by his devotees to be the rebirth of a long line of tulkus who are considered to be manifestations of the bodhisattva of compassion, Avalokiteśvara.

- An attractive Love which attracts without forcing or manipulating because it is unified and does not polarize whatever it is or whoever it is;
- A Love that has lived entirely in us since we were born, like the innocence of a child;
- A love that does not divide but unites;
- A Love that does not require anything; it is simply love;
- A non-susceptible Love, opened wide without apprehension and without the need to receive the approval of whomever;
- A Love where laughter and smiles are permanent;
- A Love from which real life comes, a love where there is only the gift of grace in ourselves, and without expectations;
- A Love where good and bad do not exist; there is only a respect for the choices of others, which makes them free to choose according to the vibrations inside them;
- A love that does not choose the words to soften or break because it is instantaneous when the opening of the heart is made;
- A Love that progresses and evolves each time the heart is opened;
- A Love of forgiveness where vengeance, hatred, and bitterness are not part of thoughts and attitudes;
- A Love whose attraction has the effect of gathering together all that is alive to become one;
- A Love unspeakable where nothing can disturb us in events that we cannot control;
- A love of compassion as we understand; we have empathy for a person or situation without judging;
- A Love of affection which feeds this love with dignity and respect;
- A Love which does not live conflicts, dualities, or bitterness because we have to transcend the fact

Chapter **17**

Charms strike the sight, but merit wins the soul.

Alexander Pope
(1688 – 1744)
He was an 18th-century English poet, best known for his satirical verse and for his translation of Homer. He is the third-most frequently quoted writer in The Oxford Dictionary of Quotations, after Shakespeare and Tennyson.

We are shaped by our thoughts; we become what we think. When the mind is pure, joy follows like a shadow that never leaves.

Gautama Buddha
or Siddhārtha Gautama Buddha
(c. 563 BCE)
He was a spiritual teacher from the Indian subcontinent, on whose teachings Buddhism was founded.

of judging whomever because we understand that it is as important to love our enemies as to love our friends;
- A Love where only the heart speaks in moments of divisions and disputes or disagreements;
- A Love where only the heart speaks, disregarding the ego and personality that try to be right or to justify themselves;
- A love of freedom where nothing can disturb the alignment that we wish to achieve with simplicity and authenticity;
- A Love where charm and seduction do not exist;
- A Simple Love where respect, understanding, and listening of the heart are ubiquitous;
- A genuine love where transparency is a purely natural reflex;
- An inner peace Love, and nothing can disturb this inner silence;
- A permanent Love of intimate heart joy which far exceeds happiness, which is only temporary, even ephemeral;
- A Love which breaks ordinary life into eternal life;
- A Love that does not condemn our errors, our faults, and our follies, but only amplifies the light of the heart with forgiveness;
- A Love that allows us to commune from our hearts with our living brothers and sisters, and the spirits of our deceased loved ones;
- A Love of Truth, where only certainty and evidence are present;
- A Love of justice which helps us not to judge beyond our knowledge but indeed to accept what others judge according to their skills and what they know in their functions or in the roles they play within the society;
- A fraternal and paternal Love which we try to live in accordance with the decisions of what others think of good or bad;

RECOGNITION & **THANKFULNESS**

Faith has to do with things that are not seen and hope with things that are not at hand.

Thomas Aquinas
(1225 – 1274)
He is held in the Catholic Church to be the model teacher for those studying for the priesthood.

Beauty without grace is the hook without the bait.

Ralph Waldo Emerson
(1803 – 1882)
He was an American essayist, lecturer, and poet, who led the Transcendentalist movement of the mid-19th century.

- A Love which multiplies on every occasion where we focus our intention, our thoughts, and our attention towards our gratitude and thankfulness, in order to constantly improve ourselves in humility and selflessness without being subjected to anyone;
- A love of frankness and sincerity where we cannot hide by lying;
- A Love where Faith is way beyond the knowledge and beliefs of any religion or philosophy whatsoever. True Faith is the abode of one who loves without fear or anxiety, having the certainty that true faith exists in itself and is something that exceeds comprehension and that we cannot touch, but only that vibrates in our hearts;
- A Love where the Light that vibrates in our hearts just transcends all our fears, our anxieties, and our shadows whatsoever.
- An Eternal Love which illuminates our shadows with Grace and makes our cells of Light shine;
- A Love that guides us to our respective paths when we pass away into death to be reborn into eternity;
- A Love which represents the perfect blend between our hearts and eternity;
- A Love which is an indescribable ecstasy, but which is in our experiential life inside;
- A Love that merges and unites our hearts with those of our brothers and sisters;
- A Love that is an Eternal Fire that dwells in our hearts;
- A Love which restitutes the autonomy of our inner life to exceed our ordinary life;
- A Love offering "marriage" within the heart between us and eternity;
- A Love where Grace shines in all its glory within us;

Chapter **17**

A journey is like marriage. The certain way to be wrong is to think you control it.

John Ernst Steinbeck, Jr.
(1902 – 1968)
He was an American writer. He is widely known for the Pulitzer Prize-winning novel *The Grapes of Wrath* (1939) and *East of Eden* (1952) - and the novella *Of Mice and Men* (1937).

- A love that has been proclaimed by the "Son of God" and God Himself: "Love one another as I have loved you".

How can I see love in the future?
When we love unconditionally, we act without expectations, without fear of being judged or judging, and without culpability, because the actions we do to help, thank and acknowledge others are made with respect, regardless of how important the situation or people involved are.

Knowing how to recognize unconditional love is an educational and detached way of seeing the future. True Love is the one of letting go, abandoning expectations, and respecting a person or a cause dear to our hearts. We do this because it is easy or simple, to be thankful to others for their value.

The ultimate lesson all of us have to learn is unconditional love, which includes not only others but ourselves as well.

Elisabeth Kübler-Ross, M.D.
(1926 – 2004)
She was a Swiss-American psychiatrist, a pioneer in near-death studies and the author of the groundbreaking book *On Death and Dying* (1969), where she first discussed what is now known as the Kübler-Ross model.

AUTHENTICITY
To manage to remain the same authentic person, it is essential to remain oneself at all times, in any place, under any circumstance and in front of everyone. Authenticity, it is being ourselves, with our qualities and our imperfections, without fear of showing our real personalities. Authenticity, above all, is transparency in what we do, in what we project, or in what we think.

To be authentic is not to lie to anyone, and not to ourselves, for any raison. We cannot acknowledge or have gratitude for people with authenticity if we are not true to ourselves. This is purely a question of honesty with ourselves first, and then with others.

RECOGNITION & THANKFULNESS

Authenticity is the alignment of head, mouth, heart, and feet - thinking, saying, feeling, and doing the same thing - consistently. This builds trust, and followers love leaders they can trust.

Lance H.K. Secretan
(1939 -)
Born in the United Kingdom. He is perhaps best known for his work in leadership theory and how to inspire teams.

Do not dwell in the past, do not dream of the future, concentrate the mind on the present moment.

Gautama Buddha
(411 - 400 BCE)

How can I stop comparing things by relying on the past?

Circumstances or events that are a part of our lives are often subject to comparison, and especially observations of our behavior in the face of certain situations.

Many people think that the past vouches for the future. As far as I am concerned, the past is gone, and it is necessary to turn to the present. But what can we do with the current tools at hand to prepare for the future? If we learn to observe ourselves, we will learn more if we do so honestly and transparently as we face problems or people. In doing so, we will become observers of our good or bad behavior; this is a clear sign of consciousness and transparency. So, we will not be able to lie or fool others or ourselves, because we will fundamentally show our true selves when we are transparent.

That we made mistakes, made wrong decisions, or had an unreasonable attitude in the face of a problem or a person does not matter if we are authentic in admitting that we did not act the right way when facing the difficulty, and it will be even easier for others to forgive us. So, from the moment we are ourselves, no matter what the circumstances, people will trust us more.

How can I be authentic when I express my gratitude and my thankfulness?

Now, after doing the above, when we express our thankfulness and gratitude, or our appreciation, people will recognize that what we say is true and authentic. The reason is simply because they know that we are basically honest and transparent in what we have expressed and we sincerely want to

Chapter **17**

The successful man will profit from his mistakes and try again in a different way.

Dale Carnegie
(1888 – 1955)
He was an American writer, lecturer, and the developer of famous courses in self-improvement, salesmanship, corporate training, public speaking, and interpersonal skills.

As we express our gratitude, we must never forget that the highest appreciation is not to utter words, but to live by them.

John F. Kennedy
(1917 – 1963)
He was the 35th President of the United States.

acknowledge them, or render a fair and equitable judgment.

When we are in the workplace and in a responsible position, it is essential to demonstrate authenticity. It is difficult to be successful with others if we are not true to them and ourselves. Keep in mind that being authentic represents success at all times. However, when we express our gratitude and thankfulness to someone, we will usually be appreciated. This kind of action will increase the confidence of the people being thanked and acknowledged by us.

The simple fact of being authentic increases our credibility, but it especially increases the respect which the others will have towards us. Transparency is the prerogative of individuals who are not afraid to show their true colors, whatever they are. To admit a mistake is to admit that sometimes we can be vulnerable and that we are always entitled to a second chance, no matter who we are.

Being true to ourselves and honest with others will make others have more confidence in us. And so we shall always be respected and acknowledged as a person who can be relied on, no matter what the situation might be.

How can I be conscious that I must be transparent, as much as possible?
As a matter of fact, the authenticity, or if you prefer the transparency, it is to be beyond appearances or conflicts of all kinds, without dualities towards ourselves or others, is to have no demands, no need of proof or evidence, and is not to resist the new which comes from the heart at all times.

Our transparency is not a projection of the personality or the ego; it is, rather, the purely transparent aspect which crosses our personality, without judgment.

To remain transparent, we have to remain humble despite the fact that we believe ourselves to be right on certain things in our lives; nobody is right, nobody is wrong; everything is a matter of perception resulting from the mind, the ego, or the personality trying to be right.

There is no persuasiveness more effectual than the transparency of a single heart, of a sincere life.

Joseph Barber Lightfoot
(1828 – 1889)
He was an English theologian and the Bishop of Durham.

We must be authentic in our comments, not attempting to add more than what is necessary. We must show our true selves, regardless of the situations or the people that we deal with. We must stop lying in our comments or our opinions. We must pay attention, as much as possible, to what the ego and the personality want to say; despicable comments might offend and hurt someone more than we might imagine. We must be true at all times with everyone.

Preferably, transparency is stopping nothing, holding nothing back of what might happen, whether it be a thought, an emotion, a physical symptom, or a relationship, but check any hostile comments which carry judgment. Transparency is simply being conscious of what is happening within us.

AUTONOMY

To appreciate and acknowledge people on both personal and organizational levels, there are mechanisms which underlie certain aspects of our personalities that we must learn to develop and manage efficiently. It is all about autonomy, not in the sense of being able to do laundry, iron clothes, cook a meal, or do any other action in ordinary life but in the sense of making decisions wisely and listening to our particular instinct or intuition, or if you prefer, our inner voice that often tells us to address a situation or a problem with intelligence, courage, and authenticity.

Why do people lack autonomy?
Most of the time, people lack autonomy because they were helped too often and did not take responsibility and make firm decisions when it was time to make them.

I've learned that in order to achieve what I wanted, it made more sense to negotiate than to defend the autonomy of my work by pounding my fist on the table.

Thom Mayne
(1944 -)
He is a Los Angeles-based architect.
Mayne received the Pritzker Architecture Prize in March 2005.

We know very well that relying constantly on others is another factor that causes lack of autonomy and does not develop responsibility. It also creates a dependency or an excessive need to always be under the responsibility or the control of somebody. It can be caused by a lack of education which makes it difficult to answer everyday questions due to the lack of schooling.

We can add to this the fear of making a mistake. In fact, various facets, which are for the greater, part difficult for the persons who experience them.

How can I express my autonomy more?
At first, feeling inferior when facing responsibilities may undermine autonomy. This may prevent someone from updating creativity due to a lack of confidence in oneself. It is also a question of putting some positive emotion in to our passions.

How can I meet my need to feed my autonomy?
First, when we have membership in an organization or are involved in some cause, this really helps to empower us to act with autonomy. We must learn to recognize this. Or we could say that self-confidence

and self-esteem are also inherent factors to acting with autonomy. Finally, our inner spiritual search could certainly also give us a boost to increase our acting with autonomy.

How can I reach autonomy while still being myself?

We can reach autonomy by remaining naturally human and authentic at all times with everyone. It helps to love life as it is, with all the good and the bad moments, and to accept and deal with all our responsibilities when we have made a commitment.

I would add that we can continue to improve ourselves in what ever fascinates us by continuing to innovate and to create. And being able to communicate and express our opinions openly, without wanting to be absolutely right, also helps, as well as taking initiatives without being afraid of making mistakes.

Finally, being resourceful, cunning, and even intelligently brilliant and constantly able to find solutions to everyday life both personally and at work is also helpful. In conclusion, it is important to innovate at every given opportunity and to create, regardless of the particular spheres of activity.

In short, autonomy is:
- Doing immediately what there is to do;
- Loving ourselves; to love others is even better;
- Feeling free to say what we think, without offending or wanting to be right;
- Freeing ourselves from our problems as soon as they show up;
- Acknowledging our strengths as well as our weaknesses;

A great many people mistake opinions for thought.

Herbert V. Prochnow
(1897 – 1998)
He was a U.S. banking executive, noted toastmaster, and author during the middle 20th-century.

As all human beings are, in my view, creatures of God's design, we must respect all other human beings. That does not mean I have to agree with their choices or agree with their opinions, but indeed I respect them as human beings.

Anonymous

Chapter 17

- Learning to manage without others and not wanting to demonstrate independence;
- Being able to learn from anyone with humility;
- Doing things seriously while having fun;
- Using our expertise to support others in order to improve ourselves;
- Speaking, writing and transferring our knowledge;
- Relying on our intuition and listen to our inner voice;
- Adapting to things that we cannot control;
- Keeping things simple and practical;
- Listening to what others have to say;
- Never judging.

"Autonomy and freedom are fundamentally inseparable!"

DETACHMENT

He who would be serene and pure needs but one thing, detachment.

Eckhart von Hochheim (c. 1260 – c. 1327) He was commonly known as Meister Eckhart and was a German theologian, philosopher, and mystic, born near Gotha, in the Landgraviate of Thuringia in the Holy Roman Empire.

Just as with our thoughts, any attachment whatsoever, even the most loving, is indisputably linked to the ego because when a friend, an animal, or even you yourself die, what will remain? All that is transitory is illusory; there is no need to reject it; there is no need to deny it; one just has to accept it and move on.

Only the ego can be attached to anything because, ultimately, it knows itself to be ephemeral, it knows itself to be condemned, and it can only give the illusion of persisting, remaining, through an attachment of some kind.

In fact, our emotional attachments are difficult to sustain because we are dependent. We must learn to rid ourselves of these emotions that are more degenerative than constructive in our consciousness.

How can I avoid indifference in detachment?

It is important never to be indifferent or insensitive to anyone, whether it be our children, our spouses, our family, our friends, or even our work colleagues; we simply need to detach ourselves from the emotions that we have and create in front of them.

It is important to feel free because we have to avoid subjecting ourselves to anyone, and even more so, anyone subjecting anyone to us. Because of this detachment, our lives will be more stable because we will feel freed from the emotional anchoring which we "feed" unconsciously in certain situations and with certain people. For us, the detachment should be a guarantee of freedom - for us and for others.

In fact, letting people live as they want; each being responsible for being true according to his or her own thoughts, beliefs, convictions, and moral codes or ethics.

How can I free myself from sad things or events that are still harmful for my mind?

It is often true that the detachment we have to apply can involve some harmful or sad events and that for the health of the mind, which takes us back to relive moments of melancholy, sorrow, a strong fury or difficulties which are psychologically difficult to manage, we must detach ourselves. Whether it is a separation, the loss of a loved one, or a job loss, we must learn to overcome the grief despite the sadness experienced.

As soon as we become aware of something sad or harmful, we need to detach ourselves from it gradually by observing the ego and the personality of the people living it. The emotion remains, but the detachment allows us not to feel it.

Our greatest happiness does not depend on the condition of life in which chance has placed us, but is always the result of a good conscience, good health, occupation, and freedom in all just pursuits.

Thomas Jefferson
(1743 – 1826)
He was an American Founding Father, the principal author of the *Declaration of Independence* (1776) and the third President of the United States.

Chapter 17

Family is the most important thing in the world.

Diana, Princess of Wales
(1961 –1997)
She was also well known for her fund-raising work for international charities, and was an eminent celebrity of the late 20th-century.

Conflict is the beginning of consciousness.

Mary Esther Harding
(1888–1971)
She was an American Jungian analyst who was the first significant Jungian psychoanalyst in the United States.

In this way, we see more and more light at the end of the tunnel instead of living nostalgia and shadow, which darkened our existence.

How can I realize the importance of detachment every day?

We must detach ourselves from all the negative emotions created by unnecessary material, members of our family, our loved ones, and also reprehensible situations that we have created over time.

This does not mean that we reject them or that we do not love them. On the contrary, it is because we love them unconditionally that we must continue on in life according to what our heart dictates us to do, rather than what our feelings of conditional love that we had formerly towards these people or things on an emotional level suggest we do. The detachment should be considered as being not only a liberation of our emotional and psychological state but an unconditional Love created towards us to transcend the sentimental illusions which tore us rather than helped us in the past.

But I am speaking in particular, about things that concern situations of conflicts, dualities, adversities, and judgments, which loaded our lives filled with distress, contempt, hatred, and sometimes even shame. We should consider that to detach ourselves from this emotional baggage represents a major relief, which will take us, sooner or later, towards the real freedom to be, towards the open-mindedness in each of us or the unlimited consciousness of the heart.

It is necessary to realize that every day we live with detachment; everything we do is beneficial to our health when we are no longer subjected to the

RECOGNITION & THANKFULNESS

punishment and the aberrations which the previous suffering caused – and which became part of an emotional burden. We have to get detached from any form of control of conditioning or of possession that is harmful to the evolution of our hearts.

Do you wish to rise? Begin by descending. You plan a tower that will pierce the clouds? Lay first the foundation of humility.

Saint Augustine (354 – 430)
He was a Latin philosopher and theologian from Roman Africa. His writings were very influential in the development of Western Christianity.

HUMILITY

The humility that I will try to explain is, by no means, based on the kind that religious institutions have created in their doctrines or their philosophies, a humility that is sometimes decadent, manipulating, and taught by imposing rules of conduct based on duality, even fear and guilt.

Rather, humility as I mean it involves accepting certain events or circumstances that we cannot always control. True humility should be seen as a letting go; in fact, as much as possible try not to control what you cannot control.

It is, in my opinion, one of the simplest, most worthy, and most authentic expressions of humility just to let things happen without trying to control them and to observe what these situations can result in emotionally, rationally and even on a moral level.

Almost any difficulty will move in the face of honesty. When I am honest I never feel stupid. And when I am honest I am automatically humble.

Hugh Prather (1938 – 2010)
He was a writer, minister, and counselor, most famous for his first book, *Notes to Myself*.

What is it to be humble in this kind of process?
Now, the humility needed to give and to be thankful to people, for example, will allow one to do things with more vision of the heart than the rationality of doing it by an obligation of imposed rules of conduct based on duality, even fear and guilt.

The humility represents the respect and the love which we have for a person, for a cause, or for an event, which will allow offering to the others our most profound gratitude without expectations of something in return.

Because when we act unconditionally, it is certain that our action towards others is always more welcomed because we do it because of who we are inside, so there is humility in our action.

How can I be humble, no matter what the circumstances?

It is essential to humbly accept our lot in life everyday, knowing that we control very few things in life. We should do what we can, what we are capable of, according to our skills, in every event or situation.

In this way, we can be attuned to all that we hear, perceive, and influence without judging. Furthermore, we can accept more easily, and with humility, what others have to live that we do not have to live or try to overcome.

We can be aware that we live constantly detached from all kinds of things, trying not to control the situations. We can humbly accept the opinions of others without judging them because we will always have something to learn from everyone; we have no inborn knowledge, and even less control over everything that happens in our environment.

One of the fundamental marks of humility is to free our friends, family members or others to live without judging them no matter what their choices or their futures.

We have to be thankful to all of those that we are surrounded by, without trying to judge them, and should, rather to understand them and to accept them as they are. Humility is accepting to live like a child

A major advantage of age is learning to accept people without passing judgment.

Mary Elizabeth "Liz" Sutherland Carpenter
(1920 – 2010)
She was a writer, feminist, former reporter, media advisor, speechwriter, political humorist, and public relations expert.

who is having fun, living in the present moment, without worrying about what tomorrow will bring. The best attitude to have is of course, the spontaneity of a child.

A child is totally immersed in the experience, without judgment, and without a point of reference, without projection. As long as there is a judgment, a mark, a projection, we are not acting like the child; we are not humble!

SIMPLICITY
Simplicity is probably one of the key things to help us remain ourselves, or if you prefer, to help us be authentic when we face situations of acknowledgement or of personal, professional, or organizational conflict.

How can I keep things simple?
Being Thankful, with simplicity, is investing in ourselves fully and wanting to show our appreciation by remaining honest, but mainly by doing so with righteousness and noble gestures of gratitude that we perform in front of people or during events.

Doing so also suggests that we are happy to show, simply and unpretentiously, that our personal values measure up to other values of thankfulness, whether they involve people or extraordinary circumstances.

Doing things in simplicity is not exaggerating or trying to make more of a situation, or trying to look as if we are above anyone or everyone else, but it is in fact, doing things modestly to emphasize with dignity the thankfulness that we have towards a person or an outstanding event.

I have just three things to teach: simplicity, patience, compassion. These three are your greatest treasures.

Lao Tzu
(6th-century BCE.)
He was a philosopher of ancient China, best known as the author of the *Tao Te Ching* (often simply referred to as *Laozi*).

Chapter 17

How can I remain composed with simplicity during the difficult situations in which we live?

In situations of conflict, it is fundamental to keep things simple. Now, when we are simple, things are always easier, more compatible, even in the eyes of others because we do not try to exploit pointlessly the rational, the logic, or to try to demonstrate that we are right.

We simply need to demonstrate that we can solve problems or conflicts as simply as possible, without endangering people or raising doubts in their minds.

So, why try overly hard to substantiate things or events with useless difficult discussions when easier, more transparent ones in which we tell the truth would be better.

How can I ensure being myself?

In this context, being simple is to remain the same at all times, under all circumstances, and in the face of everyone, whether at work, at home, or on a social and friendly level.

Exaggeration is truth that has lost its temper.

Khalil Gibran
(1883 – 1931)
He was born Gubran Khalil Gubran and was a Lebanese-American artist, poet, and writer. He is the third best-selling poet of all time, behind Shakespeare and Lao-Tzu.

An individual who is simple avoids exaggerating or doing more than what he is able to demonstrate or establish as evidence that something is. He does things according to his skills, his qualifications, and according to his lived experiences.

He tries rather to find solutions which will take only a little energy. He simplifies his schedule, his availability, and his time as much as possible, all of which he dedicates to the things that require more energy. He is simple in the face of what he wants to expose or explain, remaining himself, authentic.

RECOGNITION & THANKFULNESS

In order to succeed, people need a sense of self-efficacy, to struggle together with resilience to meet the inevitable obstacles and inequities of life.

Albert Bandura,
(1925 –)
Canadian psychologist, the David Starr Jordan Professor Emeritus of Social Science in Psychology at Stanford University.
He is widely described as the greatest living psychologist and as one of the most influential psychologists of all time.

A man is ethical only when life, as such, is sacred to him, that of plants and animals as that of his fellow men, and when he devotes himself helpfully to all life that is in need of help.

Albert Schweitzer
(1875 – 1965)
Schweitzer's passionate quest was to discover a universal ethical philosophy, anchored in a universal reality, and make it directly available to all of humanity.

He does not require anything from anyone, based on the desires or needs of his personality or his ego in order to impress anyone or be right. He tries to understand more than words, without going too far in his efforts.

He doses not waste energy on trivialities, or his own convictions by trying to justify himself or to defend the indefensible. He avoids putting himself in duality avoiding any conflicts or arguments which only reduce his credibility and take away his ability to remain simple.

When we remain simple, no matter what the event, the conflict or even the duality, it is always easier to find solutions to avoid that people involved feel the need to defend themselves. Then, the simplicity, just like the softness in any educational approach, is often the key to success and to the resolutions of the conflicts.

Resilience remains one of the most important things needed to arrive at agreements simply and suitably, agreements which allow all parties to agree mutually regardless of the level of importance of the situations. Sweetness in the comments, respect in the language, and good listening remain simple and intelligent ways to reach common ground.

PERSONAL AND PROFESSIONAL ETHICS

What are personal and professional ethics in terms of thankfulness?
Personal and professional ethics in terms of thankfulness involve living according to the personal and professional standards that we impose upon ourselves in order to love, respect, and acknowledge

Chapter 17

others and accomplish what we wish to realize for ourselves and for others afterward.

So, within the framework of thankfulness, there are fundamental principles which we have to possess in order to do things with dignity and respect given our responsibilities.

With this in mind, I offer you some principles of personal and professional ethics that you can try to use because it is important, sometimes, to learn more and have more thankfulness, which will most likely be appreciated by all those around you today and in the future.

The personal and professional ethics are important to help us learn how to acknowledge and appreciate those around us.

It is fundamental to understand that we must act according to personal and professional ethics, whether at work, at home, or in society where we live. This is key since our personality expresses itself and comes to light in various circumstances of daily life through what we do.

So, to apply these in everyday life is certainly an intelligent way to live, to respect others and to be respected, regardless of our relationships or our obligations.

What are the basic principles of personal and professional ethics?

To begin, the principle of personal and professional ethics is important to consider that to be ethical requires that one act as follows:
- Be courteous;
- Be kind and compassionate;

Be courteous to all, but intimate with few, and let those few be well tried before you give them your confidence.

George Washington
(1732 – 1799)
He was the first President of the United States of America. Washington had three roles during the war. In 1775–77, and again in 1781, he led his men against the main British forces. Although he lost many of his battles, he never surrendered his army during the war, and he continued to fight the British relentlessly until the war's end. He plotted the overall strategy of the war, in cooperation with Congress.

510 A special contribution by Yvan Poirier

- Have some form of decorum;
- Have a reasonable academic education;
- Be respectful of people, nature, and values;
- Anticipate others needs and assist them;
- Be delicate and sweet;
- Be loving and able to forgive;
- Be modest and humble.

However, it is necessary to admit that personal and professional ethics go well beyond these principles, which are only a part of what is understood as ethics. So, we shall look at what these ethics represent in our daily reality on a physical and moral level.

What can we see?

We can see by:
- understanding and respecting the laws and standards that we must follow in society. In other words, we can reveal, at the right time, things that we think are intelligent, without upsetting or insulting anyone;
- listening carefully and only with respect;
- forgiving, no matter what the situation;
- accepting that we can be wrong or make mistakes;
- providing a chance to rebuild, regardless of the situation;
- learning to mind our own business.

When people talk, listen completely. Most people never listen.

Ernest Miller Hemingway
(1899 – 1961)
He was an American author and journalist. His economical and understated style had a strong influence on 20th-century fiction, while his life of adventure and his public image influenced later generations.

How can we detach ourselves from the former to deal with the new?

We can detach ourselves from the former to deal with the new by:
- understanding that we cannot control the lives of others and let them live as they wish;
- considering that we can possess material things but never let the material possess us;

Chapter **17**

- demonstrating unconditional love by "freeing" the people we love;
- realizing that we must detach ourselves from certain people or events without remorse or guilt;
- detaching ourselves, which represents great humility because by not hanging on anymore to the former, we can make place for the new;
- detaching ourselves, whish is the gesture of humility that will help demonstrate our respect and love for ourselves and others.

How can we trust ourselves to gain the confidence of others?
We can trust ourselves to gain the confidence of others by:
- acknowledging that we can make mistakes and sometimes we have to let go of the things we can not control; that is humility;
- giving ourselves the opportunity to get help and doing so for others as well;
- realizing that if we make a mistake, we will learn to discern better thereafter;
- understanding that there are many good people around us and acknowledging them for their true value.

How can we discern what we can observe?
We can discern what we can observe by:
- looking closely at all the angles of every decision we have to make;
- differentiating between what we want and do not want;
- accepting that we can make a mistake without feeling guilty;
- learning to make sense out of things, no matter what the results;
- acknowledging that we have within us an intuition that guides us;

As long as you don't forgive, who and whatever it is will occupy rent-free space in your mind.

Isabelle Christian Holland
(1920— 2002)
She was a Swiss author of children and adult fiction. She wrote over 50 books in her lifetime and was still working at the time of her death at age 81 in New York City.

- taking the necessary time to reasonably consider what we want.

How can we forgive and to be forgiven?
We can forgive and be forgiven by:
- not feeling guilty;
- trying not to repeat the same offenses against ourselves and others;
- finding inner peace by letting go;
- discerning and acknowledging that we have the right to make mistakes and realizing that we do our best; this alone will change our lives – because of this simple act of compassion toward ourselves and others;
- healing the emotional burdens that we put on our shoulders;
- giving ourselves the chance to start anew;
- understanding that we must free ourselves of all emotional charges, that we must no longer carry them;
- forgiving an offense that we did not expect from someone – so we can heal;
- realizing that we would be happy to be forgiven by someone else;
- Have the compassion we need towards everyone;
- Make a gesture of humility which will free us from resentment and perhaps anger that poisons our health;
- Never to judge anyone, no matter what he does, thinks or says;
- Sooner or later we will face a decision that we must take, if we want to forgive.

All major religious traditions carry basically the same message, that is love, compassion and forgiveness. The important thing is they should be part of our daily lives.

Dalai Lama
(1391–1474)

How can we appreciate others – and be appreciated ourselves?
We can appreciate others – and be appreciated ourselves by:

Chapter **17**

- realizing that appreciation represents one of the most valuable actions in our lives for ourselves and others;
- having gratitude toward people who are giving of themselves and generous with their time;
- observing, without judging, the sincerity of the people when we receive appreciation;
- enjoying the people, whatever their color, their culture or their background;
- taking full advantage of the moment;
- taking a moment to look inside ourselves to see the great appreciation we have for all those around us and everything we own;
- not being afraid to show appreciation for what we accomplish ourselves and by doing the same for others.

Everyone wants to be appreciated, so if you appreciate someone, don't keep it a secret.

Mary Kay Ash
(1918 – 2001)
She was an American businesswoman and founder of Mary Kay Cosmetics, Inc. Awarded "Most Outstanding Woman in Business in the 20th-Century" from Lifetime Television in 1999.

How can we use our energy correctly for things we are involved in?

We can use our energy correctly for the things we are involved in by:

- taking the time needed to use our energy correctly when reacting to situations which are difficult and sometimes too emotional;
- balancing equally what we want to achieve in our lives according to our priorities;
- measuring what we get out of what we judge appropriate or not;
- respecting other peoples judgment; each has his or her way of reacting to any given situation;
- providing the opportunity and time for people who do not have the same thoughts or reflections that we do;
- learning to realize that we are just different and we can all learn from each other.

A special contribution by Yvan Poirier

RECOGNITION & THANKFULNESS

I think and think for months and years. Ninety-nine times, the conclusion is false. The hundredth time I am right.

Albert Einstein
(1879 – 1955)
Einstein published more than 300 scientific papers along with over 150 non-scientific works. His great intelligence and originality have made the word "Einstein" synonymous with genius.

How can we surround ourselves with people who will help us to see things more clearly?

We can surround ourselves with people who will help us to see things more clearly by:

- cleaning up our list of acquaintances, discerning the people who respect us and those who do not;
- taking measures to eliminate those who try to waste our energy;
- spending some time out, having fun with those who we influence and feel good with;
- determining what we want and what we do not want in our relationships;
- balancing and adjusting the time we spend without losing energy, regardless of the involvement;
- learning to give and receive from people, without having expectations.

How can we give our opinions without wanting to be absolutely right?

We can give our opinions without wanting to be absolutely right by:

- learning to take our place anywhere and anytime, without imposing our thoughts and reflections;
- never taking the place of or speaking for others, no matter where we are or who we are;
- talking as much as possible with our hearts, with humility and without trying to convince or to be right;
- never judging the opinions of others; they might have knowledge that you do not have;
- not being afraid to give frank opinions without offending or insulting anyone;
- avoiding being politically correct because it is the opposite of transparency;
- continually opening our minds to what's new.

Chapter **17**

How can we use our sense of humor wisely?
We can use our sense of humor wisely by:
- not taking ourselves too seriously, but by doing things seriously;
- agreeing to laugh at ourselves, but never accepting to be ridiculed, in the sense of having our dignity insulted;
- telling funny stories without saucy expressions;
- playing amusing tricks on someone without insulting or ridiculing the person in front of others;
- developing a sense of humor that makes people comfortable with us, enjoying our presence;
- keeping a smile at all times; it attracts others.

Without feelings of respect, what is there to distinguish men from beasts?

Confucius
(551 – 479 BC)
He was a Chinese teacher, editor, politician, and philosopher of the Spring and Autumn Period of Chinese history.

How can we use what we have in ourselves better?
We can use what we have in ourselves better by:
- knowing that we can not say anything to anyone, just like that, without reasonable or intelligent reason; discernment is required;
- taking the time to adjust our thinking before saying anything;
- considering that there are specific times to say things, to have good judgment and discernment;
- improving the way we communicate, if we want to be understood and not to be misinterpreted;
- learning to say and share opinions with simplicity, without exaggerating the content;
- demonstrating gratitude and respect towards people before we open our mouths to speak;
- considering it important to give our opinions, but ensuring that we do not aim at destroying or offending anyone.

How can we acknowledge ourselves in order to be acknowledged by others?
We can acknowledge ourselves in order to be acknowledged by others by:

- admitting that we have qualities, strengths, and imperfections and weaknesses;
- acknowledging that we can sometimes achieve things beyond our expectations or visions;
- learning to acknowledge that we are efficient and effective in our abilities and that we honestly do our best;
- acknowledging others' true value, if we want them to do the same for us;
- considering showing thankfulness a great way to show love, without being a profiteer;
- thanking people whenever we think of doing so, and, above all, never hesitating to do so;
- seeing the thankfulness that we receive as an educational tool that helps keep a healthy relationship, regardless of the level;
- saying THANKS no matter what the circumstances or events.

Justice consists in doing no injury to men; decency in giving them no offense.

Marcus Tullius Cicero
(106 BC – 43 BC)
He was a Roman philosopher, statesman, lawyer, orator, political theorist, Roman consul, and constitutionalist.

How can we love what we do in order to love what we wish to achieve?

We can love what we do in order to love what we wish to achieve by:

- accepting ourselves just as we are;
- loving with all our heart and without any expectations of something in return;
- accepting others regardless of their qualities or weaknesses;
- Having compassion and understanding for situations and people;
- always giving a second chance to anyone despite any mistakes or disadvantages;
- enabling others to guide us;
- letting go of wanting to control or be right;
- forgiving others and ourselves for all offenses, so that we are not overwhelmed by guilt, hatred, revenge, or resentment.

Chapter **17**

How can we choose ourselves above all in order to receive according to our true value?

We choose ourselves above all in order to receive according to our true value by:

- realizing that we are often under the impression that we choose everything - but are we aware that other factors or other people can also choose or even choose for us;
- identifying our desires and needs based on our reality:
- reviewing and analyzing our decisions when facing a choice: a relationships, work, etc.;
- giving pleasure to ourselves and to others;
- thinking that we must make choices and that they have to be assumed, respected, and upheld with dignity;
- realizing that life tells us that we must make choices every day and we have no control over anything or anybody;
- realizing that life brings us eventually to the right choices;
- realizing that the invisible is among us, in the sense of a spirit, soul, ego, subconscious, conscious, etc.; we realize that filters have sifted our choices before we make them;
- raising awareness that our choices are often made according to our discursive and analytical mind or base on our feelings which are controlled by the ego which is afraid; the good decisions, are always those of the heart;
- thinking of us by identifying and adjusting our prioritizing;
- thinking about our health above all;
- making sure that things are suitable and beneficial for us;
- thinking based on the present of what we can build in the future;

In a relationship each person should support the other; they should lift each other up.

Taylor Alison Swift
(1989 -)
She is an American singer-songwriter and occasional actress.

RECOGNITION & THANKFULNESS

- always looking at the things we enjoy and eliminating the things which do not suit us or our fundamental values.

How can we give without expecting to receive anything?

We can give without expecting to receive anything by:

- appreciating and giving unconditionally to those around us: love, attention, gentleness, etc.;
- sharing what we know best;
- sharing our energies equally, without hope of getting anything in return or with no expectations;
- raising awareness about the fact that there is always someone more needy than us;
- demonstrating that we are here to promote or to encourage others, with their needs and priorities;
- setting aside our prejudices and judgments;
- demonstrating generosity offered from the heart.

A smile is the light in your window that tells others that there is a caring, sharing person inside.

Denis E. Waitley
(1933 -)
He is an American motivational speaker and writer, consultant, and best-selling author.

How can we receive without necessarily needing to give back?

We can receive without necessarily needing to give back by:

- agreeing to accept the generosity of others;
- allowing ourselves to receive affection, attention, and gentleness for our family members;
- acknowledging that we are well supported and that there are people who love us truly and sincerely;
- appreciating everything that happens to help us keep smiling;
- enjoying every opportunity that touches our heart;
- Feeling fulfillment through situations that we were not expecting;
- realizing that we do and have done well in our environment.

Carry out a random act of kindness, with no expectation of reward, safe in the knowledge that one day someone might do the same for you.

Diana, Princess of Wales
(1961 –1997)

How can we help without any expectations?

We can help without any expectations by:

Chapter **17**

- Not being fool by the people who want our energy;
- learning to say NO at the right time or when people are trying to steal up our energy;
- understanding that we can help others, but never at the expense of our priorities, our choices, and our energies, and especially not if we feel forced;
- realizing that our assistance can be physical, material, psychic, mental, and moral, but without expectations;
- being aware that sometimes we need help but do not ask for it, at the expense of our energy;
- understanding that life gives us clear messages from people who try to help us for our personal well-being;
- not helping someone if we sense that the person has expectations beyond what reasonable or is exaggerating the assistance requested.

A creative man is motivated by the desire to achieve, not by the desire to beat others.

Ayn Rand
(born Alisa Zinov'yevna Rosenbaum)
(1905 – 1982)
She was a Russian-American novelist, philosopher, playwright, and screenwriter. She is known for her two best-selling novels *The Fountainhead* and *Atlas Shrugged* and for developing a philosophical system she called Objectivism.

How can we communicate with simplicity and humility?

We can communicate with simplicity and humility by:

- realizing that our communications are the fruit of our thoughts, our ideas, our actions, and how we react to situations;
- realizing that sharing is important, but not just with anyone or for any reason;
- realizing that our most intimate secrets may not be divulged to just anyone;
- realizing the demonstration of JOY is the greatest form of communication that exists; we should not hesitate to express it with a smile.

How can we evaluate our personal and professional ethics?

We can evaluate our personal and professional ethics by being:

- Adaptive = Adapting to unknown or different circumstances;
- Autonum = Emancipation of consciousness without being subject to the other;
- Self-educated = Learning by ourselves or while on the job;
- Brief – Having an effective Request = very little information to express the efficiency;
- Efficient = Reaching beyond our effectiveness because of our creativity;
- Able to read between the lines = Demonstrate a perception beyond the words and situations that set our course;
- Creative = Using our creativity for what we do with simplicity and humility;
- A simplifier = Simplifying everything without loosing energy;
- Innovative = We need to innovate continuously in everything we do;
- Patient and tolerant = Having an unfailing patience and tolerance for all inconsistencies, "Patience is the mother of virtues; tolerance is its complement";
- Friendly = Acting humbly with respect and love – all very freely;
- Helpful = Being a great help, while still respecting our personal choices;
- Courageous = Demonstrating courage in what we do to achieve our goals and objectives;
- Fearless = Attacking life without being too harsh;
- Persevering = Not letting go of what we begin unless we face a situation that we cannot control;
- Ecological = Respecting the environment and nature;
- A refiner = Love and refine whatever we build, regardless of its size;
- Responsible = Assuming all our responsibilities involved;

Courage is resistance to fear, mastery of fear, not absence of fear.

Samuel Langhorne Clemens (1835 – 1910)
He is better known by his pen name, Mark Twain, and was an American author and humorist. He is most noted for his novels, The Adventures of Tom Sawyer (1876) and its sequel, The Adventures of Huckleberry Finn (1885), the latter often called "the Great American Novel."

Chapter **17**

To enjoy good health, to bring true happiness to one's family, to bring peace to all, one must first discipline and control one's own mind. If a man can control his mind he can find the way to Enlightenment, and all wisdom and virtue will naturally come to him.

Gautama Buddha
(563 BCE - 483 BCE)

Once we discover how to appreciate the timeless values in our daily experiences, we can enjoy the best things in life.

Jerome Klapka Jerome
(1859 – 1927)
He was an English writer and humorist, best known for the humorous travelogue *Three Men in a Boat* (1889).

- A volunteer = Not being afraid to get involved in a project dear to our hearts;
- Authentic = True and transparent everywhere, at all times, and with everyone;
- Humble in our opinions = Sharing opinions without fear of mistake or of sounding silly;
- Humorous = Funny without being salacious;
- Reserved = Never revealing our findings, our creations, the first ideas that come to us, and remaining alert to people trying to squeeze our creative energies;
- Serious = Doing things seriously, without taking ourselves too seriously.

In Summary

Our personal and professional ethics give us the privilege to live in balance, according to our values and to the respect that we carry for ourselves and for others. They help us appreciate our lives - the good and the difficult moments. They also help us be thankful and acknowledge, at every moment of our lives, people who surround us in our families, at work, or in society as a whole.

It is important to live in the present moment every second of our lives, and especially by letting go of the thought that we control our life; it is rather our life that leads us where it wishes!

When we apply the personal and professional ethics advisedly, we manifest intelligent proof of thankfulness, and it is easier to make thankfulness a daily reality.

THE WORKPLACE

RECOGNITION & THANKFULNESS

First, I want to pay tribute to Diana myself. She was an exceptional and gifted human being. In good times and bad, she never lost her capacity to smile and laugh, nor to inspire others with her warmth and kindness.
I admired and respected her - for her energy and commitment to others, and especially for her devotion to her two boys.

Queen Elizabeth II
(1926 -)

How do I see the importance of the workplace in relation to Thankfulness?

It is imperative to realize that during our lives we spend almost two thirds of our time at work. So, if there is any place where we need to take seriously, thankfulness it is at work. Unfortunately, many companies overlook the importance of thankfulness and how it should be applied towards their employees. Private companies and government entities wonder why there are so many diseases among their executives, that is professional exhaustion, or "Burn-out ", which is a major scourge in our society. Could the lack of thankfulness be one of the reasons for this professional fatigue, something that leads people to a psychological and mental dysfunction?

This is certainly true partially. We cannot deny the fact that employees do not receive enough gratitude in their working environments, and this creates an empty space inside the work place.

I would like to make certain suggestions which would help to remedy this uncomfortable situation as quickly as possible. By offering interesting and convivial solutions to set up a system of effective thankfulness, such as a situation can be avoided or ameliorated.

It is increasingly evident that there are several important reasons for acknowledging employees in their workplace. By receiving thankfulness, employees feel:
- Appreciated;
- Loved;
- Like a part of the organization;
- Acknowledged by senior management;
- Respected for what they do;
- Respected by their colleagues;

A special contribution by Yvan Poirier

Chapter 17

- Valued because of the expressed thankfulness;
- Interested in continuing with even greater efficiency in their work;
- A desire to further improve their efficiency;
- Motivated to return to work;
- As an important part of the work, or project;
- Willing to work in new functions;
- More likely to remain in the company;
- Honored by the organization who values what they do;
- Involved in the organization and a part of the organizational "gears";
- More likely to easily accommodate changes.

Many people do not feel appreciated even at the highest levels of management. The thankfulness process should also "ascend" and "descend". Here are some important things to be applied in the workplace:

- Gratitude;
- An enhancement of value;
- Equity;
- Integrity;
- Authenticity;
- Respect;
- Appreciation;
- Impartiality;
- Observation of people from different angles.

Before continuing to discuss the working environment, allow me this brief interlude on thankfulness in general.

Three big moments of thankfulness are:

1. Birth: Coming into the world is when we are most acknowledged. Everyone wants to see the baby - its health, its beauty, and its future. In short, we

Trust is to human relationships what faith is to gospel living. It is the beginning place, the foundation upon which more can be built. Where trust is, love can flourish.

Barbara Smith
(1946 –)
She is an American, lesbian feminist who has played a significant role in building and sustaining Black Feminism in the United States.
She has also taught at numerous colleges and universities over the last twenty-five years.

consider that the child will have a future and we will do our best to help, encourage, and mentor him or her to maturity and after wards. We give the child some affection, show our feelings, caress and cherish the child.

2. Retirement: When people retire is when it is considered that a long road has been traveled, and it is then that we acknowledge that these people have worked hard to earn a living. We realize that they have accomplished a lot and that very few of them have really been well acknowledged for those accomplishments.

3. Death: This is when other people acknowledge a person best. They say he or she was beautiful, wonderful, intelligent, etc.! But how many times did they forget to say thank you or show appreciation when the person was living? We should not wait for someone's death to show our appreciation and thankfulness.

How can I promote thankfulness in the workplace?

1. Managers need to hear about the benefits of thankfulness with regard to budgeting.
2. Coordinators of thankfulness must raise the issue regularly with management.
3. It is important to understand the degrees of interaction in the workplace and in human relationships.
4. Take time at meetings to talk about everything. There will be good stimuli for thankfulness reasons to thank the employees.
5. Spend more time individually with employees.
6. For proper management of human resources, we need continuous improvement, but also to be more humane.

Correction does much, but encouragement does more.

Johann Wolfgang von Goethe
(1749 – 1832)
He was a German writer, artist, and politician. The most important of Goethe's works produced before he went to Weimar was *Götz von Berlichingen* (1773), a tragedy that was the first work to bring him recognition.

Chapter **17**

7. Remember that it is not necessarily always a gift or award that counts; it is mainly to highlight good work by constructive encouragement and sincere feedback, or with a simple thank you.
8. Transparency = respect and understanding.

According to a study made of certain major firms by the Management Organization of Health and Safety in the Work Place, the psychological distress at work among employees is quadrupled if they do not receive expressions of thankfulness.

It is recommended to connect thankfulness to the results. Someone may have dedicated a lot of time to working on a proposal but may not have obtained the contract or possibly worked hard on a project without it being accepted.

The effort must be acknowledged all the same!
The work must be considered as a source of daily motivation.

There is an increase in self-respect when the employees feel recognized for what they achieve. A word of encouragement, a sincere thank you, a gesture, or a creative remark can increase someone's self-respect in a significant way.

Some employers tend to wait such a long time before acknowledging an employee that it looks as if they always expect more from him!
Let us do the tanking now; let us not wait until the employee is tired, sick, or has left!

How can I get more motivation and satisfaction in the workplace?
1. Acknowledge that the employee has a place in the organization, regardless of his or her status.

As a people,
we know what
we can do,
we know how
to do it, and
we just want to
get on with it.
How?
By ensuring that
Canada's place
in the world is
one of influence
and pride.

Paul Edgar
Philippe Martin
PC, CC
(1938 -)
He is also known as
Paul Martin, Jr. and is a
Canadian politician who
was the 21st Prime
Minister of Canada.

RECOGNITION & THANKFULNESS

2. Appreciate him or her for the person's true values by making the person feel like part of a large chain and that each link is important.
3. Demonstrate to him or her that his or her commitment is as important as anyone else is in the organization.
4. Motivation has the effect of increasing the effectiveness and sense of belonging.
5. Thankfulness of work done with colleagues increases a person's confidence, but also his or her confidence with colleagues and the whole organization.

Here are some possible results:
1. Productivity will definitely increase.
2. Respect will increase among everyone.
3. Gradually a collaborative attitude will replace any competitive attitude.
4. The greatest gift of thankfulness in an organization is that each employee feels at ease in his or her position without wanting to take anybody else's.
5. Realize that the highest award for an employee it is to feel respected and appreciated for his or her true value.

Here are some ways to show your appreciation:
1. Do not be afraid to speak of gratitude and pride.
2. Do not rely on old stereotypes to communicate the pride of being part of the organization.
3. Demonstrate that pride must be contagious among the employees.
4. Ensure that the employees take ownership of the values and mission of the organization.
5. Provide possible solutions in order to realize the changes that are intended to improve systems and enhance the support given to the organizational values.

Life it is not just a series of calculations and a sum total of statistics, it's about experience, it's about participation, it is something more complex and more interesting than what is obvious.

Daniel Libeskind
(1946 –)
He is an architect, artist, and set designer of Polish-Jewish descent.

A special contribution by Yvan Poirier

6. Promote pride, so that it affects all the links in the organizational chain.

It is important to talk about thankfulness; it promotes the development of healthy relationships between managers and employees:
1. Promote and communicate to everyone.
2. Issue a "News Flash" once a month to maintain interest.
3. Ask for and gather the employees' ideas and suggestions for implementation.
4. Make agendas for internal committees (talk to management).
5. Share thankfulness at meetings or during training courses.
6. Do not forget to highlight the positive points of thankfulness.
7. At all times be fair and impartial.
8. Take the thankfulness seriously, but without taking yourselves too seriously; use a little humor.

Let no one think that flexibility and a predisposition to compromise is a sign of weakness or a sell-out.

Paul Kagame
(1957 -)
He is the sixth and current President of the Republic of Rwanda.

How can I obtain the participation of management and employees in the organization of ceremonies?

You can obtain the participation of management and employees in the organization of ceremonies by:
1. Finding creative communication strategies, involving managers / employees to find people who stand out.
2. Involving an advisory committee represented by managers, employees, and union representatives.
3. Leveraging the talents of employees to emcee or using their other unknown qualities.
4. Acknowledging employees who work in different spheres outside of their work.

5. Posting photos of the recipients on Honour Roll for everyone to see.
6. Achieving a substantial contribution from the division's or branch's budget.
7. Offering reasonable time for thankfulness events.
8. Sharing and promoting the thankfulness activities on the Intranet of the organization or by emailing the information to all employees.

What should I understand on a personal level about the thankfulness?

On a personal level regarding thankfulness it is important to:

1. Be sincerely grateful to everyone.
2. Have self-esteem, without boasting.
3. Accept that we can all learn from anyone, no matter who we are.
4. Avoid judgment at all costs.
5. Avoid sarcasm or vanity.
6. Demonstrate flexibility.
7. Be true everywhere, at all times, and with everyone.
8. Not to feel rejected if you are not chosen to be thanked.
9. Not to anticipate thankfulness to avoid living a delusion.
10. Not to feel guilty receiving thankfulness that others did not obtain.
11. Consider that we are all different.
12. Stop focusing on the mistakes instead of on thankfulness.
13. Understand and respect diversity, our differences.
14. Remember that nothing is permanent; nothing is guaranteed or granted.
15. Appreciate people and situations.
16. Be generous without expecting anything in return.

Expectation is the root of all heartache.

William Shakespeare
(1564 - 1616)

Chapter 17

Talent wins games, but teamwork and intelligence wins championships.

Michael Jeffrey Jordan
(1963 -)
He is a retired American professional basketball player, active entrepreneur, and majority owner of the Charlotte Bobcats.

17. Stay open to new things to change.
18. Accept that err is human and that it is perhaps a reflection of saturation, a sickness within the organization, or simply excessive fatigue.
19. Be flexible.
20. Adapt to situations, instead of waiting for situations to adapt to us.
21. Avoid taking ourselves too seriously.
22. Do what we can with the resources we have.
23. Show humility or modesty following the receipt of thankfulness for our achievements.
24. Avoid the expression of independence, perhaps even of patronizing.
25. Learn and understand about teamwork.
26. Respect each other according to our strengths and capabilities.
27. Have a winning attitude.
28. Use our knowledge and experiences without imposing them.
29. Give our opinions and ideas without requiring that they be accepted.
30. Acknowledge that we are not perfect and that we cannot demand perfection from others.
31. Admire people instead of being jealous.
32. Appreciate the moments when we receive thankfulness.
33. Rejoice over the success of others by giving them all the credit they deserve.

Besides the thankfulness that was shown towards us, we must acknowledge that we are blessed in our lives. So, we should acknowledge that:
1. We are alive;
2. We are healthy;
3. We feel good with ourselves;
4. We live in a world of peace;
5. We have a well paid job;
6. We have bread on the table every day;

7. We are privileged to see, hear, smell, taste, touch, and talk;
8. We are in a land of abundance;
9. We are loved and we feel privileged;
10. We get the thanks we deserve when it is appropriate;
11. We appreciate the smallest gestures of love shown to us;
12. Every important moment spent with those we love is one of the greatest gifts of life.

Doing what you love is the cornerstone of having abundance in your life.

Wayne Walter Dyer
(1940 -)
is an American self-help author and motivational speaker.

And there are other mechanisms that allow us to put thankfulness into practice. Everything is a question of open-mindedness for the companies that really want to apply this process, which will allow them to keep employees for a long time and to realize targeted objectives.

Congratulations to all the companies, whether governmental or private, which set up processes of thankfulness. It is always appreciated on behalf of the employees and especially profitable for the evolution of the company at all levels.

What tips and tricks should I suggest?

Although the company wants to obtain good profits, it is important to acknowledge that it can never generate substantial earnings without the indispensable contributions of the employees. However, it appears that the company's winning advantage is not only to increase its profits but also its customers and the support, and the close collaboration, of all the employees at all levels within the company.

It is essential to have different strategies of thankfulness for employees in order to increase their interest in and dedication to the development of the

Chapter 17

Politeness is the poison of collaboration.

Edwin Herbert Land
(1909 – 1991)
He was an American scientist and inventor, best known as the co-founder of the Polaroid Corporation.

Even though worker capacity and motivation are destroyed when leaders choose power over productivity, it appears that bosses would rather be in control than have the organization work well.

Margaret J. Wheatley
She is a writer and management consultant who studies organizational behavior. Her approach includes systems thinking, theories of change, chaos theory, leadership and the learning organization: particularly its capacity to self-organize.

company. We all know that recognition events are fairly valued in the organization, but it would be interesting to include another category of thankfulness, particularly one with a monetary component, which can be presented in different ways.

Here are some tips to recognize the value of employees, so they feel more involved and valued within the organization:

1. Productivity bonuses should not be given only to administrators and executives. Notice that in certain federal ministries departments or in companies, people from senior management or executives receive a bonus if they achieve the goals of their performance plan during the year. It would seem fairer for the lower levels to be able to benefit from these bonuses as well because they are working to achieve the objectives of the divisions.

2. There is also evidence that businesses operate by offering bonuses during the year or just before holidays or vacations. Some of these companies put the emphasis on sales and not on productivity. We often forget the people behind the scenes in production who can only hope to receive their salaries. Why not allow them to enjoy a certain percentage of the net profits when sales targets have been achieved? If each employee is able to benefit, only from a small portion of the net profits, productivity, and collaboration will be felt in sales. Everyone will feel involved!

3. The success of a business action plan is fundamentally a question of collaboration. If everyone gets involved, outcomes will be more fruitful for the entire organization. So why not grant employees a percentage of the profits at the end of a fiscal period. The process is simple. If

RECOGNITION & THANKFULNESS

I've always thought that people need to feel good about themselves and I see my role as offering support to them, to provide some light along the way.

Felice Leonardo "Leo" Buscaglia Ph.D.
(1924 – 1998)
He was an author and motivational speaker, and a professor in the Department of Special Education at the University of Southern California.

Goals are not only absolutely necessary to motivate us. They are essential to really keep us alive.

Robert Harold Schuller
(1926 -)
He is an American televangelist, pastor, speaker, motivator, and author. He is principally known for the weekly Hour of Power television program, which he began in 1970.

the expected percentage of the bonuses is planned in terms of the net profits, it will cost the company very little when you consider that the employees will feel valued and supported by the management. This mechanism will increase the confidence of the associates towards management, while increasing, substantially, the interest of all staff for business development. Everyone will feel like a part of a strong organization dedicated to keeping its staff in their jobs. You will realize that complicity will be introduced; your problems with employees will disappear; productivity will increase; and, subsequently, your profits will increase.

4. Contests, sweepstakes travel, and training on a personal level are also great ways to show appreciation to the staff. Admittedly, the company must find practical solutions to motivate their employees, not only to perform, but also to find a degree of affiliation deserving of recognition by the company.

5. Employees need to have effective ways to motivate themselves to succeed. If the company decides to provide training in a field other than that which the employee works in, employees will have an additional source of motivation to achieve their goals. Courses of personal motivation, self-esteem, self-confidence, painting, stamp collecting, etc. are some possible examples. In sum, these are more often than not courses or training that the employees cannot afford. With such perks, do you think that employees would not be interested in participating in the achievements set by the company?

6. Regarding the thanking of employees, we often forget that their families also support the employees. We spend almost 60 hours a week at

Chapter 17

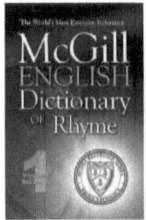

Courteousness is consideration for others; politeness is the method used to deliver such considerations.

Bryant Harrison McGill
(1969 -)
He is an American editor and author. He is the editor and author of the *McGill English Dictionary of Rhyme* and other books in the McGill Reference Series.

work; it is more time than we spend with our families. Do you not think that when a recognition event is held it would be a good idea to invite some family members to attend giveaways, events, recognition lunches/dinners, etc.? Think for a moment of how proud employees are of their work and also of how proud their family members are!

7. The company providing days off, or even hours off, is also greatly appreciated by employees. We must show appreciation to the staff in small ways that allow the employees to "breathe" a little after a busy week. This gesture is always nice, and the employees often will not hesitate to cooperate in a situation where they are asked to stay a little longer to work if there is an emergency when they normally receive such treatment.

8. Remember that salary is an important thing when trying to retain people in company positions, but recognition of all kinds will keep staff engaged, caring, and responsible. This demonstration of thankfulness goes beyond simple rewards for achievements; it is basically a fundamental respect and gratitude for the employees, something that none of them will forget when he or she leaves the job – for whatever reason. The consideration that we show to the employees is never forgotten, and it must be an intrinsic part of the company's values to have all members of the staff grow and/or advance fairly and appropriately. People must realize that it is part of the company's culture, or policy, to appreciate its staff regularly in an honest and open way.

CONCLUSION

It is essential to admit unreservedly that thankfulness, in all its forms, is key for any organization having for an objective to value its staff regularly throughout the year.

There are people and situations which must be acknowledged, on both personal and professional levels – and not just to thank them, in order to establish a climate of energetic trust and dynamic partnership.

Diversity in the world is a basic characteristic of human society, and also the key condition for a lively and dynamic world as we see it today.

Hu Jintao
(1942 -)
He is the current Paramount leader of the People's Republic of China. Hu possesses a low-key and reserved leadership style and is reportedly a firm believer in consensus-based rule. These traits have made Hu a rather bland figure in the public eye, embodying the focus in Chinese politics on technocratic competence rather than personality.

Being thankful is fundamentally a question of having respect for every person who works in an organizational environment, while knowing how to acknowledge the qualities, abilities, and success of the one or several people who "make their mark" and stand out because of what they achieve. But the recognition is not only for those who deserve it due to performance but also for those who will "take over tomorrow". If showing thanks is done with the good intention of building the future, and not only as reward for accomplished duty Being thankful is fundamentally a question of having respect for every person who works in an organizational environment, while knowing how to acknowledge the qualities, abilities, and success of the one or several people who "make their mark" and stand out because of what they achieve. But the recognition is not only for those who deserve it due to performance but also for those who will "take over tomorrow". If showing thanks is done with the good intention of building the future, and not only as reward for accomplished duty – of doing what was expected, the results and the effects will be very beneficial, both for the people who are acknowledged and for the companies that choose to emphasize thankfulness, regardless of the form used to express it.

Chapter 17

Awareness without action is worthless.

Phillip Calvin McGraw
(1950 -)
He is best known as Dr. Phil is an American television personality, author, psychologist, and the host of the television show *Dr. Phil*, which debuted in 2002.

Showing thankfulness should be treated honorably, as an incentive that benefits and motivates people to better performance, but more importantly, it should give them additional dimensions, so that they can improve their personal futures as well as the future of the company. If we acknowledge people's value fairly, the return will certainly be productive and economic for each of those involved.

Recognition, or showing thanks, in general, is probably one of the best investments any business could make if it wants the "flames of courage and motivation" of those committed people in the company to spread to the other employees, regardless of their levels within the organization or their functions.

All employers should have a permanent recognition committee in their organizations to commend employees on a regular basis. In fact, the objective is to show the staff that, as an employer, it is necessary to stand out and to maintain a high standard of performance within the company but also to make the organization progress in order to avoid any form of conflict or negative events which might occur when the company (and its employees) is faced with reorganizational change. Regularly recognizing employees will make it so much easier to find possible solutions to possible problems — and especially when the time for change comes — if there are interactions and transparent communication between the management, the employees, and the union on an ongoing basis.

In brief, when showing thanks, we should never have disagreements or biases but only clear-sighted solutions to arrive at an action in which everyone

RECOGNITION & THANKFULNESS

> An employee's motivation is a direct result of the sum of interactions with his or her manager.
>
> Germain Decelles
> *Le Changement POUR TOUS*

does his or her part to make the organization grow and develop. A company that decides to acknowledge its staff, to even make doing so a priority, is a company that promotes respect, honor, gratitude, and consideration on an individual level.

And each person within this kind of organizational system must be acknowledged according to creative and respectable models, fostering human dignity. Certainly, all this will create a climate of reliability and help maintain relationships of mutual respect, but it should also help maintain a corporate loyalty and give added value to the company, which will be established in a stable way between the employees and the employers.

A well-developed sense of humor is the pole that adds balance to your steps as you walk the tightrope of life.

Dr. William Arthur Ward

Reference: www.thequoteblog.com

CHAPTER 18

HUMOR

Humor is one of the greatest assets a person can have. Working on building your sense of humor will help you out a lot in life, including to be able to defuse difficult situations and to reduce your stress levels.

Life offers many humorous moments. You need to be watching out for them and to take notes. If you do not have a sense of humor, you may be shy. To get over this, try talking to at least ten people a day. You can even compliment them to start a conversation. If you are not comfortable talking to peers, talk to your younger sibling's friends, or your parent's friends. This will get you relaxed enough to talk more often.

The secret to humor is surprise.

Aristotle
384 BCE – 322 BCE

Watch shows, movies, comedy sketches, stand-up, or anything thing that might contain humor. If you do not understand why something is funny, try watching it again and deconstructing the humorous elements.

In addition, try to watch romantic comedies and go on websites that promote humor and comedy. Pay attention to the witty jokes. Eventually, you will understand why others think some things are so funny.

Furthermore, ask humorous friends for tips and tricks on how they improved their humor. Be aware, however, that some people are just born this way!

A man without a smiling face must not open a shop.

Chinese Proverb

Not everyone finds everything funny, but there are lots of general topics that are funny. Make a list of topics that appeal broadly in a humorous way and explore these further. Try laughing when other people do. Get into the habit. It may soon be easier for you to laugh naturally and for you to have an automatic reaction when something funny occurs. If you are

Chapter **18**

Change is such hard work.

William Edward "Billy" Crystal
(1948 -)
American actor, writer, producer, comedian, and film director.

taking things too seriously, it will be harder to be funny.

Stop viewing everything as an intelligence test, and start seeing the lighter side of life. Lighten up. Open up!

Smile more often, and laugh even when something may not be funny. When you open yourself up, you will begin to see things you have not seen before. Be ready to try out jokes on people. They will not always work, but you will soon get the hang of it and learn what makes people laugh.

Remember not to try to make people laugh with anything physical that may hurt them or yourself. Try to see the funny side of difficult or embarrassing situations. This can help to alleviate angst, fear, and unhappiness, if you can inject a little lightheartedness into such occasions.

A joke is a very serious thing.

Sir-Winston-Churchill
(1874 –1965)

Naturally, keep in good taste and do not step over the line were mourning, death, loss, and pain are involved. If you are in a special situation, such as if you are surrounded by strangers who you think want to do bad sting to you, such as kidnap you, or if you are in a court, then do not try to make the situation look funny. Making fun of life is good, but in some situations, it might get you, and/or others, into real trouble.

How can I be funny?

Having a funny disposition can prove to be a positive way to view life and your place in the world. A good sense of humor has many benefits, from personal happiness to making you the life and soul of a party. It can also help you to see the lighter side of life, and sharing your irreverent sense of challenging situations with those more seriously inclined can help others relax and enjoy life more. Being funny is recognized as an important part of job hiring, too. Many executives favor hiring someone with a sense of humor over hiring someone who does not display any humor.

Being funny is not about being flippant or frivolous. It is about being genuinely humorous and encouraging other people to have a good laugh. And while it might be a little challenging changing your outlook about the role of good humor in your life, being funny is something innate, and wanting to be funnier is the first fabulous step to becoming that way!

Being funny does not come in "one-size-fits-all"; what makes you amusing is unique to you and the way you observe the world. You should trust in your innate sense of humor. Focus first on what you find entertaining in life, and learn from your own reactions to the things that make you laugh. Trust that you do have a "funny bone."

Babies' laugh from four months of age, and all children express humor naturally from kindergarten age, using humor to entertain themselves and others, with riddles, knock-knock jokes, laughing at themselves, and even using physical slapstick humor. So, humor is already in you. You just need to bring it forth again!

Laughter is generally the desired result of anyone seeking to be funny, and usually this is because we view laughter as a sign of happiness, or as a release of or from tension.

Learn a little about what makes people laugh. Laughter itself is unconscious. While it is possible for

A person without a sense of humor is like a wagon without springs. It's jolted by every pebble on the road.

Henry Ward Beecher
(1813 –1887)
He was a prominent Congregationalist clergyman, social reformer, abolitionist, and speaker in the mid to late 19th-century. An 1875 adultery trial in which he was accused of having an affair with a married woman was one of the most notorious American trials of the 19th-century.

Chapter 18

us to inhibit our laughter consciously, although not always successfully, it is very hard for us to produce laughter on demand, and doing so will usually seem *forced*.

Fortunately, laughter is very contagious, and in a social context, it is easy to start laughing when others are laughing. Getting people to laugh, therefore, requires genuine humor, which is definitely about more than reciting hackneyed jokes!

What makes us laugh foremost includes feeling a sense of superiority over someone else behaving "dumber" than us, or being surprised by the incongruity of something, or by feeling a welcomed relief from anxiety. And for many of us, seeing our own frustrations reflected back at us by someone who clearly understands a familiar predicament or situation, and who is injecting levity into responding to it, nearly always improves our mood!

In a nutshell, as excellent comedians have already known, being humorous boils down to good timing and taking the best advantage of the context. This is why learning long lists of jokes will not necessarily make you *funny* because you still need to grasp the levity of a situation as it is unfolding before you, within the context of those present and the precise facts of each situation.

Here are some of the basic components of being funny:

Misleading the mind with surprise or cognitive incongruity: Verbal jokes use this element to the greatest level possible, trying to misdirect your attention much the same as a magic trick seeks to do. Basically, this technique relies on both cognitive

Humor is everywhere, in that there's irony in just about anything a human does.

William Sanford "Bill" Nye
(1955 -)
He is popularly known as **Bill Nye the Science Guy** and is an American science educator, comedian, television host, actor, mechanical engineer, and scientist.

Groucho Marx
(1890 – 1977)
He was an American comedian and film and television star. He is known as a master of quick wit and widely considered one of the best comedians of the modern era.

processing errors, turning assumptions upside down, and word confusion. For example: *What happens to liars when they die? Answer: They lie still.* This joke works because you have to interpret the joke in two ways, and the brain is temporarily confused by its inability to draw on usual experience. All of this happens quickly and unconsciously, and humor becomes your brains *graceful* way of coping with the mixed signals; if you *get* the joke, you will be laughing.

When writing, you can still use this technique. Write something that appears to be headed in one direction but end up in a totally different place, such as Groucho Marx' clever one-liner does "Outside of a dog, a book is man's best friend. Inside of a dog, it's too dark to read" or Rodney Dangerfield's line: "My wife met me at the door the other night in a sexy negligee. Unfortunately, she was just coming home." The aim is to keep what is coming next a total surprise!

Rodney Dangerfield
(1921 –2004)
He was an American comedian, and actor, known for the catchphrase "I don't get no respect!," and his monologues on that theme. He is also remembered for his 1980s film roles, especially in *Easy Money, Caddyshack,* and *Back To School.*

Surprising where it is least expected: On the plus side for you as an improving comical person, it is good to know that the less funny a place is, the easier it becomes to spring the element of humorous surprise.

Timing: Apt timing is as important as the surprise, because if you give the brain too much time to work out a situation or joke, the funny moment will pass by.

This is probably why jokes people have heard before do not work, as recognition dulls humor because the brain is already primed by experience. React quickly and strike while the humorous moment exists.

Using serious situations: Much humor can be derived from very grave events and situations in our daily

Chapter 18

lives. The sooner you grasp this reality and learn to bend it to your sense of humor, the better!

Thinking silly: This involves taking vital elements and not being so serious with them. Try to find the funnier, lighthearted side of what you are observing and think like a child.

Changing status: Changing a person's status, or the status of something long held to be true, can be very funny. For example, having a CEO of a company ask the receptionist for advice on how to run the company could be quite humorous.

Knowing your audience: Have a reasonable idea of what those around you find funny. When you are in a group of people you do not know, for example, just listen to what subjects they are talking about and what is making them laugh. Generally, the better you know someone, the easier it will be to make him or her laugh.

Humor is laughing at what you haven't got when you ought to have it.

James Mercer Langston Hughes (1902 –1967) American poet, social activist, novelist, playwright, and columnist. He was one of the earliest innovators of the then-new literary art form jazz poetry.

It is much easier to find funny moments in material you know well, such as your workplace attitudes, your amazing knowledge of 17th-century poetry, your familiarity with fishing trips that went wrong, etc. Whatever the material, though, it also needs to resonate with your audience, meaning that your concise ability to deconstruct a 17th-century poem might not hit its mark with somebody not familiar with the piece of writing!

As a general rule, people who are very focused on one hobby, occupation, or sitcom can be particularly amusing to other people who are also wrapped up in that particular pursuit. When they try to be funny around people who are not *in the loop*, however, their humor often falls flat. In other words, they may come off as *geeks* or *nerds*.

How do you avoid this? Broaden your horizons, so that you are "tuned-in" regardless of who you are speaking to. In a way, being funny is simply showing that you are intelligent enough to know a sufficient amount of information about something, hopefully a great many things, to be able to find the humorous nuances that others miss. Make it seem effortless. In addition, be observant. While knowing a good deal can increase your capacity for humor, there is no substitute for noticing a lot. In fact, many very knowledgeable people fail to see the humor in things. Look for the humor in everyday situations, and see what others do not.

Good comedians tend to use themselves as the principal targets for humor, presumably because they know their own foibles so well, but also because it is a means by which they show others the *warts-and-all* sides of their personalities, which instantly help us connect with ourselves, *warts-and-all*.

Do not take yourself so seriously. Remember the most embarrassing moments in your life so far and start seeing what was comical about these moments and how you can share the funny sides of them with others. Being able to laugh at yourself in a healthy, non-defensive way is good for you.

Being self-deprecating and having humble traits can make you appear approachable, and when you are being hilarious, it shows other people that you are like them; you have been through the same trials they have, and you are a *regular* person. Just make sure to play down the right things in your life though and not to make yourself appear self-destructive or to

You can turn painful situations around through laughter.
If you can find humor in anything, even poverty, you can survive it.

William Henry "Bill" Cosby, Jr.
(1937-)
American comedian, actor, author, television producer, educator, musician, and activist.

Chapter 18

have low self-esteem; these do not make you seem funny but pitiful, and sometimes pathetic. If you think your humor is self-mortifying, then it is not funny but painful for your listeners as well as for you.

Listen carefully to others and really hear them, and understand what they are about. Be an active listener and, therefore, a lifelong learner. When you are busy being focused on people other than yourself, you will get a better sense of how to help others through humor, and it will also enable you to observe and relate the small joys of life, too, making your funny self more believable and empathetic.

Furthermore, be prepared to make daily adjustments to your perspectives of the world and of other people. Your own "leaps of faith" and "changes of heart" can be very warming tales of saving face through humor for others to learn from.

> A clever, imaginative, humorous request can open closed doors and closed minds.
>
> Percy Ross
> (1916 – 2001)
> American self-made multi-millionaire.

Learn from funny people. This is a delightful part of seeking to be a funnier person. You get to watch comedians! Whether they are professional comedians, your parents, your children, or your boss, learning from the entertaining people in your life is a key step to being funny yourself. Watch the methods that they use, and see what you can adapt to your own situations and personality. Keep a record of some of the funnier things these people say or do.

And find what you admire most in these people - one admired trait from each – and if all you do is add these to your plan for being more witty, you will be improving your sense of being funny tremendously.

From a motivational point of view, as you travel along the path to becoming funnier, it is helpful to understand the extensive benefits of being a funny person. You need to focus on the benefits of being amusing. There are personal benefits for you and others to bestow on those amused by your humor.

Being funny can break down barriers between people and cause them to bond. Laughter itself is considered to be a *universal language*. Humor can play an important role during even the most serious times. For example, during both World Wars, comedians and cartoonists formed an important part of maintaining morale among both troops and citizens.

Humor can energize you and leave you feeling a lot more alert. It is like a "mind-break" without having to travel.

Being funny can make you seem a lot less scary. Have you ever experienced a moment when you have frightened a small child, but you have quickly turned the situation around by telling a joke or making fun of your scary height or appearance? It is a natural reaction when we want to make ourselves seem less frightening to others.

Humor can reduce anxiety. Using humor before an exam, test, presentation to the board, etc. is the ideal way to defuse tension and reduce anxiety levels.

Laughter can relieve pain. Numerous studies attest to the ability of laughter to relieve serious pain and illness for defined periods of time. Being funny when you visit a friend in the hospital can be a "breath of fresh air" for him or her.

Being funny can help people to learn. Whenever you are in a position to teach people, using humor can be a fantastic tool for making the learning process easier. Defusing anxiety in a classroom or workplace,

Life literally abounds in comedy if you just look around you.

Mel Brooks
(born **Melvin Kaminsky**)
(1926 -)
American film director, screenwriter, composer, lyricist, comedian, actor, and producer. He is best known as a creator of broad film farces and comic parodies.

Chapter **18**

Comedy is acting out optimism.

Robin McLaurin Williams (1951 -) American actor and comedian. Rising to fame with his role as the alien Mork in the TV series *Mork and Mindy*, and later stand-up comedy work. Williams has performed in many feature films since 1980.

Comedy is very controlling - you are making people laugh.

Gilda Susan Radner (1946 –1989) American comedian and actress, best known as one of the original cast members of the NBC sketch comedy show *Saturday Night Live*, for which she won an Emmy Award in 1978.

so that those learning are more receptive to what is being taught, is an age-old tradition that works.

What about humor in the workplace?
Being funny can boost creativity! Having a humorous side at work is beneficial for you, and understanding this can help you overcome any reservations you might feel about not always being taken seriously. In fact, if you are known as a good worker and funny, you will be the person others want to spend time around. Being amusing at work can help build teams and relieve workplace stress. In addition, funny people tend to be creative thinkers and intent on keeping an open mind about work challenges; and they often seek new ways to meet the challenges.

Give a thought to being a funny leader. A leader who loosens up allows the team to loosen up, too. If you are in a leadership or management role, set a tone that encourages good humor around the workplace, on that encourages fun to be a part of the work experience. Find out from your employees what their idea of fun is, and start to build relationships of trust based on allowing fun into the workplace.

Consider creating fun ways of tackling hard problems. Taking difficult work situations and turning them into funny ones might seem frivolous at first, but it can be an amazing way to turn around bad situations.

Know when not to be funny. Getting the balance right is important when you are trying to be amusing; there are times when being humorous about something solemn or tragic will fall flat and insult people. Rely on your common sense. Assess and know your audience before " moving forward." If your audience is likely to take a dim view of your humor under certain circumstances, know this beforehand!

HUMOR

Be extremely careful about cracking jokes or pulling pranks in the following situations: in the workplace, at funerals and weddings, in places of worship or at religious events, whenever your humor could be mistaken for harassment or discrimination, or if your humor might physically harm somebody, for example, if you pull certain kinds of pranks.

The only rules comedy can tolerate are those of taste, and the only limitations those of libel.

James Grover Thurber
(1894 –1961) American author, cartoonist, and celebrated wit. Thurber was best known for his cartoons and short stories, published mainly in *The New Yorker* magazine and then collected in his numerous books.

Sometimes a joke will fall flat, or an observation that cracks you up will just make others groan. Do not be discouraged. Learn from your comedic errors, and keep trying. Even the highest paid comedians do not always get a laugh, and no one expects anybody to be funny all the time. If you feel as if you are temporarily off the mark, just do not try to force humor.

Remember that gender matters. Men tend to tell more jokes, tease, use hostile humor, and enjoy slapstick humor, whereas women tend to prefer telling a story, usually in a self-deprecating manner, that elicits a response of group solidarity from other females. Interestingly, the roles become reversed when you stick men and women together. Men tend to tone down the teasing, while women tend to turn it up and target it at men, losing much of their self-deprecation in the process!

Everything improves with practice, but it is important to practice in a low-risk environment first and to build up your funnier self to wider audiences as you improve. Your family and friends will be most forgiving while your staff will be apprehensive if you are suddenly shape - shifting into a funnier person, and a large audience will expect you to be good at the start. Practicing with people you trust and who can give you constructive feedback is an excellent way to start.

Chapter **18**

Remember that there are times when humor is socially inappropriate: not only could someone be offended, but the person could also become hostile. As a general rule, avoid being funny at funerals, places of worship, and memorial services, or during conversations about terminal illness, race, or rape.

How can I socialize, be funny, and make friends?
Making friends is not always easy. It depends on how outgoing you are. If you are shy, then you need actually to build up your confidence in order to be popular.

Just be yourself. Do not be afraid to express your opinions. If someone insults you, just ignore him or her. The people who love you for being yourself will outnumber the people who are jealous and hate you. Even if you are feeling really down, remember that there is always something out there to smile about. Be optimistic. A positive outlook will make people want to be around you a lot more. Be cautious, however. There is a point where optimism can be annoying. Do not be too optimistic.

Having a sense of humor is important, but do not get too carried away. There are some things you have to be serious about. If you joke about your friend in a rude way, it could damage your relationship with him or her. Your thoughts can open up many doors that can lead to friendship. Share interesting/silly ideas. Listen more than you talk. Add your own thoughts into the mix, but do not hijack the conversation.

Smile as much as you can! Signs of encouragement, such as a smile, let people know you care about what they are saying. Nevertheless, have a reason to smile. Make it clear you have a reason to smile with humor or optimistic words. Smiling without a reason, or smiling too much, may creep people out.

If you're not having fun, fuggedabiutit!!! And the bonus is: fun sells!

TSufit
Canadian Author
TSufit is a Dean's List graduate from University of Toronto Law School and was once named a "Super-achiever" by *Canadian Lawyer* magazine. Her music CD *Under the Mediterranean Sky* has made Top Album lists all over North America and is played on the radio internationally.

Be patient. If you are still among strangers, the apprehension of a conversation may cause a delay in comments. Do not worry, that will go away in short order. Again, if you are shy on the outside but a little crazy on the inside, let it out once in a while. Wear your hair up high and spin around or dance. Others will laugh and find you funny and fun to be with.

Be honest. Lying will make people not want to be your friend anymore because they will not trust you anymore. Respect everyone, no matter what he or she thinks or says. Each person deserves to be treated with respect. If you treat people well, they will probably treat you the same way. Build confidence.

In addition, avoid saying something that could be taken the wrong way, but do not over-analyze what you want to say. If you think about something too much, not only will you miss out on your chance to contribute to the conversation, but what you do end up saying might sound scripted and unnatural.

Remember to avoid prejudice, even regarding age. It is not impossible for a 20-year-old to be a friend to a 70-year-old. Do not limit your possibilities. Always be nice to older people. Surround yourself with people you want to be like. Be passionate about what you believe in and keep your own opinions and ideas.

People frequently underestimate how self-conscious other people are. When you interact with other people, remember that they can often make the conversation uncomfortable because of their own insecurities. The best thing to do is to be confident. Confidence gives you a greater vantage point from which to see the social inadequacies of other people.

Cursing can be very unattractive, but at the same time, some people do not mind cursing. It is best not to curse at all. People who do not like it instantly notice it, but those who accept it do not notice it.

The duty of comedy is to correct men by amusing them.

Molière
(1622 –1673)
Les Femmes savantes (The Learned Ladies) of 1672 is considered one of Molière's masterpieces. It was born from the termination of the legal use of music in theater. Since Lully had patented the opera in France (and taken most of the best available singers for his own performances), Molière had to go back to his traditional genre. It was a great success, and it led to his last work, which is held in high esteem.

Chapter **18**

A sense of humor is a major defense against minor troubles.

Mignon McLaughlin
(1913 – 1983)
American journalist and author. She wrote two volumes entitled *Neurotic's Notebook*.

Making people laugh is magic. I feel like if you have humility, then you can do anything in comedy.

Amanda Michelle Seyfried
(1985 -)
American actress, singer-songwriter, and former child model.

Nevertheless, know the group you are with. Some groups of friends will like you better if you curse, but this can be complicated.

Remember that it might be OK to curse around your same-sex friends but not when they have an opposite-sex friend over. Simply, do not curse!

Should I smile?

Frown and you frown alone, but smile and the whole world smiles with you. Not just any smile will do, though. With 19 variations of smiles, including 16 produced by enjoyable emotions, smiling is an incredibly important part of our lives. Opportunities for smiling are all around you. Make the most of them.

Smiling is a good long-term predictor of happier life outcomes. Smiling attracts health, happiness, friends, success, and a longer life. Smiling and smiles make you feel good. Even if you are feeling a little blue, insert happy thoughts into your mind and just add that smile. The smile will trick your mind into feeling better, as endorphins are released to reduce physical or emotional stress.

Smiles make other people feel good, too. An open-mouthed smile is visible further away than a grimace and offers people reassurance that you are friendly. And it makes people feel better to see a smile, from afar or close up.

Smiles improve your appearance. Wear clothes that smile. Add to your positive body language the color of happiness. Yellow is the color for dependability. A soft yellow is non-threatening and friendly. Warm colors from the yellow family are welcoming. Gold, browns, golden-oranges, these are all dependable colors of friendship. Blues are passive and calm colors. In the visual language, soft blues project serenity and quiet peacefulness. Avoid reds that come across as aggressive and threatening.

HUMOR

Comedy has to be based on truth. You take the truth and you put a little curlicue at the end.

Isaac Sidney "Sid" Caesar
(1922 -)
He is an Emmy award winning American comic actor and writer.

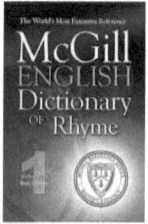

Why do we laugh at such terrible things? Because comedy is often the sarcastic realization of inescapable tragedy.

Bryant Harrison McGill
(1969 -)
American editor and author who was born in Mobile, Alabama.

Smiles make things right again and say much more than words can. If you have goofed, said something less than complimentary, feel lost or alone, or feel "down", a smile can set things right again. A smile lets other people know that you are prepared to be open to them, and that you are willingly agreeing to set things right where needed.

Smiles create trust and rapport. A smile is a great way of establishing mutual feelings of being on the same level as others, whether that is one-to-one or in front of a group giving a presentation. A smile says, "I'm OK; you're OK, and we're all going to enjoy one another's company."

Believe smiling to be arduous in some situations. Smiling on demand can be difficult, whether it is for a photo or for the sake of keeping mom happy when the relatives you cannot stand visit. This is because you are feeling self-conscious, or you lack a genuine reason for smiling. In these cases, smiling needs to come from your memory of good smiles, along with a little self-kidding or a joke in your head.

Wrinkles are better when they are smile lines, rather than frown lines. Mark Twain said: "Wrinkles should merely indicate where smiles have been". Viewed this way, smiles are an indication of your overall character, which becomes more and more outwardly telling as you age!

A smile is professional. Smiling at work or during other professional occasions is not going to make you seem unprofessional. Rather, the opposite is true a smile will humanize you and make you appear more approachable. People will appreciate your recognition of their worth, and of a job well done when you smile.

A smile makes you real. If you are afraid of appearing vulnerable when you smile, welcome the fact that any form of vulnerability suggested by a smile is precisely

Chapter 18

Comedy. It was just huge in my house. Peter Sellers and Alec Guinness, Monty Python and all those James Bond movies were highly regarded.

Michael John "Mike" Myers (1963 –) Canadian actor, comedian, screenwriter, and film producer of British parentage.

what makes it such a powerful act. You are opening yourself up to others, and people will respond better to that than to a serious, unmoving demeanor. Moreover, a smile accompanied by an assertive personality will take care of any sense that people will use your smile to walk all over you!

Make your smile natural. While it is perfectly possible to crack a smile when you feel terrible, angry, annoyed, or when you are up to something nefarious, a genuine smile is much harder to fake; indeed, only around ten percent of the population can manage that feat. A genuine smile is detectable by others because it is accompanied by a general glow, smiling eyes where the outer corners crinkle and the lower lid tightens, and a reassuring demeanor that helps the viewer to feel more at ease in your presence. A genuine smile comes from being happy and positive and from drawing your feelings from the heart.

Always smile with your eyes. A wholehearted smile will naturally draw in the eyes. The eyes are essential for a genuine, warm smile. Your eyes light up, twinkle, and reflect your happiness, and it is hard to do this unless you are really feeling it.

Practice smiling at random strangers. Make a choice to smile, make brief eye contact with a person, and smile. As you do this, think happy thoughts. It helps to choose someone attractive to begin with. Do not choose a person with sunglasses; you need to see their eyes. Not everyone will smile back, but note how you feel when they do! A lot of men feel uncomfortable about smiling at strangers, especially at other males. If that is the case, then just offer a casual "Hi!" or "Hey Man!" or "What's going on?" It works just as well, and feels less awkward for a lot of guys.

Maintain good mouth hygiene. One thing that can cause you to fear smiling is the worry that, there is

HUMOR

Comedy is exaggerated realism. It can be stretched to the almost ludicrous, but it must always be believable.

Paul Edward Lynde
(1926 –1982)
American comedian and actor. A noted character actor, Lynde was well known for his roles as Uncle Arthur on *Bewitched* and Harry MacAfee, the befuddled father in *Bye Bye Birdie* (both the musical and the film-version). He was also the regular "center square" guest on the game show *Hollywood Squares* from 1968 to 1981.

something stuck between your teeth or that you have bad breath. Eliminate these hygiene sources of worry by taking active steps to keep your mouth fresh and clean. When you smile at people, they will inevitably look at your mouth, so doing this will help you make a better impression, and, more importantly, a healthy mouth will make you feel more confident about smiling.

Remember that people will think you are a better and more fun person when you smile! Even if it is in the darkest of times, a smile can often help.

What should I consider?

Avoid self-destructive thoughts. Doing things that build talent and self-esteem will subdue such negativity. Never put yourself down.

Always be confident and other people will notice. Making a bad remark about yourself only makes it OK for other people to do so too. Be yourself. Do not think about becoming someone that you are not, as you will not get respect that way.

If you lie about something that you really do not do, people are likely to find out and maybe everyone the next week will not be into that anymore, so the best thing to do is to talk about your own interests and to ask others about theirs. Furthermore, do not put anyone down, including an older person or an ugly person. Be nice to everyone, and do not find fault in others under any circumstances

Remember not to try too hard to be funny.

Recommended Reading & References
We suggest consulting the works identified below in order to learn more about the particulars contained in this chapter.

BRICKER D. & WRIGHT J. WHAT CANADIANS THINK, about almost everything. Seal Books. ISBN 0-7704-3008-2.

SCOTT, ADAMS. THE DILBERT PRINCIPLE, THE DILBERT FUTURE, THE JOY OF WORK.
Harper Business. ISBN 0-06-018621-6

Your time is limited, so don't waste it living someone else's life. Don't be trapped by dogma - which is living with the results of other people's thinking. Don't let the noise of others' opinions drown out your own inner voice. And most important, have the courage to follow your heart and intuition.

Steven Paul Jobs

Reference: Apple Inc.

CHAPTER 19

INTUITION

No one can see into the future, yet we all must make guesses about it in order to make decisions and be better prepared for what will come our way. The guesses that we make are not based on seeing the future but on our knowledge and past experiences, with a little bit of insight mixed in.

The future is a "big place" with many eventualities, but chances are that you will want to address a specific situation, problem, or opportunity. Define this end as best as you can. Not all decisions are rational or carefully analyzed, and intuitive guesses can often be not only acceptable but quite powerful. So use your intuition!

Remember that when you use your intuition, you draw upon your experience and knowledge in a different way than when you make a rational analysis.

Pay attention to your first instinct. Intuition often works best before you have had time to study any of the details, so pay attention to it, even if you do not act on it immediately.

Intuition may clue you into emotional factors. If something feels wrong about a situation, or you just do not like somebody, do not ignore this, even if you cannot put your finger on exactly what the problem is.

Use intuition as a *lead,* rather than as a solution. Investigate what might be causing your hunch, or gut feeling, and dig deeper until you find it.

How can I develop my intuition?
Inspiration is a very hard thing to come by sometimes. Many people find that when they are trying to think,

As the old saying tells us, change is the only constant. Yet certain changes really are *different* from the rest. They are trends that offer exceptional moneymaking opportunities to wise real estate investors. Understanding and following these trends will offer you exceptional opportunities.

Barry Lenson
Insights on Moneymaking Opportunities
Trump University

Chapter **19**

Intuition becomes increasingly valuable in the new information society precisely because there is so much data.

John Naisbitt
(1929 -)
American author and public speaker in the area of futures studies. His first book, *Megatrends*, was published in 1982 and sold more than 14 million copies.

A good teacher can inspire hope, ignite the imagination, and instill a love of learning.

Charles Bradford "Brad" Henry
(1963)-
26th Governor of the U.S. state of Oklahoma.

walking helps. Walking gets more oxygen to your brain and speeds up the body's functions. It will relax you and help you think more clearly and easily. And even if you are still not inspired, you will get some exercise out of it.

If walking does not work, then chew some mint gum. Chewing has some of the same benefits as walking, and the big reason is the mint. The fragrance and taste of the mint will stimulate your brain to help you focus and think.

Look at some examples of other people's work. Observing other people's work will help influence and improve your own style and will boost the inspiration process by giving you some ideas.

Go back to what inspired you in the first place. It will remind you of why you are doing this and refresh your mind. If you are doing this for your job, then look back at what inspired you to take the job in the first place. If you are stuck halfway through your project, look through what you have done so far. Some people swear that this sparks new ideas.

Do not forget the library. This is a great place to find inspiration. Its books are gateways to your imagination. It is also a quiet place to think.

Remember that if none of this work, just go back to what you were doing later. There is no use in trying to do it now, especially if you are frustrated. Go back to it later when your mind is fresh. Go out and see people. Experience life. After all, that is where all ideas trace back to. Who knows? Maybe the people in the park or the museum will inspire you.

INTUITION

To raise new questions, new possibilities, to regard old problems from a new angle requires creative imagination and marks real advances in science.

Albert Einstein
"On the essence of scientific creativity."

Source: *Life* magazine, Jan. 2, 1939

Chapter 19

How can I follow my intuition?

Intuition is *knowing* something without being able to explain how you came to that conclusion rationally. It is that mysterious *gut feeling* or *instinct* that often turns out to be right, in retrospect. When you have narrowed down your options and are stuck at a crossroads, getting in touch with your intuition can help.

Everyone should carefully observe which way his heart draws him, and then choose that way with all his strength.

Hasidic saying

It can be difficult to depend on something that you do not understand, and you probably should not base every one of your decisions on intuition. Trust your instincts. For example, if you are hiring someone, you should look at his or her qualifications first and foremost, or else you might accidentally discriminate. But when you have weighed all the options and there is no obvious, rational choice, intuition is really all you have left.

Using intuition is basically quickly tapping into your subconscious mind, which is where you "archive" all kinds of information that you do not remember on a conscious level. Sometimes you pick up on things subconsciously without realizing it, such as body language. It registers as a certain *feeling* that you cannot articulate at that moment, but it could very well be valid.

The greatest mistake you can make in life is to be continually fearing you will make one.

Elbert Green Hubbard
(1856–1915)
American writer, publisher, artist, and philosopher.

Without intuition, you would be no different than a computer. You would only make decisions based on facts, and you would not always have all the facts. So unless you are functioning like a computer, you are already making decisions based on various factors other than logic.

Even some of the world's greatest scientists, the most logical thinkers of all time, have made their greatest discoveries based on flashes of intuition, such as Newton when the apple fell on his head.

Ask yourself questions and listen to the first answers that pop into your mind. That is not easy because several thoughts will flood your mind at once. Do not dwell on them. Just pick something, one thing. This can be scary; what if you make the wrong choice? Relax; you will be fine!

The final act of business judgment is Intuitive.

Alfred P. Sloane
(1934 – 1965)
Former president of General Motors.

Clearing your mind of repetitive thoughts and worries will make it easier for you to listen to your intuition. Meditation will help. Find a meditative technique you are comfortable using and practice it. Also, listen to your gut. There is a reason it is called a *gut feeling*. Many times, a decision that you *know* is wrong makes you feel discomfort in your stomach area.

Remember that figuring out what is really your intuition and not the rational mind or something else is a self learning process that requires trial and error. Read books about approaches and techniques that may help you discern the differences.

What can I do about fear and intuition?

Some fears are capable of causing you to put yourself down or to misinterpret danger; not all fear is realistic or beneficial. At the same time, confusing unrealistic fears with intuition can cause you to be convinced that something negative is about to take place in your life. When this happens, it can lead you to make choices and decisions that restrict, rather than broaden, your life. A fulfilling life is one of balance and your fears and intuition will serve you well when balanced, too.

If the facts don't fit the theory, change the facts.

Albert Einstein
(1878-1955)
In the period before World War II, Einstein was so well known in America that he would be stopped on the street by people wanting him to explain "that theory". He finally figured out a way to handle the incessant inquiries. He told his inquirers "Pardon me, sorry! Always I am mistaken for Professor Einstein."

Understand what happens when you mistake fear for intuition. Fear is a negative emotion that expresses

Chapter **19**

> Fear, uncertainty, and discomfort are your compasses toward growth.
>
> Anonymous

> The time to take counsel of your fears is before you make an important battle decision. That's the time to listen to every fear you can imagine! When you have collected all the facts and fears and made your decision, turn off all your fears and go ahead!
>
> George Smith Patton, Jr.
> (1885–1945)
> United States Army officer best known for his leadership while commanding corps and armies as a general during World War II.

itself through physical reactions, such as fight or flight, sweating, feeling an adrenaline rush, etc. Intuition is a positive set of feelings, or guidance that if heeded, can bring about better situations.

Fear is an emotion that causes us to want to run away, hide, and not face the oncoming negative happening, whereas intuition is about heeding the possible dangers but having the strength, resilience, and wherewithal to focus our actions and attitude in order to be able to face and deal with the negative occurrence.

As such, when you mistake fear for intuition, you are effectively telling yourself that something bad is about to occur, but that you are powerless to do anything constructive about it other than worry, fret, or pray, thereby disabling your intuition and your ability to push past the fear. This is an attempt to either sideline intuition or to change its positive effect into a negative one.

Another problem with confusing fear and intuition is that instead of living in the present, as intuition does, you are living in a worst possible future, where irrational fear resides. If you are not focusing on the present, then you are not being intuitive.

Remember that stress and anxiety can prevent you from taking time out. Without taking time out, you will find it hard to rediscover your sense of self or your *essence*. And this is when fears can dominate and take over because you are trying to protect yourself from being worn out, burned out, and used up.

Take the time to rejuvenate, so that you can let go of fears, listen to your intuition properly, and make amazing personal discoveries that won't surface without taking time to relax and regroup.

How can I think ahead?

Prior knowledge comes from many places. Consider what you already know. Have you tried something similar before? Do you know how somebody is likely to react? Have you seen something done or can you read about others' experiences with a situation? Is there something you can ask others? Can you try something out or gather data that might suggest what could happen?

Things done well and with care exempt themselves from fear.

William Shakespeare
(1564 – 1616)
English poet and playwright, widely regarded as the greatest writer in the English language and the world's pre-eminent dramatist.

People tend to bias their guesses and actions in certain predictable ways. Detect your own biases. For example, recent events may play a larger role in influencing decisions than they warrant; alternatively, you may be more likely to believe something just because everyone around you believes it. If you think this sort of thing is happening, start looking closely at hard evidence, such as facts and numbers, and question your own assumptions.

Ask yourself "what if" for various possibilities and imagine possible outcomes or courses of events that could result. In particular, think about possible consequences of different courses of action.

The winners of tomorrow will deal proactively with chaos, will look at the chaos *per se* as the source of market advantage, not a problem to be gotten around.

Thomas J. "Tom" Peters
(1942 -)
American writer on business management practices.

Consider the worst-case scenario. What is the worst thing that could possibly happen? Evaluate the possible risks!

Is the worst-case something you and others could tolerate? Could you clean up a mess, try again later, apologize, lose a bit of money, or cope with the ensuing criticism or rejection? Is the worst-case something you could plan for, avoid, or mitigate? Is the worst case too risky or undesirable? How likely is

Chapter 19

Have the courage to act instead of react.

Oliver Wendell Holmes, Sr.
(1809 –1894)
American physician, poet, professor, lecturer, and author. Regarded by his peers as one of the best writers of the 19th-century, he is considered a member of the Fireside Poets.

How people treat you is their karma; how you react is yours.

Wayne Walter Dyer
(1940 -)
American self-help advocate, author, and lecturer.

the worst case, and how likely is an undesirable outcome?

Consider the best-case scenario. What is the best thing that could possibly happen? Evaluate the possible rewards!

What can you do to bias the outcome towards the best scenario? Where should you set your goals? How likely is the best case, and how likely is a desirable outcome? If you are trying to think ahead, it is probably because you want to decide how to respond to some situation or need, so think of possible responses or actions.

Evaluate those actions. Based on your experience and knowledge about how such events usually turn out, choose or narrow down which actions to take.

Whatever you have to get ready, be it people, equipment, facilities, plans, or simply courage, get it ready. Writing can be a powerful tool for preparation. It helps you remember your plans, and it helps you to see them completely. Use a calendar, notebook, checklist, chart, or whatever helps you.

You should act according to your calculated, or anticipated, results and your plans. Then let life take its course. See what happens. By taking note of the outcome, you will have more experience and knowledge to draw from the next time you must decide about something such as this.

When you see what really does transpire, adjust your actions or responses appropriately as best as you can. You may not have the opportunity to change the course after you begin, but you do have the benefit of acquiring new information or results. Use these to

Take a step back, evaluate what is important, and enjoy life.

Terry Ann "Teri" Garr
(1947 -)
American film and television actress.

decide how to modify your actions in the present and in the future.

Remember to be honest with yourself. No amount of wishful thinking is going to stop the next natural disaster, but the realistic admission that one might happen can lead you to prepare appropriately.

How can I develop the *Sherlock Holmes* intuition? The quick wits and sharp observational skills of Sherlock Holmes used to analyze and solve the greatest mysteries is legendary. And even though Sherlock Holmes often expressed a need for the sleuthing to stick to the facts, his actions would often demonstrate that he was very reliant on his intuition as well and clearly saw both logic and intuition as equal partners in solving the mysteries before him.

While it is not possible to intuit everything in life, there are times when paying attention to our intuition is both sensible and helpful in reaching conclusions about such things as relationships, connections with others, and the suitability, or otherwise, of certain life choices.

Sir Arthur Ignatius Conan Doyle
(1859 –1930)
Scottish physician and writer, most noted for his stories about the detective Sherlock Holmes.

As for being able to work out what makes other people tick, there are some intuitive tricks you can rely upon to help you guess reasonably accurately, and your intuition can easily be developed with a little practice and perseverance by following these easy steps.

Sir Arthur Conan Doyle's fictional detective summarized his intuition thus: *It is easier to know it than to explain why I knew it. If you were asked to prove that two and two made four, you might find some difficulty, and yet you are quite sure of the fact.*

Chapter 19

Sherlock Holmes in a 1904 illustration by Sidney Paget

Everyone is entitled to his own opinion, but not his own facts.

Daniel Patrick Moynihan (1927 – 2003) American politician and Sociologist.

Yet, many people who consider themselves as *concrete* thinkers rely on evidence-based thinking processes and tend to dismiss intuition as folly and unreliable. It has not helped that intuition has long been attached to the supernatural - to the oracles, seers, witches, wizards, and other mystical sources in history.

It is unfortunate that the misuse of intuition by charlatans has tarred its reputation. But that does not mean it is not a valid part of our thinking and decision-making processes, *provided* it is balanced with an examination of the available facts and evidence.

Many human beings have experienced making decisions on a *gut feeling* from time to time and have found the outcomes to be satisfactory and sometimes even life-saving. Viewing intuition as *an educated counselor* is a helpful way to perceive it; we receive guidance from our subconscious drawing on experience accumulated over the years, often in times of danger or problem-solving.

And while the inexactitude of intuition simply means it cannot be relied upon alone as a source for reaching a conclusion, that is that all initial suppositions, theories, and hunches must be tested by logic and an analysis of the facts, intuition must not be removed altogether from our processes of deduction. Remember that the easiest person to fool is you yourself.

As such, never make unfounded accusations, allegations, or deductions at any stage in the process of reaching your conclusions about anything. It is also wise to find someone trustworthy and independently minded to bounce your conclusions off of.

INTUITION

Learn how to deduce things from studying a person. It is possible to discover quite a bit about how a person feels, whether or not they are lying, the things left unsaid, etc. by keen observation of the person.

While some people are more attuned to reading the body language of others, anyone can learn this art if he or she is willing to do so. There are plenty of books and online sites devoted to reading body language.

Check out bestsellers, such as *A Definitive Guide to Body Language* by Allan Pease and Barbara Pease, and others. Just be aware that reading body language does have its limitations because some people are good actors or deceivers, and sometimes you simply make terrible mistakes and misread the signals. Balance body language reading with other sources of intuition and the facts.

As a rule, said Holmes, the more bizarre a thing is the less mysterious it proves to be. It is your commonplace, featureless crimes which are really puzzling, just as a commonplace face is the most difficult to identify.

Watch for the signs that indicate lying and honesty. If you are going to be sleuthing or deducing like Sherlock Holmes, then you will definitely need to know how to spot the signs of a liar and a truth-teller.

Try people watching. Spending some time every week simply watching people in their daily comings and goings as you sit somewhere comfortably can teach you a great deal about people's habits, mannerisms, interactions, and personalities.

Arthur Conan Doyle
(1859 –1930)
He was also a fervent advocate of justice and personally investigated two closed cases, which led to two men being exonerated of the crimes of which they were accused. The first case, in 1906, involved a shy half-British, half-Indian lawyer named George Edalji who had allegedly penned threatening letters and mutilated animals. Police were set on Edalji's conviction, even though the mutilations continued after their suspect was jailed.

While there is a lot of guesswork involved in people watching, you can also try to hone your guesswork to being able to spot specific behavioral traits and mannerisms that can serve as future references for you.

Chapter 19

> Any truth is better than indefinite doubt.
>
> Arthur Conan Doyle
> (1859 –1930)

Sherlock Holmes (right) and Dr. Watson, by Sidney Paget.

> Depend upon it. There comes a time when for every addition of knowledge you forget something that you knew before. It is of the highest importance, therefore, not to have useless facts elbowing out the useful ones.
>
> Arthur Conan Doyle
> (1859 –1930)

Improve your powers of observation. One of the most notable things about Sherlock Holmes was that he observed things that other people missed; he often stated such things as, "You see, but you do not observe. The distinction is clear." This is not magic, and it is not psychic mumbo-jumbo. It simply requires on to be very observant and to take time to spot the things that often get overlooked when people panic, assume, or rush around without consideration for the finer details. Improving your powers of observation can be done in various ways, and each requires practice.

Moreover, if you can stay calm and think clearly when in a pressured situation, you are already well ahead of many people. This is part personality, part confidence, part common sense, and part awareness of your surroundings, and it can take time to perfect it if it does not come naturally to you.

They are other ways to improve your observation. Concentrate on improving your three most used senses: sight, smell, and sound. The very fact that these are our most used senses means that we tend to take them for granted and make assumptions about what they detect. It is here that you must become more refined and fine-tune ways in which you use these senses, in order to make better use of your powers of observation. Practice these frequently, and time yourself to find things faster and faster without panicking.

Many of us do not listen because we are too busy, smug, lazy, certain of the answers before we have learned anything, selfish, preoccupied, or insecure.

The art of listening can never be over-emphasized, and Sherlock Holmes was a master at this art. It may

INTUITION

> I never guess. It is a shocking habit destructive to the logical faculty.
>
> Arthur Conan Doyle
> (1859–1930)

Jeremy Brett at one of his performances as Sherlock Holmes in the Granada Series

> It has long been an axiom of mine that the little things are infinitely the most important.
>
> Arthur Conan Doyle
> (1859–1930)

seem like magic when someone recalls everything you have told him or her but in actual fact, it is simply good concentration, courtesy, and memorization put to excellent use. A good listener will pick up not only on what is said but also on that which is not said, the gaps that often tell the other half of the story.

Never underestimate people. Holmes recognized the complexity of others – *A complex mind. All great criminals have that.* Avoid being arrogant or simplistic in deducing the motivations of others, and give credit where it is due.

Do not disdain the information gathered from simple sources. Popular literature, such as magazines and tabloids, and daily gossip can teach you much. Listening to and reading these things will open up your mind to the ways many people "tick", and whatever is popular is what a large proportion of the population is likely to be striving to achieve or think, so you can glean much from reading about these things.

After all, Sherlock Holmes used to read the Agony Aunt columns in the paper and clearly used this as a source of information about how people tick!

Soak up everything, and do not be an intellectual snob, or you will cut off half your sources of real information.

Intuition is useful but a poor master, and it needs to be reined in by logic and factual analysis. Bring logic to the fore.

"Going with your gut" and not facing the facts is bound to lead to trouble, so be prepared to let logic

Chapter 19

> Nothing clears up a case so much as stating it to another person.
>
> Arthur Conan Doyle
> (1859–1930)

balance your intuition, making it more than mere speculation and guesswork.

Holmes advised, *It is a capital mistake to theorize before you have all the evidence. It biases the judgment.* Take heed of his words, and be sure to apply the evidence to your theories.

Analyze any situation using a step-by-step process. Holmes was good at a process of elimination by which he would discard the improbable, the illogical, the uncertain, and then whittle down his observations, deductions, and theories to reach what he believed to be the only conclusion. Indeed, he stated that: *Eliminate all other factors, and the one which remains must be the truth.*

Understand how to read a situation! There are three parts to reading a situation:
1. *See.* What do you see is happening?
2. *Observe.* What do you notice that is different - a stain, a crease?
3. *Deduce.* What does this imply?

Robert Downey, Jr. and Jude Law starred as Holmes and Watson in *Sherlock Holmes* in 2009.

In *A Study in Scarlet*, Holmes stated:
You know a conjurer gets no credit when once he has explained his trick; and if I show you too much of my method of working, you will come to the conclusion that I am a very ordinary individual after all.

> Our ideas must be as broad as Nature if they are to interpret Nature.
>
> Arthur Conan Doyle
> (1859–1930)

In other words, he did not consider that it benefited anyone to know his method or manner in great detail, and indeed, to reveal such would dispel the entertainment and effectiveness of what he did. Follow his example, and keep your intuiting and deducing methods to yourself. Avoid going around accusing people of anything until you are absolutely certain of their guilt.

INTUITION

> There is nothing more deceptive than an obvious fact.
>
> Arthur Conan Doyle
> (1859 –1930)

Benedict Cumberbatch as Holmes in *Sherlock* (BBC- 2010)

> We can't command our love, but we can our actions.
>
> Arthur Conan Doyle
> (1859 –1930)

Talk through your conclusions with a trusted person. Holmes was a guarded person and trusted people only when they had proven themselves trustworthy and loyal. Then those people, such as Watson, had Holmes' complete trust.

By the same token, as Holmes once "explained", *Nothing clears up a case so much as stating it to another person*, so be sure to open up and talk through your conclusions with someone you trust, to use them as a sounding board when you have worked through the deductions.

Things may seem as clear as day, but appearances can be deceiving in many ways. Sherlock Holmes was well aware of this and used it to his advantage in unraveling a variety of possibilities not explained openly by what the eyes see and the ears hear. He balanced intuition with logic; he drew conclusions from details; and he listened carefully.

Yet, he also kept an open mind, and accepted that some possibilities may yet be unexplained; he once said, *Life is infinitely stranger than anything which the mind of man could invent.* That does not mean that such things are not capable of explanation, but it does mean that there may be more wondrous things than those are already acquainted with in this world, and it does not pay to have a closed mind to the possibilities.

Sherlock Holmes worked hard when sleuthing, but he also loved his leisure and being languid. Deducing things and pushing your intuition to its limits can wear you down, and rejuvenation is an essential part of ensuring that you continue to stay sharp, focused, and clever. Plan downtime, party time, and leisure time into your life.

Chapter **19**

It is through science that we prove, but through intuition that we discover.

Jules Henri Poincaré
(1854 –1912)
French mathematician, theoretical physicist, engineer, and a philosopher of science.

Remember, a real decision is measured by the fact that you've taken new action. If there's no action, you haven't truly decided.

Tony Robbins
(1960 -)
His book, *Unlimited Power*, published in 1987, discusses the topics of health and energy, overcoming fears, persuasive communication, and enhancing relationships.

Remember never to take anything for granted. Even the most insignificant entity may present valuable insight into circumstances. When faced with confusion regarding to a decision that needs to be made, collect all your verbal and non-verbal facts. This may aid your decision making process. Listening to your *intuition* can be very helpful in day-to-day situations, such as predicting the outcomes of meetings and understanding the people you encounter in your everyday life.

What should I consider?

Developing your intuition can make your life more meaningful. It can also help you better understand others and yourself, as a person.

Intuition is *knowing* something without being able to explain how you came to that conclusion rationally. It is that mysterious *gut feeling* or *instinct* that often turns out to be right, in retrospect. When you have whittled down your options and are stuck at a crossroad, getting in touch with your intuition can help. Always make it a part of your decision making process.

Making a decision to do something new usually involves giving up something else. That is what makes it hard. There is a loss to deal with as well as the uncertainty of the future. We resist change when the number of positive things in our lives is equal to the number of negative things. Comparing these positives and negatives objectively helps us to move forward.

On the other hand, inaction is a possible response in many situations, but one must evaluate its merits and risks, too. It can be beneficial; more information may come later, or somebody's lack of action could harm his or her reputation. It can also cause one to risk missing deadlines or opportunities.

An in-between approach might be to wait for a little while, perhaps just long enough to learn more. Do not get so caught up in thinking ahead that you fail to act. Often, the best thing to do is to try something based on your best guess and see what happens. Treat your guesses and plans as possibilities. No one can foresee every eventuality.

Remember that whatever you do, it is not the end of the world; there is always a solution for everything. Make your own decisions. It is okay to get someone else's opinion, but the decision is yours to make. Always consider the good things and the bad things about your decision, and the possible expected results. It is natural to make a wrong decision sometimes. We learn from our mistakes, so do not get too upset about it if you do.

Recommended Reading & References
We suggest consulting the works identified below in order to learn more about the particulars contained in this chapter.

MYERS, Marc. HOW TO MAKE LUCK. 7 Secrets Lucky People Use to Succeed. Renaissance Books. ISBN 1-58063-058-8.

PETERS, Thomas J. THRIVING ON CHAOS/ A PASSION FOR EXCELLENCE. Random House. ISBN 0-517-14816-1.

PETERS, Thomas J. RE-IMAGE! Business Excellence in a Disruptive Age. Dorling Kinderly. ISBN 0-7894-9647-X.

RYE, David E. 1001 WAYS TO INSPIRE YOUR ORGANIZATION, YOUR TEAM AND YOURSELF.
Castles Books. ISBN 0-7858-2094-9.

SCHARMER, Otto C. THEORY U. Leading from the Future as it Emerges, the Social Technology of Presencing.
BK Publishers. ISBN 1-57675-763-3.

SCHMITT, Bernd H. BIG THINK STRATEGY. How to Leverage Bold Ideas and Leave Small Thinking Behind.
ISBN 1-59659-162-5.

The only true measure of success is the ratio between what we might have done and what we might have been on the one hand and the things we have done and the things we have made of ourselves on the other.

H.G. Wells

Publish: Blackford, K.M.H.: *Analyzing Character*, 1922.

SUCCESS

CHAPTER 20

Many people want to achieve success in life, but it is easier said than done. There are so many distractions that it can be challenging to discipline oneself to accomplish a monumental goal.

Einstein said that the imagination is more important than knowledge. The more vividly and accurately you imagine your success, the easier it will be for the rest of you to follow through. The same way engineers first imagine a bridge and then build it you can be the engineer of your success by dedicating a few minutes every day to the "mental movies" of your success.

> Opportunity doesn't knock. You knock and opportunity answers.
>
> Anonymous

Surround yourself with other people who are successful. When you are surrounded with people who are highly driven, it is encouraging. Start with the basics: willpower, effort, goals, and determination.

Whatever you want to accomplish requires all of these. Make a list of people you know. Include your parents, family, friends, siblings, cousins, colleagues, and classmates. List people in your social networks, such as Twitter, Facebook, LinkedIn, Google, etc. The list might even include names of people you have never met but are connected to through your social network or online group. You will be surprised to discover how many people you are connected with.

> The one sure way to success is to know everything you can about what you do.
>
> Normand Forgues
> (1940 -)
> Montreal merchant, President, Forgues Automobile inc. President, Montreal International Auto Show.

You cannot have success if you do not know what it means for you. Define the meaning of success as you see it. Everyone views success differently.

Set clear goals and be realistic. How will you know when you have achieved your goals? Your goals should be quantifiable, or else you could spend your entire life chasing after a vague idea.

Chapter 20

Action is the fundational key to all success.

Pablo Diego José Francisco de Paula Juan Nepomuceno María de los Remedios Cipriano de la Santísima Trinidad Ruiz y Picasso,
(known as Pablo Picasso.)
(1881 –1973) Spanish painter, sculptor, printmaker, ceramicist, and stage designer. One of the greatest and most influential artists of the 20th-century, he is widely known for co-founding the Cubist movement, the invention of constructed sculpture.

There are so many distractions in the world that you may not realize as such. Stay away from distractions. Whenever you feel drawn to do something which is totally not useful or productive, allot the least possible time you can to that activity. You get caught up in that activity, imagine yourself as a loser with shattered dreams and remove yourself as far from that activity as you can.

Gather as much information about anything & everything. Listen. Study. Understand. Learn. Knowledge is power. Identify the things you love to do, the things that give you satisfaction. Once you identify what you love to do, use this information to find the purpose of your life, or the objective of your life.

Donald Trumps in is book *Think Big and Kick Ass in Business and Life*, formulates an up-front definition. Another thing: *if you want to be successful, you can never, ever quit. You can never, ever give up. Now, if you love what you do, you are not to give up, because you love it. Sometimes you will feel like giving up. It may seem impossible to try again. But that is the most important time, because it is the time when you begin to learn important information about what you are doing – information you need to succeed.*

Set a time line indicating by when you want to achieve your objective. If you do not know by when you will achieve your objective, then you will never know when you have achieved it. Identify the things, skills, and material needed to achieve your objectives. Identify the skills you need to sharpen and the skills you can outsource. Then execute your small objectives and focus, at the same time, on your main objective. Yes, you need to act one what you have

SUCCESS

Without change, something sleeps inside us, and seldom awakens. The sleeper must awaken.

Franklin Patrick Herbert, Jr.
(1920 –1986)
He is a critically acclaimed and commercially successful American science fiction author. Though also a short story author, he is best known for his novels, most notably *Dune* and its five sequels.

The leader's role is most important at the moment of crisis, when the issue is in doubt. Then the leader must be visible. He must inspire confidence and impose calm and order.

Caesar's Commentaries

thought about, and you need to start realizing your dreams as soon as possible.

You need to study successful people. Look around. Who has the success that you envision for yourself? What is he or she doing? How does this person approach life?
Become an apprentice to the person if possible. Ask the person for advice. Spend time with the person, if you can. Learn as much as you can from this individual.

Step out of your comfort zone!

Successful people think big and act big. It can be a scary thing to do, but if you do not, then you will never be successful?

Do not wait for opportunities to fall into your lap. Sniff them out. Successful people make big investments, in their careers, in their businesses, in their education, and all investments involve risk. However, do not be reckless. Study your risks, make sure the odds are in your favor, and then take a leap. Be bold!

People who are successful encourage progress by solving problems and answering questions. No matter where you are or what you are doing, look around and try to think of ways you can contribute. What are people struggling with or complaining about? How can you make life easier for them in an effective way? Can you re-design or re-organize some aspect of the situation so that things run more smoothly? Can you create a product or provide a service that fills a critical gap? Be proactive and resourceful!

In contrast, not everyone will be happy for you when you succeed, or happy about your success. Some

Chapter 20

Many of life's failures are people who did not realize how close they were to success when they gave up.

Thomas Alva Edison
(1847 –1931)
He is the fourth most prolific inventor in history, holding 1,093 US patents in his name, as well as many patents in the United Kingdom, France, and Germany. He is credited with numerous inventions that contributed to mass communication and, in particular, telecommunications. These included a stock ticker, a mechanical vote recorder, a battery for an electric car, electrical power, recorded music, and motion pictures.

people are insecure and jealous. Be prepared for them, and look past them until you find the people who are happy for you and who support you in all that you do.

If your first attempt did not work, do not give up. Doing something once will not make a huge difference; it is when you do that one thing many times over that you achieve success. Success does not come through willpower alone; it takes consistency.

Success is equated with the achievement of a goal, but do not assume it will always bring happiness. Success does not guarantee happiness. Many people make the mistake of believing that if they accomplish this or that, they will be happier, but fulfillment and satisfaction have a lot more to do with how you approach life than with what you do in life. Keep things in perspective.

Accept the fact that life is unfair; some people are born with disabilities, and if you are one of them, you need to accept this fact, but remember that this also gives you an unfair advantage. You can stop wasting time about the unfairness and think about how to use the situation for your benefit.

Accept failure; understand that behind every success, there is a failure!

Remove fear and doubt from your way of thinking, and focus on staying positive in every situation.

Remember that you can be your own best friend or your worst enemy. "Pushing success" on others usually backfires. It is preferable to lead by example. If a person sees your accomplishments, he or she

SUCCESS

may start to wonder how to do more of what you are doing. Whenever you try to push yourself away from someone's, or a friend's, non-productive work, be polite. Understand that you do not have to damage relationships while becoming successful.

How can I make decisions?

We make decisions every day; everything we say and do is the result of a decision, whether we make it consciously or not. For every choice, big or small, there is no easy formula for making the right decision. The best you can do is to approach the situation, or problem, from as many perspectives as possible and then choose a course of action that seems reasonable and balanced.

First, you will need to list your options. It may appear that there is only one course of action, but that is usually not true. Even if your situation seems limited, try to make a list of alternatives. Refrain from evaluating at this point; brainstorm and write down every idea that comes to mind, as crazy as it may seem. You can always cross it off the list later, but with those crazy ideas might come some creative solutions that you might not have considered otherwise. Then ask other people for suggestions. Be succinct and ask them what they might do in your situation. Sometimes strangers can offer the most creative ideas because they do not share your assumptions or biases.

Second, for every option, list every possible outcome, and label it as positive or negative. Some people find it helpful to make a tree, which lays out every possibility in a visual format. For every scenario, think about whether the best possible outcome is worth accepting the risk of the worst possible outcome. If the worst possible outcome is completely

Sometimes it's the smallest decisions that can change your life forever.

Keri Lynn Russell
(1976 -)
American actress and dancer.
Russell appeared in the films *Eight Days a Week*, *The Curve*, and *Mad About Mambo*, all of which received only limited releases in North America.

It's a big world. There's a lot we don't know, which means there's still a lot to be discovered and a lot to be accomplished. The possibilities are always there. If you're thinking too small, you might miss them.

Donald J. Trump
with
Meredith McIver
From Trump: *How to Get Rich*.

Chapter 20

> Successful people understand that their own energy is a precious resource, and they never waste it.
>
> Mort Meyerson
> Co-Founder, Chairman of the Board and Executive of Morton H. Meyerson.

unacceptable to you, meaning that you could never forgive yourself if it happened, then you probably should not make that decision. In addition, consider which option will encounter the most resistance and why. Significant difficulty in implementing a decision can sometimes outweigh the benefits of the outcome, depending on the situation. At other times, it is the most resisted decision that would make the biggest difference.

Third, you must feel comfortable with the decision. On your list, or tree, place markings next to those decisions that are backed up by your intuition.

Fourth, this is, of course, the hardest step, but there will hopefully be a decision on your list that is backed up by both logic and intuition. It should have more plus signs than negative signs, and it should have your intuition's approval. If things do not match up clearly though, ask for advice from people you trust. No matter which decision you make, be prepared to accept responsibility for every outcome.

> It is difficult for the common good to prevail against the intense concentration of those who have a special interest, especially if the decisions are made behind locked doors.
>
> James Earl "Jimmy" Carter, Jr.
> (1924 -)
> 39th President of the United States (1977–1981), he was the recipient of the 2002 Nobel Peace Prize, the only U.S. President to have received the Prize after leaving office.

If things do not work out, it is always better to have made a conscious decision than to have been careless. At least you can say that you did the best you could. If you can, make a backup plan in preparation for any negative outcome. Think ahead. The best decision-makers are not people who never make mistakes; they are people who hope for the best and prepare for the worst.

Fifth, once you have made a decision, implement it totally. At this stage, do not be confused by thinking about the other potential alternatives that you did not pick.

Sixth, the most important step is to evaluate your

It doesn't matter which side of the fence you get off on sometimes. What matters most is getting off. You cannot make progress without making decisions.

Jim Rohn
(1930 – 2009)
American entrepreneur, author, and motivational speaker. His rags to riches story played a large part in his work, which influenced others in the personal development industry.

Luck is the sense to recognize an opportunity, and the ability to take advantage of it.

Samuel Goldwyn
(1879 –1974)
American film producer and founding contributor and executive of several motion picture studios

decision. If you do not evaluate your decision afterward, you will not learn anything from it. Ask yourself whether the outcome was what you expected. Would you do it again? What do you know now that you did not know before? How would you turn this lesson learned into advice? By drawing insight and wisdom from every decision you make, you can ensure that every choice has at least one positive outcome.

Remember to stay away from people who make it seem as though they want what is best for you but assume they know what that is, and that you do not. Their suggestions might be right, but if they refuse to account for your feelings and concerns, they might be very, very wrong as well. Recognize also that at some point, indecision becomes a decision to do nothing, which might be the worst decision of all.

How can I be bold?

Are you shy, hesitant, or passive and running the risk of leading a boring life marked by routine and unfulfilled goals? Recognize that most progress has been led by people who were bold scientists, public servants, artists, entrepreneurs, and others who did not wait for opportunities; they created opportunities.

First, pretend you are already bold. If you know someone who is bold, imagine how he or she would act. If you do not know anyone like that, think of a character from a movie or book that is daring and brave. Spend one hour a day or one day a week pretending to be that person.

When you do this, go to a place where people do not know you and will not act surprised when you do things that are out of character. Go through the motions and see what happens. You might discover

Chapter 20

> Opportunities go not to the most qualified but to the people who promote themselves the best and are in the right place at the right time. This may be unfair, but it is definitely not accidental. If you want to get anywhere, you have to learn how to promote yourself and to keep looking for the right place and time.
>
> Albert. J Bernstein. Ph.D.

that amazing things happen when you are bold, and you might be convinced to carry this "new" courageous behavior into your everyday life.

Whenever you are feeling hesitant, especially in your interactions with others, swallow your pride and make the first move. Ask your acquaintance if he or she would like to go for a cup of coffee or to the bar down the street for a drink after work.

Tell the person you favor that you have two tickets to a concert and that you would like the person to go with you. Give your significant other a big hug and apologize for that time you overreacted a few months ago. Smile and wink at the attractive cashier.

You could also do something unpredictable. What could you do that would completely surprise the people who know you? Bold people are not afraid to try new things, and one of the reasons they are so exciting to be around is that they keep you guessing.

You can start small, perhaps by wearing a color or style of clothing that you do not normally wear, or visiting a place you usually would not visit. Eventually, you may get to the point where you entertain ideas that make other people's eyes widen when you mention them or make the same people react when you talk about what you did the previous week.

Rather than wait to be recognized for your efforts, or expect someone to consider your needs, step right up to the plate and ask. Some people feel that asking for things is greedy, selfish, and rude, and it is if you are asking for something you do not deserve. However, if someone is withholding something that you have rightfully earned, they are the ones being greedy,

SUCCESS

selfish, and rude. Besides, what is the worst thing that could happen? The person could say no. Life goes on.

There is a difference between being reckless and accepting risks. Impulsive people do not accept risks; they do not even think about them. A bold person, on the other hand, is aware of the risks, and has decided to go through with the decision anyway, ready and willing to accept the consequences if things do not work out. Remember that inaction can be a mistake as well, one that leads to emptiness and regret. For many people, having taken risks and fallen flat on their faces was far more fulfilling than having done nothing at all.

Ultimately having boldness means coming from your "center", from what you believe. It is not about what you do, it is about who you are. If you do not know who you are, you can never be truly bold. Start really appreciating your uniqueness. Discover what makes you different, and then parade it around for all to see. Put flags on it; call attention to it; and love yourself for it, no matter what others think. That is the heart of boldness.

Remember not to confuse being bold with being aggressive. Aggressiveness often involves imposing your viewpoints or actions on others. Boldness has nothing to do with the people around you; it is about overcoming your fears and taking action. Furthermore, there is a difference between being bold and being suicidal. If you know doing something will hurt you, it does not matter how daring you are; do not do it.

The great end of knowledge is not knowledge but action.

Thomas Henry Huxley
(1825 –1895)
English biologist, known as "Darwin's Bulldog" for his advocacy of Charles Darwin's theory of evolution.

Every man's idea of success today is that you make a lot of money. I think success is when you really feel good about what you've done. You feel good about the accomplishment . "That's success."

Bernard "Bernie" Marcus
(1929 -)
American pharmacist and retail entrepreneur.

Chapter **20**

All that's different about me is that I still ask the questions most people stopped asking at age five.

Albert Einstein
(1879 –1955)
Throughout his life, Einstein published hundreds of books and articles. In addition to the work he did by himself, he also collaborated with other scientists on additional projects, including the Bose–Einstein statistics, the Einstein refrigerator, and others.

How can I be proactive?

Being proactive means thinking and acting in advance. This means using foresight. It is a great way to avoid more work down the road, but it can also be extremely important for averting disasters, planning well for the future and for instituting systems at work, for study, and at home, systems that will make life easier for not just you, but others as well. Many of us look to proactive people as the instigators of action and creative ideas in society.

Look at yourself, reflect, and ask yourself what kinds of tasks come or do not come your way regularly at work, at home, when you study, etc.? What kinds of tasks normally need immediate attention? How can you perform those tasks more efficiently, that is, create a plan, procedure, checklist, or routine to accomplish the task?

You should also try to prevent problems from ever arising. This means avoiding possible failure in advance and prevent the things from becoming problems. Get into the habit of taking precautions and developing fallback plans.

Develop a mindset that focuses on to solving problems instead of dwelling on them. Decide what needs to happen to overcome any given problem and how you are going to do that; and get on with it.

Write out daily "Things to Do" lists. Know which tasks are priorities and which can wait. Boldly cross off each item as it is achieved. Keep this list close at hand and let it direct your actions. If too much time passes before you cross anything off, reassess what you are doing to make sure that you do finish the tasks on the list. And be realistic about how many things you aim to accomplish in a day.

SUCCESS

In addition, get and stay ahead of less-urgent, day-to-day tasks. If you do so, they will be out of the way when deadlines, or urgent things, come up, and you will not have to worry unnecessarily.

Pay particular attention to preventative maintenance. For example, check the fluids in your car, restock your pantry, or set aside a bit of money in a savings account each week. A little effort up front could save you from a larger crisis later.

Some things do not need doing, or do not need to be done by you. Eliminate altogether any task that is truly unnecessary. Do not waste time doing it, and do not allow a misplaced sense of guilt to lead you into thinking that somehow you are responsible for its getting done. If tasks are unnecessary, they will not add anything positive to your life and are, thus, a waste of energy. Be ruthless in making this assessment about the value of a task.

What works and what does not? Evaluate your procedures as you use them. Make notes on how to improve, and incorporate those "improvements" the next time. Discard anything that does not work, but take care to note when something is only in need of tweaking, and adjust it accordingly, so that it does work.

What about seasonal rushes? Are there extra activities associated with certain times of the day, week, month, or quarter? Can you prepare for these in advance? Look ahead, and do not be afraid of the unknown!

A small amount of future stability can be self-generated by planning ahead and being ready for those things over which you do have some control.

Know your lines!
Rehearse.
In the car.
In the shower.
During sex.
Rehearse.

TSufit
Canadian Author
TSufit is a Dean's List graduate from University of Toronto Law School and was once named a "Super-achiever" by *Canadian Lawyer* magazine. Her music CD *Under the Mediterranean Sky* has made Top Album lists all over North America and is played on the radio internationally.

Chapter 20

Focus and discipline are habits that everyone can learn.

Donald J. Trump
(1946 –)

Can you learn a new skill ahead of time? Can you apply a skill you already have in a new way? Try to anticipate things you will need to know. Watch the trends around you; keep up-to-date by reading and continuous learning. Proactive people are successful because they are immersed in unfolding history and understand the lessons of the past.

Remember that although time spent specifically planning or organizing is not time spent on a necessary task, a little planning can save a lot of time down the road. Do not overlook it with the excuse that it is wasted time; you will regret not having a plan to follow later and will truly waste time going back over "old ground". But do not get so caught up in planning that you fail to act (i.e., become-paralyzed by the analysis). A plan does not need to be watertight, only indicative and motivating. You can always return to it as time goes on and add more. There is no such thing as perfection, and trying to reach this at the beginning of a plan is wasted effort. And it is only possible to anticipate so much and be ready to react if something unexpected comes up. Flexibility is a key positive trait of a proactive person, and being proactive means anticipating and preparing for all potential outcomes, not controlling your future.

All our dreams can come true – if we have the courage to pursue them.

Walter Elias "Walt" Disney
(1901 –1966)

How can I be ambitious?

Do you want to care more about your achievements, or be able to chase those dreams of yours? In other words, do you want to become more ambitious? It is very hard to be ambitious if you cannot even believe in yourself. If you have little self-confidence or self-esteem, work on developing these. Realize that you are you, and since you are never going to be anyone else, you may as well learn to love yourself. You are unique, and you have the freedom to make your own decisions. You can work hard and become whatever you want to be. Just believe in yourself, and learn to love yourself. Figure out what you are good at, and make sure other people see how good you are at whatever it is, too.

Everybody has goals, for example, to improve at a sport or to become a chemist. Once you have developed self-esteem, think about your goals and values. You might want to think about:

A wise man will make more opportunities than he finds.

Francis Bacon, 1st Viscount St Alban(s) (1561 –1626) English philosopher, statesman, scientist, lawyer, jurist, author, and pioneer of the scientific method.

- What you are good at.
- Whether you want to develop that skill our not.
- What you want to do in life.
- Whether you are willing to work to achieve your "dream".
- How you can improve at everything you do.

Then you need to decide what you want to do. Do you want to study to become an engineer? Alternatively, maybe you want to develop your natural talent and become a singer? Do not let anyone make the decision for you!

Think about how you can improve, now that you know what you want to do. Are you going to work harder at school, so you can get into medical school and become a doctor? Or are you going to practice vocalizing all day and enter competitions in order to become a singer? It is okay to be a little competitive and set challenging goals for yourself. Always dedicate some time to what you want to do, and never give up because things are not "going your way". Furthermore, nobody likes a competitive and nasty person, so keep that competitiveness friendly.

Remember not to beat yourself up if you do not quite achieve exactly what you wanted to, because you were too ambitious. Balance your work and personal life. If you work too much, you may get stressed. If your work suffers, you might risk losing your job.

Chapter 20

I have a great belief in the fact that whenever there is chaos, it creates wonderful thinking. I consider chaos a gift.

Septima Poinsette Clark
1898–1987
American educator and civil rights activist.

Develop success from failures. Discouragement and failure are two of the surest stepping stones to success.

Dale Carnegie
(1888 – 1955)

Keep organizing. It is easiest to keep goals in mind when you are not prevented from getting things done by the mess in your room or the boxes of books you have not sorted through yet. Be aware of the fact that some people may call you a workaholic. Do not believe them. Keep up with your social life, but keep chasing your dreams, and brush off any mean comments.

How can I be resourceful?

Life does not always hand us solutions to go with the problems and situations we encounter. If you are "in a pinch", sometimes you have to use what you have, along with a bit of creativity and ingenuity, to get through it. No plan can address every possible situation that might arise!

You should be prepared and remember that you cannot anticipate everything, but you can anticipate many things, and the more you can prepare for ahead of time, the more resources you will have to draw upon when faced with a problem. Find ways to minimize the number of possible future problems if you can. Prevention is better than cure.

Build a "tool kit" and learn to use it. The more tools you have to draw from when you meet with a challenge, the more resourceful you can be. Depending on where you spend your time, the tools at your disposal could take the form of a real tool kit, or they could fit in a purse, a survival kit, a workshop, a kitchen, an equipment truck, or even your selection of camping gear. Learn to use your tools. Then make sure you have them with you when you need them.

Practice and anticipation are the best tools for prevention. If you do not know how to change a tire, try it in your driveway before you get a flat tire miles away from home, in the dark, or in the rain. Learn to pitch your tent in the backyard, or take a short day's hike to get used to your backpacking gear. Refine both your tool kit and your skills before you must put them to the test.

Anticipate likely problems and deal with things before they become problems. If you worry that you might forget your keys and lock yourself out, hide a spare key in the backyard. Attach your keys to something large and visible, so you do not lose them.

Moreover, when a challenging situation does arise, try to clarify and define the problem as best, you can, simply assessing the situation. Do not spend too much time worrying about the problem. Rather, focus on finding solutions to it by training your mind each time you start worrying. Ask yourself:

- How severe is this problem?
- Is this truly a crisis, or merely an inconvenience or a setback?
- Does this need to be addressed immediately, or can it wait for an appropriate solution to be developed? The more urgent the situation, the more creative you will have to be. Calm yourself first, and think clearly before taking any action.
- What is the nature of the problem?
- What is really needed? Assess what is available to you. Being resourceful is, above all, about the clever, creative use of resources. Do not forget that resources are not all objects.
- Do I have access to what I need, or could I obtain what is necessary? Whether you need bus fare to get home, good ideas, moral support, the use of a phone, or simply extra hands, involve others if you can. Brainstorming together may result in some great, joint solutions. Ask people you know and trust to help you. Seek professional help.

The entrepreneur always searches for change, responds to it, and exploits it as an opportunity.

Peter F. Drucker
(1909-2005)
American writer and management consultant.

Chapter 20

> No one achieves career success alone. The most successful professionals nurture their networks, show support and give more than they expect to get.
>
> Anonymous

Alternatively, as appropriate, ask anybody responsible - authorities, employees, docents, ushers - since these people often have access to additional resources. Even if you end up asking for the help of strangers, you will probably be pleasantly surprised by the results. Many will take the time to help you and give you good ideas.

- Could I assemble a team or task force, if one or two people are not enough?
- Could I persuade city hall or another organization to further your cause?
- Could I contact somebody who might know the answer, lend a hand, etc.?
- Could I ask a question, get somebody or something started, coordinate, collaborate, or commiserate?
- Has somebody else solved a similar problem before?
- How does the thing, system, or situation work that I am trying to deal with?
- Whom can I contact, and how? Being resourceful is an ultimate source of knowledge!

Consider money, objects, intangibles and time. These will not get you out of every jam, but they can be pretty powerful in some situations. And if you do not have money, and you need it, being resourceful may consist either of doing without it or of raising some.

- Could I ask people for help and money, hold a fundraiser, or get a job? Do not be afraid to use some unconventional ways. Wire coat hangers can be incredibly flexible, and while screwdrivers are not really intended for chiseling, prying, pounding, scraping, etc., they will often be helpful and do what needs to be done in a pinch and intangibles, such as sunlight, gravity, and good will can all be harnessed to your advantage.

To raise new questions, new possibilities, to regard old problems from a new angle, requires creative imagination and marks real advance in science.

Albert Einstein
(1879 –1955)

If you have time, use it. Again, you may need to figure out where you can get some more. Depending on the situation you need to overcome, you may need to work longer hours, ask for more time, enlist the time of others, implement temporary measures while you can develop something more permanent, be patient, or ask for the tolerance of others.

You should also consider working backwards to find the right approach. Take stock of what is available, and then consider how you can apply it to the problem. Be creative by thinking of crazy possibilities as well as obvious or practical ones. You might find inspiration for a workable solution in one of them.

Sometimes, you will need to break the rules. Do not go around carelessly disregarding the law, but do use things in unconventional ways or go against conventional wisdom or societal norms, if it helps. Be prepared to take responsibility, redress wrongs, or explain yourself if you do overstep your bounds.

Experiment, experiment, and experiment again. Trial and error might take awhile, but if you have no experience with a particular situation, it is a very good way to begin. At the very least, you will learn what does not work. And do not forget to use the situation to your advantage, if you can, or to improvise. Do not box yourself into thinking that only a permanent solution will do. Use what you have at hand for a temporary solution.

Most importantly, be an opportunist. If an opportunity presents itself, do your best to take advantage of it. Do not over think, but act quickly. Often, an effective solution hinges on a speedy response. Be decisive, and once a conclusion is reached, do not analyze it; act.

Chapter **20**

Creativity is just connecting things.
When you ask creative people how they did something, they feel a little guilty because they didn't really do it, they just saw something.
It seemed obvious to them after a while.
That's because they were able to connect experiences they've had and synthesize new things.

Steven Paul Jobs
(1955 –2011)
Jobs was a demanding perfectionist who always aspired to position his businesses and their products at the forefront of the information technology industry by foreseeing and setting trends, at least in innovation and style.

To gain experience, learn from your mistakes. If you had to scramble to correct a problem, take steps to make sure that it does not happen again. If you tried something that did not work, try it a different way next time, and do not forget to be persistent. If you go away before the problem does, then you have not solved anything.

Keep trying, a dozen or a hundred different ways if that is what it takes. Do not give up. Never consider not succeeding immediately as a failure; consider it practice. See the positive in every situation!

Remember not to panic. Pressure may be a good motivator, but not if it is clouding your thinking. Think about why you cannot just give up on what you are doing, and that will give you the edge for the persistence you need to succeed. Practice being resourceful before the pressure is on. Do not dwell on the past. If the root cause or original problem is something you cannot fix, simply work to recover as best you can.

Furthermore, researching and reading are also very helpful. Staying up-to-date with important things can help you in the future.

Focus on something you like, and look for different links that are related to the topic or idea, so that not only do you learn about it, but you can also master it. Be informed to make sure you know what you are doing. Otherwise, you could create an entirely new problem.

Can I get the collaboration of others?
Collaboration is the act of joining together to make possible that which cannot be accomplished alone. Whether you are collaborating in the workplace, in

SUCCESS

school, or as part of a creative project, collaboration can both help and hurt a project, depending on how it is orchestrated.

Creating a collaborative climate will prove that you are trustworthy, and that you respect others. Be consistent in your behavior and the way you respond to others. In addition, be humble and open to others' ideas and suggestions.

The opposite of collaboration is a form of dictatorship, where one person tells everyone else what to do, and nothing is open for discussion. Whereas a dictatorship is ego-driven, collaboration thrives on the suppression of egos. You need to accept that while your ideas might be good, someone else's ideas might be good, too, and sometimes even better.

Task delegation is an important element of collaboration. Rather than trying to do everything yourself, it is best to "divide and conquer."

Let everyone find his or her strength and work therein to contribute to the common goal. If someone feels overwhelmed, he or she should feel comfortable enough to speak up. Furthermore, collaboration is based on the common good, and we work most effectively together when we assume we are all acting in good faith.

If someone is not acting in good faith, it will reveal itself soon enough. However, if you point a finger at someone mistakenly, the spirit of collaboration can easily turn sour.

Remember that decisions should be made based on consensus, and when you do not agree, do not get violent or angry.

A bank is a place that will lend you money if you can prove that you don't need it.

Bob Hope
(1903 –2003)
As Hope entered his ninth decade, he showed no signs of slowing down and continued appearing in numerous television specials. He was given an 80th birthday party in 1983 at the Kennedy Center in Washington, D.C. which was attended by President Ronald Reagan.

Chapter 20

How can I make money?

Use the law of supply and demand to your advantage. Most of us are familiar with the law of supply and demand. The more there is of something, the cheaper it is, and the rarer the product or service, the more expensive it is.

However, other than when we get to a toy store before sunrise to get in line for the latest fad toy that children cannot get enough of, we do not really apply the law of supply and demand to our own lives, particularly our careers.

> At a presentation I gave recently, the audience's questions were all along the same lines:
>
> " How do I get in touch with venture capitalists?"
> " What percentage of the equity do I have to give them?"
>
> No one asked me how to build a business!
>
> Arthur Rock
> (1926 -)
> American venture capitalist of Silicon Valley, California. He was an early investor in major firms including Intel, Apple Computer, Scientific Data Systems, and Teledyne.

For example, if you are aspiring to do something that many, many other people want to do, so much so that they do it for free, as a hobby, it will be far more challenging for you to make money doing it.

On the other hand, if you do something that most people do not want to do, or if you get very good at doing something that most people do not do very well, then you can make a whole lot more money.

If your goal is to make enough money to retire before the scheduled time, prioritize earning potential over job satisfaction, since you plan on getting out of the "rat race" early anyway.

Consider the types of jobs that pay extraordinarily well in exchange for hard work, little psychological satisfaction, and a punishing lifestyle, such as investment banking, sales, and engineering. If you can keep your expenses low, and do this for about 10 years, you can save a nest egg for a modest but youthful retirement, or to supplement your income while you do something you really love to do but will not get paid much for accomplishing.

SUCCESS

However, keep in mind that delayed gratification requires clear goal-setting and strong willpower. Your ability to manage your time and stop procrastinating is a critical ingredient in your ability to make money. You need to recognize that time is money. Whether you have a job or are self-employed, keep track of what you are spending your time on.

Ask yourself *Which of these activities make the most money, and which of them are a waste of time?* Simply do more of the former and less of the latter. When you are focusing on high-priority tasks, get the job done well, and get the job done fast. By working efficiently, you are giving your employer or clients more time, and they will appreciate you for it. Remember that time is a limited resource that you are always investing. Will your investments pay off?

If you are providing a skill, service, or product that is in high demand and low supply, you should be making good money. Unfortunately, there are many people who are too humble or fearful to demand that they get paid accordingly.

It is the pushovers in life who get taken advantage of and exploited, so if you think you might be one of them, learn how to stop being a people-pleaser. If you work for someone else, ask for a pay raise or get a promotion, and if none of that pans out, revisit your career options as described previously. If you are self-employed, the first thing to do is to make sure your customers and clients pay on time. This alone can substantially improve your income. Check your prices and rates against those of your competitors. Are you undercutting them? Why?

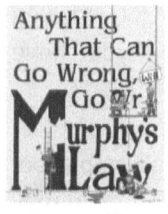

A supposed law of nature, expressed in various humorous popular sayings, to the effect that anything that can go wrong will go wrong.

Remember Murphy's Law: *Whatever can go wrong will go wrong.* Make plans, complete with as many

Chapter 20

calculations as possible, and then anticipate everything that can go wrong. Then make contingency or backup plans for each scenario. Do not leave anything to luck. If you are writing a business plan, for example, do your best to estimate when you will break even, then multiply that time frame by three to get a more realistic date; and after you have identified all the costs, add 20% to that for costs that will come up that you did not anticipate. Your best defense against Murphy's Law is to assume the worst and brace yourself. An appropriate amount of insurance may be something worth considering.

If saving money is wrong, I don't want to be right!

William Alan Shatner (1931 -) Canadian actor, musician, recording artist, author, and film director. Was born in the Côte Saint-Luc neighbourhood of Montreal, Quebec. In May 2011, he was honoured with the Governor General of Canada's Performing Arts Award for Lifetime Artistic Achievement, recording a humorous short film, *William Shatner Sings O Canada*, for the occasion. On June 2, 2011, Shatner received an honorary Doctor of Letters from McGill University, his alma mater.

It is important that you change your definition of wealth. In studies of millionaires, people are surprised to learn that most millionaires are not doctors, lawyers, and corporate leaders with big houses and fancy cars; they are people who religiously live below their means and invest the surplus into assets, rather than liabilities. As you are taking the above steps to make more money, keep in mind that increased income does not necessarily equal increased wealth.

Most people who flaunt their wealth actually have a low net worth because their debt to the asset ratio is high; in other words, they owe a whole lot more money than they, in fact, have. All the previous steps have outlined aggressive strategies for making money, but you will never get anywhere if you "have a hole in your pocket."

Take advantage of tax laws if you are self-employed. Money saved on taxes is still money saved. You may be able to deduct many of your business expenses, the use of your home, the use of your car, office supplies, etc. if you keep good records. You may also qualify for tax breaks, such as deducting your health

SUCCESS

insurance premiums on your tax return. These laws are in place to encourage commerce and business growth, so do not neglect their benefits.

If you are not self-employed but work for a company, find out if it has a retirement plan. If you are lucky, employers will sometimes match contributions you make into a retirement fund. Retirement plans also often have the benefit of being tax-deferred. The longer you get to keep your money, and make interest on it, the better your financial position will be. Whatever money you save, invest it in assets such as stocks, mutual funds, patents, copyrighted works, real-estate, anything that generates interest or royalties. Eventually, you might get to the point where your assets are doing the work for you, and all you have to do is sit there and make money!

Start analyzing your decisions from the perspective of a firm. In economics, a firm's goal is simply to maximize profit. Well-run firms spend money only if they can expect to make more money from their investment, and they allocate their resources to the most profitable uses. You are not a firm, of course, and you have other considerations, but if you make the majority of your time and money decisions by choosing the options that promise the highest return on investment, you will likely earn more money.

Watch out for inflation chipping away at your assets. We have all heard an elderly person described the purchasing power of a coin in his or her day. Inflation continues to make today's money worth less in the future. To win the race against time and inflation, learn to invest your money in the right places. A savings account might help you to keep up with inflation; however, to stay ahead of the game, you will want to invest in bonds, stocks, or some other

Remember that success is never easy.

Donald John Trump, Sr.
(1946 -)
He is an American business magnate, television personality, and author.
He is the chairman and president of The Trump Organization, and the founder of Trump Entertainment Resorts.

investment that returns interest above the average rate of inflation.

Recognize that you need to work on eliminating any debt you may have. When you have a high debt load, you are making money for someone else; what you pay in interest is their paycheck. The sooner you repay your loans and debts, the sooner you stop giving your money away.

In addition, beware of get-rich-quick schemes. Millions of people still get caught up in them. If it is too good to be true, it is truly no good. Remember that people that know how to get rich are busy getting rich. They are not advertising methods to get wealthy. Most importantly, do not lose sight of what is really important to you in your quest for money.

Success is not the key to happiness. Happiness is the key to success. If you love what you are doing, you will be successful.

Albert Schweitzer
(1875 –1965)
German and then French theologian, organist, philosopher, physician, and medical missionary.

Remember that you may be able to make more if you work longer hours, but will you and your family get to enjoy the extra money? Money can do a lot of things for you, but do not work yourself to death. You cannot take it with you!

What should I consider?

Pursue your dreams of success with passion. It is not enough just to want to become successful. A passion for success is what will make you stand out from the average person. Make sure to develop your interpersonal skills. Interpersonal skills are how you interact with people. Not only will you need these skills to manage your relationships and employees but also to negotiate deals and contracts, communicate effectively with the public, and network with others.

To become successful, make it a point to appreciate the work and input of others. Practice active listening.

SUCCESS

Be kind.

Ellen Lee
DeGeneres
(1958 –)
She is an American stand-up comedian, television host, and actress. In November 2011, Secretary of State Hillary Clinton named her a Special Envoy for Global AIDS Awareness.

This means acknowledging what other people say by repeating it back to them in your own words, as you understand it to be. Pay attention to others. Be proactive about noticing others' feelings, words, and body language. Connect people. A successful person is a hub through which other interpersonal connections are made.

Promote an environment that brings people together by treating people equally and fairly, and encouraging them to work together. Take a leadership role when it comes to resolving conflicts. Act as the mediator, rather than involving yourself personally. Furthermore, choose to develop a relationship with a successful person whose career you would like to emulate. Most of all, you must take some chances and step outside the norm in order to become a successful person that stands out. This means accepting the inevitability of small failures and learning to see them as opportunities for growth.

Remember to plan your ventures carefully and hedge as much risk as you can, but be prepared for the occasional setback.

Recommended Reading & References
We suggest consulting the works identified below in order to learn more about the particulars contained in this chapter.

BLANCHARD, Kenneth & JOHNSON, Spencer. THE ONE MINUTE MANAGER. Berkley Books. ISBN 0-425-09847-8.

BLIWAS, Ron. THE C STUDENT'S GUIDE TO SUCCESS. MJF Books. ISBN13: 978-1-56731-952-1.

PETERS, Thomas J. RE-IMAGE! Business Excellence in a Disruptive Age. Dorling Kinderly. ISBN 0-7894-9647-X.

SCHMITT, Bernd H. BIG THINK STRATEGY. How to Leverage Bold Ideas and Leave Small Thinking Behind. Your Coach in a Box. ISBN 1-59659-162-5.

The future rewards those who press on. I don't have time to feel sorry for myself. I don't have time to complain. I'm going to press on.

Barack Obama

Official photographic portrait

THE FUTURE

CHAPTER 21

In order to make your future better than your past, you first have to believe that it is possible to have a brighter future, no matter what stage you are at in life or what your circumstances are. It takes courage to think big and act upon it.

Start by making the decision to have a better future, no matter what circumstances may come your way. Obstacles are an inevitable part of life, yet it is how you respond to them that counts.

The best way to predict the future is to create it.

Peter Ferdinand Drucker
(1909 –2005)
Influential writer, management consultant, and self-described "social ecologist.

Keep in mind that small steps keep you growing for a better future. A simple way to keep moving forward is to break down your goal(s) into smaller "bite-sized" tasks that you can complete without becoming overwhelmed. Remember that it is by doing the little tasks that one is eventually led to realizing the "big picture"!

A brighter future is not necessarily about how much time you have left in your life; it is about what you choose to do with the time you have left. Regardless of your circumstances, you can always choose to make your future better than your past. It is simply a matter of choice and priorities. Always use what you have learned to build upon a better future for yourself, and never stop learning.

Your mind can build castles – just make sure the foundations are in place first.

Donald John Trump, Sr.
(1946 -)
American business magnate, television personality, and author.

Set goals: Creating goals for yourself will take you out of the past and help you create a better future. If you find it difficult to come up with meaningful goals, a great place to start is to think of a few of your accomplishments from this past year, and then think about what would represent a further achievement in each of these areas. By doing this simple exercise,

Chapter 21

you will begin to see what has been done and what you need to do next!

A better future includes anything you want to see that is an improvement on what exists now. Your future is your property. Dream big!

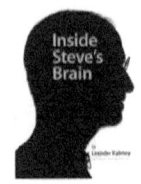

Stay Hungry.
Stay Foolish.

Steven
Paul Jobs
(1955-2011)
After Apple's founding, Jobs became a symbol of his company and industry. When *Time* named the computer as the 1982 "Machine of the Year", the magazine published a long profile of Jobs as "the most famous maestro of the micro".

Go ahead and put your vision into a form that serves you. It could be a poster collage, drawing, or painting that captures the essence of your vision; or you could write your vision as a story and read it aloud to trusted friends or partners; or it could be a mind map.

It is important to have your vision in a tangible form. Keep it accessible and visible, and notice how it inspires your daily actions. Once your vision is created, you will want it to happen.

We only have to look back in history to realize why. Most, if not all, of the greatest men and women in history in whatever field or endeavor, had healthy and creative imaginations.

Those men and women who have conquered other countries in the past have been able to see more than all those around them. They have believed in their own abilities and those of their generals to be capable of overcoming adversity. They did not allow overwhelming odds or hardships to stop them from achieving success or their "prize".

Always remember that the future comes one day at a time.

Anonymous

In their own turn, scientists, for example, have been capable of doing similar heroic exploits. They have been able to see outside the box which was limiting their vision or experience and believed that something was possible. And they then worked to achieve that.

THE FUTURE

The future starts today, not tomorrow.

Blessed Pope John Paul II
Born **Karol Józef Wojtyła**
(1920 –2005)
He reigned as Pope of the Catholic Church from 1978 until his death in 2005. He was the second-longest serving Pope in history and the first non-Italian since 1523.

All men who have achieved great things have been great dreamers.

Orison Swett Marden
(1850 – 1924)
American writer associated with the New Thought Movement. He also held a degree in medicine and was a successful hotel owner.

In addition, last but not least, just think about how our athletes prepare for their events. We can see them visualizing their run-up, leap, and successful clearance of the bar and their victorious jump.

Remember that if we learn to use some of the same methods in our own lives, perhaps we can share in the success that is available. Simply use your imagination to help improve your lot in life; envision it, and then live it!

Then in our own ways, we will be able to achieve success ourselves. We will be capable of meeting our challenges, of chasing our ambitions, and of experiencing freedom in life.

What about imagination?

Imagination is the ability to form a mental image of something that is not perceived through the senses. It is the ability of the mind to build mental scenes, objects, or events that do not exist, are not present, or have happened in the past. Memory is actually a manifestation of imagination.

Everyone possesses some imaginative ability. In some, it may be highly developed, and in others, it may be manifested in a weaker form. It manifests to various degrees in various people.

Imagination makes it possible to experience a whole world inside the mind. It gives one the ability to look at any situation from a different point of view, and it enables one mentally to explore the past and the future.

It manifests in various forms, one of which is daydreaming. Though too much idle daydreaming may make one impractical, some daydreaming, when someone is not engaged in something that requires

Germain Decelles   603

Chapter 21

In the end, the location of the new economy is not in the technology, be it the microchip or the global telecommunications network. It is in the human mind.

Alan Webber
Author, *Rules of Thumb*.
Expert on change and innovation in the knowledge economy.

We are the only beings on the planet who lead such rich internal lives that it's not the events that matter most to us, but rather, it's how we interpret those events that will determine how we think about ourselves and how we will act in the future.

Tony Robbins
(1960 -)

attention, provides some temporary happiness, calmness, and relief from stress.

In your imagination, you can travel anywhere at the speed of light without any obstacles. It can make you feel free, though temporarily, and only in the mind, from tasks, difficulties, and unpleasant circumstances.

Imagination is not limited only to seeing pictures in the mind. It includes all the five senses and the feelings. One can imagine a sound, taste, smell, a physical sensation, or a feeling or emotion.

For some people, it is easier to see mental pictures; others find it easier to imagine a feeling, and some are more comfortable imagining the sensation of one of the five senses. Training the imagination gives one the ability to combine all the senses.

A developed and strong imagination does not make you a daydreamer and impractical. On the contrary, it strengthens your creative abilities, and it is a great tool for recreating and remodeling your world and life.

This is a great power that can change your whole life. It is used extensively in creative visualization, and affirmations. It is the creator of circumstances and events. When you know how to work with it, you can make your hearts' desires come true.

Imagination plays a great role and is valuable in each one's life. It is much more than just idle daydreaming. We all use it, whether consciously or unconsciously, in most of our daily affairs. We use our imagination whenever we plan a party, a trip, our work, or a meeting. We use it when we describe an event,

THE FUTURE

explain how to arrive at a certain street, write, tell a story, or bake a cake.

Imagination is the creative power that is necessary for inventing an instrument, designing a dress or a building, painting a picture, or writing a book. The creative power of imagination plays an important role in the achievement of success in any field. What we imagine with faith and feelings comes into being. It is the power beyond creative visualization, positive thinking, and affirmations.

Visualizing an object or a situation, and repeating this mental image often, attracts the object or situation into our lives. This opens new, vast, and fascinating opportunities for us.

This means that we should think only in a positive manner about our desires; otherwise, we may create and attract into our lives events, situations, and people that we don't really want. This is actually what most of us do because we don't use the power of imagination correctly.

If you do not recognize the importance of the power of the imagination and let it have free reign in your life, your life may not be as happy and successful as you would want it to be.

A lack of understanding of the power of the imagination is responsible for the suffering, incompetence, difficulties, failures, and unhappiness people experience.

For some reason, most people are inclined to think negatively. They do not expect success. They expect the worst, and when they fail, they believe that fate is

Can you imagine what I would do if I could do all I can?

Sun Tzu
(476 BCE–221 BCE)

Ability is nothing without opportunity.

Napoléon Bonaparte
(1769-1821)

Chapter 21

against them. This attitude can be changed, and then life will improve accordingly.

Remember to use your imagination correctly, and to realize that putting this knowledge into practice, for your own and others' benefit, will put you on "the golden path" to success, satisfaction, and happiness.

Can innovation play a part in my life?
I am only a small cog in a huge wheel. How can anything I do or suggest have an impact on anything else?

They say
Improve.
I say
Re-imagine!

Tom Peters
(1942 -)

Nature is the true innovator. How can we improve upon that?

Change is inevitable, and the introduction of new things is happening all the time. These new things are sometimes called:

- Transformation.
- Novelty.
- Originality.
- Alteration.
- Revolution.

As soon as anyone starts telling you to be "realistic," cross that person off your invitation list.

John Eliot
(1604 –1690)
Puritan missionary to the American Indians. His efforts earned him the designation "the apostle to the Indians."

We have the basic elements to be innovative. We breathe and have a brain to think and abilities to act.

Maybe we need to give ourselves permission to do so? Perhaps this is the biggest hurdle. We need to believe that we can do something in a new and productive way. However, we need not try to reinvent the wheel, though many have tried. What we can do is to let ourselves think, feel, and act. We can allow our instincts to direct us, but we need to be discriminating at the same time.

THE FUTURE

He that will not apply new remedies must expect new evils; for time is the greatest innovator.

Francis Bacon, 1st Viscount St Alban(s)
(1561 1626)
English philosopher, statesman, scientist, lawyer, jurist, author, and pioneer of the scientific method.

The real danger is not that computers will begin to think like men, but that men will begin to think like computers.

Sydney J. Harris
(1917 – 1986)
American journalist for the Chicago Daily News and later the Chicago Sun-Times. His column, "Strictly Personal," was syndicated in many newspapers throughout the United States and Canada.

Recognize that planning for the future is an important step to ensure your future happiness and success. It involves taking responsibility for yourself and your actions. To do so, you will need to secure your future financially, professionally, socially, and personally.

Remember that responsibility always comes first. With every thought and action, there are ripples, consequences, action, and reaction. We do not need things to come back and haunt us, but there will be repercussions. So be alert and "stay awake", and all will go well as you delve into the unknown of the activities that you undertake.

Is creativity as good as it sounds?

We may relate to creativity in many different ways. Perhaps you may ask: How can this relate to me? I do not have a creative bone in my body I am a scientist. I have no imagination. I can paint, but I only copy nature. I design cars, but I just look at what has been developed before and modify it a little. I rely upon my mind to come up with interesting and new ideas, and then I see what I can do with them. Even so, I have no imagination you may say. Of course you do. You just do not use it that often.

Simplicity may be your thing, or you may prefer the complex. Just remember that simplicity can give strength, while the complex can only be confusing and disorienting.

By inspiration may be the way you work, always enthused with energy and purpose. You may let your inner spirit and "heart" "come forth", and enable you to create something really special, in your own way, in your given field.

Chapter 21

To think that the new economy is over is like somebody in London in 1830 saying the entire industrial revolution is over because some textile manufacturers in Manchester went broke.

Alvin Toffler
(1928 -)
He is the recipient of several prestigious prizes, including the McKinsey Foundation Book Award for Contributions to Management Literature, Officier de L'Ordre des Arts et Lettres, and appointments, including Fellow of the American Association for the Advancement of Science and the International Institute for Strategic Studies.

You may want to be productive but do not care so much about how you achieve your production. That is fine, but I am sure your method for getting your work done can be refined, improved, smoothed out – the rough edges, made sharper and yet more efficient.

Ingenuity, I hear you say, is confined to the genius and the intellectual, and is not found in the ordinary person, the man or woman on the street. However, I think we are all capable of utilizing our talents and skills beyond all recognition. Given the impulse and the chance, we only need to take that chance to be able to see just what we really can do.

Everyone has originality. Just express it!

Remember that inventiveness is not restricted to the chosen few. We can all play our part and suggest exciting and effective improvements and developments for something, given the opportunity. To be creative, we do need some imagination and some talent to let our hearts rule and not just our heads, or at least we need a combined effort. We can then all cause a change, in the way only each of us can.

How can I overcome anxiety using future visioning?

Anxiety is fear of the future. When people feel as if they do not know where they are going in life, what they want to do, or what is going to happen to them, and they believe they have no control over any of these things, they become fearful.

Understand that the way you feel right now is projecting into your future - and either creating a future that is on track with your desires or "off track".

THE FUTURE

All successful people, men and women, are big dreamers. They imagine what their future could be, ideal in every respect, and then they work every day toward their distant vision, that goal or purpose.

Brian Tracy
(1944 -)

We live in a moment of history where change is so speeded up that we begin to see the present only when it is already disappearing.

Ronald David Laing
(1927 –1989)
Scottish psychiatrist who wrote extensively on mental illness – in particular, the experience of psychosis.

You may need to get rid of any old and inaccurate programming in your head.

Any failure to believe in yourself will prevent you from achieving what you want to achieve; it acts as resistance. For example, *I don't deserve good things*, or *I can't have what I want*, these words are obstacles. So to succeed, you must get rid of any core limiting beliefs.

To help you manage your anxiety, simply retire to a comfortable place where you can relax and will not be disturbed. Lie down and shut your eyes. Visualize how your life would be if you were completely calm. Hold an image in your head of what your life would be like if you had no worries, and really feel the feelings of what it would be like.

Know that there is an end to your suffering. Ask yourself how you would feel. Is it freedom that you are looking for? We want to do things because we want to feel a certain way, so what is the feeling you want to experience? How would having more freedom make you feel? Imagine you are looking into your future. Imagine it is in a parallel world or life. Imagine every area of your life as you would like it to be. See your future self as living a joyful life, free of anxiety, feeling completely calm, and meditate on this.

Build a relationship with your future self. Notice how your future self moves, thinks and acts, differently from how you do now. Notice how their behavior is affected without anxiety. Know that you can become this calm, confident, self-assured person. Know that life can be how you want it to be, exactly how you want it.

Chapter **21**

You can use all the quantitative data you can get, but you still have to distrust it and use your own intelligence and judgment.

Alvin Toffler
(1928 -)

One doesn't discover new lands without consenting to lose sight of the shore for a very long time.

André Paul Guillaume Gide
(1869 –1951)
French author and winner of the Nobel Prize in literature in 1947. Gide's career ranged from its beginnings in the symbolist movement, to the advent of anticolonialism between the two World Wars.

Align yourself with this future. Feel it is a reality, regardless of how close to it, or far from it you feel you are at this current moment. Feel it is yours, and have faith that it will come to pass.

Write down your goals and follow them. Take inspired action. Recognize that the key to visualization is to make them feel real. Be in the visualizations. This can be a very powerful tool. Always be grateful for what you have right now.

This will make your life richer and put you on a frequency that makes you feel good. It will shift your attention to the things that you want, so that you will be able to attract them to you more easily, and it will make you feel good.

Remember not to just stop when you think you know *enough*. If you are willing to keep on learning, you will have the most amazing life, and you will know the quickest effective ways of creating that life. However, keep in mind that not everyone finds it easy or natural to connect with his or her future. It takes time, effort, and concentration, but with patience, you will see results.

How can I visualize?

Visualization is a technique used by winners in all walks of life. If you really want something to come to fruition, put your imaginative mind to work. See the result in front of you; play the game you are going to play in your mind; or watch yourself accepting your degree at college. The only limit is your own mind!

You can use visualization to acquire new habits, such as eating healthier or eating slowly, which prevent overeating and obesity. Have you ever seen an aerobatic pilot visualizing his or her routine on the ground using only his or her hands and imagination? Have you ever rehearsed a job interview in your mind? Think, *What you see is what you get*, and be ready for creativity and mind synthesis to take the lead. Dream about what you want, work it through your mind, and let it evolve in pictures. After you have spent a moment, day, month, or years visualizing the possibilities, now shift to focus mode.

Just before you engage in the activity, task, or event that will achieve an outcome, or even *the* outcome, toward your goal, focus clearly on the picture of the action you are about to perform.

You've got to think about big things while you're doing small things, so that all the small things go in the right direction.

Alvin Toffler
(1928 -)
He explains, "Society needs people who take care of the elderly and who know how to be compassionate and honest. Society needs people who work in hospitals. Society needs all kinds of skills that are not just cognitive; they're emotional; they're affectional. You can't run the society on data and computers alone." Toffler is also frequently cited as stating: "Tomorrow's illiterate will not be the man who can't read; he will be the man who has not learned how to learn."

For example, if you are trying to hit a ball, picture hitting it unmistakably in your mind, step-by-step, at the accurate height and the precise speed. Watch the ball being hit by your instrument, flying through the air, and landing wherever it is meant to land. Add all senses to the experience: hear the approaching ball; hear and feel the impact; smell the grass. Then do it for real.

Nothing is going to get better when you feel lousy about yourself and your chances in life. Always have a positive mindset to "reset" a difficult period of bad luck. It will turn that half-empty glass into the half-full glass, and the storm cloud into the silver-lined cloud. Seize opportunities to change and move on.

Anybody who wants change overnight will be disappointed. Even if you win a fortune today, you will still not be satisfied with your life in six months if you do not look inside yourself to perceive what ails you.

Instead, plan to make the realization of your hopes and dreams long term. Visualize where you will be in

Chapter 21

five, ten, and fifteen years time - and the sorts of outcomes you want.

However, do not just make a shallow photo of you in a Porsche surrounded by a large house, a massive diamond collection, and fawning friends. That is artificial and will not prove neither healthy nor satisfying in the long run. Instead, visualize what you want to achieve as a human being and what legacies you will leave your community and world.

Visualization only works when you are calm, at ease, and willing to give yourself time to focus in peace, free from immediate worries. Visualization is a technique very close to meditation, only it is more active and vivid.

In visualization, you are encouraged to think actively about the possibilities, but as with meditation, you must leave aside anything extraneous to your dreams and goals and only focus on them.

It's not so much that we're afraid of change or so in love with the old ways, but it's that place in between that we fear...
It's like being between trapezes. It's Linus when his blanket is in the dryer. There's nothing to hold on to.

Marilyn Ferguson
(1938 –2008)
American author, editor, and public speaker, best known for her 1980 book *The Aquarian Conspiracy* and its affiliation with the New Age Movement in popular culture.

Visualize the personality traits needed to get you where you want to be. It is not enough to want to be the president. You need to think about the qualities that will assist you in reaching this goal. Visualize not only the presidency but also the skills of open communication, persuasiveness, smiling, sharing, listening, discussing, being able to deflect criticism with skill and respect, etc. It is likely that there will be skills you need to work on, but again, use visualization to focus on separate skills, to bring them up to par.

What are some visualization methods you can use in your life? You can use a number of different methods to explore or describe possibilities for the future. Here are a few of the more popular ones:

THE FUTURE

The word impossible is not in my dictionary.

Napoleon III
(1808 –1873)
Napoléon Bonaparte left a Bonapartist dynasty which ruled France again; Louis became Napoleon III, Emperor of the Second French Empire and was the first President of France. In a wider sense, Bonapartism refers to a broad centrist or center-right political movement that advocates the idea of a strong and centralised state, based on populism.

One day your life will flash before your eyes. Make sure it's worth watching.

Anonymous

Environmental scanning: This is a method that looks outside of the organization's or individuals normal realm to see what changes are coming. Technology is one area that changes quickly and impacts many areas of life and business. Some futurists use the acronym "steep" to remind them of broad categories of change, which include: social, technology, economic, ecologic and political changes.

Trend identification and analysis: Trend lines indicate the direction and speed of change and are based on measurements of an indicator over multiple time periods. A line that connects the data points of population over fifty years on a graph, for example, would indicate whether the population is growing or declining and how rapidly the population is changing.

Trend extrapolation: This is an extension of a trend line into the future, usually based on the present direction of the trend line supplemented by the futurist's knowledge of related factors. In the example above of population forecasts, instead of simply extending the existing line along in the same direction, futurists and forecasters might consider factors such as declining birth rates and increasing life expectancy.

Scenario development: This is one of the best-known methods for exploring the future. The scenario method develops several stories about possible futures. These stories are based on forces, trends and other factors that exist in the present and can be projected into the future, usually including an optimistic scenario and a pessimistic scenario.

Strategic planning: This method is very common in business, and it is often used in conjunction with scenarios by futurists. In this approach, scenarios

Chapter 21

Real progress in understanding nature is rarely incremental. All-important advances are sudden intuitions, new principles, new ways of seeing.

Marilyn Ferguson,
(1938 –2008)
She was an American author, editor, and public speaker, best known for her 1980 book *The Aquarian Conspiracy* and its affiliation with the New Age Movement in popular culture.

Only your vision of the future can direct you on the rest of your journey.

Bill George
Professor of Management Practice at Harvard Business School and author of *True North*.

suggest possible futures, and strategic planning provides strategies and plans to deal with those futures. Here, we will use a version of personal strategic planning that includes creating a vision of your future, developing strategies and an action plan to achieve that vision, and contingency plans to deal with the unexpected.

Remember that visualization takes practice. Everyone has the power to visualize, but not everyone believes in doing it. If you are skeptical, you may want to convince yourself that this is a waste of time. Do not give into this temptation because everyone, skeptics included, can benefit from visualizing. It relies on our brain's ability to synthesize results, a scientifically proven fact. Beware of people who think this technique is self-deceptive. Usually, these are people embedded in negativity who could benefit from seeing the glass half full for a change. Be kind to them and listen, but do not be swayed by their fear.

How can I create a vision of my future?

Living your life without a vision leads to chaos, inaction, self-sabotage, and mindless waste. It is akin to the idea that if you do not know where you are going, you will end up in a strange place. Your life is way too valuable to allow for that scenario. Even so, I have discovered many who have difficulty getting started with a vision of what they want their lives to be.

When you sit down to create your future-life vision, start with the essence of who you are and what you value and take a stand for. A vision will not get infused with enthusiasm and possibility if it sidesteps your values. When you are in touch with what you value, your brainstorming will flow.

THE FUTURE

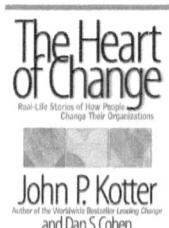

The Heart of Change
John P. Kotter
and Dan S. Cohen

In the twentieth century, the development of business professionals in the classroom and on the job focused on management – that is, people were taught how to plan, budget, organize, staff, control, and problem solve. Only in this last decade or so has much thought gone into developing leaders – people who can create and communicate visions and strategies."

John Kotter
(1947 -)
Former professor at the Harvard Business School, an acclaimed author, and now Chief Innovation Officer at Kotter International. He is regarded as an authority on leadership and change.

You might even "let yourself out of the box" of comfortable, predictable, or conventional thoughts and play a little!

You know that one secret place where your dreams have been stored. Open your dream basket. Pull out your dreams, one by one. Dream them again, and notice which ones "come alive" for you. Take those dreams seriously. Begin to regard your dreams as if they already happened and are really to be lived right now. Get in touch with the reasons for your dreams and generate some new ones. This is not about daydreaming; this is about creating your future for real.

When you create your life's vision, there is no place for judgments or limiting beliefs. You are not concerned at this point about "Who do I think I am?" or "I could never do that" or "There isn't enough money for me to..."

Once you are aligned with your values and dreams, it is time to let your vision flow without editing. Anything goes for now. Give yourself the gift of a very large vision, so you have lots to choose from. You will decide later exactly which things you want to keep and which to let go. You are the one in command of your vision.

An important key to successful visioning is for you to ignore any thoughts about how your vision will be accomplished. This is a tall order. We immediately assume that, once again, we have to deny ourselves because we cannot figure it all out ahead of time. What is important is to get a comprehensive picture of what you want, of how you want your life to be. The clear vision comes first, and then you can make it manifest.

Chapter **21**

Demonstrate your ability to listen; don't expect them to listen to you. Many people think the best way to get others to like or promote them is by dazzling them with brilliance and ability. Nobody likes to think somebody junior is brighter or more qualified than he is. Actual studies show that the way to get people to like you is by liking and showing an interest in them."

Albert J. Bernstein, Ph.D.

Capture your dreams, ideas, and yearnings on paper in whatever way feels right to you. This is the part of the creative-creation process that can get messy or chaotic. That is a good thing! Write down everything that comes to you. And then ask, *If I could have, do, or be ten times more than this, what would that look like?* or *If I could go to the place of my deepest expression with this dream, what would that be?* Do not stop until you have truly examined all possibilities, knowing you can add anything, anytime.

Remember that as you step back and consider the vision you have created for your life, it is important to take a step into the future and make believe you are already there; two, five, ten, or more years henceforth. Allow your heart to "take you" into the space of your future life. Close your eyes and feel, see, taste, smell, touch, and hear your future life in the present tense. Marvel at what your life has become, and give yourself a pat on the back. The vision you created a few years ago got you to this place. In the future, you may be able to say that the journey turned out a little differently than you had imagined it would - richer and more fun.

Can I understand the generation gap?

Today's workplace is more and more multi-generational. The influx of Generation Y into the working world is steadily growing, and its predecessors, Generation X and the Baby Boomers, are increasingly finding themselves working, or even reporting to, colleagues who have not hit age 30.

Having three generations of workers: Baby Boomers, Generation X, and Generation Y, under the same roof can be a recipe for disaster if they are managed carelessly. However, market observers and players say they are all of the strengths, innovation,

THE FUTURE

knowledge, and experience gained from having generational diversity in the workplace is greater than the sum of worries, and well worth the effort.

Born after World War II, which ended in 1945, Baby Boomers possess a "live to work" attitude and are willing to "go the extra mile" for their employer, as they appreciate job stability and security.

Boomers enjoy making decisions with clear goals and responsibilities. Boomers also tend to be task-oriented and prefer formal ways of communicating, such as in-person meetings, memos and e-mails.

Born between 1961 and 1981, Generation X^{ers} place great importance on work-life balance and are resourceful and independent. Gen X^{ers} are also highly collaborative and adaptable. They can accustom themselves to digital technologies and build interpersonal relationships through different forms of communication, be these roundtable discussions, phone calls, or e-mails.

Having grown up in the digital age, Gen Y's, born between 1982 and 2001, are also known as Millennials, and are described as being extremely tech-savvy and preferring text-based communication styles, which are vastly different from those in preceding generations. Gen Y's subscribe to text messaging, microblogging, and instant messaging (IM). Gen Y's want to be treated as equals with the rest of their older colleagues and crave a flexible working lifestyle and the freedom to develop and advance themselves, which shows that they are not intimidated by authority or afraid to speak up.

Gen Y's hold high expectations for their careers and want their work to be challenging and meaningful.

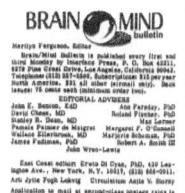

Your past is not your potential.
In any hour you can choose to liberate the future.

Marilyn Ferguson
(1938 –2008)
American Futurist
A founding member of the Association of Humanistic Psychology, Ferguson published and edited the well-regarded science newsletter *Brain/Mind Bulletin* from 1975 to 1996.

Chapter **21**

Generation Y is like Generation X but on steroids. In addition, these young adults are ideally suited for today's new corporations, as they are savvy, confident, upbeat, open-minded, creative, and independent. These qualities, however, also make Gen Y's quite a challenge to manage, as older colleagues may prefer a traditional, less collaborative style of working.

Remember that the lack of understanding of the different generations' working styles will inevitably lead to friction and clashes. To succeed in such an environment, a common business objective has to be understood by all generations. Without common sense, exacerbation will enter into all situations. For instance, Gen X and Gen Y may view Boomers' "work to live" attitude as "bootlicking," whereas the work-life balance that Gen X and Gen Y desire may seem like laziness in the eyes of Boomers.

What will the 2020 organization be like?
Less than a decade henceforth, the Millennials, or Generation Y, those born between 1982 and 2001, will be firmly entrenched within all management layers of most corporations and governmental organization around the world. As this begins to happen, it is interesting to ponder what this will mean for big business and what changes Gen Y's will bring with them as they begin to take charge and "steer the ship."

We all know who the Generation Y people are, or we think we do. They are driven, abrupt, technologically savvy, information hungry, communicative multi-takers, have short attention spans, and seek immediate gratification in everything that they do. Ironically, these personal growth seekers are also the ones who seek constant feedback and positive

Almost all quality improvement comes via simplification of design, manufacturing layout, processes, and procedures.

Tom Peters
(1942 -)
In 1990, Peters was honoured by the British Department of Trade and Industry (DTI) as one of the world's Quality Gurus.

THE FUTURE

Tom Peters

Excellent firms don't believe in excellence - only in constant improvement and constant change.

Tom Peters
(1942 -)

Test fast, fail fast, adjust fast.

Tom Peters
(1942 -)

If a window of opportunity appears, don't pull down the shade.

Tom Peters
(1942 -)

reinforcement. Stated another way, these young people are difficult to engage and nearly impossible to manage.

There is a multitude of reasons for why this may be so. Generation Y was the first wave of workers who grew up with technology. They are comfortable leveraging multiple sources of data and information simultaneously to accomplish numerous tasks. They have had ample collaborative networks available to them to help them generate ideas and identify solutions. Income, status, and financial incentives are less important to them than quality of life.

So, what happens to the organizations as Generation Y's assume control?

Today's organizational designs will likely be deemed obsolete. Millennials will demand a shift away from *command and control* reporting lines to more cooperative-based leadership models that provide greater autonomy and freedom of choice in the way work is performed.

Such a shift will stress and flex the organizations in new and challenging ways. Looser, team-based organizational designs will need to be adopted. Gone are the days of multi-layered designs characterized by managers managing managers. Rather, temporary, purpose-based worker groupings will emerge, and flatter reporting structures will increase.

The pyramid management structure that we all grew up with will slowly be replaced with a more fluid and responsive network design. A networked organizational design is the next evolutionary step for today's matrix organizations.

Chapter 21

In a network structure, work is organized into projects, and in turn, projects are grouped into portfolios of like kind. Workers who are assigned to the portfolio, in a Just-In-Time fashion, perform the execution of the projects within a portfolio.

Key knowledge workers may be permanently assigned to a portfolio, so as to allow for needed deep intimacy and understanding of a portfolio's particular subject matter, while others may be temporarily assigned to play a specific project role for a defined period of time.

This will allow an organization to better leverage its subject matter expertise across all of its portfolios. This new type of organizational design will provide the work flexibility that Generation Y staff prefers and the scalability that businesses require in order to greater manage costs and maintain quality through normal business cycles.

We found that the most exciting environments, that treated people very well, are also tough as nails. There is no bureaucratic mumbo-jumbo, excellent companies provide two things simultaneously: tough environments and very supportive environments.

The shifting of the organizational design will, in turn, lead to a new kind of operating model, one that can accommodate a more transient workforce.

Generation Y employees are very comfortable with a more integrated professional and personal life, as long as working schedules are flexible.

To this end, operating models of the future will need to contemplate and weave the freelance and contract working arrangements preferred by Millennials into the way work is performed.

Indeed, the next generation of workers is willing to trade the routine, predictability, and security which many find boring when compared to the multitasking, frenetic operating style that they tend to favor in order

Tom Peters
(1942 -)

THE FUTURE

to have the for the freedom to choose where, when, and how work is executed.

> The magic formula that successful businesses have discovered is to treat customers like guests and employees like people.
>
> Tom Peters
> (1942 -)

This type of operating model, one characterized by pulling talent in as needed and letting it go when demand is lower, fits hand and glove with the network design discussed above.

These ideas can also be institutionalized while many businesses, as well government organizations, are recognizing that the use of contracted talent is a key ingredient to establishing the much-needed agility required for success in the 21st-century organizational environment.

It is fortuitous that the types of organizational changes and the operating model evolution discussed will likely be accelerated by the need for organizations to accommodate Generation Y work-style inclinations. Several interesting implications will emerge as a result.

> Winners must learn to relish change with the same enthusiasm and energy that we have resisted it in the past.
>
> Tom Peters
> (1942 -)

Firms will have to make a conscious effort to establish programs aimed at creating a culture that attracts, develops, and retains quality Generation Y personnel.

Basic business principles concerning business ownership and profit sharing may be shaken to their roots with the result being that companies will likely be forced to increase employee-based ownership to keep Generation Y's interested.

Since collaboration and flexibility will gain prominence in established work settings, positions and job titles might need to be redefined or removed altogether, if existing titles hinder teamwork and prevent required organizational elasticity.

Chapter 21

Thought will have to be given and action taken to harness the growing use of social networks within the workplace, as Millennials will continue to call for more sophisticated means of *staying connected*.

Since many Generation Y workers will choose to be employed by more than one organization at a time, provisions will have to be made to ensure that free agent personnel are trained in the organizations' operating policies, procedures, and quality standards, so that the Generation Y's will be able to assimilate quickly and deliver desired results.

First, I believe that this nation should commit itself to achieving the goal, before this decade is out, of landing a man on the Moon and returning him safely to the Earth. No single space project in this period will be more impressive to mankind, or more important for the long-range exploration of space; and none will be so difficult or expensive to accomplish.

John Fitzgerald "Jack" Kennedy
(1917-1963)

The desire of Millennials to be employed by more than one company at a time will possibly have serious implications regarding corporate espionage and intellectual property contravention. By coupling this risk with the expanding use of social networks in the workplace, and firms will need to extend security functions to minimize intellectual property infringement risk.

Given the need for a workforce and, therefore, operational fluidity, physical location independence will need to be provided by businesses and government organizations as well. Plans to establish remote work locations that can be staffed on-demand by an assembled team of free agents will likely be part of the near-future business landscape.

Businesses will be compelled to offer more tailored and enhanced lifestyle benefits to employees. We are already seeing concierge services, childcare, and eldercare offerings emerge in benefit packages. This trend will continue as a new generation of workers seeks ways to make life easier.

THE FUTURE

Customer participation in business decisions could increase, as well, given the fact that millennial consumers will continue to call for a "voice" in the ways products and services are customized and delivered to them.

Existing older staff will have to be made aware of the trends taking shape in the employment market and the organization's desire to leverage the opportunities that exist there.

With audacity one can undertake anything, but not do everything.

Napoléon Bonaparte
(1769-1821)

Senior management teams will have to promote these cultural shifts through their actions and be prepared to manage the enterprise actively through the transitions that will be required to institutionalize these changes.

It is important to recognize that the Future organization will be one that is markedly different than what we see today. It will be a world in which the next generation of workers chooses to embrace personal independence at the risk of security, and one in which businesses and governmental organizations will have to work hard to attract this budding talent.

With all this comes a very real leadership challenge whereby organizations will need to think differently about their management structures and the skills, competences, and capabilities required to thrive in the new operating models that will result.

Clearly, a greater degree of emotional intelligence will be required by senior leaders, so that they can proactively guide organizational transformation while continuing to grow and evolve successful enterprises. Without finer insight and sensitivity, the businesses and the governmental organizations of tomorrow will be hard-pressed to create structured designs, or operating models that will consistently draw the best and brightest that Generation Y has to offer.

Remember that through open-mindedness and a willingness to break the mold, some organizations are already evolving towards the new operating models and organizational structures that will soon be needed.

What should I consider?
Who does not want to have a good future? It is something everyone desires. However, to have one, you must first accept that your future is your responsibility. The one who determines whether or not you have a good future is you. Do not expect the circumstances, or someone else, to take care of it for you. It is you who must take action!

Any thought of change frightens most people, so expect the people around you to criticize your decision to re-invent yourself. As you radically re-invent yourself and begin to pursue your dreams, many around you will try to stop you. One of the loudest voices will be your own; it will be really uncomfortable for you to step out of the place where you may not be fulfilled or happy, but which is familiar to you, into a completely new life.

Even though you have gone through the process of reflecting on the ways to change your life, and you are certain that these changes are necessary, there will be many discomforts along the way, but go ahead and change anyway. The new fulfilling and complete life you will be able to live will most certainly be worth the short-term malaise.

One important thing you should do is invest in your future. Investing in your future means making some

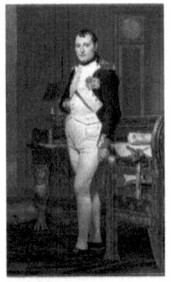

L'audace, l'audace, toujours l'audace.

(Audacity, audacity, always audacity).

Napoléon Bonaparte
(1769-1821)

THE FUTURE

Change is the law of life. And those who look only to the past or present are certain to miss the future.

John Fitzgerald "Jack" Kennedy
(1917-1963)

sacrifices in the present to reap rewards later on. It means investing your time and money in something that might not give you immediate returns but that could give you tremendous value later. It also means preparing for the uncertainties of the future. Sadly, many people do not do this. They only think about the present. Therefore, when something unexpected happens, they are not ready and get into a difficult situation.

Most of us do not improve ourselves and do not prepare for future changes. We neither learn new skills nor expand our knowledge, and then when the situation changes, our skills are no longer relevant, and we lose the opportunity of a lifetime.

Remember not to wait until something bad happens. Start now while the situation is still good! Why? Simply, because it takes time to build your future. *Change your future, now!*

Recommended Reading & References
We suggest consulting the works identified below in order to learn more about the particulars contained in this chapter.

CROSBY, B. Philip, COMPLETENESS, Quality for the 21st Century. Dutton Book. ISBN 0-525-993475-8,

MINKIN, Barry H. FUTURE IN SIGHT. 100 of the Most Important Trends, Implications, and Predictions for the New Millennium. Macmillan. ISBN 0-02-585055-5.

NAISBITT, John. GLOBAL PARADOX, The Bigger the World Economy, the More Powerful its Smallest Players. Morrow & Co. ISBN 0-688-12791-6.

PENN, Mark J. MICRO TRENDS. The Small Forces Behind Tomorrow's Big Changes. Hachette. ISBN-10 1-60024-023-2.

PETERS, Thomas J. THE LITTLE BIG THINGS. 163 Ways to Pursue Excellence. Harper Studios. ISBN 978-0-06-189408-4.

TOFFLER, Alvin. THE THIRD WAVE. Bantam Books. ISBN 0-553-14431-6.

TOFFLER, Alvin & Heidi, REVOLUTIONARY WEALTH. How it Will be Created and How it Will Change our Lives. Alfred A. Knopf. ISBN 0-3-375-40174-1.

ABOUT THE AUTHOR

In addition to writing, Germain Decelles acts as change management facilitator and project researcher.

Each year, he offers several seminars and training sessions on change management and business transformation. Additionally, he serves as Chairman of WebTech Management and Publishing Incorporated and Force Marketing Technologies, Inc.

Germain Decelles has over 30 years of business and consultation experience with local and international markets, including sectors such as: retail trade, distribution, information technology and communications, transportation, manufacturing, financial services, and government organizations.

Decelles attended the campuses of Ford Motors Management Institute, Chrysler Leasing Institute, International Forecasting Institute, McGill University, Kappa Institute, and Digital Equipment Computer Institute. He holds a Master of Business Administration from Concordia College & University and a certificate in business management and organization from the Hautes Études Commerciales de Montréal (CDN).

Decelles is a member of the Canadian Coast Guard, retired (S.A.C.S.M.), Secretary of the General Assembly, and International Advisor. He received the Admiralty service award in 1990 for promoting the service internationally. He is also a member of the Sovereign Order of Saint John of Jerusalem.

Decelles and his family live in Montreal, Quebec, Canada. You can contact him at:
gdecelles@webtechmanagement.com

ABOUT THE CONTRIBUTING AUTHOR

Yvan Poirier is involved in psychological health and personnel welfare for businesses and organizations.

He specializes in personal recognition and burn-out.

In addition, he consults in administrative organization and in the organizational planning of events. He is also a TV presenter.

From 1972 to 2005, he occupied several services' administrators' posts within various departments in the Canadian government.

Since 2005, he has offered psychological health services and personal well-being. He carried out many mandates in the manufacturing and commercial sectors, and also for non-profit institutions.

Poirier is the author of several books and conferences based on personal experiments and is very well received by the private and public sectors.

Poirier and his family live in Sainte-Anne-des-Lacs, Québec, Canada. You can contact him at:
consulting@webtechmanagement.com

SELECTED BIBLIOGRAPHY & PHOTO CREDITS

We suggest that the reader consult the works identified throughout the book and below in order to learn more about Change or certain particulars of its implementation.

The reading of these reference documents helped the author in his quest to gather information related to the various subjects contained in *Change Your Future, Now!*

By providing references throughout the book, the author strongly suggests that the reader improve even more his or her knowledge of the various subjects introduce in *Change Your Future, Now!* - We cannot guarantee the validity, accuracy, completeness, or timeliness of the information contained in the documents suggested. Most of the authors of these documents have developed international reputations in their fields.

Various books and electronic formats inspired the quotes and texts contained in this book. Biographic information and quotes are mostly original. On the other hand, we cannot guarantee their authenticity.

All the quotations, short texts, and photographs contained in the book were included to encourage the reader to reflect on the educational content provided by each author. The purpose was to provide introductory information on each subject.

All the quotations, short texts and photographs remain the property of the concerned authors. The majority of the pictures are from the Wikipedia Web site and are marked "public domain", that is,

Selected **Bibliography** &
Photo **Credits**

documents that are not eligible for copyright or for which the copyright has expired. Pictures such as book covers and official photos were extracted from various Web Sites that promote the work the authors in question. The purpose was only to identify properly the authors of quotations and short texts. Other pictures were taken from the WebTech photo's collection.

Finally, we strongly urge the reader to consult a professional or some other authority in the appropriate field before using any of the information that we provide in *Change Your Future, Now!*

The information contained in this book is provided on an information-basis only.

Recommended Reading & References
We suggest consulting the works identified below in order to learn more about the particulars contained in this chapter.

ABRASHOFF, Michael D. IT'S YOUR SHIP. Warner Books. ISBN 0-446-52911-7.

ADAM, Scott. SLAPPED TOGETHER. THE DILBERT BUSINESS ANTHOLOGY. Harper Press. ISBN 0-06-018621-6.

BLANCHARD, Kenneth & JOHNSON, Spencer. THE ONE MINUTE MANAGER. Berkley Books. ISBN 0-425-09847-8.

BLANCHARD, Ken & BOWLES, Sheldon. BIG BUCKS! How to Make Serious Money for Both You and Your Company. Morrow, Harper Collins, ISBN 0-688-17035-8.

BLANCHARD, Ken et al. KNOW CAN DO!
Audio renaissance. ISBN-10-1-4272-0251-6.

BARKLEY, Bruce T. & SAYLOR, James H. CUSTOMER-DRIVEN PROJECT MANAGEMENT: Building Quality into Project Process.
McGraw Hill. ISBN 0-07-136982-1.

BARTH, Britt-Mari. LE SAVOIR EN CONSTRUCTION.
Diffusion France Métropolitaine. 2-7256-1499-6.

BENNIS, W. & NANUS, B. LEADERS: THE STRATEGIES FOR TAKING CHARGE.
Harper Press. ISBN 0-06-015246-X.

BERNSTEIN, Albert J. PhD. DINOSAUR BRAINS: DEALING WITH ALL THOSE IMPOSSIBLE PEOPLE AT WORK. Wiley & Sons. ISBN0-471-61808-X.

BLIWAS, Ron. THE C STUDENT'S GUIDE TO SUCCESS.
MJF Books. ISBN13: 978-1-56731-952-1.

BOUCHARD, Jacques. LES 36 CORDES SENSIBLES DES QUÉBÉCOIS.
Éditions Héritage. ISBN 0-7773-3944-7.

BOUCHARD, Jacques. L'AUTRE PUBLICITÉ : La publicité sociétale.
Éditions Héritages. ISBN 0-7773-5478-0.

BOUTIN, Gérard & JULIEN, Louise. L'OBSESSION DES COMPÉTENCES.
Éditions Nouvelles. ISBN 2-921696-56-8.

BURSK, CLARK & HIDY. Harvard Business School. THE WORLD OF BUSINESS: Selected Library of the Literature of Business from the Accounting Code of Hammurabi to the 20th-century. Simon & Schuster. Library of Congress catalog card number: 62-14278

BUTLER-BOWDON, Tom. 50 PSYHOLOGY CLASSICS: Who we Are, How We Think, What We Do. Gildan Media. ISBN 1-59659-119-6.

BRIAN, Denis. A LIFE: PULITZER. Wiley & Sons. ISBN 0-471-33200-3.

BRICKER, D. & WRIGHT, J. WHAT CANADIANS THINK ABOUT ALMOST EVERYTHING. Seal Books. ISBN 0-7704-3008-2.

BRIDGES, William. MANAGING TRANSITIONS.
Perseus Group. ISBN –13: 978-0-7382-0824-4.

BRINCKERHOFF, Peter C. MISSON-BASED MANAGEMENT.
Wiley & Sons. ISBN 9-780471-390-138.

BYHAM, W. C., Ph.D. & COX, Jeff Heroz. EMPOWER YOURSELF, YOUR COWORKERS, YOUR COMPANY. Harmony Books. ISBN 0-517-59860-4.

CAMUS, William. COMMENT S'ACCOMMODER DES FEMMES.
Presse de la cité, Paris 1971.

CARDIN, Josée. L'ACCUEIL, MIROIR DE L'ENTREPRISE.
Éditions ARC. ISBN 2-89022-167-9.

CARTER, Jimmy. SOURCES OF STRENGH.
Times books. ISBN 0-8129-2944-6.

CHURCHILL, Randolph S. WINSTON S. CHURCHILL: Young Statesman 1901-1914.
Houghton, Mifflin co. 1967.

CLEMMER Jim, FIRING ON ALL CYLINDERS.
Macmillan of Canada. ISBN 0-7715-9133-0.

COHEN, Dan S. THE HEART OF CHANGE FIELD GUIDE.
Harvard Press. ISBN 1-59139-775-8.

COHEN, Herb. YOU CAN NEGOTIATE ANYTHING.
Bantam Book. ISBN 0-553-23455-2

COHEN, Herb. NEGOTIATE THIS! Warner Books. ISBN 0-446-52973-7

COLLARD, Nathalie. À LA RECHERCHE DU BONHEUR.
Le Quotidien la Presse. Forum, avril 2007. ISBN 0317-9249.

Selected **Bibliography** &
Photo **Credits**

COSETTE, C. et al. COMMUNICATION DE MASSE.
Les Éditions Boréal Express. ISBN 0-88503-046-X.

CROSBY, B. Philip. COMPLETENESS: Quality for the 21St Century.
Dutton Book, ISBN 0-525-993475-8.

CÔTÉ, Charles. PARTENARIAT ÉCOLE COMMUNAUTÉ.
Guérin. ISBN 2-7601-3357-5.

D'ADAMO, Peter Dr. LIVE RIGHT FOR YOUR TYPE.
Putman Publisher. ISBN 0-399-14673-3.

DARMON, LAROCHE & PETROF Ph.D. LE MARKETING : Fondements et applications.
McGraw-Hill. ISBN 0-07-082723-0.

DASTOT, Jean-Claude. LA PUBLICITÉ : Principes et méthodes.
Marabout service. MS219, 1973.

DAVENPORT, Thomas H. & PRUSAK, Laurence. WORKING KNOWLEDGE.
Havard Press. ISBN 1-57851-301-4.

DECKER, Bert. YOU'VE GOT TO BE BELIEVED TO BE HEARD.
St-Martin's Press. ISBN 0-312-06935-9.

DEL, Michael. DIRECT FROM DELL: Strategies That Revolutionized An Industry.
Harper. ISBN 0-694-52023-3.

DELMAR, Ken. WINNING MOVES: The Body Language of Felling.
Warner Books. ISBN 0-446-32997-5.

DE SCHIETÈRE, J.C. & TURCOTTE, P.R. LA DYNAMIQUE DE LA CRÉATIVITÉ DANS L'ENTREPRISE : Perspectives et problèmes psychologiques.
Les presses de l'université de Montréal. ISBN 0-8405 0357-1.

DER HAAS, Hans Van. LA MUTATION DE L'ENTREPRISE EUROPÉENNE.
R. Lafond. 71XI 561 000-2790.

DUCLOS, Germain, LAPORTE, Danielle & ROSS, Jacques. LES BESOINS ET LES DÉFIS, des enfants de 6 à 12 ans. Les Éditions Héritage inc. ISBN 2-7625-7790-X.

DRUCKER, Peter F. MANAGING IN TURBULENT TIMES.
Harper Business. ISBN 0-88730-616-0.

DRUCKER, Peter F. POST-CAPITALIST SOCIETY.
Harper Business. ISBN 0-88730-620-9.

ELGIN, Suzette Haden. Ph.D. HOW TO DISAGREE WITHOUT BEING DISAGREEABLE. MJF Books. ISBN-10: 1-567731-739-1.

ELGOZY, Georges. AUTOMATION ET HUMANISME.
Calmann-Lévy. Paris, 1968.

ENCYCLOPÉDIE AUTODIDACTIQUE QUILLET.
La librairie aristide Quillet, Paris.

FELDMAN, Mark. ATTENTION! LES AUTRES ÉTUDIENT VOTRE PERSONNALITÉ.
Presses Sélect. ISBN 2-89132-049-2.

FERNANDEZ-ARMESTO, Felipe. IDEAS THAT SHAPED MANKIND. Oxford University.
Barnes & Nobles Publishing. ISBN 0-7607-7826-4.

FILLIOZAT, Isabelle. L'INTELLIGENCE DU CŒUR : Confiance en soi, créativité,
aisance relationnelle, autonomie. Marabout. 40-2625-8.

FREUND, Julien. QU'EST-CE QUE LA POLITIQUE ?
Éditions du Seuil. ISBN 2-02-000325-2.

FRIEDMAN, L. Thomas. THE WORLD IS FLAT. A Brief History of the Twenty-first
Century. ISBN 1-59397-669-0.

GATES, Bill. LA ROUTE DU FUTUR.
Éditions Robert Lafond. ISBN 2-221-080559-9.

GEORGE, Bill et al. FINDING YOUR TRUE NORTH.
Jossey-Bass publisher. ISBN 928-0-470-26136-1.

GÉRARD, H. & WUNSH, G. COMPRENDRE LA DÉMOGRAPHIE : Méthode d'analyse et
problèmes de population. Marabout Université, 1973, Paris.

GILBERT, Martin. CHURCHILL.
Houghton Mifflin Co. ISBN 0-395-19405-9.

GIULIANI, Rudolph W. LEADERSHIP.
Miramax Books. ISBN 0-7868-6841-4.

GLOTTIER, Agnes & Henry et al. 1,000 YEARS, 1000 PEOPLE.
Ranking the Men and Women Who Shaped the Millennium.
Barnes & Nobles. ISBN-13: 978-0-7607-8349-8.

GOLDRATT, Eliyahu M. & COX, Jeff. LE BUT.
Québec/Amérique. ISBN 2-89037-321-5.

GOULEMOT, Jean Marie. Dossier ; ILS ONT INVENTÉ LA LIBERTÉ.
Revue l'Histoire, N° 307, mars 2006.

GRAY, Collin S. WAR, PEACE AND VICTORY: Strategy and Statecraft for the Next
Century. Simon & Schuster. ISBN 0-671-60695-6.

GRAY John, Ph.D. MEN ARE FROM MARS, WOMEN ARE FROM VENUS: A Practical
Guide for Improving Communication and Getting What You Want in Your Relationships.
Harper. ISBN 1-55994-878-7.

GREENE, Robert. THE 48 LAWS OF POWER.
Penguin Books. ISBN 978-0-14-028019-7.

HAINEAULT, Pierre. SE LIBÉRER DES GENS QUI NOUS EMPOISONNENT LA VIE.
Les Éditions Québécor. ISBN 2-7640-0889-9.

HEALD, Tim. PHILIP: A Portrait of the Duke of Edinburgh.
William Morrow & Co. ISBN 0-688-10199-2.

HÉBERT, Sylvie. LE PRIMAIRE, DES RÉPONSES À VOS QUESTIONS.
Éditions Les parents d'abord.

HENRY, Alain. RÉDIGER LES PROCÉDURES DE L'ENTREPRISE. Guide pratique.
Éditions Organisation. ISBN 2-7081-1747-2.

Selected **Bibliography** & Photo **Credits**

HINDLE, Tim. NEGOTIATING SKILLS. Fenn Publishing. ISBN 1-55168-172-2.

HINDLE, Tim. INTERVIEWING SKILLS. Fenn Publishing. ISBN 1-55168-178-2.

HINDLE, Tim. MAKING PRESENTATIONS. Fenn Publishing. ISBN 1-55168-180-2.

HINDLE, Tim. MANAGING MEETINGS. Fenn Publishing. ISBN 1-55168-182-2.

HOGUE, J-Pierre. L'HOMME ET L'ORGANISATION.
Édition Commerce, ISBN 2-7616-0048-7.

HOPKINS, Tom. HOW TO MASTER THE ART OF SELLING: How to Persuade Others Positively. Champions Press. ISBN 0-938636-03-0.

HOWARTH, David & Stephen. NELSON: The Immortal Memory.
Conway Classics. ISBN 0-85177-720-1.

HUSTON, John. 50 FAÇONS DE CHANGER VOTRE VIE.
Amerimag. ISBN 0-65385-575451-1.

IACOCCA, Lee. AN AUTOBIOGRAPHY. Bantam Press. ISBN 0-553-05067-2.

INGLE, Sud. QUALITY CIRCLES MASTER GUIDE.
Prentice-Hall. ISBN 0-13-745000-1.

INSTITUTE OF INDUSTRIAL ENGINEERS: IIE Solutions. Atlanta, 1995.

ISAACSON, Walter. EINSTEIN: His Life and Universe.
Simom & Schuster. ISBN-13-978-0-7432-6473-0.

JENNINGS, Warren. DEVENIR UN MEILLEUR LEADER; Ce que tout leader devrait savoir. Les Éditions Québecor. ISBN 2-7640-0858-9.

JONES, Arthur. MALCOM FORBES: Peripatetic Millionaire.
Harper & Row. ISBN 0-06012204-8.

JOYNER, Rick. LEADERSHIP, MANAGEMENT, And The Five Essentials For Success. Morning Star Publications. ISBN 1-878327-33-X.

KANAWATY, George. INTRODUCTION À L'ÉTUDE DU TRAVAIL ; Bureau International du Travail. Genève, 1996. ISBN 92-2-207 108-5.

KAWASAKI, Guy. THE ART OF THE START: The Time-tested, Battle-hardened Guide for Anyone Starting Anything. ISBN 1-59184-056-2.

KEEGAN, John. L'ART DU COMMANDEMENT; Alexandre, Wellington, Grant, Hitler. Editions Perrin. ISBN 2-262-00615-6.

KENNEDY, John F. PROFILE OF COURAGE.
Harper Classic. ISBN-13: 978-0-06-085493-5.

KRAUSE, G. Donald. THE ART OF WAR FOR EXECUTIVES.
Penguin Books. ISBN 0-399-53150-5.

KOTTER, John P. LEADING CHANGE.
Harvard Press. ISBN-13: 978-0-87584-747-4.

KOTTER, John P. THE HEART CHANGE.
Harvard Press. ISBN-1-57851-254-9.

KOTTER, John P. A SENSE OF URGENCY.
Brillance audio. ISBN-13: 978-1-4233-6935-0.

LAMARCHE, J. LES REQUINS DE LA FINANCE. Éditions du jour, 1962.

LAURIN, Pierre. LE MANAGEMENT; Textes et cas.
McGraw-Hill. ISBN 0-07-077581-8.

LE DICTIONNAIRE DE CITATIONS FRANÇAISES.
Le Robert. ISBN-10: 285036454.

LE DICTIONNAIRE DE CITATIONS DU MONDE ENTIER.
ISBN-10: 0785992103.

LE GROUPE INNOVATION, VERS L'ORGANISATION DU XXIE SIÈCLE.
Les presses de l'Université du Québec. ISBN 2-7605-0747-5.

LEVINSON, Jay Conrad. GUERRILLA MARKETING; Secrets for Making Big Profits from Your Small Business. Houghton Mifflin Company. ISBN 0-395-90625-3.

LICHTENBERG, Ronna. IT'S NOT BUSINESS IT'S PERSONAL: The 9 Relationship Principles that Power Your Career. Hyperion. ISBN 0-7868-6594-6.

LIEBERMAN, David J. HOW TO CHANGE ANYBODY.
Audio renaissance. ISBN 1-59397-803-8.

LIEBERMAN, David J. YOU CAN READ ANYONE: Never be Fooled, Lied to, or Taken Advantage of Again. Audi Coach. ISBN 1-59659-153-6.

LINOWES, F. DAVID. STRATEGIES FOR SURVIVAL: Using Business Know-how to Make our Social System Work.
AMACOM: American Management Association. ISBN 0-8144-5326-0.

LITTERER, Joseph A. ORGANIZATIONS: Structure and Behavior.
Wiley & Sons, New York.

LONG, James W. M.D. THE ESSENTIAL GUIDE TO CHRONIC ILLNESS.
Harper. ISBN 0-06-273137-8.

LOGAN, John R.. EVOLUTION NOT REVOLUTION: Aligning Technology with Corporate Strategy to Increase Market Value.
McGraw Hill. ISBN 0-07-138410-3.

MACHIAVELLI, Niccolo. THE PRINCE.
Penguin Classics. ISBN 0-14-044107-7.

MAURER, Rick. CHANGE WITHOUT MIGRAINES: Solving the Middle Manager's Dilemma. www.beyondresistance.com

MAURER, Rick. CAUGHT IN THE MIDDLE: For Partnership a Leadership Guide in the Workplace. Productivity Press, Oregon. Library of Congress.

MACKAY, Harvey. HOW TO BUILD A NETWORK OF POWER RELATIONSHIPS.
Conant. ISBN 0-7435-2659-7.

Selected **Bibliography** &
Photo **Credits**

MACKAY, Harvey. SWIM WITH THE SHARKS WITHOUT BEING EATEN ALIVE.
Ballantine Books. ISBN 0-8041-0426-3.

MCCORMACK, Mark H. WHAT THEY DON'T TEACH YOU AT HARVARD BUSINESS
SCHOOL. Bantam Books. ISBN 0-553-05061-3.

MEAD, Shepherd. HOW TO SUCCEED IN BUSINESS WITHOUT REALLY TRYING.
Simon & Schuster, New York. Library of Congress, 1952.

MINKIN, Barry H. FUTURE IN SIGHT: 100 of the Most Important Trends, Implications,
and Predictions for the New Millennium. Macmillan. ISBN 0-02-585055-5.

MICHAELSON, Steven W. SUN TZU FOR EXECUTION.
Adams Business. ISBN-13: 978-1-59869-052-1.

MINTZ, M. & COHEN, J. AMERICA, INC. Éditions. Spéciale, 1971.

MONTGOMERY, Douglas C. INTODUCTION TO STATISTICAL QUALITY CONTROL.
John Wiley & Sons. ISBN 0-471-51988-X.

MONTEFIORE, Simon Sebag. 101 WORLD HEROES: Great Men and Women Who
Changed History. Metro Books. ISBN-13: 978-1-4351-0509-5.

MONTIGNAC, Michel. JE MANGE, JE MAIGRIS ET JE RESTE MINCE !
Flammarion. ISBN 2-89077-187-3.

MOORE, A. Geoffrey. CROSSING THE CHASM: Marketing and Selling High-tech
Products to Mainstream Customers.
Harper Business Essentials. ISBN 0-06-051712-3.

MULRONEY, Brian. MEMOIRS.
Douglas Gibson Book. ISBN 978-0-7710-6536-1.

MYERS, Marc. HOW TO MAKE LUCK: 7 Secrets Lucky People Use to Succeed.
Renaissance Books. ISBN 1-58063-058-8.

NATIONAL LIBRARY OF QUEBEC. Consultation services.

PATTON, Arch. MEN, MONEY AND MOTIVATION. McGraw-Hill, New York, Library of
Congress Catalog card number: 61-7845.

L'OFFICIEL DES CITATIONS. Efirst. ISBN 2-75400-194-8.

NAISBITT, John. GLOBAL PARADOX: The Bigger the World Economy, the More
Powerful its Smallest Players. Morrow & Co. ISBN 0-688-12791-6.

OSTEEN, Joel. BECOME A BETTER YOU. 7 Keys to Improving Your Life Every Day.
Free Press. ISBN-13: 978-0-7432-9688-5.

PATTERSON, Kerry et al. INFLUENCER: THE POWER TO CHANGE ANYTHING.
Vital Smart. ISBN-13: 978-0-17-148499-2.

PELL. Arthur R, Dr. ENCADRER ET MOTIVER UNE ÉQUIPE.
Simon & Schuster. ISBN 2-7440-0427-8.

PENN, Mark J. MICRO TRENDS: The Small Forces Behind Tomorrow's Big Changes.
Hachette. ISBN-10 1-60024-023-2.

PETER, L. J & HULL, R. LE PRINCIPE DE PETER ; Pourquoi tout va toujours mal.
Éditions Stock, 1970. ISBN 70-11-682-850-1580.

PETERS, Thomas J. THRIVING ON CHAOS/ A PASSION FOR EXCELLENCE.
Random House. ISBN 0-517-14816-1.

PETERS, Thomas J. LE CHAOS MANAGEMENT ; Manuel pour une nouvelle prospérité de l'entreprise. Inter Éditions. ISBN 2-7296-0219-4.

PETERS, Thomas J. & WATERMAN, Robert. LE PRIX DE L'EXCELLENCE : Les secrets des meilleures entreprises. Inter Éditions. ISBN 2 7296 0025 6.

PETERS, Thomas J. RE-IMAGE! Business Excellence in a Disruptive Age.
Dorling Kinderly. ISBN 0-7894-9647-X.

PETERS, Thomas J. TALENT: Essentials. DK Publishing. ISBN 0-7566-1056-7.

PETERS, Thomas J. DESIGN: Essentials. DK Publishing. ISBN 0-7566-1054-0.

PETERS, Thomas J. TRENDS: Essentials. DK Publishing. ISBN 0-7566-1057-5.

PETERS, Thomas J. THE LITTLE BIG THINGS: 163 Ways to Pursue Excellence.
Harper Studios. ISBN 978-0-06-189408-4.

PEACH, Robert W. THE PROJECT MANAGEMENT Handbook.
CEEM Information Services, Fairfax, Virginia, 1995. ISBN 1-88333.7.

PORTNY, Stanley E. CPMP: PROJECT MANAGEMENT FOR DUMMIES.
Hungry Minds. ISBN 0-7645-5283-X.

POTTER, E.B. NIMITZ. Naval Institute Press. 1976

PYLE, Richard. SCHWARZKOPF: In His Own Words.
Signet Book. ISBN 0-451-17205-1.

PYRON, Tim et al. SPECIAL EDITION USING MICROSOFT® PROJECT 2000.
ISBN 0-7897-2253-4.

PROJECT MANAGEMENT INSTITUTE: A GUIDE TO THE PROJECT MANAGEMENT BODY OF KNOWLEDGE. PMBOK®. ISBN 1-8804110-25-7.

QUICK, Thomas L. UNDERSTANDING PEOPLE AT WORK.
Executive Enterprises Publications Co. ISBN 0-917386-17-5.

QUIRION, Claude. L'APPROCHE-SERVICE APPLIQUÉE À L'ÉCOLE ; Une gestion centrée sur les personnes. Les Éditions de la Chenelière. ISBN 2-89310-237-9.

REHKOPF, Ed. LEADERSHIP ON THE LINE.
Clarity Publications. ISBN 0-9722193-1-5.

RIES, Al & TROUT, Jack. MARKETING WARFARE.
McGraw-Hill, 1986. ISBN 0-452-25861-8.

ROBBINS, Anthony. UNLIMITED POWER.
Simon & Schuster. ISBN 0-671-62146-7.

ROBINS, Stephen. PRENEZ LA BONNE DÉCISION.
Pearson Éducation France. ISBN 2-7440-6067-4.

ROCHE, Daniel. Dossier ; UNE RÉVOLUTION TOTALE.
Revue l'Histoire, N° 307, mars 2006.

ROCK, Gilbert & COUTURIER, Gérard. COMMUNICATION ; Représentation commerciale. Chenelière-McGraw-Hill. ISBN 2-7651-0196-5.

ROGERS, David. LES STRATÉGIES MILITAIRES APPLIQUÉES AUX AFFAIRES.
Press Pocket. ISBN 2-266-03266-6.

ROHN, Jim & TRACY Brian. SMALL BUSINESS SUCCESS.
Topics. ISBN 159150915-7.

ROTHMAN, Howard. 50 COMPANIES THAT CHANGED THE WORLD: That have Shaped the Course of Modern Business. Reer Press. ISBN 1-56414-496-8-17035-8.

RYE, David E. 1001 WAYS TO INSPIRE YOUR ORGANIZATION, YOUR TEAM AND YOURSELF. Castles Books. ISBN 0-7858-2094-9.

SAMSON, Guy. L'ENFANT-TYRAN, SAVOIR DIRE NON À L'ENFANT-ROI.
Québécor. ISBN 2-7640-0851-1.

SCHARMER, Otto C. THEORY U: Leading from the Future as it Emerges, the Social Technology of Presencing. BK Publishers. ISBN 1-57675-763-3.

SCHMACHER, E.F. A GUIDE FOR THE PERPLEXED.
Harper & Row. ISBN 0-06-013859-9.

SCHWARTZ, J. LA MAGIE DE VOIR GRAND.
Éditions Sélect. ISBN 2-89132-214-2.

SELLS, Scott P. Ph.D. PARENTING YOUR OUT-OF-CONTROL TEENAGER.
St-Martin's Press. ISBN 0-312-26629-4.

SELYE, Hans, Dr. STRESS SANS DÉTRESSE.
La presse. ISBN 0-7777-0095-6.

SHOOK, L. Robert. IMAGES DE GAGNANTS.
Éditions Un monde différent. ISBN 2-90000-62-4.

SCHMITT, Bernd H. BIG THINK STRATEGY. How to Leverage Bold Ideas and Leave Small Thinking Behind. Your coach in a box. ISBN 1-59659-162-5.

SIEBEL, Thomas & MALONE, M. VIRTUAL SELLING.
The Free Press. ISBN 0-648-82287-3.

SILLS, Judith. OSER CHANGER. Stanké Publication. ISBN 2-7604-0481-1.

SIMMONS, Harry. HOW TO TALK YOUR WAY TO SUCCESS.
Prentice-Hall. 1954 – 43526.

SMITH, Hyrum W. THE 10 NATURAL LAWS OF SUCCESSFUL TIME AND LIFE MANAGEMENT. Warner Books. ISBN 0-446-51741-0.

SOMER, Elizabeth, M.A.,R.D. THE ESSENTIAL GUIDE TO VITAMINS AND MINERALS.
Harper. ISBN 0-06-273345-1.

SULLIVAN, A.M. HUMAN VALUES IN MANAGEMENT: The Business Philosophy of.
Dun & Bradstreet library. Library of Congress card number: 73-89913.

SELECTED BIBLIOGRAPHY &
PHOTO CREDITS

STACTON, David. THE BONAPARTES. Simon & Schuster. 1966.

STERNELL, Zeev. Dossier ; ILS ONT INVENTÉ LA LIBERTÉ.
Revue l'Histoire, N° 307, mars 2006.

TAYLOR, William C. MAVERICKS AT WORK. Why the Most Original Minds in Business Win. Harper. ISBN-13: 978-006-11-252-1.

THATCHER, Margaret. THE DOWNING STREET YEARS.
Harper Collins. ISBN 0-06-017056-5.

THE PHILOSOPHY BOOK. Dorling Kindersley. ISBN 978-2-7613-4125-7.

THE NEW YORK TIMES. GUIDE TO ESSENTIAL KNOWLEDGE.
St-Martin's Press. ISBN 0-312-31367-5.

THE NEW YORKER. THE COMPLETE CARTOONS OF.
Black Dog Press. ISBN 1-57912-322-8.

TSUFIT. STEP INTO THE SPOTLIGHT!
Beach View Books. ISBN 978-0-9781913-0-6.

TARDIF, Jacques. POUR UN ENSEIGNEMENT STRATÉGIQUE. L'apport de la psychologie cognitive. Logiques Écoles. ISBN 2-89381-060-8.

TIMES BOOK OF QUOTATIONS, ISBN-0-00724048-1.

TOFFLER, Alvin. LE CHOC DU FUTUR. Médiations. De Noël & Gonthier. Paris, 1971.

TOFFLER, Alvin. THE THIRD WAVE. Bantam Books. ISBN 0-553-14431-6.

TOFFLER, Alvin & Heidi. REVOLUTIONARY WEALTH: How it will be Created and how it will Change Our Lives. Alfred A. Knopf. ISBN 0-3-375-40174-1.

TOURNIER, Philippe, L'HOMME PLANÉTAIRE.
Alain Stanké. ISBN 0-88566-023-4.

TURGEON, Bernard. LA PRATIQUE DU MANAGEMENT. 2e édition.
McGraw-Hill. ISBN 0-070549606-2.

TRACY, Brian. CHANGE YOUR THINKING, CHANGE YOUR LIFE. How to Unlock Your Full Potential for Success and Achievement. Willey & sons. ISBN 0-471-73538-8.

TREMBLAY, Jacinthe. LE MYTHE DU TRAVAIL D'ÉQUIPE.
La Presse, section affaires, 30 Avril 2007. ISSN 0317-9249.

TRUDEAU, Pierre Elliott, AGAINST THE CURRENT.
McClelland & Stewart. ISBN 0-7710-6979-0.

TRUDEAU, Pierre Elliott. MEMOIRS.
McClelland & Stewart. ISBN 0-7710-8587-7.

TRUMP, Donald J. THINK BIG AND KICK ASS.
Harper Collins. ISBN 978-0-06-154783-6.

VALLÉE, Danielle. WHIZ TEENS IN BUSINESS.
Truman Publishing Co. ISBN 0-9663393-2-0.

Selected **Bibliography** &
Photo **Credits**

VALLÉE, Danielle. LEADING YOUR BUSINESS INTO THE FUTURE WITH THE INTERNET. CRC Press. ISBN 1-57444-252-X.

VALLÉE, Danielle. E-LEARNING AS A BUSINESS ASSET. Webtech Publishing. 2001.

VENTRELLA, Scott W. THE POWER OF POSITIVE THINKING IN BUSINESS. Simon & Schuster. ISBN 0-7435-1810-1.

WHITELEY, Richard C. THE CUSTOMER DRIVEN COMPANY. Perseus books. ISBN 0-201-60813-9.

WALKER, Harold Blake. POWER TO MANAGE YOURSELF. Harper & Brothers. Library of Congress catalog card number: 55-8529.

WATERMAN, Robert H. ADHOCRACY: The Power to Change. Norton & Co. ISBN 0-393-03414-3.

WEIL, Andrew, M.D. 8 WEEKS TO OPTIMUM HEALTH. Knof publisher. ISBN 0-679-44715-6.

WIKIPEDIA. wikipedia.org - Project Free Encyclopedia.

WIKIMEDIA. commons.wikimedia.org - Multimedia Database.

YEH, Raymond T. & YEH, Stephanie H. THE ART OF BUSINESS: In the Footsteps of Giants. Zero Time Publishing. ISBN 09-9754277-1-7.

ZIGLER, Philip. MOUNTBATTEN. Collins. ISBN 0-00-216543-0.

© 2013 by Germain Decelles, WebTech Management and Publishing Incorporated

CHANGE Your Future, Now!
Paperback
ISBN: ISBN 978-0-9783667-7-3

E-book format: Epub
ISBN: ISBN 978-0-9783667-8-0
E-book format : PDF
ISBN: ISBN 978-0-9783667-9-7

Copyright: first quarter 2013
National Library of Québec
National Library of Canada

17, Marien Avenue, Montréal, Québec, Canada H1 B4T8
www.webtechmanagement.com
www.webtechpublishing.com

www.ingramcontent.com/pod-product-compliance
Lightning Source LLC
Chambersburg PA
CBHW022005300426
44117CB00005B/35